THE GREAT CONVERSATION

VOLUME I
Pre-Socratics through Descartes

THE GREAT CONVERSATION

A Historical Introduction to Philosophy

VOLUME I
PRE-SOCRATICS THROUGH DESCARTES

SEVENTH EDITION

NORMAN MELCHERT

Professor Emeritus, Lehigh University

New York   Oxford
OXFORD UNIVERSITY PRESS

Oxford University Press, Inc., publishes works that further Oxford University's objective of excellence in research, scholarship, and education.

Oxford   New York
Auckland   Cape Town   Dar es Salaam   Hong Kong   Karachi
Kuala Lumpur   Madrid   Melbourne   Mexico City   Nairobi
New Delhi   Shanghai   Taipei   Toronto

With offices in
Argentina   Austria   Brazil   Chile   Czech Republic   France   Greece
Guatemala   Hungary   Italy   Japan   Poland   Portugal   Singapore
South Korea   Switzerland   Thailand   Turkey   Ukraine   Vietnam

For titles covered by Section 112 of the US Higher Education Opportunity Act, please visit www.oup.com/us/he for the latest information about pricing and alternate formats.

Published by Oxford University Press
198 Madison Avenue, New York, New York 10016
http://www.oup.com

Library of Congress Cataloging-in-Publication Data
Melchert, Norman.
The great conversation : a historical introduction to philosophy / Norman Melchert Professor Emeritus, Lehigh University.—SEVENTH EDITION.
    p. cm.
Includes bibliographical references and index.
ISBN 978-0-19-999967-5 (v. 1)
1. Philosophy—Textbooks.   I. Title.
BD21.M43 2014
190—dc23

2013043050

CONTENTS

Volume I: Pre-Socratics through Descartes

BRIEF CONTENTS TO COMPANION VOLUME

Descartes through Derrida and Quine

A WORD TO INSTRUCTORS

Philosophy is both argument and innovation. I try in this introductory text to provide students with excellent examples of both in the ongoing story of a basic part of our intellectual life. I aim to teach students how to think by apprenticing them to a succession of the best thinkers humanity has produced, thereby drawing them into this ongoing conversation. So we see how Aristotle builds on and criticizes his teacher, Plato, how Augustine creatively melds traditions stemming from Athens and Jerusalem, how Kant tries to solve "Hume's problem," and why Wittgenstein thought most previous philosophy was meaningless.

This seventh edition continues to represent the major philosophers through extensive quotations set in a fairly rich cultural and historical context. The large number of cross-references and footnotes continue to make the conversation metaphor more than mere fancy. And the four complete works—*Euthyphro, Apology, Crito,* and *Meditations*—are retained.

New to This Edition

A number of new features will be found in this edition. Throughout, the text has been tightened up and minor sections were deleted to make room for new material. In addition, several larger changes have been made. These changes include

- Two new Profiles, one on Marcus Aurelius and one on Peter Singer, have been added.
- The treatment of Descartes' *Meditations* has been rearranged to facilitate students' easier access.
- Simone deBeauvoir's *The Second Sex* is now represented in a new translation.
- The final chapter of the sixth edition has been split into two new chapters. The first, on Postmodernism, contains, in addition to the treatment of Derrida, a new section on Michel Foucault and an expanded discussion of Richard Rorty. In the second, Physical Realism and the Mind, you will find a more comprehensive treatment of consciousness, with attention to Nagel's bat example, the Chinese Room, Jackson's knowledge argument, and the debate between David Chalmers and Daniel Dennett.

Again, for this edition, a student web page is available at www.oup.com/us/melchert. Here students will find, for each chapter, essential points, vocabulary flashcards, sample multiple-choice questions, and further web resources. The latter consist mainly, though not exclusively, of original philosophical texts. This means that if you want to assign students to read, say, Hume's *Enquiry* or parts of Plato's *Republic*, these texts are easy for them to find. An Instructor's Manual is available at the same site.

The text is again available both as a single hardback edition and as two paperback volumes, so it can be used economically in either a whole-year or a single-semester course. Although the entire book contains too much material for a single semester, it provides a rich menu of choices for instructors who do not wish to restrict themselves to the earlier or later periods.

In this era, when even the educated have such a thin sense of history, teaching philosophy in this conversational, cumulative, back-and-forward-looking way can be a service not just to philosophical understanding, but also to the culture as a whole.

A WORD TO STUDENTS

Note: This is Volume I of a connected two-volume work. (It is also available as a single, complete hardback book.) This volume begins with the dawning of philosophical thought in the West and takes us up to the beginning of the modern period with Descartes' *Meditations*. The second volume starts there and moves to important twentieth-century thinkers.

We all have opinions—we can't help it. Having opinions is as natural to us as breathing. Opinions, moreover, are a dime a dozen. They're floating all around us and they're so different from each other. One person believes this, another that. You believe in God, your buddy doesn't. John thinks there's nothing wrong with keeping a found wallet, you are horrified. Some of us say, "Everybody's got their own values"; others are sure that *some* things are just plain wrong—wrong for everybody. Some delay gratification for the sake of long-term goals; others indulge in whatever pleasures happen to be at hand. What kind of world do we live in? Jane studies science to find out, Jack turns to the occult. Is death the end for us?—Some say yes, some say no.

What's a person to do?

Study Philosophy!

You don't want simply to be at the mercy of accident in your opinions—for your views to be decided by irrelevant matters such as whom you happen to know or where you were brought up. You want to believe for *good reasons*. That's the right question, isn't it? Which of these many opinions has the best reasons behind it? You want to live your life as wisely as possible.

Fortunately, we have a long tradition of really smart people who have been thinking about issues such as these, and we can go to them for help. They're called "philosophers"—lovers of wisdom—and they have been trying to straighten out all these issues. They are in the business of asking which opinions or views or beliefs there is good reason to accept.

Unfortunately, these philosophers don't all agree either. So you might ask, If these really smart philosophers can't agree on what wisdom says, why should I pay them any attention? The answer is—because it's the best shot you've got. If you seriously want to improve your opinions, there's nothing better you can do than engage in a "conversation" with the best minds our history has produced.

One of my own teachers, a short, white-haired, elderly gentleman with a thick German accent, used to say, "Whether you will philosophize or won't philosophize, you *must* philosophize." By this, he meant that we can't help making decisions about these crucial matters. We make them either well or badly, conscious of what we are doing or just stumbling along. As Kierkegaard would say, we express such decisions in the way we live, whether or not we have ever given them a moment's thought. In a sense, then, you are already a philosopher, already engaged in the business philosophers have committed themselves to. So you shouldn't have any problem in making a connection with what they write.

Does it help to think about such matters? You might as well ask whether it helps to think about the recipe before you start to cook. Socrates says that "the unexamined life is not worth living." And that's what philosophy is: an examination of opinions—and also of our lives, shaped by these opinions. In thinking philosophically, we try to sort our opinions into two baskets: the good-views basket and the trash.

We want to think about these matters as clearly and rationally as we can. *Thinking* is a kind of craft. Like any other craft, we can do it well or poorly, with shoddy workmanship or with care, and we improve with practice. It is common for people who want to learn a craft—cabinetmaking, for example—to apprentice themselves for a time to a master, doing what the master does until the time comes when they are skillful enough to set up shop on their own. You can think of reading this book as a kind of apprenticeship in thinking, with Socrates, Plato, Kant, and the rest as the masters. By thinking along with them, noting their insights and arguments, following their examinations of each other's opinions, you should improve that all-important skill of your own.

This Book

This book is organized historically because that's how philosophy has developed. It's not just a recital of this following that, however. It is also intensively *interactive* because that's what

philosophy has been. I have taken the metaphor of a conversation seriously. These folks are all talking to each other, arguing with each other, trying to convince each other—and that makes the story of philosophy a dramatic one. Aristotle learns a lot from his teacher, Plato, but argues that Plato makes one big mistake—and that colors everything else he says. Aquinas appreciates what Aristotle has done but claims that Aristotle neglects a basic feature of reality—and that makes all the difference. In the seventeenth century, Descartes looks back on his predecessors with despair, noting that virtually no agreement has been reached on any topic; he resolves to wipe the slate clean and make a new start. Beginning with an analysis of what it is to believe anything at all, C. S. Peirce argues that what Descartes wants to do is impossible. And so it goes.

This conversational and interactive aspect of philosophy is emphasized by a large number of cross-references provided in footnotes. Your understanding of an issue will be substantially enriched if you follow up on these. In order to appreciate the line one thinker is pushing, it is important to see what he is arguing against, where he thinks that others have made mistakes. No philosopher simply makes pronouncements in the dark. There is always something that bugs each thinker, something she thinks is terribly wrong, something that needs correction. This irritant may be something current in the culture, or it may be what other philosophers have been saying. Using the cross-references to understand that background will help you to make sense of what is going on—and why. The index of names and terms at the back of this book will also help you.

Philosophers are noted for introducing novel terms, or using familiar words in novel ways. They are not alone in this, of course; poets and scientists do the same. There is no reason to expect that our everyday language will be suited, just as it is, to express the truth of things, so you will have some vocabulary to master. You will find key words in **boldface** and a list of them at the end of each chapter. Use this list to help you review important concepts and arguments. Many of these boldfaced terms are given definitions in the Glossary at the back of the book.

The Issues

The search for wisdom—that is, philosophy—ranges far and wide. Who can say ahead of time what might be relevant to that search? Still, there are certain central problems that especially concern philosophers. In your study of this text, you can expect to find extensive discussions of these four issues in particular:

1. *Metaphysics,* the theory of reality. In our own day, Willard Quine has said that the basic question of metaphysics is very simple: *What is there?* The metaphysical question, of course, is not like, "Are there echidnas in Australia?" but "What kinds of things are there fundamentally?" Is the world through and through made of material stuff, or are there souls as well as bodies? Is there a God? If so, of what sort? Is the world-order itself God? Are there universal features to reality, or is everything just the particular thing that it is? Does everything happen necessarily, given what has happened before, or are fresh starts possible?

2. *Epistemology*, the theory of knowledge. We want to think not only about what there is, but also about *how we know* what there is—or, maybe, whether we can know anything at all! So we reflectively ask, What is it to know something anyway? How does that differ from just believing it? Are there different kinds of knowledge? How is knowing something related to its being true? What is truth? How far can our knowledge reach? Are there things that are just unknowable?

3. *Ethics*, the theory of right and wrong, good and bad. It is obvious enough that we aren't just knowers and believers. We are doers. The question then arises of what wisdom might say about how best to live our lives. Does the fact that something gives us pleasure make it the right thing to do? Do we need to think about how our actions affect others? If so, in what way? Are there really goods and bads, or does thinking so make it so? Do we have duties? If so, where do they come from? What is virtue and vice? What is justice? Is justice important?

4. *Human nature*—Socrates took as his motto a slogan that was inscribed in the temple of Apollo in Delphi: Know Thyself. But that has proved none too easy to do. What are we, anyway? Are we simply bits of matter caught up in the universal mechanism of the world, or do we have minds that escape this deterministic machine? What is it to have a mind? Is mind separate from body? How is it related to the brain? Do we have a free will? How important to my self-identity is my relationship to others? To what degree can I be responsible for the creation of myself?

Running through these issues is a fifth one that perhaps deserves special mention. It centers on the idea of *relativism*. The question is whether there is a way to get beyond the prejudices and assumptions peculiar to ourselves or our culture—or whether that's all there is. Are there *just* opinions, with no one opinion ultimately any better than any other? Are all views relative to time and place, to culture and position? Is there no *truth*—or, anyway, no truth that we can know to be true?

This problem, which entered the great conversation early, with the Sophists of ancient Greece, has persisted to this day. Most of the Western philosophical tradition can be thought of as a series of attempts to kill such skepticism and relativism, but this phoenix will not die. Our own age has the distinction, perhaps, of being the first age ever in which the basic assumptions of most people, certainly of most educated people, are relativistic, so this theme will have a particular poignancy for us. We will want to understand how we came to this point and what it means to be here. We will also want to ask ourselves how adequate this relativistic outlook is.

What we are is what we have become, and what we have become has been shaped by our history. In this book, we look at that history, hoping to understand ourselves better and, thereby, gain some wisdom for living our lives.

Reading Philosophy

Reading philosophy is not like reading a novel, nor is it like reading a research report in biology or a history of the American South. Philosophers have their own aims and ways of proceeding, and it will pay to take note of them at the beginning. Philosophers aim at the truth about fundamental matters, and in doing so they offer arguments.

If you want to believe for good reasons, what you are in search of is an **argument**. An argument in philosophy is not a quarrel or a disagreement, but simply this business of offering reasons to believe. Every argument, in this sense, has a certain structure. There is some proposition the philosopher wants you to believe—or thinks every rational person ought to believe—and this is called the **conclusion**. And there are the reasons he or she offers to convince you of that conclusion; these are called the **premises**.

In reading philosophy, there are many things to look for—central concepts, presuppositions, overall view of things—but the main thing to look for are the arguments. And the first thing to identify is the conclusion of the argument; what is it that the philosopher wants you to believe? Once you have identified the conclusion, you need to look for the reasons given for believing that conclusion. Usually philosophers do not set out their arguments in a formal way, with premises listed first and the conclusion last. The argument will be embedded in the text, and you need to sniff it out. This is usually not so hard, but it does take careful attention.

Occasionally, especially if the argument is complex or obscure, I give you some help and list the premises and conclusion in a more formal way. You might right now want to look at a few examples. Socrates in prison argues that it would be wrong for him to escape; that is the conclusion, and I set out his argument for it on p. 114. Plato argues that being happy and being moral are the same thing; see an outline of his argument on p. 149. Anselm gives us a complex argument for the existence of God; see my summary on pp. 262–263. And Descartes argues that we have souls that are distinct from and independent of our bodies; see p. 351.

Often, however, you will need to identify the argument buried in the prose for yourself. What is it that the philosopher is trying to get you to believe? And why does he think you should believe that? It will be helpful, and a test of your understanding, if you try to set the argument out for yourself in a more or less formal way; keep a small notebook, and list the main arguments chapter by chapter.

Your first aim should be to *understand* the argument. But that is not the only thing, because you will also want to discover how good the argument is. These very smart philosophers, to tell the truth, have given us lots of poor arguments; they're only human, after all. So you need to try to *evaluate* the arguments. In evaluating an argument, there are two things to look at: the truth or acceptability of the premises, and whether the premises actually do support the conclusion.

For an argument to be a good one, the reasons given in support of the conclusion have to at least be plausible. Ideally the premises should be known to be *true*, but that is a hard standard to meet. If the reasons are either false or implausible, they can't lend truth or plausibility to the conclusion. If there are good reasons to doubt the premises, then the argument should not convince you.

It may be, however, that all of the premises are true, or at least plausible, and yet the argument is a poor one. This can happen when the premises do not have the right kind of relation to the conclusion. Broadly speaking, there are two kinds of arguments: **deductive** and **inductive**. A good deductive argument is one in which the premises—if true—*guarantee* the truth of the conclusion. In other words, the conclusion couldn't possibly be false if the premises are true. When this condition is satisfied, we say that the argument is **valid**. Note that an argument may have validity even though the premises are not in fact true; it is enough that if the premises *were* true, then the conclusion *would have to be* true. When a deductive argument is both valid *and* has true premises, we say it is **sound**.

Inductive arguments have a looser relation between premises and conclusion. Here the premises give some support to the conclusion—the more support the better—but they fall short of guaranteeing the truth of the conclusion. Typically philosophers aim to give sound deductive arguments, and the methods of evaluating these arguments will be those of the preceding two paragraphs.

You will get some help in evaluating arguments because you will see philosophers evaluating the arguments of other philosophers. (Of course, these evaluative arguments themselves may be either good or bad.) This is what makes the story of philosophy such a dramatic and interesting one. Here are a few examples. Aristotle argues that Plato's arguments for eternal, unchanging realities (which Plato calls Forms) are completely unsound; see pp. 172–173. Augustine tries to undercut the arguments of the skeptics on pp. 232–233. And Hume criticizes the design argument for the existence of God on pp. 412–414.

Sometimes you will see a philosopher criticizing another philosopher's presuppositions (as Peirce criticizes Descartes' views about doubt, pp. 566–567), or directly disputing another's conclusion (as Hegel does with respect to Kant's claim that there is a single basic principle of morality, pp. 474–475). But even here, it is argument that is the heart of the matter.

In reading philosophy you can't just be a passive observer. It's no good trying to read for understanding while the TV is on. You need to concentrate, focus, and be actively engaged in the process. Here are a few general rules:

1. Have an open mind as you read. Don't decide after the first few paragraphs that what a philosopher is saying is absurd or silly. Follow the argument, and you may change your mind about things of some importance.
2. Write out brief answers to the questions embedded in the chapters as you go along; check back in the text to see that you have got it right.
3. Use the key words to check your understanding of basic concepts.
4. Try to see how the arguments of the philosophers bear on your own current views of things. Bring them home; apply them to the way you now think of the world and your place in it.

Reading philosophy is not the easiest thing in the world, but it's not impossible either. If you make a good effort, you may find that it is even rather fun.

Web Resources

A web site for this book is available at www.oup.com/us/melchert. Here you will find, for each chapter, the following helps:

Essential Points (a brief list of crucial concepts and ideas)
Flashcards (definitions of basic concepts)
Multiple-Choice Questions (practice tests)
Web Resources (mostly original works that are discussed in this text—e.g., Plato's *Meno*, or Nietzsche's *Beyond Good and Evil*—but also some secondary treatments)

The web also has some general resources that you might find helpful:

Stanford Encyclopedia of Philosophy: http://plato.stanford.edu
Internet Encyclopedia of Philosophy: http://www.iep.utm.edu
    Both of these encyclopedias contain reliable in-depth discussions of the philosophers and topics we will be studying.
Philosophy Pages: http://www.philosophypages.com
    A source containing a variety of things, most notably a Philosophical Dictionary.
Philosophy on the EServer: http://philosophy.eserver.org/default.htm
    A site containing original texts, critical articles, and—philosophical humor! The latter includes jokes (some not very funny), songs, poems, satires, cartoons, and proofs that *p*.
YouTube contains numerous short interviews with and about philosophers: http://www.youtube.com/results?search_query=Bryan+Magee+A.J.+Ayer+Philosophy+Logic+Logical+Positivism+Language+Vienna+Circle+Wittgenstein+Carnap+Schlick&search=related&v=DM1XmLbGKJY&page=1

ACKNOWLEDGMENTS

I want to thank those readers of the sixth edition who thoughtfully provided me with ideas for improvement. I am grateful to Dennis D. Buchholz, Tidewater Community College; Paul Harris, West Chester University of Pennsylvania; Michael Henry, St. John's University; Basil Smith, Saddleback College; Ron Schepper, Sir Sandford Fleming College; Mark Thorsby, Lone Star College; Lloyd Aultman-Moore, Waynesburg University; Aleksandr Kragh, Averett University; the adjunct faculty of a university in Arizona; Joseph Kirkland, University of Michigan-Dearborn; Nicholas Dianuzzo, Montclair State University; and Mark Alexander Horton, Western Connecticut State University.

Comments relating to this new edition may be sent to me at norm.mel@verizon.net.

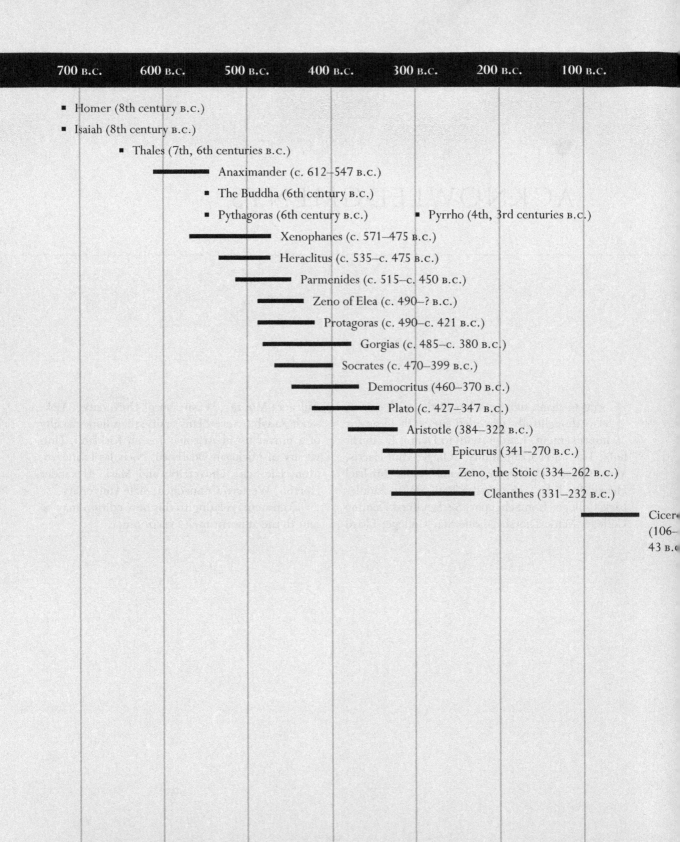

700 B.C. 600 B.C. 500 B.C. 400 B.C. 300 B.C. 200 B.C. 100 B.C.

- Homer (8th century B.C.)
- Isaiah (8th century B.C.)
- Thales (7th, 6th centuries B.C.)
Anaximander (c. 612–547 B.C.)
- The Buddha (6th century B.C.)
- Pythagoras (6th century B.C.)   - Pyrrho (4th, 3rd centuries B.C.)
Xenophanes (c. 571–475 B.C.)
Heraclitus (c. 535–c. 475 B.C.)
Parmenides (c. 515–c. 450 B.C.)
Zeno of Elea (c. 490–? B.C.)
Protagoras (c. 490–c. 421 B.C.)
Gorgias (c. 485–c. 380 B.C.)
Socrates (c. 470–399 B.C.)
Democritus (460–370 B.C.)
Plato (c. 427–347 B.C.)
Aristotle (384–322 B.C.)
Epicurus (341–270 B.C.)
Zeno, the Stoic (334–262 B.C.)
Cleanthes (331–232 B.C.)
Cicer
(106–
43 B.C

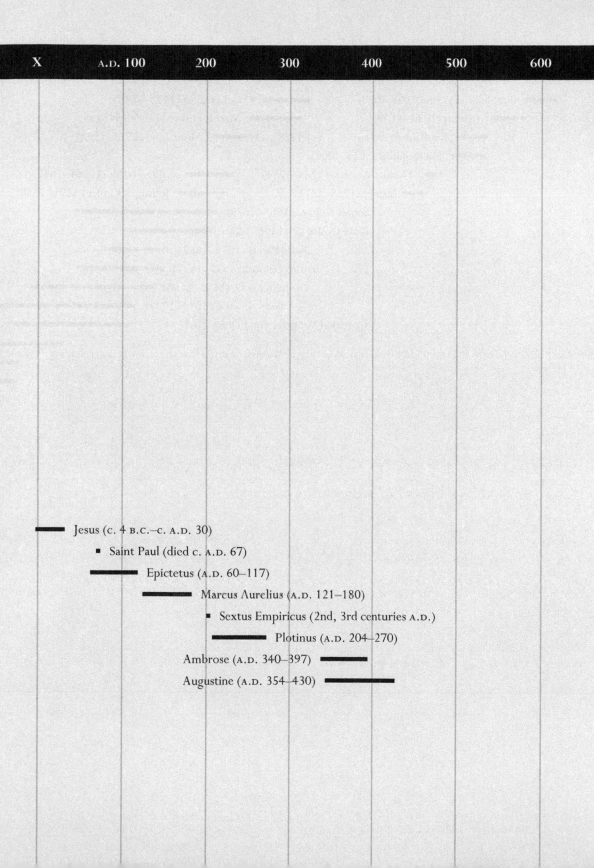

Jesus (c. 4 b.c.–c. a.d. 30)

Saint Paul (died c. a.d. 67)

Epictetus (a.d. 60–117)

Marcus Aurelius (a.d. 121–180)

Sextus Empiricus (2nd, 3rd centuries a.d.)

Plotinus (a.d. 204–270)

Ambrose (a.d. 340–397)

Augustine (a.d. 354–430)

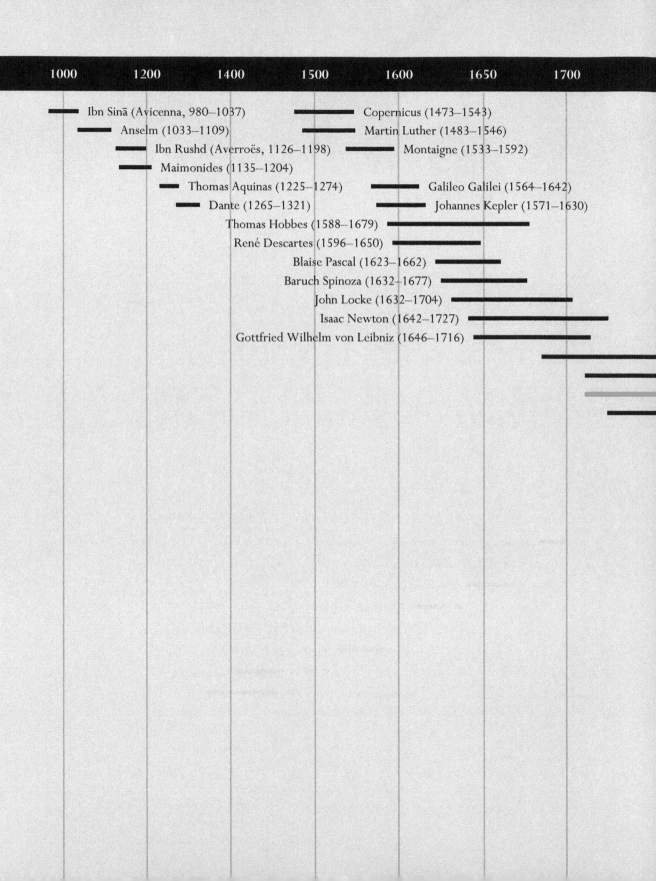

1000	1200	1400	1500	1600	1650	1700

Ibn Sinā (Avicenna, 980–1037)

Anselm (1033–1109)

Ibn Rushd (Averroës, 1126–1198)

Maimonides (1135–1204)

Thomas Aquinas (1225–1274)

Dante (1265–1321)

Thomas Hobbes (1588–1679)

René Descartes (1596–1650)

Blaise Pascal (1623–1662)

Baruch Spinoza (1632–1677)

John Locke (1632–1704)

Isaac Newton (1642–1727)

Gottfried Wilhelm von Leibniz (1646–1716)

Copernicus (1473–1543)

Martin Luther (1483–1546)

Montaigne (1533–1592)

Galileo Galilei (1564–1642)

Johannes Kepler (1571–1630)

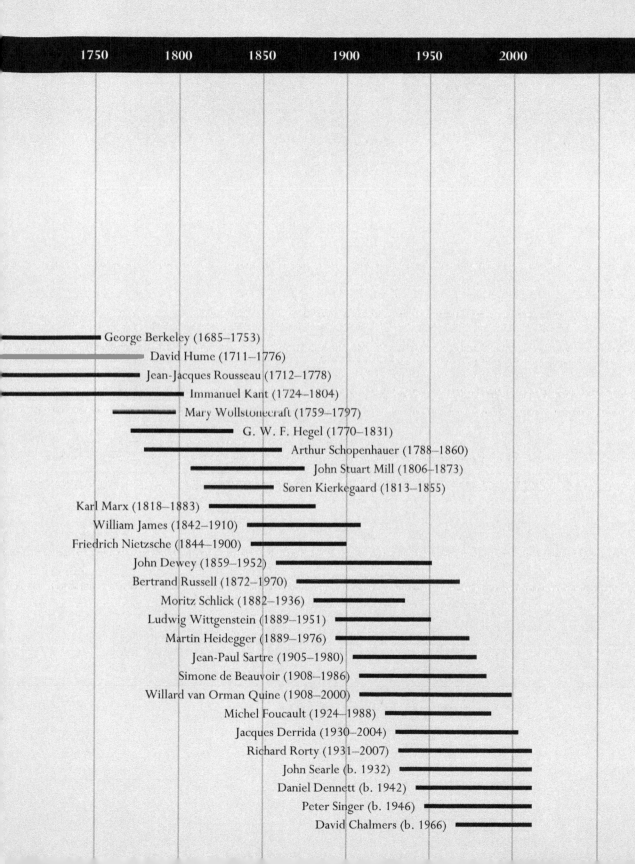

1750   1800   1850   1900   1950   2000

George Berkeley (1685–1753)
David Hume (1711–1776)
Jean-Jacques Rousseau (1712–1778)
Immanuel Kant (1724–1804)
Mary Wollstonecraft (1759–1797)
G. W. F. Hegel (1770–1831)
Arthur Schopenhauer (1788–1860)
John Stuart Mill (1806–1873)
Søren Kierkegaard (1813–1855)
Karl Marx (1818–1883)
William James (1842–1910)
Friedrich Nietzsche (1844–1900)
John Dewey (1859–1952)
Bertrand Russell (1872–1970)
Moritz Schlick (1882–1936)
Ludwig Wittgenstein (1889–1951)
Martin Heidegger (1889–1976)
Jean-Paul Sartre (1905–1980)
Simone de Beauvoir (1908–1986)
Willard van Orman Quine (1908–2000)
Michel Foucault (1924–1988)
Jacques Derrida (1930–2004)
Richard Rorty (1931–2007)
John Searle (b. 1932)
Daniel Dennett (b. 1942)
Peter Singer (b. 1946)
David Chalmers (b. 1966)

THE GREAT CONVERSATION

VOLUME I
Pre-Socratics through Descartes

I was aware that the reading of all good books is indeed like a conversation with the noblest men of past centuries who were the authors of them, nay a carefully studied conversation, in which they reveal to us none but the best of their thoughts.

—*René Descartes*

We—mankind—are a conversation.

—*Martin Heidegger*

In truth, there is no divorce between philosophy and life.

—*Simone de Beauvoir*

CHAPTER

1

BEFORE PHILOSOPHY
Myth in Hesiod and Homer

Everywhere and at all times, we humans have wondered at our own existence and at our place in the scheme of things. We have asked, in curiosity and amazement, "What's it all about?" "How are we to understand this life of ours?" "How is it best lived?" "Does it end at death?" "This world we find ourselves in—where does it come from?" "What is it, anyway?" "How is it related to us?"

These are some of the many philosophical questions we ask. Every culture offers answers, though not every culture has developed what we know as philosophy. Early answers to such questions universally take the form of stories, usually stories involving the gods—gigantic powers of a personal nature, engaged in tremendous feats of creation, frequently struggling with one another and intervening in human life for good or ill.

We call these stories *myths*. They are told and retold, elaborated and embroidered; they are taught to children as the plain facts and attain an authority by their age, by repetition, and by the apparent fact (within a given culture) that virtually everyone accepts them. They shape a tradition, and traditions shape lives.

Philosophy, literally "love of wisdom," begins when certain individuals start to ask, "Why should we believe these stories?" "How do we know they are true?"—and when they attempt to supply answers that have more going for them than antiquity and the plausibility that comes from common acceptance. Philosophers try to give us good reasons for believing one thing or another about these matters—or perhaps good reasons for thinking we can't answer such questions at all. They look at myth with a critical eye, sometimes appreciating what myths try to do, sometimes attacking myths' claims to literal truth. So there is a tension between these stories and philosophy, a tension that occasionally breaks into open conflict.

This conflict is epitomized in the execution of Socrates by his fellow Athenians in 399 B.C. Socrates was accused of not believing in the city's gods and, not coincidentally, of corrupting the young people of Athens. Socrates is a philosopher.

One might almost say he is the patron saint of philosophy, reminding us in age after age of what it means to love wisdom—in the way philosophers do.

We want to understand who Socrates is, what happened to him and why. We will also trace the story of the quest for wisdom after Socrates—in Plato and Aristotle, Augustine and Aquinas, Descartes and Hume and Kant—through our intellectual history down to the twentieth century. Myth is not dead in our day of "New Age" movements, of cults and gurus, prophets and mystics, and astrological forecasts. The conflict continues, and it is important that we understand it, for we do want to be wise.

To understand the character of this conflict, we need a sense for the nature of myth. In principle we could look at any of the great mythological traditions, in Babylon or Egypt, India or Rome. Such traditions all have a great deal in common, despite their dramatic differences of detail. But because it was the Greeks of the sixth and fifth centuries B.C. who first began to ask the questions that led to philosophical thinking, it will pay us to look at certain Greek myths. Our aim is neither a comprehensive survey nor mere acquaintance with some of these stories. We will be trying to understand something of Greek religion and culture, of the intellectual and spiritual life of the people who told these stories. As a result, we should be able to grasp why some of Socrates' contemporaries reacted to him as they did. With that in mind, we take a brief look at two of the great Greek poets: Hesiod and Homer.

Hesiod: War among the Gods

The poet we know as **Hesiod** probably composed his poem *Theogony* toward the end of the eighth century B.C. He was clearly drawing on much older traditions and seems to be synthesizing stories that have different origins and are not always consistent. The term *theogony* means "origin or birth of the gods," and the stories contained in the poem concern the beginnings of all things. He includes an immense amount of detail in this relatively short work. In this chapter, we look only at certain central events, as Hesiod relates them to us.

First, however, note that Hesiod claims to have written these lines under divine inspiration. (Suggestion: Read quotations aloud, especially poetry; you will find that they become more meaningful.)

> The Muses once taught Hesiod to sing
> Sweet songs, while he was shepherding his lambs
> On holy Helicon; the goddesses
> Olympian, daughters of Zeus who holds
> The aegis,* first addressed these words to me:
> "You rustic shepherds, shame: bellies you are,
> Not men! We know enough to make up lies
> Which are convincing, but we also have
> The skill, when we've a mind, to speak the truth."
>
> So spoke the fresh-voiced daughters of great Zeus
> And plucked and gave a staff to me, a shoot
> Of blooming laurel, wonderful to see,
> And breathed a sacred voice into my mouth
> With which to celebrate the things to come
> And things which were before.
>
> —*Theogony*, 21–35[1]

The Muses, according to the tradition Hesiod is drawing on, are nine daughters born to Zeus and Memory. In this passage, Hesiod is telling us that the stories he narrates are not vulgar shepherds' lies but are backed by the authority of the chief god and embody the remembrance of events long past. They thus represent the *truth*, Hesiod says, and are worthy of belief.

What have the Muses revealed?

> And sending out
> Unearthly music, first they celebrate
> The august race of first-born gods, whom Earth
> Bore to broad Heaven, then their progeny,
> Givers of good things. Next they sing of Zeus
> The father of gods and men, how high he is
> Above the other gods, how great in strength.
>
> —*Theogony*, 42–48

Note that the gods are themselves *born;* their origin, like our own, is explicitly sexual. Their ancestors are Earth (Gaea, or Gaia) and Heaven (Ouranos).†

---

*The *aegis* is a symbol of authority. Just so, we today may say that an event is presented "under the aegis" of an authoritative sponsor.

†Some people nowadays speak of the Gaea hypothesis and urge us to think of Earth as a living organism. Here we have a self-conscious attempt to revive an ancient way of

Note also that the gods are characterized as "givers of good things." For this, of course, they deserve our reverence and our gratitude. While there are many gods, they are not all equal in power and status. Zeus is king, the "father of gods and men."

There is confusion in the Greek stories about the very first things (no wonder), and there are contradictions among them. According to Hesiod, first of all there is *chaos,* apparently a formless mass of stuff, dark and without differentiation. Out of this chaos, Earth appears. (Don't ask how.) Earth then gives birth to starry Heaven,

> to be
> An equal to herself, to cover her
> All over, and to be a resting-place,
> Always secure, for all the blessed gods.
> —*Theogony,* 27–30

After lying with Heaven, Earth bears the first race of gods, the **Titans**, together with the Cyclops—three giants with but one round eye in the middle of each giant's forehead. Three other sons, "mighty and violent," are born to the pair, each with a hundred arms and fifty heads:

> And these most awful sons of Earth and Heaven
> Were hated by their father from the first.
> As soon as each was born, Ouranos hid
> The child in a secret hiding-place in Earth*
> And would not let it come to see the light,
> And he enjoyed this wickedness.
> —*Theogony,* 155–160

Earth, distressed and pained with this crowd hidden within her, forms a great sickle of hardest metal and urges her children to use it on their father for his shameful deeds. The boldest of the Titans, Kronos, takes the sickle and plots vengeance with his mother.

> Great Heaven came, and with him brought the night.
> Longing for love, he lay around the Earth,
> Spreading out fully. But the hidden boy

> Stretched forth his left hand; in his right he took
> The great long jagged sickle; eagerly
> He harvested his father's genitals
> And threw them off behind.
> —*Theogony,* 176–182

Where Heaven's bloody drops fall on land, the Furies spring up—monstrous goddesses who hunt down and punish wrongdoers.* Where they fall on the sea, the beautiful goddess of love and desire, Aphrodite, appears.

Hesiod tells of many other gods and goddesses, some obscure and some identifiable with features of the earth, natural forces, human passions, or moral enforcement. Most relevant to our story, however, is Hesiod's version of a characteristic theme in Greek thought, a theme repeated again and again in the great classical tragedies and also echoed in later philosophy: Violating the rule of justice—even in the service of justice—brings consequences. The Titans exact vengeance from their father for his wickedness, and they are overthrown in turn. The myths tell us: Wickedness does not pay.

Kronos, now ruler among the Titans, has children by Rhea, among them Hera, **Hades**, and **Poseidon**. Learning of a prophecy that he will be dethroned by one of these children, Kronos seizes the newborns and swallows them.† When Rhea bears yet another son, however, she hides him away in a cave on Crete and gives Kronos a stone wrapped in swaddling clothes to swallow. The hidden son, of course, is **Zeus**.

When grown to full strength, Zeus disguises himself as a cupbearer and persuades Kronos to drink a potion. This causes Kronos to vomit up his brothers and sisters—together with the stone. (The stone, Hesiod tells us, is set up at Delphi, northwest of Athens, to mark the center of the earth.) Together with his brothers and their allies, Zeus makes war on the Titans. The war drags on for ten

---

thinking about the planet we inhabit. Ideas of the Earth-mother and Mother Nature are also echoes of such early myths.

*This dank and gloomy place below the surface of the earth and sea is known as Tartarus.

---

*In contemporary literature, you can find these Furies represented in Jean-Paul Sartre's play *The Flies.*

†"Kronos" is closely related to the Greek word for time, "chronos." What might it mean that Kronos devours his children? And that they overthrow his rule to establish cities—communities of justice—that outlive their citizens?

years until Zeus frees the Cyclops from their imprisonment in Tartarus. The Cyclops give Zeus a lightning bolt, supply Poseidon with a trident, and provide Hades with a helmet that makes him invisible. With these aids, the gods overthrow Kronos and the Titans and hurl them down into Tartarus. The three victorious brothers divide up the territory: Zeus rules the sky (he is called "cloudgatherer" and "storm-bringer"); Poseidon governs the sea; and Hades reigns in Tartarus. Earth is shared by all three.

Thus, the gods set up a relatively stable order in the universe, an order both natural and moral. Although, as we will see, the gods quarrel among themselves and are not above lies, adultery, and favoritism, each of them guards something important and dear to humans. They also see to it that wickedness is punished and virtue is rewarded, just as was the case among themselves.

1. Why are philosophers dissatisfied with mythological accounts of reality?
2. What is the topic of Hesiod's *Theogony*?
3. Tell the story of how Zeus came to be king of the gods.
4. What moral runs through these early myths?

Homer: Heroes, Gods, and Excellence

Xenophanes, a philosopher we will meet later,* tells us that "from the beginning all have learnt in accordance with **Homer**."[2] As we have seen, poets were thought to write by divine inspiration, and for centuries people listened to or read the works of Homer, much as they read the Bible or the Koran today. He, above all others, was the great teacher of the Greeks. To discover what was truly excellent in battle, governance, counsel, sport, the home, and human life in general, the Greeks looked to Homer's tales. These dramatic stories offered a picture of the world and people's place in it that molded the Greek mind and

character. Philosophy begins against the Homeric background, so we need to understand something of Homer.

It is important to note that Homer simply takes for granted the tradition set down in Hesiod's *Theogony*. This religion of gods and heroes is the culture of conquerors who swept down in several waves from north and east into the Aegean area. Their sky-god tradition of Zeus, Athena, and Apollo celebrates clarity and order, mastery over chaos, intellect and beauty: fertile soil, one must think, for philosophy.

Homer's two great poems, of course, are *The Iliad* and *The Odyssey*. Here, we focus on *The Iliad,* a long poem about a brief period during the nine-year-long Trojan war.* This war came about when **Paris**, a son of **Priam**, king of **Troy**, seduced **Helen** and stole her away from her home in Achaea, in southern Greece (see Map 1). Helen was the most beautiful of women and was wife to **Menelaus**, king of Sparta. **Agamemnon**, the brother of Menelaus, was king of Argos, north of Sparta. He became commander in chief of the Greek forces that sailed across the Aegean to recover Helen, to avenge the wrong against his brother, and—not just incidentally—to gain honor, glory, and plunder. Among these forces was **Achilles**, the greatest warrior of them all, together with his formidable band of soldiers.

Here is how *The Iliad* begins.

Rage—Goddess, sing the rage of Peleus' son Achilles,
murderous, doomed, that cost the Achaeans countless losses,
hurling down to the House of Death so many sturdy souls,
great fighters' souls, but made their bodies carrion, feasts for the dogs and birds,
and the will of Zeus was moving toward its end.

---

*See "Xenophanes: The Gods as Fictions," in Chapter 2.

*The date of the war is uncertain; scholarly estimates tend to put it near the end of the thirteenth century B.C. The poems took form in song and were passed along in an oral tradition from generation to generation. They were written down some time in the eighth century B.C. Tradition ascribes them to a blind bard known as Homer, but the poems we now have may be the work of more than one poet.

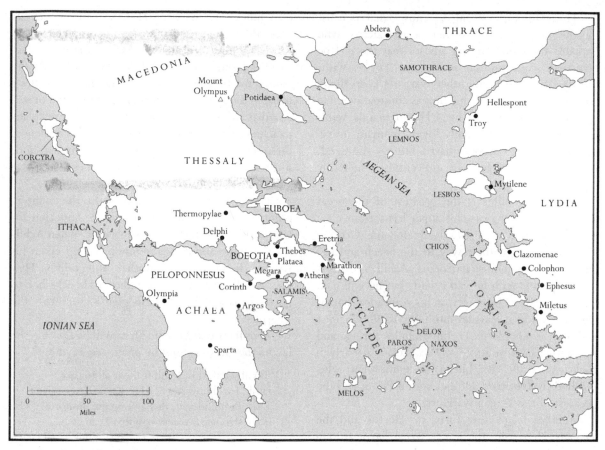

MAP 1 *The Greek Mainland*

Begin, Muse, when the two first broke and clashed,
Agamemnon lord of men and brilliant Achilles.

What god drove them to fight with such a fury?
Apollo the son of Zeus and Leto. Incensed at the
     king
he swept a fatal plague through the army—men
     were dying
and all because Agamemnon had spurned Apollo's
     priest.

—*The Iliad*, Book 1, 1–12[3]

The poet begins by announcing his theme: rage, specifically the excessive, irrational anger of Achilles—anger beyond all bounds that brings death and destruction to so many Greeks and almost costs them the war. So we might expect that the poem has a *moral* aspect. Moreover, in the sixth line we read that what happened was in accord with

the will of Zeus, who sees to it that flagrant violations of good order do not go unpunished. In these first lines we also learn of **Apollo**, the son of Zeus, who has sent a plague on the Greek army because Agamemnon offended him. We can see, then, that Homer's world is one of kings and heroes, majestic but flawed, engaged in gargantuan projects against a background of gods who cannot safely be ignored.

The story Homer tells goes roughly like this. In a raid on a Trojan ally, the Greeks capture a beautiful girl who happens to be the daughter of a priest of Apollo. The army awards her to Agamemnon as part of his spoils. The priest comes to plead for her return, offering ransom, but he is rudely rebuffed. Agamemnon will not give back the girl. The priest appeals to Apollo, who, angered by the treatment his priest is receiving, sends a plague to Agamemnon's troops.

The soldiers, wanting to know what is causing the plague, appeal to their seer, Calchas, who explains the situation and advises that the girl be returned. Agamemnon is furious. To be without his prize while the other warriors keep theirs goes against the honor due him as commander. He finally agrees to give up the girl but demands Achilles' prize, an exceptionally lovely woman, in exchange. The two heroes quarrel bitterly. Enraged, Achilles returns to his tent and refuses to fight any more.

Because Achilles is the greatest of the great among Greek warriors, his anger has serious consequences. The war goes badly for the Greeks. The Trojans fight their way to the beach and begin to burn the ships. Patroclus, Achilles' dearest friend, pleads with him to relent, but he will not. If Achilles won't have pity on his comrades, Patroclus says, then at least let him take Achilles' armor and fight in his place. To this Achilles agrees, and the tactic has some success. The Trojans are driven back toward the city, but in the fighting Patroclus is killed by **Hector**, another son of Priam and the greatest of the Trojan warriors.

Achilles' rage now turns on Hector and the Trojans. He rejoins the war to wreak havoc among them. After slaughtering many, he comes face to face with Hector. Achilles kills him and drags his body back to camp behind his chariot—a very, very bad thing to do. As the poem ends, King Priam goes alone by night into the Greek camp to plead with Achilles for the body of his son. He and Achilles weep together, for Hector and for Patroclus, and Achilles gives up the body.

🔶

"When anger rises, think of the consequences."

Confucius (537–479 B.C.)

This summary emphasizes the human side of the story. From that point of view, *The Iliad* can be thought of as the story both of the tragedy that excess and pride lead to and of the humanization

of Achilles. The main moral is the same as that expressed by a motto at the celebrated oracle at Delphi: "Nothing too much."* **Moderation** is what Achilles lacked, and his lack led to disaster. At the same time, the poem celebrates the "heroic virtues": *strength, courage, physical prowess,* and the kind of *wisdom* that consists in the ability to devise clever plans to achieve one's ends. For Homer and his audience, these characteristics, together with moderation, make up the model of human excellence. These are the virtues ancient Greeks teach their children.

Throughout the story there is also the counterpoint of the gods, who look on, are appealed to, take sides, and interfere. For instance, when Achilles is sulking about Agamemnon having taken his woman, he prays to his mother, the goddess Thetis. (Achilles has a mortal father.) He asks her to go to Zeus and beg him to give victory to—the Trojans!

Zeus frets that his wife Hera will be upset—she favors the Greeks—but he promises, saying,

"I will see to this. I will bring it all to pass.
Look, I will bow my head if that will satisfy you.
That, I remind you, that among the immortal gods
is the strongest, truest sign that I can give."
—*The Iliad,* Book 1, 625–628

Although there are numerous gods, one is supreme. If Zeus grants an appeal by bowing his head, that will be done. (Recall the sixth line of the poem.) Homeric religion, while certainly not a monotheism, is not exactly a true polytheism either. The powers that govern the world, though many, seem to be under the rule of one.† That rule gives a kind of order to the universe: Homer's world is not a chaos. There are even suggestions in Homer that Zeus himself, though the most powerful of the gods, is under the domination of Fate. Some things simply *will be,* and even Zeus cannot alter them.

---

*This was one of several mottoes that had appeared mysteriously on the temple walls. No one could explain how they got there, and it was assumed that Apollo himself must have written them.

†We shall see philosophers wrestling with this problem of "the one and the many." In what sense, exactly, is this world *one* world?

Moreover, this order is basically a just order, though it may not be designed altogether with human beings in mind. Zeus is the power who sees to it that certain customs are enforced: that oaths are kept, that suppliants are granted mercy, and that the rules governing guest and host are observed—the rules that Paris violated so grossly when he stole Helen away from her husband, Menelaus. Homer suggests that the Greeks eventually win the war because Zeus punishes the violation of these customs. On the other hand, the Greeks are punished with great losses before their eventual victory because Agamemnon had acted unjustly in taking Achilles' prize of war.

The Homeric idea of justice is not exactly the same as ours. We must see it in relation to the ambition of both mortals and gods in Homer's world. What they all covet is **honor** and glory. Agamemnon is angry not primarily because his woman was taken back to her father but because his honor has been offended. Booty is valued not for its own sake so much as for the honor it conveys—the better the loot, the greater the honor. Achilles is overcome by rage because Agamemnon has humiliated him, thus depriving him of the honor due him. That is why Thetis begs Zeus to let the Trojans prevail until the Greeks restore to Achilles "the honor he deserves."

What is just in this social world is that each person receive the honor that is due, given that person's status and position. Nestor, wise counselor of the Greeks, tries to make peace between Agamemnon and Achilles by appealing to precisely this principle.

> "Don't seize the girl, Agamemnon, powerful as
>   you are—
> leave her, just as the sons of Achaea gave her,
> his prize from the very first.
> And you, Achilles, never hope to fight it out
> with your king, pitting force against his force:
> no one can match the honors dealt a king, you
>   know,
> a sceptered king to whom Zeus gives glory.
> Strong as you are—a goddess was your mother—
> he has more power because he rules more men."
>
> —*The Iliad,* Book 1, 321–329

Nestor tries to reconcile them by pointing out what is just, what each man's honor requires. Unfortunately, neither one heeds his good advice.

The gods are also interested in honor. It has often been remarked that Homer's gods reflect the society that they allegedly govern; they are powerful, jealous of their prerogatives, quarrel among themselves, and are not above a certain deceitfulness, although some sorts of evil are simply beneath their dignity. The chief difference between human beings and the gods is that human beings are bound for death and the gods are not. Greeks often refer to the gods simply as "the immortals." Immortality makes possible a kind of blessedness among the gods that is impossible for human beings.

As immortals, the gods are interested in the affairs of mortals, but only insofar as they are entertained or their honor is touched. They are spectators of the human comedy—or tragedy; they watch human affairs the way we watch the soaps. There is a famous section in *The Iliad* where Zeus decides to sit out the battle about to rage on the plain below and simply observe. He says,

> "These mortals do concern me, dying as they are.
> Still, here I stay on Olympus throned aloft,
> here in my steep mountain cleft, to feast my eyes
> and delight my heart."
>
> —*The Iliad,* Book 20, 26–29

The gods both deserve and demand honor. We have already seen what can happen if it is not accorded. Apollo sent the plague because Agamemnon refused the ransom offered by Apollo's priest. When humans dishonor the gods or do not respect their prerogatives, they are guilty of arrogance, or **hubris.** In this state, human beings in effect think of themselves as gods, forgetting their finitude, their limitations, their mortality. Hubris is punished by the gods, as hero after hero discovers to his dismay.

The gulf between Homeric gods and mortals—even those heroes like Achilles who have one divine parent—is clear and impassable. In closing this brief survey of Greek myths, I want to emphasize two aspects of this gulf. First, those whose thoughts were shaped by Homer neither believed in nor aspired to any immortality worth prizing. True, there is a kind of shadowy existence after death, but the typical attitude toward it is expressed by Achilles when he is visited in the underworld by Odysseus.

> "No winning words about death to *me*, shining
> Odysseus!
> By god, I'd rather slave on earth for another
> man—
> some dirt-poor tenant farmer who scrapes to keep
> alive—
> than rule down here over all the breathless dead."
> —*The Odyssey*, Book 11, 555–558[4]

For these conquerors who glory in the strength of their bodies, it seems impossible to suppose that there could be anything after death to compare. They know they are destined to die, believe that death is the end of any life worth living, and take the attitude expressed by Hector when faced with Achilles:

> "And now death, grim death is looming up beside
> me,
> no longer far away. No way to escape it now. This,
> this was their pleasure after all, sealed long ago—
> Zeus and the son of Zeus, the distant deadly
> Archer—
> though often before now they rushed to my
> defense.
> So now I meet my doom. Well let me die—
> but not without struggle, not without glory, no,
> in some great clash of arms that even men to come
> will hear of down the years!"
> —*The Iliad,* Book 22, 354–362

Again, even at the end, the quest for honor is paramount.

The second aspect is a corollary to the first. It is best expressed by **Pindar**, a poet of the sixth century B.C., but the thought is thoroughly Homeric:

> Seek not to become Zeus.
> For mortals a mortal lot is best.
> Mortal minds must seek what is fitting
> at the hands of the gods,
> knowing what lies at our feet
> and to what portion we are born.
> Strive not, my soul, for an immortal life,
> but use to the full the resources
> that are at thy command.[5]

Mortal thoughts for mortals. Human beings are not divine, not gods, not immortal. Let them strive for excellence, to "use to the full the resources" at their command (and no other people, perhaps, have surpassed the Greeks in this). Let it be, however, an excellence appropriate to the "portion" allotted to humans. The deification of rulers, in Persian or Roman fashion, was not for the Greeks. They never blurred the line by worshipping living men (although dead heroes, like saints, may occasionally receive sacrifice and prayer). Here too, in its estimate of the status human beings have in the world, the Homeric tradition praises moderation.

1. Describe the main characters in Homer's poem *The Iliad*—for example, Agamemnon, Achilles, Apollo, Zeus, and Hector.
2. Retell the main outline of the story.
3. What is the theme of the poem, as expressed in the first lines?
4. How are honor and justice related in Homer's view of things?
5. What virtues are said to constitute human excellence?
6. Describe the relationship between humans and gods. In what ways are they similar, and how do they differ?
7. What is hubris, and what is its opposite?
8. Do Homer's heroes long for immortality? Explain.

FOR FURTHER THOUGHT

Gather examples of mythological thinking that are current today. What questions would a philosopher want to ask about them?

KEY WORDS

Hesiod	Helen
Theogony	Menelaus
Titans	Agamemnon
justice	Achilles
Hades	Apollo
Poseidon	Hector

Zeus   moderation
Homer   honor
Paris   hubris
Priam   Pindar
Troy

NOTES

1. Hesiod, *Theogony*, trans. Dorothea Wender, in Hesiod and Theognis (New York: Penguin Books, 1973). All quotations are taken from this translation; numbers are line numbers.

2. Kathleen Freeman, *Ancilla to the Pre-Socratic Philosophers* (Cambridge, MA: Harvard University Press, 1948), 22.

3. Homer, *The Iliad,* trans. Robert Fagles (New York: Penguin Books, 1990). All quotations are taken from this translation; references are to book and line numbers.

4. Homer, *The Odyssey,* trans. Robert Fagles (New York: Penguin Books, 1996). References are to book and line numbers.

5. Pindar, *Isthmia and Pythis III,* trans. W. K. C. Guthrie, in *The Greeks and Their Gods* (Boston: Beacon Press, 1950), 113–114.

2

PHILOSOPHY BEFORE SOCRATES

Although we can think of Hesiod and Homer as opening our conversation, this starting point is somewhat artificial, as there are other voices to be heard. Not only are there other traditions in Greece, but the Greek city-states are not the only source of this conversation. Even if philosophical thought truly begins there, we need also to pay attention to the Hebrew tradition that was taking shape while Homeric bards were singing of Troy. Because that tradition, together with its Christian successor, did not by itself lead to philosophy, despite making significant contributions to the conversation, we will consider it later (see Chapter 9).

We turn now to the first recognizably philosophical voices: those of the nature philosophers or protoscientists of Ionia (see Map 1). It is seldom entirely clear why thinkers raised in a certain tradition become dissatisfied enough to try to establish a new one. The reason is even more obscure here because we have a scarcity of information regarding these thinkers. Although most of them wrote books, these writings are almost entirely lost, some surviving in small fragments, others known only by references to them and quotations or paraphrases by later writers. As a group, these thinkers are usually known as the "pre-Socratics." This name testifies to the pivotal importance put on Socrates by his successors.*

For whatever reason, a tradition grew up in which questions about the nature of the world took center stage, a tradition that was not content with stories about the gods. For thinkers trying to *reason* their way to a view about reality, the Homeric tales, to say nothing of Hesiod's divine genealogy, must have seemed impossibly crude. Still, the questions addressed by these myths were real questions: What is the true nature of reality? What is its origin? What is our place in it? How are we related to the powers that govern it? What is the

---

*In this chapter, we look only at selected pre-Socratic thinkers. A more extensive and very readable treatment of others—including Anaximenes, Empedocles, and Anaxagoras—can be found in Merrill Ring, *Beginning with the Pre-Socratics* (Boston: McGraw-Hill, 1999).

best way to live? Philosophy is born when thinkers attempt to answer these questions more rationally than myth does.

In early philosophical thought, certain issues take center stage. There is the problem of *the one and the many*: If reality is in some sense one, what accounts for the many different individual things (and kinds of things) that we experience? Greek myth tends to answer this question in animistic or personal terms by referring either to birth or to spontaneous emergence. For instance, we find Hesiod simply asserting that "Chaos was first of all, but next appeared / Broad bosomed Earth" (*Theogony*, 116, 117). How, why, when, and by what means did it appear? On these questions the tradition is silent.

Then there is the problem of *reality and appearance*. True, things appear to change; they appear to be "out there," independent of us. But we all know that things are not always what they seem. Might reality in fact be very different from the way it appears in our experience? How could we know?

Of course, there is also the question about *human reality*: Who are we, and how are we related to the rest of what there is? These questions perplex our first philosophers. We shall see them struggling to frame ever-more satisfactory answers to them.

Thales: The One as Water

Thales (c. 625–547 B.C.) of Miletus, a Greek seaport on the shore of Asia Minor (see Map 1), seems to have been one of those dissatisfied with the traditional stories. Aristotle calls him the founder of philosophy. We know very little about Thales, and part of what we do know is arguably legendary. So, our consideration here is brief and somewhat speculative. He is said to have held (1) that the cause and element of all things is water, and (2) that all things are filled with gods. What could these two rather obscure sayings mean?

Concerning the first, it is striking that Thales supposes there is some *one* thing that is both the origin and the underlying nature of all things. It is surely not obvious that wine and bread and stones and wind are really the same stuff despite all their differences. It is equally striking that Thales chooses one of the things that occur naturally in the world of our experience to play that role. Notice that neither Zeus nor Kronos (Zeus' father, according to Hesiod) nor Rhea (the Earth-goddess mother who bore him) plays this role but water. Here we are clearly in a different thought-world from that of Homer. Thales' motto seems to be this: *Account for what you can see and touch in terms of things you can see and touch.* This idea is a radical departure from anything prior to it.

Why do you think Thales chooses water to play the role of the primeval stuff? Aristotle speculates that Thales must have noticed that water is essential for the nourishment of all things and that without moisture, seeds will not develop into plants. We might add that Thales must have noticed that water is the only naturally occurring substance that can be seen to vary from solid to liquid to gas. The fact that the wet blue sea, the white crystalline snow, and the damp and muggy air seem to be the very same thing despite their differences could well have suggested that water might take even more forms.

At first glance, the saying that all things are full of gods seems to go in a quite different direction. If we think a moment, however, we can see that it is quite consistent with the saying about water. What is the essential characteristic of the gods, according to the Greeks? Their immortality. To say that all things are full of gods, then, is to say in effect that *in* them—not, note well, outside them or in addition to them—is a principle that is immortal. But this suggests that the things of experience do not need explanations from outside themselves as to why they exist. Moreover, tradition appeals to the gods as a principle of action. Why did lightning strike just there? Because Zeus was angry with *that man*. But to say that all things are themselves full of gods may well mean that we do not have to appeal beyond them to explain why events happen. Things have the principles of their behavior within themselves.

Both sayings, then, point thought in a direction quite different from the tradition of Homer and Hesiod. They suggest that if we want to understand this world, then we should look to this world, not to another. Thales seems to have been the first to have tried to answer the question, Why do things happen as they do? in terms that are not immediately personal. In framing his answer this way, Thales is not only the first philosopher, but the first scientist as well. It is almost impossible to overestimate the significance of this shift for the story of Western culture.

---

1. In what way are the two sayings attributed to Thales consistent?
2. Contrast the view suggested by Thales' sayings with that of Homer.

Anaximander: The One as the Boundless

Let's grant that Thales produced a significant shift in Western thought. What next? Although he may have done so, we have no evidence that Thales addresses the question of *how* water accounts for everything else. If everything is water, why does it seem as though so many things are *not* water, that water is just one kind of thing among many? Thales leaves us with a puzzle for which he offers no solution.

There is something else unsatisfactory about his suggestion: Even though water has those unusual properties of appearing in several different states, water itself is not unusual. It is, after all, just one of the many things that need to be explained. If we demand explanations of dirt and bone and gold, why should we not demand an explanation for water as well?

Ancient Greeks would have found a third puzzling feature in Thales' idea. They tended to think in terms of opposites: wet and dry, hot and cold. These pairs are opposites because they cancel each other out. Where you have the wet, you can't have the dry, and so on. Water is wet, yet the dry also exists. If the origin of things had been water, how could the dry have ever come into existence? It seems impossible.

Although again we are speculating, it is reasonable to suppose that problems such as these led to the next stage in our story. We can imagine **Anaximander**, a younger fellow citizen from

Miletus born about 612 B.C., asking himself—or perhaps asking Thales—these questions. How does water produce the many things of our experience? What makes water so special? So the conversation develops.

Like Thales, Anaximander wants an account of origins that does not appeal to the gods of Homer and Hesiod, but as we'll see, he does not reject the divine altogether. We can reconstruct Anaximander's reasoning thus:

1. Given any state of things *X,* it had a beginning.
2. To explain its beginning, we must suppose a prior state of things *W.*
3. But *W* also must have had a beginning.
4. So we must suppose a still prior state *V.*
5. Can this go on forever? No.
6. So there must be something that itself has no beginning.
7. We can call this "the infinite" or "**the Boundless**."

It is from this, then, that all things come.

We are ready now to appreciate a passage of Aristotle's, in which he looks back and reports the views of Anaximander.

> Everything either is a beginning or has a beginning. But there is no beginning of the infinite; for if there were one, it would limit it. Moreover, since it is a beginning, it is unbegotten and indestructible. . . . Hence, as we say, there is no source of this, but this appears to be the source of all the rest, and "encompasses all things" and "steers all things," as those assert who do not recognize other causes besides the infinite. . . . And this, they say, is the divine; for it is "deathless" and "imperishable" as Anaximander puts it, and most of the physicists agree with him. (DK 12 A 15, *IEGP,* 24)[1]

Only the Boundless, then, can be a beginning for all other things. It *is* a beginning, as Aristotle puts it; it does not *have* a beginning. Because it is infinite, moreover, it has not only no beginning but also no end—otherwise it would have a limit and not be infinite.

It should be no surprise that the infinite is called "divine." Recall the main characteristic of the Greek gods: They are immortal; they cannot die. As Anaximander points out, this is precisely the key feature of the Boundless.

Here we have the first appearance of a form of reasoning that we will meet again when later thinkers try to justify belief in a god (or God) conceived in a much richer way than Anaximander is committed to.* Yet even here some of the key features of later thought are already present. The Boundless "encompasses all things" and "steers all things." Those familiar with the New Testament will be reminded of Paul's statement that in God "we live and move and have our being" (Acts 17:28).[2]

We should note that Aristotle remarks almost casually that those who use this language "do not recognize other causes besides the infinite." Here he hints at what he considers a defect in the view of Anaximander: It is too abstract to account in detail for the nature and behavior of the many species and individuals we actually find in the world. What we need is not one big cause but many little causes.† But that is getting ahead of our story.

We have seen how Anaximander deals with one of the puzzles bequeathed to him by Thales. It is not water but the Boundless that is the source and element of all things. What about the other problem? By what process does the Boundless produce the many individual things of our experience?

Here we have to note that the Boundless is thought of as indefinite in character, neither clearly this nor that. If it had a clear nature of its own, it would already exclude everything else; it would be, for instance, water but not fire, so it would have limits and not be infinite. Therefore, it must contain all things, but in a "chaotic" mixture.‡ The hot, the cold, the dry, and the wet are all present in the Boundless, but without clear differentiation.

How, then, does the process of differentiation from the Boundless work? If Anaximander could show how these basic four elements (hot, cold, dry, and wet) separate out from the chaos, his basic problem would be solved. The *one* would generate *many* things. The question of how particular things are formed could be solved along similar lines. Note that at this early stage of thought, no clear

distinction is made between heat as a property of a thing and the thing that is hot. There is just "the hot" and "the cold," what we might think of as hot stuff and cold stuff. In fact, these stuffs are virtually indistinguishable from earth (the cold), air (the dry), fire (the hot), and water (the wet). The universe as we experience it seems to be composed of various mixtures of these elemental stuffs.*

To solve his problem, Anaximander uses an analogy: Fill a circular pan with water; add some bits of limestone, granite, and lead (what you need is a variety of different weights); and then swirl the water around. You will find that the heavier bits move toward the middle and the lighter bits to the outside. Like goes to like; what starts as a jumble, a chaos, begins to take on some order. Anaximander is apparently familiar with this simple experiment and makes use of it to explain the origin of the many.

If the Boundless were swirling in a **vortex motion,** like the water in the pan, then what was originally indistinguishable in it would become separated out according to its nature. You might ask: Why should we think that the Boundless engages in such a swirling, vortex motion? Anaximander would simply ask you to look up. Every day we see the heavenly bodies swirl around the earth: the sun, the moon, and even the stars. Did you ever lie on your back in a very dark, open spot (a golf course is a good place) for a long time and look at the stars? You can see them move, although it takes a long while to become conscious of their movement.†

Furthermore, it seems clear that the motions we observe around us exemplify the vortex principle that like goes to like. What is the lightest of the elements? Anyone who has stared at a camp fire for a few moments will have no doubt about the answer. The sticks stay put, but the fire leaps up, away from the cold earth toward the sky—toward

---

*For examples, see Thomas Aquinas' proofs of the existence of God (Chapter 11).

†See pp. 168–169.

‡Remember that Hesiod tells us that "Chaos was first of all."

*Much of Greek medicine was based on these same principles. A feverish person, for instance, has too much of the hot, a person with the sniffles too much of the wet, and so on. What is required is to reach a balance among the opposite elements.

†Copernicus, of course, turns this natural view inside out. The stars only *appear* to move; in actuality, Copernicus suggests, it is *we* who are moving. See pp. 306–307.

the immensely hot, fiery sun and the other bright but less hot heavenly bodies.

According to the geography accepted at the time, moreover, the habitable earth was surrounded by an ocean of water, which was surrounded in turn by the air. Thus, we have an ordered, sorted world: earth (cold and heavy) in the middle, water next (wet and not quite so heavy), then air, and in an outermost ring the fiery element—all in a continuous vortex motion that both produces and sustains the order. This explanation seems plausible and fits the observable data. What more could one ask?

Anaximander has other interesting ideas, too.[3] He explains why we do not see a blaze of fiery light covering the sky but bright spots: The blaze is mostly hidden by an opaque covering. He calculates (inaccurately) the orbits of the sun and the moon. He offers an explanation of why the earth stays where it does (it rides on air—what we might call the Frisbee principle). He gives us a non-Zeusian explanation of thunder and lightning (caused by the wind compressed in clouds). He suggests that humans originated inside other animals (fish, in particular). We needn't stop to discuss most of these points, but we need to give some attention to one more principle.

Anaximander tells us that existing things "make reparation to one another for their injustice according to the ordinance of time" (DK 12 B 1, *IEGP*, 34). Several questions arise here. What existing things? No doubt it is the opposites of hot and cold, wet and dry that Anaximander has in mind, but why does he speak of injustice? How can the hot and cold do each other injustice, and how can they "make reparation" to each other?

There can be little doubt of the answer. He presupposes a principle of balance in nature that must ultimately be served, however much one or the other element seems to have gotten the upper hand. The hot summer is hot at the expense of the cold; it requires a cold winter to right the balance. A too dry winter, we still tend to think, will have to be paid for by a too wet spring. Thus, each season encroaches on the "rights" due to the others and does them an injustice, but reparation is made in turn when each gets its due—and more. This keeps the cycle going.

Notice two points in particular. First, this view is, in its own way, an extension of the Homeric view that requires a certain moderation in human behavior. Too much of anything—too much anger, too much pride—brings down the wrath of the gods. Anaximander imagines a cosmic principle of moderation at work in the elements of the world. It is as if he were saying to Homer, "You are right, but your view is too limited; the principle applies not only within the human world but also in the universe at large."

The second point, however, is equally important. This principle is not imposed on reality from without; it is not applied by the gods. Anaximander conceives it as immanent in the world process itself. Thus, he says, does the world work. In this he is faithful to the spirit of Thales, and in this both of them depart from the tradition of Homer, the first and foremost teacher of the Greeks. Anaximander's explanations are framed impersonally. It is true that the Boundless "steers all things," but the Homeric gods who intervene at will in the world have vanished. To explain particular facts in the world, no will, no purpose, no intention is needed. The gods turn out to be superfluous.

You can easily see that a cultural crisis is on the way. If the Homeric tradition is still alive and flourishing in the religious, artistic, political, and social life of Greek cities, what will happen when this new way of thinking begins to take hold? Our next thinker begins to draw some conclusions.

---

1. What puzzling features of Thales' view seem to have stimulated Anaximander to revise it?
2. State Anaximander's argument for the Boundless.
3. How, according to Anaximander, does the Boundless produce the many distinct things of our experience?
4. What evidence do we have in our own experience for a vortex motion?
5. How is the injustice that Anaximander attributes to existing things related to the Homeric virtue of moderation?
6. What sort of crisis is brewing?

Xenophanes: The Gods as Fictions

From what we know about Anaximander, it seems that his criticism of the mythological tradition was implicit rather than explicit. He was intent on solving his problems about the nature and origins of the world. Although his results were at odds with tradition, we have no record that he took explicit notice of this. Not so with **Xenophanes**. A native of Colophon, about forty miles north of Miletus (see Map 1), he was, like Thales and Anaximander, an Ionian Greek living on the eastern shores of the Aegean Sea. We are told that he fled in 546 B.C., when Colophon was taken by the Persians, and that he lived at least part of his life thereafter in Sicily. Xenophanes was a poet and apparently lived a long life of more than ninety-two years.

Xenophanes is important to our story because he seems to have been the first to state clearly the religious implications of the new nature philosophy. He explicitly criticizes the traditional conception of the gods on two grounds. First, the way Hesiod and Homer picture the gods is unworthy of our admiration or reverence:

> Homer and Hesiod have attributed to the gods all those things which in men are a matter for reproach and censure: stealing, adultery, and mutual deception. (DK Z1 B11, *IEGP,* 55)*

What he says is true, of course. It has often been remarked that Homer's gods are morally no better (and in some ways may be worse) than the band of ruthless warrior barons on whom they are so clearly modeled. They are magnificent in their own fashion, but flawed, like a large and brilliant diamond containing a vein of impurities. What is significant about Xenophanes' statement is that he not only notices

this but clearly expresses his disapproval.* He thinks it is *shameful* to portray the gods as though they are no better than human beings whom good men regard with disgust. That Homer, to whom all Greeks of the time look for guidance in life, should give us this view of the divine seems intolerable to Xenophanes. This moral critique is further developed by Plato.† For both of them, such criticism is the negative side of a more exalted idea of the divine.

This kind of criticism makes sense only on the basis of a certain assumption: that Homer is not simply mirroring the truth for us but is inventing stories. Several sayings of Xenophanes make this assumption clear.

> The Ethiopians make their gods snub-nosed and black; the Thracians make theirs gray-eyed and red-haired. (DK 21 B 16, *IEGP,* 52)

> And if oxen and horses and lions had hands, and could draw with their hands and do what man can do, horses would draw the gods in the shape of horses, and oxen in the shape of oxen, each giving the gods bodies similar to their own. (DK 21 B 15, *IEGP,* 52)

Here we have the first recorded version of the saying that god does not make man in his own image but that we make the gods in our image. This, Xenophanes tells us, is what Homer and Hesiod have done. Atheists and agnostics have often made this point since Xenophanes' time. Was Xenophanes, then, a disbeliever in the divine? No, not at all. No more than Anaximander, who says the infinite sees all and steers all. Xenophanes tells us there is

> one god, greatest among gods and men, in no way similar to mortals either in body or mind. (DK 21 B 23, *IEGP,* 53)

Several points in this brief statement stand out. There is only **one god**.‡ Xenophanes takes pains to stress how radically different this god is from anything

---

*When the Greeks talk about "men," they may not have been thinking about women. Women were not citizens, for example, in ancient Athens. It does not follow, of course, that what the Greeks say about "men" has no relevance for women of today. Here is a useful way to think about this. Aristotle formulated the Greek understanding of "man" in terms of *rational animal,* a concept that can apply to human beings generally. What the Greeks say about "man" may well apply to women, too, although one should be on guard lest they sneak masculinity too much into this generic "man." Their mistake (and not theirs alone!) was to have underestimated the rationality and humanity of women.

I will occasionally use the term "man" in this generic sense, but I will often paraphrase it with "human being" or some other substitute. Rather than the awkward "he or she," I will sometimes use "he" and sometimes "she," as seems appropriate.

---

*For a contrary evaluation, see Nietzsche, p. 530.

†See *Euthyphro* 6a, for instance. This criticism is expanded in Plato's *Republic,* Book II, where Plato explicitly forbids the telling of Homeric and Hesiodic tales of the gods to children in his ideal state.

‡It may seem that Xenophanes allows the existence of other gods in the very phrase he uses to praise this one god. Scholars disagree about the purity of his monotheism. In the context of other things he says, however, it seems best to understand this reference to "gods" as a reference to "what tradition takes to be gods."

PYTHAGORAS

A figure about whom there are as many legends as facts, Pythagoras (b. 570 B.C.) lived most of his adult life in Croton in southern Italy (see Map 2 on page 28). He combined mathematics and religion in a way strange to us and was active in setting up a pattern for an ideal community. The Pythagorean influence on Plato is substantial.

Pythagoras and his followers first developed geometry as an abstract discipline, rather than as a tool for practical applications. It was probably Pythagoras himself who discovered the "Pythagorean theorem" (the square of the hypotenuse of a triangle is equal to the sum of the squares on the other two sides), as well as the principle that the interior angles of a triangle are equal to two right angles.

He also discovered the mathematical ratios of musical intervals: the octave, the fifth, and the fourth. Because mathematics informs these intervals, the Pythagoreans held, somewhat obscurely, that *all things are numbers*. They also believed that the sun, the moon, and other heavenly bodies make a noise as they whirl about, much as a piece of wood whirled on a string produces noise. They believed that these sounds produce a cosmic harmony, the "music of the spheres."

Pythagoras believed that the soul is a distinct and immortal entity, "entombed" for a while in the body. After death, the soul migrates into other bodies, sometimes the bodies of animals. To avoid both murder and cannibalism, the Pythagoreans were vegetarians. Xenophanes tells the story, probably apocryphal, that Pythagoras saw a puppy being beaten and cried out, "Do not beat it; I recognize the voice of a friend."

Mathematics was valued not just for itself but as a means to purify the soul, to disengage it from bodily concerns. In mathematical pursuits the soul lives a life akin to that of the gods.

It is said that Pythagoras was the first to call himself a philosopher, a *lover* of wisdom. No one, he said, is wise except the god. Compare Socrates (*Apology* 23a).

---

in the Homeric tradition. It is "in no way similar to mortals." This point is brought out in some positive characterizations he gives of this dissimilar god.

> He sees all over, thinks all over, hears all over. (DK 21 B 24, *IEGP,* 53)
>
> He remains always in the same place, without moving; nor is it fitting that he should come and go, first to one place and then to another. (DK 21 B 26, *IEGP,* 53)
>
> But without toil, he sets all things in motion by the thought of his mind. (DK 21 B 25, *IEGP,* 53)

This god is very different from human beings indeed. We see with our eyes, think with our brain, and hear with our ears. We seldom remain in the same place for more than a short time; indeed, if we are strict enough about what constitutes the "same place," we might come to agree with Heraclitus, who argues that we and all things are constantly moving from one place to another.* Furthermore, if we want to set anything besides ourselves in motion, just thinking about it or wishing for it isn't enough. In all these ways we are different from the one god.

Yet there is a similarity after all, and Xenophanes' "in no way similar" must be qualified. The one god sees and hears and thinks; so do we. He does not do it in the way we do it; the way the god does it is indeed "in no way similar." But god is intelligent, and so are we.

Here is a good place to comment on an assumption that seems to have been common among the Greeks. Where there is order, there is intelligence. Order, whether in our lives or in the world of nature, is not self-explanatory; only intelligence can explain order. This assumption doesn't seem to be explicitly argued for. It lies in the background as something almost too obvious to comment on. We can find experiences to give it some support, and perhaps these are common enough to make it *seem* self-evident—but it is not. For example, consider the state of papers on your desk or tools in your workshop. If you are like me, you find that

---

*See pp. 19–20.

these things, if left to their own devices, degenerate slowly into a state of chaos. Soon it is impossible to find what you want when you need it and it becomes impossible to work. What you need to do then is *deliberately* and with some *intelligent plan in mind* impose order on the chaos. Order is the result of intelligent action, it seems. It doesn't just happen.

Whether this assumption is correct is an interesting question, one about which modern physics and evolutionary biology have had interesting things to say.* Modern mathematicians tell us that however chaotic the jumble of books and papers on your desk, there exists some mathematical function according to which they are in perfect order. But for these ancient Greeks, the existence of order always presupposes an ordering intelligence. We find this assumption at work in the idea of god that Anaximander and Xenophanes have given us.

Consider now a saying that shows how closely Xenophanes' critique of the traditional gods relates to the developing nature philosophy:

> She whom men call "Iris," too, is in reality a cloud, purple, red, and green to the sight. (DK 21 B 32, *IEGP,* 52)

In *The Iliad,* Iris is a minor goddess, a messenger for the other gods. For instance, after Hector has killed Patroclus, Iris is sent to Achilles to bid him arm in time to rescue Patroclus' body (Book 18, 192–210). She seems to have been identified with the rainbow, which many cultures have taken as a sign or message from the gods. (Compare its significance to Noah, for example, after the flood in Genesis 9:12–17.)

Xenophanes tells us that rainbows are simply natural phenomena that occur in natural circumstances and have natural explanations. A rainbow, he thinks, is just a peculiar sort of cloud. This idea suggests a theory of how gods are invented. Natural phenomena, especially those that are unusual, particularly striking, or

important to us, are personified and given lives that go beyond what is observable. Like the theory that the gods are invented, this theory has often been held. It may not be stretching things too far to regard Xenophanes as its originator.

It is clear that there is a kind of natural unity between nature philosophy and criticism of Homer's gods. They go together and mutually reinforce one another. Together they are more powerful than either could be alone. We will see that they come to pose a serious threat to the integrity of Greek cultural life.

There is one last theme in Xenophanes that we should address. Poets in classical times typically appealed to the Muses for inspiration and seemed often to think that what they spoke or wrote was not their own—that it was literally in-spired, breathed into them, by these goddesses. Remember Hesiod's claim that he was taught to sing the truth by the Muses. Similarly, Homer begins *The Iliad* by inviting the goddess to sing through him the rage of Achilles.* No doubt this is more than a literary conceit, many writers have experiences of inspiration when they seem to be no more than a mouthpiece for powers greater and truer than themselves. Hesiod and Homer may well have had such experiences. Whether such experiences guarantee the *truth* of what the writer says in such ecstatic states is, of course, another question. Listen to Xenophanes:

> The gods have not revealed all things from the beginning to mortals; but, by seeking, men find out, in time, what is better. (DK 21 B 18, *IEGP,* 56)

> No man knows the truth, nor will there be a man who has knowledge about the gods and what I say about everything. For even if he were to hit by chance upon the whole truth, he himself would not be aware of having done so, but each forms his own opinion. (DK 21 B 38, *IEGP,* 56)

> Let these things, then, be taken as like the truth. (DK 21 B 35, *IEGP,* 56)

This is a very rich set of statements. Let us consider them in six points.

---

*See p. 316 for an example. Here Descartes claims that a chaos of randomly distributed elements, if subject to the laws of physics, would by itself produce an order like that we find in the world. For more recent views, see the fascinating book by James Gleick, *Chaos: Making a New Science* (New York: Penguin Books, 1987). The dispute over "intelligent design" shows that this is still a live issue.

---

*Look again at these claims to divine inspiration on pp. 2 and 5.

1. Xenophanes is deliberately, explicitly, denying our poets' claims of inspiration. The gods have *not* revealed to us in this way "from the beginning" what is true, Xenophanes says. If we were to ask him why he is so sure about this, he would no doubt remind us of the unworthy picture of deity painted by the poets and of the natural explanations that can be given for phenomena they ascribe to the gods. Xenophanes' point is that a poet's claim of divine revelation is no guarantee of her poem's truth.

2. How, then, is it appropriate to form our beliefs? By "**seeking**," Xenophanes tells us. This idea is extremely vague. How, exactly, are we to seek? No doubt he has in mind the methods of the Ionian nature philosophers, but we don't have a very good idea of just what they were, so we don't get much help at this point.

Still, his remarks are not entirely without content. He envisages a process of moving toward the truth. If we want the truth, we should face not the past but the future. It is no good looking back to the tradition, to Homer and Hesiod, as though they had already said the last words. We must look to ourselves and to the results of our seeking. He is confident, perhaps because he values the results of the nature philosophers, that "in time"—not all at once—we will discover "what is better." We may not succeed in finding the truth, but our opinions will be "better," or more "like the truth." *

3. It may be that we know some **truth** already. Perhaps there is even someone who knows "the whole truth." But even if he did, that person could not know for certain that it is the truth. To use a distinction Plato later makes much of, the person would not be able to distinguish his knowledge of the truth from mere opinion.† (Plato, as we'll see, does not agree.) There is, Xenophanes means to tell us, no such thing as *certainty* for limited human beings such as ourselves. Here is a theme that later skeptics take up.‡

4. It does not follow from this somewhat skeptical conclusion that all beliefs are equally good. Xenophanes is very clear that although we may not ever be certain we have reached the truth, some beliefs are better or more "like the truth" than others. Unfortunately, he does not tell us how we are to tell which are more truthlike. Again we have a problem that many later thinkers take up.

5. Here we have a new direction for thought. Until now, thought has basically been directed outward—to the gods, to the world of human beings, to nature. Xenophanes directs thought back upon itself. His questioning questions itself. How much can we know? How can we know it? Can we reach the truth? Can we reach certainty about the truth? These are the central questions that define the branch of philosophy called **epistemology,** the theory of knowledge. It seems correct to say that Xenophanes is its father.

"I was born not knowing and have only had a little time to change that here and there."

Richard Feynman (1918–1988)

---

6. If we ask, then, whether there is anyone who can know the truth *and* know that he knows it, what is the answer? Yes. The one god does, the one who "sees all over, thinks all over, hears all over." In this answer, Xenophanes carries forward that strain of Homeric tradition emphasizing the gulf between humans and gods. The most important truth about humans is that they are not gods.* Xenophanes' remarks about human knowledge seem designed to drive that point home once and for all.

---

1. What are Xenophanes' criticisms of the Homeric gods?
2. What is his conception of the one god?
3. Can we know the truth about things, according to Xenophanes? If so, how?
4. Relate his sayings about knowing the truth to the idea of hubris and to claims made by Hesiod and Homer.

---

*In recent philosophy these themes have been taken up by the *fallibilists.* See C. S. Peirce (p. 571).

†See pp. 119–121.

‡See, for instance, the discussions by Sextus Empiricus (pp. 209–215) and Montaigne (pp. 303–306). Similar themes are found in Descartes' first *Meditation.*

---

*Compare the poem of Pindar, part of which is quoted on p. 8.

Heraclitus: Oneness in the *Logos*

Heraclitus is said to have been at his peak (probably corresponding to middle age) shortly before 500 B.C. A native of Ephesus (see Map 1), he was, like the others we have considered, an Ionian Greek living on the shores of Asia Minor. We know that he wrote a book, of which about one hundred fragments remain. He had a reputation for writing in riddles and was often referred to in Roman times as "Heraclitus the obscure." His favored style seems to have been the epigram, the short, pithy saying that condenses a lot of thought into a few words. Despite his reputation, most modern interpreters find that the fragments reveal a powerful and unified view of the world and man's place in it. Furthermore, Heraclitus is clearly an important influence on subsequent thinkers such as Plato and the Stoics.

One characteristic feature of his thought is that reality is a flux.

> All things come into being through opposition, and all are in flux, like a river. (DK 22 A 1, *IEGP,* 89)

There are two parts to this saying, one about **opposition** and one about **flux**. Let's begin with the latter and discuss the part about opposition later.

Plato ascribes to Heraclitus the view that "you cannot step twice into the same river." If you know anything at all about Heraclitus, it is probably in connection with this famous saying. What Heraclitus actually says, however, is slightly different.

> Upon those who step into the same rivers flow other and yet other waters. (DK 22 B 12, *IEGP,* 91)

You can, he says, step several times into the same river. Yet it is not the same, for the waters into which you step the second time are different waters. So, you both can and cannot.

This oneness of things that are different—even sometimes opposite—is a theme Heraclitus plays in many variations:

> The path traced by the pen is straight and crooked. (DK 22 B 59, *IEGP,* 93)

> Sea water is very pure and very impure; drinkable and healthful for fishes, but undrinkable and destructive to men. (DK 22 B 61, *IEGP,* 93)

> The way up and the way down are the same. (DK 22 B 60, *IEGP,* 94)

The road from Canterbury to Dover is the road from Dover to Canterbury. They are "the same," just as it is the same water that is healthful and destructive, the same movement of the pen that is crooked (when you consider the individual letters) but also straight (when you consider the line written).

Consider the river. It is the same river, although the water that makes it up is continually changing. A river is not identical with the water that makes it up but is a kind of structure or pattern that makes a unity of ever-changing elements. It is a *one* that holds together the *many*. So it is, Heraclitus tells us, with "all things." All things are in flux, like the river: ever-changing, yet preserving an identity through the changes. The river is for that reason a fit symbol for reality.

Another appropriate symbol for this flux is fire.

> This world-order, the same for all, no god made or any man, but it always was and is and will be an ever-lasting fire, kindling by measure and going out by measure. (DK 22 B 30, *IEGP,* 90)

Is Heraclitus here expressing disagreement with Thales? Is he telling us Thales is wrong in thinking that water is the source of all things—that it isn't water, but fire? Not exactly.

Remember that at this early stage of thought the very language in which thoughts can be expressed is itself being formed. This means that thought is somewhat crude, as we observed earlier. Thinkers have not yet made a distinction between "hot-stuff" and "fire that is hot." Heraclitus is reaching for abstractions that he hasn't quite got and cannot quite express. What he wants to talk about is the "world-order." This is, we would say, not itself a thing but an abstract pattern or structure in which the things of the world are displayed. Heraclitus, though, hasn't quite got that degree of abstraction, so he uses the most ethereal, least solid thing he is acquainted with to represent this world-order: fire.

We can be certain, moreover, that Heraclitus does not have ordinary cooking fires primarily in mind. Recall the view of Anaximander that the outermost sphere of the universe, in which the sun and stars are located, is a ring of fire. If you have ever been to Greece on a particularly clear day, especially on or near the sea, you can see even through our polluted atmosphere that not only the sun but also the entire sky shines. The heavens are luminous, radiant. It is not too much to say the sky blazes. In this luminous *aether,* as it was called, the gods are supposed to live. Olympus is said to be their home because its peak is immersed in this fiery element. Notice the epithet Heraclitus gives to fire: He calls it "ever-lasting." What, for the Greeks, deserves this accolade? Only, of course, the divine.

It is, then, the world-order itself that is immortal, divine. Heraclitus represents it as fire, the most ethereal and least substantial of the elements. No god made *that,* of course, for the world-order is itself eternal and divine.

This divine fire is both the substance of the world and its pattern. In its former aspect it is ever "kindling by measure and going out by measure." This thought is also expressed in the following fragments:

> The changes of fire: first sea, and of sea half is earth, half fiery thunderbolt. . . . (DK 22 B 31, *IEGP,* 91)

> All things are an exchange for fire, and fire for all things; as goods are for gold, and gold for goods. (DK 22 B 90, *IEGP,* 91)

The sea, we learn, is a mixture, half earth and half fire. All things are in continuous exchange. Earth is washed into the sea and becomes moist; sea becomes air, which merges with the fiery heavens, from which rains fall and merge again with earth. If Heraclitus were able to use the distinction between things and patterns, he might say that *as substance* fire has no priority over other things. It is just one of the four elements taking part with the others in the constant cycles of change. But *as pattern,* as world-order, it does have priority, for this pattern is eternal and divine. He does not, of course, say this; he can't. If he were able to, he might be less obscure to his successors.

We need now to go back to the first part of our original fragment, where Heraclitus says that "all things come into being through opposition." What can this mean? Compare the following statements:

> War is the father and king of all. . . . (DK 22 B 53, *IEGP,* 93)

> It is necessary to understand that war is universal and justice is strife, and that all things take place in accordance with strife and necessity. (DK 22 B 80, *IEGP,* 93)

Strife, opposition, war. Why are these elevated into universal principles? To see what Heraclitus is saying, think about some examples. A lyre will produce music, but only if there is a tension on the strings. The arms of the lyre pull in one direction, the strings in the opposite. Without this opposition, there is no music. Consider the river. What is it that makes a river a river? It is the force of the flowing water struggling with the opposing forces of the containing banks. Without the opposition between the banks and the water, there would be no river. Think of a sculpture. It is the result of the efforts of the artist and the chisel fighting the resistance of the stone.

Here's another example, showing two of Heraclitus' themes: A bicycle wheel is *one* thing, though it is composed of *many* parts: hub, spokes, and rim. What makes these many items into one wheel? The tension that truing the wheel puts on the spokes, so that the hub and rim are pulling in opposite directions.

Now, if we think not about physical phenomena but about society, we see that the same is true. What is justice, Heraclitus asks, but the result of the conflict between the desires of the wealthy and the desires of the poor? Were either to get the upper hand absolutely, there would be no justice. Tension, opposition, and conflict, he tells us, are *necessary.* Without them the universe could not persist. If we look carefully at each of these examples, we see that each consists of a unity of diverse elements. The lyre, the river, the statue, the bicycle wheel, and justice are each a one composed in some sense of many. In every "one," "many" strive.

In *The Iliad,* Achilles laments the death of Patroclus, saying,

> "If only strife could die from the lives of gods and men."

> —*The Iliad,* Book 18, 126

To this cry, Heraclitus responds,

He did not see that he was praying for the destruction of the whole; for if his prayers were heard, all things would pass away. (DK 22 A 22, *IEGP*, 93)

Strife, then, is necessary. It produces not chaos but the opposite; in fact, the divine world-order is the guarantee that a balance of forces is maintained. The result is this:

To god all things are beautiful and good and just; but men suppose some things to be just and others unjust. (DK 22 B 102, *IEGP*, 92)

Again we see the Homeric contrast between gods and mortals, and again the contrast is to the disadvantage of mortals. God, the divine fire, the world-order, sees things as they are; and they are good. Strife is not opposed to the good; strife is its necessary presupposition. Mortals, such as Achilles, only "suppose," and what they suppose is false.

It is not characteristic of men to be intelligent; but it is characteristic of god. (DK 22 B 78, *IEGP*, 98)

We are now ready to consider the most explicit version of Heraclitus' solution to the problem of the one and the many. To do that, I must introduce a term that I will usually leave untranslated. It is a term that has numerous meanings in Greek and has had a long and important history, stretching from Heraclitus to the Sophists, to Plato and Aristotle, into the writings of the New Testament and the Christian church fathers, and beyond. The term is *logos*.*

Logos is derived from a verb meaning "to speak" and refers first of all to the word or words that a speaker says. As in English, however, a term is easily stretched beyond its simple, literal meaning. As we can ask for the latest word about the economy, the Greek can ask for the *logos* about the economy, meaning something like "message" or "discourse." This meaning easily slides into the *thought* expressed in a discourse. Because such thought is typically backed up by reasons or has a rationale behind it, *logos* also

comes to mean "rationale" or "argument." Arguments are composed of conclusions and the reasons offered for those conclusions. So, an argument has a typical pattern or structure to it, which is the job of *logic* to display. (Our term "logic" is derived from the Greek *logos*.) *Logos*, then, can also mean a structure or pattern, particularly if the pattern is a rational one.

You can see that *logos* is a very rich term, containing layers of related meanings: word, message, discourse, thought, rationale, argument, pattern, structure. When the word is used in Greek, it reverberates with all these associations. We have no precise equivalent in English, and for that reason I usually do not translate it.

As we have seen, Heraclitus claims that all things are in a process of continual change and that part of what makes them the things they are is a tension between opposite forces. This world of changes is not a chaos but is structured by a world-order that is divine in nature; in itself, therefore, it is good and beautiful. Unfortunately,

the many do not understand such things.* (DK 22 B 17, *IEGP*, 94)

Though the *logos* is as I have said, men always fail to comprehend it, both before they hear it and when they hear it for the first time. For though all things come into being in accordance with this *logos*, they seem like men without experience. (DK 22 B 1, *IEGP*, 94)

Now Heraclitus tells us that there is a *logos* by which "all things come into being." What else is this but the structure or pattern of the world-order that we have met before? But now the conception is deepened. The *logos* is not just accidentally what it is. There is a logic to it that can be seen to be reasonable and right. It is not understood, however, by "the many." As Socrates does later, Heraclitus contrasts the few who are wise, who listen to the *logos*, with the many who are foolish.

Why is it that the many do not understand the *logos*? Is it so strange and distant that only a few people ever have a chance to become acquainted with it? Not at all.

---

*Postmodern critics of the Western philosophic tradition often call it "logocentric," meaning that it privileges rationality and assumes that words—especially spoken discourse—can adequately mirror reality. See Jacques Derrida, p. 681.

---

*His term "the many" usually applies to all the individual things of which the world is composed; here, of course, it means "most people."

Though they are in daily contact with the *logos* they are at variance with it, and what they meet appears alien to them. (DK 22 B 73, *IEGP*, 94)

To those who are awake the world-order is one, common to all; but the sleeping turn aside each into a world of his own. (DK 22 B 89, *IEGP*, 95)

We ought to follow what is common to all; but though the *logos* is common to all, the many live as though their thought were private to themselves. (DK 22 B 2, *IEGP*, 95)

All people are "in daily contact" with this *logos*. It is all about us, present in everything that happens. You can't do or say anything without being immersed in it. Yet we ignore it. We are like sleepers who live in private dreams rather than in awareness of this rational pattern of things that "is common to all." We each manufacture a little world of our own, no doubt distorted by our own interests, fears, and anxieties, which we take for reality.

In so doing, we miss the *logos* and become foolish rather than wise. What is it, after all, to be wise?

Wisdom is one thing: to understand the thought which steers all things through all things. (DK 22 B 41, *IEGP*, 88)

The one and only wisdom is willing and unwilling to be called Zeus. (DK 22 B 32, *IEGP*, 88)

To be wise is to understand the nature and structure of the world. To be wise is to see that all is and must be ever-changing, that strife and opposition are necessary and not evil, and that if appreciated apart from our narrowly construed interests, they are good and beautiful. To be wise is to grasp the *logos,* the "thought which steers all things."* To be wise is to participate in the perspective of Zeus.

Why is this **wisdom** both "willing and unwilling" to be called by the name of Zeus? We can assume it is willing because Zeus is the common name for the highest of the gods, for the divine; to have such wisdom makes one a participant in the divine. Acting according to the *logos* is manifesting in one's life the very principles that govern the universe. However, such wisdom refuses the name of Zeus as

---

*Compare Anaximander, p. 12. Heraclitus here identifies that which "steers all things" as a thought. This theme is later developed by the Stoics. See pp. 205–207.

Homer pictures him: immoral, unworthy, and no better than one of the many who do not understand the *logos*. Heraclitus, we see, agrees with the criticisms of traditional religion offered by Xenophanes.

Hesitant to reinforce these traditional pictures of deity, Heraclitus tells us,

Thunderbolt steers all things. (DK 22 B 64, *IEGP*, 89)

As we have just seen, there is a "thought" (a *logos*) that steers all things. Now we are told it is "thunderbolt." Thus we are brought back to the idea that a divine fire both *is* the world-order and manifests itself *in* that world-order. Reluctant to use the name of Zeus, Heraclitus chooses the most dramatic form of fire familiar to early humans: lightning, the weapon Zeus supposedly uses to enforce his will. This "fire" is also the *logos,* the pattern or structure providing the unity of the world. This is what makes one world out of the many things.

Perhaps people are not to be too much blamed, however, for their lack of wisdom. For

Nature loves to hide. (DK 22 B 123, *IEGP*, 96)

and

The lord whose oracle is at Delphi neither speaks out nor conceals, but gives a sign. (DK 22 B 93, *IEGP*, 96)

Even though the *logos* is common to all, even though all our experience testifies to it, discerning this *logos* is difficult. It is rather like a riddle; the answer may be implicit, but it is still hard to make out. Solving the problem is like interpreting the ambiguous pronouncements of the famous oracle at Delphi, located north and west of Athens (see Map 1). People could go there and ask the oracle a question, as Croesus, king of the Lydians (see Map 1), once did. He wanted to know whether to go to war against the Persians. He was told that if he went to war a mighty empire would fall. Encouraged by this reply, he set forth, only to find the oracle's pronouncement validated by his own defeat.

How, then, is the riddle to be unraveled? How can we become wise, learning the secrets of the *logos*? This is a question, remember, that we have asked before. Xenophanes has told us that by

THE TAO

One sometimes finds that similar thoughts are expressed at about the same time in areas of the world that are widely separated in space. So it is with Heraclitus and the author of the *Tao Te Ching*. This Chinese classic is traditionally ascribed to Lao Tzu, said to be an older contemporary of Confucius in the sixth century, B.C., although the text as we have it is from a later date. It is a small book of eighty-one chapters, each containing a set of brief, aphoristic sayings, often obscure to the casual reader. The term "Tao" means "the way."* "Te," variously translated as "nature," "power," or "virtue," is the way the Tao manifests itself in human life. The term "Ching" means a sacred text.

Our lives are usually pretty frantic. We desire some things and fear losing others. We spend energy worrying about deteriorating relationships, trying to understand why others don't like us. We think more knowledge will help and find only new problems. Our changeable feelings drive us first this way, then that. We feel like we have lost our way. We have lost our way. We have lost *the* way, the **Tao**.

> There was something formless and perfect
> Before the universe was born.
> It is serene. Empty.
> Solitary. Unchanging.
> Infinite. Eternally present.
> It is the mother of the universe.
> For lack of a better name,
> I call it the Tao.
>
> *TTC*, 25

> It has no desires for itself;
> Thus it is present for all beings.
>
> *TTC*, 7

The origin of all things, the Tao, cannot properly be named or described; what can be named are the ten thousand things that arise out of it and flow back into it in a ceaseless process. Look out the window; do you see those trees, the pines, the oaks? Each

expresses the Tao in its own way—comes into being, lives for a time, and passes away again, without anxiety, without fear or desire. ("Consider the lilies of the field," Jesus said.)

A friend of mine emailed me on a dark day of high winds and much rain. "A yucky day," he said. I wrote back: "I thought the rain was glorious; and now the sun is breaking through the clouds. It's all good." That's close, but not quite right.

> When people see some things as beautiful,
> other things become ugly.
> When people see some things as good,
> other things become bad.
>
> *TTC*, 2

The terms "beautiful" and "ugly," "good" and "bad" express desires we have. My friend didn't like the day, didn't want it to be that way, wanted it to be different. So he called it "yucky." But the Tao "has no desires for itself"; that is why it can be "present for all beings."

> The great Tao flows everywhere.
> All things are born from it,
> yet it doesn't create them.
> It pours itself into its work,
> yet it makes no claim.
> It nourishes infinite worlds,
> yet it doesn't hold on to them.
> Since it is merged with all things
> and hidden in their hearts,
> it can be called humble.
> Since all things vanish into it
> and it alone endures,
> it can be called great.
> It isn't aware of its greatness;
> thus it is truly great.*
>
> *TTC*, 34

If the Tao "flows everywhere," then it flows also in us. If "all things are born from it," then so are we. But our problem is the same as that diagnosed by

---

*It is of interest to note that early Christianity was known simply as "the Way." And in his book *The Abolition of Man*, the Christian writer, C. S. Lewis, refers to the pattern of objective values in reality as "*the Tao*."

*Compare Plotinus on the emanation of all things from the One (pp. 235–236). And contrast this with Augustine's concept of creation out of nothing (pp. 236–237).

(continued)

THE TAO   *(continued)*

Heraclitus: Though we are in daily contact with it (he calls it the *logos*), we are "at variance with it," and it appears alien to us. Though it is "common to all," yet we live in worlds private to ourselves. Unlike the Tao, we make claims, hold on to things, want to be called great. Thus we miss true greatness and are lost in the swamps of comparison, contempt, and violence.

When goodness doesn't flow naturally, people feel the need for rules, so they try to legislate goodness. When piety is not natural, it must be imposed. We feel that we have to *make* people good and pious. Or we try to *make ourselves* just and good. But this never really works; it only produces arrogance and self-righteousness.

> The more prohibitions you have,
> the less virtuous people will be.*
>
> *TTC, 57*

About this sort of "goodness," the *Tao Te Ching* says,

> Throw away holiness and wisdom,
> and people will be a hundred times happier.
> Throw away morality and justice,
> and people will do the right thing.
>
> *TTC, 19*

When will they do the right thing? When they live in the Tao. Paradoxically, however,

> The Tao never does anything,
> yet through it all things are done.
>
> *TTC, 37*

And that is precisely the secret. When we live in the Tao, it is the Tao itself that accomplishes what we do. That is the Way.

> Less and less do you need to force things,
> until finally you arrive at non-action.
> When nothing is done,
> nothing is left undone.
>
> *TTC, 48*

> The Master allows things to happen.
> She shapes events as they come.

---

*Compare St. Paul in Romans 2:16. "By works of the law shall no one be justified."

> She steps out of the way
> And lets the Tao speak for itself.*
>
> *TTC, 45*

Non-action, that's the key. Watch Roger Federer, one of the world's top tennis players. Fluidly, almost effortlessly, he's where he needs to be for the next shot. Shaping events as they come, he "steps out of the way" and lets the game play itself. Life can be like that, the Taoist says.

> The Master . . . doesn't think about his
>   actions;
> they flow from the core of his being.
>
> *TTC, 50*

> The Master can keep giving
> because there is no end to her wealth.
> She acts without expectation,
> succeeds without taking credit,
> and doesn't think that she is better
> than anyone else.
>
> *TTC, 77*

We are usually so full of self that we see everything in terms of benefit or harm to ourselves. We hope for this and fear that. But

> Hope and fear are both phantoms
> that arise from thinking of the self.
> When we don't see the self as self,
> what do we have to fear?

> See the world as your self.
> Have faith in the way things are.
> Love the world as your self;
> then you can care for all things.†
>
> *TTC, 13*

Sometimes, of course, things do not go as we expect. Even Roger Federer loses occasionally.

---

*The translator, Stephen Mitchell, sometimes uses the masculine, sometimes the feminine form to refer to human beings—just like the author of this book! Compare again St. Paul at Galatians 2:20: "It is no longer I who live, but Christ who lives in me."

†Compare the Stoics on keeping our wills in harmony with nature (p. 205).

(continued)

THE TAO (continued)

What then?

> Failure is an opportunity.
> If you blame someone else,
> there is no end to the blame.
>
> Therefore the Master
> fulfills her own obligations
> and corrects her own mistakes.
> She does what she needs to do
> and demands nothing of others.
>
> *TTC,* 79

In sum,

> If you don't realize the source,
> You stumble in confusion and sorrow.
> When you realize where you come from,

> You naturally become tolerant,
> Disinterested, amused,
> Kindhearted as a grandmother,
> Dignified as a king.
> Immersed in the wonder of the Tao,
> you can deal with whatever life brings you,
> and when death comes, you are ready.
>
> *TTC,* 16

NOTE:

There are more than forty English translations of the *Tao Te Ching.* This one, translated by Stephen Mitchell (New York: HarperCollins, 1988), is more free than some, but captures the spirit of the text very well. For a charming introduction to the Tao, see *The Tao of Pooh,* Benjamin Hoff (New York: Penguin Books, 1982).

"seeking" we can improve our opinions, but that is pretty uninformative.* Does Heraclitus advance our understanding any? To some degree he does. Two fragments that seem to be in some tension with each other address this issue:

> Those things of which there is sight, hearing, understanding, I esteem most. (DK 22 B 55, *IEGP,* 96)
>
> Eyes and ears are bad witnesses to men if they have souls that do not understand their language. (DK 22 B 107, *IEGP,* 96)

We can come to understand the world-order, then, not by listening to poets, seers, or self-proclaimed wise men but by using our eyes and ears. Yet we must be careful, for the senses can deceive us, can be "bad witnesses." They must be used critically, and not everyone "understands their language." These few remarks do not, of course, take us very far. Later philosophers will fill in this picture.

Finally, Heraclitus draws from his view of the *logos* some significant conclusions for the way humans should live:

> It is not good for men to get all they wish. (DK 22 B 110, *IEGP,* 97)

> If happiness consisted in bodily pleasures we ought to call oxen happy who find vetch to eat. (DK 22 B 4, *IEGP,* 101)
>
> It is hard to fight against impulse; for what it wants it buys at the expense of the soul. (DK 22 B 85, *IEGP,* 101)
>
> Moderation is the greatest virtue, and wisdom is to speak the truth and to act according to nature, giving heed to it. (DK 22 B 112, *IEGP,* 101)

Why is it not good for men to get all they wish? If they did so, they would destroy the necessary tensions that make possible the very existence of both themselves and the things they want. They would overstep the bounds set by the *logos,* which allows the world to exist at all—a "many" unified by the "one." We must limit our desires, not for prudish or puritanical reasons, but because opposition is the very life of the world-order. Suppose I have a taste for sweets and indulge that taste without limit. I soon find myself ill or, if I persist, dead. Suppose, instead, you want at any cost to be thin like the supermodels. We know what sad consequences such unlimited desires bring. Similarly, Achilles indulges his impulse to anger with disastrous results. Of course, such impulses are "hard to fight against." Why? Because indulging them at

---

*See p. 18.

all strengthens them, and we cannot help indulging them to some degree. Indulging an impulse seems to diminish the resources of the soul to impose limits on that impulse. Such indulgence is bought "at the expense of the soul."*

That is why wisdom is difficult and why it is missed by the many. They, like cattle, seek to maximize their bodily pleasures. In doing so, they are "at variance" with the *logos,* which requires of every force that it be limited. That is why "moderation is the greatest virtue"—and why it is so rare.

Note that Heraclitus ties his ethics intimately to his vision of the nature of things. The *logos* without is to be reflected in the *logos* within. Wisdom is "to speak the truth and to act according to nature." To speak the truth is to let one's words (one's *logos*) be responsive to the *logos* that is the world-order. To speak falsely is to be at variance with that *logos.* All one's actions should reflect that balance, the moderation nature displays to all who understand its ways. In the plea for moderation, Heraclitus reflects the main moral tradition of the Greeks since Homer, but he sets it in a larger context and justifies it in terms of the very nature of the universe itself and its divine *logos.*

In his exaltation of the few over the many, Heraclitus also reflects Homeric values.

> One man is worth ten thousand to me, if only he be best. (DK 22 B 49, *IEGP,* 104)

> For the best men choose one thing above all the rest: everlasting fame among mortal men. But the many have glutted themselves like cattle. (DK 22 B 29, *IEGP,* 104)

The Homeric heroes seek their "everlasting fame" on the field of battle. Heraclitus, we feel, would seek it on the field of virtue.

In Heraclitus, then, we have a solution to the problem of the one and the many. We do live in one world, a *uni-*verse, despite the multitude of apparently different and often conflicting things we find in it. It is made one by the *logos,* the rational, divine, firelike pattern according to which things

---

*For a more recent semi-Heraclitean view of the need to be hard on oneself, see Nietzsche, p. 553.

behave. Conflict does not destroy the unity of the world; unless it goes to extremes, such tension is a necessary condition of its very existence. And if we see and hear and think rightly, we can line up our own lives according to this same *logos,* live in a self-disciplined and moderate way, and participate in the divine wisdom.

---

1. What does Heraclitus mean when he says that all things are "in flux"? Give your own examples.
2. In what sense is the "world-order" fire? Why was it not made by any god?
3. Explain the saying "War is the father and king of all."
4. What is the *logos?*
5. How is it that we "fail to comprehend" the *logos?*
6. What is wisdom? Why is it "willing and unwilling" to be called Zeus?
7. Why is it not good for us to get all we wish? Why is it "hard to fight against impulse"? Why should we fight against it anyway?
8. Sum up Heraclitus' solution to the problem of the one and the many.

Parmenides: Only the One

Parmenides introduces the strangest thought so far. His view is hard for us to grasp. Once we see what he is saying, moreover, we find it hard to take seriously. So we need to make a special effort to understand. It helps to keep in mind that Parmenides is not an isolated figure independent of any context; he is a participant in the great conversation and constantly has in mind the views of his predecessors and contemporaries, some of whom are familiar to us.

What makes the argument of Parmenides so alien to us is its conclusion; most people simply cannot believe it. The conclusion is that there is no "many"; only "**the One**" exists. We find this hard to believe because our experience is so obviously manifold. There is the desk, and here is the chair. They are two; the chair is not the desk and the desk is not the chair. So, at least, it seems. If Parmenides is to convince us otherwise, he has his work cut out for him. He is well aware of this situation and addresses the problem explicitly.

Parmenides was not an Ionian, as were Thales, Anaximander, Xenophanes, and Heraclitus. This fact is significant because, in a sense, geographical location is not intellectually neutral. Different places develop different traditions. Parmenides lived at the opposite edge of Greek civilization in what is now the southern part of Italy, where there were numerous Greek colonies. He came from a city called Elea (see Map 2), which, according to tradition, was well governed in part through Parmenides' efforts. Plato tells us that Parmenides once visited Athens in his old age and conversed with the young Socrates. If this is so, Parmenides must have been born about 515 B.C. and lived until at least the year 450 B.C.

Parmenides wrote a book, in verse, of which substantial parts have come down to us. In the prologue, he claims to have been driven by horse and chariot into the heavens and escorted into the presence of a goddess who spoke to him, saying,

> Welcome, youth, who come attended by immortal charioteers and mares which bear you on your journey to our dwelling. For it is no evil fate that has set you to travel on this road, far from the beaten paths of men, but right and justice. It is meet that you learn all things—both the unshakable heart of well-rounded truth and the opinions of mortals in which there is no true belief. (DK 28 B 1, *IEGP,* 108–109)

Such language might seem to be a throwback to the kinds of claims made by Hesiod.* Parmenides is telling us that the content of his poem has been revealed to him by divine powers. Is this philosophy? In fact, it is. The content of the revelation is an **argument,** and the goddess admonishes him to

> judge by reasoning the much-contested argument that I have spoken. (DK 28 B 7, *IEGP,* 111)

The claim that this argument was revealed to him by a goddess may reflect the fact that the argument came to him in an ecstatic or inspired state. Or it may just be a sign of how different from ordinary mortal thought the "well-rounded truth" really is. In either case, the claim that the poem is a

revelation is inessential. We are invited to *judge* it, not just to accept it; we are to judge it "by reasoning." This is the key feature of philosophy.*

Note that the goddess reveals to him two ways: the truth and the "opinions of mortals," which deal not with truth but with **appearance.** His poem is in fact set up in two parts, "The Way of Truth" and "The Way of Opinion." Because it is the former that has been influential, we'll concentrate on it.

What, then, is this argument that yields such strange conclusions? It begins with something Parmenides thought impossible to deny.

> Thinking and the thought that it is are the same; for you will not find thought apart from what is, in relation to which it is uttered. (DK 28 B 8, *IEGP,* 110)

When you *think,* the content of your thinking is a *thought.* And every thought has the form: It *is* so and so. If you think, "This desk is brown," you are thinking what *is,* namely, the desk and its color. If you think "This desk is not brown," once more you are thinking of what *is,* namely, the desk. Suppose you say, "But I am thinking that it is *not brown;* so I am thinking of what is *not.*" Parmenides will reply that "not brown" is just an unclear way of expressing the real thought, which is that the desk *is,* let us say, gray. If you are thinking of the desk, you are thinking of *it* with whatever color it has. Suppose you say, "But I am thinking of a unicorn, and there aren't any unicorns; so am I not thinking of what is not?" No, Parmenides might say, for what is a unicorn? A horse with a single horn, and horses and horns both *are.*† So once again we do not "find thought apart from what is." To think at all, he tells us, is to think that something *is.*

> For thought and being are the same. (DK 28 B 3, *IEGP,* 110)

They are "the same" in much the same way that for Heraclitus the way up and the way down are

---

*Look again at Hesiod's description of his inspiration by the Muses, p. 2.

---

*Socrates insists that when a statement is made, we must "examine" it. See pp. 64–67.

†Actually, it is not entirely clear how Parmenides deals with thoughts that are apparently about nonexistent things. This is a puzzle that is not cleared up until the twentieth century by Bertrand Russell. See the brief treatment of his celebrated Theory of Definite Descriptions on p. 590.

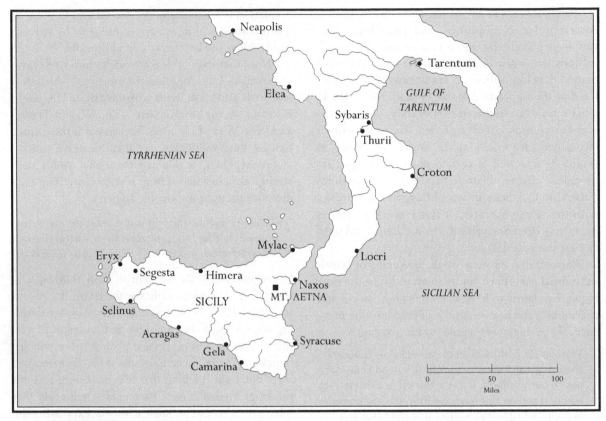

MAP 2 Southern Italy and Sicily

the same. If you have the one, you also have the other. The concept of "being" is just the concept of "what is," as opposed to "what is not." Whenever you think, you are thinking of what is. Thinking and being, then, are inseparable.

This is Parmenides' starting point. It seems rather abstract and without much content. How can the substantial conclusions we hinted at be derived from such premises? The way to do it is to derive a corollary of this point.

> It is necessary to speak and to think what is; for being is, but nothing is not. (DK 28 B 6, *IEGP,* 111)

You cannot think "nothing." Why not? Because nothing *is not,* and to think is (as we have seen) to think of what *is.* If you could think of nothing, it would (by the first premise) be *something.* But that is contradictory. Nothing cannot be something! Nothing "is not."

That still does not seem very exciting. Yet from this point remarkable conclusions follow (or seem to follow; whether the argument is a sound one we will examine later).* In particular, all our beliefs about *the many* must be false. You believe, for example, that this book you are reading is one thing and the hand you are touching it with is another, so you believe that there are *many* things. If Parmenides' argument is correct, however, that belief is false. In reality there is no distinction between them. Parmenides describes ordinary mortals who do not grasp that fact in this way:

> Helplessness guides the wandering thought in their breasts; they are carried along deaf and blind alike, dazed, beasts without judgment, convinced that to be and not to be are the same and not the same, and that the road of all things is a backward-turning one. (DK 28 B 6, *IEGP,* 111)

---

*See the critique by Democritus on pp. 33–34.

This is harsh! The language he uses makes it clear that he has in mind not only common folks but also philosophers—Heraclitus in particular. It is Heraclitus who insists more rigorously than anyone else that "to be and not to be are the same" (to be straight, for instance, and not straight).* Whatever is, Heraclitus tells us, is only temporary; all is involved in the universal flux, coming into being and passing out of being. In that sense, "the road of all things" is indeed "a backward-turning one." You may be reminded of the phrase common in funeral services: "Ashes to ashes, dust to dust."

Parmenides tells us, however, that to think in this way is to be blind, deaf, helpless, dazed—no better than a beast. Things cannot be so. To say that something "comes into being" is to imply that it formerly *was not*. But this is something that you can neither imply, nor say, nor even think sensibly, for it involves the notion of **"not-being."** And we have already seen that not-being cannot be thought. It is inconceivable, for "thought and being are the same." So we are confused when we speak of something coming into being. We do not know what we are saying.

The same argument holds for passing away. The fundamental idea involved in passing away is that something leaves the realm of being (of what is) and moves into the realm of not-being (of what is not). My dog dies and *is no more*—or so it seems. But Parmenides argues that this is really inconceivable. Passing away would involve the notion of what is not, but *what is not* cannot be thought. If it cannot be thought, it cannot be. There is no "realm of not being." There couldn't be.

Parmenides summarizes the argument:

How could what is perish? How could it have come to be? For if it came into being, it is not; nor is it if ever it is going to be. Thus coming into being is extinguished, and destruction unknown. (DK 28 B 8, *IEGP,* 113)

But if there can be no coming into being and passing away, then there can be no Heraclitean flux.

Indeed, the common experience that things do have beginnings and endings must be an illusion. **Change** is impossible!

For never shall this prevail: that things that are not, are. But hold back your thought from this way of inquiry, nor let habit born of long experience force you to ply an aimless eye and droning ear along this road; but judge by reasoning the much-contested argument that I have spoken. (DK 28 B 7, *IEGP,* 111)

We have already examined the last part of this passage, but it is important to see what contrasts with the "reasoning" that Parmenides commends. We are urged not to let our thought be formed by "habit born of long experience." Parmenides acknowledges that experience is contrary to the conclusions he is urging upon us. Of course the senses tell us that things change, that they begin and end, but Parmenides says not to rely on sensory experience. You must rely on reasoning alone. You must *go wherever the argument takes you,* even if it contradicts common sense and the persuasive evidence of the senses.*

In urging us to follow reason alone, Parmenides stands at the beginning of one of the major traditions in Western philosophy. Although we shouldn't take such "isms" too seriously, it is useful to give that tradition a name. It is called **rationalism.** Parmenides is rightly considered the first rationalist philosopher.

Notice the contrast to the Ionian nature philosophers. They all try to explain the nature of the things we observe; they start by assuming that the world is composed of many different things changing in many different ways, and it never occurs to them to question this assumption. Heraclitus, remember, says that he esteems most the things we can see and hear and understand.† Parmenides resolutely rejects this reliance on the senses.

---

*See the remark on p. 19 about the path traced by the pen.

*We will see this theme repeated by Socrates; if it is true that as a young man Socrates conversed with Parmenides (as Plato tells us), it is likely that he learned this principle from him. For an example, see *Crito* 46b, p. 107.

†In the seventeenth and eighteenth centuries, such reliance on sensory data is called *empiricism* and is starkly contrasted to rationalism. For an example, see pp. 397–398.

He has not finished, however, deriving surprising conclusions from his principles. If we grant his premises, he tells us, we must also acknowledge that what exists

> is now, all at once, one and continuous. (DK 28 B 8, *IEGP,* 113)

> Nor is it divisible, since it is all alike; nor is there any more or less of it in one place which might prevent it from holding together, but all is full of what is. (DK 28 B 8, *IEGP,* 114)

What is must exist "all at once." This means that time itself must be unreal, an illusion. Why? Because the present can only be identified as the present by distinguishing it from the past (which is *no longer*) and from the future (which is *not yet*), and this shows that the notions of past and future both involve the unthinkable notion of "what is not." So "what is" must exist all at once in a continuous present. This thought is later exploited by St. Augustine in his notion of God.*

Moreover, *what is* must be indivisible; it cannot have parts. Why? Well, what could separate one thing from another? Only *what is not,* and what is not *cannot be.* You might be inclined to object at this point and say that one thing can be separated from another by some third thing. But the question repeats itself: What separates the first thing from the third? There can't be an infinite number of things between any two things, so at some point you will have to say that the only difference between them is that the one just *is not* the other. But, if Parmenides is right, that's impossible. So all is "full of what is."

It follows, of course, that there cannot be a vortex motion, as Anaximander thought, scattering stuff of different kinds to different places, because there cannot be things of different kinds. It is "all alike." There is not "any more or less of it in one place which might prevent it from holding together."† Why not? Because if there were "less" in

some place, this could only be because it is mixed with some nonbeing. Because there is no nonbeing, there cannot be a "**many**." The problem of the one and the many should never have come up!

It also follows that being must be uncreated and imperishable, without beginning or end. If *what there is* had come into being, it must have come from not being—but this is impossible. To perish, it would have to pass away into nothingness—but nothingness is not. So being can neither begin nor end. "For never shall this prevail: that things that are not, are."

We can characterize *what is* in the following terms. It is one, eternal, indivisible, and unchanging. If experience tells you otherwise, Parmenides says, so much the worse for experience.

If you think about it for just a moment, you can see that Parmenides has thrust to the fore one of the basic philosophical problems. It is called the problem of **appearance and reality.** Parmenides readily admits that the world *appears* to us to be many and to change continuously and that the things in it seem to move about. What he argues is that it is not so *in reality.* In reality, he holds, there is just the one. Any convictions we have to the contrary are just "the opinions of mortals in which there is no true belief."

We are all familiar with things not really being what they appear to be. Sticks in water appear to be bent when they are not. Roads sometimes appear to be wet when there is no water on them, and so on. The distinction is one we can readily understand. What is radical and disturbing about Parmenides' position is that everything our senses acquaint us with is allocated to the appearance side of the dichotomy. Nowhere do we sense what really is. Can this be right? This problem puzzles many a successor to Parmenides—or at least *appears* to do so!

Because these views are so strange, so alien to the usual ways of thinking, it is worth noting the response of Parmenides' contemporaries and successors. Do

---

*For Augustine, however, it is only God who enjoys this atemporal kind of eternity; time has a certain reality for Augustine—created and dependent, but not ultimate. See pp. 239–242.

†Anaximenes, a nature philosopher we are not considering, holds that air, when compressed, becomes cloud, then

---

water, then earth and stone. When more rarefied, it becomes fire. Parmenides argues that such an explanation for the many kinds of things we seem to experience is impossible, because such compression and rarefaction implicitly involve nonbeing.

they dismiss him as "that crazy Eleatic" who denies multiplicity and change? Do they think of him as a fool and charlatan? No, they take him very seriously. Plato, for example, always treats Parmenides with respect. Why? Because he, more successfully than anyone else up to his time, does what they are all trying to do: to follow reason wherever it leads. If his conclusions are uncongenial, that means only that his arguments must be examined carefully for any errors. Parmenides provides for the first time a coherent, connected argument—something you can really wrestle with. Succeeding philosophers have to come to terms with Parmenides in one way or another. Even though few accept his positive views, his influence is great, and his impact is still felt today.

1. What does Parmenides mean when he says that "thought and being are the same"?
2. What is the argument that there are not, in reality, *many* things?
3. If Parmenides is right, why must Heraclitus be wrong about all things being in flux?
4. Doesn't the testimony of our senses prove that there are many things? Why does Parmenides maintain that it does not?
5. How must reality (as opposed to appearance) be characterized?
6. In what sense is Parmenides a rationalist?

Zeno: The Paradoxes of Common Sense

In response to Parmenides' strange argument, you may be tempted to slice an apple in two just to prove that there really are many things, or wiggle your ears to show change actually happens. Of course, that won't do, because Parmenides has arguments to show that all this is merely appearance, not reality. Still, his conclusion is so at odds with common sense that we feel there must be something wrong with it.

One of Parmenides' pupils, **Zeno** by name, claims to have arguments showing that there is something even more wrong with common sense (and the natural science developing out of it) than simple falsity: It generates logical contradictions. It

is bad enough if a view conflicts with deeply held convictions, but it is even worse if those convictions turn out to be contradictory in themselves. So, Zeno holds, his arguments not only counter those who abuse his teacher, but also "pay them back with interest" (Plato, *Parmenides,* 128d).

Some of Zeno's arguments concern the many, but his most famous arguments concern change —in particular, the sort of change that we call "motion." Common sense assumes that motion is something real. The question is, however, Can we understand in a consistent way what common sense assumes? Let us look at three of Zeno's arguments.

1. Suppose Achilles were to enter a race with a tortoise. Being honorable and generous, the great runner would offer the tortoise a head start. The tortoise would lumber laboriously along, and after a suitable interval Achilles would spring from the starting blocks. But surprise! He would be unable, despite his utmost efforts, to catch the tortoise. Why?

Consider this: when Achilles begins to run, the tortoise is already at some point down the race course, call it A. In order to catch him, Achilles must first reach that point. That seems obvious. By the time Achilles has reached A, however, the tortoise has moved on to some further point, B. That also seems obvious. So Achilles needs to race to point B. He does so. Of course, by the time Achilles has attained B, the tortoise is at C. Another effort, this time to get to C, and again the tortoise is beyond him—at D. You can see that no matter how long the race goes on, Achilles will not catch the tortoise. So much for all that training!

This looks like a perfectly fair deduction from commonsense principles. So common sense holds both that one runner can catch another (because we see it done) *and* that one runner cannot catch another (as the argument shows). This is self-contradictory.

2. Consider an arrow in flight. Common sense holds that the arrow moves. Where does it move? Once this question is asked, it looks as though there are just two possibilities. Either the arrow moves in the space where it is, or it moves in some space where it is not—but neither is possible.

It obviously cannot move in a space it does not occupy, because it simply isn't there. Nor can it move in the space it occupies at any given moment, because at that moment it takes up the whole of that space, and there is no place left for it to move into. So the arrow cannot move at all. Once again, this seems a commonsense deduction; however, once again it is at odds with common sense itself, because nothing is more common than believing you can shoot an arrow at a target.

3. You no doubt believe that you can move from where you are now sitting to the door of the room. If you get a sudden yen for a pizza, you might just do it. Before you could get to the door, however, there is something else you would have to do first. You would have to get to the midpoint between where you are now and the door. That seems obvious—but consider: Before you could get to that point, there is something else you would have to do first. You would have to get to the midpoint between *that* point and where you are sitting. You can see how it goes. If you always have to get to one point before getting to a second, you will not even be able to get out of your chair!

Once again we see common sense in conflict with itself. If our common belief in motion contains self-contradictions, it cannot possibly be true; therefore, it cannot describe reality. You can see why Zeno thought these arguments paid back Parmenides' opponents "with interest."

Let us pause a moment to reflect on what kind of argument Zeno is using here. Logicians call it a **reductio ad absurdum** argument, or a reduction to absurdity. It has a form like this. (Let's take the arrow case as an example.)

Assume the truth of a proposition.

1. The arrow can move.

Deduce consequences from that assumption.

2. a. It must move either where it is or where it is not.
   b. It can do neither.

Draw the conclusion.

3. The arrow cannot move.

Display the contradiction.

4. The arrow can move (by 1), and the arrow cannot move (by 3).

Draw the final conclusion.

5. Motion is impossible because assuming it yields a contradiction—in 4—and no contradiction can possibly be true.

Reductio arguments are **valid** arguments.* They are very powerful arguments. That is why Zeno's arguments are so disturbing, and that is why articles trying to resolve the **paradoxes** still appear today in philosophical and scientific journals.

These are serious paradoxes. Their importance for our story is that they present examples of rigorous argument that opponents had to imitate to refute—another push toward rationalism. They also force a reconsideration of the basic notions of space, time, and motion—a process still going on in contemporary physics.

---

1. State Zeno's arguments against motion, and explain how they support Parmenides.
2. What is the pattern of a reductio ad absurdum argument?

Atomism: The One and the Many Reconciled

Anaximander and other nature philosophers proceed on the assumption that the world is pretty much as it seems. We learn of it, as Heraclitus tells us, by sight, hearing, and understanding. We need only to set forth the elements of which it is made, its principles of organization, and why it changes. This might be difficult to do because the world is complex and human minds are limited, but there doesn't seem to be a shadow of suspicion that sight and hearing on the one hand (the senses) and understanding (reasoning) on the other hand might come into conflict. Yet that is precisely the outcome of Parmenidean logic. The world as revealed

---

*See the discussion of validity in the discussion of Aristotle's logic, Chapter 7, and the definition in the Glossary.

by our senses *cannot* be reality, and the force of that "cannot" is the force of reason itself. Parmenides has *proved* it. These arguments of Parmenides shake Ionian nature philosophy to its core.

Clearly, it is difficult simply to acquiesce in these results. It is not easy to say that our sensory convictions about the manyness of things, their changeableness, and their motion are all illusory. Several notable thinkers attempt to reconcile the arguments of Parmenides and his pupil Zeno with the testimony of the senses. Empedocles and Anaxagoras, in particular, struggle with these problems, but it is generally agreed that neither of them really resolves the issue. It is not until we come to the atomists that we find, in principle, a satisfactory solution.

Two figures are important in developing atomist thought: Leucippus and **Democritus**. About the former we know very little; two ancient authorities doubt even that he existed. Others, however, attribute to Leucippus the key idea that allows the Parmenidean argument to be met. About Democritus we know much more. He lived in Abdera, a city of Thrace in northern Greece (see Map 1), during the middle of the fifth century B.C. He wrote voluminously, perhaps as many as fifty-two books, of which well over two hundred fragments are preserved. He is also thoroughly discussed by later philosophers such as Aristotle, so we have a fairly complete notion of his teachings.

We need not try to sort out the separate contributions of Leucippus and Democritus. (We can't do so with certainty in any case.) They seem together to have developed the view known as **atomism,** to which we now turn.

THE KEY: AN AMBIGUITY

In a work titled *Of Generation and Corruption* (concerned with coming into being and passing away), Aristotle summarizes the Parmenidean arguments against these kinds of changes and then says,

> Leucippus, however, thought he had arguments which, while consistent with sense perception, would not destroy coming into being or passing away or the multiplicity of existing things. These he conceded to be appearances, while to those who upheld the "one" he conceded that there can be no

motion without a void, that the void is not-being, and that not-being is no part of being; for what is, in the strict sense, is completely full. But there is not one such being but infinitely many, and they are invisible owing to the smallness of their bulk. They move in the void (for void exists) and, by coming together and separating, effect coming into being and passing away. (DK 67 A 7, *IEGP,* 196)

Notice that Aristotle does not say simply that Leucippus disagrees with Parmenides. To disagree with an opinion is easy—too easy. What is needed is a *reason* to disagree. Aristotle says that Leucippus has, or thinks he has, *arguments.* These arguments concede some things to the *monists* (the believers in the "one"), but they show that these concessions are not as damaging to common sense as the monists had thought. The acceptable parts of the monistic argument can be reconciled with sense perception, with beginning and ending, and with multiplicity. What are these arguments?

Surprisingly, a follower of Parmenides, Melissus, gives us a hint toward an adequate solution:

> If there were a many, they would have to be such as the one is. (DK 30 B 8, *IEGP,* 148)

Melissus does not accept that there is a many. He just tells us that *if* there were a many, each thing would have to have the characteristics Parmenides ascribes to the one. Each would have to be all-alike, indivisible, full, and eternal. What Leucippus does is to accept this principle and to say there are many such "ones." There are, in fact, an infinite number of them. Democritus was to call them "**atoms.**"

From all we have seen so far, however, this is mere assertion; we need an argument. It goes like this. We must grant to Parmenides that being and not-being are opposites, and of course not-being *is not.* It doesn't follow from these concessions, though, that there is no such thing as empty space. Space can be empty in precisely this sense: It contains no *things* or *bodies.* Nonetheless, space may have *being.* Empty space, which Democritus calls "**the void,**" is *not* the same as not-being. It only seems so if you do not distinguish *being* from *body.* Being a body or a thing may be just one *way* of being something. There may be others. Moreover, *what-does-not-contain-any-body* need not be the same as *what-is-not-at-all.*

Once that distinction is recognized, we can see that Parmenides' argument confuses the two. He argues that there can be only a "one" because if there were "many" they would have to be separated by *what is not;* and what is not *is not.* So there cannot be a many; what is must be all full and continuous. The atomists argue that there is an ambiguity here. Some of what is *can* be separated from other parts of what is—by the void. So there *can* be a many. The void does not lack being altogether. It only lacks the kind of being characteristic of *things.* Democritus also calls the void "no-thing"—not, note carefully, "nothing" (nothing at all), which he acknowledges *is not.* No-thing (the void) is a kind of being in which no body exists. He puts the point this way:

> No-thing exists just as much as thing. (DK 68 B 156, *IEGP,* 197)

A diagram may help to make this clear.

Parmenides

Being   Not-being

is   is not

Democritus

Being

Thing   No-thing   Not-being

(Body)   (Void)   is not

is

We noted earlier the struggle to develop a language adequate to describe reality. Language begins, as the language of children does, tied to the concrete. Only with great difficulty does it develop enough abstraction—enough distance, as it were, from concrete things—to allow for the necessary distinctions. The language of Parmenides simply lacks the concepts necessary to make these crucial distinctions. Leucippus and Democritus are in effect forging new linguistic tools for doing the job of describing the world. This is a real breakthrough: It makes possible a theory that does not deny the evidence of the senses and yet is rational (that is, does not lead to contradictions).

THE WORLD

Reality, then, consists of atoms and the void. Atoms are so tiny that they are mostly, perhaps entirely, invisible to us. Each of them is indivisible (the word "atom" comes from roots that mean "not cuttable").* Because they are indivisible, they are also indestructible; they exist eternally. Atoms are in constant motion, banging into each other and bouncing off, or maybe just vibrating like motes of dust in a stream of sunlight. Such motion is made possible by the existence of the void; the void provides a place into which a body can move. Their motion, moreover, is not something that must be imparted to them from outside. It is their nature to move.

These atoms are not all alike, although internally each is homogeneous, as Melissus argues it must be. Atoms differ from each other in three ways: in shape (including size), in arrangement, and in position. Aristotle gives us examples from the alphabet to illustrate these ways. *A* differs from *N* in shape, *AN* differs from *NA* in arrangement, and *Z* differs from *N* in position. As the atoms move about, some of them hook into others, perhaps of the same kind, perhaps different. If enough get hitched together, they form bodies that are visible to us. In fact, such compounds or composites are what make up the world of our experience. Teacups and sparrow feathers differ from each other in the kinds of atoms that make them up and in the way the atoms are arranged. Light bodies differ from heavy bodies, for example, because the hooking together is looser and there is more void in them. Soft bodies differ from hard ones because the connections between the atoms are more flexible.

The atomists can explain coming into being and passing away as well. A thing comes into being when the atoms that make it up get hooked together in the appropriate ways. It passes away again when its parts disperse or fall apart.

These principles are obviously compatible with much of the older nature philosophy, and the atomists adopt or adapt a good bit of that tradition.

---

*What we call "atoms" nowadays are not, as we well know, indivisible. We also know, since Einstein, that matter and energy are convertible. Nonetheless, physicists are still searching for the ultimate building blocks of nature. Perhaps they are what scientists call "quarks." Whether that is so or not, however, the ancient atomists' assumption that there are such building blocks and that they are very tiny indeed is alive and well in the twenty-first century.

The structure of the universe, for instance, is explained by a vortex motion or whirl that separates out the various kinds of compounds. Like tends to go to like, just as pebbles on a seashore tend to line up in rows according to their size. In this way, we get a picture of the world that is, in its broad features, not very different from that of Anaximander. There is, however, one crucial and very important difference.

Anaximander said that the Boundless "encompasses all things" and "steers all things." Xenophanes claims that the one god "sets all things in motion by the thought of his mind." Heraclitus identifies the principle of unity holding together the many changing things of the world as a divine *logos,* or thought. In contrast, Democritus' principles leave no room for this kind of intelligent direction to things. Remember: What exist are atoms and the void. Democritus boldly draws the conclusions from this premise. If we ask why the atoms combine to form a world or why they form some particular thing in this world, the only answer is that they *just do.* The only reason that can be given is that these atoms happened to be the sort, and to be in the vicinity of other atoms of a sort, to produce the kind of thing they did produce. There is no further reason, no intention or purpose behind it.*

> Nothing occurs at random, but everything occurs for a reason and by necessity. (DK 67 B 2, *IEGP,* 212)

By this, Democritus means that events don't just happen, but neither do they occur in order to reach some goal or because they were planned or designed to happen that way. If we are asked why so and so occurred, the proper answer will cite previously existing material causes. In one sense, this is the final destination of pre-Socratic speculation about nature. It begins by casting out the Homeric gods. It ends by casting out altogether intelligence and purpose from the governance of the world. Everything happens according to laws of motion that govern the wholly mechanical interactions of the atoms. In these happenings, mind has no place.

This account has—or seems to have—serious consequences for our view of human life. We normally think that we are pretty much in control of our lives, that we can make decisions to do one thing or another, go this way or that. It's up to us. If everything occurs "by necessity," however, as Democritus says, then each of these decisions is itself determined by mechanical laws that reach back to movements of atoms that long preceded our birth. It begins to look as if we are merely cogs in the gigantic machine of the world, no more really in control of our actions than the clouds are in control of (can choose) when it is going to rain. Supposing Democritus (or his modern followers) are right, what happens to our conviction that we have a free will? Democritus does not solve this problem, but he is the first to set out the parameters of the problem with some clarity.*

The Soul

If mind or intelligence cannot function as an explanation of the world-order, it is nonetheless obvious that it plays a role in human life. Democritus owes us an explanation of human intelligence that is compatible with his basic principles. His speculations are interesting and suggestive, though still quite crude. This problem is one we cannot claim to have solved completely even in our own day.

Atomistic accounts of **soul** and mind must, of course, be compatible with a general materialist view of reality: What exist are atoms and the void. According to Democritus, the soul is composed of exceedingly fine and spherical atoms; in this way, soul interpenetrates the whole of the body. Democritus holds that

> spherical atoms move because it is their nature never to be still, and that as they move they draw the whole body along with them, and set it in motion. (DK 68 A 104, *IEGP,* 222)

Soul-atoms are in this sense akin to fire-atoms, which are also small, spherical, and capable of

---

*Compare the nonpurposive character of evolutionary accounts of the origin of species with creationist accounts.

*Concerning free will, see the discussions by Epicurus (p. 200), the Stoics (pp. 205–207), Augustine (pp. 247–248), Descartes (*Meditation IV*), Hume (pp. 408–410), Kant (pp. 440–442), Hegel (p. 474), Nietzsche (pp. 548–549), and de Beauvoir (pp. 667–668).

penetrating solid bodies and (as Heraclitus has observed) are strikingly good examples of spontaneous motion. The soul or principle of life is, like everything else, *material*.

Living things, of course, have certain capacities that nonliving things do not: They experience sensations (tastes, smells, sights, sounds, pains). Some, at least, are capable of thought, and humans seem to have a capacity to know. Can Democritus explain these capacities using his principles regarding atoms and the void?

Think first about sensations. There doesn't seem to be too much difficulty in explaining tastes. Sweet and sour, salt and bitter are just the results of differently shaped atoms in contact with the tongue. The sweet, Democritus says, consists of atoms that are "round and of a good size," the sour of "bulky, jagged, and many-angled" atoms, and so on (DK 68 A 129, *IEGP*, 200). These speculations are not grounded in anything like modern experimental method, but the kind of explanation is surely familiar to those who know something of modern chemistry.

Smells are explained along analogous lines, and sounds, too, are not difficult; Democritus explains them in terms of air being "broken up into bodies of like shape . . . rolled along with the fragments of the voice."[4] Vision is the sense most difficult to explain in terms of an atomistic view. Unlike touch, taste, and even hearing, it is a "distance receptor." With sight, it is as though we were able to reach out to the surfaces of things at some distance from us without any material means of doing so. In this respect, the eye seems quite different from the hand or the tongue.

Democritus, however, holds that sight is not really different. Like the other senses, it works by contact with its objects, only in this case the contact is more indirect than usual. The bodies made up of combined atoms are constantly giving off "images" of themselves, he tells us. These images are themselves material, composed of exceptionally fine atoms. These "effluences" strike the eye and stamp their shape in the soft and moist matter of the eye, whereupon it is registered in the smooth and round atoms of soul present throughout the body.

This kind of explanation is regarded by most of his Greek successors as very strange. Aristotle even

calls it a great absurdity. It may not strike us as absurd. Indeed, it seems somewhere near the truth.

It does have a paradoxical consequence, though, which Democritus recognizes and is willing to accept. It means that our senses *do not give us direct and certain knowledge of the world*. If you think a moment, you will see that this is indeed an implication of his view. Our experience of vision is a product, in the mathematical sense. It is the outcome of a complex set of interactions between the object seen, the intervening medium, and our sensory apparatus. Exactly what our experience is when we look at a distant mountain is not a simple function of the characteristics of the mountain. That experience depends also on whether the air is clear or foggy, clean or polluted. It depends on whether it is dawn, dusk, or noon. Moreover, what we experience depends on what kinds and proportions of rods and cones we have in our eyes, on complex sending mechanisms in the optic nerve, and the condition of the visual center in the brain.

Democritus cannot express his point in these contemporary terms, of course. Nonetheless, this is exactly his point. Similar explanations also apply to the other senses. It was recognized in ancient times that honey, for example, can taste sweet to a healthy person and bitter to a sick one. Clearly, the difference depends on the state of the receptor organs. What is the character of the honey itself? Is it both sweet and bitter? That seems impossible. Democritus draws the conclusion that it is neither. Sweetness and bitterness, hot and cold, red and blue exist only in us, not in nature.

> Sweet exists by convention, bitter by convention, color by convention; but in reality atoms and the void alone exist. (DK 68 B 9, *IEGP*, 202)

To say that something exists by **convention** is to say that its existence depends upon us.* In nature alone, it is not to be found. If our sense experience is conventional in this sense, then we cannot rely on it to tell us what the world is really like. In a way, Parmenides was right after all!†

---

*For a fuller discussion of the distinction between nature and convention, see "*Physis* and *Nomos*" in Chapter 3.
†See pp. 29–30.

It is necessary to realize that by this principle man is cut off from the real. (DK 68 B 6, *IEGP,* 203)

We are "cut off from the real" because whatever impact the real has on us is in part a product of our own condition. This is true not only of the sick person but also of the well one. The sweetness of the honey to the well person depends on sensory receptors just as much as the bitterness to the sick one. Neither has a direct and unmediated avenue to what honey really is.

Later philosophers exploit these considerations in skeptical directions, doubting that we can have any reliable knowledge of the world at all. For Democritus, however, they do not lead to utter skepticism:

There are two forms of knowledge: one legitimate, one bastard. To the bastard sort belong all the following: sight, hearing, smell, taste, touch. The legitimate is quite distinct from this. When the bastard form cannot see more minutely, nor hear nor smell nor taste nor perceive through the touch, then another, finer form must be employed. (DK 68 B 11, *IEGP,* 203–204)

He seems to be telling us that the senses can take us only so far, because they have a "bastard" parentage (that is, they are the products of both the objects perceived and the perceiving organs). But there is "another, finer" and "legitimate" form of knowledge available to the soul. This knowledge is no doubt based on reasoning. Its product is the knowledge that what really exist are atoms and the void. At this point, we would like reasoning itself to be explained in terms of the atomistic view, as the senses have been explained. No such explanation is offered. This is not surprising; indeed, many think that a satisfactory account of reasoning on these materialistic principles is only now, after the invention of the computer, beginning to be constructed—but that, of course, is reaching far ahead of our story.*

How to Live

Democritus wrote extensively on the question of the best life for a human being, but only fragments remain. Many of them are memorable, however,

---

*But take a look at "The Matter of Minds" in Chapter 25, pp. 717–728.

and I simply list without comment a number of his most lively aphorisms.

- Disease occurs in a household, or in a life, just as it does in a body. (DK 68 B 288, *IEGP,* 221)
- Medicine cures the diseases of the body; wisdom, on the other hand, relieves the soul of its sufferings. (DK 68 B 31, *IEGP,* 222)
- The needy animal knows how much it needs; but the needy man does not. (DK 68 B 198, *IEGP,* 223)
- It is hard to fight with desire; but to overcome it is the mark of a rational man. (DK 68 B 236, *IEGP,* 225)
- Moderation increases enjoyment, and makes pleasure even greater. (DK 68 B 211, *IEGP,* 223)
- It is childish, not manly, to have immoderate desires. (DK 68 B 70, *IEGP,* 225)
- The good things of life are produced by learning with hard work; the bad are reaped of their own accord, without hard work. (DK 68 B 182, *IEGP,* 226)
- The brave man is he who overcomes not only his enemies but his pleasures. There are some men who are masters of cities but slaves to women. (DK 68 B 214, *IEGP,* 228)
- In cattle excellence is displayed in strength of body; but in men it lies in strength of character. (DK 68 B 57, *IEGP,* 230)
- I would rather discover a single cause than become king of the Persians. (DK 68 B 118, *IEGP,* 229)

Many of the themes expressed here should be familiar by now. We will see them worked out more systematically in later Greek philosophy, particularly by Plato and Aristotle.

---

1. State as clearly as you can the argument by which the atomists defeat Parmenides and reconcile the one and the many.
2. How would atomists explain the difference between, say, chalk and cheese? How do they explain coming into being and passing away again?
3. On atomistic principles, what happens to the notion of a cosmic intelligence?
4. What is the atomist's account of soul?
5. What does it mean to say that sweet and bitter exist "by convention"?

6. Why does Democritus say that our senses cut us off from the real? Why are we not absolutely cut off?

7. What problem does atomism pose for the idea that we have a free will?

FOR FURTHER THOUGHT

1. Twentieth-century philosopher of science Karl Popper quotes Xenophanes approvingly and asserts that the development of thought we can trace in the pre-Socratics exemplifies perfectly the basic structure of scientific thinking. He calls it the "rational critical" method and says it works through a sequence of bold conjectures and incisive refutations. Can you identify such moves in the thinking of the philosophers we have studied so far? (See Popper's *Conjectures and Refutations: The Growth of Scientific Knowledge* [New York: Harper and Row, 1968].)

2. What sort of defense could you mount against the attacks on common sense put forth by rationalists such as Parmenides and Zeno? Is there something you could do to show that the world of our sense experience is, after all, the real world?

3. Here is an argument to prove that a ham sandwich is better than perfect happiness: (1) A ham sandwich is better than nothing; (2) nothing is better than perfect happiness; therefore (3) a ham sandwich is better than perfect happiness. Will untangling this fallacy throw light on the atomists' critique of Parmenides?

4. If you know something about the physiology of the central nervous system, try to determine whether modern accounts of that system also "cut us off from the real."

KEY WORDS

Thales	Xenophanes
Anaximander	one god
the Boundless	seeking
vortex motion	truth
epistemology	change
Heraclitus	rationalism
opposition	many
flux	appearance/reality
logos	Zeno
wisdom	reductio ad absurdum
Tao	valid
non-action	paradox
Parmenides	Democritus
the One	atomism
argument	atoms and the void
appearance	soul
not-being	convention

NOTES

1. Quotations from the pre-Socratic philosophers are in the translation by John Manley Robinson, *An Introduction to Early Greek Philosophy* (Boston: Houghton Mifflin, 1968). They are cited by the standard Diels/Kranz number, followed by *IEGP* and the page number in Robinson.

2. Biblical quotations in this text are taken from the Revised Standard Version, 1946/1971, National Council of Churches.

3. If you would like to pursue these details, the books by Robinson (see Note 1) and Ring (cited in a footnote at the beginning of this chapter) are excellent sources. A more extensive treatment with original Greek texts is found in G. S. Kirk and J. E. Raven, *The Presocratic Philosophers* (Cambridge, England: Cambridge University Press, 1957).

4. Quoted in G. S. Kirk and J. E. Raven, *The Presocratic Philosophers* (Cambridge: Cambridge University Press, 1960), 423.

CHAPTER

3

THE SOPHISTS

Rhetoric and Relativism in Athens

When we think of "the glory that was Greece," we think inevitably of **Athens** (see Map 1). To this point, however, we have mentioned Athens scarcely at all. Greek culture, as we have seen, ranged from the southern parts of Italy and Sicily in the west to the Ionian settlements on the shores of Asia Minor and to Thrace in the north. In the fifth and fourth centuries B.C., however, Greek culture came more and more to center in one city: Athens. The story of how this came about is a fascinating tale related for us by the Greek historian Herodotus and pieced together by modern writers from his history and many other sources. For our purposes, we need to understand several key elements of the rise of Athens. What kind of city was Athens in that time, what was it like to live in Athens, and how was it different from other cities?[1]

Although we have used the terms "Greece" and "Greek culture," there was at the beginning of the fifth century (around 500 B.C.) nothing like a unified Greek state. People lived in or owed allegiance to a large number of city-states. A city-state (a *polis*) was an area—an island, perhaps, or an arable plain

with natural boundaries of mountains and the sea—in which one city was dominant. The city was usually fortified and offered protection to the farmers, who sometimes lived within the walls and sometimes outside in smaller villages. The prominent city-states of that time were Thebes, Corinth, Argos, Sparta, and Athens, but there were many more. Among these city-states there were often rivalries, quarrels, shifting alliances, and wars.

Two things happened around the beginning of the fifth century that contributed to the preeminence of Athens among the city-states: the beginnings of **democracy** in government and the **Persian wars.**

Democracy

For nearly a century, ever since the reforms of Solon, the common people had had some voice in the government of Athens. According to the constitution of Solon, the powers of government were divided among several bodies. Among them were the Council, which was composed of "the best men" (aristocrats), and the Assembly, to which all free men belonged. Important decisions were made by the Council, but the Assembly could veto measures that were excessively unpopular. This structure was modified over the years, but it took on the character of an ideal; again and again reforms of various kinds were justified as being a return to the constitution of Solon.*

During a large part of the sixth century, Athens was ruled by "tyrants." This word did not originally have all the negative connotations it now has. It simply meant "boss" or "chief" and was applied to a ruler who was not a hereditary king but had seized power some other way. Some of the tyrants of Athens more or less respected Solon's constitution, but at least one tyrant was killed to restore the democracy.

In 508 B.C., a quarrel arose concerning citizenship for a large influx of immigrants to the city. The aristocrats, fearful for their power, tried to purge the citizenship rolls, but the Assembly passed a proposal to extend citizenship to many of the new residents. After a three-day siege of the Acropolis by the people, the aristocrats—who had been backed by a king of Sparta and his soldiers—capitulated. Citizenship was broadened, though not so far as to include women and slaves, and thereafter the citizens had control of major decisions. It was to be so for the next hundred years and, with a few exceptions, for some time after that.

The Persian Wars

The Greek colonies on the shores of Asia Minor were always in a precarious state. Their language and heritage bound them to the Greek mainland, but their geographical situation made them of natural interest to whatever power was dominant to the east. These Greek cities paid taxes to the rising Persian power, but in 499 B.C. they rebelled. Athens sent twenty ships to aid these Greeks, and in the fighting they burnt Sardis, one of the principal Persian cities. The rebellion was put down by Persia, and anxiety began to increase among mainland

Greeks. The Persians now had reason to take revenge and, having reasserted their control over the Asian Greek cities, were free to concentrate on the mainland.*

In 490 B.C., the Persians came in force across the Aegean, conquered a coastal island, and landed at Marathon. In a famous battle on the plain twenty-six miles north and east of Athens, the Greeks under Miltiades, an Ionian general, defeated the Persians, killing 6,400 of them. The victory had an exhilarating effect on the democratic city of Athens, which had supplied most of the soldiers for the battle.

It was clear to the Athenians, however, that the Persians were not about to be stopped by the loss of one battle, no matter how decisive at the time. Herodotus represents the Persian monarch Xerxes, who had recently succeeded his father Darius, as saying:

> I will bridge the Hellespont [see Map 1] and march an army through Europe into Greece, and punish the Athenians for the outrage they committed upon my father and upon us. As you saw, Darius himself was making his preparations for war against these men; but death prevented him from carrying out his purpose. I therefore on his behalf, and for the benefit of all my subjects, will not rest until I have taken Athens and burnt it to the ground, in revenge for the injury which the Athenians without provocation once did to me and my father [the burning of Sardis]. . . . If we crush the Athenians and their neighbours in the Peloponnese, we shall so extend the empire of Persia that its boundaries will be God's own sky, so that the sun will not look down upon any land beyond the boundaries of what is ours. (*Histories* 7.8)[2]

There was much debate in Athens about how to meet the danger. One party favored land-based defenses, citing the former victory at Marathon. The other party, led by Themistocles, favored building up the navy and a defense by sea. After much infighting, the Athenians decided on a large increase in fighting ships of the latest style—and just in time. In the year 480 B.C., Xerxes, lashing ships together

---

*For democracy in Athens, see http://en.wikipedia.org/wiki/Athenian_democracy.

*For Persian Wars, see http://lilt.ilstu.edu/drjclassics/lectures/history/PersianWars/persianwars.shtm.

to make a bridge, led an army of perhaps 200,000 men across the Hellespont (which separates Asia from Europe), brought Thrace under submission, and began to advance south toward Athens. Advice was sought, in time-honored fashion, from the Oracle at Delphi (see Map 1). The oracle was not favorable. A second plea brought this response:

> That the wooden wall only shall not fall, but help you and your children. (*Histories* 7.141)

How should this opaque answer be interpreted? Some believed that wooden walls on the hill of the Acropolis would withstand the aggressor. Themistocles argued that the "wooden wall" referred to the ships that had been built and that they must abandon Athens and try to defeat the Persians at sea. Most of the Athenians followed Themistocles, though some did not.

First, however, it was necessary to stop the advance of the Persian army. Many saw it as a threat against Greece as a whole, not just against Athens. A force led by Spartan soldiers under the Spartan king Leonidas met the Persians at Thermopylae, eighty miles northwest of Athens (see Map 1). Greatly outnumbered, the Greeks fought valiantly, inflicting many deaths, but were defeated. Leonidas was killed.*

The Persians took Athens, overwhelmed the defenders on the Acropolis, and burned the temples. However, the main Athenian forces, in ships off the nearby island of Salamis, were still to be dealt with. On a day splendid in Greek history, Xerxes sat on a mountain above the bay of Salamis (see Map 1) and saw the Greeks tear apart his navy. Themistocles' strategy had worked. The next spring (479 B.C.), however, the Persians occupied Athens again. It took a great victory by the combined Athenian and Spartan armies at Plataea to expel the Persians for good.

These victories had several results. Athens, which had borne the brunt of the defense of Greece, became preeminent among the city-states. The city had displayed its courage and prowess for all to see and took the lead in forming a league for the future

---

*This battle is celebrated in the movie *300*.

defense of the Greek lands. In time, the league turned into an Athenian empire. Other states paid tribute to Athens, which saw to their protection, and Athens became a great sea power.

Athens also became very wealthy. It was not only the tribute from the allies, although that was significant. With their control of the sea, Athenians engaged in trading far and wide. A large and wealthy merchant class grew up, and Athens became the center of Greek cultural life. Under **Pericles**, the most influential leader of the democratic city in the middle of the fifth century B.C., the city built the magnificent temples on the Acropolis. Pericles was influential in encouraging Greek art and sculpture, supported the new learning, and was a close associate of certain philosophers. A speech of his, commemorating fallen soldiers in the first year of the tragic war with Sparta, gives a sense of what it meant to Athenians to be living in Athens at that time. Only part of it, as represented for us by the historian Thucydides, is quoted here. (Suggestion: Read it aloud.)

> Let me say that our system of government does not copy the institutions of our neighbours. It is more a case of our being a model to others, than of our imitating anyone else. Our constitution is called a democracy because power is in the hands not of a minority but of the whole people. When it is a question of settling private disputes, everyone is equal before the law; when it is a question of putting one person before another in positions of public responsibility, what counts is not membership of a particular class, but the actual ability which the man possesses. No one, so long as he has it in him to be of service to the state, is kept in political obscurity because of poverty. And, just as our political life is free and open, so is our day-to-day life in our relations with each other. We do not get into a state with our next-door neighbour if he enjoys himself in his own way, nor do we give him the kind of black looks which, though they do no real harm, still do hurt people's feelings. We are free and tolerant in our private lives; but in public affairs we keep to the law. This is because it commands our deep respect.
>
> We give our obedience to those whom we put in positions of authority, and we obey the laws

themselves, especially those which are for the protection of the oppressed, and those unwritten laws which it is an acknowledged shame to break.

And here is another point. When our work is over, we are in a position to enjoy all kinds of recreation for our spirits. There are various kinds of contests and sacrifices regularly throughout the year; in our own homes we find a beauty and a good taste which delight us every day and which drive away our cares. Then the greatness of our city brings it about that all the good things from all over the world flow in to us, so that to us it seems just as natural to enjoy foreign goods as our own local products.

Then there is a great difference between us and our opponents in our attitude towards military security. Here are some examples: Our city is open to the world, and we have no periodical deportations in order to prevent people observing or finding out secrets which might be of military advantage to the enemy. This is because we rely, not on secret weapons, but on our own real courage and loyalty. . . .

Our love of what is beautiful does not lead to extravagance; our love of the things of the mind does not make us soft. We regard wealth as something to be properly used, rather than as something to boast about. As for poverty, no one need be ashamed to admit it: the real shame is in not taking practical measures to escape from it. Here each individual is interested not only in his own affairs but in the affairs of the state as well. . . . We do not say that a man who takes no interest in politics is a man who minds his own business; we say that he has no business here at all. . . .

Again, in questions of general good feeling there is a great contrast between us and most other people. We make friends by doing good to others, not by receiving good from them. . . . We are unique in this. When we do kindnesses to others, we do not do them out of any calculations of profit or loss: we do them without afterthought, relying on our free liberality. Taking everything together then, I declare that our city is an education to Greece, and I declare that in my opinion each single one of our citizens, in all the manifold aspects of life, is able to show himself the rightful lord and owner of his own person, and do this, moreover, with exceptional grace and exceptional versatility. . . . Mighty indeed are the marks and monuments of our empire which we have left. Future ages will wonder at us, as the present age wonders

at us now. We do not need the praises of a Homer, or of anyone else whose words may delight us for the moment, but whose estimation of facts will fall short of what is really true. For our adventurous spirit has forced an entry into every sea and into every land; and everywhere we have left behind us everlasting memorials of good done to our friends or suffering inflicted on our enemies. [3]

Such was the spirit of the Golden Age of classical Athens: proud, confident, serenely convinced that the city was "an education to Greece"—and not without reason. Twenty-five hundred years later, we still are moved by their tragedies, laugh at their comedies, admire their sculpture, are awed by their architecture, revere their democracy, and study their philosophers.

---

1. How did Athens come to preeminence among Greek cities?
2. For what qualities does Pericles praise Athens?

The Sophists

The social situation in fifth-century B.C. Athens called for innovations in education. The "best men" in the old sense no longer commanded a natural leadership. What counted was actual ability, as Pericles said, so men sought to develop their abilities. Aristocratic education centering on Homer was no longer entirely adequate. Most citizens received an elementary education that made them literate and gave them basic skills. If a father wanted his son to succeed in democratic Athens, however, more was needed.

To supply this need, there arose a class of teachers offering what we can call higher education. Many of these teachers were itinerant, moving from city to city as the call for their services waxed and waned. They were professionals who charged for their instruction. The best of them became quite wealthy, because there was a substantial demand for their services. We can get a sense of what they claimed to provide for their students and of the eagerness with which they were sought out from the beginning of Plato's dialogue *Protagoras*. As we'll see, Protagoras was one of the greatest of these teachers.* Socrates is the speaker.

> Last night, just before daybreak, Hippocrates, the son of Apollodorus and brother of Phason, began knocking very loudly on the door with his stick, and when someone opened it he came straight in in a great hurry, calling out loudly, "Socrates, are you awake or asleep?" I recognized his voice and said, "It's Hippocrates; no bad news, I hope?" "Nothing but good news," he said. "Splendid," I said; "what is it, then? What brings you here so early?" He came and stood beside me; "Protagoras has come," he said. "He came the day before yesterday," I said; "have you only just heard?" "Yes, indeed," he said; "yesterday evening. . . . Late as it was, I immediately got up to come and tell you, but then I realized that it was far too late at night; but as soon as I had had a sleep and got rid of my tiredness, I got up straight away and came over here, as you see."
>
> I knew him to be a spirited and excitable character, so I said, "What's all this to you? Protagoras hasn't done you any wrong, has he?"
>
> He laughed. "By heavens, he has, Socrates. He is the only man who is wise, but he doesn't make me wise too."
>
> "Oh yes, he will," I said; "If you give him money and use a little persuasion, he'll make you wise as well."
>
> "I wish to God," he said, "that that was all there was to it. I'd use every penny of my own, and of my friends too. But it's just that that I've come to you about now, so that you can put in a word for me with him. First of all, I'm too young, and then I've never seen Protagoras." (*Protagoras* 310a–e)[4]

Note the eagerness expressed by Hippocrates— and for education, too! What could this education be that excited such desire? What did the **Sophists,** as these teachers were called, offer?

While they wait for day to dawn, Socrates tries in his questioning fashion to see whether Hippocrates really knows what he is getting into. Not surprisingly, it turns out that he doesn't. Undaunted, they set off and go to the home where Protagoras is staying. After some difficulty (the servant at the door is sick of Sophists and slams the door in their faces), they meet Protagoras, who is in the company of a number of other young men and fellow Sophists. Socrates makes his request:

> Hippocrates here is anxious to become your pupil; so he says that he would be glad to know what benefit he will derive from associating with you. (*Protagoras* 318a)

Protagoras answers,

> Young man, . . . if you associate with me, this is the benefit you will gain: the very day you become my pupil you will go home a better man, and the same the next day; and every day you will continue to make progress. (*Protagoras* 318a)

Socrates, of course, is not satisfied with this answer. If Hippocrates were to associate with a famous painter, then each day his painting might improve. If he studied with a flutist, his flute playing would get better. But in what respect, exactly, will associating with Protagoras make Hippocrates "a better man"?

> You have put a good question, Socrates, and I like answering people who do that. . . . What I teach is the proper management of one's own affairs, how best to run one's household, and the management of public affairs, how to make the most effective contribution to the affairs of the city both by word and action. (*Protagoras* 318d–319a)

Here we have the key to the excitement of Hippocrates and to the demand for this instruction from the rising middle class of Athens. The Sophists claim to be able to teach the things that foster success, both personal and political, in this democratic city. Many of them also teach specialized subjects such as astronomy, geometry, arithmetic, and music. Nearly all are committed to the new learning developed by the nature philosophers. They are self-consciously "modern," believing they represent progress and enlightenment as opposed to ignorance and superstition.

However, it is their claim to teach "excellence" or "virtue" (the Greek word ***areté*** can be translated

---

*Protagoras was paid in the following way. Before the instruction, he and his pupil would go to the temple; there the student would vow to pay, when the course was finished, whatever he then thought Protagoras' instruction was worth. It is said that when he died, Protagoras was wealthier than five Phidiases. (Phidias was the most famous sculptor in Athens.)

either way) both in mastering one's own affairs and in providing leadership in the city that makes them popular.* The excellences they claim to teach are the skills, abilities, and traits of character that make one competent, successful, admired, and perhaps even wealthy.

The term "sophist" has rather negative connotations for us. A *sophism,* for instance, is a fallacious argument that looks good but isn't, and *sophistry* is verbally pulling the wool over someone's eyes. The term did not always have such connotations. "Sophist" comes from the Greek *sophos,* meaning wise. The term was applied in the fifth century to many earlier wise men, including Homer and Hesiod. Undoubtedly, the best of the Sophists, such as Protagoras, were neither charlatans nor fools. In connection with their teaching the young, they also made important contributions to the great conversation. They were philosophers who had to be taken seriously; for this reason, they are of interest to us.

RHETORIC

All of the Sophists taught **rhetoric,** the principles and practice of persuasive speaking. Some of the Sophists, Gorgias for example, claimed to teach nothing but that. Clearly, in democratic Athens this art would be very valuable. Suppose, for instance, that you are brought into court by a neighbor. If you hem and haw, utter only irrelevancies, and cannot present the evidence on your side in a coherent and persuasive way, you are likely to lose whether you are guilty or not. Or suppose you feel strongly about some issue that affects the welfare of the city; only if you can stand up in the Assembly of citizens and speak persuasively will you have any influence. You must be able to present your case, marshal your arguments, and appeal to the feelings of the audience. This is the art the Sophists developed and taught.

---

*The Greek *areté* (ahr-e-tay) can apply to horses and knives, to flutists and cobblers, as well as to human beings as such. It has to do with the excellence of something when it does well what it is supposed to do. So it goes beyond the sphere of morality but includes it. Though usually translated "virtue," this English word is really too narrow. I will often use the broader term "excellence," and especially "human excellence," when what is in question is not someone's excellence as a teacher or sailor but as a human being.

In one of his dialogues, Plato represents Gorgias as claiming to teach

> the ability to use the spoken word to persuade the jurors in the courts, the members of the Council, the citizens attending the Assembly—in short, to win over any and every form of public meeting. (*Gorgias* 452e)[5]

A rhetorician is capable of speaking effectively against all comers, whatever the issue, and can consequently be more persuasive in front of crowds about . . . anything he likes. (*Gorgias* 457b)

We need to understand what rhetoric means to the Sophists because its philosophical consequences are deep. The central idea is that by using the principles of persuasive speaking, one can make a case for any position at all. It follows that if there are, as we often say these days, two sides to every issue, someone skilled in rhetoric should be able to present a persuasive argument for each side. In fact, this idea was embodied in one of the main teaching tools of the Sophists.

A student was encouraged to construct and present arguments on both sides of some controversial issue. He was not judged to be proficient until he could present a case as persuasive on one side as on the other. This method, presumably, was designed to equip a student for any eventuality; one never knew on what side of some future issue one's interests would lie.

A humorous story about Protagoras and one of his students illustrates this method. Protagoras agreed to teach a young man how to conduct cases in the courts. Because the young man was poor, it was agreed that he would not have to pay his teacher until he won his first case. Some time elapsed after the course of instruction was over, and the student did not enter into any cases. Finally Protagoras himself brought the student to court, prosecuting him for payment. The student argued thus: If I win this case, I shall not have to pay Protagoras, according to the judgment of the court; if I lose this case, I will not yet have won my first case, and so I will not have to pay Protagoras according to the terms of our agreement; since I will either win or lose, I shall not have to pay the sum. Protagoras, not to be outdone by his student, argued as follows: If he loses this case, then by the judgment of the court he must pay me; if he wins it, he will have won his first case and therefore will have to pay me; so, in either case, he will have to pay me.

The story is probably apocryphal, and the arguments may be "sophistical" in the bad sense, but it is not easy to see what has gone wrong. The example is not far from the flavor of much of the Sophists' teaching.

The philosophical interest of this technique can be seen if we recall certain meanings of the term *logos,* which connotes speech, thought, argument, and discourse. What the Sophists were training their students to do was to present opposite *logoi.* There was the *logos* (what could be said) on one side, and there was the *logos* on the other. The presumption was that for every side of every issue a persuasive *logos* could be developed. Some Sophists seem to have written works consisting of just such opposed *logoi,* presumably as examples and practice pieces for their students.

In this connection, we must note a phrase that became notorious later on. It seems to have expressed a boast made by Protagoras and some of the other Sophists. They claimed to teach others *how to make the weaker argument into the stronger.* Suppose you are in court with what looks like a very weak case. The principles of rhetoric, if cleverly applied, could turn your argument into the stronger one—in the sense that it would be victorious.

Such a technique has profoundly skeptical implications. Think back to Heraclitus.* He believes that there is one *logos* uniting the many changing things of the world into one world-order. This *logos* is "common to all." Although many deviate from the *logos,* it is there and available to everyone. The wise are those who "listen to the *logos*" and order their own lives in accord with the pattern of the world-order. Think of Parmenides, who acknowledges that there is such a thing as the way of opinion but holds that it is quite distinct from the way of truth, in which "thought and being are the same."†

The practice of the Sophists seems to show that thought and being are *not* the same. Thought and

being fall apart; there is no necessary correlation at all. No matter what the reality is, thought can represent it or misrepresent it with equal ease. If a *logos* that will carry conviction can be constructed on any side of any issue, how is one to tell when one is in accord with Heraclitus' *logos* and when one is not? How is one to discriminate the truth from mere opinion?

The Sophists' answer is that one cannot. All we have—and all we ever can have—are opinions. Parmenides writes of two ways, the way of truth and the way of opinion. The former represents the way things *are,* whereas the latter sets forth the way things *appear.* The practice of rhetoric raises doubts about our ability to discern reality. It suggests that human beings are confined to appearances; truth is beyond us. For human beings, things are as they seem to be. No more can be said.

So the Sophists agree with Democritus that we are "cut off from the real" by the conventional nature of our sense experience.* But unlike Democritus, they hold that there is no other avenue to the truth. Democritus thinks that intelligence or mind can penetrate where the senses fail us; he holds that reasoning can reveal what the eyes and ears cannot—that reality is composed of atoms and the void. However, if the Sophists are right in their conviction that an equally persuasive *logos* can be constructed on every side of every issue, then the appeal to reasoning cannot be sustained. For one can reason equally well for and against atoms and the void—or, indeed, anything else!

As you can see, the Sophists tend to be skeptical about their predecessors' claims to reveal the truth, skeptical of human ability to come to know truth at all. You should be able to see how this **skepticism** is intimately related to the way they conceive and teach rhetoric. If rhetoric can make a convincing case for absolutely anything, then what can one know?

Such skepticism does not reduce them to silence, however. A person can still talk intelligibly about how things seem, even if not about how they really are. No doubt many of the theories of the nature philosophers are understood in just this way; they

---

*See especially p. 22.
†See pp. 27–28.

---

*See pp. 36–37.

are plausible stories that represent the way the world seems to be. These stories represent probabilities at best, not the truth; but probabilities are the most that human beings can hope to attain. Without trying to penetrate to the core of reality, the Sophists are content with appearances. Without insisting on certainty, they are content with plausibility. Without knowledge, they are content with opinion.

The skeptical attitude is displayed in a statement by Protagoras concerning the gods. He is reported to have said:

> Concerning the gods I am not in a position to know either that they are or that they are not, or what they are like in appearance; for there are many things that are preventing knowledge, the obscurity of the matter and the brevity of human life. (DK 80 B 4, *IEGP*, 269)[6]

This statement seems to have been the basis for an accusation that Protagoras was an atheist. We know that he was at one time banished from Athens and that certain of his books were burned; it is likely that such statements were among those that aroused the anger of the citizens. (We will see a parallel in the case of Socrates.) Protagoras does not, however, deny the existence of the gods. He says that in light of the difficulty of the question and because life is short, we are prevented from knowing about the gods. His view is not that of the atheist, then, but that of the **agnostic**. The only reasonable thing to do, he says, is to suspend judgment on this issue. This is the view of the skeptic.

---

1. What do the Sophists claim to teach? How do they understand *areté*?
2. What is rhetoric? How was it taught?
3. How does the concept of a *logos* come into Sophist teaching?

RELATIVISM

The Sophists' point of view is best summed up in a famous saying by Protagoras. It is the first sentence of a book titled *On Truth*. Unfortunately, it is the only part of the book that has come down to us.

> Of all things the measure is man: of existing things, that they exist; of non-existing things, that they do not exist. (DK 80 B 1, *IEGP*, 245)

A "measure" is a standard or criterion to appeal to when deciding what to believe. Protagoras' statement that man is the measure of all things means that there is no criterion, standard, or mark by which to judge, except ourselves. We cannot jump outside our skins to see how things look independently of how they appear to us. *As they appear to us, so they are.*

Clearly, he means, in the first instance at least, that things are as they appear to the individual. A common example is the wind. Suppose to one person the wind feels cold and to another it feels warm. Can we ask whether the wind is cold or warm in itself—apart from how it seems? How could that be settled? Protagoras draws the conclusion that this question has no answer. If the wind seems cold to the first one, then to that person it *is* cold; and if it seems warm to the second, then it *is* warm—to that person. About the warmth or coldness of the wind, no more than this can be said. The first person cannot correct the second, and the second cannot correct the first. Each is the final judge of how the wind seems. Since it is not possible to get beyond such seemings, each individual is the final judge of how things *are* (to that individual, of course).

This doctrine is the heart of a viewpoint known as **relativism.** Here is the first appearance of one of the focal points of this book. From this point on, we see the major figures in our tradition struggling with the problems raised by relativism and the skepticism about our knowledge that attends it. Most of them oppose it. Some are willing to make certain concessions to it. But it has never been banished for long, and in one way or another it reappears throughout our history to pose its disturbing questions. In our own century, many have adopted some form of it. It is the merit of the Sophists that they set out the question in the clearest of terms and force us to come to grips with it.

We have now its essence. We need yet to understand what recommends it and what its implications are.

One implication that must have been obvious is that well-meaning citizens, not clearly prejudiced by self-interest, could disagree about the course the city should take. Another is that a well-wrought and persuasively delivered speech on any side of an issue could in fact convince a court or assembly of citizens. If you put these two observations together, it is not hard to draw the conclusion that the *best logos* about an issue is simply the one that does the best job of convincing. How can one judge which of two opposing *logoi* is the best, if not in terms of success? (An independent "logic," in terms of which one might judge that a certain persuasive device was "fallacious," had not yet been developed.) However, if there is no way to tell which *logos* is best except by observing which one *seems* best, then knowledge cannot be distinguished from opinion.* The best opinion is simply that which is generally accepted. But that means it may differ from culture to culture, from time to time, and even from individual to individual. There is no truth independent of what seems to be true. What seems true to one person or at one time may not seem true to another person or at another time. The best *logos* (what passes for truth) is relative to the individual, the culture, or the time. These observations and arguments were surely among those that motivated the Sophists to adopt their relativism.

💮

"Relativists tend to understate the amount of attunement, recognition, and overlap that actually obtains across cultures."

Martha Nussbaum (b. 1947)

There was another factor. Greeks in general, and Athenians in particular, had expanded their horizons. They continued to distinguish, as Greeks always had done, between themselves and "barbarians," whom they took to be inferior to themselves. But the more they traveled and became acquainted with the customs and characters of other nations,

the harder it became to dismiss them as stupid and uncivilized. This exposure to non-Greek ways of doing things exerted a pressure on thought. These ways came to be seen not as inferior but as just different. There is a famous example given by the historian Herodotus, who was himself a great traveler and observer.

> Everyone without exception believes his own native customs, and the religion he was brought up in, to be the best. . . . There is abundant evidence that this is the universal feeling about the ancient customs of one's country. One might recall, in particular, an anecdote of Darius. When he was king of Persia, he summoned the Greeks who happened to be present at his court, and asked them what they would take to eat the dead bodies of their fathers. They replied that they would not do it for any money in the world. Later, in the presence of the Greeks, and through an interpreter, so they could understand what was said, he asked some Indians, of the tribe called Callatiae, who do in fact eat their parents' dead bodies, what they would take to burn them. They uttered a cry of horror and forbade him to mention such a dreadful thing. One can see by this what custom can do, and Pindar, in my opinion, was right when he called it "king of all."[7]

PHYSIS AND NOMOS

The Sophists developed this notion that custom was "king of all" in terms of a distinction between *physis* and *nomos*. The word **physis** is the term for what the nature philosophers were studying. It is usually translated as "nature" and means the characteristics of the world, or things in general, independent of what human beings impose on it. As you can see, it is the word from which our "physics" is derived.

Nomos is the word for custom or convention, for those things that are as they are because human beings have decided they should be so. In America cars are driven on the right side of the road, in England on the left. Neither practice is "natural," or by *physis*. This is a clear example of convention. We drive on one side in America and on the other side in England simply because we have agreed to. In the case Herodotus refers to, it is not so clear that an explicit decision is responsible for how the Greeks and the Indians care for their dead. These

_____

*See "Knowledge and Opinion" in Chapter 6 to see how Plato struggles against this view.

are practices that probably go back into prehistory. Still, it is clear enough that neither practice is "by nature." Herodotus assigns the difference to custom, which is certainly *nomos,* for it is possible that, difficult as it might be, Greeks and Indians alike might take thought and change their practices. The mark of what is true by *physis* is that it is not up to us to decide, nor can we change the pattern if we want to. If by agreement we can change the order of certain things (for example, which side of the road to drive on), then these things exist by *nomos,* not by *physis.*

Let us talk in terms of "the way things are." The way things are may be due to *physis* or to *nomos.* If they are due to *physis,* then we cannot go against them. For instance, it is part of the way things are that taking an ounce of strychnine will, unless immediate remedies are taken, cause one to die. It is not possible to swallow an ounce of strychnine, take no remedy, and continue to live. The connection between taking strychnine and death is a matter of *physis.* It does not depend on our decisions.

It is also part of the way things are that poisoning another human being is punished in some way. Yet it is possible (and it has happened) that someone might poison another and not receive punishment. Perhaps the killer is never discovered, or perhaps his lawyer is particularly skilled in rhetoric. If the way things are can be evaded, provided one is lucky or clever enough, then those connections are established by *nomos* and not by *physis.* It is for this reason that in cases of *nomos* we are likely to talk in terms of what a person "ought" to do: what is "right" or "appropriate," or "good" to do. It is neither right nor appropriate to follow the laws of nature. With respect to them, we have no choice. But conventions, customs, or laws that exist by *nomos* have a "normative" character to them. They state what we should do but may fail to do. It is possible to go against them. We should not, in England, drive on the right, but we can. Murderers should be punished, but they sometimes are not.

The distinction is an important one, and the credit for making it clearly must go to the Sophists. But how, you might ask, did they use it?

The question about the gods can be put clearly using this terminology. Do the gods exist by *physis* or by *nomos?* To answer that they exist by nature is to claim that their existence is quite independent of whatever humans believe about them. To say that the gods exist only by *nomos* amounts to saying that they are dependent on our belief; they have no reality independent of what we happen to believe about them. It is clear that the skeptical and relativistic nature of Sophist thought favors the latter alternative. Certain Sophists may have said that if it seems to you the gods exist, then they do exist— for you. But the agnosticism of Protagoras is probably more representative.

The distinction between *nomos* and *physis* is also applied to the virtues and, in particular, to justice. If a settled community like a city-state is to survive, then it is necessary that a certain degree of justice should prevail. Agreements must be kept, deceptions must be exceptions, and each individual must be able to count on others to keep up their end of things. So much is clear.* But is justice, which demands these things, something good by nature? Or is it merely a convention, foisted on individuals perhaps against their own best interest? Is justice a matter of *physis,* or is it entirely *nomos?* This question is important. It is extensively debated by the Sophists and, as we will see, by Plato and his successors.

It is clear what answer the Sophists must give to this question. They can look back to the institution of democracy, which is obviously a change made by human beings. They can see the process of laws being debated and set down. They observe decisions being made and sometimes reversed again. Clearly, forms of government, laws, and customs are matters of *nomos.* They are made by and can be altered by human decisions.

From the Sophists' point of view, if you want to know what is right or just, consult the laws. Is it

---

*Justice in this context is clearly something more than the justice of Homeric heroes giving one another the honor due to each (see p. 7). What is needed in settled city-states is more extensive than what is needed by warrior bands. Some notion of fair play or evenhandedness seems to be involved. The nature of justice is a perennial problem, and we will return to it.

just to keep agreements made? Then the laws will say so. How much tax is owed? The laws will tell you. For matters not covered explicitly by law, you must look to the customs of the people. Where else can one look? Just as there is no sense in asking whether the wind in itself is either cold or warm (apart from the way it seems to those who feel it), so is there no sense in asking whether a given law is really just. If it seems just to the people of Athens, say, then it is just (for the Athenians).

For clarity's sake, let's call this sense of justice conventional justice. Conventional justice is defined as whatever the conventions (the *nomoi*) of a given society lay down as just.

We can contrast with this the idea of natural justice. Heraclitus, for instance, holds that

> all human laws are nourished by the one divine law.
> For it governs as far as it will, and is sufficient for all
> things, and outlasts them. (DK 22 B 114, *IEGP,* 103)

His idea is that human laws do not have their justification in themselves. They are "nourished," or get their sustenance, from a "divine law." This divine law, of course, is "common to all," the one *logos,* which is the same as the world-order. So human laws are not self-sufficient, in Heraclitus' view. Because people are often "at variance" with the *logos,* we can infer that human law, too, may diverge from the *logos.* It makes sense for Heraclitus to contrast conventional justice with real or natural justice. He believes not only that there is a court of appeal from a possibly unjust human law, but also that human beings can know what divine law requires.

An example of such an appeal is found in **Sophocles'** play *Antigone.* Following a civil war, Creon, king of Thebes, proclaims that the body of Polyneices, leader of the opposition, remain unburied. This was, in Greek tradition, a very bad thing; only if one's body was buried could the spirit depart for Hades. Polyneices' sister, **Antigone**, defies the decree and covers the body with dirt. Before the king she acknowledges that she knew of the king's order and defends her action in these words.

> It was not Zeus who published this decree,
> Nor have the Powers who rule among the dead

> Imposed such laws as this upon mankind;
> Nor could I think that a decree of yours—
> A man—could override the laws of Heaven
> Unwritten and unchanging. Not of today
> Or yesterday is their authority;
> They are eternal; no man saw their birth.
> Was I to stand before the gods' tribunal
> For disobeying them, because I feared
> A man?[8]

Both Heraclitus and Antigone suggest that beyond conventional justice there is another justice. If the laws established by convention violate these higher laws, it may be permissible to violate the conventions.* For the Sophists, however, no such appeal is possible. One might not like a law and therefore work to change it, but there is no appeal to another kind of law to justify its violation. Their skepticism about any reality beyond appearances and their consequent relativism rule out any such appeal.

A certain conservatism seems to be a consequence of this way of looking at justice. Protagoras, for instance, in promising to make Hippocrates a "better man," one able to succeed in Athenian society, would scarcely teach him that Athens is profoundly mistaken in her ideas of justice. He certainly would not turn him into a rebel and malcontent, or even into a reformer. That is no way to attain the admiration of one's fellow citizens; that is the way to earn their hostility and hatred. So it is likely that the Sophists taught their students to adapt to whatever society they found.

Some of the Sophists, though, draw different conclusions. They agree with Heraclitus that there is a natural justice, but they disagree completely about its content. Natural justice, they hold, is not the "nourisher" of conventional justice, but its enemy. A Sophist named **Antiphon** writes,

> Life and death are the concern of nature, and living creatures live by what is advantageous to them and die from what is not advantageous; and the advantages which accrue from law are chains upon nature, whereas those which accrue from nature are free. (DK 87 B 44, *IEGP,* 251)

---

*Note that we have here a justification for civil disobedience. A more recent example is Martin Luther King, Jr.'s, 1963 "Letter from Birmingham Jail."

Antiphon is telling us that if we only observe, we can see that a *natural* law governs the affairs of men and other living creatures: the law of self-preservation. Like all laws, it carries a punishment for those who violate it: death. Unlike conventional laws, this punishment necessarily follows the violation of the law. That is what makes it a natural law rather than a matter of convention. All creatures, he says, follow this law by seeking what is "advantageous" to themselves.

In contrast to *this* natural law, the restraints conventional justice places on human behavior are "chains upon nature." Antiphon goes as far as to claim that

> most of the things which are just by law [in the conventional sense] are hostile to nature. (DK 87 B 44, *IEGP,* 251)

It is natural, then, and therefore right or just (in the sense of *physis*) to pursue what is advantageous. Some of the time your advantage may coincide with the laws of the city. But because there is a tension between conventional law and your advantage, and because seeking your advantage is in accord with a natural law, Antiphon gives us this remarkable piece of advice:

> A man will be just, then, in a way most advantageous to himself if, in the presence of witnesses, he holds the laws of the city in high esteem, and in the absence of witnesses, when he is alone, those of nature. For the laws of men are adventitious, but those of nature are necessary; and the laws of men are fixed by agreement, not by nature, whereas the laws of nature are natural and not fixed by agreement. He who breaks the rules, therefore, and escapes detection by those who have agreed to them, incurs no shame or penalty; if detected he does. (DK 87 B 44, *IEGP,* 250–251)

If you incur no "shame or penalty" by breaking the conventional laws (that is, if you are not caught), then you have not brought any disadvantage upon yourself by doing so. Furthermore, the law of self-preservation takes precedence over the conventional laws because it is "necessary" and "natural." Only *its* prescriptions cannot be evaded. Antiphon drives the point home:

> If some benefit accrued to those who subscribed to the laws, while loss accrued to those who did not

subscribe to them but opposed them, then obedience to the laws would not be without profit. But as things stand, it seems that legal justice is not strong enough to benefit those who subscribe to laws of this sort. For in the first place it permits the injured party to suffer injury and the man who inflicts it to inflict injury, and it does not prevent the injured party from suffering injury nor the man who does the injury from doing it. And if the case comes to trial, the injured party has no more of an advantage than the one who has done the injury; for he must convince his judges that he has been injured, and must be able, by his plea, to exact justice. And it is open to the one who has done the injury to deny it; for he can defend himself against the accusation, and he has the same opportunity to persuade his judges that his accuser has. For the victory goes to the best speaker. (DK 87 B 44, *IEGP,* 252–253)

"For the victory goes to the best speaker": We come around again to rhetoric. No matter which of the sophistic views of justice you take, rhetoric is of supreme importance. Whether you say that conventional justice is the only justice there is or hold that there is a natural justice of self-preservation, it is more important to *appear* just than to *be* just. According to the former view, appearances are all anyone can know; according to the latter, the way you appear to others determines whether you obtain what is most advantageous to yourself.

The Sophists produced a theory of the origins of conventional justice as well. It is not clear how widespread it was; there was no unified sophistic doctrine. But it is of great interest and was picked up in the nineteenth century by Friedrich Nietzsche, who made it a key point in his attempt at a "revaluation of values." * It is represented for us in Plato's *Gorgias,* where it is presented by **Callicles**.

> In my opinion it's the weaklings who constitute the majority of the human race who make the rules. In making these rules, they look after themselves and their own interest, and that's also the criterion they use when they dispense praise and criticism. They try to cow the stronger ones—which is to say, the ones who are capable of increasing their share of things—and to stop them getting an increased share, by saying that to do so is wrong and contemptible and by defining injustice in precisely those terms, as the

---

*See Chapter 20, especially pp. 548–549.

attempt to have more than others. In my opinion, it's because they're second-rate that they're happy for things to be distributed equally. Anyway, that's why convention states that the attempt to have a larger share than most people is immoral and contemptible; that's why people call it doing wrong. But I think we only have to look at nature to find evidence that it is *right* for better to have a greater share than worse, more capable than less capable. The evidence for this is widespread. Other creatures show, as do human communities and nations, that right has been determined as follows: the superior person shall dominate the inferior person and have more than him. By what right, for instance, did Xerxes make war on Greece or his father on Sythia, not to mention countless further cases of the same kind of behaviour? These people act, surely, in conformity with the natural essence of right and, yes, I'd even go so far as to say that they act in conformity with natural *law,* even though they presumably contravene our man-made laws.

What do we do with the best and strongest among us? We capture them young, like lions, mould them, and turn them into slaves by chanting spells and incantations over them which insist that they have to be equal to others and that equality is admirable and right. But I'm sure that if a man is born in whom nature is strong enough, he'll shake off all these limitations, shatter them to pieces, and win his freedom; he'll trample all our regulations, charms, spells, and unnatural laws into the dust; this slave will rise up and reveal himself as our master; and then natural right will blaze forth. (*Gorgias* 483b–484a)

Callicles' basic idea is that we are by nature equipped with certain passions and desires. It is natural to try to satisfy these. Although the weak may try to fetter those who are strong by imposing a guilty conscience on them, the strong do nothing contrary to nature if they exert all their power and cleverness to satisfy whatever desires they have. Such behavior may be conventionally frowned upon, but it is not, in itself, unjust.

Note how dramatically this contrasts with the ethics of the Greek tradition. Compare it, for instance, to Heraclitus, who holds that it is not good for men to get all they wish, that "moderation is the greatest virtue."*

Callicles holds that enjoyment consists not in moderating one's desires but in satisfying them to the fullest extent. The really happy man is the one who is strong enough to do this without fear of retaliation. Here we have the very opposite of the "nothing too much" doctrine at Delphi—a negation of the tradition of self-restraint.

The views of the Sophists are bold and innovative, a response to the changing social and political situation, particularly in democratic Athens. But they are more than just reflections of a particular society at a given time. They constitute a serious critique of the beliefs of their predecessors and a challenge to those who come after them. These views force us to face the question: Why shouldn't we be Sophists too?

---

1. Explain Protagoras' saying "Man is the measure of all things."
2. What in the Sophists' teaching tends toward relativism?
3. Contrast *physis* with *nomos.*
4. Contrast conventional justice with natural justice. What two different concepts of natural justice can be distinguished?
5. How could the *physis/nomos* distinction be turned toward an antisocial direction?
6. Would a Sophist say that it is more important to be just or to appear just? Why?

Athens and Sparta at War

In the context of the sophistic movement, we are philosophically prepared to understand Socrates and his disciple, Plato. But to understand why Socrates was brought to trial, we need to know something of the war. It was called the **Peloponnesian War** by Thucydides, who lived through it and wrote its history in a fascinating book by that title.* The Peloponnesus is the large peninsula at the southern tip of mainland Greece, connected by the narrow Isthmus of Corinth to Greece proper. It was named for

---

*See p. 25.

*For Peloponnesian War, see http://en.wikipedia.org/wiki/Peloponnesian_War.

a largely mythical ancestor, Pelops, supposedly the grandson of Zeus and the grandfather of Agamemnon and Menelaus of Trojan War fame. In the fifth century B.C., the dominant power on the peninsula was the city-state of Sparta (see Map 1).

Sparta was quite unlike Athens. The Spartans had taken an important role in the defeat of the Persians, but thereafter, unlike Athens, they had followed a more cautious and defensive policy. Sparta was primarily a land power; Athens ruled the seas. Although the Spartans had allies, mostly in the Peloponnesus, Athens had created an empire dominating most of the north of Greece and most of the islands in the Aegean. Sparta was not democratic. Rule in Sparta was in the hands of a relatively small portion of the population, in effect a warrior class. Their way of life was austere and, as we say, spartan—devoted not to wealth and enjoyment but to rigorous training and self-discipline. They were supported by a large slave population called Helots and by other subject peoples in the area who paid tribute.

Perhaps it was inevitable that two such formidable powers in close proximity and so different would clash. They cooperated well enough in repelling the Persian invasion, but when that danger was past, their interests diverged. As Thucydides tells us,

> What made war inevitable was the growth of Athenian power and the fear which this caused in Sparta. (*HPW* 1.23)[9]

War may indeed have been inevitable, but its coming was tragic. In the end, it led to the defeat of Athens and to the weakening of Greece in general. It meant the beginning of the end of the Golden Age of Greece.

The war itself was long and drawn out, lasting from 431 to 404 B.C., with an interval of seven years of relative peace in the middle. It was immensely costly to both sides, both in terms of men lost and wealth squandered. We will not go into the details of the war; they can be found in Thucydides or any of a number of modern histories.* But war does things to a people, especially a long and

inconclusive war fought with increasing desperation. And we need to have a sense for the temper of the times.

Athens encouraged the development of democracy in her allies and appealed to the people (as opposed to the aristocrats) in cities she hoped to bring into her empire. These moves were resisted by the aristocratic or oligarchical parties in these states, who were often supported by Sparta. Thucydides records the events in Corcyra (see Map 1) after the victory of the democratic side over the oligarchs.

> They seized upon all their enemies whom they could find and put them to death. They then dealt with those whom they had persuaded to go on board the ships, killing them as they landed. Next they went to the temple of Hera and persuaded about fifty of the suppliants there to submit to a trial. They condemned every one of them to death. Seeing what was happening, most of the other suppliants, who had refused to be tried, killed each other there in the temple; some hanged themselves on the trees, and others found various other means of committing suicide. During the seven days that Eurymedon [an Athenian naval commander] stayed there with his sixty ships, the Corcyreans continued to massacre those of their own citizens whom they considered to be their enemies. Their victims were accused of conspiring to overthrow the democracy, but in fact men were often killed on grounds of personal hatred or else by their debtors because of the money they owed. There was death in every shape and form. And, as usually happens in such situations, people went to every extreme and beyond it. There were fathers who killed their sons; men were dragged from the temples or butchered on the very altars; some were actually walled up in the temple of Dionysus and died there. . . .
>
> Later, of course, practically the whole of the Hellenic world was convulsed, with rival parties in every state—democratic leaders trying to bring in the Athenians, and oligarchs trying to bring in the Spartans. (*HPW* 3.81–3.83)

We can see here the disintegration of the traditional Greek ideal of moderation; people "went to every extreme and beyond it." Moreover, the arguments of the more extreme Sophists found a parallel in concrete political undertakings. Naked

---

*See suggestions in Note 1, at the close of this chapter.

self-interest came more and more to play the major role in decisions no longer even cloaked in terms of justice. Perhaps worst of all, Thucydides says, the very meaning of the words for right and virtue changed. When that happens, confusion reigns while moral thought and criticism become impossible.

After the death of Pericles in the early years of the war, Athens had no natural leader. Leadership tended to flow to those who could speak persuasively before the Assembly. These leaders were called "demagogues," those who could lead (*agoge*) the *demos*. Policy was inconstant and sometimes reversed, depending on who was the most persuasive speaker of the day. Dissatisfaction with democracy began to grow, especially in quarters traditionally allied with the "best people." When Athens was finally defeated in 404, treachery on the part of these enemies of democracy was suspected but could not be proved.

According to the terms of the peace treaty imposed on Athens, she had to receive returning exiles (most of whom were antidemocratic), agree to have the same friends and enemies as Sparta, and accept provisional government by a Council that came to be known as **the Thirty.** A new constitution was promised, but naturally the Thirty were in no hurry to form a new government. Supported by a cohort of Spartan men-at-arms, they carried out a purge of "wrongdoers," executing criminals and those who had opposed surrender. But their rule soon involved the persecution of any dissidents, as well as people they just didn't like, and the expropriation of their property to support the new system. They claimed, of course, to be enforcing virtue. In classic fashion, they tried to involve as many Athenian citizens as possible in their adventures to prevent them from making accusations later. Socrates, as we learn, was one of five persons summoned to arrest a certain Leon of Salamis. (He refused.) The rule of the Thirty became, in short, a reign of terror. Ever after, Athenians could not hear the words "the Thirty" without a shudder.

This rule lasted less than a year. Exiles, joined by democratic forces within the city, attacked and defeated the forces backing the Thirty. Their leader **Critias** was killed in the fighting, the others

were exiled, and democracy was restored. Though a bloodbath was resisted, bad feelings on all sides continued for many years.

Because of the war and its aftermath, Athenians lost confidence in their ability to control their own destiny. The satisfaction in their superiority expressed so well by Pericles disintegrated. Men seemed torn by forces beyond their ability to control in a world that was not well ordered, whether by the gods or by something like the Heraclitean *logos.* The world and human affairs seemed chaotic, beyond managing.

The Greeks had always believed, of course, that humans were not complete masters of their own fate. This belief was expressed in the ideas that the gods intervene in human affairs for their own ends and that none of us can escape our fate. We find such ideas in the works of Homer and in the tragedies of Aeschylus and Sophocles. But in the time of the war, these notions were tinged with a new sense of bitterness and despair. The third of the great Greek tragedians, **Euripides,** expresses the new mood.

Hippolytus, in the play by that name, is devoted to Artemis (the Roman Diana), goddess of the woodlands, of the hunt, and of chastity. **Phaedra,** his father's second wife, falls passionately in love with him under the influence of Aphrodite (Venus). She is literally sick with love—sick, she says, to death. Her nurse first admonishes her in classic fashion.

> The ways of life that are most fanatical
> trip us up more, they say, than bring us joy.
> They're enemies to health. So I praise less
> the extreme than temperance in everything.
> The wise will bear me out.
>
> —*Hippolytus 261–266*[10]

Temperance, moderation in all things, is her message. It is not wise to let one's passions get out of control. It is the old message that comes down through the philosophers from Homer. Her words suggest that Phaedra should give up her passion.

But upon learning the object of Phaedra's love and her inability or unwillingness to give it up, the nurse changes her mind:

> In this world second thoughts, it seems, are best.
> Your case is not so extraordinary,

beyond thought or reason. The Goddess in her anger has smitten you, and you are in love. What wonder is this? . . .

> The tide of love,
> at its full surge, is not withstandable. . . .
> He who has read the writings of the ancients
> and has lived much in books, he knows
> that Zeus once loved the lovely Semele. . . .
>   Yet all these dwell in heaven.
> They are content, I am sure, to be subdued
> by the stroke of love. . . .
> We should not in the conduct of our lives
> be too exacting.
>
> ——*Hippolytus* 436–468

Here we have the nurse as rhetorician, constructing a plausible *logos* to suit the one who hears her. She even appeals to the example of the gods; if they give in to their passions, she says, why should you think it wrong for you to do the same? Phaedra, hanging on to her virtue as best she can despite her acknowledged love, gives this reply:*

> This is the deadly thing which devastates
> well-ordered cities and the homes of men—
> that's it, this art of oversubtle words.
> It's not the words ringing in the ear
> that one should speak, but those that have the power
> to save their hearer's honorable name.
>
> ——*Hippolytus* 486–489

The nurse responds:

> This is high moralizing! What you want is not fine
>   words, but the man!
>
> ——*Hippolytus* 490–491

To Phaedra's protests that this is "wicked, wicked!" and her refusal to listen to such "shameful" words, the nurse admits,

> O, they are shameful! But they are better than
> your noble-sounding moral sentiments.
> "The deed" is better if it saves your life:
> than your "good name" in which you die exulting.
>
> ——*Hippolytus* 500–503

Here again we have the morality of certain Sophists. What is important is that you save your life. Considerations of honor and morality must be held

---

*Is it necessary to point out that we have here a critique of the practice of rhetoric?

strictly in second place. It is quite the opposite of the Homeric morality; Achilles, for instance, and Hector too, are quite ready to die for honor and glory; death is, by comparison, unimportant.

As the play develops, the nurse tells Hippolytus of Phaedra's love for him. He rejects it and vows to tell his father, Theseus, who is out of the city at the time. When Phaedra learns of this, she kills herself and leaves a note (to save her good name) accusing Hippolytus of rape. Theseus returns, reads the note, and curses his son. The consequence is Hippolytus' death in a chariot accident; only then does Theseus learn of his son's innocence.

The play is framed at beginning and end by speeches of the two goddesses, Aphrodite and Artemis, respectively. Aphrodite vows to take vengeance on Hippolytus because he despises her and worships only chastity. This she does, using Phaedra as her tool. Artemis at the end vows to avenge Hippolytus by destroying some favorite of Aphrodite's. (Some vengeance!) The impression left by the play is that humans are mere pawns in the hands of greater powers—powers that are in opposition to each other, that make no sense, and have no rhyme or reason in some higher unity of purpose. Led this way or that by passions we cannot control, we are bound for destruction.

The chorus laments near the end:

> The care of God for us is a great thing,
> if a man believe it at heart:
> it plucks the burden of sorrow from him.
> So I have a secret hope
> of someone, a God, who is wise and plans;
> but my hopes grow dim when I see
> the deeds of men and their destinies.
> For fortune is ever veering, and the currents of life
>   are shifting,
> shifting, wandering forever.
>
> ——*Hippolytus* 1102–1110

We have the hope, the chorus says, that our lives are more than "sound and fury, signifying nothing."* We would like to believe that there is a wise plan to our lives, but if we look about us at the world—and, the Sophists would say, what else can we do?—we find no such reason to hope. Men's

---

*Shakespeare's *Macbeth*, act 5, scene 5.

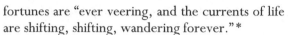

fortunes are "ever veering, and the currents of life are shifting, shifting, wandering forever."*

So things must have looked in the last decades of the fifth century B.C. in Athens.

Aristophanes and Reaction

Although the Sophists were obviously popular in some circles, they were hated and feared in others. They were a phenomenon that both depended on and fostered the kind of democracy Athens practiced: direct democracy where decisions were made by whichever citizens were present in the Assembly on a given day. Political power rested directly with the people in this system, but the masses, of course, tended to be at the mercy of those who possessed the rhetorical skills to sway them in the direction of their own interests: the demagogues. The old families who could look back to the "good old days" when the "best people" made the decisions were never happy in this state of affairs. As we have seen, they tried, when they could, to reverse the situation—not always with better results!

Among those who were unhappy were certain intellectuals, including a writer of comedies named **Aristophanes.** One of his plays, **The Clouds,**† is a satire on the new education provided by the Sophists and on the sophistic movement in general. It is worth a look not only because it gives us another point of view on the Sophists but also because he makes Socrates a principal character in the play. In fact, Socrates is presented in *The Clouds* as the leading Sophist, who runs a school called the "Thinkery" to which students come to learn—provided they pay. When we first see Socrates, he is hanging in the air, suspended in a basket.

> You see,
> only by being suspended aloft, by dangling
> my mind in the heavens and mingling my rare
>   thought
> with the ethereal air, could I ever achieve strict

scientific accuracy in my survey of the vast
  empyrean.
Had I pursued my inquiries from down there on
  the ground,
my data would be worthless. The earth, you see,
  pulls down
the delicate essence of thought to its own gross
  level.

> —*Clouds,* p. 33[11]

This is, of course, attractive nonsense. As we'll see, Socrates neither had a Thinkery, charged for instruction, nor was interested in speculations about the heavens and earth. Most important, although he did share the Sophists' interest in human affairs, Socrates was one of their most severe critics. Aristophanes' picture of Socrates is satire painted with a broad brush.

Socrates' students are represented as engaging in scientific studies to determine, for example, how far a flea can jump and out of which end does a gnat tootle. But that is not the main interest of the play. Strepsiades, a man from the country who has married an extravagant city wife and has a son who loves horse racing, is worried about the debts they have piled up. In particular, several of his son's debts are coming due and he hasn't the money to pay them. So he decides to send his son to the Thinkery to learn the new sophistic logic, which can make the weaker argument into the stronger. He thinks that by getting his son to learn these rhetorical tricks he may be able to avoid paying back the money.

Strepsiades is at first unable to persuade his son to go. So he becomes a student himself. He does not prove an apt pupil, however, and Socrates eventually kicks him out, but not before he has learned a thing or two. When he meets his son, Pheidippides, he again tries to force him to go to the school.

PHEIDIPPIDES: But Father,
  what's the matter with you? Are you out of your
  head?
  Almighty Zeus, you must be mad!
STREPSIADES: "Almighty Zeus!"
  What musty rubbish! Imagine, a boy your age still
  believing in Zeus!
P: What's so damn funny?
S: It tickles me when the heads of toddlers like you are
  still stuffed with such outdated notions.

---

*A somewhat altered version of the play is available in the movie *Phaedra*, starring Melina Mercouri and Anthony Perkins.

†First performed in Athens in 423 B.C., the eighth year of the war.

Now then,
listen to me and I'll tell you a secret or two that
might make an intelligent man of you yet. But remember. You mustn't breathe a word of this.

P: A word of what?

S: Didn't you just swear by Zeus?

P: I did.

S: Now learn what Education can do for you: Pheidippides, there is no Zeus.

P: There is no Zeus?

S: No Zeus. Convection-Principle's in power now.
Zeus has been banished.

—*Clouds,* pp. 75–76

The "convection principle" is our old friend the
vortex motion or cosmic whirl, by means of which
the nature philosophers explain the structure of the
world. In the form given this principle by the atomists, as we have seen, there is no need for—indeed,
no room for—any intelligent purpose at all. Everything is caused to happen necessarily, in a completely mechanical fashion. Zeus has indeed been
"banished."

Aristophanes, far from conceding that this is
progress, deplores the new thought. The old methods of education are farcically confronted with the
new by means of two characters, dressed in the
masks of fighting cocks, called the just *logos* and
the unjust *logos.* (In this translation, they are called
"Philosophy" and "Sophistry," respectively.) After
some preliminary sparring and insult trading, the
just *logos* speaks first.

PHILOSOPHY: Gentlemen,
I propose to speak of the Old Education, as it
flourished once
beneath my tutelage, when Homespun Honesty,
Plainspeaking, and Truth
were still honored and practiced, and throughout
the schools of Athens
the regime of the three D's—DISCIPLINE, DECO-
RUM, and DUTY—
enjoyed unchallenged supremacy.
Our curriculum was Music and Gymnastics, enforced by that rigorous discipline summed up in the
old adage:
BOYS SHOULD BE SEEN BUT NOT HEARD. . . .

SOPHISTRY: Ugh, what musty, antiquated rubbish.
. . .

P: Nonetheless, these were the precepts on which I
bred a generation of heroes, the men who fought at
Marathon. . . .
No, young man, by your courage I challenge you.
Turn your back upon his blandishments of vice,
the rotten law courts and the cheap, corrupting
softness of the baths.
Choose instead the Old, the Philosophical Education. Follow me
and from my lips acquire the virtues of a man:—
A sense of shame, that decency and innocence of
mind that shrinks from doing wrong.
To feel the true man's blaze of anger when his
honor is provoked.
Deference toward one's elders; respect for one's
father and mother.

—*Clouds,* pp. 86–89

This speech is applauded roundly by the chorus,
who say that the unjust *logos* will have to produce
"some crushing *tour de force,* some master stroke" to
counter these persuasive comments. The unjust *logos*
is not at a loss.

SOPHISTRY: Now then, I freely admit
that among men of learning I am—somewhat
pejoratively—dubbed
the Sophistic, or Immoral Logic. And why?
Because I first
devised a Method for the Subversion of Established
Social Beliefs
and the Undermining of Morality. Moreover, this
little invention of mine,
this knack of taking what might appear to be the
worse argument
and nonetheless winning my case, has, I might add,
proved to be
an *extremely* lucrative source of income. . . .
—Young man,
I advise you to ponder this life of Virtue with scru-
pulous care,
all that it implies, and all the pleasures of which its
daily practice
must inevitably deprive you. Specifically, I might
mention these:

Sex. Gambling. Gluttony. Guzzling. Carousing.
Etcet.
And what on earth's the point of living, if you leach
your life
of all its little joys?

 Very well then, consider your natural needs.
Suppose, as a scholar of Virtue, you commit
 some minor peccadillo,
a little adultery, say, or seduction, and suddenly
find yourself
caught in the act. What happens? You're ruined,
you can't defend yourself
(since, of course, you haven't been taught). But follow me, my boy,
and obey your nature to the full; romp, play, and
laugh
without a scruple in the world. Then if caught in
flagrante,
you simply inform the poor cuckold that you're utterly innocent
and refer him to Zeus as your moral sanction.
After all, didn't he,
a great and powerful god, succumb to the love of
women?
Then how in the world can you, a man, an ordinary
mortal,
be expected to surpass the greatest of gods in moral
self-control?
Clearly, you can't be.

       —*Clouds, pp. 91–94*

To his father's satisfaction, Pheidippides is persuaded to study with the Sophists. But the climax
comes when the son turns what he has learned, not
on the creditors, but on his father. After a quarrel, he
begins to beat his father with a stick. This is not bad
enough; he claims to be able to *prove* that he is right to
do so!

PHEIDIPPIDES: Now then, answer my question: did
 you lick me when I was a little boy?
STREPSIADES: Of course I licked you.
 For your own damn good. Because I loved you.
P: Then *ipso facto,*
 since you yourself admit that loving and lickings are
synonymous, it's only fair that I—for your own
damn good,

you understand—whip you in return.
 In any case by what right do you whip me but
claim exemption for yourself?
 What do you think I am? A slave?
Wasn't I born as free a man as you?
 Well?
S: But . . .
P: But what?
Spare the Rod and Spoil the Child?
Is that your argument?
 If so,
then I can be sententious too. *Old Men Are Boys
Writ Big,*
as the saying goes.
 A fortiori then, old men logically deserve to be
beaten more, since at their age they have clearly less
excuse for the mischief that they do.
S: But it's unnatural! It's . . . . *illegal!*
Honor your father and mother.
 That's the law.
 Everywhere.
P: The *law?*
And who made the law?
 An ordinary man. A man like you or me.
A man who lobbied for his bill until he persuaded
the people to make it law.
 By the same token, then, what prevents me now
from proposing new legislation granting sons the
 power to
inflict corporal punishment upon wayward fathers?
 . . .
 However, if you're still unconvinced, look to
 Nature for a sanction. Observe the roosters,
for instance, and what do you see?
A society
whose pecking order envisages a permanent state
 of open
warfare between fathers and sons. And how do
 roosters
differ from men, except for the trifling fact that
 human
society is based upon law and rooster society isn't?
       —*Clouds, pp. 122–124*

Strepsiades is forced by the "persuasive power" of
this rhetoric to admit defeat: "The kids," he says,
"have proved their point: naughty fathers should
be flogged." But when Pheidippides adds that since

"misery loves company" he has decided to flog his *mother,* too, and can prove "by Sokratic logic" the propriety of doing so, that's the last straw. Strepsiades cries out:

> By god, if you prove *that,*
> then for all I care, you heel,
> you can take your stinking Logics
> and your Thinkery as well
> with Sokrates inside it
> and damn well go to hell!
>
> —*Clouds,* p. 126

Disillusioned by the promise of sophistry, Strepsiades admits he was wrong to try to cheat his son's creditors. Convinced that the new education is, as the just *logos* has put it, the "corrupter and destroyer" of the youth, he ends the play by burning down the Thinkery. The moral is drawn, as it typically is, by the chorus—in this case a chorus of Clouds representing the goddesses of the new thought:

> This is what we are,
> the insubstantial Clouds men build their hopes upon,
> shining tempters formed of air, symbols of desire;
>   and so we act, beckoning, alluring foolish men
> through their dishonest dreams of gain to
>   overwhelming
> ruin. There, schooled by suffering, they learn at last
> to fear the gods.
>
> —*Clouds,* p. 127

The Clouds is surely not a fair and dispassionate appraisal of the sophistic movement. It is partisan in the extreme, a caricature by a traditionalist deeply antagonistic to the changes Athenian society was going through. And yet it poses some serious questions. Is there a way to distinguish between *logoi* independently of their persuasiveness? If not, is argument just a contest that the most persuasive must win? And if Strepsiades can think of no logical rejoinder to his son's sophisms, what is the outcome? Are arson and violence the only answer? But if that is so, in what sense is that answer superior to the rhetoric that it opposes? Isn't it just employing another tool of force, less subtle than the verbal manipulations of the rhetorician?

What is put in question by the Sophists and Aristophanes' response to them is this: Is there any technique by which people can discuss and come to agree on matters important to them that does not reduce to a power struggle in the end? Is there something that can be identified as being reasonable, as opposed to being merely persuasive? Can human beings, by discussing matters together, come to know the truth? Or is it always just a question of who wins?

This is the question that interests Socrates.

1. Sketch the argument between Phaedra and the Nurse in Euripides' *Hippolytus.*
2. What philosophical question is posed by Aristophanes' play *The Clouds*?

KEY WORDS

Athens	Sophocles
democracy	Antigone
Persian wars	Antiphon
Pericles	Callicles
Sophists	Peloponnesian War
areté	The Thirty
rhetoric	Critias
skepticism	Euripides
agnostic	Hippolytus
relativism	Phaedra
physis	Aristophanes
nomos	*The Clouds*

FOR FURTHER THOUGHT

1. Sophist/relativist views about the good or the true are often expressed by the question "Who's to say?" Is that a good question? If not, why not?
2. What do you think? Is it more important to *be* just or to *appear* just? Why?

NOTES

1. *The Pelican History of Greece* by A. R. Burn (New York: Penguin Books, 1984) is a lively treatment of these matters. A standard source is J. B. Bury, *A History of Greece* (London: Macmillan and Co., 1951). The Greek historians Herodotus, Thucydides, and Xenophon are also quite readable.

2. Quotations from Herodotus, *The Histories* (New York: Penguin Books, 1972), are cited in the text by title, book number, and section number.

3. Thucydides, *History of the Peloponnesian War,* trans. Rex Warner (New York: Penguin Books, 1954), 2.35–41.

4. Quotations from Plato's *Protagoras,* trans, C. C. W. Taylor (Oxford: Oxford University Press, 1996), are cited in the text by title and section numbers.

5. Quotations from Plato's *Gorgias,* trans. Robin Waterfield (Oxford: Oxford University Press, 1994), are cited in the text by title and section number.

6. Quotations from John Manley Robinson's *An Introduction to Early Greek Philosophy* (Boston: Houghton Mifflin Co., 1968) are cited in the text using the standard Diels/Kranz numbers, followed by the page number in *IEGP*.

7. Herodotus, *The Histories* (Penguin Books, 1972), bk. 3, sec. 38.

8. Sophocles, *Antigone,* trans. H. D. F. Kitto, in *Sophocles: Three Tragedies* (London: Oxford University Press, 1962), ll. 440–450.

9. Quotations from Thucydides, *History of the Peloponnesian War,* trans. Rex Warner (New York: Penguin Books, 1954), are cited in the text using the abbreviation *HPW.* References are to book and section numbers.

10. Quotations from Euripides' *Hippolytus,* trans. David Grene, in *Euripides I,* ed. David Grene and Richmond Lattimore (Chicago: University of Chicago Press, 1965), are cited in the text by title and line numbers.

11. Quotations from Aristophanes' *Clouds,* trans. William Arrowsmith (New York: New American Library, 1962), are cited in the text by title and page numbers.

4

SOCRATES

To Know Oneself

Some philosophers are important just for what they say or write. Others are important also for what they are—for their personality and character. No better example of the latter exists than **Socrates.**

Socrates wrote nothing, save some poetry written while he was waiting to be executed; he is said to have written a hymn to Apollo and to have put the fables of Aesop into verse. But those have not survived. His impact on those who knew him, however, was extraordinary, and his influence down to the present day has few parallels.

The fact that he wrote nothing poses a problem, of course. We have to look to other writers for our knowledge of him. Aristophanes is one source, but such farce must be taken with more than one grain of salt. Another source is **Xenophon,** who tells numerous stories involving Socrates but is philosophically rather unsophisticated.* Aristotle,

too, discusses him. But our main source is Plato, a younger companion of Socrates and a devoted admirer.

Plato didn't, however, write a biography, nor did he write a scholarly analysis of his master's thought. He has left us a large number of dialogues, or conversations, in most of which Socrates is a participant, often the central figure. These might be very reliable, if Plato had carried with him a tape recorder and then transcribed the conversations, but of course he couldn't have. These dialogues were all written after Socrates' death, many of them long after. And there can be no doubt that in the later dialogues Plato is putting ideas of his own into the mouth of Socrates. We should not think there is anything dishonest about this practice. The ancient world would have accepted it as perfectly in order; Plato surely believed that his own ideas were a natural development from those of Socrates and that in this way he was honoring his master. But it does pose a problem if we want to discuss the historical Socrates rather than Plato's Socrates.

---

*Note: This is not Xenophanes, the pre-Socratic philosopher discussed in Chapter 2.

No definitive solution to this problem may ever be found. One scholar has acknowledged that "in the end we must all have to some extent our own Socrates."[1] Still, some things are reasonably certain.

The dialogues of Plato can pretty well be sorted into three periods, as follows.

1. The early dialogues, such as *Euthyphro, Crito,* and the *Apology,* are thought to represent quite accurately Socrates' own views and ways of proceeding. They seem to have been written soon after his death. In these dialogues, Socrates questions various individuals about the nature of piety, courage, justice, or virtue/excellence (*areté*).* The outcome of the conversation is usually negative in just this sense: No agreed-upon solution is reached. The participant, who at the dialogue's beginning claims to know the answer, is forced to admit ignorance. You might ask, Is there any point to such conversations? Well, the participants do learn something—that is, how little they really know. In this way the ground is cleared of at least some intellectual rubbish.

2. In the middle dialogues, such as *Meno, Phaedo, Symposium,* and the monumental *Republic,* Socrates is still the main protagonist. Here, however, we find positive doctrines aplenty, supported by many arguments. Here Plato is working out his own solutions to the problems that the Sophists posed and trying to go beyond the negative outcomes of Socratic questioning. What Plato is doing here will be the main subject of Chapter 6.

3. The late dialogues contain further developments and explore difficulties discovered in the doctrines of the middle period. Here Socrates begins to play a lesser role; in the very late *Laws,* he disappears altogether.

In this chapter and the next, we discuss Socrates primarily as he appears in the early works of Plato, and we read in their entirety three short dialogues. Before reading those, however, we need to learn something about Socrates' character and person.

---

*The meaning of this important word is discussed in Chapter 3, on p. 44.

Character

Socrates was born in 470 or 469 B.C. His father was a stonemason and perhaps a minor sculptor. It is thought that Socrates pursued this same trade as a young man. He was married to Xanthippe, a woman with a reputation for shrewishness, and had three sons, apparently rather late in life.

Of some importance is the fact that his mother was a midwife. Socrates calls himself a "midwife" in the realm of thought. It is interesting to note that one of the duties of a Greek midwife in classical times was to determine whether the child was a bastard (presumably by way of resemblance to the purported father). A midwife does not give birth herself, of course. In a similar way, Socrates makes no claim to be able to give birth to true ideas but says he can help deliver the ideas of others and determine their truth. He does this by "examining" them, trying to discover their "resemblance" or consistency with other ideas expressed in the conversation. The question is always this: Do the answers to Socrates' questions fit together with the original claim that what was said is true? (Compare: Does the baby the midwife delivers accord with the claim that so and so is the father?) As we read the three dialogues, we will see numerous examples of his "midwifery."*

No one ever claimed that Socrates was good looking, except in a joke. In a charming work designed to let us see "great and good men" in their "lighter moods," Xenophon reports on an impromptu "beauty contest" held at a banquet. The contestants are Critobulus, a good-looking young man, and Socrates. Socrates is challenged to prove that he is the more handsome.

SOCRATES: Do you think beauty exists in man alone, or in anything else?

CRITOBULUS: I believe it is found in horse and ox and many inanimate things. For instance, I recognize a beautiful shield, sword or spear.

S: And how can all these things be beautiful when they bear no resemblance to each other?

---

*You might like to look at the actual words in which Socrates claims this role of midwife for himself. See Chapter 5, p. 104.

c: Why, if they are well made for the purposes for which we acquire them, or well adapted by nature to our needs, then in each case I call them beautiful.

s: Well then, what do we need eyes for?

c: To see with of course.

s: In that case my eyes are at once proved to be more beautiful than yours, because yours look only straight ahead, whereas mine project so that they can see sideways as well.

c: Are you claiming that a crab has the most beautiful eyes of any animal?

s: Certainly, since from the point of view of strength also its eyes are best constructed by nature.

c: All right, but which of our noses is the more beautiful?

s: Mine, I should say, if the gods gave us noses to smell with, for your nostrils point to earth, but mine are spread out widely to receive odours from every quarter.

c: But how can a snub nose be more beautiful than a straight one?

s: Because it does not get in the way but allows the eyes to see what they will, whereas a high bridge walls them off as if to spite them.

c: As for the mouth, I give in, for if mouths are made for biting you could take a much larger bite than I.

s: And with my thick lips don't you think I could give a softer kiss?[2]

"I do not even have any knowledge of what virtue itself is."
—SOCRATES

After this exchange, the banqueters take a secret ballot to determine who is the more handsome. Critobulus gets every vote, so Socrates exclaims that he must have bribed the judges! It must have been nearly impossible to resist caricaturing this odd-looking man who shuffled about Athens barefoot and peered sideways at you out of his bulging eyes when you spoke to him. Aristophanes was not the only writer of comedies to succumb to the temptation.

We see several things about Socrates in this little excerpt: (1) It was not for his physical attractiveness that Socrates was sought after as a companion; he was acknowledged on all sides to be extraordinarily ugly, though it seems to have been an interesting kind of ugliness; (2) we see something of Socrates' humor; here it is light and directed at himself, but it could also be sharp and biting; (3)

we have our first glimpse of the typical Socratic method, which proceeds by question and answer, not by long speeches; and (4) we see that Socrates here identifies the good or the beautiful in terms of usefulness or advantage, and this is typical of his views on these questions of value.

He served in the army several times with courage and distinction. In Plato's *Symposium,* the story of an all-night banquet and drinking party, **Alcibiades,** a brilliant young man we shall hear more of, gives the following testimony:

Now, the first thing to point out is that there was no one better than him in the whole army at enduring hardship: it wasn't just me he showed up. Once, when we were cut off (as happens during a campaign), we had to do without food and no one else could cope at all. At the same time, when there *were* plenty of provisions, he was better than the rest of us at making the most of them, and especially when it came to drinking: he was reluctant to drink, but when pushed he proved more than a match for everyone. And the most remarkable thing of all is that no one has ever seen Socrates drunk. . . .

Once—and this was the most astonishing thing he did—the cold was so terribly bitter that everyone was either staying inside or, if they did venture out, they wore an incredible amount of clothing, put shoes on, and then wrapped pieces of felt and sheepskin around their feet. Socrates, however, went out in this weather wearing only the outdoor cloak he'd usually worn earlier in the campaign as well, and without anything on his feet; but he still made his way through the ice more easily than the rest of us with our covered feet. . . .

One morning, a puzzling problem occurred to him and he stayed standing where he was thinking about it. Even when it proved intractable, he didn't give up: he just stood there exploring it. By the time it was midday, people were beginning to notice him and were telling one another in amazement that Socrates had been standing there from early in the morning deep in thought. Eventually, after their evening meal, some men from the Ionian contingent took their pallets outside—it was summer at the time—so that they could simultaneously sleep outside where it was cool and watch out for whether he'd stand there all night as well. In fact, he stood there until after sunrise the following morning, and then he greeted the sun with a prayer and went on his way. (*Symposium* 219e–220d)[3]

Alcibiades goes on to tell how Socrates saved his life and in a retreat showed himself to be the coolest man around, so that

anyone could tell, even from a distance, that here was a man who would resist an attack with considerable determination. And that's why he and Laches got out of there safely, because the enemy generally don't take on someone who can remain calm during combat. (*Symposium* 221b)e

He sums up his view by saying that

there's no human being, from times past or present, who can match him. . . .

The first time a person lets himself listen to one of Socrates' arguments, it sounds really ridiculous. . . . He talks of pack-asses, metal-workers, shoemakers, tanners; he seems to go on and on using

the same arguments to make the same points, with the result that ignoramuses and fools are bound to find his arguments ridiculous. But if you could see them opened up, if you can get through to what's under the surface, what you'll find inside is that his arguments are the only ones in the world which make sense. And that's not all: under the surface, his arguments abound with divinity and effigies of goodness. They turn out to be extremely far-reaching, or rather they cover absolutely everything which needs to be taken into consideration on the path to true goodness. (*Symposium* 221c–222a)

It is somewhat ironic to hear Alcibiades talking of "true goodness" here. He was for a time a close associate of Socrates but in later life became notorious for lechery and lust for power. He was suspected of being responsible for the mutilation of statues of Hermes (often set by the gates or doors of Athenian houses) and was put on trial while he was away on a military mission. Eventually he deserted and offered his services as a general to the Spartans! The common opinion was that Alcibiades was handsome and brilliant but also treacherous and despicable. Nonetheless, there is no reason to doubt the testimony to Socrates that Plato here puts into his mouth.

The party is invaded by a bunch of revelers; everyone drinks a great deal, many leave, and some fall asleep. Near morning, only three persons are still awake: Agathon the host, Aristophanes (yes, the comic playwright), and Socrates. They are still drinking and arguing, now about whether one and the same person could write both tragedies and comedies.

They were coming round to his point of view, but they were too sleepy to follow the argument very well; Aristophanes fell asleep first and Agathon joined him after daybreak.

Now that he'd put them to sleep, . . . Socrates went to the Lyceum for a wash, spent the day as he would any other, and then went home to sleep in the evening. (*Symposium* 223d)

He "spent the day as he would any other." How was that? Socrates' days seem to have been devoted mainly to conversations in the public places of Athens. He was not independently wealthy, as you might suspect. Xenophon tells us that he schooled his body and soul by following a system which . . . would make it easy to meet his expenses. For he was so frugal that it is hardly possible to imagine a man doing so little work as not to earn enough to satisfy the needs of Socrates. (*Memorabilia* 1.3.5)[4]

●

"That man is richest whose pleasures are the cheapest."

Henry David Thoreau (1817–1862)

He was temperate in his desires and possessed remarkable self-control with regard not only to food and drink but also to sex. He apparently refrained from the physical relationship that was a fairly common feature of friendships between older men and their young protégés in ancient Athens.* Although he used the language of "love" freely, he held that the proper aim of such friendships was to make the "beloved" more virtuous, self-controlled, and just. No doubt he believed that the young could not learn self-control from someone who did not display it. By common consent the judgment of Alcibiades was correct: Socrates was unique.

Is Socrates a Sophist?

In *The Clouds,* Aristophanes presents Socrates as a Sophist. There are undeniable similarities between Socrates and the Sophists, but there are also important differences. We need to explore this a bit.

Socrates clearly moves in the same circles as the Sophists; he converses with them eagerly and often, and his interests are similar. His subject matter is human affairs, in particular *areté*—excellence or virtue. As we have seen, the Sophists set themselves up as teachers of such excellence. Socrates does not. He cannot do so, he might insist, because he does not rightly know what it is, and no one can teach what he doesn't understand. Nonetheless, he explores this very area, trying to clarify what human excellence consists in, whether it is one thing

---

*See, for example, the complaint of Alcibiades in *Symposium* 217a–219d.

or many (for example, courage, moderation, wisdom, justice), and whether it is the kind of thing that can be taught at all.

We have noted that many of the Sophists also teach specialized subjects, including geometry, astronomy, and nature philosophy in general. Socrates apparently was interested in nature philosophy as a youth but gave it up because it could not answer the questions that really intrigue him, such as, Why are we here? and What is the best kind of life? Human life is what fascinates him. So he and the Sophists share a community of interest.

Young men associate themselves with Socrates, too, sometimes for considerable periods of time, and consider him their teacher. He does not, as we noted in connection with Aristophanes' "Thinkery," have a school. And he does not consider himself a teacher. In fact, we will hear his claim that he has never taught anyone anything. (This takes some explaining, which we will do later.) So he is unlike the Sophists in that regard, for they do consider that they have something to teach and are proud to teach it to others.

Socrates is unlike the Sophists in another regard. He takes no pay from those who associate themselves with him. This is, of course, perfectly consistent with his claim that he has nothing to teach. Xenophon adds that Socrates "marvelled that anyone should make money by the profession of virtue, and should not reflect that his highest reward would be the gain of a good friend" (*Memorabilia* 1.2.7).

Like the Sophists, Socrates is interested in the arts of communication and argument, in techniques of persuasion. But it is at just this point that we find the deepest difference between them, the difference that perhaps allows us to deny that Socrates is a Sophist at all. For the Sophists, these arts (rhetoric) are like strategies and tactics in battle. The whole point is to enable their practitioner to win. Argument and persuasion are thought of as a kind of strife or contest where, as Antiphon put it, "victory goes to the best speaker." No concern for *truth* underlies the instruction of the Sophists; the aim is *victory*. This is wholly consistent with their denial that truth is available to human beings, with their skepticism and relativism. If all you can get are opinions anyway, then you might as well try to make things appear to others as they appear to you. That is what serves your self-interest. And rhetoric, as they conceive and teach it, is designed to do just that.*

For Socrates, on the other hand, the arts of communication, argument, and persuasion have a different goal. His practice of them is designed not to win a victory over his opponent but to advance toward the truth. He is convinced that there is a truth about human affairs and that we are capable of advancing toward it, of shaping our opinions so that they are more "like truth," to use that old phrase of Xenophanes.† Socrates could never agree that if a man *thinks* a certain action is just, then it *is* just—not even "for him." So he is neither a relativist nor a skeptic. Justice, Socrates believes, is something quite independent of our opinions about it. And what it is needs investigation.

Socrates' way of proceeding coheres well with this conviction about truth. He usually refrains from piling up fine phrases in lengthy speeches that might simply overwhelm his listeners; he does not want them to agree with his conclusions for reasons they do not themselves fully understand and agree to. So he asks questions. He is very insistent that his listeners answer in a sincere way, that they say what they truly believe. Each person is to speak for himself. In the dialogue *Meno,* for instance, Socrates professes not to know what virtue is. Meno expresses surprise, for surely, he says, Socrates listened to Gorgias when he was in town. Yes, Socrates admits, but he does not altogether remember what Gorgias said; perhaps Meno remembers and agrees with him. When Meno admits that he does, Socrates says,

> Then let's leave him out of it; he's not here, after all. But in the name of the gods, Meno, please do tell me in your own words what you think excellence is. (*Meno* 71d)[5]

So Meno is put on the spot and has to speak for himself. Again and again Socrates admonishes his hearers not to give their assent to a proposition unless they really agree.

The course of Socrates' conversations generally goes like this. Someone, often Socrates himself, asks a question: "What is piety?" or "Can human excellence be taught?" In response to the question, an answer is put forward, usually by someone other than Socrates. Socrates in turn proposes they "examine" whether they agree or disagree with this proposition. The examination proceeds by further questioning, which leads the person questioned to realize that the first answer is not adequate. A second answer that seems to escape the difficulties of the first is put forward, and the pattern repeats itself. A good example is found in *Euthyphro,* to which we'll turn shortly. In the early, more authentically Socratic dialogues, we are usually left at the end with an inconsistent set of beliefs; it is clear that we cannot accept the whole set, but neither Socrates nor his partner knows which way to go. Thus the participant is brought to admit that he doesn't understand the topic at all—although he thought he did when the conversation began.

This technique of proposal–questions–difficulties–new proposal–questions is a technique that Plato calls **dialectic.** Socrates thinks of it as a way, the very best way, of improving our opinions and perhaps even coming to knowledge of the truth. What is the connection between dialectic and truth? The connection is this: So long as people sincerely say

---

*See the Antiphon quote on p. 50.

†Look again at the fragment from Xenophanes on pp. 17–18.

what they believe and are open to revising this on the basis of good reasons, people can *together* identify inadequate answers to important questions. There really can be no doubt that certain answers won't do. But if you can be sure that some opinions aren't right, what remains unrefuted may well be in the vicinity of the truth. It is important, however, to note that even in the best case this sort of examination cannot *guarantee* the truth of what is left standing at the end. Socrates apparently knows this; that's why he so often confesses his ignorance.

This dialectical procedure, then, is better at detecting error than identifying truth, and for it to do even that certain conditions must be met. Each participant must say what he or she really believes, and no one must be determined to hang on to a belief "no matter what." In other words, the aim must be, not victory over the other speaker, but progress toward the truth. Dialectic is the somewhat paradoxically cooperative enterprise in which each *assists* the others by *raising objections* to what the others say.

We should reflect a moment on how odd this seems. We usually think we are being helped when people agree with us, support us in our convictions, and defend us against attacks. Socrates, however, thinks the best help we can get—what we really need—is given by questions that make us think again, questions that make us uncomfortable and inclined to be defensive. Again like Xenophanes, Socrates does not think that truth is evident or obvious; he does not agree that if something is widely accepted, this is a good reason to believe it. We sometimes even get the impression that if everybody believes it, it *must* be suspect! It is by "seeking" that we approach the truth, and that's neither easy nor comfortable. Socrates' technique for seeking the truth is this dialectic of question and answer.

That this is a cooperative enterprise and not merely a competition to see who wins is displayed in the fact that communication is not one way. Socrates does not deliver sermons; he does not lecture, at least not in the early dialogues. Also, anyone can ask the questions. In Plato's dialogues, it is usually Socrates who asks, but not always. Sometimes he gives his partner a choice of either asking or answering questions.

As you can imagine, this rather antagonistic procedure was not always understood or appreciated by Socrates' compatriots. It was certainly one of the factors that generated hostility toward him. In fact, you had to be a certain kind of person to enjoy talking with Socrates and to benefit from a conversation with him, as a passage from the *Gorgias* makes clear. Here the topic is rhetoric, or the art of persuasion. At issue is whether persuasion can lead to knowledge of truth or whether it is restricted to opinion. Socrates says to Gorgias, who teaches rhetoric,

> If you're the same kind of person as I am, I'd be glad to continue questioning you; otherwise, let's forget it. What kind of person am I? I'm happy to have a mistaken idea of mine proved wrong, and I'm happy to prove someone else's mistaken ideas wrong, I'm certainly not *less* happy if I'm proved wrong than if I've proved someone else wrong, because, as I see it, I've got the best of it: there's nothing worse than the state which I've been saved from, so that's better for me than saving someone else. You see, there's nothing worse for a person, in my opinion, than holding mistaken views about the matters we're discussing at the moment. (*Gorgias* 458a)[6]

This is a crucial passage for understanding Socrates' technique. He is in effect telling us that he will converse only with those who have a certain *character*. Progress in coming to understand the truth is as much a matter of character as intelligence. If you care more for your reputation, for wealth, for winning, or for convincing others that your opinion is the right one, Socrates will leave you alone. Or, if you insist on talking with him, you are bound to leave feeling humiliated rather than enlightened; for your goals will not have been reached. In order to make progess, he says, you must be such a person as he himself claims to be. What sort of person is that? You must be just as happy to be shown wrong as to show someone else to be wrong. No—you must be even *happier,* for if you are weaned from a false opinion, you have escaped a great evil.

It is worth expanding on this point a bit. To profit from a conversation with Socrates, you must (1) be open and honest about what you really do believe; and (2) not be so wedded to any one of your beliefs that you consider an attack on it as an attack on yourself. In other words, you must have a certain objectivity with respect to your own opinions. You must be able to say, "Yes, that is indeed an opinion of mine, but I shall be glad to exchange it for another if there is good reason to do so." This outlook skirts two dangers: wishy-washiness and **dogmatism.** People with these Socratic virtues are not wishy-washy, because they really do have opinions. But neither are they dogmatic, because they are eager to improve their opinions. We might ask to what extent people must have this attitude if they are to be able to learn at all.

This attitude does, in any case, seem to characterize Socrates. At this point, the character and aims of Socrates stand as a polar opposite to those of the Sophists. There could never have been a day on which Socrates taught his students "how to make the weaker argument into the stronger." To take that as one's aim is to show that one cares not for the truth but only for victory. To teach the techniques that provide victory is to betray one's character, to show that one is looking for the same thing oneself: fame, wealth, and the satisfaction of one's desires. That is why the Sophists taught for pay and grew wealthy. That is why Socrates refused pay and remained poor. And that is why the portrait Aristophanes gives us in *The Clouds* is only a caricature—not the real Socrates.

What Socrates "Knows"

Socrates' most characteristic claim concerns his ignorance. In his conversations, he claims not to know what human excellence, courage, or piety is. He begs to be instructed. Of course, it is usually the instructors who get instructed, who learn that they don't know after all. How shall we understand Socrates' claim not to know?

In part, surely, he is being ironic, especially in begging his partner in the conversation to instruct him. It is a role that Socrates is playing, the role of ignorant inquirer. But there is more to it than that. With respect to those large questions about the nature of human excellence, it is fairly clear that Socrates never does get an answer that fully satisfies

him. In the sense of "know" which implies you can't be wrong, Socrates does not claim to know these things. Only "the god," he says in the *Apology,* is truly wise. Even on points he might be quite confident about, he must allow that the next conversation could contain questions or objections that raise new difficulties—difficulties he cannot overcome. In this respect, his confession of ignorance is quite sincere.

"The wisest man is he who does not fancy that he is so at all."

Nicolas Boilean Despreau (1636–1711)

Nonetheless, there are things that are *as good as known* for Socrates, things he is so confident about that he is even willing to die for them. When we read his defense before the jury, we will see him affirm a number of things—remarkable things—with the greatest confidence. He will say, for instance, that a good man cannot be harmed—something, I wager, that you don't believe. This combination of ignorance and conviction seems paradoxical. How can we understand it?

As Socrates continues to examine his convictions and the beliefs of others, discarding what is clearly indefensible, certain affirmations survive all the scrutiny and rude questions. These are claims that neither Socrates nor any of his conversational partners have been able to undermine; these claims have *stood fast*. You can imagine that as the years go by and his convictions come under attack from every conceivable quarter, those few principles that withstand every assault must come to look more and more "like the truth," to recall that phrase from Xenophanes, so much like the truth that it becomes almost inconceivable that they should be upset in the future. These convictions Socrates is willing to bet on, even with his life.

Before we examine some of the early dialogues, it will be useful to identify several of them.*

---

*Because in this section I make use of material from several of the middle dialogues, I cannot claim with certainty to be representing the historical Socrates. In line with the earlier remark that each of us must to some degree construct our own Socrates, you might think of the picture painted here as Melchert's Socrates.

WE OUGHT TO SEARCH FOR TRUTH

In his conversation with Meno, Socrates says that

> there's one proposition that I'd defend to the death, if I could, by argument and by action: that as long as we think we should search for what we don't know we'll be better people—less fainthearted and less lazy—than if we were to think that we had no chance of discovering what we don't know and that there's no point in even searching for it. (*Meno* 86b–c)

This remark occurs in the context of an argument we will examine later* that the soul is directly acquainted with truth before it enters a human body. This argument has the practical consequence that we may hope to recover the knowledge we had before birth. Socrates says that although he is not certain about every detail of this argument, he is sure that we will be better persons if we do not give up hope of attaining the truth.

Again we can see the Sophists lurking in the background; for it is they who claim that knowledge of truth is not possible for human beings, each of us being the final "measure," or judge, of what seems so to us. Socrates believes that this doctrine (relativism) will make us worse persons, fainthearted and lazy. After all, if we can dismiss any criticism by saying, "Well, it's true for *me*," then our present beliefs are absolutely secure; so why should we undertake the difficult and dangerous task of examining them? The Sophist point of view seems to Socrates like a prescription for intellectual idleness and cowardice. And he is certain that to be idle and cowardly is to be a worse person rather than a better one. So one thing that "stands fast" for Socrates is that we ought to search for the truth and not despair of finding it.

HUMAN EXCELLENCE IS KNOWLEDGE

Socrates seems to have held that human excellence consists in knowledge. No doubt this strikes us as slightly odd; it seems overintellectualized, somehow. Knowledge, we are apt to think, may be one facet of being an excellent human being, but how could it be the whole of it?

The oddness is dissipated somewhat when we note what sort of knowledge Socrates has in mind. He is constantly referring us to the craftsmen—to "metal-workers, shoe-makers, tanners," as Alcibiades said—and to such professions as horse training, doctoring, and piloting a ship. In each case, what distinguishes the expert from a mere novice is the possession of knowledge. Such knowledge is not just having abstract intellectual propositions in your head, however; it is knowledge of *what* to do and *how* to do it. The Greek word here is **techne,** from which our word "technology" comes. This *techne* is a kind of applied knowledge. What distinguishes the competent doctor, horse trainer, or metal-worker, then, is that they possess a *techne*. The amateur or novice does not.

Socrates claims that human excellence is a *techne* in exactly this same sense. What does the doctor know? She knows the human body and what makes for its health—its physical excellence. What does the horse trainer know? He knows horses—their nature and how they can be made to respond so that they will turn into excellent beasts. In a quite parallel fashion, the expert in human excellence (or virtue)—if there is one—would have to know human nature, how it functions, and wherein its excellence consists.*

Just as the shoemaker must understand both his materials (leather, nails, thread) and the use to which shoes are put—the point of having shoes—so those who wish to live well must understand themselves and what the point of living is. And just as one who has mastered the craft of shoemaking will turn out fine shoes, Socrates thinks, so one who has mastered the craft of living will live well. In the *Gorgias,* for instance, Socrates argues in this way:

s: Now, isn't a person who's come to understand building a builder?

G: Yes.

s: While a person who's come to understand music is a musician. Yes?

G: Yes.

---

*See pp. 103–104.

*See Aristotle's development of just this point, pp. 186–187.

s: And a person who's come to understand medicine is a doctor, and so on and so forth. By the same token, anyone who has come to understand a given subject is described in accordance with the particular character his branch of knowledge confers. Do you agree?

G: Yes.

s: So doesn't it follow that someone who has come to understand morality is moral?

G: Definitely. No doubt about it.

—*Gorgias* 460b

Knowledge in this *techne* sense, Socrates holds, is both a necessary condition for human excellence (without it you cannot be a good person) and a sufficient condition (when it is present, so are all the excellent qualities of human life).

In the *Meno* we find another argument with the same conclusion. Socrates gets agreement that human excellence must be something beneficial. But, he argues, things that are generally beneficial need not always be so. For instance, whether wealth, health, and strength are an advantage to the possessor depends on whether they are used wisely or foolishly. And the same goes for what people generally call virtues.

s: Now, among these qualities, take those that you think aren't knowledge—those that are different from knowledge—and let me ask you whether they're sometimes harmful and sometimes beneficial. Take courage, for instance, when it isn't wisdom but is something like recklessness. Isn't it the case that unintelligent recklessness harms people, while intelligent boldness does them good?

M: Yes.

s: And does the same go for self-control and cleverness? Are intelligent learning and training beneficial, while unintelligent learning and training are harmful?

M: Most definitely.

s: In short, then, mental endeavour and persistence always end in happiness when they are guided by knowledge, but in the opposite if they are guided by ignorance.

—*Meno* 88b–c

The conclusion that human excellence consists in knowledge faces a difficulty. If it is knowledge, then it should be teachable. Recall Socrates' conversation with Protagoras. He points out that if a father wanted his son to be a painter, he would send him to someone who knew painting. If he wanted him to learn the flute, he would send him to someone who was an expert in flute playing. But where are the teachers of human excellence? Socrates could not allow that the Sophists were such. And he disclaims any knowledge of what such excellence consists in, so he can't teach it. But if there are no teachers, perhaps it isn't knowledge after all.

Socrates is able to resist this conclusion by a device that we'll examine soon.* For now, it is enough to note that this is one thing that "stands fast" for him: that human excellence is wisdom or knowledge.†

ALL WRONGDOING IS DUE TO IGNORANCE

This thesis is a corollary to the claim that virtue is knowledge. If to know the right is to do the right, then failing to do the right must be due to not knowing it. Not to know something is to be ignorant of it. So whoever acts wrongly does so out of ignorance. If we knew better, we would do better.

Socrates holds, in fact, that we always act out of a belief that what we are doing is good. At the least, we think that it will produce good in the long run. We never, Socrates thinks, intend to do what we *know* is wrong or bad or evil or wicked. So if we do things that are wrong, it must be that we are not well-informed. We believe to be good what is in fact evil—but that is to believe something false, and to believe the false is to be ignorant of the true.

---

*See pp. 102–103.

†There is a kind of paradox here, as you may already suspect. Socrates claims (1) that human excellence is knowledge, (2) that he lacks this knowledge, and yet (3) that he is a good man. It seems impossible to assert all three consistently; to assert any two seems to require the denial of the third. Socrates, however, has a way out. In Chapter 5, we address this Socratic paradox. See p. 100.

Here we have a strong argument for the importance of moral education for the young. They can be brought up to be excellent human beings if only they come to learn what is in fact good and right and true.

For a comparison, let us look again to Euripides' *Hippolytus,* where Phaedra (who is, you remember, in love with her stepson) struggles with her passion.

> We know the good, we apprehend it clearly. But we can't bring it to achievement. Some are betrayed by their own laziness, and others value some other pleasure above virtue.[7]

Here Phaedra expresses an opinion opposed to that of Socrates: We do sometimes "know the good," she says, and yet fail to do it. One can imagine Euripides and Socrates debating this point over a glass of wine. Perhaps Euripides even writes this play as he does and puts these words into Phaedra's mouth as part of an ongoing argument. Socrates does not agree; he believes it is not possible to apprehend the good clearly and not do it. Neither laziness nor pleasure can stand in the way. For human excellence *is* knowledge.

This view is connected intimately to Socrates' practice. He is not a preacher exhorting his fellow men to live up to what they know to be good. He is an inquirer trying to discover exactly what human excellence is. All people, he assumes, do the best they know. If people can be brought to understand what human excellence consists in, an excellent life will follow.

This view has seemed mistaken to many people. Not only Euripides disagrees. Among others, so do Aristotle, Saint Paul, and Augustine.

THE MOST IMPORTANT THING OF ALL IS TO CARE FOR YOUR SOUL

There is a final cluster of things Socrates seems to "know." They all hang together and are represented in the dialogues we'll be reading, so I'll just mention several of them briefly here.

Among the striking and unusual propositions that Socrates thinks have survived all the examination are these:

- It is better to suffer injustice than to commit injustice.
- A good person cannot be harmed in either life or death.

These have to do with the soul. The most important part of a human being, Socrates believes, is not the body but the soul; from convictions in the soul flow all those actions that reveal what a person really is. Indeed, Socrates even seems to identify himself with his soul.* For that reason, the most important task any person has is to care for the soul. And to that end nothing is more crucial than self-knowledge. Just as the shoemaker cannot make good shoes unless he understands his material, you cannot construct a good life unless you know yourself.

In the *Apology,* Socrates says that for a human being "the unexamined life is not worth living." In particular, we need to know what we *do* know and what we *do not* know so that we can act wisely, and not foolishly. For foolishness is behavior based on false opinions. As you can see, this concern with the soul animates Socrates' practice; it is in pursuit of such self-knowledge that he questions his contemporaries—both for their sake and for his. One of the two mottoes at the Delphic Oracle might be the motto for Socrates' own life and practice: "Know Thyself."

"Ful wys is he that can himselven knowe."

Geoffrey Chaucer (1343–1400)

---

1. Describe briefly the character of Socrates, as we know it from the testimony of his friends.
2. In what ways is Socrates like the Sophists?
3. In what ways is he different?

---

*See the jest Socrates makes just before he drinks the hemlock in *Phaedo* 115c, p. 115.

4. How does Socrates proceed in his "examination" of his fellow citizens?
5. What is the connection between dialectic and truth?
6. What kind of a person do you have to be to profit from a conversation with Socrates?
7. A number of things seem to have "stood fast" for Socrates in the course of all his examinations, things that in some sense we can say he "knows." What are they?

FOR FURTHER THOUGHT

Here are several convictions Socrates thinks have withstood all the criticisms to which they have been exposed:

- That the most important thing in life is to care for the well-being of the soul
- That a good person cannot be harmed by a worse person
- That it is better to suffer injustice than to commit it

Choose one to consider. If you agree, try to say why. If you disagree, try to come up with a critique that might get Socrates to change his mind.

KEY WORDS

Socrates   dialectic
Xenophon   dogmatism
Alcibiades   *techne*

NOTES

1. W. K. C. Guthrie, *Socrates* (Cambridge: Cambridge University Press, 1971), 4.
2. Xenophon, *Symposium V,* trans. W. K. C. Guthrie, in *Socrates,* 67–68.
3. Quotations from Plato's *Symposium,* trans. Robin Waterfield (Oxford: Oxford University Press, 1994), are cited in the text by title and section number.
4. Quotations from Xenophon, *Memorabilia,* in *Xenophon: Memorabilia and Oeconomicus,* ed. E. C. Marchant (London: Heinemann, 1923), are cited in the text by title and book and section number.
5. Quotations from Plato's *Meno,* trans. Robin Waterfield in *Meno and Other Dialogues* (Oxford: Oxford University Press, 2005), are cited in the text by title and section number.
6. Quotations from Plato's *Gorgias,* trans. Robin Waterfield (Oxford: Oxford University Press, 1994), are cited by title and section number.
7. Euripides, *Hippolytus,* trans. David Grene, in *Euripides I,* ed. David Grene and Richmond Lattimore (Chicago: University of Chicago Press, 1965), ll. 380–384.

5

THE TRIAL AND DEATH OF SOCRATES

We are now ready to read several of Plato's early dialogues. In each of them Socrates is the major figure. They must have been written soon after Socrates' death. Because many people witnessed the trial and would have known of his conduct while awaiting execution, scholars think they present as accurate a picture of the historical Socrates as we can find. We'll read *Euthyphro, Apology,* and *Crito* in their entirety, and a selection from *Phaedo.*

This chapter is partitioned into two parts for each dialogue. The text of the dialogue is printed first; this is followed by a section of commentary and questions. Here is a suggestion for you. Begin by giving each dialogue in turn a quick reading (they are all quite short). Don't try to understand everything the first time through; just get a feel for it. It would be ideal to read them aloud with a friend, each taking a part. After you have done the quick read-through, go to the commentary and questions that follow. Using these as a guide, re-read each dialogue section by section, trying this time to understand everything and answering the questions as you go along. A good plan is to write out brief answers. You will be amazed at how rich these brief works are.

References are to page numbers in a standard Greek text of Plato.[1] These numbers are printed in the margins and are divided into sections *a* through *e.*

EUTHYPHRO

Translator's Introduction

Euthyphro is surprised to meet Socrates near the king-archon's court, for Socrates is not the kind of man to have business with courts of justice. Socrates explains that he is under indictment by one Meletus for corrupting the young and for not believing in the gods in whom the city believes. After a brief discussion of this, Socrates inquires about Euthyphro's business at court and is told that he is prosecuting his own father for the murder of a laborer who is himself a murderer. His family and friends believe his course of action to be impious, but Euthyphro explains that in this they are mistaken and reveal their ignorance of the nature of piety. This naturally leads Socrates to ask, What is piety? and the rest of the dialogue is devoted to a search for a definition of piety, illustrating the Socratic search for universal definitions of ethical terms, to which a number of early Platonic dialogues are devoted. As usual, no definition is found that satisfies Socrates.

The Greek term hosion *means, in the first instance, the knowledge of the proper ritual in prayer and sacrifice, and of course its performance (as Euthyphro himself defines it in 14b). But obviously Euthyphro uses it in the much wider sense of pious conduct generally (e.g., his own) and in that sense the word is practically equivalent to righteousness (the justice of the Republic), the transition being by way of conduct pleasing to the gods.*

Besides being an excellent example of the early, so-called Socratic dialogues, Euthyphro *contains several passages with important philosophical implications. These include those in which Socrates speaks of the one Form, presented by all the actions that we call pious (5d), as well as the one in which we are told that the gods love what is pious because it is pious, it is not pious because the gods love it (10d). Another passage clarifies the difference between genus and species (11e). The implications are discussed in the notes on those passages.*

The Dialogue

2   EUTHYPHRO:[1] What's new, Socrates, to make you leave your usual haunts in the Lyceum

and spend your time here by the king-archon's court? Surely you are not prosecuting anyone before the king-archon as I am?

SOCRATES: The Athenians do not call this a prosecution but an indictment, Euthyphro.

b   E: What is this you say? Someone must have indicted you, for you are not going to tell me that you have indicted someone else.

S: No indeed.

E: But someone else has indicted you?

S: Quite so.

E: Who is he?

S: I do not really know him myself, Euthyphro. He is apparently young and unknown. They call him Meletus, I believe. He belongs to the Pitthean deme, if you know anyone from that deme called Meletus, with long hair, not much of a beard, and a rather aquiline nose.

E: I don't know him, Socrates. What charge does he bring against you?

c   S: What charge? A not ignoble one I think, for it is no small thing for a young man to have knowledge of such an important subject. He says he knows how our young men are corrupted and who corrupts them. He is likely to be wise, and when he sees my ignorance corrupting his contemporaries, he proceeds

d   to accuse me to the city as to their mother. I think he is the only one of our public men to start out the right way, for it is right to care first that the young should be as good as possible, just as a good farmer is likely to take care of the young plants first, and of the others later. So, too, Meletus first gets rid of us who corrupt the young shoots, as he says, and then

3   afterwards he will obviously take care of the

---

[1]We know nothing about Euthyphro except what we can gather from this dialogue. He is obviously a professional priest who considers himself an expert on ritual and on piety

generally, and, it seems, is generally so considered. One Euthyphro is mentioned in Plato's *Cratylus* (396d) who is given to *enthousiasmos*, inspiration or possession, but we cannot be sure that it is the same person.

older ones and become a source of great blessings for the city, as seems likely to happen to one who started out this way.

E: I could wish this were true, Socrates, but I fear the opposite may happen. He seems to me to start out by harming the very heart of the city by attempting to wrong you. Tell me, what does he say you do to corrupt the young?

b S: Strange things, to hear him tell, for he says that I am a maker of gods, and on the ground that I create new gods while not believing in the old gods, he has indicted me for their sake, as he puts it.

E: I understand, Socrates. This is because you say that the divine sign keeps coming to you.[2] So he has written this indictment against you as one who makes innovations in religious matters, and he comes to court to slander you, knowing that such things are easily misrep-

c resented to the crowd. The same is true in my case. Whenever I speak of divine matters in the assembly and foretell the future, they laugh me down as if I were crazy; and yet I have foretold nothing that did not happen. Nevertheless, they envy all of us who do this. One need not worry about them, but meet them head-on.

S: My dear Euthyphro, to be laughed at does not matter perhaps, for the Athenians do not mind anyone they think clever, as long as he does not teach his own wisdom, but if they think that he makes others to be like himself they get angry,

d whether through envy, as you say, or for some other reason.

E: I have certainly no desire to test their feelings towards me in this matter.

S: Perhaps you seem to make yourself but rarely available, and not to be willing to teach your own wisdom, but I'm afraid that my liking for people makes them think that I pour out to anybody anything I have to say, not only without charging a fee but even glad to reward anyone who is willing to listen. If then they were

e intending to laugh at me, as you say they laugh at you, there would be nothing unpleasant in

their spending their time in court laughing and jesting, but if they are going to be serious, the outcome is not clear except to you prophets.

E: Perhaps it will come to nothing, Socrates, and you will fight your case as you think best, as I think I will mine.

S: What is your case, Euthyphro? Are you the defendant or the prosecutor?

E: The prosecutor.

S: Whom do you prosecute?

4 E: One whom I am thought crazy to prosecute.

S: Are you pursuing someone who will easily escape you?

E: Far from it, for he is quite old.

S: Who is it?

E: My father.

S: My dear sir! Your own father?

E: Certainly.

S: What is the charge? What is the case about?

E: Murder, Socrates.

S: Good heavens! Certainly, Euthyphro, most men would not know how they could do this

b and be right. It is not the part of anyone to do this, but of one who is far advanced in wisdom.

E: Yes, by Zeus, Socrates, that is so.

S: Is then the man your father killed one of your relatives? Or is that obvious, for you would not prosecute your father for the murder of a stranger.

E: It is ridiculous, Socrates, for you to think that it makes any difference whether the victim is a stranger or a relative. One should only watch whether the killer acted justly or not; if he acted justly, let him go, but if not, one should

c prosecute, even if the killer shares your hearth and table. The pollution is the same if you knowingly keep company with such a man and do not cleanse yourself and him by bringing him to justice. The victim was a dependent of mine, and when we were farming in Naxos he was a servant of ours. He killed one of our household slaves in drunken anger, so my father bound him hand and foot and threw him in a ditch, then sent a man here to enquire from the priest what should be done. During

d that time he gave no thought or care to the bound man, as being a killer, and it was no matter if he died, which he did. Hunger and cold and his bonds caused his death before the messenger came back from the seer. Both my father and my other relatives are angry that I

---

[2] In Plato, Socrates always speaks of his divine sign or voice as intervening to prevent him from doing or saying something (e.g., *Apology* 31d), but never positively. The popular view was that it enabled him to foretell the future, and Euthyphro here represents that view. Note, however, that Socrates dissociates himself from "you prophets" (3e).

am prosecuting my father for murder on behalf of a murderer when he hadn't even killed him, they say, and even if he had, the dead man does not deserve a thought, since he was a killer.

e For, they say, it is impious for a son to prosecute his father for murder. But their ideas of the divine attitude to piety and impiety are wrong, Socrates.

s: Whereas, by Zeus, Euthyphro, you think that your knowledge of the divine, and of piety and impiety, is so accurate that, when those things happened as you say, you have no fear of having acted impiously in bringing your father to trial?

e: I should be of no use, Socrates, and Euthyphro
5 would not be superior to the majority of men, if I did not have accurate knowledge of all such things.

s: It is indeed most important, my admirable Euthyphro, that I should become your pupil, and as regards this indictment challenge Meletus about these very things and say to him: that in the past too I considered knowledge about the divine to be most important, and that now that he says I am guilty of improvising and innovating about the gods I have become

b your pupil. I would say to him: "If, Meletus, you agree that Euthyphro is wise in these matters, consider me, too, to have the right beliefs and do not bring me to trial. If you do not think so, then prosecute that teacher of mine, not me, for corrupting the older men, me and his own father, by teaching me and by exhorting and punishing him." If he is not convinced, and does not discharge me or indict you instead of me, I shall repeat the same challenge in court.

e: Yes, by Zeus, Socrates, and, if he should try to indict me, I think I would find his weak spots

c and the talk in court would be about him rather than about me.

s: It is because I realize this that I am eager to become your pupil, my dear friend. I know that other people as well as this Meletus do not even seem to notice you, whereas he sees me so sharply and clearly that he indicts me for ungodliness. So tell me now, by Zeus, what you just now maintained you clearly knew: what

d kind of thing do you say that godliness and ungodliness are, both as regards murder and other things; or is the pious not the same and alike in every action, and the impious the opposite of all that is pious and like itself, and everything

that is to be impious presents us with one form[3] or appearance in so far as it is impious?

e: Most certainly, Socrates.

s: Tell me then, what is the pious, and what the impious, do you say?

e: I say that the pious is to do what I am doing now, to prosecute the wrongdoer, be it about murder or temple robbery or anything else,

e whether the wrongdoer is your father or your mother or anyone else; not to prosecute is impious. And observe, Socrates, that I can quote the law as a great proof that this is so. I have already said to others that such actions are right, not to favour the ungodly, whoever they are. These people themselves believe that Zeus is the best and most just of the gods, yet

6 they agree that he bound his father because he unjustly swallowed his sons, and that he in turn castrated his father for similar reasons. But they are angry with me because I am prosecuting my father for his wrongdoing. They contradict themselves in what they say about the gods and about me.

s: Indeed, Euthyphro, this is the reason why I am a defendant in the case, because I find it hard to accept things like that being said about the gods, and it is likely to be the reason why I shall be told I do wrong. Now, however, if you, who have full knowledge of such things, share their opinions, then we must agree with

b them too, it would seem. For what are we to say, we who agree that we ourselves have no knowledge of them? Tell me, by the god of friendship, do you really believe these things are true?

e: Yes, Socrates, and so are even more surprising things, of which the majority has no knowledge.

---

[3]This is the kind of passage that makes it easier for us to follow the transition from Socrates' universal definitions to the Platonic theory of separately existent eternal universal Forms. The words *eidos* and *idea,* the technical terms for the Platonic Forms, commonly mean physical stature or bodily appearance. As we apply a common epithet, in this case pious, to different actions or things, these must have a common characteristic, present a common appearance or form, to justify the use of the same term, but in the early dialogues, as here, it seems to be thought of as immanent in the particulars and without separate existence. The same is true of 6d where the word "form" is also used.

s: And do you believe that there really is war among the gods, and terrible enmities and battles, and other such things as are told by

c the poets, and other sacred stories such as are embroidered by good writers and by representations of which the robe of the goddess is adorned when it is carried up to the Acropolis? Are we to say these things are true, Euthyphro?

e: Not only these, Socrates, but, as I was saying just now, I will, if you wish, relate many other things about the gods which I know will amaze you.

s: I should not be surprised, but you will tell me these at leisure some other time. For now, try to tell me more clearly what I was asking just

d now, for, my friend, you did not teach me adequately when I asked you what the pious was, but you told me that what you are doing now, prosecuting your father for murder, is pious.

e: And I told the truth, Socrates.

s: Perhaps. You agree, however, that there are many other pious actions.

e: There are.

s: Bear in mind then that I did not bid you tell me one or two of the many pious actions but that form itself that makes all pious actions pious, for you agreed that all impious actions are

e impious and all pious actions pious through one form, or don't you remember?

e: I do.

s: Tell me then what this form itself is, so that I may look upon it, and using it as a model, say that any action of yours or another's that is of that kind is pious, and if it is not that it is not.

e: If that is how you want it, Socrates, that is how I will tell you.

s: That is what I want.

7 e: Well then, what is dear to the gods is pious, what is not is impious.

s: Splendid, Euthyphro! You have now answered in the way I wanted. Whether your answer is true I do not know yet, but you will obviously show me that what you say is true.

e: Certainly.

s: Come then, let us examine what we mean. An action or a man dear to the gods is pious, but an action or a man hated by the gods is impious. They are not the same, but quite opposite, the pious and the impious. Is that not so?

e: It is indeed.

s: And that seems to be a good statement?

b e: I think so, Socrates.

s: We have also stated that the gods are in a state of discord, that they are at odds with each other, Euthyphro, and that they are at enmity with each other. Has that, too, been said?

e: It has.

s: What are the subjects of difference that cause hatred and anger? Let us look at it this way. If you and I were to differ about numbers as to which is the greater, would this difference make us enemies and angry with each other, or would we proceed to count and soon re-

c solve our difference about this?

e: We would certainly do so.

s: Again, if we differed about the larger and the smaller, we would turn to measurement and soon cease to differ.

e: That is so.

s: And about the heavier and the lighter, we would resort to weighing and be reconciled.

e: Of course.

s: What subject of difference would make us angry and hostile to each other if we were unable to come to a decision? Perhaps you do not

d have an answer ready, but examine as I tell you whether these subjects are the just and the unjust, the beautiful and the ugly, the good and the bad. Are these not the subjects of difference about which, when we are unable to come to a satisfactory decision, you and I and other men become hostile to each other whenever we do?

e: That is the difference, Socrates, about those subjects.

s: What about the gods, Euthyphro? If indeed they have differences, will it not be about these same subjects?

e: It certainly must be so.

e s: Then according to your argument, my good Euthyphro, different gods consider different things to be just, beautiful, ugly, good, and bad, for they would not be at odds with one another unless they differed about these subjects, would they?

e: You are right.

s: And they like what each of them considers beautiful, good, and just, and hate the opposites of these?

e: Certainly.

s: But you say that the same things are considered just by some gods and unjust by others, and as

8

they dispute about these things they are at odds and at war with each other. Is that not so?

E: It is.

S: The same things then are loved by the gods and hated by the gods, and would be both god-loved and god-hated.

E: It seems likely.

S: And the same things would be both pious and impious, according to this argument?

E: I'm afraid so.

S: So you did not answer my question, you surprising man. I did not ask you what same thing is both pious and impious, and it appears that

b what is loved by the gods is also hated by them. So it is in no way surprising if your present action, namely punishing your father, may be pleasing to Zeus but displeasing to Kronos and Ouranos, pleasing to Hephaestus but displeasing to Hera, and so with any other gods who differ from each other on this subject.

E: I think, Socrates, that on this subject no gods would differ from one another, that whoever has killed anyone unjustly should pay the penalty.

c S: Well now, Euthyphro, have you ever heard any man maintaining that one who has killed or done anything else unjustly should not pay the penalty?

E: They never cease to dispute on this subject, both elsewhere and in the courts, for when they have committed many wrongs they do and say anything to avoid the penalty.

S: Do they agree they have done wrong, Euthyphro, and in spite of so agreeing do they nevertheless say they should not be punished?

E: No, they do not agree on that point.

S: So they do not say or do anything. For they do not venture to say this, or dispute that they must not pay the penalty if they have done

d wrong, but I think they deny doing wrong. Is that not so?

E: That is true.

S: Then they do not dispute that the wrongdoer must be punished, but they may disagree as to who the wrongdoer is, what he did and when.

E: You are right.

S: Do not the gods have the same experience, if indeed they are at odds with each other about the just and the unjust, as your argument maintains? Some assert that they wrong one another, while others deny it, but no one

e among gods or men ventures to say that the wrongdoer must not be punished.

E: Yes, that is true, Socrates, as to the main point.

S: And those who disagree, whether men or gods, dispute about each action, if indeed the gods disagree. Some say it is done justly, others unjustly. Is that not so?

E: Yes, indeed.

9 S: Come, now, my dear Euthyphro, tell me, too, that I may become wiser, what proof you have that all the gods consider that man to have been killed unjustly who became a murderer while in your service, was bound by the master of his victim, and died in his bonds before the one who bound him found out from the seers what was to be done with him, and that it is right for a son to denounce and to prosecute his father on behalf of such a man. Come, try to show me a clear sign that all the gods definitely be-

b lieve this action to be right. If you can give me adequate proof of this, I shall never cease to extol your wisdom.

E: This is perhaps no light task, Socrates, though I could show you very clearly.

S: I understand that you think me more dull-witted than the jury, as you will obviously show them that these actions were unjust and that all the gods hate such actions.

E: I will show it to them clearly, Socrates, if only they will listen to me.

c S: They will listen if they think you show them well. But this thought came to me as you were speaking, and I am examining it, saying to myself: "If Euthyphro shows me conclusively that all the gods consider such a death unjust, to what greater extent have I learned from him the nature of piety and impiety? This action would then, it seems, be hated by the gods, but the pious and the impious were not thereby now defined, for what is hated by the gods has also been shown to be loved by them." So I will not insist on this point; let us assume, if you wish, that all the gods consider this unjust and that they all hate it. However,

d is this the correction we are making in our discussion, that what all the gods hate is impious, and what they all love is pious, and that what some gods love and others hate is neither or both? Is that how you now wish us to define piety and impiety?

E: What prevents us from doing so, Socrates?

s: For my part nothing, Euthyphro, but you look whether on your part this proposal will enable you to teach me most easily what you promised.

e E: I would certainly say that the pious is what all the gods love, and the opposite, what all the gods hate, is the impious.

s: Then let us again examine whether that is a sound statement, or do we let it pass, and if one of us, or someone else, merely says that something is so, do we accept that it is so? Or should we examine what the speaker means?

E: We must examine it, but I certainly think that this is now a fine statement.

10 s: We shall soon know better whether it is. Consider this: Is the pious loved by the gods because it is pious, or is it pious because it is loved by the gods?

E: I don't know what you mean, Socrates.*

11 s: I'm afraid, Euthyphro, that when you were asked what piety is, you did not wish to make its nature clear to me, but you told me an affect or quality of it, that the pious has the quality of being loved by all the gods, but you

b have not yet told me what the pious is. Now, if you will, do not hide things from me but tell me again from the beginning what piety is, whether loved by the gods or having some other quality—we shall not quarrel about that—but be keen to tell me what the pious and the impious are.

E: But Socrates, I have no way of telling you what I have in mind, for whatever proposition we put forward goes around and refuses to stay put where we establish it.

s: Your statements, Euthyphro, seem to belong

c to my ancestor, Daedalus. If I were stating them and putting them forward, you would perhaps be making fun of me and say that because of my kinship with him my conclusions in discussion run away and will not stay where one puts them. As these propositions are yours, however, we need some other jest, for they will not stay put for you, as you say yourself.

E: I think the same jest will do for our discussion, Socrates, for I am not the one who makes them go round and not remain in the same place; it

d is you who are the Daedalus; for as far as I am concerned they would remain as they were.

s: It looks as if I was cleverer than Daedalus in using my skill, my friend, in so far as he could only cause to move the things he made himself, but I can make other people's move as well as my own. And the smartest part of my skill is that I am clever without wanting to be, for I would rather have your statements to me

e remain unmoved than possess the wealth of Tantalus as well as the cleverness of Daedalus. But enough of this. Since I think you are making unnecessary difficulties, I am as eager as you are to find a way to teach me about piety, and do not give up before you do. See whether you think all that is pious is of necessity just.

E: I think so.

s: And is then all that is just pious? Or is all that

12 is pious just, but not all that is just pious, but some of it is and some is not?

E: I do not follow what you are saying, Socrates.

s: Yet you are younger than I by as much as you are wiser. As I say, you are making difficulties because of your wealth of wisdom. Pull yourself together, my dear sir, what I am saying is not difficult to grasp. I am saying the opposite of what the poet said who wrote:

> You do not wish to name Zeus, who had done it, and who made all things grow, for where there is fear there is also shame.

b I disagree with the poet. Shall I tell you why?

E: Please do.

s: I do not think that "where there is fear there is also shame," for I think that many people who fear disease and poverty and many other such things feel fear, but are not ashamed of the things they fear. Do you not think so?

E: I do indeed.

s: But where there is shame there is also fear. For is there anyone who, in feeling shame and embarrassment at anything, does not also at

c the same time fear and dread a reputation for wickedness?

E: He is certainly afraid.

s: It is then not right to say "where there is fear there is also shame," but that where there is shame there is also fear, for fear covers a larger area than shame. Shame is a part of fear just as odd is a part of number, with the result that it is not true that where there is number there is also

---

*From 10a to 11a, there appears a complex and rather confusing argument. I omit it here and supply a paraphrase in the commentary section that follows the dialogue.—N.M.

oddness, but that where there is oddness there is also number. Do you follow me now?

E: Surely.

S: This is the kind of thing I was asking before, whether where there is piety there is also justice, but where there is justice there is not always piety, for the pious is a part of justice. Shall we say that, or do you think otherwise?

E: No, but like that, for what you say appears to be right.

S: See what comes next: if the pious is a part of the just, we must, it seems, find out what part of the just it is. Now if you asked me something of what we mentioned just now, such as what part of number is the even, and what number that is, I would say it is the number that is divisible into two equal, not unequal, parts. Or do you not think so?

E: I do.

S: Try in this way to tell me what part of the just the pious is, in order to tell Meletus not to wrong us any more and not to indict me for ungodliness, since I have learned from you sufficiently what is godly and pious and what is not.

E: I think, Socrates, that the godly and pious is the part of the just that is concerned with the care of the gods, while that concerned with the care of men is the remaining part of justice.

S: You seem to me to put that very well, but I still need a bit of information. I do not know yet what you mean by care, for you do not mean the care of the gods in the same sense as the care of other things, as, for example, we say, don't we, that not everyone knows how to care for horses, but the horse breeder does.

E: Yes, I do mean it that way.

S: So horse breeding is the care of horses.

E: Yes.

S: Nor does everyone know how to care for dogs, but the hunter does.

E: That is so.

S: So hunting is the care of dogs.

E: Yes.

S: And cattle raising is the care of cattle.

E: Quite so.

S: While piety and godliness is the care of the gods, Euthyphro. Is that what you mean?

E: It is.

S: Now care in each case has the same effect; it aims at the good and the benefit of the object

cared for, as you can see that horses cared for by horse breeders are benefited and become better. Or do you not think so?

E: I do.

S: So dogs are benefited by dog breeding, cattle by cattle raising, and so with all the others. Or do you think that care aims to harm the object of its care?

E: By Zeus, no.

S: It aims to benefit the object of its care?

E: Of course.

S: Is piety then, which is the care of the gods, also to benefit the gods and make them better? Would you agree that when you do something pious you make some of the gods better?

E: By Zeus, no.

S: Nor do I think that this is what you mean—far from it—but that is why I asked you what you meant by the care of gods, because I did not believe you meant this kind of care.

E: Quite right, Socrates, that is not the kind of care I mean.

S: Very well, but what kind of care of the gods would piety be?

E: The kind of care, Socrates, that slaves take of their masters.

S: I understand. It is likely to be a kind of service of the gods.

E: Quite so.

S: Could you tell me to the achievement of what goal service to doctors tends? Is it not, do you think, to achieving health?

E: I think so.

S: What about service to shipbuilders? To what achievement is it directed?

E: Clearly, Socrates, to the building of a ship.

S: And service to housebuilders to the building of a house?

E: Yes.

S: Tell me then, my good sir, to the achievement of what aim does service to the gods tend? You obviously know since you say that you, of all men, have the best knowledge of the divine.

E: And I am telling the truth, Socrates.

S: Tell me then, by Zeus, what is that excellent aim that the gods achieve, using us as their servants?

E: Many fine things, Socrates.

S: So do generals, my friend. Nevertheless you could easily tell me their main concern, which is to achieve victory in war, is it not?

E: Of course.

S: The farmers too, I think, achieve many fine things, but the main point of their efforts is to produce food from the earth.

E: Quite so.

S: Well then, how would you sum up the many fine things that the gods achieve?

b E: I told you a short while ago, Socrates, that it is a considerable task to acquire any precise knowledge of these things, but, to put it simply, I say that if a man knows how to say and do what is pleasing to the gods at prayer and sacrifice, those are pious actions such as preserve both private houses and public affairs of state. The opposite of these pleasing actions are impious and overturn and destroy everything.

c S: You could tell me in far fewer words, if you were willing, the sum of what I asked, Euthyphro, but you are not keen to teach me, that is clear. You were on the point of doing so, but you turned away. If you had given that answer, I should now have acquired from you sufficient knowledge of the nature of piety. As it is, the lover of inquiry must follow his beloved wherever it may lead him. Once more then, what do you say that piety and the pious are? Are they a knowledge of how to sacrifice and pray?

E: They are.

S: To sacrifice is to make a gift to the gods, whereas to pray is to beg from the gods?

E: Definitely, Socrates.

d S: It would follow from this statement that piety would be a knowledge of how to give to, and beg from, the gods.

E: You understood what I said very well, Socrates.

S: That is because I am so desirous of your wisdom, and I concentrate my mind on it, so that no word of yours may fall to the ground. But tell me, what is this service to the gods? You say it is to beg from them and to give to them?

E: I do.

S: And to beg correctly would be to ask from them things that we need?

E: What else?

e S: And to give correctly is to give them what they need from us, for it would not be skillful to bring gifts to anyone that are in no way needed.

E: True, Socrates.

S: Piety would then be a sort of trading skill between gods and men?

E: Trading yes, if you prefer to call it that.

S: I prefer nothing, unless it is true. But tell me, what benefit do the gods derive from the gifts they receive from us? What they give us is

15 obvious to all. There is for us no good that we do not receive from them, but how are they benefited by what they receive from us? Or do we have such an advantage over them in the trade that we receive all our blessings from them and they receive nothing from us?

E: Do you suppose, Socrates, that the gods are benefited by what they receive from us?

S: What could those gifts from us to the gods be, Euthyphro?

E: What else, do you think, than honour, reverence, and what I mentioned just now, gratitude?

b S: The pious is then, Euthyphro, pleasing to the gods, but not beneficial or dear to them?

E: I think it is of all things most dear to them.

S: So the pious is once again what is dear to the gods.

E: Most certainly.

S: When you say this, will you be surprised if your arguments seem to move about instead of staying put? And will you accuse me of being Daedalus who makes them move, though you are yourself much more skillful than Daedalus and make them go round in a circle? Or do you not realize that our argument has moved around and come again to the same place? You

c surely remember that earlier the pious and the god-beloved were shown not to be the same but different from each other. Or do you not remember?

E: I do.

S: Do you then not realize now that you are saying that what is dear to the gods is the pious? Is this not the same as the god-beloved? Or is it not?

E: It certainly is.

S: Either we were wrong when we agreed before, or, if we were right then, we are wrong now.

E: That seems to be so.

S: So we must investigate again from the beginning what piety is, as I shall not willingly give up before I learn this. Do not think me d unworthy, but concentrate your attention and tell the truth. For you know it, if any man does, and I must not let you go, like Proteus, before you tell me. If you had no clear knowledge of piety and impiety you would never have ventured to prosecute your old father for murder on behalf of a servant. For fear of the gods you would have been afraid to take the risk lest you should not be acting rightly, and would have been ashamed before men, but now I know well that you believe you have

e clear knowledge of piety and impiety. So tell me, my good Euthyphro, and do not hide what you think it is.

E: Some other time, Socrates, for I am in a hurry now, and it is time for me to go.

S: What a thing to do, my friend! By going you have cast me down from a great hope I had, that I would learn from you the nature of the

16 pious and the impious and so escape Meletus' indictment by showing him that I had acquired wisdom in divine matters from Euthyphro, and my ignorance would no longer cause me to be careless and inventive about such things, and that I would be better for the rest of my life.

COMMENTARY AND QUESTIONS

Read 2a–5a   Note that **Euthyphro** is surprised to find Socrates at court. His surprise indicates that Socrates is neither the sort who brings suit against his fellow citizens nor the sort one would expect to be prosecuted.

Q1. Why does Socrates say that **Meletus** is likely to be wise? (2c)

Q2. What sort of character does Socrates ascribe to Meletus here? Is Socrates sincere in his praise of Meletus?

Q3. There seem to be two charges against Socrates. Can you identify them? (2c, 3b)

It is well known that Socrates claims to have a **"divine sign"** that comes to him from time to time. We hear of it again in the *Apology*. That the gods should speak to mortals in signs does not strike the ancient Greeks as a strange notion. Usually the gods speak through oracles, prophets, or seers. When Agamemnon wants to know why his troops are being wasted with plague, he calls on Calchas, who is described as

> the clearest by far of all the seers
> who scan the flight of birds. He knew all things that are,
> all things that are past and all that are to come.
>
> —*The Iliad*, Book 1, 80–82

When Oedipus seeks the cause for his city's distress, he calls the blind seer Tiresias. So the idea that the gods make their will known to mortals is a familiar one.

Euthyphro claims this ability for himself, saying that he "foretells the future." He assumes (mistakenly) that Socrates too claims this ability, and he concludes that it is out of envy for this talent that Meletus and the others are pressing charges. Moreover, Socrates' "sign" from the gods, Euthyphro thinks, would also explain the accusation that Socrates is introducing "new gods."

Does Socrates believe in the "old gods"? There can be little doubt that his view of the Olympians is much the same as that of Xenophanes or Heraclitus: The stories of Homer cannot be taken literally. (See *Euthyphro* 6a.) Yet he always speaks reverently of "god" or "the god" or "the gods" (these three terms being used pretty much interchangeably). And he feels free to use traditional language in speaking about the divine, so he writes that last hymn to Apollo and would probably have agreed with Heraclitus that the divine is "willing and unwilling to be called Zeus."*

Moreover, Xenophon tells us that Socrates behaves in accord with the advice given by the Priestess at Delphi when asked about sacrifice and ritual matters: "Follow the custom of the State: that is the way to act piously." Xenophon goes on to tell us,

> And again, when he prayed he asked simply for good gifts, "for the gods know best what things are good." Though his sacrifices were humble, according to his means, he thought himself not a whit inferior to those who made frequent and magnificent sacrifices out of great possessions. . . . No, the greater the piety of the giver, the greater (he thought) was the delight of the gods in the gift.[2]

---

*See p. 22.

There seems every reason to suppose that Socrates is pious in the conventional sense. Still, he would not have held back his beliefs if asked directly about the gods; as he says in 3d, his "liking for people" makes it seem that he pours out to anybody what he has to say. And traditionalists might well take exception to some of that.

What of the "sign"? Was that an introduction of new gods? There is no reason to believe that Socrates ever thought of it as such. It seems to be analogous to what we would call the voice of conscience, though clearly it was much more vivid to him than to most of us. It never, he tells us, advises him positively to do something; it only prevents him, and it is clearly not anything like Euthyphro's future-telling. (Note that in 3e he separates himself from "you prophets.") But he clearly thinks of the sign as a voice of the divine, however that is best conceived.

Q4.　Why is Euthyphro in court?
Q5.　What does Euthyphro claim to know?

Read 5a–6e　We now know what the topic of this conversation is to be. Socrates says he is "eager" to be Euthyphro's pupil.

Q6.　Why does Socrates say he wants Euthyphro to instruct him? Do you think he really expects to be helped?
Q7.　Do you think this is going to be a serious inquiry? Or is Socrates just having some sport with Euthyphro?

Notice in 5d the three requirements that must be met to satisfy Socrates. He wants to know what **the "pious"** or the "holy" or the "godly" is (all these words may translate the Greek term).

1. A satisfactory answer will pick out some feature that is the same in every pious action.
2. This feature will not be shared by any impious action.
3. It will be that feature (or the lack of it) that *makes* an action pious (or impious).

What Socrates is searching for, we can say, is a **definition** of piety or holiness.* He wants to know what it is so that it can be recognized when it appears. It is like wanting to know what a crow is: We want to know what features all crows have that are not shared by eagles and hedgehogs, the possession of which ensure that this thing we see before us is indeed a crow.

Would a knowledge of what piety is be useful if one were on the brink of being brought to trial for impiety? A Sophist might not think so at all. At that point, the typical Sophist would construct a dazzling rhetorical display that would emotionally engage the jury on his side. But Socrates, as always, wants to know the truth. He wants to know the truth even more than he wants to be acquitted. We can think of this as one aspect of his persistent search to know himself. Who is he? Has he been guilty of impiety? Only an understanding of what piety truly is will tell.

Q8.　What does Euthyphro say piety is?
Q9.　What does Socrates focus on as the likely reason he is on trial?
Q10.　What is Socrates' objection to the definition Euthyphro has proposed?

Note particularly the term **"form"** in 6d–e. It clearly does not mean "shape," except perhaps in a most abstract sense. The form of something is whatever makes it the kind of thing it is. The form may sometimes be shape, as the "form" of a square is to be an area bounded by equal straight lines and right angles, but it need not be. When we ask in this sense for the "form" of an elephant, we are asking for more than an outline drawing, and for more than even a photograph can supply. What we want is what the biologist can give us; we are asking what an elephant is. Notice that the biologist can do this not only for elephants but also for mammals—and no one can draw the geometrical shape of a mammal. (True, you can draw a picture of *this* mammal or *that* mammal, but not a picture of a mammal *as*

---

*There are a number of different kinds of definition. For a critique of Socrates' kind, see Wittgenstein's notion of "family resemblances" in Chapter 22.

such. Yet it can be given a definition.) In the same way, it is perfectly in order to ask for the "form" of abstract qualities such as justice, courage, or piety.

Read 7a–9b   Here we have Euthyphro's second attempt at answering Socrates' question.

Q11.   What is Euthyphro's second answer?
Q12.   Why does Socrates exclaim, "Splendid!"?
Q13.   What is the difference between answering "in the way" he wanted and giving a "true" answer?

Note Socrates' characteristic invitation in 7a: "Let us examine what we mean." How does this examination proceed? He reminds Euthyphro of something he admitted earlier—that there is "war among the gods" (6b)—and wonders whether that is *consistent* with the definition Euthyphro now proposes; do the two fit together, or do they clash?

Q14.   How does Socrates derive the conclusion (8a) that "the same things then are loved by the gods and hated by the gods"? Is this a correct deduction from the statements Euthyphro previously agreed to?
Q15.   What further conclusion follows? Why is that disturbing?

In 8b, Socrates drives the disturbing consequence home by applying it to Euthyphro's own case. Socrates is never one to leave things up in the air, unconnected to practical life. If this is a good understanding of piety, then it ought to illumine the matter at hand. But of course, Euthyphro cannot admit that his own prosecution is loved by some of the gods and hated by others—that it is both pious and impious. He protests that *none* of the gods would disagree that "whoever has killed anyone unjustly should pay the penalty."

Now, this is sneaky. Can you see why? It is a move that might slide past a lesser antagonist, but Socrates picks it up immediately.

Q16.   What do people dispute about concerning wrongs and penalties? And what not?

So Socrates drives Euthyphro back to the issue: In light of the admission that the gods quarrel, what reason is there to think that prosecuting his father is an instance of what the gods love and thus an example of piety?

Q17.   Do you believe that Socrates has put Euthyphro in an untenable position here?

Read 9c–11d   Socrates takes the lead here and proposes a modification to the earlier definition. Euthyphro embraces the suggestion with enthusiasm in 9e. Be sure you are clear about the new definition. Write it down.

Again we get the invitation to examine this new attempt. In 9e, Socrates backs it up with this question: "Or do we let it pass, and if one of us, or someone else, merely says that something is so, do we accept that it is so?" Are there reasons why this should not be accepted? The mere fact that someone—anyone—says it is so does not make it so. Do you agree with Socrates here?

In 10a, we get an important question, one that reverberates through later Christian theology and has a bearing on whether there can be an **ethics** independent of what God or the gods approve. Is a secular ethics possible? Suppose we agree that in normal circumstances it is wrong to lie (allowing that a lie may be justified, for example, if it is the only way to save a life). And suppose, for the sake of the argument, we also agree that God or the gods hate lying (in those normal circumstances). What is it, we still might ask, that *makes* lying wrong? Is it the fact that it is hated by the divine power(s)? Or is there something about lying itself that makes it wrong—and that is why the gods hate it? To ask these questions is a way of asking for the "form" of wrongness. (Look again at the three requirements for a satisfactory definition in 5d and on page 82; it is the third requirement that is at issue.)

Suppose we agree, Socrates says, that what all the gods love is pious and what they all hate is impious; the question remains whether it is this love and hate that explains the piety of the pious. Suppose it is. Then a behavior is pious or holy *simply because* that behavior pleases the gods. It follows that if the gods loved lying, stealing, or adultery, that would make it right to lie, steal, or sleep with your neighbor's spouse. In this case, ethics is tied intrinsically to religion.

The alternative is that there is something about these actions that makes them wrong—and that is why the gods hate them. If this alternative is correct, then a secular ethics is possible. If we could identify what it is about lying that makes it wrong, we would have a reason not to lie whether we believe in the gods or not. Those who think that God's command (or love) is what *makes* lying wrong will be likely to say, if they lose faith in God, that "everything is permitted."* But on the alternative to divine command theory, this radical consequence does not follow. The question Socrates raises is an important one.

Assuming that the alternatives are clear, which one should we prefer? There is no doubt about Socrates' answer: the pious is pious *not* because the gods love it; rather, the gods love what is pious because of what it is. In the omitted section (10a–11a), Socrates piles up analogies to explain this. Let's try to simplify. Suppose that Henry, a gardener, loves his roses. The roses are loved, then, because Henry loves them. But he doesn't love them because they are loved by him! That would be absurd. He loves them because of something in the roses, something that makes them worthy of his love—their fragrance, perhaps, or their beauty.

In the same way, Socrates argues, if the gods love piety in humans, it must be because there is something lovable about it. Socrates wants to understand what it is. That is why he complains in 11a that Euthyphro has not answered his question. He says that Euthyphro has told him only "an affect or quality" of the pious—namely, that it is loved by the gods. But, he claims, Euthyphro has not yet made its "nature" or "form" clear. To be told only

that the pious is what all the gods love is to learn only about how it is regarded by them. Euthyphro has spoken only of something quite external; he has not revealed a single thing about what it really is!

Q18.　Is this a good argument? Suppose, in response to the question, "Why do the gods love the pious?" one were to reply, "They just do!" Is Socrates assuming that there must be a reason? Is he assuming what he needs to prove? Think about this.

Socrates probably calls Daedalus (in 11c) his "ancestor" because Daedalus was the mythical "patron saint" of stonemasons and sculptors. He was reputed to be such a cunning artisan that his sculptures took life and ran away.

Q19.　Why is Socrates reminded of Daedalus here?

Read 11e–end　Again Socrates makes a suggestion, this time that piety and justice are related somehow. It seems a promising line to investigate, but some clarifications are needed. Are they identical? Or is one a part of the other? And if the latter, which is part of which?

Q20.　What answer do the two settle on? Why?
Q21.　In what way are the fear/shame and odd/number distinctions analogous?
Q22.　What are the two kinds of "care" that are distinguished? (13a–c and 13d–e)
Q23.　Which one is the relevant one? Why?

In 14c we reach a crucial turning point in the dialogue. Note that Socrates here says they were on the verge of solving the problem, but Euthyphro "turned away." If only he had answered a certain question, Socrates says, he "should now have acquired . . . sufficient knowledge of the nature of piety." But Euthyphro didn't answer it.

Apparently Socrates feels that they were on the right track. Let us review. Piety is part of justice. It is that part consisting in **care of the gods.**

---

*This formula, "Everything is permitted," is that of Ivan Karamazov, the atheist in Dostoyevsky's novel, *The Brothers Karamazov.* The servant of the family, Smerdyakov, is persuaded that this is so, and on these grounds he murders the brothers' father.

The kind of care at issue is the kind that slaves offer their masters. Such service on the part of slaves is always directed to some fine end (for example, health, ships, houses). The question arises, to what fine end is service to the gods devoted? To put it another way, what is the point of piety? What is it *for*? What is "that excellent aim that the gods achieve, using us as their servants?" Remember that for Socrates the good is always something useful or advantageous. He is here asking—on the tacit assumption that piety is something good—what the advantage is that piety produces. We can identify the good things produced by service to doctors. What good things are produced by service to the gods? If one could answer this question, the nature of piety might finally be clarified. It would be service to the gods for the sake of *X*. All we need to know is what *X* is.

Unfortunately, all Euthyphro can say with regard to *X* is that it is "many fine things." When pressed harder, he in effect changes the subject, although he probably doesn't realize he is doing so. He says in 14b that "to put it simply," piety is knowing "how to say and do what is pleasing to the gods at prayer and sacrifice." This certainly does not answer the question of what aim the gods achieve through our service!

Let us, however, briefly consider Euthyphro's statement. First, it does go some way toward answering the question of what we should do to be pious. Euthyphro's answer is in fact the traditional answer common to most religions: pray and offer sacrifice. That answer would have been the standard one in Athens, and it is a little surprising that it comes out so late in the dialogue. It corresponds to the advice of the Delphic Oracle to "follow the custom of the state."

Second, Euthyphro's statement mentions some advantages to being pious in this way: preserving "both private houses and public affairs of state." But this is puzzling. Why does Socrates not accept this as an answer to the question about the nature of *X,* for the sake of which we ought to be pious in just this way?

No answer is given in the dialogue; perhaps it must just remain puzzling. But here is a suggestion. Socrates, at the end of the Peloponnesian War,

may simply be unable to believe this is true. No doubt Athens had offered many prayers and had made all the required sacrifices during the war. Athens had prayed for victory, just as Sparta must have prayed for victory. Yet Athens not only lost, she did irreparable damage to herself; such piety, it seemed, did *not* preserve private houses and public affairs. If the promised advantages do not materialize, Socrates would conclude, this kind of piety is not after all a good thing. Perhaps the exasperation evident in 14c expresses Socrates' view that by this time in history it is all too clear piety can't be that. It can't be a kind of "trading skill" between gods and mortals. And on the assumption that piety is a good thing, it must be something quite different from Euthyphro's version of it. So the nature of *X* remains unclarified.

Well, this is rather speculative but not, I think, implausible. As we'll see, Jesus and the Christians have an answer about the nature of *X*. We find it clearly, for instance, in St. Augustine.* It is an answer that Socrates is close to but does not quite grasp. It demands that we rethink the nature of

---

*See p. 250.

God and the relations of man to God altogether. But that is a story for later.

Socrates, regretfully, feels it is necessary to follow his "teacher," and once more takes up his questioning in 14c. There is a fairly simple argument running through these exchanges, but it is not easy to pick it out. Let me try to identify the steps; check the text to see that I am getting it right.

1. Piety is prayer and sacrifice. (This is Euthyphro's latest definition, now up for examination.)
2. Prayer and sacrifice are begging from the gods and giving to the gods.
3. The giving must, to be "skillful," be giving what they need.
4. To give what they need would be to benefit them.
5. But we cannot benefit the gods.
6. If our giving does not benefit the gods, the only alternative is that this giving "pleases" them.
7. But that is just to say that they like it, it is dear to them—it is what they love.
8. And that returns us to the earlier definition: that piety is what all the gods love. (And we already know that this is not satisfactory. So we are going in a circle.)

The crux of the argument is, no doubt, Premise 5. It is expressed by Euthyphro in a surprised question in 15a and accepted by Socrates. Why can't we benefit the gods? No reasons are given here, but they are not hard to find. The gods, recall, are the immortals; as such they are also the happy ones. To think of them as having needs that mere mortals could supply would have seemed to many Greeks—especially to those who had the "high" view of "the god" characteristic of Xenophanes, Heraclitus, and Socrates—as impious in the extreme. We receive all our benefits from them. To think that we could benefit them would be arrogance and hubris of the first rank.

Q24. Do you agree with this view? What do you think of this argument? Has the discussion really come full circle?

Q25. What characteristic of Socrates do you think Plato means to impress upon us in Socrates' next-to-last speech?

Q26. Has Euthyphro learned anything in the course of this discussion?

Q27. Have you? If so, what?

At the end of the dialogue, Euthyphro escapes, we are left without an answer to the question examined, and Socrates must go to his trial still ignorant of the nature of piety.

APOLOGY

Translator's Introduction

The Apology[1] professes to be a record of the actual speech that Socrates delivered in his own defence at the trial. This makes the question of its historicity more acute than in the

dialogues in which the conversations themselves are mostly fictional and the question of historicity is concerned only with how far the theories that Socrates is represented as expressing were those of the historical Socrates. Here, however, we are dealing with a speech that Socrates made as a matter of history. How far is Plato's account accurate? We should always remember that the ancients did not expect historical accuracy

---

[1]The word _apology_ is a transliteration, not a translation, of the Greek _apologia,_ which means defense. There is certainly nothing apologetic about the speech.

in the way we do. On the other hand, Plato makes it clear that he was present at the trial (34a, 38b). Moreover, if, as is generally believed, the Apology was written not long after the event, many Athenians would remember the actual speech, and it would be a poor way to vindicate the Master, which is the obvious intent, to put a completely different speech into his mouth. Some liberties could no doubt be allowed, but the main arguments and the general tone of the defence must surely be faithful to the original. The beauty of language and style is certainly Plato's, but the serene spiritual and moral beauty of character belongs to Socrates. It is a powerful combination.

Athenian juries were very large, in this case 501, and they combined the duties of jury and judge as we know them by both convicting and sentencing. Obviously, it would have been virtually impossible for so large a body to discuss various penalties and decide on one. The problem was resolved rather neatly, however, by having the prosecutor, after conviction, assess the penalty he thought appropriate, followed by a counter-assessment by the defendant. The jury would then decide between the two. This procedure generally made for moderation on both sides.

Thus the Apology is in three parts. The first and major part is the main speech (17a–35a), followed by the counter-assessment (35a–38c), and finally, last words to the jury (38c–42a), both to those who voted for the death sentence and those who voted for acquittal.

The Dialogue

17 I do not know, men of Athens, how my accusers affected you; as for me, I was almost carried away in spite of myself, so persuasively did they speak. And yet, hardly anything of what they said is true. Of the many lies they told, one in particular surprised me, namely that you should be careful not to be deceived by an accomplished speaker like

b me. That they were not ashamed to be immediately proved wrong by the facts, when I show myself not to be an accomplished speaker at all, that I thought was most shameless on their part— unless indeed they call an accomplished speaker the man who speaks the truth. If they mean that, I would agree that I am an orator, but not after their manner, for indeed, as I say, practically nothing they said was true. From me you will hear the

c whole truth, though not, by Zeus, gentlemen, expressed in embroidered and stylized phrases like theirs, but things spoken at random and expressed in the first words that come to mind, for I put my trust in the justice of what I say, and let none of

you expect anything else. It would not be fitting at my age, as it might be for a young man, to toy with words when I appear before you.

One thing I do ask and beg of you gentlemen: if you hear me making my defence in the same kind of language as I am accustomed to use in the market place by the bankers' tables,[2] where many of you have heard me, and elsewhere, do not be surprised or create a disturbance on that account.

d The position is this: this is my first appearance in a law-court, at the age of seventy; I am therefore simply a stranger to the manner of speaking here. Just as if I were really a stranger, you would certainly excuse me if I spoke in that dialect and

18 manner in which I had been brought up, so too my present request seems a just one, for you to pay no attention to my manner of speech—be it better or worse—but to concentrate your attention on whether what I say is just or not, for the excellence of a judge lies in this, as that of a speaker lies in telling the truth.

It is right for me, gentlemen, to defend myself first against the first lying accusations made against me and my first accusers, and then against the later accusations and the later accusers. There have

b been many who have accused me to you for many years now, and none of their accusations are true. These I fear much more than I fear Anytus and his friends, though they too are formidable. These earlier ones, however, are more so, gentlemen; they got hold of most of you from childhood, persuaded you and accused me quite falsely, saying that there is a man called Socrates, a wise man, a student of all things in the sky and below the earth, who

c makes the worse argument the stronger. Those who spread that rumour, gentlemen, are my dangerous accusers, for their hearers believe that those who study these things do not even believe in the gods. Moreover, these accusers are numerous, and have been at it a long time; also, they spoke to you at an age when you would most readily believe them, some of you being children and adolescents, and they won their case by default, as there was no defence.

What is most absurd in all this is that one can-

d not even know or mention their names unless one

---

[2]The bankers or money-changers had their counters in the market place. It seems that this was a favourite place for gossip.

of them is a writer of comedies.[3] Those who maliciously and slanderously persuaded you—who also, when persuaded themselves then persuaded others—all those are most difficult to deal with: one cannot bring one of them into court or refute him; one must simply fight with shadows, as it were, in making one's defence, and cross-examine when no one answers. I want you to realize too that my accusers are of two kinds: those who have accused me recently, and the old ones I mention; and to think that I must first defend myself against the latter, for you have also heard their accusations

e   first, and to a much greater extent than the more recent.

Very well then. I must surely defend myself and
19   attempt to uproot from your minds in so short a time the slander that has resided there so long. I wish this may happen, if it is in any way better for you and me, and that my defence may be successful, but I think this is very difficult and I am fully aware of how difficult it is. Even so, let the matter proceed as the god may wish, but I must obey the law and make my defence.

Let us then take up the case from its beginning.
b   What is the accusation from which arose the slander in which Meletus trusted when he wrote out the charge against me? What did they say when they slandered me? I must, as if they were my actual prosecutors, read the affidavit they would have sworn. It goes something like this: Socrates is guilty of wrongdoing in that he busies himself studying things in the sky and below the earth; he makes the worse into the stronger argument, and he teaches these same things to others. You have seen
c   this yourselves in the comedy of Aristophanes, a Socrates swinging about there, saying he was walking on air and talking a lot of other nonsense about things of which I know nothing at all. I do not speak in contempt of such knowledge, if someone is wise in these things—lest Meletus bring more cases against me—but, gentlemen, I have no part in it, and on this point I call upon the majority of you as witnesses. I think it right that all those of you who have heard me conversing, and many of you
d   have, should tell each other if anyone of you have ever heard me discussing such subjects to any extent

at all. From this you will learn that the other things said about me by the majority are of the same kind.

Not one of them is true. And if you have heard from anyone that I undertake to teach people and
e   charge a fee for it, that is not true either. Yet I think it a fine thing to be able to teach people as Gorgias of Leontini does, and Prodicus of Ceos, and Hippias of Elis.[4] Each of these men can go to any city and persuade the young, who can keep company with anyone of their own fellow-citizens
20   they want without paying, to leave the company of these, to join with themselves, pay them a fee, and be grateful to them besides. Indeed, I learned that there is another wise man from Paros who is visiting us, for I met a man who has spent more money on Sophists than everybody else put together, Callias, the son of Hipponicus. So I asked him—he has two sons—"Callias," I said, "if your sons were colts or calves, we could find and engage a supervisor for them who would make them excel
b   in their proper qualities, some horse breeder or farmer. Now since they are men, whom do you have in mind to supervise them? Who is an expert in this kind of excellence, the human and social kind? I think you must have given thought to this since you have sons. Is there such a person," I asked, "or is there not?" "Certainly there is," he said. "Who is he?" I asked, "What is his name, where is he from? and what is his fee?" "His name, Socrates, is Evenus, he comes from Paros, and his
c   fee is five minas." I thought Evenus a happy man, if he really possesses this art, and teaches for so moderate a fee. Certainly I would pride and preen myself if I had this knowledge, but I do not have it, gentlemen.

One of you might perhaps interrupt me and say: "But Socrates, what is your occupation? From where have these slanders come? For surely if you did not busy yourself with something out of the common, all these rumours and talk would not

---

[3]This refers in particular to Aristophanes, whose comedy, *The Clouds,* produced in 423 B.C., ridiculed the (imaginary) school of Socrates.

[4]These were all well-known Sophists. Gorgias, after whom Plato named one of his dialogues, was a celebrated rhetorician and teacher of rhetoric. He came to Athens in 427 B.C., and his rhetorical tricks took the city by storm. Two dialogues, the authenticity of which has been doubted, are named after Hippias, whose knowledge was encyclopedic. Prodicus was known for his insistence on the precise meaning of words. Both he and Hippias are characters in the *Protagoras* (named after another famous Sophist).

have arisen unless you did something other than most people. Tell us what it is, that we may not

d speak inadvisedly about you." Anyone who says that seems to be right, and I will try to show you what has caused this reputation and slander. Listen then. Perhaps some of you will think I am jesting, but be sure that all that I shall say is true. What has caused my reputation is none other than a certain kind of wisdom. What kind of wisdom? Human wisdom, perhaps. It may be that I really possess this, while those whom I mentioned just now are

e wise with a wisdom more than human; else I cannot explain it, for I certainly do not possess it, and whoever says I do is lying and speaks to slander me. Do not create a disturbance, gentlemen, even if you think I am boasting, for the story I shall tell does not originate with me, but I will refer you to a trustworthy source. I shall call upon the god at Delphi as witness to the existence and nature of my wis-

21 dom, if it be such. You know Chairephon. He was my friend from youth, and the friend of most of you, as he shared your exile and your return. You surely know the kind of man he was, how impulsive in any course of action. He went to Delphi at one time and ventured to ask the oracle—as I say, gentlemen, do not create a disturbance—he asked if any man was wiser than I, and the Pythian replied that no one was wiser. Chairephon is dead, but his brother will testify to you about this.

b Consider that I tell you this because I would inform you about the origin of the slander. When I heard of this reply I asked myself: "Whatever does the god mean? What is his riddle? I am very conscious that I am not wise at all; what then does he mean by saying that I am the wisest? For surely he does not lie; it is not legitimate for him to do so." For a long time I was at a loss as to his meaning; then I very reluctantly turned to some such investigation as this: I went to one of those reputed

c wise, thinking that there, if anywhere, I could refute the oracle and say to it: "This man is wiser than I, but you said I was." Then, when I examined this man—there is no need for me to tell you his name, he was one of our public men—my experience was something like this: I thought that he appeared wise to many people and especially to himself, but he was not. I then tried to show him

d that he thought himself wise, but that he was not. As a result he came to dislike me, and so did many of the bystanders. So I withdrew and thought to myself: "I am wiser than this man; it is likely that

neither of us knows anything worthwhile, but he thinks he knows something when he does not, whereas when I do not know, neither do I think I know; so I am likely to be wiser than he to this small extent, that I do not think I know what I do not know." After this I approached another man,

e one of those thought to be wiser than he, and I thought the same thing, and so I came to be disliked both by him and by many others.

After that I proceeded systematically. I realized, to my sorrow and alarm, that I was getting unpopular, but I thought that I must attach the greatest importance to the god's oracle, so I must go to all those who had any reputation for knowledge to examine its meaning. And by the dog,[5] gentlemen

22 of the jury—for I must tell you the truth—I experienced something like this: in my investigation in the service of the god I found that those who had the highest reputation were nearly the most deficient, while those who were thought to be inferior were more knowledgeable. I must give you an account of my journeyings as if they were labours I had undertaken to prove the oracle irrefutable. After the politicians, I went to the poets, the writers

b of tragedies and dithyrambs and the others, intending in their case to catch myself being more ignorant than they. So I took up those poems with which they seemed to have taken most trouble and asked them what they meant, in order that I might at the same time learn something from them. I am ashamed to tell you the truth, gentlemen, but I must. Almost all the bystanders might have explained the poems better than their authors could.

c I soon realized that poets do not compose their poems with knowledge, but by some inborn talent and by inspiration, like seers and prophets who also say many fine things without any understanding of what they say. The poets seemed to me to have had a similar experience. At the same time I saw that, because of their poetry, they thought themselves very wise men in other respects, which they were not. So there again I withdrew, thinking that I had the same advantage over them as I had over the politicians.

Finally I went to the craftsmen, for I was con-

d scious of knowing practically nothing, and I knew that I would find that they had knowledge of many

_____

[5] A curious oath, occasionally used by Socrates, it appears in a longer form in the *Gorgias* (482b) as "by the dog, the god of the Egyptians."

fine things. In this I was not mistaken; they knew things I did not know, and to that extent they were wiser than I. But, gentlemen of the jury, the good craftsmen seemed to me to have the same fault as the poets: each of them, because of his success at his craft, thought himself very wise in other most important pursuits, and this error of

e theirs overshadowed the wisdom they had, so that I asked myself, on behalf of the oracle, whether I should prefer to be as I am, with neither their wisdom nor their ignorance, or to have both. The answer I gave myself and the oracle was that it was to my advantage to be as I am.

As a result of this investigation, gentlemen of

23 the jury, I acquired much unpopularity, of a kind that is hard to deal with and is a heavy burden; many slanders came from these people and a reputation for wisdom, for in each case the bystanders thought that I myself possessed the wisdom that I proved that my interlocutor did not have. What is probable, gentlemen, is that in fact the god is wise and that his oracular response meant that human wisdom is worth little or nothing, and that when

b he says this man, Socrates, he is using my name as an example, as if he said: "This man among you, mortals, is wisest who, like Socrates, understands that his wisdom is worthless." So even now I continue this investigation as the god bade me—and I go around seeking out anyone, citizen or stranger, whom I think wise. Then if I do not think he is, I come to the assistance of the god and show him that he is not wise. Because of this occupation, I do not have the leisure to engage in public affairs to any extent, nor indeed to look after my own, but I live in great poverty because of my service to the god.

c Furthermore, the young men who follow me around of their own free will, those who have most leisure, the sons of the very rich, take pleasure in hearing people questioned; they themselves often imitate me and try to question others. I think they find an abundance of men who believe they have some knowledge but know little or nothing. The result is that those whom they question are angry,

d not with themselves but with me. They say: "That man Socrates is a pestilential fellow who corrupts the young." If one asks them what he does and what he teaches to corrupt them, they are silent, as they do not know, but, so as not to appear at a loss, they mention those accusations that are available against all philosophers, about "things in the sky and things below the earth," about "not

believing in the gods" and "making the worse the stronger argument;" they would not want to tell the truth, I'm sure, that they have been proved to lay claim to knowledge when they know nothing. These people are ambitious, violent and numer-

e ous; they are continually and convincingly talking about me; they have been filling your ears for a long time with vehement slanders against me. From them Meletus attacked me, and Anytus and Lycon, Meletus being vexed on behalf of the poets, Anytus on behalf of the craftsmen and the politicians, Lycon on behalf of the orators, so that, as

24 I started out by saying, I should be surprised if I could rid you of so much slander in so short a time. That, gentlemen of the jury, is the truth for you. I have hidden or disguised nothing. I know well enough that this very conduct makes me unpopular, and this is proof that what I say is true, that such is the slander against me, and that such

b are its causes. If you look into this either now or later, this is what you will find.

Let this suffice as a defence against the charges of my earlier accusers. After this I shall try to defend myself against Meletus, that good and patriotic man, as he says he is, and my later accusers. As these are a different lot of accusers, let us again take up their sworn deposition. It goes something like this: Socrates is guilty of corrupting the young and of not believing in the gods in whom the city believes, but in other new divinities. Such is their

c charge. Let us examine it point by point.

He says that I am guilty of corrupting the young, but I say that Meletus is guilty of dealing frivolously with serious matters, of irresponsibly bringing people into court, and of professing to be seriously concerned with things about none of which he has ever cared, and I shall try to prove that this is so. Come here and tell me, Meletus.

d Surely you consider it of the greatest importance that our young men be as good as possible?[6] —— Indeed I do.

Come then, tell the jury who improves them. You obviously know, in view of your concern. You say you have discovered the one who corrupts them, namely me, and you bring me here and accuse me to the jury. Come, inform the jury and

_____

[6]Socrates here drops into his usual method of discussion by question and answer. This, no doubt, is what Plato had in mind, at least in part, when he made him ask the indulgence of the jury if he spoke "in his usual manner."

tell them who it is. You see, Meletus, that you are silent and know not what to say. Does this not seem shameful to you and a sufficient proof of what I say, that you have not been concerned with any of this? Tell me, my good sir, who improves

e our young men?   ——The laws.

That is not what I am asking, but what person who has knowledge of the laws to begin with? ——These jurymen, Socrates.

How do you mean, Meletus? Are these able to educate the young and improve them?
——Certainly.

All of them, or some but not others?   ——All of them.

Very good, by Hera. You mention a great

25 abundance of benefactors. But what about the audience? Do they improve the young or not? ——They do, too.

What about the members of Council?   ——The Councillors, also.

But, Meletus, what about the assembly? Do members of the assembly corrupt the young, or do they all improve them?   ——They improve them.

All the Athenians, it seems, make the young into fine good men, except me, and I alone corrupt them. Is that what you mean?   ——That is most definitely what I mean.

b You condemn me to a great misfortune. Tell me: does this also apply to horses do you think? That all men improve them and one individual corrupts them? Or is quite the contrary true, one individual is able to improve them, or very few, namely the horse breeders, whereas the majority, if they have horses and use them, corrupt them? Is that not the case, Meletus, both with horses and all other animals? Of course it is, whether you and Anytus say so or not. It would be a very happy state of affairs if only one person corrupted our youth, while the others improved them.

c You have made it sufficiently obvious, Meletus, that you have never had any concern for our youth; you show your indifference clearly; that you have given no thought to the subjects about which you bring me to trial.

And by Zeus, Meletus, tell us also whether it is better for a man to live among good or wicked fellow-citizens. Answer, my good man, for I am not asking a difficult question. Do not the wicked do some harm to those who are ever closest to them, whereas good people benefit them?   ——Certainly.

d And does the man exist who would rather be

harmed than benefited by his associates? Answer, my good sir, for the law orders you to answer. Is there any man who wants to be harmed?   ——Of course not.

Come now, do you accuse me here of corrupting the young and making them worse deliberately or unwillingly?   ——Deliberately.

What follows, Meletus? Are you so much wiser at your age than I am at mine that you understand that wicked people always do some harm to their

e closest neighbours while good people do them good, but I have reached such a pitch of ignorance that I do not realize this, namely that if I make one of my associates wicked I run the risk of being harmed by him so that I do such a great evil deliberately, as you say? I do not believe you, Meletus, and I do not think anyone else will. Either I do not

26 corrupt the young or, if I do, it is unwillingly, and you are lying in either case. Now if I corrupt them unwillingly, the law does not require you to bring people to court for such unwilling wrongdoings, but to get hold of them privately, to instruct them and exhort them; for clearly, if I learn better, I shall cease to do what I am doing unwillingly. You, however, have avoided my company and were unwilling to instruct me, but you bring me here, where the law requires one to bring those who are in need of punishment, not of instruction.

And so, gentlemen of the jury, what I said is clearly true: Meletus has never been at all con-

b cerned with these matters. Nonetheless tell us, Meletus, how you say that I corrupt the young; or is it obvious from your deposition that it is by teaching them not to believe in the gods in whom the city believes but in other new divinities? Is this not what you say I teach and so corrupt them? ——That is most certainly what I do say.

Then by those very gods about whom we are

c talking, Meletus, make this clearer to me and to the jury: I cannot be sure whether you mean that I teach the belief that there are some gods—and therefore I myself believe that there are gods and am not altogether an atheist, nor am I guilty of that—not, however, the gods in whom the city believes, but others, and that this is the charge against me, that they are others. Or whether you mean that I do not believe in gods at all, and that this is what I teach to others.   ——This is what I mean, that you do not believe in gods at all.

d You are a strange fellow, Meletus. Why do you say this? Do I not believe, as other men do, that the sun and the moon are gods? ——No, by Zeus, jurymen, for he says that the sun is stone, and the moon earth.

My dear Meletus, do you think you are prosecuting Anaxagoras? Are you so contemptuous of the jury and think them so ignorant of letters as not to know that the books of Anaxagoras[7] of Clazomenae are full of those theories, and further, that the young men learn from me what they can
e buy from time to time for a drachma, at most, in the bookshops, and ridicule Socrates if he pretends that these theories are his own, especially as they are so absurd? Is that, by Zeus, what you think of me, Meletus, that I do not believe that there are any gods? ——That is what I say, that you do not believe in the gods at all.

You cannot be believed, Meletus, even, I think, by yourself. The man appears to me, gentlemen of the jury, highly insolent and uncontrolled. He seems to have made this deposition out of inso-
27 lence, violence and youthful zeal. He is like one who composed a riddle and is trying it out: "Will the wise Socrates realize that I am jesting and contradicting myself, or shall I deceive him and others?" I think he contradicts himself in the affidavit, as if he said: "Socrates is guilty of not believing in gods but believing in gods," and surely that is the part of a jester!

Examine with me, gentlemen, how he appears
b to contradict himself, and you, Meletus, answer us. Remember, gentlemen, what I asked you when I began, not to create a disturbance if I proceed in my usual manner.

Does any man, Meletus, believe in human affairs who does not believe in human beings? Make him answer, and not again and again create a disturbance. Does any man who does not believe in horses believe in equine affairs? Or in flute music but not in flute-players? No, my good sir, no man could. If you are not willing to answer, I will tell
c you and the jury. Answer the next question, however. Does any man believe in divine activities who does not believe in divinities? ——No one.

Thank you for answering, if reluctantly, when the jury made you. Now you say that I believe in divine activities and teach about them, whether new or old, but at any rate divine activities according to what you say, and to this you have sworn in your deposition. But if I believe in divine activities I must quite inevitably believe in divine beings. Is that not so? It is indeed. I shall assume that you
d agree, as you do not answer. Do we not believe divine beings to be either gods or the children of gods? Yes or no? ——Of course.

Then since I do believe in divine beings, as you admit, if divine beings are gods, this is what I mean when I say you speak in riddles and in jest, as you state that I do not believe in gods and then again that I do, since I believe in divine beings. If on the other hand the divine beings are children of the gods, bastard children of the gods by nymphs or some other mothers, as they are said to be, what man would believe children of the gods to exist, but not gods? That would be just as absurd as
e to believe the young of horses and asses, namely mules, to exist, but not to believe in the existence of horses and asses. You must have made this deposition, Meletus, either to test us or because you were at a loss to find any true wrongdoing of what to accuse me. There is no way in which you could persuade anyone of even small intelligence that it is not the part of one and the same man to be-
28 lieve in the activities of divine beings and gods, and then again the part of one and the same man not to believe in the existence of divinities and gods and heroes.

I do not think, gentlemen of the jury, that it requires a prolonged defence to prove that I am not guilty of the charges in Meletus' deposition, but this is sufficient. On the other hand, you know that what I said earlier is true, that I am very unpopular with many people. This will be my undoing, if I am undone, not Meletus or Anytus but the slanders and envy of many people. This has destroyed many
b other good men and will, I think, continue to do so. There is no danger that it will stop at me.

Someone might say: "Are you not ashamed, Socrates, to have followed the kind of occupation that has led to your being now in danger of death?" However, I should be right to reply to him: "You are wrong, sir, if you think that a man who is any good at all should take into account the risk of life or death; he should look to this only in his actions, whether what he does is right or wrong, whether

---

[7]Anaxagoras of Clazomenae, born about the beginning of the fifth century B.C., came to Athens as a young man and spent his time in the pursuit of natural philosophy. He claimed that the universe was directed by Nous (Mind), and that matter was indestructible but always combining in various ways. He left Athens after being prosecuted for impiety.

c he is acting like a good or a bad man." According to your view, all the heroes who died at Troy were inferior people, especially the son of Thetis who was so contemptuous of danger compared with disgrace.[8] When he was eager to kill Hector, his goddess mother warned him, as I believe, in some such words as these: "My child, if you avenge the death of your comrade, Patroclus, and you kill Hector, you will die yourself, for your death is to follow immediately after Hector's." Hearing this, he despised death and danger and was much more afraid to live a coward who did not avenge his
d friends. "Let me die at once," he said, "when once I have given the wrongdoer his deserts, rather than remain here, a laughingstock by the curved ships, a burden upon the earth." Do you think he gave thought to death and danger?

   This is the truth of the matter, gentlemen of the jury: wherever a man has taken a position that he believes to be best, or has been placed by his commander, there he must I think remain and face danger, without a thought for death or anything
e else, rather than disgrace. It would have been a dreadful way to behave, gentlemen of the jury, if, at Potidaea, Amphipolis and Delium, I had, at the risk of death, like anyone else, remained at my post where those you had elected to command had ordered me, and then, when the god ordered me, as I thought and believed, to live the life of a philosopher, to examine myself and others, I had aban-
29 doned my post for fear of death or anything else. That would have been a dreadful thing, and then I might truly have justly been brought here for not believing that there are gods, disobeying the oracle, fearing death, and thinking I was wise when I was not. To fear death, gentlemen, is no other than to think oneself wise when one is not, to think one knows what one does not know. No one knows whether death may not be the greatest of all blessings for a man, yet men fear it as if they knew that it is the greatest of evils. And surely it is
b the most blameworthy ignorance to believe that one knows what one does not know. It is perhaps on this point and in this respect, gentlemen, that I differ from the majority of men, and if I were to claim that I am wiser than anyone in anything, it would be in this, that, as I have no adequate knowledge of things in the underworld, so I do not

think I have. I do know, however, that it is wicked and shameful to do wrong, to disobey one's superior, be he god or man. I shall never fear or avoid things of which I do not know, whether they may not be good rather than things that I know
c to be bad. Even if you acquitted me now and did not believe Anytus, who said to you that either I should not have been brought here in the first place, or that now I am here, you cannot avoid executing me, for if I should be acquitted, your sons would practise the teachings of Socrates and all be thoroughly corrupted; if you said to me in this regard: "Socrates, we do not believe Anytus now; we acquit you, but only on condition that you spend no more time on this investigation and do not practise philosophy, and if you are caught
d doing so you will die," if, as I say, you were to acquit me on those terms, I would say to you: "Gentlemen of the jury, I am grateful and I am your friend, but I will obey the god rather than you, and as long as I draw breath and am able, I shall not cease to practise philosophy, to exhort you and in my usual way to point out to any one of you whom I happen to meet: Good Sir, you are an Athenian, a citizen of the greatest city with the
e greatest reputation for both wisdom and power; are you not ashamed of your eagerness to possess as much wealth, reputation and honours as possible, while you do not care for nor give thought to wisdom or truth, or the best possible state of your soul?" Then, if one of you disputes this and says he does care, I shall not let him go at once or leave him, but I shall question him, examine him and test him, and if I do not think he has attained the goodness that he says he has, I shall reproach him because he attaches little importance to the
30 most important things and greater importance to inferior things, I shall treat in this way anyone I happen to meet, young and old, citizen and stranger, and more so the citizens because you are more kindred to me. Be sure that this is what the god orders me to do, and I think there is no greater blessing for the city than my service to the god. For I go around doing nothing but persuading both young and old among you not to care for
b your body or your wealth in preference to or as strongly as for the best possible state of your soul as I say to you: "Wealth does not bring about excellence, but excellence brings about wealth and all other public and private blessings for men."

---

[8] The scene between Thetis and Achilles is from *The Iliad* (18, 94ff.).

Now if by saying this I corrupt the young, this advice must be harmful, but if anyone says that I give different advice, he is talking nonsense. On this point I would say to you, gentlemen of the jury: "Whether you believe Anytus or not, whether you acquit me or not, do so on the understanding

c that this is my course of action, even if I am to face death many times." Do not create a disturbance, gentlemen, but abide by my request not to cry out at what I say but to listen, for I think it will be to your advantage to listen, and I am about to say other things at which you will perhaps cry out. By no means do this. Be sure that if you kill the sort of man I say I am, you will not harm me more than yourselves. Neither Meletus nor Anytus can harm me in any way; he could not harm me, for I do not

d think it is permitted that a better man be harmed by a worse; certainly he might kill me, or perhaps banish or disfranchise me, which he and maybe others think to be great harm, but I do not think so. I think he is doing himself much greater harm doing what he is doing now, attempting to have a man executed unjustly. Indeed, gentlemen of the jury, I am far from making a defence now on my own behalf, as might be thought, but on yours, to prevent you from wrongdoing by mistreating the

e god's gift to you by condemning me; for if you kill me you will not easily find another like me. I was attached to this city by the god—though it seems a ridiculous thing to say—as upon a great and noble horse which was somewhat sluggish because of its size and needed to be stirred up by a kind of gadfly. It is to fulfill some such function that I believe the god has placed me in the city. I never cease to rouse each and every one of you, to persuade and reproach you all day long and every-

31 where I find myself in your company.

Another such man will not easily come to be among you, gentlemen, and if you believe me you will spare me. You might easily be annoyed with me as people are when they are aroused from a doze, and strike out at me; if convinced by Anytus you could easily kill me, and then you could sleep on for the rest of your days, unless the god, in his care for you, sent you someone else. That I am the kind of person to be a gift of the god to the city you might realize from the fact that it does not seem

b like human nature for me to have neglected all my own affairs and to have tolerated this neglect now for so many years while I was always concerned with you, approaching each one of you like a father

or an elder brother to persuade you to care for virtue. Now if I profited from this by charging a fee for my advice, there would be some sense to it, but you can see for yourselves that, for all their shameless accusations, my accusers have not been

c able in their impudence to bring forward a witness to say that I have ever received a fee or ever asked for one. I, on the other hand, have a convincing witness that I speak for truth, my poverty.

It may seem strange that while I go around and give this advice privately and interfere in private affairs, I do not venture to go to the assembly and there advise the city. You have heard me give the reason for this in many places. I have a divine sign

d from the god which Meletus has ridiculed in his deposition. This began when I was a child. It is a voice, and whenever it speaks it turns me away from something I am about to do, but it never encourages me to do anything. This is what has prevented me from taking part in public affairs, and I think it was quite right to prevent me. Be sure, gentlemen of the jury, that if I had long ago attempted to take part in politics, I should have died

e long ago, and benefited neither you nor myself. Do not be angry with me for speaking the truth; no man will survive who genuinely opposes you or any other crowd and prevents the occurrence of many

32 unjust and illegal happenings in the city. A man who really fights for justice must lead a private, not a public, life if he is to survive for even a short time.

I shall give you great proofs of this, not words but what you esteem, deeds. Listen to what happened to me, that you may know that I will not yield to any man contrary to what is right, for fear of death, even if I should die at once for not yielding. The things I shall tell you are commonplace and smack of the lawcourts, but they are true. I

b have never held any other office in the city, but I served as a member of the Council, and our tribe Antiochis was presiding at the time when you wanted to try as a body the ten generals who had failed to pick up the survivors of the naval battle.[9]

---

[9]This was the battle of Arginusae (south of Lesbos) in 406 B.C., the last Athenian victory of the war. A violent storm prevented the Athenian generals from rescuing their survivors. For this they were tried in Athens and sentenced to death by the assembly. They were tried in a body, and it is this to which Socrates objected in the Council's presiding committee which prepared the business of the assembly. He obstinately persisted in his opposition, in which he stood alone, and was overruled by the majority. Six generals who were in Athens were executed.

This was illegal, as you all recognized later. I was the only member of the presiding committee to oppose your doing something contrary to the laws, and I voted against it. The orators were ready to prosecute me and take me away, and your shouts were egging them on, but I thought I should run

c   any risk on the side of law and justice rather than join you, for fear of prison or death, when you were engaged in an unjust course.

This happened when the city was still a democracy. When the oligarchy was established, the Thirty[10] summoned me to the Hall, along with four others, and ordered us to bring Leon from Salamis, that he might be executed. They gave many such orders to many people, in order to

d   implicate as many as possible in their guilt. Then I showed again, not in words but in action, that, if it were not rather vulgar to say so, death is something I couldn't care less about, but that my whole concern is not to do anything unjust or impious. That government, powerful as it was, did not frighten me into any wrongdoing. When we left the Hall, the other four went to Salamis and brought in Leon, but I went home. I might have been put to death for this, had not the government fallen

e   shortly afterwards. There are many who will witness to these events.

Do you think I would have survived all these years if I were engaged in public affairs and, acting as a good man must, came to the help of justice and considered this the most important thing? Far from it, gentlemen of the jury, nor would any other man.

33   man. Throughout my life, in any public activity I may have engaged in, I am the same man as I am in private life. I have never come to an agreement with anyone to act unjustly, neither with anyone else nor with any one of those who they slanderously say are my pupils. I have never been anyone's teacher. If anyone, young or old, desires to listen to me when I am talking and dealing with my own concerns, I have never begrudged this to anyone, but I do not converse when I receive a fee and not

b   when I do not. I am equally ready to question the rich and the poor if anyone is willing to answer my questions and listen to what I say. And I cannot justly be held responsible for the good or

bad conduct of these people, as I never promised to teach them anything and have not done so. If anyone says that he has learned anything from me, or that he heard anything privately that the others did not hear, be assured that he is not telling the truth.

Why then do some people enjoy spending con-

c   siderable time in my company? You have heard why, gentlemen of the jury, I have told you the whole truth. They enjoy hearing those being questioned who think they are wise, but are not. And this is not unpleasant. To do this has, as I say, been enjoined upon me by the god, by means of oracles and dreams, and in every other way that a divine manifestation has ever ordered a man to do anything. This is true, gentlemen, and can easily be established.

d   If I corrupt some young men and have corrupted others, then surely some of them who have grown older and realized that I gave them bad advice when they were young should now themselves come up here to accuse me and avenge themselves. If they are unwilling to do so themselves, then some of their kindred, their fathers or brothers or other relations should recall it now if their family had been harmed by me. I see many of these present here, first Crito, my contempo-

e   rary and fellow demesman, the father of Critoboulos here; next Lysanias of Sphettus, the father of Aeschines here; also Antiphon the Cephisian, the father of Epigenes; and others whose brothers spent their time in this way; Nicostratus, the son of Theozotides, brother of Theodotus, and Theodotus has died so he could not influence him; Paralios

34   here, son of Demodocus, whose brother was Theages; there is Adeimantus, son of Ariston, brother of Plato here; Acantidorus, brother of Apollodorus here.

I could mention many others, some one of whom surely Meletus should have brought in as witness in his own speech. If he forgot to do so, then let him do it now; I will yield time if he has anything of the kind to say. You will find quite the contrary, gentlemen. These men are all ready to come to the help of the corruptor, the man who

b   has harmed their kindred, as Meletus and Anytus say. Now those who were corrupted might well have reason to help me, but the uncorrupted, their kindred who are older men, have no reason to help me except the right and proper one, that they know that Meletus is lying and that I am telling the truth.

---

[10]This was the harsh oligarchy that was set up after the final defeat of Athens in 404 B.C. and that ruled Athens for some nine months in 404–3 before the democracy was restored.

Very well, gentlemen of the jury. This, and maybe other similar things, is what I have to say in my defence. Perhaps one of you might be angry as c he recalls that when he himself stood trial on a less dangerous charge, he begged and implored the jury with many tears, that he brought his children and many of his friends and family into court to arouse as much pity as he could, but that I do none of these things, even though I may seem to be running the ultimate risk. Thinking of this, he might d feel resentful toward me and, angry about this, cast his vote in anger. If there is such a one among you—I do not deem there is, but if there is—I think it would be right to say in reply: My good sir, I too have a household and, in Homer's phrase, I am not born "from oak or rock" but from men, so that I have a family, indeed three sons, gentlemen of the jury, of whom one is an adolescent while two are children. Nevertheless, I will not beg you to acquit me by bringing them here. Why do I do none of these things? Not through arrogance, e gentlemen, nor through lack of respect for you. Whether I am brave in the face of death is another matter, but with regard to my reputation and yours and that of the whole city, it does not seem right to me to do these things, especially at my age and with my reputation. For it is generally believed, whether it be true or false, that in 35 certain respects Socrates is superior to the majority of men. Now if those of you who are considered superior, be it in wisdom or courage or whatever other virtue makes them so, are seen behaving like that, it would be a disgrace. Yet I have often seen them do this sort of thing when standing trial, men who are thought to be somebody, doing amazing things as if they thought it a terrible thing to die, and as if they were to be immortal if you did not execute them. I think these men bring b shame upon the city so that a stranger, too, would assume that those who are outstanding in virtue among the Athenians, whom they themselves select from themselves to fill offices of state and receive other honours, are in no way better than women. You should not act like that, gentlemen of the jury, those of you who have any reputation at all, and if we do, you should not allow it. You should make it very clear that you will more readily convict a man who performs these pitiful dramatics in court and so makes the city a laughingstock, than a man who keeps quiet.

Quite apart from the question of reputation,

c gentlemen, I do not think it right to supplicate the jury and to be acquitted because of this, but to teach and persuade them. It is not the purpose of a juryman's office to give justice as a favour to whoever seems good to him, but to judge according to law, and this he has sworn to do. We should not accustom you to perjure yourselves, nor should you make a habit of it. This is irreverent conduct for either of us.

Do not deem it right for me, gentlemen of the d jury, that I should act towards you in a way that I do not consider to be good or just or pious, especially, by Zeus, as I am being prosecuted by Meletus here for impiety; clearly, if I convinced you by my supplication to do violence to your oath of office, I would be teaching you not to believe that there are gods, and my defence would convict me of not believing in them. This is far from being the case, gentlemen, for I do believe in them as none of my accusers do. I leave it to you and the god to judge me in the way that will be best for me and for you.

[The jury now gives its verdict of guilty, and Meletus asks for the penalty of death.]

e There are many other reasons for my not being angry with you for convicting me, gentlemen of the jury, and what happened was not unexpected. 36 I am much more surprised at the number of votes cast on each side, for I did not think the decision would be by so few votes but by a great many. As it is, a switch of only thirty votes would have acquitted me. I think myself that I have been cleared on Meletus' charges, and not only this, but it is clear b to all that, if Anytus and Lycon had not joined him in accusing me, he would have been fined a thousand drachmas for not receiving a fifth of the votes.

He assesses the penalty at death. So be it. What counter-assessment should I propose to you, gentlemen of the jury? Clearly it should be a penalty I deserve, and what do I deserve to suffer or to pay because I have deliberately not led a quiet life but have neglected what occupies most people: wealth, household affairs, the position of general or public orator or the other offices, the political clubs and factions that exist in the city? I thought myself too honest to survive if I occupied myself with those c things. I did not follow that path that would have made me of no use either to you or to myself, but I went to each of you privately and conferred upon him what I say is the greatest benefit, by trying to persuade him not to care for any of his belongings

before caring that he himself should be as good and as wise as possible, not to care for the city's possessions more than for the city itself, and to care
d for other things in the same way. What do I deserve for being such a man? Some good, gentlemen of the jury, if I must truly make an assessment according to my deserts, and something suitable. What is suitable for a poor benefactor who needs leisure to exhort you? Nothing is more suitable, gentlemen, than for such a man to be fed in the Prytaneum,[11] much more suitable for him than for any of you who has won a victory at Olympia with a pair or a team of horses. The Olympian victor
c makes you think yourself happy; I make you be happy. Besides, he does not need food, but I do. So if I must make a just assessment of what I deserve,
37 I assess it at this: free meals in the Prytaneum.

When I say this you may think, as when I spoke of appeals to pity and entreaties, that I speak arrogantly, but that is not the case, gentlemen of the jury; rather it is like this: I am convinced that I never willingly wrong anyone, but I am not convincing you of this, for we have talked together but a short time. If it were the law with us, as it is
b elsewhere, that a trial for life should not last one but many days, you would be convinced, but now it is not easy to dispel great slanders in a short time. Since I am convinced that I wrong no one, I am not likely to wrong myself, to say that I deserve some evil and to make some such assessment against myself. What should I fear? That I should suffer the penalty Meletus has assessed against me, of which I say I do not know whether it is good or bad? Am I then to choose in preference to this something that I know very well to be an evil
c and assess the penalty at that? Imprisonment? Why should I live in prison, always subjected to the ruling magistrates? A fine, and imprisonment until I pay it? That would be the same thing for me, as I have no money. Exile? for perhaps you might accept that assessment.

I should have to be inordinately fond of life, gentlemen of the jury, to be so unreasonable as to suppose that other men will easily tolerate my company and conversation when you, my fellow
d citizens, have been unable to endure them, but found them a burden and resented them so that you are now seeking to get rid of them. Far from it, gentlemen. It would be a fine life at my age to be driven out of one city after another, for I know very well that wherever I go the young men will
e listen to my talk as they do here. If I drive them away, they will themselves persuade their elders to drive me out; if I do not drive them away, their fathers and relations will drive me out on their behalf.

Perhaps someone might say: But Socrates, if you leave us will you not be able to live quietly, without talking? Now this is the most difficult point on which to convince some of you. If I say
38 that it is impossible for me to keep quiet because that means disobeying the god, you will not believe me and will think I am being ironical. On the other hand, if I say that it is the greatest good for a man to discuss virtue every day and those other things about which you hear me conversing and testing myself and others, for the unexamined life is not worth living for man, you will believe me even less.

What I say is true, gentlemen, but it is not easy
b to convince you. At the same time, I am not accustomed to think that I deserve any penalty. If I had money, I would assess the penalty at the amount I could pay, for that would not hurt me, but I have none, unless you are willing to set the penalty at the amount I can pay, and perhaps I could pay you one mina of silver.[12] So that is my assessment.

Plato here, gentlemen of the jury, and Crito and Critoboulus and Apollodorus bid me put the penalty at thirty minae, and they will stand surety for the money. Well then, that is my assessment, and they will be sufficient guarantee of payment.

[The jury now votes again and sentences Socrates to death.]

c It is for the sake of a short time, gentlemen of the jury, that you will acquire the reputation and the guilt, in the eyes of those who want to denigrate the city, of having killed Socrates, a wise man, for they who want to revile you will say that I am wise even if I am not. If you had waited but a little while, this would have happened of its own accord. You see my age, that I am already advanced in years and close to death. I am saying this not

---

[11]The Prytaneum was the magistrates' hall or town hall of Athens in which public entertainments were given, particularly to Olympian victors on their return home.

---

[12]One mina was 100 drachmas, equivalent to, say, twenty-five dollars, though in purchasing power probably five times greater. In any case, a ridiculously small sum under the circumstances.

d to all of you but to those who condemned me to death, and to these same jurors I say: Perhaps you think that I was convicted for lack of such words as might have convinced you, if I thought I should say or do all I could to avoid my sentence. Far from it. I was convicted because I lacked not words but boldness and shamelessness and the willingness to say to you what you would most gladly have heard from me, lamentations and tears and

e my saying and doing many things that I say are unworthy of me but that you are accustomed to hear from others. I did not think then that the danger I ran should make me do anything mean, nor do I now regret the nature of my defence. I would much rather die after this kind of defence than live after making the other kind. Neither I nor any

39 other man should, on trial or in war, contrive to avoid death at any cost. Indeed it is often obvious in battle that one could escape death by throwing away one's weapons and turning to supplicate one's pursuers, and there are many ways to avoid death in every kind of danger if one will venture to do or say anything to avoid it. It is not difficult to avoid death, gentlemen of the jury, it is much more dif-

b ficult to avoid wickedness, for it runs faster than death. Slow and elderly as I am, I have been caught by the slower pursuer, whereas my accusers, being clever and sharp, have been caught by the quicker, wickedness. I leave you now, condemned to death by you, but they are condemned by truth to wickedness and injustice. So I maintain my assessment, and they maintain theirs. This perhaps had to happen, and I think it is as it should be.

c Now I want to prophesy to those who convicted me, for I am at the point when men prophesy most, when they are about to die. I say gentlemen, to those who voted to kill me, that vengeance will come upon you immediately after my death, a vengeance much harder to bear than that which you took in killing me. You did this in the belief that you would avoid giving an account of your life, but I maintain that quite the opposite will happen to you. There will be more people to test you,

d whom I now held back, but you did not notice it. They will be more difficult to deal with as they will be younger and you will resent them more. You are wrong if you believe that by killing people you will prevent anyone from reproaching you for not living in the right way. To escape such tests is neither possible nor good, but it is best and easiest not to discredit others but to prepare oneself to be as

good as possible. With this prophecy to you who convicted me, I part from you.

e I should be glad to discuss what has happened with those who voted for my acquittal during the time that the officers of the court are busy and I do not yet have to depart to my death. So, gentlemen, stay with me awhile, for nothing prevents us from talking to each other while it is allowed. To

40 you, as being my friends, I want to show the meaning of what has occurred. A surprising thing has happened to me, judges—you I would rightly call judges. At all previous times my usual mantic sign frequently opposed me, even in small matters, when I was about to do something wrong, but now that, as you can see for yourselves, I was faced with what one might think, and what is generally thought to be, the worst of evils, my divine sign has not opposed me, either when I left home

b at dawn, or when I came into court, or at any time that I was about to say something during my speech. Yet in other talks it often held me back in the middle of my speaking, but now it has opposed no word or deed of mine. What do I think is the reason for this? I will tell you. What has happened to me may well be a good thing, and those of us who believe death to be an evil are certainly mis-

c taken. I have convincing proof of this, for it is impossible that my customary sign did not oppose me if I was not about to do what was right.

Let us reflect in this way, too, that there is good hope that death is a blessing, for it is one of two things: either the dead are nothing and have no perception of anything, or it is, as we are told, a change and a relocating for the soul from here to another place. If it is complete lack of percep-

d tion, like a dreamless sleep, then death would be a great advantage. For I think that if one had to pick out that night during which a man slept soundly and did not dream, put beside it the other nights and days of his life, and then see how many days and nights had been better and more pleasant than that night, not only a private person but the great king would find them easy to count com-

e pared with the other days and nights. If death is like this I say it is an advantage, for all eternity would then seem to be no more than a single night. If, on the other hand, death is a change from here to another place, and what we are told is true and all who have died are there, what greater

41 blessing could there be, gentlemen of the jury? If anyone arriving in Hades will have escaped from

those who call themselves judges here, and will find those true judges who are said to sit in judgement there, Minos and Radamanthus and Aeacus and Triptolemus and the other demi-gods who have been upright in their own life, would that be a poor kind of change? Again, what would one of you give to keep company with Orpheus and Musaeus, Hesiod and Homer? I am willing to die many times if that is true. It would be a won-

b derful way for me to spend my time whenever I met Palamedes and Ajax, the son of Telamon, and any other of the men of old who died through an unjust conviction, to compare my experience with theirs. I think it would be pleasant. Most important, I could spend my time testing and examining people there, as I do here, as to who among them is wise, and who thinks he is, but is not.

What would one not give, gentlemen of the jury, for the opportunity to examine the man who led the great expedition against Troy, or Odys-

c seus, or Sisyphus, and innumerable other men and women one could mention. It would be an extraordinary happiness to talk with them, to keep company with them and examine them. In any case, they would certainly not put one to death for doing so. They are happier there than we are here in other respects, and for the rest of time they are deathless, if indeed what we are told is true.

You too must be of good hope as regards death, gentlemen of the jury, and keep this one truth in mind, that a good man cannot be harmed either

d in life or in death, and that his affairs are not neglected by the gods. What has happened to me now has not happened of itself, but it is clear to me that it was better for me to die now and to escape from trouble. That is why my divine sign did not oppose me at any point. So I am certainly not angry with those who convicted me, or with my accusers. Of course that was not their purpose when they accused and convicted me, but they

e thought they were hurting me, and for this they deserve blame. This much I ask from them: when my sons grow up, avenge yourselves by causing them the same kind of grief that I caused you, if you think they care for money or anything else more than they care for virtue, or if they think they are somebody when they are nobody. Reproach them as I reproach you, that they do not care for the right things and think they are worthy

42 when they are not worthy of anything. If you do

this, I shall have been justly treated by you, and my sons also.

Now the hour to part has come. I go to die, you go to live. Which of us goes to the better lot is known to no one, except the god.

COMMENTARY AND QUESTIONS

As we delve into the character of Socrates as Plato portrays it in this dialogue, we should be struck by his single-mindedness. If it should turn out that death is a "change from here to another place," how would Socrates spend his time there? He would continue precisely the activities that had occupied him in this life; he would "examine" all the famous heroes to see which of them is wise. And why does he think such examination is so important, a "service to the god"? No doubt because it undermines hubris, that arrogance of thinking one possesses "a wisdom more than human."

Read 17a–18a In this short introductory section, Socrates draws a contrast between himself and his accusers, characterizes the kind of man he is, and reminds the jury of its duty.

Q1. What is the function of Socrates' contrast between **persuasion** and **truth?** List the terms in which each is described.
Q2. What kind of man does Socrates say that he is?
Q3. What is his challenge to the jury?

"As scarce as truth is, the supply has always been in excess of the demand."
Josh Billings (1818–1885)

Read 18b–19a Socrates makes a distinction between two sets of accusers.

Q4. Identify the **earlier accusers** and the later accusers. How do they differ?
Q5. Why is it going to be very difficult for Socrates to defend himself against the earlier accusers?

Read 19b–24b　Here we have Socrates' defense against the "earlier accusers." He tries to show how his "unpopularity" arises from his practice of questioning. He describes the origins of this occupation of his and discusses the sort of wisdom to which he lays claim.

Q6.　What are the three points made against him in the older accusations?

Q7.　What does Socrates say about each of these accusations?

Q8.　How does Socrates distinguish himself from the Sophists here?

We have mentioned the **Oracle at Delphi** before. One could go there and, after appropriate sacrifices, pose a question. The "Pythian" (21a) was a priestess of Apollo who would, in the name of the god, reply to the questions posed. We have noted that it was characteristic of the Oracle to reply in a riddle, so it is not perverse for Socrates to wonder what the answer to Chairephon's question means. What sort of wisdom is this in which no one can surpass him? He devises his questioning technique to clarify the meaning of the answer.

Note that several times during his speech Socrates asks the jury not to create a disturbance (20e, 27b, 30c). We can imagine that he is interrupted at those points by hoots, hissing, catcalls, or their ancient Greek equivalents.

Q9.　Which three classes of people did Socrates question? What, in each case, was the result?

Q10.　What conclusion does Socrates draw from his investigations?

Here we can address that paradox noted earlier (page 69) arising out of Socrates' simultaneous profession of ignorance, his identification of virtue with knowledge, and the claim (obvious at many points in the *Apology*) that he is both a wise and a good man. In light of his confessed ignorance and the identification of knowledge with virtue, it seems he should conclude that he *isn't* virtuous. But it is the distinction drawn in 22e–23b between a

wisdom appropriate for "the god" on the one hand and "**human wisdom**" on the other that resolves this paradox. The god, Socrates assumes, actually knows the forms of piety, justice, *areté,* and the other excellences proper to a human being. Humans, by contrast, do not; and this is proved, Socrates thinks, by the god's declaration that there is no man wiser than he—who knows that he doesn't know!

"Knowledge is proud that he has learned so much; Wisdom is humble that he knows no more."

William Cowper (1731–1800)

Because humans do not know what makes for virtue and a good life, the best they can do is subject themselves to constant dialectical examination. This searching critique will tend to rid us of false opinions and will also cure us of the hubris of thinking that we have a wisdom appropriate only to the god. The outcome of such examination, acknowledging our ignorance, Socrates calls "human wisdom," which by comparison with divine wisdom is "worth little or nothing." Still, it is the sort of wisdom, Socrates believes, that is appropriate to creatures like us. And that is why "the unexamined life is not worth living" for a human being (38a). And that is why there is "no greater blessing for the city" than Socrates' never-ending examination of its citizens (30a). Such self-examination is the way for us to become as wise and good as it is possible for human beings to be.

Read 24b–28a　At this point, Socrates begins to address the "**later accusers.**" He does so in his usual question-and-answer fashion. Apparently, three persons submitted the charge to the court: Meletus, Anytus, and Lycon. Meletus seems to have been the primary sponsor of the charge, seconded by the other two. So Socrates calls Meletus forward and questions him. As in the *Euthyphro,* two charges are mentioned. Be sure you are clear about what they are.

In 24c Socrates tells the jury his purpose in cross-examining Meletus. He wants to demonstrate that Meletus is someone who ought not to be taken seriously, that he has not thought through the meaning of the charge, and that he doesn't even care about these matters.* In short, Socrates is about to demonstrate before the jury—before their very eyes!—not only what sort of man Meletus is, and that he is not wise, but also what sort of man Socrates is. It is the truth, remember, that Socrates is after; if the jury is going to decide whether Socrates is impious and a corrupter of youth, they should have the very best evidence about what sort of man they are judging. Socrates is going to oblige them by giving them a personal demonstration.

He begins by taking up the charge of corrupting the youth. If Meletus claims that Socrates corrupts the youth, he must understand what corrupting is. To understand what it is to corrupt, one must also understand what it is to improve the youth. And so Socrates asks him, "Who improves them?"

Q11.   Does Meletus have a ready answer? What conclusion does Socrates draw from this? (24d)

When Meletus does answer, Socrates' questions provoke him to say that all the other citizens improve the youth and only Socrates corrupts them!

Q12.   How does Socrates use the analogy of the horse breeders to cast doubt on Meletus' concern for these matters?

Starting in 25c, Socrates presents Meletus with a **dilemma**. The form of a dilemma is this: Two alternatives are presented between which it seems necessary to choose, but each alternative has consequences that are unwelcome, usually for different reasons. The two alternatives are called the "horns" of a dilemma, and there are three ways to deal with them. One can grasp one of the horns (that is, embrace that alternative with its consequences); one can grasp the other horn; or one can (sometimes,

*Compare *Apology* 24c, 25c, 26a,b with *Euthyphro* 2c–d, 3a.

but not always) "go between the horns" by finding a third alternative that has not been considered.

Q13.   What are the horns of the dilemma that Socrates presents to Meletus?
Q14.   How does Meletus respond?
Q15.   How does Socrates refute this response?
Q16.   Supposing that this refutation is correct and that one cannot "pass through" the horns, what is the consequence of embracing the other horn? How does Socrates use the distinction between punishment and instruction?

Again Socrates drives home the conclusion that Meletus has "never been at all concerned with these matters." If he had been, he surely would have thought these things through. As it is, he cannot be taken seriously.

At 26b, the topic switches to the other charge. As the examination proceeds, we can see Meletus becoming angrier and angrier, less and less willing to cooperate in what he clearly sees is his own destruction. No doubt this is an example—produced right there for the jury to see—of the typical response to Socrates' questioning. We might think Socrates is not being prudent here in angering Meletus and his supporters in the jury. But again, it is for Socrates a matter of the truth; this is the kind of man he is. And the jury should see it if they are going to judge truly.

Q17.   Socrates claims that Meletus contradicts himself. In what way?
Q18.   What "divine activities" must the jury have understood him to be referring to? (27d–e)
Q19.   What does Socrates claim will be his undoing, if he is undone?

Read 28b–35d   Socrates is now finished with Meletus, satisfied that he has shown him to be thoughtless and unreliable. Notice that at this point he claims to have proved that he is "not guilty" of the charges Meletus has brought against him. No doubt Socrates believes that one cannot be rightly convicted on charges that are as vague and undefined as these have proved to be. Do you think this suffices for a defense?

Socrates then turns to more general matters relevant to his defense. He first imagines someone saying that the very fact that he is on trial for his life is shameful. How could he have behaved in such a manner as to bring himself to this?

Q20. On what principle does Socrates base his response? Do you agree with this principle? (Compare the speech of the nurse in *Hippolytus* on page 54.)

Q21. To whom does Socrates compare himself? Do you think the comparison is apt? How do you think this would have struck an Athenian jury?

Q22. Socrates refers to his military service; in what respects does he say his life as a philosopher is like that?

Q23. Why does he say that to fear death is to think oneself wise when one is not? Do you agree with this? If not, why not?

In 29c–d Socrates imagines that the jury might offer him a "deal," sparing his life if only he ceased practicing philosophy. Xenophon tells us that during the reign of the Thirty, Critias and another man, Charicles, demanded that Socrates cease conversing with the young. If this story is accurate, it may be that Socrates has this demand in mind. Or it may be that there had been talk of such a "deal" before the trial.

Q24. What does Socrates say his response would be? (Compare Acts 5:29 in the Bible.)

Q25. Why does he say that "there is no greater blessing for the city" than his service to the god? What are "the most important things"? Do you agree?

In the section that begins in 30b, Socrates makes some quite astonishing claims:

- If they kill him, they will harm themselves more than they harm him.
- A better man cannot be harmed by a worse man.
- He is defending himself not for his own sake but for theirs.

These claims seem to turn the usual ways of thinking about such matters completely upside down. Indeed, to our natural common sense, they seem incredible. Surely they must have seemed so to the jury as well. We usually think, don't we, that others can harm us. So we are on our guard. Socrates tells us, however, that this natural conviction of ours is false. It's not that we cannot be harmed at all, however. Indeed, we can be harmed—but only if we do it to ourselves! How can we harm ourselves? By making ourselves into worse persons than we otherwise would be. We harm ourselves by acting unjustly. That is why Socrates says that if his fellow citizens kill him they will harm themselves more than they will harm him. They will be doing injustice, thereby corrupting their souls; and the most important thing is care for the soul.

Q26. Socrates claims throughout to be concerned for the souls of the jury members. Show how this is consistent with his daily practice in the streets of Athens.

Q27. What use does Socrates make of the image of the "gadfly"?

Socrates feels a need to explain why, if he is so wise, he has not entered politics. There are two reasons, one being the nature of his "wisdom." He focuses here on the other reason: his "sign" prevented it. If it had not, he says, there is little doubt that he would "have died long ago" and could not have been a "blessing to the city" for all these years.

He cites two incidents as evidence of this, one occurring when the city was democratic, one under the rule of the Thirty. He is trying to convince the jury that he is truly apolitical because he was capable of resisting both sorts of government. In both cases, he resisted alone because the others were doing something contrary to law, and in both cases he was in some danger. Why should he feel the need to establish his political neutrality? Surely because there was a political aspect to the trial—not explicit, but in the background.

In 33a, he gets to what many people feel is the heart of the matter. Let us ask: Why was Socrates brought to trial at all? There was his reputation as a Sophist, of course—all those accusations of the "earlier accusers." There was the general hostility that his questioning generated. There was his "divine sign." But it is doubtful that these alone would have sufficed to bring him to court. What probably tipped the balance was the despicable political career of some who had at one time been closely associated with him, in particular Critias, leader of the Thirty, and Alcibiades, the brilliant and dashing young traitor. This kind of "guilt by association" is very common and very hard to defend against. If these men had spent so much time with Socrates, why hadn't they turned out better? Socrates must be responsible for their crimes! This could not be mentioned in the official charge because it would have violated the amnesty proclaimed by the democracy after the Thirty were overthrown. But it is hard not to believe that it is lurking in the background.

How does Socrates defend himself against this charge? He makes another remarkable claim. He has *never*, he says, "been anyone's teacher." For that reason, he cannot "be held responsible for the good or bad conduct of these people, as I never promised to teach them anything and have not done so." This requires some explaining.

In the *Meno*, where the topic is whether virtue can be taught, Socrates invites **Meno** to join in a search for the nature of virtue. Meno asks,

> And how will you search for something, Socrates, when you don't know what it is at all? I mean, which of the things you don't know will you take in advance and search for, when you don't know what it is? Or even if you come right up against it, how will you know that it's the unknown thing you're looking for? (*Meno* 80d)[3]

In response to this puzzle, Socrates calls over a slave boy who has never studied geometry. He draws a square on the ground and divides it equally by bisecting the sides vertically and horizontally. (Draw such a square yourself.) He then asks the boy to construct another square with an area twice the original area. This is a nice problem. Clearly, if the original area is four, we want a square with an area of eight. But how can we get it? (Before you go on, think a minute and see if you can solve it.)

Socrates proceeds by asking the boy questions. The first, rather natural suggestion is to double the length of the sides. But on reflection, the boy can see (as you can, too) that this gives a square of sixteen. Wanting something between four and sixteen, the boy tries making the sides of the new square one and one-half times the original. But this gives a square of nine, not eight. Finally, at a suggestion from Socrates, the boy sees that taking the diagonal of the original square as one side of a new square solves the problem. (Do you agree that this solves the problem? How can you be sure?)*

What is the relevance of this to Meno's puzzle? And what does it have to do with Socrates' claim never to have been anyone's teacher? The crucial point is that the boy can just "see" that the first two solutions are wrong. And when the correct solution is presented, he "recognizes" it as correct. But he has never been taught geometry! Moreover, his certainty about the correct solution does not now rest on the authority of Socrates. For one thing, Socrates doesn't *tell* him that this is a correct solution. For another, even if he did, why should the boy believe him? No, the boy sees the truth for himself. So Socrates doesn't teach him this truth!

This leaves us with another puzzle. How could the boy have recognized the true solution as the true one? Consider this analogy. You are walking down the street and see someone approaching. At first she is too far away to identify, but as she gets nearer you say, "Why, that's Joan!" Now, what must be the case for you to "recognize" Joan truly? There can be no doubt: You must already have been acquainted with Joan in some way. That alone is the condition under which recognition is possible.

Socrates thinks the slave boy's case must be similar. He must already have been acquainted with this truth; otherwise, it is not possible to explain how he recognizes it when it is present before him. But when? Clearly not in this life. Socrates draws what seems to be the only possible conclusion: that he was acquainted with this truth before birth and that it was always within him. (This is taken as evidence that the soul exists before the body, but that is not our present concern.) Coming to know is just recognizing

---

*A fuller explanation with a diagram of the square can be found on p. 121.

what, in some implicit sense, one has within one-self all along. What Socrates does is ask the right questions or present the appropriate stimuli. But he doesn't "implant" knowledge; he doesn't teach.

In the dialogue *Theatetus,* Plato represents Socrates as using a striking image:

> I am so far like the midwife that I cannot myself give birth to wisdom, and the common reproach is true, that, though I question others, I can myself bring nothing to light because there is no wisdom in me. . . . Those who frequent my company at first appear, some of them, quite unintelligent, but, as we go further with our discussions, all who are favored by heaven make progress at a rate that seems surprising to others as well as to themselves, although it is clear that they have never learned any-thing from me. The many admirable truths they bring to birth have been discovered by themselves from within. But the delivery is heaven's work and mine. (*Theatetus* 150c–d)[4]

Here, then, is the background for the claim that Socrates has never taught anyone anything. His role is not that of teacher or imparter of knowledge and wisdom but that of "midwife" (recall that this was his mother's profession), assisting at the birth of ideas which are within the "learner" all along and identifying those that are "illegitimate." This is why he says—though he could not have explained all this to the jury—that he cannot be held responsible for the behavior of men like Critias and Alcibiades.

Q28. What additional arguments does Socrates use in 33d–34b?

Q29. Why does he refuse to use the traditional "appeal to pity"? See particularly 35c.

Read 35e–38b The verdict has been given, and now, according to custom, both the prosecution and the defense may propose appropriate penalties. Meletus, of course, asks for death.

Q30. What penalty does Socrates first suggest? Why?

Along the way, Socrates says something most interesting. "The Olympian victor makes you think yourself happy; I make you be happy." What could this mean? Compare health. Is it possible to feel healthy, think yourself healthy, while actually being unhealthy? Of course. A beginning cancer hurts not at all; in that condition, one can feel perfectly all right. No one, however, would say that a person in whom a cancer is growing is healthy. In the same way Socrates suggests that feeling happy is not the same thing as actually being happy. Think of a city the night after its major league team brings back the championship. People are dancing in the streets, hugging each other, laughing and celebrating. They are feeling happy. Are these happy people? Not necessarily. When the euphoria wears off, they may well return to pretty miserable lives. Happiness, Socrates suggests, is a condition or state of the soul, not a matter of how you feel.* This condition, he claims, his questioning about virtue can produce.

Q31. Why does Socrates resist exile as a penalty?

Q32. What does he say is "the greatest good" for a man? Why?

Q33. What penalty does he finally offer?

Read 38c–end After being sentenced to death, Socrates addresses first those who voted to condemn him and then his friends. To both he declares himself satisfied. He has presented himself for what he is; he has not betrayed himself by saying only what they wanted to hear in order to avoid death.

Q34. What does Socrates say is more difficult to avoid than death? And who has not avoided it?

Q35. What does he "prophesy"?

Q36. What "surprising thing" does he point out to his friends? What does he take it to mean?

Q37. What two possibilities does Socrates consider death may hold? Are there any he misses?

Q38. What is the "one truth" that Socrates wishes his friends to keep in mind? How does he try to comfort them?

---

*If Socrates is right, our contemporary, endless fascination with how we feel about things—especially how we feel about ourselves—is a mistake we could have learned to detect long ago, from him.

CRITO

Translator's Introduction

About the time of Socrates' trial, a state galley had set out on an annual religious mission to Delos and while it was away no execution was allowed to take place. So it was that Socrates was kept in prison for a month after the trial. The ship has now arrived at Cape Sunium in Attica and is thus expected at the Piraeus momentarily. So Socrates' old and faithful friend, Crito, makes one last effort to persuade him to escape into exile, and all arrangements for this plan have been made. It is this conversation between the two old friends that Plato professes to report in this dialogue. It is, as Crito plainly tells him, his last chance, but Socrates will not take it, and he gives his reasons for his refusal. Whether this conversation took place at this particular time is not important, for there is every reason to believe that Socrates' friends tried to plan his escape, and that he refused. Plato more than hints that the authorities would not have minded much, as long as he left the country.

The Dialogue

43 SOCRATES: Why have you come so early, Crito? Or is it not still early?

CRITO: It certainly is.

S: How early?

C: Early dawn.

S: I am surprised that the warder was willing to listen to you.

C: He is quite friendly to me by now, Socrates. I have been here often and I have given him something.

S: Have you just come, or have you been here for some time?

C: A fair time.

b S: Then why did you not wake me right away but sit there in silence?

C: By Zeus no, Socrates. I would not myself want to be in distress and awake so long. I have been surprised to see you so peacefully asleep. It was on purpose that I did not wake you, so that you should spend your time most agreeably. Often in the past throughout my life, I

have considered the way you live happy, and especially so now that you bear your present misfortune so easily and lightly.

S: It would not be fitting at my age to resent the fact that I must die now.

c C: Other men of your age are caught in such misfortunes, but their age does not prevent them resenting their fate.

S: That is so. Why have you come so early?

C: I bring bad news, Socrates, not for you, apparently, but for me and all your friends the news is bad and hard to bear. Indeed, I would count it among the hardest.

d S: What is it? Or has the ship arrived from Delos, at the arrival of which I must die?

C: It has not arrived yet, but it will, I believe, arrive today, according to a message brought by some men from Sunium, where they left it. This makes it obvious that it will come today, and that your life must end tomorrow.

S: May it be for the best. If it so please the gods, so be it. However, I do not think it will arrive today.

C: What indication have you of this?

44 S: I will tell you. I must die the day after the ship arrives.

C: That is what those in authority say.

S: Then I do not think it will arrive on this coming day, but on the next. I take to witness of this a dream I had a little earlier during this night. It looks as if it was the right time for you not to wake me.

C: What was your dream?

S: I thought that a beautiful and comely woman dressed in white approached me. She called me and said: "Socrates, may you arrive at fer-

b tile Phthia[1] on the third day."

---

[1] A quotation from the ninth book of *The Iliad* (363). Achilles has rejected all the presents of Agamemnon for him

c: A strange dream, Socrates.

s: But it seems clear enough to me, Crito.

c: Too clear it seems, my dear Socrates, but listen to me even now and be saved. If you die, it will not be a single misfortune for me. Not only will I be deprived of a friend, the like of whom I shall never find again, but many people who do not know you or me very well will think that I could have saved you if I were willing to spend money, but that I did not care

c   to do so. Surely there can be no worse reputation than to be thought to value money more highly than one's friends, for the majority will not believe that you yourself were not willing to leave prison while we were eager for you to do so.

s: My good Crito, why should we care so much for what the majority think? The most reasonable people, to whom one should pay more attention, will believe that things were done as they were done.

d   c: You see, Socrates, that one must also pay attention to the opinion of the majority. Your present situation makes clear that the majority can inflict not the least but pretty well the greatest evils if one is slandered among them.

s: Would that the majority could inflict the greatest evils, for they would then be capable of the greatest good, and that would be fine, but now they cannot do either. They cannot make a man either wise or foolish, but they inflict things haphazardly.

e   c: That may be so. But tell me this, Socrates, are you anticipating that I and your other friends would have trouble with the informers if you escape from here, as having stolen you away, and that we should be compelled to lose all our property or pay heavy fines and suffer other

45   punishment besides? If you have any such fear, forget it. We would be justified in running this risk to save you, and worse, if necessary. Do follow my advice, and do not act differently.

———————

to return to the battle, and threatens to go home. He says his ships will sail in the morning, and with good weather he might arrive on the third day "in fertile Phthia" (which is his home). The dream means, obviously, that on the third day Socrates' soul, after death, will find its home. As always, counting the first member of a series, the third day is the day after tomorrow.

s: I do have these things in mind, Crito, and also many others.

c: Have no such fear. It is not much money that some people require to save you and get you out of here. Further, do you not see that those informers are cheap, and that not much money would be needed to deal with them? My money is available and is, I think, sufficient. If,

b   because of your affection for me, you feel you should not spend any of mine, there are those strangers here ready to spend money. One of them, Simmias the Theban, has brought enough for this very purpose. Cebes, too, and a good many others. So, as I say, do not let this fear make you hesitate to save yourself, nor let what you said in court trouble you, that you would not know what to do with yourself if

c   you left Athens, for you would be welcomed in many places to which you might go. If you want to go to Thessaly, I have friends there who will greatly appreciate you and keep you safe, so that no one in Thessaly will harm you.

Besides, Socrates, I do not think that what you are doing is right, to give up your life when you can save it, and to hasten your fate as your enemies would hasten it, and indeed have hastened it in their wish to destroy you. Moreover, I think you are betraying your sons

d   by going away and leaving them, when you could bring them up and educate them. You thus show no concern for what their fate may be. They will probably have the usual fate of orphans. Either one should not have children, or one should share with them to the end the toil of upbringing and education. You seem to me to choose the easiest path, whereas one should choose the path a good and courageous man would choose, particularly when one claims throughout one's life to care for virtue.

e   I feel ashamed on your behalf and on behalf of us, your friends, lest all that has happened to you be thought due to cowardice on our part: the fact that your trial came to court when it need not have done so, the handling of the trial itself, and now this absurd ending which will be thought to have got beyond our control through some cowardice and unmanliness

46   on our part, since we did not save you, or you save yourself, when it was possible and could be done if we had been of the slightest

use. Consider, Socrates, whether this is not only evil, but shameful, both for you and for us. Take counsel with yourself, or rather the time for counsel is past and the decision should have been taken, and there is no further opportunity, for this whole business must be ended tonight. If we delay now, then it will no longer be possible, it will be too late. Let me persuade you on every count, Socrates, and do not act otherwise.

s: My dear Crito, your eagerness is worth much
b if it should have some right aim; if not, then the greater your keenness the more difficult it is to deal with. We must therefore examine whether we should act in this way or not, as not only now but at all times I am the kind of man who listens only to the argument that on reflection seems best to me. I cannot, now that this fate has come upon me, discard the arguments I used; they seem to me much the same. I value and respect the same principles
c as before, and if we have no better arguments to bring up at this moment, be sure that I shall not agree with you, not even if the power of the majority were to frighten us with more bogeys, as if we were children, with threats of incarcerations and executions and confiscation of property. How should we examine this matter most reasonably? Would it be by taking up first your argument about the opinions of men, whether it is sound in every case that one should pay attention to some opinions,
d but not to others? Or was that well-spoken before the necessity to die came upon me, but now it is clear that this was said in vain for the sake of argument, that it was in truth play and nonsense? I am eager to examine together with you, Crito, whether this argument will appear in any way different to me in my present circumstances, or whether it remains the same, whether we are to abandon it or believe it. It was said on every occasion by those who thought they were speaking sensibly, as I
e have just now been speaking, that one should greatly value some people's opinions, but not others. Does that seem to you a sound statement?

You, as far as a human being can tell, are exempt from the likelihood of dying tomorrow, so the present misfortune is not likely to lead
47 you astray. Consider then, do you not think it

a sound statement that one must not value all the opinions of men, but some and not others, nor the opinions of all men, but those of some and not of others? What do you say? Is this not well said?

c: It is.

s: One should value the good opinions, and not the bad ones?

c: Yes.

s: The good opinions are those of wise men, the bad ones those of foolish men?

c: Of course.

s: Come then, what of statements such as this:
b Should a man professionally engaged in physical training pay attention to the praise and blame and opinion of any man, or to those of one man only, namely a doctor or trainer?

c: To those of one only.

s: He should therefore fear the blame and welcome the praise of that one man, and not those of the many?

c: Obviously.

s: He must then act and exercise, eat and drink in the way the one, the trainer and the one who knows, thinks right, not all the others?

c: That is so.

c s: Very well. And if he disobeys the one, disregards his opinion and his praises while valuing those of the many who have no knowledge, will he not suffer harm?

c: Of course.

s: What is that harm, where does it tend, and what part of the man who disobeys does it affect?

c: Obviously the harm is to his body, which it ruins.

s: Well said. So with other matters, not to enumerate them all, and certainly with actions just and unjust, shameful and beautiful, good and bad, about which we are now deliberat-
d ing, should we follow the opinion of the many and fear it; or that of the one, if there is one who has knowledge of these things and before whom we feel fear and shame more than before all the others. If we do not follow his directions, we shall harm and corrupt that part of ourselves that is improved by just actions and destroyed by unjust actions. Or is there nothing in this?

c: I think there certainly is, Socrates.

s: Come now, if we ruin that which is improved

by health and corrupted by disease by not following the opinions of those who know, is life

e   worth living for us when that is ruined? And
that is the body, is it not?

c: Yes.

s: And is life worth living with a body that is corrupted and in bad condition?

c: In no way.

s: And is life worth living for us with that part of
us corrupted that unjust action harms and just
action benefits? Or do we think that part of us,
whatever it is, that is concerned with justice

48   and injustice, is inferior to the body?

c: Not at all.

s: It is more valuable?

c: Much more.

s: We should not then think so much of what the
majority will say about us, but what he will
say who understands justice and injustice, the
one, that is, and the truth itself. So that, in the
first place, you were wrong to believe that we
should care for the opinion of the many about
what is just, beautiful, good, and their opposites. "But," someone might say "the many are
able to put us to death."

b   c: That too is obvious, Socrates, and someone
might well say so.

s: And, my admirable friend, that argument that
we have gone through remains, I think, as before. Examine the following statement in turn
as to whether it stays the same or not, that the
most important thing is not life, but the good
life.

c: It stays the same.

s: And that the good life, the beautiful life, and
the just life are the same; does that still hold,
or not?

c: It does hold.

s: As we have agreed so far, we must examine

c   next whether it is right for me to try to get out
of here when the Athenians have not acquitted me. If it is seen to be right, we will try to
do so; if it is not, we will abandon the idea.
As for those questions you raise about money,
reputation, the upbringing of children, Crito,
those considerations in truth belong to those
people who easily put men to death and would
bring them to life again if they could, without
thinking; I mean the majority of men. For us,
however, since our argument leads to this, the

only valid consideration, as we were saying just
now, is whether we should be acting rightly in
giving money and gratitude to those who will

d   lead me out of here, and ourselves helping
with the escape, or whether in truth we shall
do wrong in doing all this. If it appears that
we shall be acting unjustly, then we have no
need at all to take into account whether we
shall have to die if we stay here and keep quiet,
or suffer in another way, rather than do wrong.

c: I think you put that beautifully, Socrates, but
see what we should do.

e   s: Let us examine the question together, my dear
friend, and if you can make any objection while
I am speaking, make it and I will listen to you,
but if you have no objection to make, my dear
Crito, then stop now from saying the same
thing so often, that I must leave here against
the will of the Athenians. I think it important
to persuade you before I act, and not to act
against your wishes. See whether the

49   start of our enquiry is adequately stated, and
try to answer what I ask you in the way you
think best.

c: I shall try.

s: Do we say that one must never in any way do
wrong willingly, or must one do wrong in one
way and not in another? Is to do wrong never
good or admirable, as we have agreed in the
past, or have all these former agreements been
washed out during the last few days? Have we

b   at our age failed to notice for some time that
in our serious discussions we were no different from children? Above all, is the truth such
as we used to say it was, whether the majority
agree or not, and whether we must still suffer worse things than we do now, or will be
treated more gently, that nonetheless, wrongdoing is in every way harmful and shameful to
the wrongdoer? Do we say so or not?

c: We do.

s: So one must never do wrong.

c: Certainly not.

s: Nor must one, when wronged, inflict wrong in
return, as the majority believe, since one must
never do wrong.

c   c: That seems to be the case.

s: Come now, should one injure anyone or not,
Crito?

c: One must never do so.

s: Well then, if one is oneself injured, is it right, as the majority say, to inflict an injury in return, or is it not?

c: It is never right.

s: Injuring people is no different from wrong-doing.

c: That is true.

s: One should never do wrong in return, nor injure any man, whatever injury one has suffered at his hands. And Crito, see that you do

d not agree to this, contrary to your belief. For I know that only a few people hold this view or will hold it, and there is no common ground between those who hold this view and those who do not, but they inevitably despise each other's views. So then consider very carefully whether we have this view in common, and whether you agree, and let this be the basis of our deliberation, that neither to do wrong or to return a wrong is ever right, not even to injure in return for an injury received. Or do you disagree and do not share this view as a

e basis for discussion? I have held it for a long time and still hold it now, but if you think otherwise, tell me now. If, however, you stick to our former opinion, then listen to the next point.

c: I stick to it and agree with you. So say on.

s: Then I state the next point, or rather I ask you: when one has come to an agreement that is just with someone, should one fulfill it or cheat on it?

c: One should fulfill it.

s: See what follows from this: if we leave here

50 without the city's permission, are we injuring people whom we should least injure? And are we sticking to a just agreement, or not?

c: I cannot answer your question, Socrates. I do not know.

s: Look at it this way. If, as we were planning to run away from here, or whatever one should call it, the laws and the state came and confronted us and asked: "Tell me, Socrates, what are you intending to do? Do you not by this action you are attempting intend to

b destroy us, the laws, and indeed the whole city, as far as you are concerned? Or do you think it possible for a city not to be destroyed if the verdicts of its courts have no force but are nullified and set at naught by private individuals?" What shall we answer to this and

other such arguments? For many things could be said, especially by an orator on behalf of this law we are destroying, which orders that

c the judgments of the courts shall be carried out. Shall we say in answer, "The city wronged me, and its decision was not right." Shall we say that, or what?

c: Yes, by Zeus, Socrates, that is our answer.

s: Then what if the laws said: "Was that the agreement between us, Socrates, or was it to respect the judgments that the city came to?" And if we wondered at their words, they would perhaps add: "Socrates, do not wonder at what we say but answer, since you are ac-

d customed to proceed by question and answer. Come now, what accusation do you bring against us and the city, that you should try to destroy us? Did we not, first, bring you to birth, and was it not through us that your father married your mother and begat you? Tell us, do you find anything to criticize in those of us who are concerned with marriage?" And I would say that I do not criticize them. "Or in those of us concerned with the nurture of babies and the education that you too received?

e Were those assigned to that subject not right to instruct your father to educate you in the arts and in physical culture?" And I would say that they were right. "Very well," they would continue, "and after you were born and nurtured and educated, could you, in the first place, deny that you are our offspring and servant, both you and your forefathers? If that is so, do you think that we are on an equal footing as regards the right, and that whatever we do to you it is right for you to do to us? You were not on an equal footing with your father as regards the right, nor with your master if

51 you had one, so as to retaliate for anything they did to you, to revile them if they reviled you, to beat them if they beat you, and so with many other things. Do you think you have this right to retaliation against your country and its laws? That if we undertake to destroy you and think it right to do so, you can undertake to destroy us, as far as you can, in return? And will you say that you are right to do so, you who truly care for virtue? Is your wisdom such as not to realize that your country is to be honoured more than your mother, your father and

b all your ancestors, that it is more to be revered and more sacred, and that it counts for more among the gods and sensible men, that you must worship it, yield to it and placate its anger more than your father's? You must either persuade it or obey its orders, and endure in silence whatever it instructs you to endure, whether blows or bonds, and if it leads you into war to be wounded or killed, you must obey. To do so is right, and one must not give way or retreat or leave one's post, but both in war and in courts and everywhere else, one

c must obey the commands of one's city and country, or persuade it as to the nature of justice. It is impious to bring violence to bear against your mother or father, it is much more so to use it against your country." What shall we say in reply, Crito, that the laws speak the truth, or not?

c: I think they do.

s: "Reflect now, Socrates," the laws might say "that if what we say is true, you are not treating us rightly by planning to do what you are planning. We have given you birth, nurtured you, educated you, we have given you and all

d other citizens a share of all the good things we could. Even so, by giving every Athenian the opportunity, after he has reached manhood and observed the affairs of the city and us the laws, we proclaim that if we do not please him, he can take his possessions and go wherever he pleases. Not one of our laws raises any obstacle or forbids him, if he is not satisfied with us or the city, if one of you wants to go and live in a colony or wants to go anywhere else, and keep his property. We say, however, that whoever

e of you remains, when he sees how we conduct our trials and manage the city in other ways, has in fact come to an agreement with us to obey our instructions. We say that the one who disobeys does wrong in three ways, first because in us he disobeys his parents, also those who brought him up, and because, in spite of his agreement, he neither obeys us nor, if we do something wrong, does he try to persuade

52 us to be better. Yet we only propose things, we do not issue savage commands to do whatever we order; we give two alternatives, either to persuade us or to do what we say. He does neither. We do say that you too, Socrates, are

open to those charges if you do what you have in mind; you would be among, not the least, but the most guilty of the Athenians." And if I should say "Why so?" they might well be right to upbraid me and say that I am among the Athenians who most definitely came to that agreement with them. They might well say:

b "Socrates, we have convincing proofs that we and the city were congenial to you. You would not have dwelt here most consistently of all the Athenians if the city had not been exceedingly pleasing to you. You have never left the city, even to see a festival, nor for any other reason except military service; you have never gone to stay in any other city, as people do; you have had no desire to know another city or other

c laws; we and our city satisfied you.

"So decisively did you choose us and agree to be a citizen under us. Also, you have had children in this city, thus showing that it was congenial to you. Then at your trial you could have assessed your penalty at exile if you wished, and you are now attempting to do against the city's wishes what you could then have done with her consent. Then you prided yourself that you did not resent death, but you chose, as you said, death in preference to exile. Now, however, those words do not make you ashamed, and you pay no heed to us, the

d laws, as you plan to destroy us, and you act like the meanest type of slave by trying to run away, contrary to your undertakings and your agreement to live as a citizen under us. First then, answer us on this very point, whether we speak the truth when we say that you agreed, not only in words but by your deeds, to live in accordance with us." What are we to say to that, Crito? Must we not agree?

c: We must, Socrates.

s: "Surely," they might say, "you are breaking the undertakings and agreements that you made with us without compulsion or deceit,

e and under no pressure of time for deliberation. You have had seventy years during which you could have gone away if you did not like us, and if you thought our agreements unjust. You did not choose to go to Sparta or to Crete,

53 which you are always saying are well governed, nor to any other city, Greek or foreign. You have been away from Athens less

than the lame or the blind or other handicapped people. It is clear that the city has been outstandingly more congenial to you than to other Athenians, and so have we, the laws, for what city can please without laws? Will you then not now stick to our agreements? You will, Socrates, if we can persuade you, and not make yourself a laughingstock by leaving the city.

"For consider what good you will do yourself or your friends by breaking our agreements and committing such a wrong? It is pretty obvious that your friends will themselves be in danger of exile, disfranchisement and loss of property. As for yourself, if you go to one of the nearby cities—Thebes or Megara, both are well governed—you will arrive as an enemy to their government; all who care for their city will look on you with suspicion, as a destroyer of the laws. You will also strengthen the conviction of the jury that they passed the right sentence on you, for anyone who destroys the laws could easily be thought to corrupt the young and the ignorant. Or will you avoid cities that are well governed and men who are civilized? If you do this, will your life be worth living? Will you have social intercourse with them and not be ashamed to talk to them? And what will you say? The same as you did here, that virtue and justice are man's most precious possession, along with lawful behaviour and the laws? Do you not think that Socrates would appear to be an unseemly kind of person? One must think so. Or will you leave those places and go to Crito's friends in Thessaly? There you will find the greatest license and disorder, and they may enjoy hearing from you how absurdly you escaped from prison in some disguise, in a leather jerkin or some other things in which escapees wrap themselves, thus altering your appearance. Will there be no one to say that you, likely to live but a short time more, were so greedy for life that you transgressed the most important laws? Possibly, Socrates, if you do not annoy anyone, but if you do, many disgraceful things will be said about you.

"You will spend your time ingratiating yourself with all men, and be at their beck and call. What will you do in Thessaly but feast, as if you had gone to a banquet in Thessaly? As for those conversations of yours about justice and the rest of virtue, where will they be? You say you want to live for the sake of your children, that you may bring them up and educate them. How so? Will you bring them up and educate them by taking them to Thessaly and making strangers of them, that they may enjoy that too? Or not so, but they will be better brought up and educated here, while you are alive, though absent? Yes, your friends will look after them. Will they look after them if you go and live in Thessaly, but not if you go away to the underworld? If those who profess themselves your friends are any good at all, one must assume that they will.

"Be persuaded by us who have brought you up, Socrates. Do not value either your children or your life or anything else more than goodness, in order that when you arrive in Hades you may have all this as your defence before the rulers there. If you do this deed, you will not think it better or more just or more pious here, nor will any one of your friends, nor will it be better for you when you arrive yonder. As it is, you depart, if you depart, after being wronged not by us, the laws, but by men; but if you depart after shamefully returning wrong for wrong and injury for injury, after breaking your agreement and contract with us, after injuring those you should injure least— yourself, your friends, your country and us— we shall be angry with you while you are still alive, and our brothers, the laws of the underworld, will not receive you kindly, knowing that you tried to destroy us as far as you could. Do not let Crito persuade you, rather than us, to do what he says."

Crito, my dear friend, be assured that these are the words I seem to hear, as the Corybants seem to hear the music of their flutes, and the echo of these words resounds in me, and makes it impossible for me to hear anything else. As far as my present beliefs go, if you speak in opposition to them, you will speak in vain. However, if you think you can accomplish anything, speak.

c: I have nothing to say, Socrates.

s: Let it be then, Crito, and let us act in this way, since this is the way the god is leading us.

COMMENTARY AND QUESTIONS[5]

Read 43a–44b   Plato opens the dialogue with a scene designed to emphasize yet again how different Socrates is from most men. The time is approaching for his execution, yet he sleeps peacefully—as though he had not a care in the world. His dream confirms what he had concluded at the end of the trial: Death is not an evil to be feared but is more like the soul coming home again after many hardships.

Read 44b–46a   **Crito** loses no time in trying to persuade Socrates to escape. He piles reason upon reason.

Q1.   List at least seven reasons Crito urges upon Socrates for making his escape.

Most of these reasons are prudential in nature, not moral. The one that does appeal to "what is right" seems to come right out of the Sophist's playbook: What is right, Crito says, is to preserve one's own life whenever one can.* Several of the reasons appeal to "what people will think" or "how things will look" if Socrates does not take this opportunity. This leads Socrates to ask why one should pay any attention at all to what the majority of people say.

Q2.   What does Crito say in response to this question, and what is Socrates' reply?

Q3.   What does Socrates indicate as "the greatest good"?

Read 46b–49a   Characteristically, Socrates says they must "examine" whether to act in this way.

Q4.   What kind of man does Socrates here say that he is?

Socrates reminds Crito that he has always maintained that one should pay attention only to the opinions of some people, the "most reasonable"

---

*See the quotations from Antiphon, pp. 49–50.

people. He then invites Crito to reexamine this conviction in the light of his present situation—his facing imminent death. Does it "stand fast" even now? Perhaps it will now appear unserious, nothing more than "play and nonsense," and Socrates will want to change his mind.

The examination is conducted, as so often, in terms of an analogy; Socrates draws a comparison between the health of the body and the health of the soul. He points out that you don't listen to just anybody when it comes to matters of bodily health. The same must also be true when it is a matter of the soul's well-being. You want to listen to those who are wise, not to the opinions of the many. So what most people might think if Socrates escapes or does not escape is, strictly speaking, irrelevant. It should be set aside. Reluctantly perhaps, Crito agrees.

Socrates adds that life is really not worth living when the body is corrupted by disease and ruined; the important thing is "not life, but the good life." The same must then be true of the soul.

Q5.   What corrupts and ruins the soul, according to Socrates? What benefits it?

Q6.   Which, body or soul, is most valuable? Why do you think he says that?

Q7.   Socrates says that three kinds of life are "the same": The good life, the beautiful life, and the just life. Think about the lives you are familiar with. Do you agree? Is it really the just people whose lives are beautiful and good?

They agree, then, that the right thing to do is the only thing they should have in mind when making the decision. The question is simply this: Is it just or unjust to escape? Will escaping bring benefit or harm to the soul?

Read 49a–50a   The next principle Socrates brings up for reexamination is this: that one should never willingly do wrong. Why not? Because doing wrong is "harmful and shameful to the wrongdoer." Again we see Socrates emphasizing that we harm ourselves by harming our souls, and we harm our souls by doing wrong, which makes us into worse people than we otherwise would be.

Note that injuring is not the same as inflicting harm. Remember, Socrates was a soldier, and a good one. He even cited his military experience with pride in his defense before the jury. But soldiers inflict damage on other soldiers, perhaps even kill them. Moreover, Athens is about to execute Socrates, but he says nothing to suggest that capital punishment is wrongdoing or injury. It may, then, be justifiable—in war or according to law— to inflict harm. Still, we must never injure each other. Injury is *unjust* harming of another.

What is wrong, Socrates says, is doing injustice in return for an injustice done to you. Wrong done to you never justifies your doing wrong. The reason is simply that doing injustice is *always* wrong, always a corruption of the soul. When you consider how to act, according to Socrates, you should never think about revenge, or paying back, or getting even. All these motivations look to the past, to what has happened to you, and you should look only to actions that will promote excellence—in your soul and in others. That is the way to care for your soul, and Crito says that he agrees.

Socrates says they should examine next whether one should always keep agreements made, providing they are just agreements (49e). Crito agrees immediately, so we come to the major part of the argument.

Read 50a–54d In this section, we have a dramatic piece of rhetoric. Plato gives us a dialogue within the dialogue in the form of an imaginary "examination" of Socrates by the laws of Athens. It is rhetoric all right; but, like Parmenides' poem, it contains an argument. Socrates will look to this argument, this *logos,* in making his decision. Remember that Socrates says he is the kind of man who listens only to the best *logos.* So it is the argument that we must try to discern.

Socrates indicates the conclusion of the argument right off: that escaping will constitute an attempt to injure the laws, and indeed the whole city, insofar as it is in Socrates' power to do so. It is this proposition that the laws have to prove. If they can do so, it will follow immediately that Socrates must not escape, because an escape attempt will amount to doing injury. It will also be no good for Socrates to reply, "Well, the laws injured me by convicting me unjustly!" because we have already agreed that one must not return injury for injury.

How will escaping injure the laws of Athens? This part of the argument begins with the laws claiming that they are to be honored more than mother, father, or all one's ancestors.

So the situation is this: In virtue of his long residence in Athens, Socrates has agreed to be a citizen under the laws, to accept their benefits and "live in accordance" with them. This agreement was made without any compulsion and in full knowledge of what was involved. There can be no doubt that it is a just agreement. Further, Socrates and Crito have already agreed that just agreements must be kept. But it is not yet clear how breaking this agreement will injure the laws and the city of Athens.

A clue is found in 54b, where the laws say that Socrates was wronged not by them, but by men. No legal order can exist without application and enforcement, courts and punishments, and part of voluntarily accepting citizenship is agreeing to abide by decisions of the legally constituted courts. There can be no doubt that the court that convicted Socrates was a legal court. It should also be noted that Socrates does not criticize the Athenian law against impiety on which he was tried. If the jury made a mistake and decided the case unjustly, that cannot be laid at the door of the laws. Such things can always happen. So the laws did Socrates no injustice. (Though even if they had, that would not, on Socrates' principles, justify his doing wrong in return.)

The situation then is this: To escape would be tantamount to an attack on the authority of this court to decide as it did. If *this* court lacks authority over its citizens, what court has such authority? To attack the authority of the courts is to attempt, insofar as it is possible for one man, to destroy the legal system, and the city, as a whole. "Or do you think it is possible for a city not to be destroyed if the verdicts of its courts have no force but are nullified and set at naught by private individuals?" (50b)

The argument is complex, and it may be useful to set it out in skeleton form.

1. One must never do wrong.
   a. Because to do wrong is "in every way harmful and shameful to the wrongdoer." (49b)
   b. Because doing wrong harms the part of ourselves that is "more valuable." (48a)
2. One must never return wrong for wrong done. (This follows directly from 1.)
3. To injure others (treat them unjustly) is to do wrong.
4. One must never injure others. (This follows from 1 and 3.)
5. To violate a just agreement is to do injury.
6. To escape would be to violate a just agreement with the laws. (Here we have the argument presented in the dialogue between Socrates and the laws.)
7. To escape would be an injury to the laws. (This follows from 5 and 6.)
8. To escape would be wrong. (This follows from 3 and 7.)
9. Socrates must not escape. (This follows from 1 and 8.)

This *logos* is one that Socrates finds convincing, and Crito has nothing to say against it. So it is the one Socrates will be content to live—and die—by. Once again, it is better to *suffer* injustice than to *do* it, even if that means losing one's life to avoid committing an unjust act.

There remains the task of countering the considerations Crito has put forward in favor of escape. In 53a–54a, the laws address these arguments point by point.

Q14. Go back to your list in Q1, and state the rebuttal offered by the laws. Who is more persuasive—Crito or the laws?

Read 54d–e Corybants are priests of Earth and the fertility goddess Cybele, who express their devotion in ecstatic dances, oblivious to what is going on around them. The dialogue ends with Plato once again emphasizing the very real piety of Socrates. He quietly accepts the verdict of the *logos* as guidance from the god. The voice of reason, as far as it can be discerned, is the voice of the divine.*

---

*Remember that human reason, for Socrates, is not the same as divine wisdom. We are not gods. That is why continual examination of ourselves is in order; and that is why his "voice" is significant; it supplies something human *logoi* could not. Compare what Heraclitus says about wisdom, the *logos*, and the divine, p. 22.

PHAEDO (DEATH SCENE)

Translator's Introduction

In the Phaedo, a number of Socrates' friends have come to visit him in prison on the last day of his life, as he will   *drink the hemlock at sundown. The main topic of their conversation is the nature of the soul and the arguments for its immortality. This takes up most of the dialogue. Then Socrates tells a rather elaborate myth on the shape of the earth in a hollow of which we live, and of which we know nothing of the splendours of its surface, the purer air and brighter heavens. The myth then deals with the dwelling places of various kinds of souls after death. The following passage immediately follows the conclusion of the myth.*

The Dialogue (Selection)

No sensible man would insist that these things are as I have described them, but I think it

114d is fitting for a man to risk the belief—for the risk is a noble one—that this, or something like this, is true about our souls and their dwelling places, since the soul is evidently immortal, and a man should repeat this to himself as if it were an incantation, which is why I have been prolonging my tale. That is the reason why a man should be of good cheer about his own soul, if during life he has ignored the pleasures

e of the body and its ornamentation as of no concern to him and doing him more harm than good, but has seriously concerned himself with the pleasures of learning, and adorned his soul not with alien but with its own ornaments, namely moderation, righteousness, courage,

115 freedom, and truth, and in that state awaits his journey to the underworld.

Now you, Simmias, Cebes, and the rest of you, Socrates continued, will each take that journey at some other time but my fated day calls me now, as a tragic character might say, and it is about time for me to have my bath, for I think it better to have it before I drink the poison and save the women the trouble of washing the corpse.

When Socrates had said this Crito spoke:

b Very well, Socrates, what are your instructions to me and the others about your children or anything else? What can we do that would please you most? —Nothing new, Crito, said Socrates, but what I am always saying, that you will please me and mine and yourselves, by taking good care of your own selves in whatever you do, even if you do not agree with me now, but if you neglect your own selves, and are un-

c willing to live following the tracks, as it were, of what we have said now and on previous occasions, you will achieve nothing even if you strongly agree with me at this moment.

We shall be eager to follow your advice, said Crito, but how shall we bury you?

In any way you like, said Socrates, if you can catch me and I do not escape you. And laughing quietly, looking at us, he said: I do not convince Crito that I am this Socrates talking to you here

d and ordering all I say, but he thinks that I am the thing which he will soon be looking at as a corpse, and so he asks how he shall bury me. I have been saying for some time and at some length that after I have drunk the poison I shall no longer be with you but will leave you to go and enjoy some good fortunes of the blessed, but it seems that I have said all this to him in vain in an attempt to reassure you and myself too. Give a pledge to Crito on my behalf, he said, the opposite pledge to that he gave to the jury. He pledged that I would stay, you must

e pledge that I will not stay after I die, but that I shall go away, so that Crito will bear it more easily when he sees my body being burned or buried and will not be angry on my behalf, as if I were suffering terribly, and so that he should not say at the funeral that he is laying out, or carrying out, or burying Socrates. For know you well, my dear Crito, that to express oneself badly is not only faulty as far as the language goes, but does some harm to the soul. You must be of good cheer, and say you are burying my body, and bury it in any way you like and think

116 most customary.

After saying this he got up and went to another room to take his bath, and Crito followed him and he told us to wait for him. So we stayed, talking among ourselves, questioning what had been said, and then again talking of the great misfortune that had befallen us. We all felt as if we had lost a father and would be

b orphaned for the rest of our lives. When he had washed, his children were brought to him— two of his sons were small and one was older— and the women of his household came to him. He spoke to them before Crito and gave them what instructions he wanted. Then he sent the women and children away, and he himself joined us. It was now close to sunset, for he had stayed inside for some time. He came and sat down after his bath and conversed for a short

c while, when the officer of the Eleven came and stood by him and said: "I shall not reproach you as I do the others, Socrates. They are angry with me and curse me when, obeying the orders of my superiors, I tell them to drink the poison. During the time you have been here I have come to know you in other ways as the noblest, the gentlest, and the best man who has ever come here. So now too I know that you will not make trouble for me; you know who is responsible and you will direct your anger against them. You know what message I bring. Fare you well, and try to endure what you must as easily as possible." The officer was **d** weeping as he turned away and went out. Socrates looked up at him and said: "Fare you well also, we shall do as you bid us." And turning to us he said: How pleasant the man is! During the whole time I have been here he has come in and conversed with me from time to time, a most agreeable man. And how genuinely he now weeps for me. Come, Crito, let us obey him. Let someone bring the poison if it is ready; if not, let the man prepare it.

e But Socrates, said Crito, I think the sun still shines upon the hills and has not yet set. I know that others drink the poison quite a long time after they have received the order, eating and drinking quite a bit, and some of them enjoy intimacy with their loved ones. Do not hurry; there is still some time.

It is natural, Crito, for them to do so, said **117** Socrates, for they think they derive some benefit from doing this, but it is not fitting for me. I do not expect any benefit from drinking the poison a little later, except to become ridiculous in my own eyes for clinging to life, and be sparing of it when there is none left. So do as I ask and do not refuse me.

Hearing this, Crito nodded to the slave who was standing near him; the slave went out and after a time came back with the man who was to administer the poison, carrying it made ready in a cup. When Socrates saw him he said: Well, my good man, you are an expert in this, what must one do? —"Just drink it and walk **b** around until your legs feel heavy, and then lie down and it will act of itself." And he offered the cup to Socrates who took it quite cheerfully, . . . without a tremor or any change of feature or colour, but looking at the man from under his eyebrows as was his wont, asked: "What do you say about pouring a libation from this drink? Is it allowed?" —"We only

mix as much as we believe will suffice," said the man.

c I understand, Socrates said, but one is allowed, indeed one must, utter a prayer to the gods that the journey from here to yonder may be fortunate. This is my prayer and may it be so.

And while he was saying this, he was holding the cup, and then drained it calmly and easily. Most of us had been able to hold back our tears reasonably well up till then, but when we saw him drinking it and after he drank it, we could hold them back no longer; my own tears came in floods against my will. So I covered my face. I was weeping for myself—not for him, but for my misfortune in being deprived of such a com- **d** rade. Even before me, Crito was unable to restrain his tears and got up. Apollodorus had not ceased from weeping before, and at this moment his noisy tears and anger made everybody present break down, except Socrates. "What is this," he said, "you strange fellows. It is mainly for this reason that I sent the women away, to **e** avoid such unseemliness, for I am told one should die in good omened silence. So keep quiet and control yourselves."

His words made us ashamed, and we checked our tears. He walked around, and when he said his legs were heavy he lay on his back as he had been told to do, and the man who had given him the poison touched his body, and after a **118** while tested his feet and legs, pressed hard upon his foot and asked him if he felt this, and Socrates said no. Then he pressed his calves, and made his way up his body and showed us that it was cold and stiff. He felt it himself and said that when the cold reached his heart he would be gone. As his belly was getting cold Socrates uncovered his head—he had covered it—and said—these were his last words— "Crito, we owe a cock to Asclepius;[1] make this offering to him and do not forget." —"It shall be done," said Crito, "tell us if there is anything else," but there was no answer. Shortly afterwards Socrates made a movement; the man uncovered him and his eyes were fixed. Seeing this Crito closed his mouth and his eyes.

---

[1] A cock was sacrificed to Asclepius by the sick people who slept in his temples, hoping for a cure. Socrates obviously means that death is a cure for the ills of life.

Such was the end of our comrade, . . . , a man who, we would say, was of all those we have known the best, and also the wisest and the most upright.

COMMENTARY AND QUESTIONS

Read 114d–115e About fifteen people were present for this last conversation. Plato, it is said, was absent because he was ill. By this point, they have agreed that the soul is immortal and that the souls of the just and pious, especially if they have devoted themselves to wisdom, dwell after death in a beautiful place.

Q1. What are said to be the "ornaments" of the soul?
Q2. What harm, do you think, can it do the soul to "express oneself badly"?

Read 116–end Socrates seems to have kept his calm and courage to the end—and his humor. There is a little joke about burial at 115c. Xenophon, too, records this:

> A man named Apollodorus, who was there with him, a very ardent disciple of Socrates, but otherwise simple, exclaimed, "But Socrates, what I find it hardest to bear is that I see you being put to death unjustly!" The other, stroking Apollodorus' head, is said to have replied, "My beloved Apollodorus, was it your preference to see me put to death justly?" and smiled as he asked the question.[6]

The simple majesty of the final tribute is, perhaps, unmatched anywhere.

FOR FURTHER THOUGHT

1. Socrates believes that acts of injustice cannot be wrong simply because the gods disapprove of them. There must be something about such acts themselves, he claims, that makes them wrong. If you agree, try to say what that is. If you disagree, argue for that conclusion.

2. Imagine that you are a member of the Athenian jury hearing the case of Socrates. How would you vote? Why?
3. How might constant resort to the F-word harm the soul?
4. Should Socrates have accepted Crito's offer of escape? Construct a *logos* that supports your answer.

KEY WORDS

Euthyphro	truth
Meletus	earlier accusers
divine sign	Oracle at Delphi
the pious	human wisdom
definition	later accusers
form	dilemma
ethics	Meno
care of the gods	Crito
persuasion	

NOTES

1. The dialogues and translator's introductions in this chapter are from Plato, *The Trial and Death of Socrates*, 2d ed., trans. G. M. A. Grube (Indianapolis: Hackett, 1975).
2. Xenophon, *Memorabilia*, trans. E. C. Marchant, in *Xenophon IV*, ed. E. C. Marchant and O. J. Todd (Cambridge, MA: Harvard University Press, 1979), bk. 1, 3, 2–3.
3. Plato, *Meno*, trans. Robin Waterfield, in *Meno and Other Dialogues* (Oxford: Oxford University Press, 2005).
4. Plato, *Theatetus*, in *The Collected Dialogues of Plato*, ed. E. Hamilton and H. Cairns (Princeton: Princeton University Press, 1961).
5. I am indebted to R. E. Allen's interpretation of the *Crito* in his *Socrates and Legal Obligation* (Minneapolis: University of Minnesota Press, 1980).
6. Xenophon, *Apology 28*, trans. O. J. Todd, in *Xenophon IV*, ed. E. C. Marchant and O. J. Todd (Cambridge, MA: Harvard University Press, 1979).

CHAPTER

6

PLATO

Knowing the Real and the Good

When Socrates died in 399 B.C., his friend and admirer Plato was just thirty years old. He lived fifty-two more years. That long life was devoted to the creation of a philosophy that would justify and vindicate his master, "the best, and also the wisest" man he had ever known (*Phaedo* 118). It is a philosophy whose influence has been incalculable in the West. Together with that of his own pupil Aristotle, it forms one of the two foundation stones for nearly all that is to follow; even those who want to disagree first have to pay attention. In a rather loose sense, everyone who thinks about philosophy at all is either a Platonist or an Aristotelian.

"The safest general characterization of the
European philosophical tradition is that it
consists of a series of footnotes to Plato."
Alfred North Whitehead (1861–1947)

In Raphael's remarkable painting *The School of Athens* (see the cover of this book), all the sight lines draw the eye toward the two central figures. Plato is the one on the left, pointing upward. Aristotle is on the right with a hand stretched out horizontally. We will not be ready to appreciate the symbolism of these gestures until we know something of both, but that these two occupy center stage is entirely appropriate.

Plato apparently left Athens after Socrates' death and traveled quite widely. About 387 B.C., he settled again in his home town and established a school near a grove called "Academus," from which comes our word "academy." There he inquired, taught, and wrote the dialogues.

Let us briefly review the situation leading up to Socrates' death. These are extremely troubled times. An ugly, drawn-out war with Sparta ends in humiliation, accompanied by internal strife between democrats and oligarchs, culminating in the tyranny of the Thirty, civil war, and their overthrow. The Sophists, meanwhile, have been teaching doctrines that seem to undermine all the traditions and cast doubt on everything people hold sacred. And the intellectual situation in general, though it will look active and fruitful from a future vantage point, surely looks chaotic and unsettled from close up. It is a war of ideas no one has definitely won. You have Parmenides' One versus Heraclitus' flux, Democritus' atomism versus the skepticism of the Sophists, and the controversy over *physis* and *nomos.* Some urge conformity to the laws of the city; others hold that such human justice is inferior to the pursuit of self-interest, which can rightly override such "mere" conventions.

In this maelstrom appears Socrates—ugly to look at, fascinating in character, incredibly honest, doggedly persistent, passionately committed to a search for the truth, and convinced that *none* of his contemporaries know what they are talking about. Plato is not the only one entranced. But clearly Plato has genius of his own, and he takes the Socratic task on his own shoulders. Animating Socrates' practice, as we have seen, is the conviction that there is a *truth* about the matters he investigates, but he seldom feels he has found it. Plato sets for himself the goal—nothing less!—of refuting skepticism and relativism. He intends to *demonstrate,* contrary to the Sophists, that there is a truth about reality and that it can be known. And he intends to show, contrary to Democritus, that this reality is not indifferent to moral and religious values.

His basic goal, and in this he is typically Greek, is to establish the pattern for a good state.* If you were to ask him, "Plato, exactly what do you mean by 'a good state'?" he would have a ready answer. He would say that a good state is one in which a good person can live a good life. And if you pressed him about what kind of person was a good person, he would acknowledge that here was a hard question, one needing examination. But he would at least be ready with an example. And by now you know who the example would be. It follows that Athens as it existed in 399 B.C. was not, despite its virtues, a good state, for it had executed Socrates.

To reach this goal of setting forth the pattern of a good state, Plato has to show that there is such a thing as goodness—and not just by convention. It couldn't be that if Athens *thought* it was a good

thing to execute Socrates then it *was* a good thing to execute Socrates. Plato knew in his heart that was wrong. But now he has to *show* it was wrong. Mere assertion was never enough for Socrates, and it won't do for Plato, either. He will construct a *logos,* a true *logos,* a *dialectic,* to show us the goodness that exists in *physis,* not just in the opinions of people or the conventions of society. And he will show us how we can come to know what this goodness is and become truly wise. These, at least, are his ambitions.

Knowledge and Opinion

We sometimes make the following contrast: Do you only believe that, or do you know it? This contrast between mere belief, or opinion, and knowledge is important for Plato. Indeed, he uses it to derive surprising conclusions—conclusions that make up the heart and center of his philosophy. It is on this distinction that his critique of the sophistic relativism and skepticism turns.

The Sophists argue, you will recall, that if someone thinks the wind is cold, then it is cold—for that person.* And they generalize this claim. "Of *all* things, the measure is man," asserts Protagoras. In effect, all we can have are opinions or beliefs. If a certain belief is satisfactory to a certain person, then no more can be said. We are each the final authority of what seems right to us. We are restricted to appearance; knowledge of reality is beyond our powers. This is the heart of their skepticism and relativism.

Plato tries to meet this challenge in three steps. First, he has to clarify the distinction between opinion and knowledge. Second, he has to show that we do have knowledge. Third, he needs to explain the nature of the objects that we can be said to know. As we will see, Plato's **epistemology** (his theory of knowledge) and his **metaphysics** (his theory of reality) are perfectly knit together in his unique solution to these problems.

MAKING THE DISTINCTION

What is the difference between **knowing** something and just **believing** it? The key seems to be

---

*His *Republic* is an attempt to define an ideal state. The *Laws,* perhaps his last work, is a long and detailed discussion trying to frame a realistic constitution for a state that might actually exist.

---

*See p. 46.

this: You can believe falsely, but you can't know falsely. Suppose that at a certain time, call it T1, you claim to know that John is Kate's husband. Later, at T2, you find out that John is really unmarried and has never been anyone's husband. What will you then say about yourself at T1? Will you say, "Well, I used to know (at T1) that John was married, but now I know he is not"? This would be saying, "I did know (falsely) that John was married, but now I know (truly) that he is not." Or will you say, "Well, I *thought* I knew (at T1) that John was married, but I *didn't* know it at all"? Surely you will say the latter. If we become convinced that something we claim to know is false, we retract that claim. We do not claim to know things we believe are false. We can put this in the form of a principle: Knowledge involves truth.

Believing or having opinions is quite the opposite. If at T1 you *believe* that John is married to Kate and you later find out he isn't, you won't retract the claim that you did believe that at T1. You will simply say, "Yes, I did believe that; but now I believe (or know) it isn't so." It is quite possible to believe something false; it happens all the time. Believing does not necessarily involve truth.

We can, of course, believe truly. But even so, belief and knowledge are not the same thing. In the *Meno,* Plato has Socrates say,

> As long as they stay put, true beliefs too constitute a thing of beauty and do nothing but good. The problem is that they tend not to stay for long; they escape from the human soul and this reduces their value, unless they're anchored by working out the reason. . . . When true beliefs are anchored, they become pieces of knowledge and they become stable. That's why knowledge is more valuable than true belief, and the difference between the two is that knowledge has been anchored. (*Meno* 98a)[1]

In the *Republic,* Plato compares people who have only true opinions to blind people who yet follow the right road (*R* 506c).[2] Imagine a blind woman who wanders along, turning this way and that. It just happens that each of her turnings corresponds to a bend in the road, but her correct turnings are merely an accident. She might equally well go straight over the cliff at the next bend. By contrast, we who can

see the road, have a reason why we turn as we do; we can see that the road bends here to avoid the precipice. We know that we must turn left here precisely because we can give an account of why we turn as we do. Our belief that we must turn left here is "anchored" by our "reason" that there is a cliff dead ahead.

We can connect this contrast between true belief and knowledge with the practice of Socrates. It is his habit, as we have seen, to examine others about their beliefs. And we can now say that surviving such examination is a necessary condition for any belief to count as knowledge. It is only a negative condition, however, because such survival doesn't guarantee truth; perhaps we simply have not yet come across the devastating counterexample. But Plato wants more than survival. In addition to surviving criticism, he wants to supply positive reasons for holding on to a belief. What he hopes to supply is a *logos* that gives *the reason why.*

We have here a second and a third point of distinction between knowledge and belief (even true belief). Not only does knowledge invariably involve truth, but it also "stays put." And it endures in this way because it involves the reason why.

And this leads to a final difference. In the *Timaeus,* Plato tells us that

> the one is implanted in us by instruction, the other by persuasion; . . . the one cannot be overcome by persuasion, but the other can. (*Timaeus* 51e)[3]

The instruction in question will be an explanation of the reason why. But what is persuasion? Can there be any doubt that Plato has in mind here all the tricks and techniques of rhetoric? If you truly know something, he is saying, you will understand why it is so. And that understanding will protect you from clever fellows (advertisers, politicians, public relations experts) who use their art to "make the weaker argument appear the stronger." Opinion or mere belief, by contrast, is at the mercy of every persuasive talker that comes along. If you believe something but don't clearly understand the reason why it is so, your belief will easily be "overcome" by persuasion. Compare yourself, for instance, to the blind woman at the bend of the road just before the cliff. She might easily be persuaded to go straight ahead; no one could persuade you to do so.

As you can see, Plato draws a sharp and clear line between opinion and knowledge. We can summarize the distinction in a table.

Opinion	Knowledge
is changeable	endures or stays put
may be true or false	is always true
is not backed up by reasons	is backed up by reasons
is the result of persuasion	is the result of instruction

So far even Sophists need not quarrel; they could agree that such a distinction can be made. But they would claim that it cannot be *applied* because all we ever have are opinions. We can perhaps understand what it would be like to have knowledge, but it doesn't follow that we actually have any. So Plato has to move to his second task; he has to demonstrate that we can in fact know certain things.

WE DO KNOW CERTAIN TRUTHS

Plato's clearest examples are the truths of mathematics and geometry. Think back to the slave boy and the problem of doubling the area of a square.* The correct solution is to take the diagonal of the original square as a side of the square to be constructed. That solution can be seen to be

*See pp. 103–104.

correct because an "account" or explanation can be given: the reason why. Now look at the following diagram.

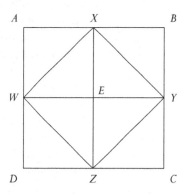

The reason why the square *WXYZ* is double the original square *WEZD* is that it is made up of four equal triangles, each of which is the same size as one-half the original. Because four halves make two wholes, we have a square twice the size of *WEZD*. This *logos* gives the reason why this is the correct solution. Once you (or the slave boy) understand this rationale, it will not be easier to persuade you otherwise than to persuade you to go straight over the cliff edge. What we have here, then, is an opinion that is true, will stay put, is backed up by reason, and is the result of instruction. In other words, we have not just opinion—we have knowledge.

"Knowledge, in truth, is the great sun in the Firmament. Life and power are scattered with all its beams."

Daniel Webster (1782–1852)

This example (and innumerable others of the same kind can be constructed) is absolutely convincing to Plato. There can be no doubt, he thinks, that this solution is not just a matter of how it seems to one person or another. About these matters cultures do not differ.* There is no sense in which man is the "measure" of this truth. It is not conventional or up

*Compare Socrates on what the gods do not quarrel about (*Euthyphro* 7 b,c).

to us to decide; we *recognize* it. Relativism, at least as a general theory, is mistaken. Skepticism is wrong. We do have knowledge of the truth.

But two important questions are still unsettled. First, what exactly do we have knowledge about when we know that this is the correct solution to the problem? Socrates probably drew the squares in the sand. Are we to suppose that he drew so accurately that the square made on the diagonal was really twice the area of the original? Not likely. The truth the slave boy came to know, then, is not a truth about that sand drawing. What is it about, then? Here is a puzzle. And Plato's solution to this puzzle is the key to understanding his whole philosophy.

The second question is whether this kind of knowledge can be extended to values and morality. Can we know that deception is unjust with the same certainty as that a square on the diagonal is twice the size of an original square? We address the first of these questions now and come back to the second later.

---

1. What are Plato's goals? What does he aim to do?
2. Distinguish knowledge from opinion.

The Objects of Knowledge

Plato would say that Socrates' sand drawing is not the object of the slave boy's knowledge. Let's make sure we see Plato's point here. "I agree," you might say, "that Socrates' sand drawing is not exact. But we can do much better than sand drawings nowadays. Surely we can draw, or construct, a square exactly double the size of a given square!" Ah, but can we? Suppose the area of the original square is 4; then we want a square that is 8—not, note well, 7.999999999. And not 8.000000001 either.

There are two interesting points here. One is that we could not draw or make such a square, except perhaps by accident. Our instruments are not precise enough for that. The second is that even if we had such a square before us, we could not know that it was such a square, for all our measurements are valid only within a certain range of error. The slave boy's knowledge (and yours), it seems, cannot be derived from the drawing you see before

"So the philosopher, who consorts with what is divine and ordered, himself becomes godlike and ordered as far as a man can see. . . ."

—Plato

you; and neither is it about that drawing. Yet it is true, and it does constitute knowledge. Plato puts the point in this way:

> Do sight and hearing afford mankind any truth, or aren't even the poets always harping on such themes, telling us that we neither hear nor see anything accurately? And yet if those of all the bodily senses are neither accurate nor clear, the others will hardly be so; because they are, surely, all inferior to those. Don't you think so?
>
> Certainly.
>
> So when does the soul attain the truth? Because plainly, whenever it sets about examining anything in company with the body, it is completely taken in by it.
>
> That's true.
>
> So isn't it in reasoning, if anywhere at all, that any realities become manifest to it?
>
> Yes. (*Phaedo*, 65b–c)[4]

The senses (sight, hearing, and the rest) never get it right, Plato tells us; they are not "clear" or "accurate." We grasp the truth only through a *logos* that "works out the reason."

Here Plato agrees with Parmenides, who admonishes us not to trust our senses but to follow reasoning alone.* In this sense, Plato too is a rationalist. You should be able to see, from the example we have considered, why he thinks this is the only way to proceed. (There is a role for the senses in the formulation of opinion about the world of experience, as we'll see, but they cannot give us *knowledge*.)

You should also be able to see that Plato agrees with Heraclitus about the world revealed to us through the senses.† Consider the drawing of the square again. Suppose we did get it just right; the area is exactly 8. But of course we drew it with a pencil, pen, or laser—with some physical material. What is to prevent it, once drawn correctly, from turning incorrect in the very next moment? Suppose a molecule of ink or a particle of light gets displaced? It might bounce in and out of correctness from nanosecond to nanosecond. It seems like a continual flux. And that is just what Heraclitus thinks it is. But our solution doesn't bounce in and out of truth that way. It "stays put." Once again, the truth we know cannot be about the world disclosed to our senses. Nothing in that world "stays put."

Interestingly, Plato holds that both Parmenides and Heraclitus are correct. They aren't in fact contradicting each other, even though one holds that reality is unchangeable and the other that reality is continually changing. Both are correct because each is talking about a different reality. The one is revealed to us through the senses, the other through reasoning. You are familiar with the reality of Heraclitus; it is just the everyday world we see, hear, smell, taste, and touch. The other world is not so ordinary, and we must say more about it.

We need to go back to the question, what is our truth about the square *true of?* If it is not about any square you could see or touch, what then? Plato's answer is that it is a truth about the Square Itself. This is an object that can be apprehended only by the intellect, by thinking and reasoning. Still, it is an object, a reality; why should we suppose that the senses are our only avenue to what there is? It is, moreover, a public object, for you and I (and indeed anyone) can know the same truths about it. In fact, it is more public than sense objects. The square I see as red you may see as green, but everyone agrees that a square may be doubled by taking its diagonal as the base of another square.

Here is another feature of the Square Itself. It is not some particular square or other. It is not, for instance, one with an area of 4 rather than 6 or 10 or 19⅝. The doubling principle works for *any* square. So if our truth is a truth about the Square Itself, this must be a very unusual object! It must be an object that in some sense is *shared* by all the particular squares that ever have been or ever will be.

Here we are reminded of what Socrates is looking for. Remember that when Socrates questions Euthyphro, he isn't satisfied when presented with an *example* of piety. What he wants is something common to all pious actions, present in no impious actions, and which accounts for the fact that the pious actions are pious. He wants, he says, the "form" of piety.* Plato takes up the term **Form** and uses it as the general term for the objects of knowledge. In our example, what we know is something about the Form of the Square. We may use the terms "Form of the Square" and "the Square Itself" interchangeably. What we can know, then, are Forms (the Square Itself, the Triangle Itself) and how they are related to each other.

About the world of the senses, Plato tells us, no knowledge in the strict sense is possible. Here there are only opinions. Because the Square Itself does not fluctuate like visible and tangible squares, it can qualify as an object of knowledge.

Up to this point we have traced Plato's reasoning about the Forms on the basis of the assumption that we do have some knowledge. Let us recapitulate the major steps.

---

*You might like to review briefly what Parmenides says; see p. 29.

†See p. 19–21.

---

*See *Euthyphro* 6d–e.

- Knowledge is enduring, true, rational belief based on instruction.
- We do have knowledge.
- This knowledge cannot be about the world revealed through the senses.
- It must be about another world, one that endures.
- This is the world of Forms.

Let us call this the **Epistemological Argument** for the Forms. Epistemology, you may recall, is the fancy term for the theory of knowledge—what knowledge is and what it is about.* And Plato has here concluded from a theory of what knowledge is that its objects must be realities quite different from those presented by the senses. These are realities that, like Parmenides' One, are eternal and unchanging, each one forever exactly what it is.

This very statement, however, reveals that Parmenides was not wholly right. For there is not just One Form—or the Form of the One—but many. There is the Square Itself, the Triangle Itself, the Equal Itself, and indeed, as we shall see, the Just Itself, the Good Itself, and the Form of the Beautiful as well. The reality that is eternal is not a blank One but a most intricately related, immensely complex pattern of Forms. This pattern is reflected partly in our mathematical knowledge. It is what mathematics is about.

This Epistemological Argument is one leg supporting the theory of Forms, but it is not the only one. Before we consider further the nature of Forms and their function in Plato's thought, let us look briefly at two more reasons why Plato believes in their reality.

In a late dialogue where Socrates is no longer the central figure, Plato has Parmenides say:

> I imagine your ground for believing in a single form in each case is this. When it seems to you that a number of things are large, there seems, I suppose, to be a certain single character which is the same when you look at them all; hence you think that largeness is a single thing. (*Parmenides* 132a)

Socrates agrees. What we might call the **Metaphysical Argument**† for the Forms goes like this.

Consider two things that are alike. Perhaps they are both large or white or just. Think of two large elephants, Huey and Gertrude. They have a certain "character" in common. Each is large. Now, what they have in common (largeness) cannot be the same as either one; largeness is not the same as Huey and it is not the same as Gertrude. Nor is it identical with the two of them together, since their cousin Rumble is also large. What they share, then, must be a reality distinct from them. Let us call it the Large Itself. Alternatively, we could call it the Form of the Large.

This argument starts not from the nature of knowledge and its difference from opinion, but from the nature of *things*. That is why we can call it a "metaphysical" argument. A similarity among things indicates that they have something in common. What they have in common cannot be just another thing of the same sort as they are. Gertrude, for example, is not something that other pairs of things could share in the way they can share largeness; each of two other things can be large, but it is nonsense to suppose that each can be Gertrude. What Gertrude and Huey have in common must be something of another sort altogether. It is, Plato holds, a Form.

Finally, let us look at a **Semantic Argument** for the Forms. Semantics is a discipline that deals with words, in particular with the meanings of words and how words are related to what they are about. In the *Republic* we read that

> any given plurality of things which have a single name constitutes a specific type [Form]. (*R* 596a)

The interesting phrase here is "have a single name." What Plato has in mind here is the fact that we have names of several different kinds. "Gertrude" is a name, and it stands for a certain elephant—for Gertrude, in fact. But "elephant" also seems to be a name, yet it functions quite differently from "Gertrude." A proper name like "Gertrude" names or picks out or stands for one particular thing in the world. But we give the name "elephant" to Gertrude and Huey and Rumble and

---

*See "A Word to Students."

†For an explanation of the term "metaphysics," see "A Word to Students."

all the other elephants there ever have been or ever will be. Why? Because, Plato suggests, we are assuming that one Form is common to them all. Just as the name "Gertrude" names some particular elephant, the name "elephant" names the Form Elephant—what all elephants have in common. Whenever we give the same name to a plurality of things, Plato tells us, it is legitimate to assume that we are naming a Form.

This line of reflection offers an answer to a somewhat puzzling question: how do *general* words get their meaning? What we call "proper names" seem to get their meaning by standing for or naming some object. "Socrates" is meaningful (not just a noise) because it stands for Socrates, and "Gertrude" gets its meaning by naming Gertrude. Plato's theory tells us that general terms such as "man" or "elephant" get their meaning in the same basic way. They too stand for something; they too are names. But they are the names of Forms, not of particular things that our senses could allow us to meet.

What we have in Plato's philosophy is a single answer to three problems that any philosophy striving for completeness must address. Let us summarize.

- *Problem One.* Assuming that we do have some knowledge, what is our knowledge about? What are the objects of knowledge? Plato's answer is that what we know are the Forms of things.

- *Problem Two.* The particular things that we are acquainted with can be grouped into kinds on the basis of what they have in common. How are we to explain these common features? Plato tells us that what they have in common is a Form.

- *Problem Three.* Some of our words apply not to particular things but to all things of a certain kind. How are we to understand the meaning of these general words? Plato's theory is that these general terms are themselves names, and that what they name is not a particular sensible thing but a Form.

THE REALITY OF THE FORMS

We have, then, a number of lines of investigation—epistemological, metaphysical, and semantic—all of which seem to point in the same direction: In addition to the world of sense so familiar to us, there is another world, the world of Forms. The Forms are not anything we can smell, taste, touch, or see, but that is not to say they are unreal or imaginary. To suppose that they must be unreal if our senses do not make contact with them is just a prejudice; we could call it the Bias Toward the Senses. But Plato believes he has already exposed this as a mere bias.*

Consider again the problem of doubling the size of a square. In the *Republic* Socrates imagines that he is questioning someone who only has opinion but thinks it is knowledge:

> "But can you tell us please, whether someone with knowledge knows something or nothing?" You'd better answer my questions for him.
> My answer will be that he knows something. . . .
> Something real or something unreal?
> Real. How could something unreal be known?
> (R 476e)

You can't know what *isn't,* Plato tells us, for the simple reason that in that case there isn't anything there to know. You can only know what *is.*† In other words, if you do know something, there must be something in reality for you to know. In the case of doubling the square, what you know concerns a set of Forms and their relations to each other. So there must be Forms; they cannot be merely unreal and imaginary.

There is a further and more radical conclusion. The Forms are not only real; they are more real than anything you can see or hear or touch. What is Plato's argument for this surprising conclusion? Recall the distinction between knowledge and opinion.‡ If we reflect a little, we can see that we ought to have a threefold division rather than a twofold one; in addition to Knowledge and Opinion, there is Invincible Ignorance. As Plato says, "Something

---

*Here again Plato agrees with Parmenides. For Parmenides' critique of the senses, see pp. 28–29.

†This is a narrower version of the Parmenidean principle that thought and being always go together (see p. 27). Plato accepts that *thought* might diverge from being, but the thought that meets the tests of *knowledge* will not. That is why we value it.

‡Review the table on p. 121.

completely real is completely accessible to knowledge, and something utterly unreal is entirely inaccessible to knowledge" (R 477a). About the unreal we are ignorant—not just ignorant for the time being or in such a way that we might learn, but *invincibly* ignorant. We then have three capacities to correlate with their objects.

Knowledge	Opinion	Invincible Ignorance
—of what is—	—?—	—of what is not—

What corresponds to opinion in the same way as reality and nothingness correspond to knowledge and ignorance? Opinion, Plato suggests, stands midway between knowledge and ignorance. It is more than ignorance but less than knowledge. Because it is a capacity of ours, there must be objects that answer to it; when we have an opinion, it is always an opinion *about something*. The natural solution is to find something midway between *what is* on the one hand and *what is not* on the other hand. Can we find something of which it is accurate to say that it both *is* and *is not*?

Yes, Plato tells us, there do exist things that both are and are not. What things? None other than those items embedded in the Heraclitean flux, the visible world of our experience. For nothing in this sensible world of ours is unqualifiedly beautiful. There are beautiful things, to be sure, but they are beautiful for a time, or beautiful in these circumstances but not in those. Even the beauty of Helen of Troy faded with age. It would be true to say that Helen both was and was not beautiful. Gertrude the elephant is large, but not in comparison to Mount Everest. In comparison to Mount Everest, Gertrude is small, even tiny. So Gertrude is both large and not large. And this kind of reflection applies to absolutely everything in the sensory world.* How these things are regarded depends on the perspective taken, the aspect considered, the comparisons in mind. Moreover, all of them come into being and pass away again. None just *is*. Each of them can *appear* now this way, now that.

So we can now fill in the question mark in the foregoing chart: Opinion is about

—the world of experience—

Notice that we have reached the conclusion that Plato wants us to reach. The Forms are more real than anything you can experience by means of your senses. Unlike sensible things, they are unchangeably what they are—forever. Even if every square thing ceased to exist, the Square Itself would remain. In comparison to the Forms, Helen and Gertrude—and just and pious actions, too—are only partly real. They surely have some reality; they are not nothing. But they are less real than the Forms, for they do not endure. For that reason we can have no knowledge of them; about them the best we can hope for is opinion. They don't "stay put" long enough to be known. As Plato charmingly puts it, these things "mill around somewhere between unreality and perfect reality" (R 479d).

Plato thinks that in a sense there are two worlds. There is the world of the Forms, which can be known, but only by reasoning, by the intellect. This is the most real world. And there is the world of the many particular, ever-changing things that make up the flux of our lives. These can be sensed; about them we may have opinions, but they cannot be known. This world is real, but less real than the world of the Forms.

It is clear that Plato needs to go on. No one could be satisfied to stop at this point. Even if we grant that he is right to this point (and let us grant it provisionally), we now must insist on an answer to a further question: How are the two worlds related? With this question we arrive at the most interesting part of Plato's answer to sophistic skepticism and relativism.

1. In what way does Plato agree with Parmenides? With Heraclitus?
2. Be sure you can sketch the three lines of argument for the reality of the Forms: epistemological, metaphysical, and semantic.
3. If the objects of knowledge are the Forms, what are the objects of opinion?
4. Why does Plato think the Form of Bicycle is *more real* than the bicycle I ride to work?

---

*Compare Heraclitus, p. 19.

The World and the Forms

If Plato is right, reality is not at all what it seems to be. What we usually take as reality is only partly real; reality itself is quite different. For convenience' sake, let us use the term "the world" to refer to this flux of things about us that appear to our senses: rivers, trees, desks, elephants, men and women, runnings, promisings, sleepings, customs, laws, and so on. This corresponds closely enough to the usual use of that term; however, the world must now be understood as less than the whole of reality, and none of it entirely real. We can then put Plato's point in this way: In addition to the world, there are also the Forms, and they are what is truly real. This much, he would add, we already know. For we have given an account (a *logos*) of the reason why we must believe in the reality of the Forms.

How Forms Are Related to the World

We must now examine the relationship between the two realities. Let us begin by thinking about shadows. We could equally well consider photographs, mirror images, and reflections in a pool of water. A shadow is in a certain sense less real than the thing that casts it. It is less real because it doesn't have any independent existence; its shape depends wholly on the thing that it is a shadow of (and of course the light source). Think about the shadow shapes you can make on a wall by positioning your hands in various ways in front of a strong lamp. Shaping your hands one way produces the shape of a rabbit; another way, an owl. What the shadow is depends on the shape of your hands. The shape of your hands does *not,* note well, depend on the shape of the shadow. If you put your hands in your pockets, your hands and their shape still exist, but the shadows vanish. This is the sense in which shadows are less real; your hands have an independent existence, but the shadows do not.

Both shadows and hands are parts of the world. So there are different degrees of reality *within* the world, too. Could we use the relationship between shadows and hands to illuminate the relationship

between world and Forms? This is in fact what Plato does in a famous diagram called the **Divided Line**. Plato here calls the world "**the visible**" and the Forms "**the intelligible**," according to how we are acquainted with them.

> Well, picture them as a line cut into two unequal sections and, following the same proportions, subdivide both the section of the visible realm and that of the intelligible realm. Now you can compare the sections in terms of clarity and unclarity. The first section in the visible realm consists of likenesses, by which I mean a number of things: shadows, reflections . . . and so on.
> And you should count the other section of the visible realm as consisting of the things whose likenesses are found in the first section: all the flora and fauna there are in the world, and every kind of artefact, too. (R 509e–510a)

Let us draw Plato's line, labeling as much of it as he has so far explained (p. 128).

It is important for the symbolism that the lengths of the various sections are *not equal*. These lengths are related to each other by a certain ratio or proportion: As B is related to A, and D to C, so is (C + D) related to (A + B). Plato intends this proportionality between the line segments to represent the fact that the intelligible world of the Forms is related to the entire visible world in exactly the same way as things within the visible world are related to their likenesses. (Note that the actual length of the sections is irrelevant; we could draw the line with D being the longest just as well. All that counts is how they are related to each other.)

Let's construct a more realistic example than shadows of arbitrarily shaped hands. Imagine that we live at the bottom of a canyon. Our society has a very strong taboo against looking up, which has been handed down by our earliest ancestors from generation to generation. We do not look up to the rim of the canyon and the sky beyond. The sun shines down into the canyon during the middle part of each day, and we can see the shadows of the canyon walls move across the canyon floor from west to east. Eagles live high up in the canyon wall, but they never come down to the canyon floor,

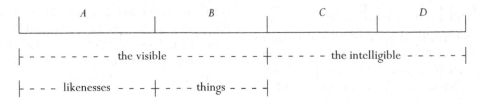

preferring to forage for their food in the richly supplied plains above. We have never seen an eagle, nor are we likely to.

We do see the shadows of eagles as they glide from one wall of the canyon to the other. Sometimes the eagles perch directly on the edge of the canyon wall and cast shadows of a very different shape, of many different shapes, in fact; sometimes they perch facing west, sometimes north, and so on. We do not know that these are eagle shadows, of course, for we are not acquainted with eagles. All we know are the shadows.

Could we have any reliable beliefs about eagles? We could. If we collected all the shadow shapes that we had seen, we could get a pretty good idea of what an eagle looks like and at least some idea of its behaviors. We might even get a kind of science of eagles on this basis; from certain shadows we might be able to make predictions about the shapes of others, and these predictions might often turn out to be true. The concept "eagle" would be merely a construct for us, of course; it would be equivalent to "that (whatever it is) which accounts for shadows of this sort." We would think of eagles as the things that explain such shadows, the things making the shadow-patterns intelligible. But we would never have any direct contact with eagles.

One day, an eagle is injured in a fight and comes fluttering helplessly down to the canyon floor. This has never happened before. We catch the injured bird and nurse it back to health. While we have it in our care, we examine it carefully. We come to realize that this is the creature responsible for the shadows we have been observing with interest all these generations. We already know a good bit about it, but now our concept of "eagle" is no longer just a construct. Now we have the *thing* in our sight, and we can see just what features of an eagle account for that shadow science we have constructed.

We can say that this creature explains the shadows we were familiar with; it makes it intelligible that our experience of those shadows was what it was; now we understand why those shadows had just the shapes they did have and no others.

We can also say that this great bird is what produces these shadows; we now see that the shadows are caused by creatures like this; birds of this kind are responsible for the existence of those shadows. So we are attributing two kinds of relations between eagles themselves and their shadows, which we'll call the relations of **Making Intelligible** and of **Producing.**

Remember now that our example has been framed entirely within the sphere of the world, what Plato calls "the visible." So we have been discussing what falls only within the *A* and *B* portions of the Divided Line. Now we need to apply the relations between *A* and *B* to the relations between (*A* + *B*) and (*C* + *D*). In other words, we need now to talk about the relationship between the world and the Forms, between "the visible" and "the intelligible."

Let us return to our example. While we have the eagle in our care, we examine it carefully, take measurements and X rays (imagine that although we know nothing of astronomy because we never look up, our science is otherwise quite advanced), do behavioral testing, and come to understand the bird quite thoroughly. What do we learn? We learn a lot, of course, about this particular eagle (we have named him "Charlie"), but we are also learning about the *kind* of creature that produces and makes intelligible the shadows we have long observed. So we are learning about eagles in general. It is true that if we generalize from this one case only, we may make some mistakes. Charlie may in some respects not be a typical eagle, but we can ignore this complication for the moment.

If we are learning about eagles, not just about Charlie, then we could put it this way: We are getting acquainted with what makes an eagle an eagle (as opposed to an owl or an egret). This is very much like, we might reflect, coming to understand what makes pious actions pious. Socrates says that he wants to know not just which actions are pious, you remember, but what it is that *makes* them pious rather than impious. He wants to understand the Form of the Pious. So we can say that we are coming to know the Form of the Eagle. This Form is what explains or makes intelligible the fact that this particular bird is an eagle. We might go as far as to say that it is what makes Charlie an eagle; his having this Form rather than some other produces Charlie-as-eagle—is responsible for the fact that Charlie is an eagle.

It may be that Charlie is not a perfect eagle. And further acquaintance with eagles would doubtless improve our understanding of what makes an eagle an eagle, of those characteristics that constitute "eaglehood." If we were to improve our understanding of the Eagle Itself, we might well reach the same conclusion we reached about squares: that no visible eagle is a perfect example of the type or Form. Still, any particular eagle must have the defining characteristics of the species; it must, Plato says, *participate* in the Form Eagle, or it wouldn't be an eagle at all.

What is this "participation" in a Form? We can now say that it is strictly analogous to the relationship between eagle shadows and actual eagles. Actual eagles participate in the Form Eagle in this sense: The Form makes the actual eagle intelligible and accounts for its existence as an eagle. So again there are two kinds of relationships, this time between the Form Eagle and particular eagles: the relationships of Making Intelligible and of Producing. The relationship on the Divided Line between (A + B) and (C + D) is indeed analogous to the relationship between A and B.

We should remind ourselves, too, that Forms have a kind of independence actual eagles lack. Should an ecological tragedy kill all the eagles in the world, the Form Eagle would not be affected. We might never again see an eagle, but we could perfectly well still think about eagles; we could, for instance, regret their passing and recall what magnificent birds they were.* The intelligible has this kind of superiority to the visible: It endures. And this, Plato would conclude, is a sign that the Form (the object of thought) is more real than those things (the objects of sight) that participate in it. In Forms we have the proper objects of knowledge, which must itself endure.

LOWER AND HIGHER FORMS

Let us return to the Divided Line. We need to note that the section of the Line representing the Forms is itself divided. There are, it seems, two kinds of Forms, just as there are two kinds of things in the visible world (likenesses and things). We need to understand why Plato thinks so and why he thinks this distinction is important.

He takes an example from mathematics to explain the leftward portion of the intelligible section of the line (C).

> I'm sure you're aware that practitioners of geometry, arithmetic, and so on take for granted things like numerical oddness and evenness, the geometrical figures, the three kinds of angle, and any other things of that sort which are relevant to a given subject. They act as if they know about these things, treat them as basic, and don't feel any further need to explain them either to themselves or to anyone else, on the grounds that there is nothing unclear about them. They make them the starting points for their investigations. (*R* 510c, d)

The important idea here is "taking for granted." When we thought about doubling the square, we took the ideas of Square, Triangle, Double, and Equal for granted. Operating in the leftward reaches of the right "half" of the divided line (section C), we used these Forms as "starting points" for thinking about the square Socrates drew in the sand.

Actually, the movements go like this: Beginning with the sand square, we hypothetically posit Forms to account for it. That is, we move *rightward* on the line from the visible to the intelligible. Then, taking these Forms for granted, we produce

---

*Those of you familiar with *Star Trek IV: The Voyage Home* may recall that Kirk and Spock in the twenty-third century could still think about humpback whales, long after they became extinct.

an explanation of the visible phenomenon. Explanation moves *leftward*. But we can now see that the Forms we posit as hypotheses—the Square, the Triangle, etc.—themselves need to be explained. And so we need to move rightward again, this time into the highest section of the line. Think about the Square again. The Square is *explained and produced* by Forms like Plane, Line, Straight, Angle, and Equal. (A square is a plane figure bounded by four equal straight lines joined by right angles.) In this kind of reasoning, reasoning that explains a Form, there is no reliance on sensory input. In moving to section *D* we move from Forms to more basic Forms in a purely intelligible fashion.

So the Forms in *D* make intelligible the Forms in *C*. Again, explanation goes right to left. But there must come a point where this pattern of explanation cannot be used anymore, where making intelligible can't operate by appealing to something still more basic. When you get to the end of the Divided Line, whatever is there will serve as the explanation for everything to the left of it. But that must be intelligible in itself.

Plato calls the construction of lower Forms "science." The scientist examines the actual things in the visible world (Charlie or the sand square) and posits explanations of them in terms of hypothetical Forms. Things that explain shadows are now treated by the scientist just as the shadows were—as likenesses of something still more real, to be explained by appeal to Forms. A Form loses its merely hypothetical character when it is explained in terms of higher Forms. We then understand why that Form must be as it is. And this purely conceptual process of moving from Forms to Forms, and eventually to the highest Form—the First Principle—Plato calls "dialectic."* (see *R* 511b, c)

Dialectic, then, is a purely intellectual discipline, no longer relying on the world of sense at all. It is a search for the ultimate presuppositions of all our hypothetical explanations and proceeds solely through awareness of Forms. If by such dialectical

reasoning we should come to an ultimate presupposition, we will, Plato assures us, have discovered "the starting point for everything" (*R* 511b).

We obviously need to explore what Plato has to say about this Starting Point. But first let us amplify our understanding of the Divided Line (see the following chart) by adding some further characterizations. Notice the difference in labels given to the sections of the line on the second and third levels down. The second level characterizes reality in terms of what it is. These labels are *metaphysical* in nature. The third level (written in capital letters) characterizes reality in terms of how it is apprehended, so these labels have an *epistemological* flavor to them. (The first level is also epistemological, but less fine-grained than the third.) Here we see how intimately Plato's theory of knowledge is related to his theory of reality. We add two directional indicators to show that things get more real as you progress along the line from *A* to *D*, and that items to the right are responsible for the existence of items to the left and provide explanations for them.

The sciences, we can now say, are only stages on the way to true and final understanding. They are not yet "that place which, once reached, is traveller's rest and journey's end" (*R* 532e). The sciences do grasp reality to some extent; but because they do not themselves lead us to the Starting Point, Plato thinks scientists still live in a kind of dream world. "There's no chance of their having a conscious glimpse of reality as long as they refuse to disturb the things they take for granted and remain incapable of explaining them" (*R* 533c).

It is for dialectic to give this reasoned account of first things. Its

> quest for certainty causes it to uproot the things it takes for granted in the course of its journey, which takes it towards an actual starting-point. When the mind's eye is literally buried deep in mud, far from home, dialectic gently extracts it and guides it upwards. (*R* 533c–d)

Let us note that dialectic, in leading us to the Starting Point, is supposed to give us certainty. This is very important to Plato; indeed, the quest for certainty is a crucial theme in most of Western philosophy. Why should Plato suppose that acquaintance with

---

*Note that the term "dialectic" is used in a narrower sense here than that discussed in connection with Socratic question-and-answer method. For a comparison, see pp. 65–66.

```
           A                 B                 C                 D
  |────────────────|─────────────────|─────────────────|─────────────────|

  ├ - - - - - - - the visible - - - - - - - - ┼ - - - - - the intelligible - - - - - ┤

  ├ - - - likenesses - - - ┼ - - - things - - - ┼ - -lower forms- - ┼ - - higher - - ┤

  ├ - -IMAGINATION- - ┼ - - OPINION - - ┼ - -SCIENCES- - ┼ -DIALECTIC· ┤
```

────────────────────────────► BEING MORE REAL ────────────────────────────►
◄──────────────── PRODUCING AND EXPLAINING ◄────────────────

the Starting Point will be accompanied by certainty, by "traveller's rest and journey's end"? Because it is no longer hypothetical. The truth of the Starting Point need no longer be supported by principles beyond itself. It does not cry out for explanation; it does not beckon us on beyond itself. Its truth is evident. To see it—with "the mind's eye"—is to understand. Here we need no longer anxiously ask, "But is this really true?" Here we know we are not just dreaming. Here the soul can "rest."*

The Form of the Good

The examples we have considered recently—doubling the square, Charlie, and the Forms they participate in—are examples from mathematics and the world of natural science. But we should not forget that there are other Forms as well: Piety, Morality, Beauty, and the Good. We'll soon explore the dialectic showing that the Form of Morality participates in the Form of the Good and say at least something about Beauty. But if we want to illuminate Plato's Starting Point, it is to the Form of the Good that we shall have to look directly.

Let us begin by asking why Plato should think of Goodness Itself as that Form to which dialectic will lead us in our search for the ultimate presupposition. As we consider this, we should remember that in moving higher and higher on the Divided Line we are always gaining clearer, less questionable explanations of why something is the way it is.

In the dialogue *Phaedo,* Plato relates a conversation that Socrates had with his friends on the day of his death. At one point Socrates says,

> When I was young . . . I was remarkably keen on the kind of wisdom known as natural science; it seemed to me splendid to know the reasons for each thing, why each thing comes to be, why it perishes, and why it exists. (*Phaedo* 96a)

He relates that he was unable to make much progress toward discovering those causes and became discouraged until hearing one day someone read from a book of Anaxagoras.* Socrates heard that Mind directs and is the cause of everything.

> Now this was a reason that pleased me; it seemed to me, somehow, to be a good thing that intelligence should be the reason for everything. And I thought that, if that's the case, then intelligence in ordering all things must order them and place each individual thing in the best way possible; so if anyone wanted to find out the reason why each thing comes to be or perishes or exists, this is what he must find out about it: how is it best for that thing to exist, or to act or be acted upon in any way? (*Phaedo* 97c–d)

Socrates procured the books of Anaxagoras and read them eagerly. But he was disappointed. For when it came down to cases, Anaxagoras cited as causes the standard elements of Greek nature philosophy—air and water and such.

> In fact, he seemed to me to be in exactly the position of someone who said that all Socrates' actions were performed with his intelligence, and who

─────────

*Compare Heraclitus on how the many who do not recognize the *logos* live as though they were asleep, lost in a dream-world of their own making. See p. 22.

─────────

*A pre-Socratic nature philosopher. You may recall that Socrates mentions him in the speech at his trial: *Apology* 26d.

then tried to give the reasons for each of my actions by saying, first, that the reason why I'm now sitting here is that my body consists of bones and sinews, and the bones are hard and separated from each other by joints, whereas the sinews, which can be tightened and relaxed, surround the bones, together with the flesh and the skin that holds them together; so that when the bones are turned in their sockets, the sinews by stretching and tensing enable me somehow to bend my limbs at this moment, and that's the reason why I'm sitting here bent this way. (*Phaedo* 98c–d)

Are these facts about his body the true explanation of why Socrates is sitting there in prison? It does not seem to Socrates to even be the right kind of explanation. These considerations do not even mention

the true reasons: that Athenians judged it better to condemn me, and therefore I in my turn have judged it better to sit here, and thought it more just to stay behind and submit to such penalty as they may ordain. . . . Fancy being unable to distinguish two different things: the reason proper, and that without which the reason could never be a reason! (*Phaedo* 98c–99b)

Why is Socrates sitting in prison? The true explanation is that the Athenians decided it was better to condemn him and that Socrates has decided that not escaping was for the best. The behaviors of the various bodily parts are not irrelevant, but they are not the "true reason." They are just conditions necessary for that real reason to have its effect. We do not get a satisfactory explanation until we reach one that mentions what is *good,* or *better,* or *best.*

This suggests that explanations in which we can "rest" must be framed in terms of what is good. Because explanations proceed by citing Forms, the ultimate explanation of everything must be in terms of the **Form of the Good**. The Form of the Good, then, must play the part of the Starting Point. In the final analysis, to understand why anything is as it is, we must see that it is so because it participates in this Form, because it is good for it to be so.

That is why Plato thinks the Form of the Good is the Starting Point. But what is it? To call this Starting Point the Form of the Good is not very illuminating. It doesn't tell us any more than Socrates

knows about the pious at the beginning of his examination of Euthyphro. Socrates knows that he is looking for the Form of the Pious, but he also knows that he doesn't know what that is. In just this sense, we might now ask Plato, "What is this Form which plays such a crucial role? Explain it to us."

At this point, Plato disappoints us; he tells us plainly that he cannot give such an explanation.* He says that "our knowledge of goodness is inadequate" (*R* 505a). When he is pressed to discuss it, he says, "I'm afraid it'll be more than I can manage" (*R* 506d). But he does agree to describe "something which seems to me to be the child of goodness and to bear a very strong resemblance to it" (*R* 506e).

Consider sight, Plato suggests. What makes sight possible? Well, the eyes, for one thing. But eyes alone see nothing; there must also be the various colored objects to be seen. Even this is not enough, for eyes do not see colors in the dark. To eyes and objects we must add light. Where does light come from? From the sun. It is the sun, then, that is

the child of goodness I was talking about. . . . It is a counterpart to its father, goodness. As goodness stands in the intelligible realm to intelligence and the things we know, so in the visible realm the sun stands to sight and the things we see. . . .

What I'm saying is that it's goodness which gives the things we know their truth and makes it possible for people to have knowledge. It is responsible for knowledge and truth, and you should think of it as being within the intelligible realm, but you shouldn't identify it with knowledge and truth, otherwise you'll be wrong: for all their value, it is even more valuable. (*R* 508b–509a)

Knowledge, truth, and beauty are all good things. For Plato this means that they participate in the Form of the Good. This Form alone makes it intelligible that there should be such good things. You might ask in wonderment, why is there such a thing as knowledge at all? What accounts for that? If Plato is right here, you will not find a satisfactory answer to your question until you discover why it

---

*This reticence on Plato's part contrasts dramatically with the confidence many have since displayed in giving us their accounts of what is good. These accounts, of course, do not all agree with one another.

is for the best that knowledge should exist; and discovering that is equivalent to seeing its participation in the Form of Goodness Itself.

However, although knowledge is a good thing, Plato cautions us that it must not be thought of as identical with Goodness. It is no more identical with Goodness than Charlie is identical with the Form Eagle. That Form explains Charlie, but, as we saw, it has an existence quite independent of Charlie. The Form of the Good surpasses all the other Forms as well as the visible world in beauty and honor. If we think again about the Divided Line, we can now say that the Form of the Good is at the point farthest to the right of that Line, at the very end of section *D*. It makes intelligible everything to the left of it.

This ultimate Form not only makes everything else intelligible, it also is responsible for the very existence of everything else.

> I think you'll agree that the ability to be seen is not the only gift the sun gives to the things we see. It is also the source of their generation, growth, and nourishment. . . .
>
> And it isn't only the known-ness of the things we know which is conferred upon them by goodness, but also their reality and their being, although goodness isn't actually the state of being, but surpasses being in majesty and might. (*R* 509b)

Just as the sun is responsible for the world of sight, is actually its cause, so the Form of the Good is the cause of the reality of everything else; it both *produces* and *makes intelligible* everything that is. To emphasize the uniqueness of this Form, Plato goes so far as to say that it "surpasses being." Since we usually understand what is beyond being to be nothing at all, this is a dark saying. And Plato does not do much to make it clear.*

Let us pause and see what Plato claims to have accomplished. He has proved, he believes, that we

do have knowledge; so, wholesale skepticism is a mistake. This knowledge is not dependent on what individuals or cultures happen to think; so, relativism is a mistake. Moreover, knowledge must have objects that endure; so, this knowledge must be of realities other than those in the world. So, there are Forms, whose being is eternal and unchanging. Knowledge of these Forms enables us to understand not only them and their relations to each other but also the things in the world, which owe their being and characteristics to participation in these Forms. And supreme among the Forms is that of Goodness. Therefore, atomism is a mistake.

But how does it follow that atomism is a mistake? Recall the central claim of the atomists: What exists is made up of atoms and the void. Nothing else. Plato, however, thinks he has proved that there are Forms, indeed, that these are the most real things of all. And Forms are radically different from atoms because each atom is a tiny particular thing and a Form can be shared by many particulars.

Moreover, Democritus holds that events happen necessarily, mechanically, according to how the atoms happen to combine and fall apart again. No purpose, no goal, no direction toward the best can be discerned in the world.* But Plato believes he has shown us that a complete explanation must be like the one given by Socrates in prison; it will have to explain why what happens is for the best and so will involve the Form of the Good. Science, pursued to its basic presuppositions, reveals a world with a moral and religious dimension.

It follows that reality is not, as Democritus thinks, indifferent to values; a kind of piety toward reality is quite in order. Democritus would overthrow the traditional religion altogether. Plato is no happier than his philosophical predecessors with the Homeric picture of the gods; belief in such gods is insupportable. Yet religious attitudes can be preserved. We shall soon see how Plato's metaphysical viewpoint—that values are realities, too—affects what he says about practical matters such as morality and the good state. But first we need to conclude this part of our consideration with his most famous story, the **Myth of the Cave**.

---

*It is as if the Form of the Good were not the point farthest to the right on the Divided Line but were pushed right off the end. Plato seems to be saying that this Form is strictly incomparable to everything else, both other Forms and the world. Yet it is responsible for them all. Later Christian thinkers took this as an "anticipation" of the Judeo–Christian concepts of God and creation. See, for instance, St. Augustine, pp. 235–238.

---

*See pp. 34–35.

1. Draw Plato's Divided Line and explain what each of its parts represents. (Close the book, then try to draw and label it.)
2. What two relationships exist between a Form and some visible thing that "participates" in it?
3. What is the distinction Plato draws between "science" and "dialectic," and how does this relate to the distinction between hypotheses and first principles?
4. What is the argument that purports to show that the Starting Point—the rightmost point on the Divided Line—is the Form of the Good?
5. How do Plato's arguments up to this point help him achieve his aims?

The Love of Wisdom

There is a progress in the soul that corresponds to the degrees of reality in things. This idea is indicated in the various sections of the Divided Line. Contemplating the images of worldly things is analogous to the use of *imagination;* indeed, mental images are quite like shadows and mirror images in their dependence on things. About things and events in the world we can have probable beliefs or *opinions.* When we reason about them we are hypothesizing Forms; here is the domain of *science.* Finally, we reach *understanding* through the process of dialectic, which takes us upward to the highest Forms on which all the others depend.

We can think of this progress as progress toward **wisdom**.

WHAT WISDOM IS

A wise person would understand everything in the light of the Forms, particularly the Form of the Good. To produce such wise individuals is the aim of education. The progress toward wisdom is illustrated for us in a dramatic myth told in the seventh book of the *Republic.* As you read it, keep the Divided Line and the analogy of the sun in mind.

"Imagine people living in a cavernous cell down under the ground; at the far end of the cave, a long way off, there's an entrance open to the outside world. They've been there since childhood, with their legs and necks tied up in a way which keeps them in one place and allows them to look only straight ahead, but not to turn their heads. There's firelight burning a long way further up the cave behind them, and up the slope between the fire and the prisoners there's a road, beside which you should imagine a low wall has been built—like the partition which conjurors place between themselves and their audience and above which they show their tricks."

"All right," he said.

"Imagine also that there are people on the other side of this wall who are carrying all sorts of artefacts, human statuettes, and animal models carved in stone and wood and all kinds of materials stick out over the wall; and as you'd expect, some of the people talk as they carry these objects along, while others are silent."

"This is a strange picture you're painting," he said, "with strange prisoners."

"They're no different from us," I said. "I mean, in the first place, do you think they'd see anything of themselves and one another except the shadows cast by the fire on to the cave wall directly opposite them?"

"Of course not," he said. "They're forced to spend their lives without moving their heads."

"And what about the objects which were being carried along? Won't they only see their shadows as well?"

"Naturally."

"Now, suppose they were able to talk to one another: don't you think they'd assume that their words applied to what they saw passing by in front of them?"

"They couldn't think otherwise."

"And what if sound echoed off the prison wall opposite them? When any of the passers-by spoke, don't you think they'd be bound to assume that the sound came from a passing shadow?"

"I'm absolutely certain of it," he said.

"All in all, then," I said, "the shadows of artefacts would constitute the only reality people in this situation would recognize."

"That's absolutely inevitable," he agreed.

"What do you think would happen, then," I asked, "if they were set free from their bonds and cured of their inanity? What would it be like if they found that happening to them? Imagine that one of them has been set free and is suddenly made to stand up, to turn his head and walk, and to look towards the firelight. It hurts him to do all this and he's too dazzled to be capable of making out the objects whose shadows he'd formerly been look-ing at. And suppose someone tells him that what he's been seeing all this time has no substance, and that he's now closer to reality and is seeing more accurately, because of the greater reality of the things in front of his eyes—what do you imagine his reaction would be? And what do you think he'd say if he were shown any of the passing objects and had to respond to being asked what it was? Don't you think he'd be bewildered, and would think that there was more reality in what he'd been seeing be-fore than in what he was being shown now?"

"Far more," he said.

"And if he were forced to look at the actual firelight, don't you think it would hurt his eyes? Don't you think he'd turn away and run back to the things he could make out, and would take the truth of the matter to be that these things are clearer than what he was being shown?"

"Yes," he agreed.

"And imagine him being dragged forcibly away from there up the rough, steep slope," I went on, "without being released until he's been pulled out into the sunlight. Wouldn't this treatment cause him pain and distress? And once he's reached the sunlight, he wouldn't be able to see a single one of the things which are currently taken to be real, would he, because his eyes would be overwhelmed by the sun's beams?"

"No, he wouldn't," he answered, "not straight away."

"He wouldn't be able to see things up on the surface of the earth, I suppose, until he'd got used to his situation. At first, it would be shadows that he could most easily make out, then he'd move on to the reflections of people and so on in water, and later he'd be able to see the actual things themselves. Next he'd feast his eyes on the heavenly bodies and the heavens themselves, which would be easier at night: he'd look at the light of the stars and the moon, rather than at the sun and sunlight during the daytime."

"Of course."

"And at last, I imagine, he'd be able to discern and feast his eyes on the sun—not the displaced im-age of the sun in water or elsewhere, but the sun on its own, in its proper place."

"Yes, he'd inevitably come to that," he said.

"After that, he'd start to think about the sun and he'd deduce that it is the source of the seasons and the yearly cycle, that the whole of the visible realm is its domain, and that in a sense everything which he and his peers used to see is its responsibility."

"Yes, that would obviously be the next point he'd come to," he agreed.

"Now, if he recalled the cell where he'd origi-nally lived and what passed for knowledge there and his former fellow prisoners, don't you think he'd feel happy about his own altered circumstances, and sorry for them?"

"Definitely."

"Suppose that the prisoners used to assign pres-tige and credit to one another, in the sense that they rewarded speed at recognizing the shadows as they passed, and gain the ability to remember which ones normally come earlier and later and at the same time as which other ones, and expertise at using this as a basis for guessing which ones would ar-rive next. Do you think our former prisoner would covet these honours and would envy the people who had status and power there, or would he much prefer, as Homer describes it, 'being a slave labour-ing for someone else—someone without property', and would put up with anything at all, in fact, rather than share their beliefs and their life?"

"Yes, I think he'd go through anything rather than live that way," he said.

"Here's something else I'd like your opinion about," I said. "If he went back underground and sat down again in the same spot, wouldn't the sud-den transition from the sunlight mean that his eyes would be overwhelmed by darkness?"

"Certainly."

"Now, the process of adjustment would be quite long this time, and suppose that before his eyes had settled down and while he wasn't seeing well, he had once again to compete against those same old prisoners at identifying those shadows. Wouldn't he make a fool of himself? Wouldn't they say that he'd come back from his upward journey with his eyes ruined, and that it wasn't even worth trying to go up there? And wouldn't they—if they could—grab hold of anyone who tried to set them free and take them up there, and kill him?"

"They certainly would," he said. (R 514a–517a)

Any such myth is subject to multiple interpreta-tions. But let us see if we can, in light of what we know of Plato so far, identify the various stages of the ascent to wisdom. The people fettered in the cave, seeing only the shadows of things, are like those who gain their understanding of things from the poets, from Homer and Hesiod. Or, in our day, they are like those who get their impressions of the world by paying attention to the media—to movies, to the soaps, to television news programs. They see only images of reality—reflections, interpretations.

Those who climb up to the wall, on which are carried various items casting the shadows, are like those who can look directly on things in the visible world. The fire, I think, represents the physical sun, lighting up these perceptible realities so they can be apprehended. Looking on them directly reveals how fuzzy and indistinct the shadows of them on the wall actually were.

But to really understand these things it is necessary to climb higher, out of the cave altogether. This move is like the transition on the Divided Line between the visible world and the intelligible world; it is the transition from things to Forms. The sun outside the cave represents the Form of the Good, just as it does in the **Analogy of the Sun**. First our adventurer can only see the lower Forms, reflections of the "Sun." But gradually, through dialectic, he can come to see the Form of the Good itself.

And what would happen if someone like that, who had come to understand things to that extent, who saw things as they really were and understood their participation in Goodness—what would happen if that person were to return to the cave? Can there be any doubt that Plato is thinking of Socrates here?

To love wisdom is to be motivated to leave the Cave. At each stage, Plato emphasizes how difficult, even painful, the struggle for enlightenment is. It is much easier, much more comfortable, to remain a prisoner in relative darkness and occupy oneself with what are, in reality, only shadows—content to be entertained by the passing show of images.

The Divided Line

A   B   C   D

The myth gives us an interesting picture of education. **Education**, Plato says, is not

> capable of doing what some people promise. They claim to introduce knowledge into a mind which doesn't have it, as if they were introducing sight into eyes which are blind. . . .
>
> An implication of what we're saying at the moment, however, . . . is that the capacity for knowledge is present in everyone's mind. If you can imagine an eye that can turn from darkness to brightness only if the body as a whole turns, then our organ of understanding is like that. Its orientation has to be accompanied by turning the mind as a whole away from the world of becoming, until it becomes capable of bearing the sight of real being and reality at its most bright, which we're saying is goodness. . . .
>
> That's what education should be, . . . the art of orientation. Educators should devise the simplest and most effective methods of turning minds around. It shouldn't be the art of implanting sight in the organ, but should proceed on the understanding that the organ already has the capacity, but is improperly aligned and isn't facing the right way.
> (R 518b–d)

We should be reminded here of Socrates and the slave boy. The capacity to understand is already there. Socrates just needs to point the boy in the right direction, and that he does with his questions. Education is not stuffing the mind with facts, Plato tells us, but turning the soul to face reality, trusting that the student will recognize the truth when confronted by it. Recall Socrates' claim that he has never *taught* anyone anything.* Here is a whole philosophy of education in a nutshell.

This "turning minds around" is not easy to do, however. The prisoners in the cave are not happy to be told that they suffer from an illusion. Wisdom can be resisted. If we can resist this turning of the soul and be comfortable in the cave, focused on the pleasures of feasting, drinking, and so on, what motivation is there to engage in a struggle that Plato insists is both difficult and dangerous? We need now to talk not just of what wisdom is, but of the **love of wisdom**.

LOVE AND WISDOM

The theme of Plato's dialogue *Symposium,* from which Alcibiades' tribute to the character of Socrates was taken,* is love. After dinner each guest is obliged to make a speech in praise of love. When Socrates' turn comes, he protests that he cannot make such a flattering speech as the others have made, but he can, if they like, tell the truth about love.† They urge him to do so.

Socrates claims to have learned about love from a wise woman named **Diotima**, who instructed him by the same question-and-answer method he now uses on others.‡ I'll abbreviate the speech in which Socrates relates her instruction, keeping the question-and-answer mode. This very rich discussion of love is found in *Symposium* 198a–212b.

Q: Is love the love of something or not?

A: Of something.

Q: Does love long for what it loves?

A: Certainly.

Q: Is this something that love has, or something love lacks?

A: It must be what love lacks, for no one longs for what he or she has.

Q: What does love love?

A: Beauty.

Q: Then love must lack beauty?

A: Apparently so.

Q: Is love ugly, then?

A: Not necessarily. For just as opinion is a middle term between ignorance and knowledge, so love may be between beauty and ugliness.

---

*See *Apology* 33b and Chapter 5, pp. 103–104.

*Review pp. 62–63.

†This should remind you of the contrast Socrates draws between rhetoric and his own plain speaking at the very beginning of the *Apology*. About love, it must be noted that the Greeks had distinct words for several different kinds of love; in this their language was more discriminating than ours. The kind of love Socrates is here discussing is *eros,* from which our term "erotic" is drawn.

‡Although women are not prominent among the ancient philosophers whose works have been preserved, there are hints here and there that they played a larger role in the pursuit of wisdom than is superficially apparent. See Kathleen Wider, "Women Philosophers in the Ancient Greek World: Donning the Mantle," *Hypatia* 1, no. 1 (Spring 1986).

Q: Is love a god?

A: No. For the gods lack nothing in the way of beauty or happiness. For that reason, the gods do not love beauty or happiness either. Nor do the gods love wisdom, for they are wise and do not lack it.

Q: What is love, then?

A: Midway between mortals and the gods, love is a spirit that connects the earthly and the heavenly. [Think of the world and the Forms.]

Q: What is the origin of love?

A: Love is the child of Need and Resourcefulness (the son of Craft). It is a combination of longing for what one does not have and ingenuity in seeking it.

Q: But what, more exactly, is it that love seeks?

A: Love seeks the beautiful. And the good.

Q: To what end?

A: To make them its own.

Q: And what will the lover gain by making the beautiful and the good his own?

A: Happiness.

Q: Does everyone seek happiness?

A: Of course.

Q: Then is everyone always in love?

A: Yes and no. We tend to give the name of love to only one sort of love. Actually, love "includes every kind of longing for happiness and the good." So those who long for the good in every field—business, athletics, philosophy—are also lovers.

Q: For how long does a lover want to possess that good that he or she longs for?

A: Certainly not for a limited time only. To think so would be equivalent to wanting to be happy for only a short time. So the lover must want the good to be his or hers forever.

Q: How could a mortal attain this?

A: By becoming immortal.

Q: So a mortal creature does all it can "to put on immortality"?

A: Evidently.

Q: Could this be why lovers are interested not just in beauty but in procreation by means of such beauty?

A: Yes. It is by breeding another individual as like itself as possible that mortal creatures like animals and humans attain as much of immortality as is possible for them. Such a creature cannot, like the gods, remain the same throughout eternity; it can only leave behind new life to fill the vacancy that is left in its species by its death.

Q: Is there any other way to approach immortality?

A: Yes, by attaining the "endless fame" that heroes and great benefactors of humankind attain. Think, for example, of Achilles and Homer and Solon.

Q: So some lovers beget children and raise a family, and others "bear things of the spirit . . . wisdom and all her sister virtues," especially those relevant to "the ordering of society, . . . justice and moderation"?

A: Yes. And the latter will be especially concerned to share these goods with friends and, with them, to educate each other in wisdom.

Q: Is there a natural progression of love?

A: Yes.

At this point, we need to hear Plato's words themselves. Diotima is speaking as if someone were to be initiated into a cult devoted to love.

> Well then, she began, the candidate for this initiation cannot, if his efforts are to be rewarded, begin too early to devote himself to the beauties of the body. First of all, if his preceptor instructs him as he should, he will fall in love with the beauty of one individual body, so that his passion may give life to noble discourse. Next he must consider how nearly related the beauty of any one body is to the beauty of any other, when he will see that if he is to devote himself to loveliness of form it will be absurd to deny that the beauty of each and every body is the same. Having reached this point, he must set himself to be the lover of every lovely body, and bring his passion for the one into due proportion by deeming it of little or of no importance.
>
> Next he must grasp that the beauties of the body are as nothing to the beauties of the soul, so that wherever he meets with spiritual loveliness, even in the husk of an unlovely body, he will find it beautiful enough to fall in love with and to cherish—and beautiful enough to quicken in his heart a longing for such discourse as tends toward the building of a noble nature. And from this he will be led to contemplate the beauty of laws and institutions. And when he discovers how nearly every kind of beauty is akin to every other he will conclude that the beauty of the body is not, after all, of so great moment.
>
> And next, his attention should be diverted from institutions to the sciences, so that he may know the beauty of every kind of knowledge. . . . And,

turning his eyes toward the open sea of beauty, he will find in such contemplation the seed of the most fruitful discourse and the loftiest thought, and reap a golden harvest of philosophy, until, confirmed and strengthened, he will come upon one single form of knowledge, the knowledge of the beauty I am about to speak of.

And here, she said, you must follow me as closely as you can.

Whoever has been initiated so far in the mysteries of Love and has viewed all these aspects of the beautiful in due succession, is at last drawing near the final revelation. And now, Socrates, there bursts upon him that wondrous vision which is the very soul of the beauty he has toiled so long for. It is an everlasting loveliness which neither comes nor goes, which neither flowers nor fades, for such beauty is the same on every hand, the same then as now, here as there, this way as that way, the same to every worshiper as it is to every other. (*Symposium* 210a–211a)

These are the steps, Plato tells us, that a resourceful lover takes. It is important to recognize that he sees these as making up a natural progression; there is nothing arbitrary about this series. In discussing these stages, let us remember that one can love in ways other than sexual. A lover, then, is someone who lacks that which will make him or her happy. What will make the lover happy is to possess the beautiful and the good—forever. For that the lover yearns. It is the lover's resourcefulness, propelled by longing, that moves the lover up the ladder of love. At each rung the lover is only partially satisfied and is therefore powerfully motivated to discover whether there might be something still more satisfying.

Being in the world, the lover naturally begins in the world. His or her first object is some beautiful body. But he or she will soon discover that the beauty in this body is not unique to that individual. It is shared by every beautiful body. What shall the lover do then? Although Plato does not say so explicitly, we might conjecture that at this point it is easy for the lover to go wrong by trying to possess each of these bodies in the same way as he or she longed to possess the first one—like Don Juan. We might think of it like this. Don Juan (with 1,003 conquests in Spain alone) has moved beyond the first stage of devotion to just one lovely body. He now tries to devote to each the same

love that he devoted to the one. This is bound to be unsatisfying; if a single one does not satisfy, there is no reason to think that many ones will satisfy.

How does Plato describe the correct step at this point? The lover of "every lovely body" must "bring his passion for the one into due proportion by deeming it of little or of no importance." Rather than trying to multiply the same passion many times, the discovery of beauty in many bodies must occasion what we might call a "sublimation" of the original passion. It must be transferred to a more appropriate kind of object. Indeed, it is at this point that the lover first becomes dimly aware of the Form of Beauty.* The resourcefulness of love makes it clear that only this sort of object is going to satisfy; only this sort of object endures.

The lover, moreover, discovers that a beautiful soul is even more lovely than a beautiful body, finding it so much more satisfying that he or she will "fall in love with" and "cherish" a beautiful soul even though it is found "in the husk of an unlovely body." (Could Plato here be thinking of the physical ugliness of Socrates?) The lover will then come to love *all* beautiful souls.

The next step is to "contemplate the beauty of laws and institutions." Presumably the transition from lovely individual souls to a pleasing social order is a small one. What explains, accounts for, the existence of lovely souls? They must have been well brought up. And that can happen only in a moderate, harmonious, and just social order. The beauty of a good state comes into view, and we move one more step away from the original passion for an individual beautiful body; when this stage is reached, the lover "concludes that beauty of the body is not, after all, of so great moment."

Once in the sphere of "spiritual loveliness," the lover comes to long for knowledge. Why? It is not difficult to see why if you keep the Divided Line in mind. What is it that makes intelligible and produces good social institutions? Surely they must be

---

*Recall the doctrine of learning by recollection (p. 103). The beautiful individual is the "occasion" for recollecting what the soul previously knew, Beauty Itself. Only by a prior acquaintance with this Form can the lover recognize the beloved as beautiful.

founded, not on opinion, but on knowledge. Plato speaks movingly here of "the beauty of every kind of knowledge," and supposes that the lover—not yet satisfied—will explore all the sciences. Here the lover will find an "open sea of beauty," in contemplation of which he or she will be able to bring forth "the most fruitful discourse and the loftiest thought, and reap a golden harvest of philosophy."

But even this is not the last stage. And we must note that Diotima cautions Socrates at this point to "follow . . . as closely as you can." The final stage, then, must be difficult to grasp. Indeed, those who have not attained it might well be unable to appreciate it fully. It is, in fact, a kind of mystical vision of the Form of Beauty Itself.* Note the rapturously emotional language Plato uses here. There can be little doubt that he is describing an experience that he himself had, one to which he ascribes a supreme value.

It is called a "wondrous vision," an "everlasting loveliness." Like all the Forms, the Form of Beauty is eternal. The religious character of the vision is indicated by the term "worshiper," which Plato applies to the lover who attains this "final revelation."

"Beauty crowds me till I die.
    Beauty mercy have on me
But if I expire today
    Let it be in sight of thee—"
                Emily Dickinson (1830–1886)

A diagram may make the stages of love more vivid (see "The Ladder of Love"). Note that the steps of the ladder are related to each other in precisely the same way as the sections of the Divided Line or the ascent from the Cave. Climbing the ladder gets the lover more and more reality, and the higher rungs explain the lower.

We began this discussion of love in order to find an answer to a question. Why, we wondered, would anyone be motivated to leave the Cave and

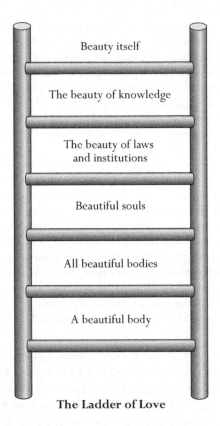

Beauty itself

The beauty of knowledge

The beauty of laws and institutions

Beautiful souls

All beautiful bodies

A beautiful body

The Ladder of Love

make the difficult ascent to the sunlight, leaving behind the easy pleasures of worldly life? We now have Plato's answer. It is because we are all lovers.* We all want to be happy, to possess the beautiful and the good, forever. This is what we lack and long for. And to the extent of our resourcefulness, we will come to see that this passion cannot be satisfied by the possession of one beautiful body or even of many. We will be drawn out of the Cave toward the sun, toward the beautiful and the good in themselves, by the very nature of love. Plato is convinced that within each of us there is motivation that, if followed, will lead us beyond shadows to the Forms. The educator does not need to implant that in us; it is already there. All the educator needs to do is point us in the right direction.

In Plato's discussion of the love of wisdom we have an example of dialectic at work—the very

---

*The language Plato uses to describe this experience is remarkably similar to the language of Christian mystics describing the "beatific vision" of God.

---

*Actually, this is not quite Plato's view. He thinks there are distinctly different sorts of people, and only some of them are lovers of wisdom. But I take here the more democratic view and give you all the benefit of the doubt!

dialectic that occupies the fourth section on the Divided Line. We see Plato exploring the nature of *eros,* teasing out of the Form of Love its intimate connections with the Forms of Knowledge and Beauty. In one sense we all know beauty when we see it; the wolf whistle of the construction worker when the attractive woman passes by is proof of that. But if we truly understand *eros,* Plato tells us, we will see that its combination of need and resource must lead us beyond its immediate objects to the highest levels of intellectual activity and spirituality.

Wisdom, which for Plato is equivalent to seeing everything in the light of the Forms, particularly in the light of the highest Forms of Beauty and Goodness, is something we all need, lack, and want. Wisdom alone will satisfy. Only wisdom, where the soul actually participates in the eternality of the Forms, will in the end bring us as close to immortality as mortals can possibly get.

But this conclusion is not yet quite accurate. As stated, it assumes the Homeric picture of human beings as mortal through and through. This is not Plato's considered view, and we need now to inquire into his theory of the soul.

---

1. Relate the Myth of the Cave.
2. What does an educator do for those he or she "teaches"?
3. What is love (*eros*)?
4. Sketch the "ladder" of love.

The Soul

Plato thought about his central problems throughout a long life. And it is apparent, particularly in his doctrine of the **soul,** that his thought developed complexities unimagined early on. Scholars dispute whether this development involves some inconsistency, whether his later thought is in conflict with the earlier. Some say yes, some say no. There is no doubt that there is at least a tension between the earlier and the later views of the soul. In this introductory treatment I will ignore these problems, presenting a picture of the soul that will be oversimplified and less than complete but true in essentials to Plato's views on the subject.[5]

THE IMMORTALITY OF THE SOUL

At the end of his defense before the jury, Socrates concludes that "there is good hope that death is a blessing." He thinks one of two things must be true: Either death is a dreamless sleep, or we survive the death of the body and can converse with those who died before. But he does not try to decide between them.*

Plato offers arguments to demonstrate that the latter is the true possibility—that the soul is immortal. We find such an argument in the story of Socrates and the slave boy.† According to Socrates, the boy is able to recognize the truth when it is before him because he is remembering or recollecting what he was earlier acquainted with. But if that is so, then he—or rather his soul—must have existed before he was born, and in such a state that he was familiar with the Forms. Similarly, in judging two numbers to be equal we are using a concept that we could not have gained from experience, for no two worldly things are ever exactly equal. Plato concludes that

> it must, surely, have been before we began to see and hear and use the other senses that we got knowledge of the equal itself, of what it is, if we were going to refer the equals from our sense-perceptions to it, supposing that all things are doing their best to be like it, but are inferior to it. (*Phaedo* 75b)

If we had knowledge of the Equal "before we began to see and hear and use the other senses," then we must have been acquainted with this Form before our birth.

We may have doubts about the adequacy of this argument for the preexistence of the soul; if we could give another explanation of how we come to know the truth or of how we develop ideal concepts such as "equal," it might be seriously undermined. But even if it were a sound argument, it would not yet prove that the soul is immortal. For even if our souls do antedate the beginnings of our bodies, it is still possible that they dissipate when

---

*See *Apology* 40a–41c.
†In *Meno* 82b–86b.

our bodies do (or some time after). In that case, the soul would still be mortal.

Plato considers this possibility, but he has other arguments. Recall Socrates in his prison cell. Why is he there? As we have seen, it is not because his body has made certain movements rather than others—or at least this is a very superficial explanation. Socrates is still in prison because he has thought the matter through (with Crito) and as a result has decided not to escape.

Now Plato contrasts two kinds of things: those that move only when something else moves them and those that move themselves. To which class does the body belong? It must, Plato argues, belong to the first class; for a corpse is a body, but it doesn't move itself. The difference between living and nonliving bodies is that the former possess a principle of activity and motion within themselves. Such a principle of energy, capable of self-motion is exactly what we call a soul.

> Any body that has an external source of motion
> is soulless, but a body deriving its motion from
> a source within itself is animate or besouled.
> (*Phaedrus* 245e)

So a soul is essentially a self-mover, a source of activity and motion. It is because Socrates is "besouled," capable of moving himself, that he remains in prison. No explanation that does not involve Socrates' soul can be adequate. Therefore, his remaining in prison cannot be explained by talking only about his body, for the body is moved only by something other than itself.

It is precisely because the body is not a self-mover that it can die. The body must be moved either by a soul or by some other body. But if the soul is a self-mover, if it is inherently a source of energy and life, if it does not depend on something outside itself to galvanize it into action—then the soul cannot die.

> All soul is immortal, for that which is ever in mo-
> tion is immortal. But that which while imparting
> motion is itself moved by something else can cease
> to be in motion, and therefore can cease to live; it
> is only that which moves itself that never intermits
> its motion, inasmuch as it cannot abandon its own
> nature; moreover this self-mover is the source and
> first principle of motion for all other things that are
> moved. (*Phaedrus* 245c)

The argument seems to be that life—a principle of self-motion—is the very essence of the soul. Because nothing can "abandon its own nature," the soul cannot die.

If the soul is a source of energy distinct from the body, if it survives the body's decay, and if the soul is the essential self, then Socrates was right in not being dismayed at death. But Plato goes further. It must be the task of those who love wisdom to maximize this separation of soul from body even in this life. As we have seen, it is not through the body that we can come to know the reality of the Forms. The body confuses and distracts us. Only the intellect can lead us through the sciences, via dialectic, to our goal: the Beautiful and the Good. And intellect is a capacity of the soul.

It follows that those who seek to be wise should aim at

> the parting of the soul from the body as far as possi-
> ble, and the habituating of it to assemble and gather
> itself together, away from every part of the body,
> alone by itself, and to live, so far as it can, both in
> the present and in the hereafter, released from the
> body, as from fetters. (*Phaedo* 67c–d)

Pursuing philosophy, loving wisdom, means wanting to free the soul, to release it from its bondage to the body. But if the separation of the soul from the body is death, it follows that

> those who practise philosophy aright are cultivating
> dying, and for them, least of all men, does being
> dead hold any terror. (*Phaedo* 67e)

If we understand by "the world" what we indicated previously, then it is accurate to say that Plato's philosophy contains a drive toward otherworldliness. Raphael was thus right to paint Plato pointing upward. Our true home is not in this world but in another. The love of wisdom, as he understands it, propels us out and away from the visible, the changeable, the bodily—out and away from the world. The most extreme expression of this drive is the assertion that the philosopher cultivates dying. It is true that one who has climbed out of the Cave into the sunlight of the Forms may return to the darkness below, but only for the purpose of encouraging others to turn their souls, too, toward the eternal realities.

Yet this is not a philosophy of pure escape from the world. The otherworldly tendency is balanced by an emphasis on the practical, this-worldly usefulness of acquaintance with the Forms. In order to see this practical side of Plato at work, we must talk about the internal structure of the soul.

THE STRUCTURE OF THE SOUL

When a subject is both difficult and important, Plato often constructs an analogy or a myth. The analogy of the sun presented the Form of the Good. The struggle toward wisdom is the subject of the Myth of the Cave. And to help us comprehend the soul, Plato tells the **Myth of the Charioteer**.*

As to soul's immortality then we have said enough, but as to its nature there is this that must be said. What manner of thing it is would be a long tale to tell, and most assuredly a god alone could tell it, but what it resembles, that a man might tell in briefer compass. Let this therefore be our manner of discourse. Let it be likened to the union of powers in a team of winged steeds and their winged charioteer. Now all the gods' steeds and all their charioteers are good, and of good stock, but with other beings it is not wholly so. With us men, in the first place, it is a pair of steeds that the charioteer controls; moreover, one of them is noble and good, and of good stock, while the other has the opposite character, and his stock is opposite. Hence the task of our charioteer is difficult and troublesome. (*Phaedrus* 246a–b)

Now of the steeds, so we declare, one is good and the other is not, but we have not described the excellence of the one nor the badness of the other, and that is what must now be done. He that is on the more honorable side is upright and clean-limbed, carrying his neck high, with something of a hooked nose; in color he is white, with black eyes; a lover of glory, but with temperance and modesty; one that consorts with genuine renown, and needs no whip, being driven by the word of command alone. The other is crooked of frame, a massive jumble of a creature, with thick short neck, snub nose, black skin, and gray eyes; hot-blooded, consorting with wantonness and vainglory; shaggy of ear, deaf, and hard to control with whip and goad. (*Phaedrus* 253d–e)

We are presented with a picture of the soul in three parts, two of which contribute to the motion of the whole and one whose function is to guide the ensemble. The soul is not only internally complex, however; it is beset by internal conflict. The two horses are of very different sorts and struggle against each other to determine the direction the soul is to go. For this reason, "the task of our charioteer is difficult and troublesome."

In the *Republic,* Plato tells a story to illustrate one type of possible conflict in the soul.

Leontius the son of Aglaeon was coming up from the Piraeus, outside the North Wall but close to it, when he saw some corpses with the public executioner standing near by. On the one hand, he experienced the desire to see them, but at the same time he felt disgust and averted his gaze. For a while, he struggled and kept his hands over his eyes, but finally he was overcome by the desire; he opened his eyes wide, ran up to the corpses, and said, "There you are, you wretches! What a lovely sight! I hope you feel satisfied!"

Now what it suggests . . . . is that it's possible for anger to be at odds with the desires, as if they were different things. (*R* 439e–440a)

This story also gives us a clue to further identification of the two horses in the Myth of the Charioteer. The black, unruly, and hot-blooded steed is desire, or appetite. Leontius *wants* to look at the corpses. Though he struggles against it, he is finally "overcome by the desire."

This desire is opposed by what Plato calls the "spirited" part of the soul, which corresponds to the white horse. When we call someone "animated" (in the sense this has in ordinary speech), we are calling attention to the predominance of "spirit" in that person. Children "are full of spirit from birth," Plato tells us. Spirit puts sparkle in the eyes and joy in the heart. Spirit makes us angry at injustice; it drives the athlete to victory and the soldier to battle. It is, Plato tells us, "an auxiliary of the rational part, unless it is corrupted by bad upbringing" (*R* 440e–441a).

The two horses, then, represent desire and spirit. What of the charioteer? Remember that the function of the charioteer is to guide the soul. What else could perform this guiding function, from Plato's point of view, but the rational part of the soul? Think of a desperately thirsty man in the desert. He sees a pool of

---

*The image Plato uses here may well have been suggested by chariot racing in the Olympic games.

water and approaches it with all the eagerness that deprivation can create. But when he reaches the pool, he sees a sign: "Danger: Do not drink. Polluted." He experiences conflict within. His *desire* urges him to drink. But *reason* tells him that such signs usually indicate the truth, that polluted water will make him very ill and may kill him, and that if he drinks he will probably be worse off than if he doesn't. He decides not to drink. In this case, it is the rational part of him that opposes his desire. His reason guides him away from the water and tries to enlist the help of spirit to make that decision effective.

Desire, spirit, and reason, then, make up the soul. Desire *motivates,* spirit *animates,* and reason *guides.* In the gods, these parts are in perfect harmony. The charioteer in a god's soul has no difficulty in guiding the chariot. In humans, though, there is often conflict, and the job of the rational charioteer is hard.*

"Where id was, there shall ego be."
                            Sigmund Freud (1856–1939)

Plato supposes that any one of these parts may be dominant in a given person. This allows for a rough division of people into three sorts, according to what people take pleasure in:

> We found that one part is the intellectual part of a person, another is the passionate [spirited] part, and the third has so many manifestations that we couldn't give it a single label which applied to it and it alone, so we named it after its most prevalent and powerful aspect: we called it the desirous part, because of the intensity of our desires for food, drink, sex, and so on, and we also referred to it as the mercenary part, because desires of this kind invariably need money for their fulfilment. . . .
>
> Now, sometimes this intellectual part is the motivating aspect of one's mind; sometimes—as circumstances dictate—it's one of the other two. . . .
>
> Which is why we're also claiming that there are three basic human types—the philosophical, the competitive, and the avaricious. (*R* 580d–581c)

Plato uses the idea of three kinds of human beings in his plan for an ideal state, as we'll see. But first we need to examine his views on how the various parts of the soul *should* be related. This will allow us to see the practical use to which Plato thinks the Forms can be put.

---

1. What argument is offered for the soul's immortality?
2. Why does Plato consider philosophy as "training for dying"?
3. What are the parts of the soul? What are their functions?

Morality

Plato believes that he has met the challenge of skepticism. We do have knowledge; knowing how to double the square is only one example of innumerable other things we either know or can come to know. Relativism is also a mistake, he thinks; for the objects of such knowledge are public and available to all. It is by introducing the Forms that he has solved these problems. They are the public, enduring objects about which we can learn through reasoning and instruction. They are the realities that make intelligible all else and give even the fluctuating things of the world such stability as they do have.

We might not be satisfied yet, however. We might say, "That's all very well in the sphere of geometry and the like, but what about ethics and politics? Is there knowledge here, too?" And we might remind Plato of Socrates reminding Euthyphro that even the gods dispute with each other—not about numbers, lengths, and weights, but about "the just and the unjust, the beautiful and the ugly, the good and the bad" (*Euthyphro* 7d). If we are to meet the challenge of skepticism and relativism, we must do it in this sphere, too. Can we *know,* for instance, that justice is good rather than bad? Are there public objects in this sphere, too, about which rational persons can come to agreement? Or, in this aspect of human life, is custom "king of all"?* Is it true here, as the Sophists argue, that *nomos* rules entirely, that morality, for example,

---

*Recall the saying by Democritus, the atomist: "It is hard to fight with desire; but to overcome it is the mark of a rational man." See p. 37.

*Quoted by Herodotus from Pindar, after he tells the story of the Greeks and Indians before Darius (p. 47). Review the *nomos/physis* controversy that follows.

is merely conventional? Unless this challenge can be met, Plato has not succeeded. Skepticism and relativism, ruled out of the theoretical sphere, will reappear with renewed vigor in our practical life. And Plato will neither be able to prove that Athens was wrong to have executed Socrates nor be convincing about the structure of a good state.

Plato makes the problem of morality one of the main themes in the *Republic*. He is asking the Socratic question: What is morality? For Plato, this is equivalent to asking about the Form of Morality. The particular question is this: Is the **Form of the Moral** related to the Form of the Good? And if so, how? To put it in more familiar terms, is morality something good or not?* Remembering that for Socrates the good is always some sort of *advantage,* we can ask: Will I be *better off* being moral than being immoral? Again Plato takes us up the Divided Line, this time with a dialectic designed to show us that the answer is yes, that being moral is indeed something good—and good by nature, not by convention.

As we have seen, Antiphon argues that conventional morality, which forbids deception, stealing, and breaking contracts, may not be in the interest of the individual. When it is not to his advantage, he says, there is nothing wrong with violating the conventional rules, following the law of self-preservation, and being (in the conventional sense) immoral. If you can deceive someone and get away with it when it is to your advantage, that is what you should do.

Plato always tries to present his opponents' views in a strong way, and in the *Republic* we find **Thrasymachus**, another Sophist, arguing the case. Because, he claims, the rules of morality are purely conventional and are made by those with the power to make them, it will seldom be to the advantage of an individual to be moral.† Thrasymachus addresses Socrates:

> You're so far off understanding right and wrong, and morality and immorality, that you don't even realize that morality and right are actually good for

*This is Nietzsche's question, too. But unlike Plato, he answers no. See pp. 546–549.

†This principle is sometimes humorously called "The Golden Rule: He who has the gold, makes the rule." Another version of it is the principle that might makes right.

someone else—they are the advantage of the stronger party, the ruler—and bad for the underling at the receiving end of the orders. . . .

> In any and every situation, a moral person is worse off than an immoral one. Suppose, for instance, that they're doing some business together, which involves one of them entering into association with the other: by the time the association is dissolved, you'll never find the moral person up on the immoral one—he'll be worse off. Or again, in civic matters, if there's a tax on property, then a moral person pays more tax than an immoral one even when they're both equally well off; and if there's a hand-out, then the one gets nothing, while the other makes a lot. And when each of them holds political office, even if a moral person loses out financially in no other way, his personal affairs deteriorate through neglect, while his morality stops him making any profit from public funds, and moreover his family and friends fall out with him over his refusal to help them out in unfair ways; in all these respects, however, an immoral person's experience is the opposite. . . .

> So you see, Socrates, immorality—if practised on a large enough scale—has more power, licence, and authority than morality. And as I said at the beginning, morality is really the advantage of the stronger party, while immorality is profitable and advantageous to oneself. (*R* 343c–344c)

From Thrasymachus' point of view, being moral is "sheer simplicity," whereas being immoral is "sound judgment" (*R* 348c–d). When the question is, "How anyone can live his life in the most rewarding manner?" (*R* 344e), Thrasymachus answers: Be immoral!

Now Plato accepts this as the right question, but he thinks Thrasymachus gives the wrong answer. Which life is the most worthwhile? Which kind of life is advantageous to the one who lives it? That is indeed the question. But how shall we answer it?

Here is a clue. As we saw in our discussion of love, everyone desires to be happy. No one doubts that what makes you truly happy (enduringly happy) is good. So it looks like **happiness** is one thing that everyone admits is good by nature (*physis*); it isn't just by convention (*nomos*) that we agree on that. This suggests a strategy that could counter the argument of Thrasymachus. If Plato could show that being moral is in your long-term interest because it is the only way to be truly happy, Thrasymachus would be defeated.

But is the moral person the happy person? That question is posed in a radical way by another participant in the dialogue of the *Republic*, **Glaucon**, who tells the following story. It is about an ancestor of **Gyges**.

> He was a shepherd in the service of the Lydian ruler of the time, when a heavy rainstorm occurred and an earthquake cracked open the land to a certain extent, and a chasm appeared in the region where he was pasturing his flocks. He was fascinated by the sight, and went down into the chasm and saw there, as the story goes, among other artefacts, a bronze horse, which was hollow and had windows set in it; he stopped and looked in through the windows and saw a corpse inside, which seemed to be that of a giant. The corpse was naked, but had a golden ring on one finger; he took the ring off the finger and left. Now, the shepherds used to meet once a month to keep the king informed about his flocks, and our protagonist came to the meeting wearing the ring. He was sitting down among the others, and happened to twist the ring's bezel in the direction of his body, towards the inner part of his hand. When he did this, he became invisible to his neighbours, and to his astonishment they talked about him as if he'd left. While he was fiddling about with the ring again, he turned the bezel outwards, and became visible. He thought about this and experimented to see if it was the ring which had this power; in this way he eventually found that turning the bezel inwards made him invisible, and turning it outwards made him visible. As soon as he realized this, he arranged to be one of the delegates to the king; once he was inside the palace, he seduced the king's wife and with her help assaulted and killed the king, and so took possession of the throne. (*R* 359d–360b)*

Would you want a ring like this? How would you use it? You are invited to imagine a situation in which you could avoid any nasty consequences for behaving unjustly; all you have to do is use the ring. You could behave as badly as you like while invisible and no one could pin it on you. You would never be caught or punished. If you took a fancy

to something, you could just take it. If you wanted to do something, nothing would prevent you. In a situation like this, what would be the best thing to do? What use of the ring would bring the greatest advantage?

On the one hand, if being moral is worthwhile only because of its consequences, then removing the consequences would diminish the worth of being a moral person; you might as well be unjust and satisfy your desires. On the other hand, if being moral is the true good, good in itself, then it would be better to refrain from unjust actions; it would be more advantageous not to steal, kill, or commit adultery, even if you could get away with it. Your life would be better being moral, even though you would have to do without some of the things that would please you.

Glaucon challenges Socrates to prove that being a moral person is something good in itself, not good just because it usually brings good consequences in its wake. He imagines two extreme cases:

> Our immoral person must be a true expert. . . . [He] must get away with any crimes he undertakes in the proper fashion, if he is to be outstandingly immoral; getting caught must be taken to be a sign of incompetence, since the acme of immorality is to give an impression of morality while actually being immoral. So we must attribute consummate immorality to our consummate criminal, and . . . we should have him equipped with a colossal reputation for morality even though he is a colossal criminal. He should be capable of correcting any mistakes he makes. He must have the ability to argue plausibly, in case any of his crimes are ever found out, and to use force wherever necessary, by making use of his courage and strength and by drawing on his fund of friends and his financial resources.
>
> Now that we've come up with this sketch of an immoral person, we must conceive of a moral person to stand beside him—someone who is straightforward and principled, and who . . . wants genuine goodness rather than merely an aura of goodness. So we must deprive him of any such aura, since if others think him moral, this reputation will gain him privileges and rewards, and it will become unclear whether it is morality or the rewards and privileges which might be motivating him to

---

*This ring is obviously an ancestor to the One Ring that plays a central role in Tolkien's *The Lord of the Rings*.

be what he is. We should strip him of everything except morality, then, and our portrait should be of someone in the opposite situation to the one we imagined before. I mean, even though he does no wrong at all, he must have a colossal reputation for immorality, so that his morality can be tested by seeing whether or not he is impervious to a bad reputation and its consequences; he must unswervingly follow his path until he dies—a saint with a lifelong reputation as a sinner. When they can both go no further in morality and immorality respectively, we can decide which of them is the happier. (R 361a–d)

Perhaps the just man languishes in prison, dirty, cold, and half-starved; all he has is justice. The unjust man, meanwhile, revels in luxuries and the admiration of all. The challenge is to show that the one who does right is, despite all, the happier of the two—the one who has the best life. If Plato can demonstrate this, he will have shown that morality, not immorality, participates in the Form of the Good. It is this bit of dialectic we now want to understand.

We should note at this point, however, that we have so far been discussing whether being moral has the advantage over being immoral without being very clear about the nature of morality. We have assumed we know what it is we are talking about; as Socrates makes clear, however, this is often an unwarranted assumption. So we now have to address this Socratic question directly: What is it to be moral? Only if we are clear about that can we hope to answer the question whether it is something good, even apart from its consequences.

To answer this question, Plato draws on his description of the soul. As we have seen, there are three parts to the soul: reason, spirit, and appetite. Each has a characteristic function. In accord with its function, each has a peculiar excellence. Just as the function of a knife is to cut, the best knife is the one that cuts smoothly and easily; so the excellence of anything is the best performance of its function. What are the functions of the various parts of the soul?

The function of appetite or desire is to motivate a person. It is, if you like, the engine that supplies the energy driving the whole mechanism. If you never *wanted* anything, it is doubtful that you would ever *do* anything. Your heart might beat and your lungs take in air, but there would be no actions on your part. So appetite is performing its function and doing it well when it motivates you strongly to achievement.

Spirit's function is to animate life, so that it is more than the dull drudgery of satisfying wants. Without spirit, life would perhaps go on, but it wouldn't be enjoyable; it might not even be worth living. Spirit is "doing its thing" if it puts sparkle into your life, determination into your actions, and courage into your heart. It supplies the pride and satisfaction that accompany the judgment that you have done well, and it is the source of indignation and anger when you judge that something has been done badly.

It is the task of the rational part of the soul to pursue wisdom and to make judgments backed by reasons. It performs this task with excellence when it judges in accord with knowledge. The rational part of the soul, then, works out by reasoning the best course of action. Its function is to guide or rule the other two parts. Desire, one could say, is blind; reason gives it sight. Spirit may be capricious; reason gives it sense.

Just as the body is in excellent shape when each of its parts is performing its function properly—heart, lungs, digestive system, muscles, nerves, and so on—so the whole soul is excellent when desire, spirit, and reason are all functioning well. The excellent human being is one who is strongly motivated, emotionally vivacious, and rational. Such a person, Plato believes, will also be happy.

For what is the source of unhappiness? Isn't it precisely a lack of harmony among the various parts of the soul? Desire wants what reason says it may not have. Spirit rejoices at what reason advises against. These are cases in which the parts of the soul are not content to perform their proper function. One wants to usurp the function of another. When, for example, you want what reason says is not good for you, it may be that your desire is so great that it overrides the advice given. In that case, desire takes over the guiding function that properly belongs to reason. But then you will do something unwise; and if it is unwise, you will suffer for it. And that is no way to be happy.

On the assumption that we all want to be happy and that being happy is what is good, the good life for human beings must be one in which each part of the soul performs its functions excellently—where reason makes the decisions, supported by spirit, and desire is channeled in appropriate directions. The good and happy person is the one who is internally harmonious. Though we do not all realize it, this internal harmony is what we all most want; for that is the only way to be happy.

Do you remember what Socrates said at his trial—that "the Olympian victor makes you think yourself happy; I make you happy" (*Apology* 36e)? We said then that Socrates thinks happiness is not *feeling* happy, but *being* happy, and that *being* happy is a condition of the soul. We now know more clearly what that condition is: harmony among the parts of the soul.

But what does this have to do with morality? We can answer this question if we think again of an unharmonious soul. Suppose that desire, for instance, overrides reason. It wrongs reason, displacing it from its rightful place as a guide. It is not too much to say that it does reason an *injustice*. So there is a kind of justice and injustice in the individual soul, having to do with the way its parts relate to each other. Let us then speak of *justice in the soul*. In a just soul desire, spirit, and reason all do their thing without overreaching their proper bounds.

Given what we have just said about happiness, it is clear that justice in the soul correlates with happiness and injustice (internal conflict) with unhappiness. Insofar as we are internally just we will be happy. Now happiness, we said, is something good by nature; everyone naturally desires to be happy. It follows that justice in the soul is also something good by nature. If we were wise, we would seek our happiness by trying to keep our souls harmonious, by promoting justice in the soul.

What Thrasymachus claims, of course, is not that injustice in the soul is a good thing but that our lives will be better if we are unjust in the community. He no doubt thinks that you can be internally happy and externally immoral. What Plato needs to demonstrate is that this combination won't work, that there is a strict correlation between *justice in the soul* and *morality in the community*. Will the internally just person also be externally just? Will a just soul naturally express itself by keeping promises,

refraining from stealing and deception, respecting the rights of others? That's the question. To put it another way, Will the person who behaves immorally in the community find it impossible to be just (and therefore happy) within herself?

Near the end of the *Republic* Plato has Socrates construct an imaginary model of the mind to address this question.

"Make a model, then, of a creature with a single—if varied and many-headed—form, arrayed all around with the heads of both wild and tame animals, and possessing the ability to change over to a different set of heads and to generate all these new bits from its own body."

"That would take some skilful modelling," he remarked, "but since words are a more plastic material than wax and so on, you may consider the model constructed."

"A lion and a man are the next two models to make, then. The first of the models, however, is to be by far the largest, and the second the second largest."

"That's an easier job," he said. "It's done."

"Now join the three of them together until they become one, as it were."

"All right," he said.

"And for the final coat, give them the external appearance of a single entity. Make them look like a person, so that anyone incapable of seeing what's inside, who can see only the external husk, will see a single creature, a human being."

"It's done," he said.

"Now, we'd better respond to the idea that this person gains from doing wrong, and loses from doing right, by pointing out to its proponent that this is tantamount to saying that we're rewarded if we indulge and strengthen the many-sided beast and the lion with all its aspects, but starve and weaken the man, until he's subject to the whims of the others, and can't promote familiarity and compatibility between the other two, but lets them bite each other, fight, and try to eat each other."

"Yes, that's undoubtedly what a supporter of immorality would have to say," he agreed.

"So the alternative position, that morality is profitable, is equivalent to saying that our words and behaviour should be designed to maximize the control the inner man has within us, and should enable him to secure the help of the leonine quality and then tend to the many-headed beast as a farmer tends to his crops—by nurturing and cultivating its tame aspects, and by stopping the wild ones growing. Then he can ensure that they're all compatible with one another, and with himself, and can look after them all equally, without favouritism."

"Yes, that's exactly what a supporter of morality has to say," he agreed. (R 588b–589b)

Plato uses this image to show the *identity* of the harmonious, internally just person and the moral person who does what is right. To do wrong to others is to allow the beast within to rule, to allow it to overwhelm the man within (who represents reason). But that means that the internal parts of the soul are no longer doing their own thing, but struggling for dominance. Harmony, and therefore happiness, is destroyed and the good is lost.*

The internally just person, on the other hand, fostering the excellent functioning of each part of the soul in inner harmony, allows the man within to master the beast and tame the lion. The various parts are "compatible with one another." The external result of this inner harmony is a moral life, for the beast will not wildly demand what reason says it is not proper to want.

> Can there be any profit in the immoral acquisition of money, if this entails the enslavement of the best part of oneself to the worst part? . . .
>
> [And] do you think the reason for the traditional condemnation of licentiousness is the same—because it allows that fiend, that huge and many-faceted creature, greater freedom than it should have? . . .
>
> And aren't obstinacy and bad temper considered bad because they distend and invigorate our leonine . . . side to a disproportionate extent? . . .
>
> Whereas a spoilt, soft way of life is considered bad because it makes this part of us so slack and loose that it's incapable of facing hardship? (R 589da–590b)

You can go through a list of the vices and show, Plato believes, that in each case they result from

feeding the monster or from letting the lion run amok. The moral virtues, on the other hand, are exactly the opposite.

"It is with our passions, as it is with fire and water, they are good servants but bad masters."

Aesop (620–560 B.C.)

Here, then, is Plato's answer to Thrasymachus, and to the challenge posed by Glaucon. The immoral man does not have the advantage after all. If we reason carefully about it, Plato says, we can see that it is more profitable to be moral because immorality entangles one's soul in disharmony. And disharmony in the soul is unhappiness. And a life of unhappiness is not the good life.

Justice in the soul, then, is correlated with a moral life. When each part of the soul is justly "doing its thing"—reason making the decisions, supported by the lion of the spirit and a domesticated appetite—a person's external actions will be morally acceptable actions. As we have seen, justice in the soul is happiness, and happiness is a natural good—good by *physis,* not just by *nomos.* So an attempt to understand the Form of Morality takes us necessarily to the Form of the Good. It is best to be moral, even though we suffer for it. And Plato can think he has given us a *logos* that supports Socrates' claim that it is worse to *do* injustice than to *suffer* it. Socrates believed this with full conviction; Plato thinks we can know it is true. The advantage lies with the moral person.

The argument is complex, but the heart of it is straightforward. Let us set down the key notions in this bit of dialectic.

1. Moral actions flow from a soul in harmony.
2. A harmonious soul is a happy soul.
3. Happiness is a natural good.
4. So morality is itself a natural good. (This follows from 1, 2, and 3.)
5. So acting morally is not good simply for its consequences, but is something good in itself. (The Form of the Moral participates in the Form of the Good.)

---

*Compare this to Heraclitus' aphorism on p. 25, where he says that what impulse wants it buys "at the expense of the soul." Giving in to impulse is—in terms of Plato's image—feeding the beast. The beast grows strong at the expense of the lion and the man.

Plato claims that by such dialectical reasoning we can have knowledge in the sphere of practice as well as in the theoretical sphere. Such dialectic, he believes, has defeated the skepticism and relativism of the Sophists and vindicated the practice of his master, who went around "doing nothing but persuading both young and old among you not to care for your body or your wealth in preference to or as strongly as for the best possible state of your soul" (*Apology* 30b).

---

1. What question does the Ring of Gyges story pose?
2. What is happiness? Unhappiness?
3. What is the psychology of the just person? Of the unjust person?
4. How is justice in the soul related to moral behavior in the community? Relate this to the image of the man, the lion, and the monster.

The State

We will not discuss Plato's views of the ideal state in any detail, but we must note several political implications of doctrines we have already canvassed. Like his views on the soul, his views on an ideal community developed throughout his lifetime, and his later thought manifests some deep changes in attitude and outlook. We will simplify by focusing on several famous doctrines of the middle-period *Republic*.

Plato sees a parallel between the internal structure of a soul and the structure of a community. Just as the parts of the soul have distinctive functions, individual men and women differ in their capacities and abilities. They can be grouped into three classes: (1) Some will be best fitted to be laborers, carpenters, plumbers, stonemasons, merchants, or farmers; these can be thought of as the *productive* part of the community; they correspond to the part of the soul called "appetite." (2) Others, who are adventurous, strong, brave, and in love with danger, will be suited to serve in the army and navy; these form the *protective* part of the state, and they correspond to spirit in the soul. (3) Some, a very few, who are intelligent, rational, self-controlled, and in love with wisdom, will be suited to make decisions for the community; these

are the *governing* part; and obviously their parallel in the soul is reason.

Up to this point, we have more or less been taking for granted that the search for wisdom is open to everyone. But this is not in fact Plato's view. Like Socrates, he contrasts the few who know with the many who do not. A basic principle for Plato's ideal state is that there are, and always will be, only a few who are fit to rule. Obviously, Plato is consciously and explicitly rejecting the foundations of Athenian democracy as it existed in his day, where judges were selected by lot rather than by ability and where laws could be passed by a majority of the citizens who happened to show up in the Assembly on any given day. It is *not* the case, Plato urges, that everyone is equally fit to govern. Where democracy is the rule, rhetoric and persuasion carry the day, not reason and wisdom.

He is not, of course, in favor of tyranny or despotism, either; we can think of these as forms of government where the strong rule—that is, whoever has the power to seize the reins. Nor does he favor oligarchy, or rule by the wealthy. Who, then, are these "few" who are fit to be rulers? Consider again the harmonious, internally just soul. In such a soul, reason rules. So in the state,

> Unless communities have philosophers as kings, . . .
> or the people who are currently called kings and rulers
> practise philosophy with enough integrity . . . there
> can be no end to political troubles, . . . or even to human
> troubles in general, I'd say. (*R* 473c–d)

The **philosopher kings** will be those who love wisdom and are possessed of the ability to pursue it, those who have the ability to *know*. Because, as we have seen, knowledge is always knowledge of the Forms, philosopher kings will be those who have attained such knowledge, especially knowledge of the Forms of Justice and Morality and the Form of the Good. For how can one rule wisely unless one knows what is good for the community and what is right?

This is supported by an analogy, some form of which Plato uses again and again:

> Imagine the following situation on a fleet of ships,
> or on a single ship. The owner has the edge over
> everyone else on board by virtue of his size and

strength, but he's rather deaf and short-sighted, and his knowledge of naval matters is just as limited. The sailors are wrangling with one another because each of them thinks that he ought to be the captain, despite the fact that he's never learnt how, and can't name his teacher or specify the period of his apprenticeship. In any case, they all maintain that it isn't something that can be taught, and are ready to butcher anyone who says it is. They're for ever crowding closely around the owner, pleading with him and stopping at nothing to get him to entrust the rudder to them. Sometimes, if their pleas are unsuccessful, but others get the job, they kill those others or throw them off the ship, subdue their worthy owner by drugging him or getting him drunk or something, take control of the ship, help themselves to its cargo, and have the kind of drunken and indulgent voyage you'd expect from people like that. And that's not all: they think highly of anyone who contributes towards their gaining power by showing skill at winning over or subduing the owner, and describe him as an accomplished seaman, a true captain, a naval expert; but they criticize anyone different as useless. They completely fail to understand that any genuine sea-captain has to study the yearly cycle, the seasons, the heavens, the stars and winds, and everything relevant to the job, if he's to be properly equipped to hold a position of authority in a ship. . . . When this is what's happening on board ships, don't you think that the crew of ships in this state would think of any true captain as nothing but a windbag with his head in the clouds, of no use to them at all?

   . . . I'm sure you don't need an analysis of the analogy to see that it's a metaphor for the attitude of society towards true philosophers. (R 488a–489a)

It is indeed a fairly transparent analogy, the details of which do not need much comment. But we need to make explicit something that Plato takes for granted here. The analogy assumes that there is a body of knowledge available to the statesman similar to that utilized by the navigator. It assumes that this can be taught and learned and that it involves some theory that can be applied by the skilled practitioner. Clearly, the knowledge of statecraft involves acquaintance with the Forms.

In a similar way, Plato compares the statesman to a doctor (*Gorgias* 463a–465e). We would never entrust the health of our bodies to just anybody.

We rely on those who have been trained in that craft by skilled teachers. Furthermore, just as not everyone is by nature qualified to be a doctor, not everyone is fit to rule. Because the education necessary to reach the higher level of the Forms is rigorous and demanding, only a few will be able to do it. And for that reason, government in the best state will be by the few: the few who are wise.

A large part of the *Republic* is devoted to a description of the social and educational arrangements that will make it possible to produce philosophers who are kings and kings who are philosophers. Though these discussions are interesting, we omit them here. We still need, however, to ask about the many. If only the few will ever make it to wisdom, what are the many to do? If they cannot *know* the good, how can they be depended on to *do* the good? And if they do not do the good, won't the state fall apart in anarchy and chaos?

The state can be saved from this fate by the principle that, for purposes of action, right opinion is as effective as knowledge. If you merely believe that the cliff is directly ahead and as a result turn left, you will avoid falling over just as surely as if you knew that it was. The problem then, is to assure that the large majority has correct beliefs. They may not be able to follow the complicated dialectical reasoning demonstrating the goodness of morality, but they should be firmly persuaded that it pays to be moral.

Such right opinion is inculcated in the young by education, which is directed by the guardians or rulers, who know what is best. There are detailed discussions in the *Republic* about what sort of stories the young should be told and what sort of music should be allowed. Consider music. It is clear that the young cannot be allowed to listen to whatever kind of music they desire; for there is music that feeds the many-headed beast within and encourages passions that will destroy the harmony of a good state. (You might ask yourself what Plato would say about the popular music of today.) Music and stories should both encourage the belief— which Plato thinks can be demonstrated dialectically to the few—that the best and happiest life is a life of moderation and rational self-control, a moral life.

There is in Plato's state, then, a distinct difference between the few and the many. The latter are brought up on a carefully censored educational regime; it would not be unfair to call the diet offered to the many propaganda, for it is persuasive rather than rational. The few, of course, are those who know what is best, for they have attained knowledge of the Forms. They arrange the education of the others so that they will attain as much goodness as they are capable of.

"But who is to guard the guards themselves?"
Juvenal (late first, early second century)

With respect to knowledge, Plato is both an optimist and a pessimist: an optimist about the few, a pessimist about the many. It is worth noting that Plato is in effect jettisoning one of the basic principles of his master, Socrates: that "the unexamined life is not worth living for a man" (*Apology* 38a). Plato seems to have concluded that for most people this sets the standard too high. They will do best not under Socratic "examination," but conditioned by censorship, propaganda, indoctrination, and persuasion under the guidance of those for whom such dialectical examination leads to a knowledge of the Forms.

Those who find these antidemocratic consequences disturbing have reason to go back to their presuppositions. We will find subsequent philosophers raising serious questions both about the Forms and about Plato's view that some—but not all—of us are capable of knowing them.

---

1. Who should rule in the state? And why?
2. Explain the analogy of the navigator.
3. How will "the many" be "educated" in Plato's ideal republic?

Problems with the Forms

Plato offers a complete vision of reality, including an account of how knowledge is possible, an ethics that guides our practical lives, and a picture of an ideal community. As we have seen, all these aspects of reality involve the Forms. The Forms are the most real of all the things there are. They serve as the stable and enduring objects of our knowledge. The Forms of Goodness, Morality, and Beauty function as guides to our goals, our behaviors, and our creative drives. And knowledge of them is the foundation for a good state.

But are there such realities? It is not only the political consequences that lead people to raise this question. It is raised in Plato's own school, and serious objections are explored—and not satisfactorily answered—by Plato himself in a late dialogue, the *Parmenides*. Here the leading character is made out to be Parmenides himself, the champion of the One, from whom Plato undoubtedly derives his inspiration in devising the doctrine of the eternal and unchanging Forms.

Parmenides examines the young Socrates:

> I imagine your ground for believing in a single form in each case is this. When it seems to you that a number of things are large, there seems, I suppose, to be a certain single character which is the same when you look at them all; hence you think that largeness is a single thing.
>
> True, he replied.
>
> But now take largeness itself and the other things which are large. Suppose you look at all these in the same way in your mind's eye, will not yet another unity make its appearance—a largeness by virtue of which they all appear large?
>
> So it would seem.
>
> If so, a second form of largeness will present itself, over and above largeness itself and the things that share in it, and again, covering all these, yet another, which will make all of them large. So each of your forms will no longer be one, but an indefinite many. (*Parmenides* 131e–132b)

The argument begins with a statement we used before when the Forms were introduced.* But then an unacceptable conclusion is derived. Let us see if we can follow the argument.

Think again about Gertrude and Huey, the two elephants. Both are large. Let the small letters *g* and *h* represent Gertrude and Huey. Let the capital

---

*See p. 124.

letter *L* represent the property they share of being large.* Then we have

$$Lg \qquad Lh$$

According to Plato's view of the Forms, this common feature means that Gertrude and Huey "participate" in a Form—the Large. Let's represent this Form by *F*. So we add the following to our diagram:

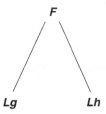

It is the Form *F* that *makes* the two elephants large and makes it intelligible that they are just what they are—that is, large.

Now Plato also regularly thinks of the Forms as *possessing* the very character that they engender in the particulars. Or, to put it the other way around, he says that individual things "copy" or "imitate" the Form. When writing about the Form of Beauty, for example, Plato says that it is in itself beautiful, that it exemplifies "the very soul of the beauty he has toiled for so long," that it possesses "an everlasting loveliness."† Particular individuals are beautiful just to the extent that they actually have that Beauty which belongs in preeminent fashion to the Form.

If that is right, then Largeness must itself be large. So we have to add this feature to our representation:

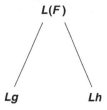

*We here use a convention of modern logicians, for whom small letters symbolize individuals and large letters represent properties or features. The property symbols are written to the left of the individual symbols.

†See p. 139.

But now a problem stares us in the face: Now the Form and the two elephants all have something in common—Largeness. And according to the very principle Plato uses to generate the *F* in the first place, there will now have to be a *second F* to explain what the first *F* shares with the individuals! And that, of course, will also be Large. So we will have to put down:

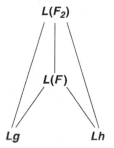

And now you can probably see how this is going to go. There will have to be a third *F*, a fourth, a fifth, and so on and on and on. We will no longer have just one Largeness, but two, three, four. . . . As Plato acknowledges through the character of Parmenides, each Form "will no longer be one, but an indefinite many." We are on the escalator of an *infinite regress*.

Moreover, at any stage of the regress what is real is supposed to depend on there already being a level above it, which explains the features at that stage. So this is what philosophers call a *vicious* infinite regress. For any stage to exist, there must actually be an infinite number of stages in reality, on which its existence depends. We thought we were explaining something about Gertrude and Huey. But this explanation now dissipates itself in the requirement for a never-ending series of explanations—and all of exactly the same sort. This is bad news for Plato's theory of Forms.

Still further, this argument can be applied to any characteristic whatever. It is traditionally formulated in terms of the Form of Man. Heraclitus and Socrates are both men; so there must be a Form of Man to explain this similarity. If that Form is itself a man, you have a third man. In this guise the argument has a name. It is called the **Third Man Argument**. It could as well be called the Third, Fourth, Fifth, Sixth . . . Man Argument.

The Forms are posited to explain the fact of knowledge, the meaning of general terms, and the common features of individuals.* But the Third Man Argument shows that—on principles accepted by Plato himself, at least in his middle period—the Forms do *not* explain what they are supposed to explain.

Like all such paradoxes derived from a set of premises, this indicates that something is wrong. But it does not itself tell us *what* is wrong. Some solution to the problem is needed. As we will see, Aristotle offers a solution.

Explain the threat posed to Plato's philosophy by the Third Man Argument.

FOR FURTHER THOUGHT

1. How persuaded are you by Plato's arguments for the reality of intelligible Forms? If you are not convinced, try to formulate your objections to these arguments in such a way that Plato would have to pay attention.
2. Consider someone you know whom you regard as an exceptionally good person. How much does this person resemble Plato's portrait of the just person? How is he or she different?
3. Would you characterize Plato's views about a good state as elitist, or just realist? Justify your answer with a bit of dialectical reasoning.

KEY WORDS

epistemology	knowing
metaphysics	believing

Form	education
Epistemological Argument	love of wisdom
	Diotima
Metaphysical Argument	ladder of love
Semantic Argument	soul
Divided Line	Myth of the Charioteer
the visible	Form of the Moral
the intelligible	Thrasymachus
Producing	happiness
dialectic (Plato's)	Making Intelligible
Form of the Good	Glaucon
Myth of the Cave	Gyges
wisdom	philosopher kings
Analogy of the Sun	Third Man Argument

NOTES

1. Plato, *Meno*, trans. Robin Waterfield, in *Meno and Other Dialogues* (Oxford: Oxford University Press, 2005).
2. Quotations from Plato's *Republic*, trans. Robin Waterfield (Oxford: Oxford University Press, 1993), are cited in the text using the abbreviation *R*. References are to section numbers.
3. Quotations from Plato's *Timaeus, Parmenides, Symposium,* and *Phaedrus,* in *The Collected Dialogues of Plato,* ed. E. Hamilton and H. Cairns (Princeton: Princeton University Press, 1961), are cited in the text by title and section numbers.
4. Quotations from Plato's *Phaedo*, trans. David Gallop (Oxford: Oxford University Press, 1993), are cited in the text by title and section numbers.
5. A discussion of these problems may be found in W. K. C. Guthrie, "Plato's Views on the Nature of the Soul," in *Plato II: A Collection of Critical Essays,* ed. Gregory Vlastos (Notre Dame, IN: University of Notre Dame Press, 1978), 230–243.

---

*Review pp. 124–125.

ARISTOTLE

The Reality of the World

The year was 384 B.C. Socrates had been dead for fifteen years; Plato had begun his Academy three years earlier. In northern Thrace, not far from the border of what Athenians called civilization, a child was born to a physician in the royal court of Macedonia. This child, named Aristotle, was destined to become the second father of Western philosophy.

At the age of eighteen Aristotle went to Athens, where bright young men from all over desired to study, and enrolled in the Academy. He stayed there for twenty years, as a student, researcher, and teacher, until the death of Plato in 347 B.C. He then spent some time traveling around the Greek islands, pursuing research in what we would call marine biology. For a short time he went back to Macedonia, where he had a position at court as a tutor to the young Alexander, later known as "The Great," who was shortly to complete his father's ambition of conquering and unifying the known world.

By 335, Aristotle was back in Athens, where he founded a school of his own, the Lyceum. He remained there until 323, when he was apparently forced to flee—lest, he said, the Athenians "should sin twice against philosophy."[1] He died the following year at the age of sixty-three.

Aristotle and Plato

Let us begin by drawing some comparisons between Aristotle and his teacher, Plato.[2] First, Plato was born into an aristocratic family with a long history of participation in the political life of the city. Aristotle's father was a doctor. These backgrounds can serve as symbols of their different interests and outlook. The influence of Plato on Aristotle's thought is marked; still, Aristotle is a quite different person with distinct concerns, and his philosophy in some respects takes quite a different turn. That Aristotle's hand is stretched out horizontally in Raphael's painting symbolizes perfectly the contrast with Plato. Here are some comparisons.

OTHERWORLDLINESS

As we see, there is a strong drive toward other-worldliness in Plato.* One feels in Plato a profound dissatisfaction with the familiar world of sense, which is to him no more than a pale shadow of reality. The real is quite different—unchanging, eternal, and unperceivable. The aim of philosophy, the love of wisdom, is to grasp by intellect this otherworldly reality, the Forms, and ultimately to be so caught up in contemplating the True, the Good, and the Beautiful as to escape the Heraclitean flux altogether. To philosophize is to die away from sense and desire.

Aristotle, by contrast, does not seem to suffer the same discontents. While he develops a profound view of the divine and its relation to the world, he does not seem driven to denigrate life in this world as something to be fled from. Life in this world, if not perfect, is as good as one could reasonably expect. The snails and octopuses he studies so avidly, dissects, classifies, and writes about are nothing if not real things. And philosophy is not an escape from them, but a way of comprehending them.

THE OBJECTS OF KNOWLEDGE

Plato is a combination of rationalist and mystic. He is committed to the idea that reality is ultimately rational. The Forms are perfectly definite realities, hanging together in perfectly rational ways, just as geometrical forms make up a perfectly systematic whole. Mathematics, in fact, seems to embody the ideal of knowledge, and reasoning is the way to discover truth. Yet it seems that even reason is not ultimately sufficient. Eventually, when you get far enough up the hierarchy of the Forms, you just have to "see" the truth (with "the mind's eye"). Thus Diotima in the *Symposium* is supposed to have spoken about the "vision" of Beauty when the lover comes to "see the heavenly beauty face to face."[†]

It is perhaps for this reason that Plato—unable to describe what must be seen—offers us in crucial places his memorable myths and analogies. These fit with the idea that teaching is "turning the soul toward reality." The myths point us in a direction

where we might be able to see for ourselves what language is inadequate to describe.

Aristotle, much more down to earth, is convinced that language is quite capable of expressing the truth of things. This truth concerns the sensible world, and our knowledge of it begins with actually seeing, touching, and hearing the things of the world. The senses, although not sufficient in themselves to lead us to knowledge, are the only reliable avenues along which to pursue knowledge. We must be careful, of course, and mistakes are easy to make. But we can come to both know and adequately express this knowledge of the changing world about us.

HUMAN NATURE

Plato is sure that the real person is the soul, not the body. Souls inhabit bodies for a time but are neither bound to nor dependent on them for their existence. The body is nothing more than a temporary and ultimately unreal prison. Our souls possess knowledge of the Forms before we are born, and with determination, intelligence, and virtue, we can enjoy a blessed communion with the Forms after death.

Aristotle's view of human beings is more complicated. There is some question whether the things he says about this topic can all be harmonized into one account. But the main theme is simple. Man is a "rational animal." The person is not identical with a soul-thing distinct from the body; a person is an animal of a certain special sort. As such, a person has a soul of a certain, very special sort. But the soul is not a thing; it is simply the "form" of the particular sort of body that a man has. Human beings are not "tandem" creatures composed of a "stoker" and a "captain." A person is one unified creature. What we get in Aristotle is a (basically) this-worldly account of the soul.*

RELATIVISM AND SKEPTICISM

Plato is preoccupied, one might even say obsessed, with the problem of refuting Protagorean relativism and skepticism. This is terribly important to him; it matters enormously. We can sense in his

---

*See p. 142.

[†]*Symposium* 211e; see the discussion on pp. 137–139.

*There is a complication here that should be noted. See the discussion of *nous*, later in this chapter.

writing the passionate concern to prove these doctrines wrong. Its urgency is the motivational source behind his introduction of the Forms to serve as the unchanging, public objects of knowledge.

Plato is convinced that it was sophistic relativism and skepticism that had really killed Socrates, not the particular members of that jury. It is the views they had come to hold—that every opinion is as true as every other, that what seems good to someone *is* good (for that person), that if it seems right for Athens to condemn Socrates, then it is right. Plato knows in his heart that this is not right. So there must be standards that are more than conventional, standards that are not just *nomos* but have a reality in *physis*. Hence the Forms, the dialectic about morality, the subordination of everything else to the Form of the Good, and his outline of an ideal state. In a sense, this is Plato's *one* problem; it almost seems as if everything else in Plato gets its sense from that one center.

To that problem Aristotle seems almost oblivious, as though it were not on his horizon at all. The explanation may be partly that he believes Plato has succeeded in refuting the skeptics, so it doesn't have to be done again. But there is probably more to it. As a biologist, he knows that not every opinion about crayfish, for example, is equally good, so he isn't overwhelmed by the arguments of the skeptics. So he pursues his research and writes up his results, which, he believes, do constitute knowledge of the sensory world. The only problem, philosophically speaking, is to analyze the processes by which we attain such knowledge and to set out the basic features of the realities disclosed.

ETHICS

Plato wants and thinks we can get the same kind of certainty in rules of behavior that we have in mathematics. Dialectic, reasoning about the Forms, can lead us to moral truths. And the ultimate vision of the Form of the Good will provide a single standard for deciding practical questions. Apprehension of the latter seems to promise, in a flash of insight, the solution for all questions of value—but only for the few specially qualified individuals able to make the tortuous journey out of the Cave.

"It is those who act rightly who get the rewards and the good things in life."

—ARISTOTLE

Characteristically, Aristotle is less inclined to make such grandiose claims. We ought not, he advises, to ask for more certainty in a given subject matter than the subject matter allows. In matters of practical decision, we are not likely to get the same certainty we can get in mathematics. He proceeds, therefore, in a more cautious and specific way, discussing particular virtues and the conditions under which it is and isn't reasonable to hold people responsible for the exercise of these virtues. There is no suggestion that ethical knowledge is something restricted to a small coterie of specially trained experts. The ordinary citizen, he holds, is quite able to make good decisions and to live a good life.* Appeal to the Form of the Good is in any case useless in these matters.

—————

*Here it must be remembered that in Athens there were many slaves and that women were not citizens.

The Greek poet Archilochus had written in the seventh century,

> The fox knoweth many things, the hedgehog one great thing.[3]

Two quite different intellectual styles are exemplified by Plato and Aristotle. Plato is a man with one big problem, one passion, one concern; everything he touches is transformed by that concern. Aristotle has many smaller problems. These are not unrelated to each other, and there is a pattern in his treatment of them all. But he is interested in each for its own sake, not just in terms of how they relate to some grand scheme. Plato is a hedgehog. Aristotle is a fox.

It is quite possible to overdraw this contrast, however. There is a very important respect in which Aristotle is a "Platonist" from beginning to end. He agrees with his teacher without qualification that knowledge—to be knowledge—must be certain and enduring. And for that to be so, knowledge must be of objects that are themselves free from the ravages of time and change. For both Plato and Aristotle, knowledge is knowledge of forms.* But they understand the forms differently—and thereon hangs the tale to come.

Logic and Knowledge

The Sophists' claim to teach their pupils "to make the weaker argument appear the stronger" has been satirized by Aristophanes, scorned by Socrates, and repudiated by Plato. But until Aristotle does his work in logic, no one gives a good answer to the question, Just what makes an argument weaker or stronger anyway? An answer to this question is absolutely essential for appraising the success of either the Sophists or those who criticize them. Unless you have clear criteria for discriminating weak from strong arguments, bad arguments from good, the whole dispute remains in the air. Are there standards by which we can divide arguments

into good ones and bad ones? Aristotle answers this question.

He does not, of course, answer it once and for all—though for two thousand years many people will think he very nearly has. Since the revolution in logic of the last hundred years, we can now say that Aristotle's contribution is not the last word. But it is the first word, and his achievement remains a part of the much expanded science of logic today.

It is undoubtedly due in part to Aristotle's ability to produce criteria distinguishing sound arguments from unsound ones that he can take the sophistic challenge as lightly as he does. To Aristotle, the Sophists can be dismissed as the perpetrators of "sophisms," of bad arguments dressed up to look good. They are not such a threat as they seem, because their arguments can now be *shown* to be bad ones.

But it is not mainly as an unmasker of fraudulent reasoning that Aristotle values logic.* Aristotle thinks of logic as a *tool* to be used in every intellectual endeavor, allowing the construction of valid "accounts" and the criticism of invalid ones. As his universal intellectual tool, logic is of such importance that we need to understand at least the rudiments of Aristotle's treatment of the subject.

It will be useful, however, to work toward the logic from more general considerations. Why should we care about logic? What can it do for us? We need to think again about *wisdom*.

Aristotle begins the work we know as *Metaphysics* with these memorable words:

> All men by nature desire to have knowledge. An indication of this is the delight that we take in the senses; quite apart from the use that we make of them, we take delight in them for their own sake, and more than of any other this is true of the sense of sight. . . . The reason for this is that, more than any other sense, it enables us to get to know things, and it reveals a number of differences between things. (*M* 1.1)[4]

This delight is characteristic even of the lower animals, Aristotle tells us, though their capacities

---

*Note that "form" is here uncapitalized. I will use the capitalized version, Form, only when referring to Plato's independent, eternal reality. For Aristotle's forms, an uncapitalized version of the word will do.

*Aristotle does not himself use the term "logic," which is of a later origin. What we now call "logic" is termed by his successors the "organon," or "instrument" for attaining knowledge.

for knowledge are more limited than ours. They are curious and take delight in the senses and in such knowledge as they are capable of. Some of the lower animals, though not all, seem to have *memory*, so that the deliverances of their senses are not immediately lost. Memory produces *experience*, in the sense that one can learn from experience. (We have learned that taking aspirin relieves a headache; we do not totally understand why.) Some of the animals are quite good at learning from experience. Humans, however, are best of all at this; in humans, *universal judgments* can be framed in *language* on the basis of this experience. We not only see numerous black crows and remember them but also form the judgment that all crows are black and use this statement together with others to build up a knowledge of that species of bird.

We regard those among us as wisest, Aristotle says, who know not only that crows are black but also why they are so. Those who are wise, then, have knowledge of the *causes* of things, which allows them to use various arts for practical purposes (as the doctor is able to cure the sick because she knows the causes of their diseases). Knowing the causes, moreover, allows the wise person to teach others how and why things are the way they are.

Wisdom, then, either is or at least involves knowledge. And knowledge involves both *statements* (*that* something is so) and *reasons* (statements *why* something is so). Furthermore, for the possession of such statements to qualify as wisdom, they must be true. As Plato has pointed out, falsehoods cannot constitute knowledge.

It is Aristotle's intention to clarify all this, to sort it out, put it in order, and show how it works. So he has to do several things. He has to (1) explain the nature of *statements*—how, for instance, they are put together out of simpler units called *terms;* (2) explain how statements can be *related* to each other so that some can give "the reason why" for others; and (3) give an account of what makes statements *true* or *false*. These tasks make up the logic.

TERMS AND STATEMENTS

When Aristotle discusses **terms**, the basic elements that combine to form **statements**, he is also discussing the world. In his view, the terms we use can be classified according to the kinds of things they pick out. He insists that things in the world can *be* in a number of different ways.* Correlated with the different kinds of things there are—or different ways things can be—are different kinds of terms. These kinds, called **categories**, are set out this way:

> Every uncombined term indicates substance or quantity or quality or relationship to something or place or time or posture or state or the doing of something or the undergoing of something. (*C* 4)

Aristotle gives some examples:

- Substance—man or horse
- Quantity—two feet long, three feet high
- Quality—white or literate
- Relationship—double, half, or greater
- Place—in the Lyceum, in the marketplace
- Time—yesterday or last year
- Posture—reclining at table, sitting down
- State—having shoes on, being in armor
- Doing something—cutting, burning
- Undergoing something—being cut, being burnt

He does not insist that this is a complete and correct list. But you can see that categories are very general concepts, expressing the various *ways* in which being is manifested. Such distinctions exist and must be observed.

> None of these terms is used on its own in any statement, but it is through their combination with one another that a statement comes into being. For every statement is held to be either true or false, whereas no uncombined term—such as "man," "white," "runs," or "conquers"—is either of these. (*C* 4)

Neither "black" nor "crow" is true or false. But "That crow is black" must be one or the other. Terms combine to make statements. For example, we might combine terms from the preceding list to make statements such as these:

- A man is in the Lyceum.
- A white horse was in the marketplace yesterday.
- That man reclining at a table was burning rubbish last year.

---

*One of the mistakes made by Parmenides and others, he claims, is failing to recognize that being comes in kinds.

Terms can be combined in a wide variety of ways, but there are, Aristotle believes, certain standard and basic forms of combination to which all other combinations can be reduced. This means there is a limited number of basic forms that statements can take.

The clue to discovering these basic forms is noting that every statement is either true or false. Not every *sentence* we utter, of course, is either true or false. "Close the door, please," is neither. It may be appropriate or inappropriate, wise or foolish, but it isn't the right kind of thing to be true or false. It is not, Aristotle would say, a *statement*. Aristotle's own example is a prayer; it is, he says, "a sentence, but it is neither true nor false" (*I* 4).

Statements (the kinds of things that can be true or false) *state* something. And they state something *about* something. We can then analyze statements in two parts: there is the part indicating what we are talking about, and there is the part indicating what we are saying about it. Call the first part the *subject* and the second part the *predicate*. Every statement, Aristotle believes, displays (or can be reformulated to display) a pattern in which some term plays the role of subject and another term the role of predicate. It will be convenient to abbreviate these parts as *S* and *P*, respectively.

Not every term, however, can play both roles. And this fact is of very great importance for Aristotle, for it allows him to draw the most fundamental distinction on which his whole view of reality is based.

> What is most properly, primarily, and most strictly spoken of as a substance is what is neither asserted of nor present in a subject—a particular man, for instance, or a particular horse. (*C* 5)

Look back to the list of terms on page 159. There is one kind of term that stands out from the rest: **substance**. Although there are several kinds of substance (as we shall see), the kind that is "properly, primarily, and most strictly" called substance is distinguishable by the kind of role the term for it can play in statements—or rather, the kind of role it *cannot* play. Terms designating such substances can play the role only of subject, never of predicate. They can take only the *S* role in statements, not the *P* role.

Consider the term "Socrates." This term indicates one particular man, namely Socrates himself. And it cannot take the *P* place in a statement; we can say things about Socrates—that he is wise, or snub-nosed—but we cannot use the term "Socrates" to say something about a subject. We cannot, for example, say "Snub-nosed is Socrates," except as a fancy and poetic expression for "Socrates is snub-nosed." In both of these expressions, "Socrates" is in the *S* place and "is snub-nosed" in the *P* position. In both, "is snub-nosed" is used to say something about Socrates. It is not *spatial* position in the sentence that counts, then, but what we could call *logical* position. In a similar way, it is clear that Socrates cannot be "present in" a subject, in the way the color blue can be present in the water of the Aegean Sea or knowledge of Spanish can be present in those who know the language.

Things *are*, Aristotle holds, in all these different ways. Some things have being as qualities, some as relations, some as places, and so on. But among all these, there is one *basic* way in which a thing can be: being an individual substance, a thing, such as Socrates. All the other ways of being are parasitic on this. They are all characteristics of these basic substances; our terms for them express things we can say *about* these primary substances. For example, we can say that Socrates is five feet tall (Quantity), that he is ugly (Quality), that he is twice as heavy as Crito (Relationship), that he is in prison (Place), and so on. But that about which we say all these things, of which they all are (or may be) true, is some particular individual. And that Aristotle calls **primary substance**.

> The reason why primary substances are said to be more fully substances than anything else is that they are subjects to everything else and that all other things are either asserted of them or are present in them. (*C* 5)

It is clear that Aristotle will reject the Platonic Forms. We shall explore what he says about the Forms more fully later, but here he says that those things which are "more fully substances than anything else" are particular, individual entities such as this man, this horse, this tree, this snail. These are not shadows of more real things, as Plato held;

they are the most real things there are. Everything else is real only in relation to them.

For now, however, we want to concentrate not on this metaphysical line of reasoning, but on the logical. Let us review. The wise person is the one who knows—both what is and why it is. Such knowledge is expressed in statements. Statements are composed of terms put together in certain definite ways. All of them either are already or can be reformulated to be subject–predicate statements, in which something is said about something. And the ultimate subjects of statements are primary substances.

Before we leave this topic, we need to note a complication. We can say, "Socrates is a *man*." This conforms to our S–P pattern. But we can also say, "*Man* is an animal." This seems puzzling. How could "man" play the role of both P (in the first statement) and S (in the second)? If primary substances (individual things) are the ultimate subjects of predication, shouldn't we rule out "Man is an animal" as improper? Yet it is a very common kind of thing to say; indeed, biology is chock full of such statements!

Aristotle solves this problem by distinguishing two senses of "substance."

> But people speak, too, of secondary substances, to which, as species, belong what are spoken of as the primary substances, and to which, as genera, the species themselves belong. For instance, a particular man belongs to the species "man," and the genus to which the species belongs is "animal." So it is these things, like "man" and "animal," that are spoken of as secondary substances. (*C* 5)

Individual humans, he notes, belong to a *species:* the species man. And each man, each human, is a kind of animal. So "animal" is a *genus*, under which there are many species: humans, lions, whales, and so on. In a sense, then, species and genera are substances, too. They are substances by virtue of expressing the essential nature of primary substances (the individual people, lions, whales). A genus or species, Aristotle holds, has no reality apart from the particular things that make it up, but we can think of it as a derivative kind of substance about which we can say lots of interesting things. Terms

for **secondary substances**, then, can also play the *S* role in a statement.

---

1. What is logic *for*?
2. What is a "category"? Give some examples.
3. What makes a statement different from a term?
4. What two roles can terms play in statements?
5. What distinguishes primary substance from all the other categories?
6. What kind of thing is *most real* for Aristotle? Contrast with Plato.

TRUTH

So far Aristotle has been dealing with issues of *meaning*. We turn now to what he has to say about **truth**. In one of the most elegant formulations in all philosophy, using only words any four-year-old can understand, Aristotle defines truth.

> To say that what is is not, or that what is not is, is false and to say that what is is, or that what is not is not, is true. (*M* 4.7)

Note that truth pertains to what we say. Grass is green. To say of it that it is green is to say something true about it. To say that it is not green—red or blue, perhaps—is to say something false. Contrariwise, the snail in my garden is not a mathematician. If I say that it is not a mathematician, I speak truthfully, whereas if I say that it is a mathematician, I speak falsely. Truth represents things as they are. Falsehood says of them that they are other than they are. This view of truth is not the only possible one.* We should, therefore, have a name for it. Let us call it the **correspondence** theory of truth, because it holds that a statement is true just when it "corresponds" to the reality it is about. We can also call it the classical view of truth.

---

*For other views of truth, see Hegel's claim that the truth is not to be found in isolated statements, but is only the *whole* of a completed system of knowledge ("Reason and Reality: The Theory of Idealism," in Chapter 17), and the pragmatist view that truth consists of all that a community of investigators would agree upon if they inquired sufficiently long (Chapter 21, pp. 567–569).

> *"Truth is truth to the end of reckoning."*
> *William Shakespeare, Measure for Measure, act 5,*
> *scene 1.*

REASONS WHY: THE SYLLOGISM

We can now say that the wise person is able to make true statements about whatever subject she discusses. But she is able to do more than that; she is able to "give an account" of *why* what she says is true. In Aristotle's terminology, she is able to specify the *causes* of things.

With this we come to logic proper, the study of *reason-giving*. In giving the cause why a certain statement is true, the wise person offers other statements. Will these constitute good reasons for what she claims to know or not? If she is truly wise, they presumably will; but to discover whether someone is wise, we may have to decide (1) whether what she says is true and (2) whether the reasons she offers for what she says actually support her claim. Giving a reason is giving an **argument:** offering premises for a conclusion. Perhaps it will be only a weak argument, perhaps a strong one. How can we tell? Aristotle is committed to the view that we cannot determine the strength of an argument on the basis of how far it convinces us, or even most people. To Aristotle, the Sophist's reliance on persuasiveness as the key to goodness in argument must seem like Euthyphro's third answer to Socrates' questions about piety—that it gives at best a property of good arguments, not the essence of the matter. Aristotle is trying to find what it is about an argument that explains why people should—or should not—be convinced.

Remember that for Aristotle all statements have an *S–P* form; they all say something about something. Such statements may either affirm that something is the case ("Grass is green") or deny it ("My snail is not a mathematician"). Call the former affirmative statements and the latter negative statements.

Moreover, *S–P* statements may either be about *all* of the subject ("All whales are mammals") or only about *some* of the subject ("Some dogs are

vicious"). The former statements can be called *universal*, because they predicate something of each and every item talked about; each and every whale, for instance, is said to be a mammal. The latter statements can be called *particular;* our example does not say something about each and every dog, only about this or that dog or some collection of dogs. These distinctions give us a fourfold classification of statements. It will be useful to draw a chart, with some examples of each.

	Affirmative	Negative
Universal	All men are mortal. (All *S* is *P*)	No men are mortal. (No *S* is *P*)
Particular	Some men are mortal. (Some *S* is *P*)	Some men are not mortal. (Some *S* is not *P*)

There are some interesting logical relationships among these statement forms. For example, a universal affirmative statement is the *contradictory* of a particular negative statement. To say that these are contradictories is to say that if either of them is true, the other must be false; and if either is false, the other must be true. (Look at the following chart and check whether this is so.) Universal negatives and particular affirmatives are likewise contradictories. The two statements at the top of the Square of Opposition (universal affirmative and negative) cannot be true together, but they can both be false. Analogously, the two statements at the bottom (particular affirmative and negative) can be true together, but they cannot both be false. For ease of reference each of the statement forms is assigned a letter: *A, E, I,* or *O.*

Inferences in this square are called "immediate" inferences because they go from one statement directly or immediately to another. There are also "mediate" inferences, and to these we must now turn. Such inferences constitute arguments in

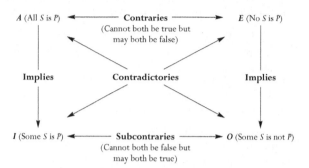

SQUARE OF OPPOSITION
(assuming at least one *S* exists)

A (All *S* is *P*) ◄——— **Contraries** ———► *E* (No *S* is *P*)
(Cannot both be true but
may both be false)

Implies   **Contradictories**   **Implies**

I (Some *S* is *P*) ◄——— **Subcontraries** ———► *O* (Some *S* is not *P*)
(Cannot both be false but
may both be true)

which reasons are given to support a conclusion. Again, an example is useful. Suppose that someone claiming to be wise asserts, "All men are mortal." Remembering that wisdom includes not only knowing truths but also knowing their causes or reasons, we ask her why this is so. In response, she says, "Because animals are mortal, and all men are animals." She has given us an argument.

> All animals are mortal.
> All men are animals.
> Therefore: All men are mortal.

Aristotle calls this kind of argument a **syllogism**. Every syllogism is made up of three statements. In the three statements are three terms (here the terms are "man," "animal," and "mortal"), two terms in each statement. Two of the statements function as reasons for the third. These are the **premises**, and what is to be proved is the **conclusion**.

Consider the terms that occur in the conclusion; each of these occurs also in just one of the premises. And the third term, which Aristotle calls the **middle term**, occurs once in each of the premises. It is the middle term that links the two terms in the conclusion. The fact that the middle term is related to each of the others in a certain specific way is supposed to be the *cause* or the *reason why* the conclusion is true.

One of Aristotle's greatest achievements is the realization that what makes a syllogism good or bad not only has nothing to do with its persuasiveness, but it also has nothing to do with its subject matter.

Its goodness or badness as a piece of reason-giving is completely independent of what it is about. It is not because it is about men and animals rather than gods and spirits that it either is or is not successful. Its success is wholly a matter of its form.* In evaluating a syllogism, we might as well use letters of the alphabet in place of meaningful terms. In fact, this is exactly what Aristotle does. How good an argument is, then, depends only on how terms are related to each other, not on what they are about.

We can represent the relevant structure or form of this example in the following way, using *S* for the subject of the conclusion, *P* for its predicate, and *M* for the middle term that is supposed to link these together.

> All *M* is *P*.
> All *S* is *M*.
> Therefore: All *S* is *P*.

Remember, all that matters is how the terms are related to each other. What the terms mean doesn't matter. This suggests that if our original argument was a good one, any other argument that has this same form will also be a good one. What counts is form, not content.

But what is it for *any* argument to be good? Let us remind ourselves of the point and purpose of giving arguments in the first place. The point is to answer *why*. Any good argument, then, must satisfy two conditions: (1) The reasons offered (the premises) must be *true;* and (2) the *relation* between the premises and the conclusion must be such that *if* the premises are true, the conclusion can't possibly be false.† When an argument satisfies the second condition (if the premises are true, the conclusion *must* be true) it is **valid**. (Note that an argument may have that part of logical goodness

---

*Form is here contrasted with content, or subject matter; it is not the Platonic contrast between the ultimate reality and the world of the senses.

†Note that we are talking about *deductive* arguments here. There are also *inductive* arguments, in which the tie between the premises and the conclusion is a looser one; the premises in an inductive argument give some reason to believe the conclusion, but they fall short of guaranteeing its truth.

we call validity even though its premises are false.) A poor argument fails to satisfy at least one of these conditions: Either (1) the premises are *not true*, or (2) the relation between premises and conclusion is not such as to *guarantee* the truth of the conclusion when the premises are true. Poor arguments give poor reasons, then, either in the sense that you shouldn't even believe the reasons (because they aren't true) or in the sense that although the reasons are true they do not provide a *reason why* the conclusion is true.

Now we can ask, is the syllogism above a good argument? It should be obvious that it is. (Not all syllogisms are so obviously either bad or good; Aristotle uses obviously good ones like this as axioms to prove the goodness of less obvious ones.) If it is not obvious, it can easily be made so. Remembering that correctness is a matter of *form*, not content, let us take the terms as names for shapes. Then we can represent the argument in the following way:

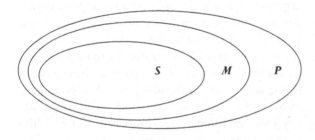

Simply by looking at these shapes, we can now see that if all of *S* is included in *M*, and all of *M* is included in *P*, then all of *S* must be included in *P*. It couldn't be any other way. But that is exactly what a good argument is supposed to do: to show you that, given the truth of the premises, the conclusion must also be true. It gives you a reason why the conclusion is true. So this argument form is a valid one. Since our original argument (1) is an instance of this valid form and (2) has true premises, it is a good argument.

Let us consider another syllogism:

No sparrows are mammals.
No mammals are plants.
Therefore: No sparrows are plants.

Each of these statements is true. But is this a *valid* argument? Do the reasons offered *make true* the conclusion? No. It has this form:

No *S* is *M*.
No *M* is *P*.
Therefore: No *S* is *P*.

If that is a correct argument form, then any other argument having that form must be correct. This suggests a method of testing for goodness in arguments. Try to find another argument that has the same form as this one but that has true premises and a false conclusion. If you can, you have shown that these reasons do *not* guarantee the truth of the conclusion. The middle term is not doing its job of linking the subject and the predicate of the conclusion. So the argument is not a good one. Can we find such an argument? Easy.

No Toyotas are Ferraris.
No Ferraris are inexpensive.
Therefore: No Toyotas are inexpensive.

You can see (check to be sure you do) that this argument has the same form as the argument about sparrows. But here, although the premises are both true, the conclusion is false. In a valid argument, however, the conclusion *must* be true if the premises are true. So this argument is not valid. The reasons offered do not give us the *reason why* the conclusion is true (since it *isn't* true). Since it is form that accounts for goodness in arguments, then if this argument is no good, neither is the one about sparrows—even though the conclusion in that example happens to be true. That is the problem; it just *happens* to be true; it is not true *because* the premises are true. So the argument doesn't do the job that arguments are supposed to do. It doesn't give the *reason why*. It is an *invalid* argument.

On the basis of fairly simple examples such as these, Aristotle develops a complex system of logic. He tries to set out all the correct and all the incorrect forms of reasoning.* The result is a powerful

---

*Aristotle is mistaken in thinking that syllogisms of this sort exhaust the forms of correct reasoning; we now know that there are many more correct forms. He also neglects, or gives an inadequate picture of, so-called inductive reasoning. But his achievement is impressive nonetheless.

tool both for testing arguments and for constructing arguments that tell us the cause or reason why things are as they are. In its latter use, logic is called *demonstration*. What can be demonstrated, we can know.

KNOWING FIRST PRINCIPLES

Can everything knowable be demonstrated? Can we give reasons for everything? Aristotle's answer is no:

> For it is altogether impossible for there to be proofs of everything; if there were, one would go on to infinity, so that even so one would end up without a proof. (*M* 4.4)

Giving a proof for a statement, as we have seen, means constructing a syllogism; that means finding premises from which the statement logically follows. But we can ask whether there is also a proof for these premises. (Why should we believe *them?*) If so, other syllogisms can be constructed with these premises as their conclusions. But then, what about the premises of these syllogisms? This kind of questioning, like the child's "why?" can go on indefinitely. And so we will continue to be unsatisfied about the truth of the statement we were originally seeking reasons to believe. But this means, as Aristotle says, that "it is impossible for there to be proofs for everything."

The chain of demonstrations must come to an end if we are to have knowledge. But where can it end? Socrates has an answer to this question.* If, as he thinks, our souls existed before we were born and had lived in the presence of the truth, then we might be able to "recollect" the truth when we were reminded of it. This recollection would not be demonstrative, needing argument and premises and such; it would be an immediate recognition of the truth. But Aristotle cannot use this Socratic solution. As we'll discover, he can see no reason to believe that our souls existed before we were born, nor does he think there are independently existing Forms we could have been acquainted with.

So Aristotle is faced with this problem: Since not everything can be known by demonstration,

how do we come to know that which cannot be demonstrated? If we are to avoid an infinite regression, there must be starting points for our proofs.

> The starting point of demonstration is an immediate premise, which means that there is no other premise prior to it. (*PA* 1.2)

We can call these immediate premises **first principles**. If we are to have knowledge by demonstration, our knowledge of these starting points must not be inferior to what we prove from them. In fact, Aristotle says, they must be even better known. About them we must have the most certainty of all.

> Since we know and believe through the first, or ultimate, principles, we know them better and believe in them more, since it is only through them that we know what is posterior to them. . . . This is because true, absolute knowledge cannot be shaken. (*PA* 1.2)

This means that we must be more certain about what makes something an animal than about what makes something a monkey; in geometry, we must know the definition of line with greater clarity than that of isosceles triangle.

But how are such principles to be known? We can't just start from nothing and—by a leap—get to knowledge. In this respect Socrates was right.

> All instruction and all learning through discussion proceed from what is known already. (*PA* 1.1)

This seems paradoxical. It is as though we were required to know *something* prior to our coming to know *anything*. But this is impossible.

The key to resolving the paradox, Aristotle holds, is not the preexistence of the soul but the recognition that things may be "known" in several senses. What Aristotle does is to show how knowledge of these first principles *develops*. This is a characteristically Aristotelian tactic. Instead of saying that we either know or we don't know, Aristotle shows us how knowledge develops from implicit to more and more explicit forms. What is presupposed is not full-blown, explicit, and certain knowledge (such as Socrates supposed the soul had in its preexistence), but a series of stages, beginning in a *capacity* of a certain sort. Though it is

---

*Discussed on pp. 103–104.

incredible to think that we are born knowing how to double a square (and just can't remember it), it makes good sense to think we are born with capacities of various kinds. One relevant capacity, moreover, human knowers share with other animals. Knowing begins in perceiving.

Aristotle agrees with Plato that perceiving something is not the same as knowing it. The object of perception is always an individual thing, but knowledge is of the universal; perception can be mistaken, but knowledge cannot. But these facts don't lead Aristotle, as they lead Plato, to disparage the senses, to cut them off from reality, and to install knowledge in another realm altogether. Perception is not knowledge, but it is where knowledge begins. (It is surely of crucial importance to note here that when Plato thinks of knowledge, his first thought is of mathematics; when Aristotle thinks of knowledge, his first thought is of biology.)

We noted earlier that some animals have memory in addition to their faculties of sense perception. Thus they can retain traces of what they perceive in their encounters with the environment. These traces build up into what Aristotle calls "experience." And experience is the source of a *universal*, a sense of the unity of the many things encountered.

> Clearly it must be by induction that we acquire knowledge of the primary premises, because this is also the way in which sense-perception provides us with universals.[5]

How do we come to know the first principles, from which demonstrations may then proceed? By **induction**, Aristotle tells us. Imagine the biologist observing creatures in a tidal pool. At first, she can distinguish only a few kinds, those very different from each other. As she keeps watching very closely, new differences (as well as new similarities) become apparent. She begins to group these creatures according to their similarities, bringing the Many under a variety of Ones. Then all these Ones are united under further universal principles, until finally all are classified under the One heading of "animals." "Is this like the one I saw a moment ago? Yes. So there is that kind; and that is different from this kind. Still, they are alike in a certain respect, so they may be species of the same genus. . . ." "Eventually, the biologist comes to group the creatures according to characteristics they do and do not share with each other. Her perception provides her with "universals" under which she groups or organizes the various kinds of things that she has been observing.

These universals provide something like definitions of the natural kinds of things that exist. The wider one's experience of a certain field, the more firmly these inductive definitions are grounded. The first principles of any field are arrived at in this way. Thus we can come to know what a plant is, what an animal is, what a living being is. And these definitions can serve as the starting points, the ultimate principles of any science.

Not everything, as we have seen, can be known by demonstration. What cannot be demonstrated must be grasped some other way. That way is induction from sense perceptions. But what is there in us that is capable of such a grasp? It is clearly not the senses, nor memory, nor even experience. On the other hand, it is not our reasoning ability, for the capacity in question has nothing to do with proof. Aristotle uses a term for this capacity of ours that has no very adequate English counterpart: *nous*. It is sometimes translated as "mind" and sometimes as "intuition"; the English term "mind" seems too broad and "intuition" too vague. *Nous* is the name for that ability we have to grasp first principles by abstracting what is essential from many particular instances present to our senses.*

1. What is truth?
2. What is an argument? A syllogism? A middle term?
3. What is required in a good argument?
4. What is a first principle? Why are first principles needed? How are they known?
5. Do Aristotle's reflections on first principles do anything to resolve the puzzle about the slave boy and the preexistence of the soul? Explain.

---

*Do we really have such a faculty? Can we get certainty about premises from which the rest of our knowledge can be logically derived? Modern philosophy from the seventeenth century on will be preoccupied with these questions. What if we can't? Are we thrown back again into that sophistic skepticism and relativism from which both Plato and Aristotle thought they had delivered us? See, for example, Montaigne, who thinks we are ("Skeptical Thoughts Revived," in Chapter 12) and Descartes, who is certain we are not (*Meditations*).

The World

Aristotle discusses his predecessors often and in detail.* He believes that something can be learned from all of them and that by showing where they go wrong we can avoid their mistakes and take a better path. Such a dialectical examination of the older philosophers does not amount to knowledge, for it is neither demonstration of a truth nor insight into first principles. But it clears the ground for both and is therefore of considerable importance.

His fundamental conviction about the work of his predecessors is that they go wrong by not *observing* closely enough. With the possible exception of Socrates and certain of the Sophists who were interested in other things, they had all been searching for explanations that would make the world intelligible. But these explanations either are excessively general (Thales' water, Anaximander's Boundless, and the rather different *logos* of Heraclitus), or seem to conclude that there is no intelligibility in the world at all (Parmenides condemns the world to the status of mere appearance, and Plato believes only the Forms are completely intelligible). Even Democritus, who was from a theoretical point of view superior to all but Plato, misses the intelligibility in the observable world and tries to find it in the unobservable atoms.

Aristotle, drawing on his own careful observations, is convinced that the things that make up the world have principles of intelligibility *within* them.† In order to explain their nature, their existence, and the changes they regularly undergo, it is necessary only to pay close attention to *them*. The world as it offers itself to our perception is not an unintelligible, chaotic flux from which we must flee to find knowledge. It is made up of things—the primary substances—that are ordered; the principles of their order are internal to them, and these principles, through perception, can be known.

---

*In, for example, *Physics* I and *Metaphysics* I: The book you are now reading is itself an example of the Aristotelian conviction expressed in the next sentence.

†In this regard, Aristotle is carrying on the tradition begun by Thales but improving on it by making explanations more specific and detailed. See the discussion of Thales' remark, "All things are full of gods," p. 11.

NATURE

What Aristotle calls **"nature"** is narrower than what we have been calling "the world." Within the world there are two classes of things: *artifacts*, which are things made for various purposes by people (and by some animals), and *nature-facts*. There are beds, and there are boulders. These two classes differ in important respects. The basic science concerned with the world (what Aristotle calls "physics") deals with boulders, but only in a derivative sense with beds. Aristotle draws the distinction in the following way:

> Of the things that exist, some exist by nature, others through other causes. Those that exist by nature include animals and their parts, plants, and simple bodies like earth, fire, air, and water—for of these and suchlike things we do say that they exist by nature. All these obviously differ from things that have not come together by nature; for each of them has in itself a source of movement and rest. This movement is in some cases movement from place to place, in others it takes the forms of growth and decay, in still others of qualitative change. But a bed or a garment or any other such kind of thing has no natural impulse for change—at least, not insofar as it belongs to its own peculiar category and is the product of art. (*PH* 2.1)

Of course, beds and garments change, too. But they change not because they are beds and garments but because they are made of natural things such as wood and wool. It is by virtue of being wood that the bedstead develops cracks and splinters, not by virtue of being a bedstead. The sword rusts not because it is a sword but because it is made of iron.

Nature, then, is distinguished from art and the products of art because it "has in itself a source of movement and rest." We should note that Aristotle understands "movement" here in a broad sense: there is (1) movement from place to place, also called local motion; (2) growth and decay; and (3) change in qualities. (We usually call only the first of these "movement.") Natural things, then, change in these ways because of what they are. An artifact like a bed may move from place to place, but only if someone moves it; it does not grow or decay; and any change in its qualities is due either to some external activity (I paint my bed red) or to a property of the natural substance it is made of (the wood in the bedstead fades from dark to light brown). By contrast, a beaver moves about from place to place on its own, is born, matures, becomes wiser with age, and dies because this is the *nature* of beavers.

Nature, then, is the locus of change. Aristotle is convinced that if we only observe closely enough, we can understand the principles governing these changes. Nature is composed of primary substances that are the *subjects* of change. They change in two ways: (1) they come into being and pass away again; (2) while in existence, they vary in quality, quantity, relation, place, and so on. About natural substances we can have knowledge. And because Aristotle agrees with his teacher Plato that knowledge is always knowledge of the real, it follows that nature is as real as anything could be!

The Four "Becauses"

The wise person, as we have seen, knows not only what things are but also why. Aristotle sees that all his predecessors are asking why things are the way they are and giving these answers: because of water, because of the Boundless, because of opposition and the *logos*, because of atoms and the void, because of the Forms. What none of them sees is that this is not one question but four distinct questions.

> Some people regard the nature and substance of things that exist by nature as being in each case the proximate element inherent in the thing, this being itself unshaped; thus, the nature of a bed, for instance, would be wood, and that of a statue bronze. (*PH* 2.1)

People who think this way identify the substance of a thing—its nature—with the element or elements it is made of. Thales, for instance, thinks that the nature of all things is water; everything else is nonessential, just accidental ways in which the underlying substance happens, for a time, to be arranged. The underlying substratum, however, is eternal; that is the real stuff!

Those who think this way are taking the why-question in one very specific sense. They answer,

"Because it is made of such and such stuff." Aristotle does not want to deny that this is one very proper answer to the why-question. Why is this statue what it is? Because it is made of bronze. The answer points to the *matter* from which it is made. Let us call this kind of answer to the why-question the **material cause**. Material causes, then, are one type of causation.

But citing a material cause does not give a complete answer to the why-question. That should be obvious enough; lots of bronze is not formed into statues. Consider some wood that has not been made into a bed. We could call such wood a "potential bed," but it is not yet a *bed*. It is the same, he says,

> with things that come together by nature; what is potentially flesh or bone does not yet have its own nature until it acquires the form that accords with the formula, by means of which we define flesh and bone; nor can it be said at this stage to exist by nature. So in another way, nature is the shape and form of things that have a principle of movement in themselves—the form being only theoretically separable from the object in question. (*PH* 2.1)

Bone is what accords with "the formula" for bone—the definition that sets out the essential characteristics of bone. The elements of which bone is composed are not yet themselves bone; they are at best potential bone and may be formed into bone. In the case of bronze, there is no statue until it takes the shape of a statue. So here is another reason why a thing is the thing it is: It satisfies the requirements for being that sort of thing.

Aristotle here uses the term "form" both for the shape of something simple like a statue and for the definition of more complex things like bone. This is in accord with the usage for the term that comes down from Socrates and Plato. However, Aristotle adds this qualification: "the form being only theoretically separable from the object in question." He means that we can consider just the form of some substance independently of the material stuff that makes it up; but we must not suppose on that account that the form really is separable from the thing. Aristotle's forms are not Plato's Forms.

The form of a thing is not an independent object, but just its-having-the-characteristics-that-make-it-the-thing-that-it-is.

So we can answer the why-question in a second way by citing the form. Why is this bit of stuff bone? Because it has the characteristics mentioned in the definition of bone. Aristotle calls this the **formal cause**.

But there must be something else, particularly in cases where a substance such as a mouse or a man comes into being. There is the material stuff out of which mice and men are made, and each has its proper form. But what explains the fact of their *coming to be?*

> Thus, the answer to the question "why?" is to be given by referring to the matter, to the essence, and to the proximate mover. In cases of coming-to-be it is mostly in this last way that people examine the causes; they ask what comes to be after what, what was the immediate thing that acted or was acted upon, and so on in order. (*PH* 2.7)

Here is a third answer to the why-question. This answer names whatever triggered the beginning of the thing in question, what Aristotle calls the "proximate mover." This sense of cause comes closest to our modern understanding of causes. For Aristotle, though, such causes are always themselves substances ("man generates man"), whereas for us causes tend to be conditions, events, or happenings. This cause is often called the **efficient cause**.

There is one more sense in which the why-question can be asked. We might be interested in the "what for" of something, particularly in the case of artifacts. Suppose we ask, "Why are there houses?" One answer is that cement and bricks and lumber and wallboard exist. Without them (or something analogous to them) there wouldn't be any houses. This answer cites the material cause. Another answer is that there are things which satisfy the definition for a house, an answer naming the formal cause. A third answer cites the fact that there are house builders—the efficient cause. But even if we had all these answers, we would not be satisfied. What we want to know is why there are houses in the sense of what purpose they serve, what ends they satisfy.

Why are there houses? To provide shelter from the elements for human beings. If it were not for this purpose they serve, there would be no such things; the materials for houses might exist, but they would not have come together in the sort of form that makes a house a house. When we answer the why-question in this way, Aristotle says we are giving the **final cause**.*

> It is clear, then, that there are causes, and that they are as many in number as we say; for they correspond to the different ways in which we can answer the question "why?" The ultimate answer to that question can be reduced to saying what the thing is . . . or to saying what the first mover was . . . or to naming the purpose . . . or, in the case of things that come into being, to naming the matter. . . . Since there are these four causes, it is the business of the natural scientist to know about them all, and he will give his answer to the question "why?" in the manner of a natural scientist if he refers what he is being asked about to them all—to the matter, the form, the mover, and the purpose. (*PH* 2.7)

IS THERE PURPOSE IN NATURE?

The most controversial of the four "becauses" is the last. We say there is a purpose for artifacts (houses, for example), but only because human beings have

---

*Compare Socrates' answer to the question about why he is in prison, pp. 131–132.

purposes. We need, want, desire shelter; so we form an intention that shelters should exist. We think, plan, and draw up a blueprint, then gather the materials together and assemble a house. But the crucial thing here is the intention—without that, no houses. To say that there are final causes in nature seems like imputing intentions to nature. We might be able to answer the question, What is a sheep dog for? because sheep dogs serve our purposes. But does it even make sense to ask what *dogs* are for?[6] In a humorous sketch Bill Cosby asks, "Why is there air?" He answers: to have something to blow up basketballs with. But that is obviously a joke.

Yet Aristotle holds seriously that the question about final causes applies to nature-facts just as much as to artifacts. There may be some things that are accidental by-products (two-headed calves and such), and they may not have a purpose. Such accidents, he says, occur merely from "necessity." But accidents apart, he thinks nature-facts are inherently purposive.

Aristotle does not think that there are *intentions* resident in all things; intentions are formed after deliberation, and only rational animals can deliberate. But that does not mean that nature in general is devoid of *purposes*, for the concept of purpose is broader than that of intention.

> Things that serve a purpose include everything that might have been done intentionally, and everything that proceeds from nature. When such things come to be accidentally, we say that they are as they are by chance. (*PH* 2.5)

But why couldn't everything in nature happen by chance, without purpose, according to sheer necessity? This is what Democritus thinks the world is like—the accidental product of the necessary hooking up of atoms.* Why is that a mistake?

Aristotle has two arguments. (1) He draws on his close observations of nature to conclude that

> all natural objects either always or usually come into being in a given way, and that is not the case with anything that comes to be by chance. (*PH* 2.8)

Chance or accident makes sense only against a background of regularity, of what happens "either always or usually." Roses come from roses and not from grains of wheat; therefore, a rose coming from a rose is no accident. But since everything must occur either by chance or for a purpose, it must happen for some purpose. (2) Art (meaning something like the art of the physician or house builder) either completes nature or "imitates nature." But there is purpose in art, so there must be purpose in nature as well.*

TELEOLOGY

The idea that natural substances are *for* something is called **teleology**, from the Greek word *telos*, meaning end or goal. We can get a better feel for this by thinking about a concrete example. Consider a frog. Let it be a common leopard frog such as children like to catch by the lake in the summertime. We can consider the frog from two points of view: (1) at a given time we can examine a kind of cross section of its history, and (2) we can follow its development through time.

At the moment when he is caught by little Johnny, the frog has certain characteristics. Johnny might list them as spottedness, four-leggedness, and hoppiness. A biologist would give us a better list amounting to a definition of what a frog is. This "what-it-is" the frog shares with all other frogs; it is what makes it a frog rather than a toad or a salamander. This is what Aristotle calls its form.

But of course it is one particular frog, the one Johnny caught this morning. It is not "frog in general," or "all the frog there is." What makes it the particular individual that it is? Surely it is the matter composing it; this frog is different from the one Sally caught, because even though they share the same form, each is made up of different bits of matter.

So in a cross section it is possible to distinguish form from matter. But now let us look at the history of the frog. Each and every frog develops from a fertilized egg into a tadpole and then into an

---

*Are these sound arguments? A key move in the development of modern science is their rejection. See pp. 309–310.

adult frog. At each of these temporal stages, more-over, one can distinguish form and matter. The egg is matter that satisfies the definition for eggs; the tadpole has the form for tadpoles; the frog satisfies the formula for frogs. These stages are related in a regular, orderly way. As Aristotle puts it, this development is something that happens "always or usually." There is a determinate pattern in this history. And it is always the same.

In the egg, Aristotle will say, there is a potentiality to become a frog. It won't become a toad. It has, so to speak, a direction programmed into it. There is a goal or end *in* the egg, which is what determines the direction of development. The term for this indwelling of the goal is **entelechy**. The goal, or *telos*, is present in the egg. The goal (being a frog) is not present in actuality, of course—otherwise, the egg would not be an egg but already a frog. The egg has *actually* the form for an egg, but the form frog is there *potentially*. If it were not, Aristotle would say, the egg might turn into anything! (Note that the final cause toward which the egg and tadpole develop is itself a form; the goal is to actualize the form of a frog.)

This indwelling of the end, entelechy, is what Aristotle means by the purpose that is in natural things. Such things have purpose in the sense that there is a standard direction of development for them; they move toward an end. Natural things, particularly living things, look in two directions. They look back to earlier forms (which contained the later forms potentially) and forward to still later forms (which they contain potentially). Earlier forms of a substance are already potentially what they will actually become only later. The tadpole is the potentiality of there being an actual frog. The frog is the actuality the tadpole tends toward.

Science, Aristotle says, can grasp not only the nature of static and eternal things, such as Plato's Forms, but also the natural laws of development. These laws are universals, too. Knowledge is always of the universal, of forms; in this Plato was right. But the forms are not outside the natural world; they are within it, guiding and making intelligible the changes that natural substances undergo either always or usually. The concepts of the four causes, plus actuality and potentiality, are the

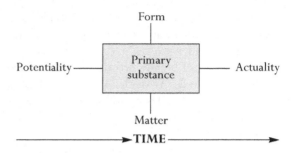

tools by which science can succeed in its task of understanding the natural world.

Once again we see a philosopher forging linguistic tools to make intelligible what seemed unintelligible to earlier thinkers. Parmenides, working only with concepts of being and not being, argued that change was impossible.* Aristotle uses the concepts of potentiality and actuality to discern universal laws governing orderly and intelligible change. Philosophy is argument and reason-giving. But it is also creation and invention, requiring the imagination to envision new conceptual possibilities.

1. How do nature-facts differ from artifacts? In what ways are they similar?
2. Explain each of the four causes.
3. How are Aristotle's forms both like and unlike Plato's Forms?
4. Describe how Aristotle uses the concepts of form/matter and actuality/potentiality to gain an understanding of the natural world, for example, of a frog.

First Philosophy

It is from a feeling of wonder that men start now, and did start in the earliest times, to practice philosophy. (*M* 1.2)

Practicing philosophy, Aristotle makes clear, is not the basic activity of human beings. They must first see to the necessities of life, and only when these are reasonably secure will they have the leisure to pursue wisdom. The wise person, as we have seen,

---

*See p. 29.

wishes to know, wishes to know everything, and wishes to know the causes in every case. So far does human wonder go.

There need not be any practical payoff to such knowledge. Indeed, Aristotle is quite convinced that there will not be. There are, of course, practical sciences such as medicine, which do have practical consequences. But the most uniquely human pursuit of knowledge is characterized by a delight in knowing "for its own sake." In a certain sense, Aristotle says, this pursuit is "more than human, since human nature is in many respects enslaved" (*M* 1.2). So much of our activity is devoted to the necessities of just staying alive that we are enslaved to the needs of our own nature. The knowledge that does nothing more than satisfy wonder, in contrast, is more than human because it would be free from this bondage. It is akin to the knowledge god would have. In our quest for such "divine" knowledge, we would have as our main concern those things that are "first" or "primary" or independent of everything else. We could call such a search "**first philosophy**."

Familiar as we are with the world of nature, we wonder now whether that is all there is.

> If there is no other substance apart from those that have come together by nature, natural science will be the first science. But if there is a substance that is immovable, the science that studies it is prior to natural science and is the first philosophy. . . .
> It is the business of this science to study being qua being, and to find out what it is and what are its attributes qua being. (*M* 6.1)

Biology, we might say, studies *being qua* (as) *living being;* or to put it another way, the biologist is interested in *what there is* just insofar as it is *alive.* There are in fact a variety of sciences, theoretical and practical, each of which cuts out a certain area of what there is—of being—for study. Each such science brings its subject matter together under some unifying first principles. And this question must inevitably arise: Is there some still higher unity to what there is? Is being *one?* Is it unified by some principles that are true of it throughout?

If so, this too must be an area of knowledge, and the wise person's wonder will not be satisfied

until it is canvassed and understood. This science would be concerned with the characteristics or attributes of being in an unqualified sense: of being qua being. If there is such a science, it is "first" in the sense that it would examine the principles taken for granted by all the special sciences. It would ask about the ultimate causes of all things. If, says Aristotle, natural substances are the only ones there are, then natural science will be this first science or philosophy. But if there are other substances—ones not subject to change—then the science that studies those will be first philosophy.* So first philosophy, also called **metaphysics**, looks for the ultimate principles and causes of all things. What are they?

NOT PLATO'S FORMS

As we have seen, Plato gives an answer to this very question. The ultimate realities are the Forms, he says, and ultimately the Form of the Good. But Aristotle criticizes this answer severely. Not only are the Forms subject to the Third Man problem, they present many other difficulties.† Let us briefly explore some of them.

1. The things of this world are supposed to derive their reality from their "participation" in the Forms. But nowhere does Plato explain just what this "participation" amounts to. Without such an account, however, all we have are "empty phrases" and "poetic metaphors" (*M* 1.9).

2. The Forms are themselves supposed to be substantial realities—indeed, the most real of all the things there are. Aristotle's comment is this:

> In seeking to find the causes of the things that are around us, they have introduced another lot of

---

*Aristotle seems to be assuming here that the cause that accounts for the entire world of changing substances cannot itself just be a changing substance; if it were, it would itself need accounting for. So it must be—if it exists—something unchanging. If nature is defined as the sphere of those things that change because of a source of movement or change within them, an ultimate, unchanging cause of natural things would be beyond nature.

†Review the Third Man Argument on pp. 152–154.

objects equal in number to them. It is as if someone who wanted to count thought that he would not be able to do so while the objects in question were relatively few, and then proceeded to do so when he had made them more numerous. (*M* 1.9)

To say that the Form Human is the cause of humans is simply to multiply the entities needing explanation. If it is difficult to explain the existence and nature of human beings, it is certainly no easier to explain the existence and nature of humans-plus-the-Form-Human.

3. The Forms are supposed to be what many individuals of the same kind have in common. Yet they are also supposed to be individual realities in their own right. But, says Aristotle, these requirements conflict. If the Forms are indeed individual substances, it makes no sense to think of them being shared out among other individual substances.* If, on the other hand, they are universal in character (nonindividual), there is no sense in thinking of them as things that exist separately from particulars. Being-a-man, Aristotle holds, is realized not in a substantial Form independently of all men, but precisely and only in *each individual man*. Because the "friends of the Forms" are unable to explain how such substances are both individual and universal,

> they make them the same in form as perishable things (since we know them), talking of "the man himself" and "the horse itself," just adding the word "self" to the names of sensible objects. (*M* 7.16)

But this is completely useless as an explanation.

4. Finally, there is no way to understand how the Forms, eternally unchanging, account for changes. They are supposed to be the first principles and causes of whatever happens in the world. But

> one is most of all bewildered to know what contribution the forms make either to the sensible things that are eternal or to those that come into being and perish; for they are not the cause of their movement or of any change in them. (*M* 1.9)

By "the sensible things that are eternal," Aristotle means the things in the natural world whose movement is (as he thought) regular and everlasting: the sun, moon, and the fixed stars. How can eternally stable Forms explain change either in these things or in the even more unstable items on earth?

The outcome of Aristotle's critical appraisal of his master's metaphysics is a thoroughgoing rejection of the Forms. The fundamental things that exist have to be things that are *individual* and can exist *independently* of other things. Plato's Forms do not satisfy either requirement. The Forms are supposed to be the common features of things that are individual, but such features, Aristotle believes, have no independent being; they depend for such being as they have on individual substances (of which they are the qualities, relations, and so on). The sensible things of nature, humans and beavers, surely exist; but being mortal and having a broad, flat tail are qualities existing only as modifications of these. Whether anything beyond these individual entities exists is still an open question. But if it does, it too will be substantial, individual, and capable of independent existence. It will not be a "common feature" of individual things.*

WHAT OF MATHEMATICS?

The most convincing arguments for the Forms seem to be mathematical in nature. Socrates is not talking about his sand figure, so Plato concludes that Socrates is talking about the Square Itself, the Triangle Itself, and the Equal. Aristotle wishes to avoid drawing this conclusion. So how does he deal with mathematics?

The natural scientist, in studying changeable things, deals with subjects like the shape of the moon and the sphericity of the earth.

> Such attributes as these are studied by mathematicians as well as by natural scientists, but not by virtue of their being limits of natural bodies. The

---

*Review the discussion of substance on pp. 160–161.

*We can think of these reflections as a critique of Plato's metaphysical argument for the Forms (see p. 124). In the following section, Aristotle examines the epistemological argument.

mathematician is not interested in them as attributes of whatever they are attributes of, and so he separates them. For these attributes can be conceptually separated from movement, without this separation making any difference or involving any false statement. (*PH* 2.2)

The crucial point is that we can "conceptually" separate attributes of things and consider them on their own, without supposing that they must be independent things. To use one of Aristotle's favorite examples, consider a snub nose. As a natural thing, a nose is a compound made up of form and matter; as such, it is of interest to the natural scientist but not to the mathematician. What makes it "snub," though, is its being curved in a certain way. And we can consider the curve alone, abstracting away from the matter in the nose. When we do this, we are taking up the mathematician's point of view. But the fact that we can adopt this viewpoint does not mean that Curvedness exists independently of noses. There need be no Form of the Curve to make mathematics intelligible.

There is no argument, Aristotle holds, from knowledge in mathematics to the reality of Platonic Forms independent of the world of nature. Mathematics is a science that, like natural science, has the world of nature as its only object. But it does not study it *as nature;* it studies only certain abstractions from natural things, without supposing that such abstractions are themselves things.

SUBSTANCE AND FORM

When we considered Aristotle's categories, it was already apparent that certain terms were more basic than others.* These terms picked out substances and could play only the subject role in a statement. Now Aristotle reinforces this conclusion, looking more directly at things themselves.

> There are many ways in which the term "being" is used, corresponding to the distinctions we drew earlier, when we showed in how many ways terms are used. On the one hand, it indicates what a thing is and that it is this particular thing; on the other, it indicates a thing's quality or size, or whatever else is

asserted of it in this way. Although "being" is used in all these ways, clearly the primary kind of being is what a thing is; for it is this alone that indicates substance. . . . All other things are said to be only insofar as they are quantities, qualities, affections, or something else of this kind belonging to what is in this primary sense. (*M* 7.1)

We can ask many different questions about any given thing: How old is it? How large is it? What color is it? What shape is it? Is it alive? Does it think? Answers to each of these questions tell us something about the thing in question, describing a way the thing *is*, saying something about its *being*. But one question, Aristotle argues, is basic, namely, *What is it?* We may learn that it is thirty years old, six feet tall, white, fat, and thinking of Philadelphia, but until we learn that it is a *man* all these answers hang in the air. Aristotle puts it this way: that answer gives us the "substance." And substance is *what is*, in the basic, fundamental, primary sense.

This is the first answer to the metaphysical question about being qua being. For something to be, in the primary sense, is for it to be a substance. Whatever exists is dependent on substance. But more must be said. What is it that makes a given object a substance?

If we think back to the discussion of nature, we recall that natural things are composed of matter and form (the latter being expressed in a formula or definition). Could it be the matter that makes an object a substance? No. Matter, considered apart from form, is merely potentially something. If you strip off all form, you are tempted to say that what is left is sheer, undifferentiated, characterless something. But even that would be wrong, because every "something" has some character or form that differentiates it from something else. This "prime matter" can't be anything at all, on its own. It cannot have an independent existence; it exists only *as formed*. So matter cannot be what accounts for, or what makes or causes, something to be a substance. For what accounts for something being a substance must be at least as substantial as the substances it produces.

What of the other alternative? Could it be form that makes a portion of being into a substance? In a series of complex arguments, Aristotle argues

---

*See pp. 160–161.

that this is in fact the case. But not just any form makes the substance *what it is*. The form responsible for the substantiality of substances he calls the **essence** of the thing. *Essences* are expressed by definitions telling us *what things are*.

Johnny's frog may weigh five ounces, but weighing five ounces is not part of the essence of that frog. The proof is that if the frog eats well and gains weight, it does not cease to be a frog. What makes it a frog remains the same whether it weighs five, six, or seven ounces. The definition of frog allows a variation in many of the qualities and quantities Johnny's frog might have. But not in all. It could not cease to be amphibious and still be a frog. Amphibiousness is part of the essence of what it is to be a frog. All natural things (and artifacts, too), Aristotle holds, have an essence: a set of characteristics without which they would not be the things they are.

> Why, for instance, are these materials a house? Because of the presence of the essence of house. One might also ask, "Why is this, or the body containing this, a man?" So what one is really looking for is the cause—that is, the form—of the matter being whatever it is; and this in fact is the substance. (*M* 7.17)

We are, remember, looking for first principles and causes. We want to know what it is that makes a bit of matter what it is. We know that natural things are substances; they can exist independently and individually. But what makes this bunch of bricks a house, this mass of protoplasm a human? The answer is that each satisfies the definition of the essence of that thing. The presence of the essence house in the one case and the essence human in the other is the *cause* of each one being what it is.

So here we come to a second answer. Even more basic than substances composed of form and matter is the form itself. The cause of something could not be less real than the thing itself. So we find Aristotle asserting that this form—essence— is the very substance of substance itself.

In a way, this should be no surprise. Thinking back to the account Aristotle gives of natural substances, we can see how prominent form is. There are four causes, four explanations of why

something is the particular substance it is. The material cause cannot be fundamental, as we have seen. But think about the other three: the form or essence of the thing; the final cause or goal, which is itself a form; and the efficient cause. Even this latter must involve a form, for it must be something actual, and actualities always embody form; as Aristotle likes to say, "man begets man." From all three points of view, then, form is the principal cause of the substantiality of things.

Aristotle gives us a simple example. Consider a syllable, *ba*. What makes this a syllable? There is the "matter" that makes it up: the elements *b* and *a*. But it is not the matter that makes these into the syllable *ba*, for these elements might also compose *ab*. So it must be the form. Moreover, the form cannot itself be an element, or we would need to explain how it is related to the *b* and the *a* (that is, we would have the Third Man problem). So the form must be something else.

> But this "something else," although it seems to be something, seems not to be an element; it seems in fact to be the cause of . . . that [the *b* and the *a*] being a syllable . . . ; in each case it is the thing's substance, since that is the ultimate cause of a thing's being. (*M* 7.17)

So form is the substance of things. But substance is what can exist independently and as an individual entity. This raises a very interesting possibility. Might there be substances that are not compounds of matter and form? Might there be substances that are *pure forms*?

All of nature is made up of material substances in which matter is made into something definite by the presence of form within it. But might there be something more fundamental than nature itself, in just the way that form is more basic than the compounds it forms? If there were any such substances, knowledge of them might be what the wise person seeks. Wisdom is knowing the being and causes of things. If there were substances of pure form, they would be less dependent and more basic than the things of nature, since even natural things depend on form for their substantiality. Knowledge of such "pure" substances would therefore be the knowledge most worth having, the most divine knowledge; it would satisfy our wonder in the highest degree. We need now to explore this possibility.

PURE ACTUALITIES

One thing is clear. If there are such purely formal substances, without any matter, they would be pure *actualities* as well. They couldn't involve any "might bes," for the principle of potentiality is matter and they would have no matter. Nor could such substances admit of any change, for every change is a movement from something potential to something actual (for example, from tadpole into frog). But then it would be *eternal* as well.

A second thing is also clear. These would be the *best* things. Why? Think again about natural things, for example, the frog that Johnny caught. When is that frog at its very best? Surely when it is most froggy—hopping around, catching flies, doing all the things frogs most typically do. It is not at its best when it has a broken leg, nor when it is feeling listless, nor when it is a mere tadpole. In Aristotle's terms, the frog is best when the form that makes it a frog (the essence) is most fully actualized in the matter—when it most fully is *what it is*. If there are substances lacking matter and potency altogether, substances that are fully actual, then they must be the best substances. For they cannot fail to display all the perfection of their form.

But are there any such substances—perfect, immaterial, and eternal—pure actualities without the possibility of change? If so, what are they like?

GOD

In the world of nature, the best things would be those that come closest to these ideals. Aristotle believes these are the heavenly bodies that move eternally in great circles. They change their positions constantly, but in a perfectly regular way, without beginning or ending.* But even such eternal motion is not self-explanatory.

There is something that is always being moved in an incessant movement, and this movement is circular . . . : and so the first heaven will be eternal. There must, then, be something that moves it. But since that which is moved, as well as moving things, is intermediate, there must be something that moves things without being moved; this will be something eternal, it will be a substance, and it will be an actuality. (*M* 12.7)

Think about baseball. A bat may impart movement to a ball, but only if put into movement by a batter. The bat is what Aristotle calls an "intermediate" mover; it moves the ball and is moved by the batter. The batter himself is moved to swing the bat by his desire to make a hit. Aristotle would put it this way: Making a hit is the final cause (the goal) that moves him to swing as he does. So the batter himself is only an "intermediate" mover. He moves as he does for the sake of making a hit. The goal of making a hit in turn exists for the sake of winning the game, which has as *its* goal the league championship. In the world of baseball, the ultimate final cause putting the whole season in motion is the goal of winning the World Series. Each batter is striving to embody the form: Member of a Team That Wins the World Series.

Let's return to the world of nature, containing the eternal movements of the heavenly bodies. Is there any final or ultimate mover here? There must be, Aristotle argues; otherwise we could not account for the movement of anything at all. Not all movers can be "intermediate" movers. If they were, that series would go on to infinity, but there cannot be any actually existing collection of infinitely many things. There must, then, be "something that moves things without being moved."*

Moreover, we can know certain facts about it. It must itself be eternal because it must account for the eternal movement of the heavenly bodies and

---

*His reasons for thinking so are complex, involving a theory of the nature of time; we will not discuss that theory here. It can be found in *Physics* IV, 10–14. His theory was combined with the astronomy of the second-century Alexandrian, Ptolemy, and was to dominate scientific

thinking until the beginnings of modern science in the sixteenth century. For a fuller discussion of this Aristotelian/Ptolemaic theory of the universe, see "The World God Made for Us," in Chapter 12.

*This is a form of argument that looks back to Anaximander (see p. 12) and forward to Saint Thomas Aquinas (see his first and second arguments for the existence of God, pp. 271–273).

so cannot be less extensive than they. It must be a substance, for what other substances depend on cannot be less basic than they. And, of course, it must be fully actual; otherwise, its being what it is would cry out for further explanation—for a mover for it.

What kind of cause could this **unmoved mover** be? Let's review the four causes. It clearly couldn't be a material cause, since that is purely potential. It couldn't be an efficient cause, for the eternal movement of the heavens does not need a temporal trigger. It is not the formal cause of a compound of form and matter because it contains no matter. It could only be a *final cause*. This conclusion is driven home by an analogy.

> Now, the object of desire and the object of thought move things in this way: they move things without being moved. (*M* 12.7)

Our baseball example already indicated this. What sets the whole baseball world in motion is a goal, namely, winning the World Series. Within the world of baseball, there is no further purpose. It moves the players, managers, umpires, and owners, but without being moved itself.* It is "the object of desire and thought," and functions that way as a final cause. It is what they all "love."

> The final cause then moves things because it is loved, whereas all other things move because they are themselves moved. . . . The first mover, then, must exist; and insofar as he exists of necessity, his existence must be good; and thus he must be a first principle. . . .
>
> It is upon a principle of this kind, then, that the heavens and nature depend. (*M* 12.7)

The ultimate cause of all things is a final cause; it is what all other things love. Their love for it puts them in motion, just as the sheer existence of a bicycle stimulates a boy or girl into activity, delivering papers, mowing lawns, and saving to buy it. As the object of desire and love, this first mover must be something good. Can we say anything more about the nature of this unmoved mover?

———

*You may object that there are further goals: fame, money, and so on. And you are right. But that just shows that the "world" of baseball is not a self-contained world; it is not *the* world, but has a place in a wider setting.

Its life is like the best that we can enjoy—and we can enjoy it only a short time. It is always in this state (which we cannot be), since its actuality is also pleasure. . . . If, then, God is always in the good state which we are sometimes in, that is something to wonder at; and if he is in a better state than we are ever in, that is to be wondered at even more. This is in fact the case, however. Life belongs to him, too; for life is the actuality of mind, and God is that actuality; and his independent actuality is the best life and eternal life. We assert, then, that God is an eternal and most excellent living being, so that continuous and eternal life and duration belong to him. For that is what God is. (*M* 12.7)

There must be such an actuality, Aristotle argues, to explain the existence and nature of changing things. As the final cause and the object of the "desire" in all things, it must be the best. What is the best we know? The life of the mind.* So God must enjoy this life in the highest degree.

God, then, is an eternally existing, living being who lives a life of perfect thought. But this raises a further problem. What does God think about? Aristotle's answer to this question is reasonable, but puzzling, too.

> Plainly, it thinks of what is most divine and most valuable, and plainly it does not change; for change would be for the worse. . . . The mind, then, must think of itself if it is the best of things, and its thought will be thought about thought. (*M* 12.9)

It would not be appropriate for the best thought to be about ordinary things, Aristotle argues. It must have only the best and most valuable object. But that is itself! So God will think only of himself. He will not, in Aristotle's view, have any concern or thought for the world. He will engage eternally in a contemplation of his own life—which is a life of contemplation. His relation to the world is not that of *creator* (the world being everlasting needs no efficient cause), but of *ideal*, inspiring each thing in the world to be its very best in imitation of the divine perfection. God is not the origin of the world, but its goal. Yet he is and must be an actually existing, individual substance, devoid of matter, and the best in every way.

———

*This is discussed in more detail later in this chapter. See "The Highest Good."

God, then, is to *the* world as winning the World Series is to the "world" of baseball. He functions as the unifying principle of reality, that cause to which all other final causes must ultimately be referred. There is no multitude of ultimate principles, no polytheism. The world is one world. As Aristotle puts it,

> The world does not wish to be governed badly. As Homer says: "To have many kings is not good; let there be one." (*M* 12.10)

1. What is "first" philosophy? Is there another name for it?
2. List four criticisms of Plato's doctrine that the Forms are the most real of all things.
3. How does Aristotle's understanding of mathematics tend to undermine Plato's epistemological argument for the Forms?
4. In what way is substance the primary category of being?
5. What is an essence?
6. In what ways is form the most basic thing in substances?
7. What is God like? What kind of cause is God?

The Soul

Plato holds that the essence of a person is found in the soul, an entity distinct from the body. Souls exist before their "imprisonment" in a body and survive the death of the body. The wise person tries to dissociate himself as much as possible from the obscure and harmful influences of the body. The practice of philosophy, the love of wisdom, is a kind of purification making a soul fit for blessedness after death.

Aristotle argues against the otherworldliness implicit in such views. One of the causes of such otherworldliness, Aristotle holds, is a too narrow focus.

> Till now, those who have discussed and inquired about the soul seem to have considered only the human soul; but we must take care not to forget the question of whether one single definition can be given of soul in the way that it can of animal, or whether there is a different one in each case—for horse, dog, man, and god, for instance. (*PS* 1.1)

The term "soul" is the English translation of the Greek *psyche*. And that is the general word applied to life. So, things with *psyche*—ensouled things—are living things. But not only humans are alive. Aristotle is raising the question whether soul or life or *psyche* is something shared in common among all living things. If you think only about the life characteristic of humans, you might well think of soul as something quite other than nature; but if you pay attention to the broader context, you may find that you have to give a very different account of soul. Again we see Aristotle the biologist at work, trying to organize and classify all living things, humans being just one species among many.

LEVELS OF SOUL

There is "one definition of soul in the same way that there is one definition of shape" (*PS* 2.3). Just as there are plane figures and solid figures, and among the latter there are spheres and cubes, so souls come in a variety of kinds.

> We must, then, inquire, species by species, what is the soul of each living thing—what is the soul of a plant, for instance, or what is that of a man or a beast. (*PS* 2.3)

The general definition of soul involves life: "that which distinguishes what has a soul from what has not is life" (*PS* 2.2). But souls may differ from each other as triangles differ from rectangles; the latter are constructed on the basis of triangles, which are more fundamental (every rectangle is composed of two triangles). Similarly, there are more primitive souls (or forms of life) and more complex forms built upon them. Aristotle distinguishes three general levels of soul: that of plants, that of beasts, and that of humans.

The most fundamental of these forms is that of the plants,

> for clearly they have within themselves a faculty and principle such that through it they can grow or decay in opposite directions. For they do not just grow upwards without growing downwards; they grow in both directions alike, and indeed in every direction . . . for as long as they can receive

nourishment. This nutritive faculty can be separated from the other faculties, but the other faculties cannot exist apart from it in mortal creatures. This is clear in the case of plants, since they have none of the other faculties of the soul. (PS 2.2)

Nutritive soul, the capacity to take in nourishment and convert it to life, is basic to living things and is found in plants and animals alike. Plants, however, do not share the higher levels of soul. They live and reproduce and so have a kind of soul, but without the capacities of movement, sensation, and thought.

We should pause a moment to consider reproduction. Why do plants (as well as animals) reproduce? We know that for Aristotle the answer is incomplete if it makes no mention of the final cause. What is the final cause for reproduction?

> The most natural function of any living being that is complete, is not deformed, and is not born spontaneously is to produce another being like itself . . . so that it may share, as far as it can, in eternity and divinity; that is what they all desire, and it is the purpose of all their natural activities. (PS 2.4)

This is an application of the principle uncovered in first philosophy. There is an unmoved mover, existing eternally in perfect independence and actuality—the final cause of whatever else exists. So the fact that plants and animals reproduce can be explained by their "desire" to share, as far as possible, the eternity and divinity that caps off the universe. Each thing imitates God in the way possible for it. God's eternal existence is responsible for the fact that the mature pine tree drops its cones and new plants of that very same species grow up, for the reproduction of beings like themselves is as close as mortal beings can come to a kind of eternity.*

More complex forms of soul are built upon the nutritive soul and are never found in nature without it. The next level can be called the level of **sensitive soul**; it belongs to the animals.

_____
*Compare Plato's discussion of love, pp. 137–140.

Plants possess only the nutritive faculty, but other beings possess both it and the sensitive faculty; and if they possess the sensitive faculty, they must also possess the appetitive; for appetite consists of desire, anger, and will. All animals possess at least one sense, that of touch; anything that has a sense is acquainted with pleasure and pain, with what is pleasant and what is painful; and anything that is acquainted with these has desire, since desire is an appetite for the pleasant. (PS 2.3)

Animals, then, have sensations and desires in addition to the faculties of nutrition and reproduction. Some animals, though not all, also have the capacity for locomotion.

Finally, there is **rational soul**, soul that has the capacity to think. Among naturally existing species, it seems to be characteristic only of human beings. Whether there is something unique and special about this kind of soul we'll consider in due course.

In general, then, there are three kinds or levels of soul: nutritive, sensitive, and rational. They correspond to three great classes of living things: plants, animals, and human beings. They are related in such a way that higher kinds of soul incorporate the lower, but the lower can exist without the higher.

Soul and Body

We need now to ask how souls are related to bodies. Can we give the same sort of answer for each of the kinds of soul? Plato, concentrating on human beings, holds that souls are completely distinct entities, capable of existence on their own. That is not so plausible in the case of plant and animal souls. What does Aristotle say?

Actually, Aristotle gives two answers, and that fact has been the cause of much subsequent debate. There is a general answer and an answer that pertains specifically to the rational form of soul. Let's look first at the general answer. The scene is set by a remark about the proper way to talk about soul.

> It is probably better to say not that the soul feels pity or learns or thinks, but that man does these things with his soul; for we should not suppose that the movement is actually in the soul, but that in some cases it penetrates as far as the soul, in others it starts from it; sensation, for instance, starts from

the particular objects, whereas recollection starts from the soul and proceeds to the movements or their residues in the sense organs. (*PS* 1.4)

This view of soul is one that firmly embeds soul in the body and makes us unitary beings. It is not the case that certain operations can be assigned to the soul and certain others to the body. It is not the soul that feels or learns or thinks while the body eats and walks; it is the *person* that does all these things. It would be no more sensible, Aristotle holds, to say that the soul is angry than that the body weaves or builds. Neither souls nor bodies do these things; human beings do them all. Sensation is not something the soul accomplishes; it cannot occur at all without a body, sense organs, and objects to which those sense organs are sensitive. Recollection has its effects in bodily movements (remembering an appointment makes you run to catch the bus). A person is *one being* with *one essence*.

But what exactly is a soul, and how is it related to a body? We must remind ourselves of the results of Aristotle's investigations of being qua being. The basic things that exist are substances, and in natural substances there is a material substratum that is actualized—made into the substance it is—by a form.

> The soul, then, must be a substance inasmuch as it is the form of a natural body that potentially possesses life; and such substance is in fact realization, so that the soul is the realization of a body of this kind. (*PS* 2.1)

Suppose you have before you a living being (whether plant, animal, or human makes no difference just now). Subtract from it—in thought—its life. What you have left is a body that *could* be alive, but isn't—a body that is potentially alive. In one sense it is just a body, like a stone or a stove. But in another sense it isn't, for stones and stoves are not even potentially alive; they are not organized in the right way to be alive. Walt Disney can make stoves talk, perhaps, but only in cartoons. There are no talking stoves in reality, precisely because a stove is not the sort of body that is potentially alive.* The

body from which we have in thought abstracted life, however, is such a body. It cannot now engage in nutrition or sensation or thought, but it could. It is a kind of "substratum" that could support life—*matter* that could have the *form* of a living thing.

Remember that "form" does not stand for shape (except in very simple cases) but for the essence, the definition, the satisfaction of which makes a thing the substance it is. Remember also that form is the principle of actualization or realization; it is what makes a bit of matter into an actual thing. And remember that form is itself substance: the very substance of substances.

Now you can understand Aristotle's view of soul as "the form of a natural body that potentially possesses life" and as the "realization of a body of this kind." Restore—in thought—life to that body from which you earlier abstracted it. Now it is capable of performing all the activities that are appropriate to that kind of being; it feeds itself and perhaps sees, desires, and thinks. And its being capable of those activities is the *same* as its having certain essential characteristics. Having those characteristics is having a form of a certain kind; having that form is having a soul.

> We have, then, said in general what the soul is: it is a formal substance. That means that it is the essence of a body of a particular kind. (*PS* 2.1)

Aristotle offers us several examples. Suppose that an axe were a natural body. Then its "formal substance" would be "being an axe." And that would be its soul. But axes are not alive, any more than stones or stoves. They don't actually have souls because the soul is the principle of life in living things. The analogy should show you, though, what *kind* of thing a soul is—a *form* for a *primary substance*. Similarly, Aristotle says, "If the eye were an animal, its soul would be sight; for sight is the formal substance of the eye" (*PS* 2.1). From these examples it should be clear that the soul, so conceived, is not a separable entity; for neither "being an axe" nor sight have any existence independent of actual axes and eyes.

It should be no surprise, then, to hear Aristotle say rather offhandedly,

---

*From Aristotle's point of view, the reincarnationist idea that a human soul might enter into the body of a lower animal is absurd. Cows and dogs do not have the right sorts of bodies (including brains) to support human souls.

We do not, therefore, have to inquire whether the soul and body are one, just as we do not have to inquire whether the wax and its shape, or in general the matter of any given thing and that of which it is the matter, are one. (*PS* 2.1)

This problem, which so occupies Plato and for which he constructs so many proofs, is simply one that we do not have to inquire into! The answer is *obvious*, as obvious as the answer to the question whether the shape of a wax seal can exist independently of the wax.

Aristotle gives a brief indication of how this view works in practice. Consider anger. Some people define anger as a disposition to strike out or retaliate in response to some perceived wrong. Its definition therefore involves beliefs, desires, and emotions— all mental states of one sort or another. Others say that anger is just a bodily state involving heightened blood pressure, tensing of muscles, the flow of adrenaline, and so on. Nothing mental needs to be brought into its explanation. What would Aristotle say? He contrasts the viewpoint of the natural scientist with that of the "logician," by which he means one who seeks the definition of such states.

> The natural scientist and the logician would define all these affections in different ways; if they were asked what anger is, the one would say that it was a desire to hurt someone in return, or something like that, the other that it was a boiling of the blood and the heat around the heart. Of these, one is describing the matter, the other the form and the definition; for the latter is indeed the definition of the thing, but it must be in matter of a particular kind if the thing is going to exist. (*PS* 1.1)

If Aristotle is right, psychology and physiology in fact study the same thing. The former studies the form, and the latter the matter. From one point of view anger is a mental state, from the other a physical state. There need be no quarrel between the psychologist and the physiologist. Certain kinds of physical bodies have capacities for certain kinds of activities, and the exercise of those activities is their actuality and form; it is their life—their soul.*

Think of the body of Frankenstein's monster before it was jolted into life. What the tragic doctor provided for the body was a soul. But what is that? He didn't plug a new thing into that body; he just actualized certain potentialities the body already had. The doctor made it able to walk and eat, to see and talk, to think. Having a soul is just being able to do those kinds of things.

This, then, is Aristotle's general account of the relation of soul and body. Souls are the forms (the essential characteristics) of certain kinds of bodies, and as such they do not exist independently of bodies. This means, of course, that a soul cannot survive the death of the body to which it gives form any more than sight can survive the destruction of the eyes.

This general account, however, stands in tension with his account of the rational soul, or perhaps just a part of the rational soul, to which we now turn.

Nous

For the most part, Aristotle's account of the soul is thoroughly "naturalistic." Soul is just how naturally existing, living bodies of a certain kind function; it is not an additional part separable from such bodies. In this regard, things with souls are thoroughly embedded in the world of nature. But can this naturalistic form-of-the-body account be the *complete* story about soul? Or could it be that a part of some souls—of rational souls—has an independent existence after all?

Sensation is passive, simply registering the characteristics of the environment, but thinking seems to be more active; otherwise mirrors and calm pools would be thinking about what they reflect. Consider, for example, using induction to grasp the first principles of natural kinds.* We aren't simply absorbing what comes in through the senses (as cream cheese might absorb the odor of garlic left nearby), but are actively observing, noting, classifying things. Thinking is *doing* something. Aristotle's word for this active capacity of ours is *nous*. And the question is whether *nous* (translated

---

*This paragraph has a very contemporary ring to it. It expresses a view called "functionalism," the dominant theory of mind in recent cognitive science. See pp. 718–721.

---

*Review the discussion of induction on pp. 165–166.

below as "mind") can be adequately understood as nothing more than one aspect of the human form.

> There is the mind that is such as we have just described by virtue of the fact that it becomes everything; then, there is another mind, which is what it is by virtue of the fact that it makes everything; it is a sort of condition like light. For in a way light makes what are potentially colors become colors in actuality. This second mind is separable, incapable of being acted upon, mixed with nothing, and in essence an actuality. (*PS* 3.5)

Here Aristotle distinguishes between two aspects of *nous* itself. There is the side of *nous* that "becomes everything." What he means by this is that the mind can adapt to receive the form of just about anything; it is flexible, malleable, open to being written upon. But there is also the side of *nous* that "makes everything." Mind lights things up, makes them stand out clearly. Here is an example that may help. Think of daydreaming. Your eyes are open, and there is in your consciousness a kind of registration of everything in your visual field, but you aren't paying it any heed. Your mind is "elsewhere," and you don't *know* what is before you. Suddenly, however, your attention shifts and what has been present all along is noted. Actively paying attention makes what was just potentially knowable into something actually known—just as light makes colors visible, although the colors were there all along before they were lighted up.

According to Aristotle's principles, only an actuality can turn something that is potentially *X* into something actually *X*. So active *nous* must be an actual power to produce knowledge from the mere registrations of passive *nous*. In fact Aristotle concludes that the active and passive powers of *nous* are distinct and separable. Sometimes he goes so far as to speak not just of two powers, but of two minds.

The second mind, he says, is "mixed with nothing" and "separable" from the first. To say it is mixed with nothing must mean that it is a pure form unmixed with matter. If you think a moment, you should be able to see that it must be a pure form if it can actualize *everything;* if it were mixed with matter, it would be some definite thing and

would lack the required plasticity. The eye, for instance, is a definite material organ. As such, its sensitivity is strictly limited; it can detect light and colors, but not sounds or tastes. The ear is tuned to sounds alone and the tongue restricted to tastes. If *nous* is not limited in this way, it seems that it cannot be material. If it is not material, it cannot be a part of the body. And if it is not part of the body, it must be a separable entity.

There is another reason Aristotle believes that active *nous* must be an actuality separate from the body. He cannot find any "organ" or bodily location for this activity. Sight is located in the eyes, hearing in the ears, and so on. But where could the faculty of knowing be? Reflecting on his general view of the soul, Aristotle writes,

> Clearly, then, the soul is not separable from the body; or, if it is divisible into parts, some of the parts are not separable, for in some cases the realization is just the realization of the parts. However, there is nothing to prevent some parts being separated, insofar as they are not realizations of any body. (*PS* 2.1)

Sight is the "realization" of the eye. But what part of the body could have as its function something as infinitely complex as thinking and knowing? The seat of sensation and emotions, Aristotle thinks, is the heart. When we are afraid or excited we can feel our heart beating fast. The brain he considers an organ for cooling the body. (This is wrong, but not implausible; one of the best ways to keep warm on a cold day is to wear a hat.) Without a knowledge of the microstructure of the brain, it must have seemed to him that there is nothing available in the body to serve as the organ of thought, so the active part of *nous* must be separable from the body.

It is not only separable, Aristotle holds; it is

> immortal and eternal; we do not remember this because, although this mind is incapable of being acted upon, the other kind of mind, which is capable of being acted upon, is perishable. But without this kind of mind nothing thinks. (*PS* 3.5)

Why should active *nous* be eternal? Because it is not material; it is not the form of a material substance (i.e., of part of the body). It is rather one of those substantial forms that can exist separately. Lacking matter, it also lacks potentiality for change and is fully and everlastingly what it is. If *nous* is eternal and immortal, it must, like the soul of Socrates and Plato, have existed prior to our birth. But, Aristotle insists, we do not *remember* anything we know before birth—because there is nothing there to remember. Active *nous*, remember, is like the light. It lights up what the senses receive, making actual what is so far only a potentiality for knowledge. But it is not itself knowledge; it only produces knowledge from material delivered by the senses.* And before birth there were no senses or sense organs to produce this material. Aristotle cannot accept the Socratic and Platonic doctrine of recollection as an explanation of knowing.

For similar reasons, it does not seem that *nous* can be anything like personal immortality, in which an individual human being survives death and remembers his life. Active *nous*, in fact, seems impersonal.

A number of questions arise, but Aristotle does not give us answers. Is *nous* numerically the same thing in all individuals, or is there a distinct *nous* for each person? What is the relation between *nous* and God, to which it bears some striking resemblances? How, if *nous* is independent and separable, does it come to be associated with human souls at all?

These questions give rise to a long debate, partly about what Aristotle means, partly about what truth there is to all this. In the Middle Ages, for instance, Jewish, Muslim, and Christian thinkers, trying to incorporate Aristotle into a broader theological context, wrestle determinedly with these problems. But for our purposes it is enough

to register his conviction that there is something about human beings, and particularly about them as knowers, that cannot be accounted for in purely naturalistic terms. There is a part of the soul that is, after all, otherworldly.

---

1. What is Aristotle's objection to Plato's account of the soul?
2. Characterize the three levels of soul.
3. Why do living things reproduce? (Compare Plato on love.)
4. How is a soul related to a body? Be sure you understand the concepts of "substratum," "realization," and "formal substance."
5. Why does Aristotle think there is something (*nous*) about human souls that is eternal?

The Good Life

Because Aristotle's views of knowledge, reality, and human nature are so different from Plato's, we might expect his views of the good for human beings to differ as well. So they do. They do not disagree much over specific goods; both, for instance, defend the traditional virtues of moderation, justice, and courage. Moreover, Aristotle is as insistent as Plato that adherence to such virtues can be rationally justified. And the general form of justification is the same; both strive to show that the virtuous person is the happy person. So there is a large measure of agreement. But the whole approach to ethics is quite different, for in repudiating the Forms, Aristotle denies the claim of Socrates and Plato that knowledge—in the strict, scientific sense—is possible in this sphere. He makes this quite explicit in the following paragraphs:

> Our treatment will be adequate if we make it as precise as the subject matter allows. The same degree of accuracy should not be demanded in all inquiries any more than in all the products of craftsmen. Virtue and justice—the subject matter of politics—admit of plenty of differences and uncertainty. . . .
>
> Then, since our discussion is about, and proceeds from, matters of this sort, we must be content with indicating the truth in broad, general

---

*Immanuel Kant's view of the relation between concepts and percepts is very similar to this account of *nous.* Like *nous,* concepts alone cannot give us any knowledge; they structure, or interpret, or "light up" the deliverances of the senses; knowledge is a product of the interplay of "spontaneous" conceptualization and "receptive" sensation. (See pp. 435–436.) It is also interesting to compare this discussion of *nous* with Heidegger's view of the "clearing" in which things become present. See "Modes of Disclosure" in Chapter 23.

outline. . . . The educated man looks for as much precision in each subject as the nature of the subject allows. (*NE* 1.3)

When he talks about knowledge of the natural world, Aristotle always insists that it is knowledge of its universal and unchanging aspects. Aristotle never repudiates Plato's principle that knowledge in the strict sense (science) must be certain; and to be certain, its objects must be eternal and unchanging. We can know the essences of natural things and their laws of development because these patterns never change. Members of a species may vary within limits, and each individual is born, changes, and dies. But the universal and unchanging character of the species persists.*

Theoretical knowledge like this, when disciplined by demonstration and insight into first principles, is different from what we can expect in the realm of ethics. The subject matter in ethics is practical—choice, character, and action. Ethics is a practical art; it is better not to call it a science. It is more like navigation than astronomy. It aims at wisdom about what to do and how to live. We always act in some particular situation or other, so ethics must pay attention to particulars as well as universals. Therefore, we "must be content with indicating the truth in broad, general outline" and look only "for as much precision . . . as the nature of the subject allows."

There are two consequences of looking at ethics this way. First, we should not be surprised if those who are ignorant of science sometimes make better decisions than those who are more knowledgeable. What counts here is experience of particulars, not just knowledge of what is universally true. Second, we ought not to expect young people to be very good at these matters, for "they are inexperienced in the practical side of living" and tend to be "ruled by their emotions" (*NE* 1.3). There may be child prodigies in music and mathematics, but there are no child prodigies in ethics.

This focus on the practical and particular is the reason why Aristotle rejects Plato's Form of the Good as the apex of wisdom. If Plato were right here, not only should there be a science of the good, it should be one unified science. But, Aristotle says, there is no single science of the good. What we find instead is a multitude of goods; there is a good of medicine, a good of generalship, a good pertaining to politics, and so on. Each has its own end (health, victory, and well-being, for example) and must be judged in terms of the good it aims at.

Worse yet, even if there were a single unique Form of the Good, knowledge of it would be useless. Aristotle tells us that in all the arts and sciences

> people aim at some good and try to find where they fall short; yet they leave aside knowing this Idea [Form]! It would be unreasonable for all craftsmen to be unaware of it, if it is so useful, and not even try to find it. It is hard to see how a weaver or builder will benefit in his art, by knowing this Idea [Form] of the good.* (*NE* 1.6)

It is not, then, by a theoretical knowledge of the highest realities that we should try to address our practical problems of choice and action. Yet we must try to be as rational as possible. We can think of Aristotle as making the attempt to apply reason to the somewhat recalcitrant facts of human nature, in order to shape it into the best that it can be. The aim of ethics is not, after all, purely "theoretical." It should have a practical payoff.

> We are not studying in order to know what virtue is, but to become good, for otherwise there would be no profit in it. (*NE* 2.2)

What is it, then, to "become good," and how can we do so?

HAPPINESS

Aristotle begins his main treatise on ethics, the *Nicomachean Ethics*, with these words:

> Every skill and every inquiry, and similarly, every action and choice of action, is thought to have some

---

*Aristotle has no theory of the evolution of species. There were hints of such a view in at least one of the pre-Socratic philosophers (Empedocles), but Aristotle explicitly repudiates it.

*The term *Eidos,* which we have been translating as "Form," is sometimes also rendered "Idea." This is all right, but we must remember that such Platonic "Ideas" are not subjectively located in our minds.

good as its object. This is why the good has rightly been defined as the object of all endeavor. (*NE* 1.1)

Whenever we do something, we have some end in view. If we exercise, our end is health; if we study, our end is knowledge or a profession; if we earn money, our end is security. And we consider that end to be good; no one strives for what he or she considers bad.*

> Now, if there is some object of activities that we want for its own sake (and others only because of that), and if it is not true that everything is chosen for something else—in which case there will be an infinite regress, that will nullify all our striving—it is plain that this must be the good, the highest good. Would not knowing it have a great influence on our way of living? Would we not be better at doing what we should, like archers with a target to aim at? (*NE* 1.2)

We often do one thing for the sake of another. But this cannot go on forever, or there will be no point to anything we do. What we want to find is some end that we want, but not for the sake of anything else: something we prize "for its own sake." That would be the highest good, since there is nothing else we want that *for*. If we can identify something like that and keep it clearly before our eyes, as an archer looks at the target while shooting, we will be more likely to attain what is truly good.

Is there anything like that?

> What is the highest good in all matters of action? As to the name, there is almost complete agreement; for uneducated and educated alike call it happiness, and make happiness identical with the good life and successful living. They disagree, however, about the meaning of happiness. (*NE* 1.4)

Aristotle's term for happiness is *eudaemonia.* Whether "happiness" is the best English translation

for this term is unclear. A better alternative might be "well-being," and some speak of human "flourishing." In any case, it is clear that *eudaemonia* is not merely a matter of *feeling* happy; Aristotle, as much as Socrates, wants to distinguish being happy from just feeling happy.* In this book, we will follow the major tradition, however, and speak of what all of us desire as happiness.

Everyone wants to be happy. And the question, "Why do you want to be happy—for what?" seems to be senseless. This is the end, the final goal. Money we want for security, but happiness for its own sake. Yet, for us as well as for Aristotle, there is something unsatisfying about this answer, something hollow. For we immediately want to ask: "What is happiness, anyway?"

Many people, Aristotle notes, think that happiness is pleasure; in fact, they live as though that were so. But that cannot be correct. For the good of every creature must be appropriate to that creature's nature; it couldn't be right that the good life for human beings was the same as "the kind of life lived by cattle" (*NE* 1.4). It is true that "amusements" are pleasant, and that they are chosen for their own sake. Within limits, there is nothing wrong with that. But

> it would be absurd if the end were amusement and if trouble and hardship throughout life would be all for the sake of amusing oneself. . . . It would be stupid and childish to work hard and sweat just for childish amusement. (*NE* 10.6)†

Other people think that happiness is a matter of fame and honor. Again, there is something to be said for that; it is more characteristically human than mere pleasure. Aristotle does not want to deny that honor is something we can seek for its own sake; still

> it seems to be more superficial than what we are looking for, since it rests in the man who gives the honor rather than in him who receives it, whereas

---

*This is true in general. Both Socrates and Plato, however, hold it is universally true. For that reason, they hold that if we know what is good, we will do what is good. But Aristotle believes there are exceptions when people can act contrary to what they themselves consider to be their best judgment. See the view expressed in Euripides' *Hippolytus,* quoted on p. 70. Saint Paul and Augustine both agree with Aristotle that such inner conflict is possible. See pp. 225 and 242–248.

---

*See Socrates making this distinction in his trial speech, *Apology* 36e, and p. 104.

†Contemporary American culture sometimes makes one think that we are making this Aristotelian mistake on a massive scale.

our thought is that the good is something proper to the person, and cannot be taken away from him. (*NE* 1.5)

Here Aristotle is surely drawing on the tradition of Socrates, who believes that "the many" could neither bestow the greatest blessings nor inflict the greatest harms.* The highest good, happiness, must be something "proper to the person" that "cannot be taken away." The problem with honor and fame—or popularity—is that you are not in control of them; whether they are bestowed or withdrawn depends on others. If what you most want is to be popular, you are saying to others: "Here, take my happiness; I put it into your hands." This seems unsatisfactory to Aristotle.

"Popularity? It is glory's small change."

Victor Hugo (1802–1885)

How, then, shall we discover what happiness is?

We might achieve this by ascertaining the specific function of man. In the case of flute players, sculptors, and all craftsmen—indeed all who have some function and activity—"good" and "excellent" reside in their function. Now, the same will be true of man, if he has a peculiar function to himself. Do builders and cobblers have functions and activities, but man not, being by nature idle? Or, just as the eye, hand, foot, and every part of the body has a function, similarly, is one to attribute a function to man over and above these? In that case, what will it be? (*NE* 1.7)

The eye is defined by its **function**. It is a thing for seeing with; an eye is a good one if it performs that function well—gives clear and accurate images. A woman is a flutist by virtue of performing a certain function: playing the flute. A good flutist is one who plays the flute with excellence, and that is in fact what each flutist aims at. Again we see that the good of a thing is relative to its proper function. Moreover—and this will be important—the flutist is *happy* when she plays with excellence.

This suggests to Aristotle that if human beings had a function—not as flutists or cobblers, but just

in virtue of being human—we might be able to identify the good appropriate to them. He thinks we can discover such a function.

The function of man is activity of soul in accordance with reason, or at least not without reason. (*NE* 1.7)

Let's examine this statement. Aristotle is claiming that there is something in human beings analogous to the function of a flutist or cobbler: "activity of soul in accordance with reason."* What does that mean? And why does he pick on that, exactly?

If we are interested in the function of a human being, we must focus on what makes a human being human: the soul. As we have seen, soul is the realization of a certain kind of body; it is its life and the source of its actuality as an individual substance. It is the *essence* of a living thing. A dog is being a dog when it is doing essentially doglike things. And human beings are being human when they are acting in essentially human ways. Now what is peculiarly characteristic of humans? We already know Aristotle's answer to that: Humans are different from plants and the other animals because they have the *rational* level of soul. So the function of a human being is living according to reason, or at least, Aristotle adds, "not without reason." This addition is not insignificant. It means that although an excellent human life is a rational one, it is not limited to purely intellectual pursuits. There are excellences (virtues) that pertain to the physical and social aspects of our lives as well. The latter he calls the *moral virtues*.

Furthermore, although the function of the cobbler is simply to make shoes, the best cobbler is the one who makes excellent shoes. As Aristotle says, "Function comes first, and superiority in excellence is superadded." If that is so, then

the good for man proves to be activity of soul in conformity with excellence; and if there is more than one excellence, it will be the best and most complete of these. (*NE* 1.7)

Doing what is characteristic of humans to do, living in accord with reason, and in the most

---

*See *Apology* 30d, *Crito* 44d.

*In one important respect, Aristotle is Plato's faithful pupil. Look again at the functions of the soul for Plato (pp. 143–144). Which one is dominant?

The things thought pleasant by the vast majority of people are always in conflict with one another, because it is not by nature that they are pleasant; but those who love goodness take pleasure in what is by nature pleasant. This is the characteristic of actions in conformity with virtue, so that they are in themselves pleasant to those who love goodness. Their life has no extra need of pleasure as a kind of wrapper; it contains pleasure in itself. (*NE* 1.8)

"In the long run men hit only what they aim at."
Henry David Thoreau (1817–1862)

Does a happy life "incorporate external goods as well," as some say? Aristotle's answer is, yes—at least in a moderate degree.

It is impossible (or at least not easy) to do fine acts without a supply of "goods." Many acts are done through friends, or by means of wealth and political power, which are all, as it were, instruments. When people are without some of these, that ruins their blessed condition—for example, noble birth, fine children, or beauty. The man who is quite hideous to look at or ignoble or a hermit or childless cannot be entirely happy. Perhaps this is even more so if a man has really vicious children or friends or if they are good but have died. So, as we have said, happiness does seem to require this external bounty. (*NE* 1.8)

A certain amount of good fortune is a necessary condition for happiness. One would not expect the Elephant Man, for example, to be entirely happy, nor a person whose children have become thoroughly wicked. This means, of course, that your happiness is not entirely in your own control. To be self-sufficient in happiness may be a kind of ideal, but in this world it is not likely to be entirely realized.

One point needs special emphasis. The happy life, which is one and the same with the good life, is a life of *activity*. Happiness is not something that happens to you. Even though it may require a foundation in moderate good fortune, winning the lottery will not guarantee happiness. Happiness is not something the world owes you or can give you. It

excellent kind of way, is the good for humans. And if that is the human being's good, then it also constitutes human happiness. I used to have a big black Newfoundland dog named Shadow, a wonderful dog. When was Shadow happiest? When he was doing the things that Newfoundlands characteristically do—running along between the canal and the river, retrieving sticks thrown far out into the water. He loved that, he was *good* at it, and you could see it made him happy. It is the same with human beings, except that humans have capacities that my dog didn't have.

It seems as though everything that people look for in connection with happiness resides in our definition. Some think it to be excellence or virtue; others wisdom; others special skill; whereas still others think it all these, or some of these together with pleasure, or at least not without pleasure. Others incorporate external goods as well. (*NE* 1.8)

Happiness is not possible without excellence or virtue (*areté*), any more than a flutist is happy over a poor performance. It surely includes wisdom, for excellent use of one's rational powers is part of being an excellent human being. Special skills are almost certainly included, for there are many necessary and useful things to be done in a human life, from house building to poetry writing. And it will include pleasure, not because pleasure is itself the good—we have seen it cannot be that—but because the life of those who live rationally with excellence is in itself pleasant.

is not passive. It is not rest. Think about the following analogy:

> At the Olympic games, it is not the handsomest and strongest who are crowned, but actual competitors, some of whom are the winners. Similarly, it is those who act rightly who get the rewards and the good things in life. (*NE* 1.8)

Happiness is an *activity* of soul in accord with excellence.

And finally, Aristotle adds, "in a complete life." Just as one swallow does not make a summer, so "a short time does not make a man blessed or happy" (*NE* 1.7). There is a certain unavoidable fragility to human happiness.

> There are many changes and all kinds of chances throughout a lifetime, and it is possible for a man who is really flourishing to meet with great disaster in old age, like Priam of Troy. No one gives the name happy to a man who meets with misfortune like that and dies miserably. (*NE* 1.9)

1. Why does Aristotle say that ethics cannot be an exact science?
2. Give two criticisms of the Form of the Good as a basis for ethics.
3. Why does Aristotle think happiness is the highest good?
4. Why cannot pleasure be the essence of happiness? Why not honor or fame?
5. How does the idea of function help in determining the nature of happiness?
6. What is the function of human beings? What is their good?
7. How does pleasure come into the good life?

VIRTUE OR EXCELLENCE (*Areté*)

The good for human beings, then, is happiness, and happiness is the full development and exercise of our human capacities "in conformity with excellence." But what kind of thing is this excellence? How is it attained? Is there just one excellence which is appropriate to human beings, or are there many? We often speak of the "virtues" in the plural—courage, moderation, justice, temperance, and so on; are these independent of one another, or can you be an

excellent human being only if you have them all? These are the questions we now address. (I shall speak in terms of "**virtues**" for the time being and postpone the question about their unity.)

1. In considering what kind of thing a virtue is, Aristotle notes that it is for our virtues and vices that we are praised and blamed. A virtue, then, cannot be a simple emotion or feeling, for two reasons: (1) we are blamed not for being angry, but for giving in to our anger, for nursing our anger, or for being unreasonably angry, and those things are in our control; and (2) we feel fear and anger without choosing to, but the virtues "are a sort of choice, or at least not possible without choice" (*NE* 2.5). Nor can the virtues be capacities we have by nature; again, we are called good or bad not because we are *capable* of feeling angry or *capable* of reasoning, but because of the ways we use these capacities.

But if the virtues are not emotions or capacities, what can they be? Aristotle's answer is that they are *dispositions* or **habits**. To be courageous is to be disposed to do brave things. To be temperate is to have a tendency toward moderation in one's pleasures. These dispositions have intimate connections with choice and action. People who never do the brave thing when they have the opportunity are not brave, no matter how brave they happen to feel. And the person who just happens to do a brave thing, in a quite accidental way, is not brave either. The brave person acts bravely whenever the occasion calls for it; and the more the person is truly possessed of that virtue, the more easily and naturally courageous actions come. There is no need to engage in fierce internal struggles to screw up the courage to act rightly.

So this is the answer to the first question. To have a virtue of a certain kind is to have developed a habit of choosing and behaving in ways appropriate to that virtue.

2. How are the virtues attained? They are not innate in us, though we have a natural capacity for them. They are, Aristotle tells us, learned. And they are learned as all habits are learned, by practice.

> Where doing or making is dependent on knowing how, we acquire the know-how by actually doing. For example, people become builders by actually

building, and the same applies to lyre players. In the same way, we become just by doing just acts; and similarly with "temperate" and "brave." (*NE* 2.1)

This leads, moreover, to a kind of "virtuous circle."

> We become moderate through abstaining from pleasure, and when we are moderate we are best able to abstain. The same is true of bravery. Through being trained to despise and accept danger, we become brave; we shall be best able to accept danger once we are brave. (*NE* 2.2)

So we learn these excellences by practicing behavior that eventually becomes habitual in us. And if they can be learned, they can be taught. Socrates seems forever unsure whether human excellence is something that can be taught.* Aristotle is certain that it can be and tells us how.

> The point is that moral virtue is concerned with pleasures and pains. We do bad actions because of the pleasure going with them, and abstain from good actions because they are hard and painful. Therefore, there should be some direction from a very early age, as Plato says, with a view to taking pleasure in, and being pained by, the right things. (*NE* 2.3)

A child can be taught virtue—moderation, courage, generosity, and justice—by associating pleasures with them and pains with their violation—by rewarding and punishing. A child needs to be taught to find pleasure in virtuous behavior and shame in vice. If we can teach a person to build well or to play the lyre well in this way, we can also teach the more specifically human excellences. Why should we teach these virtues to our children? Aristotle has a clear answer: If they find pleasure in the most excellent exercise of their human nature, they will be happier people. Such happy people are also the virtuous and good, for the good person is the one who takes pleasure in the right things.

3. Our third question is whether virtue is one or many. Can a person be partly good and partly bad, or is goodness all or nothing? Plato and Socrates are both convinced that goodness is one. For Plato, knowledge of the Form of the Good is the

only secure foundation for virtue; and that Form is *one*. Whoever grasped it fully would be good through and through. We might expect Aristotle to be more pluralistic. In fact, he says that Socrates and Plato are in one sense right and in one sense wrong. There are indeed many virtues, and they can perhaps even exist in some independence of each other. Often, a brave man is not particularly moderate in choosing his pleasures; James Bond would be an example. But in their perfection, Aristotle holds, you can't have one virtue without having them all. What will the brave man without moderation do, for example, when he is pulled in one direction by his bravery and in another by some tempting pleasure? Won't his lack of moderation hamper the exercise of his courage?

The unity of human excellence in its perfection is a function of the exercise of reason. If you follow reason, you will not be able to develop only one of these virtues to the exclusion of others. This use of reason Aristotle calls *practical sense* or **practical wisdom**. "Once the single virtue, practical sense, is present, all the virtues will be present" (*NE* 6.13).

To this "single virtue," which provides the foundation and unity of all the rest, we now turn.

THE ROLE OF REASON

Happiness is living the life of an excellent human being; you can't be an excellent human being unless you use your rational powers. But how, exactly, does Aristotle think that rationality helps in living an excellent life?

> Let us consider this first: it is in the nature of things for the virtues to be destroyed by excess and deficiency, as we see in the case of health and strength—a good example, for we must use clear cases when discussing abstruse matters. Excessive or insufficient training destroys strength, just as too much or too little food and drink ruins health. The right amount, however, brings health and preserves it. So this applies to moderation, bravery, and the other virtues. The man who runs away from everything in fear, and faces up to nothing, becomes a coward; the man who is absolutely fearless, and will walk into anything, becomes rash. It is the same with the man who gets enjoyment from all the

---

*See *Meno* and Chapter 5, pp. 69 and 103.

pleasures, abstaining from none: he is immoderate; whereas he who avoids all pleasures, like a boor, is a man of no sensitivity. Moderation and bravery are destroyed by excess and deficiency, but are kept flourishing by the mean. (*NE* 2.2)

We can think of an emotion or an action tendency as laid out on a line, the extremes of which are labeled "too much" and "too little." Somewhere between these extremes is a point that is "just right." This point Aristotle calls **"the mean."** It is at this "just right" point that human excellence or virtue flourishes. To possess a virtue, then, is to have a habit that keeps impulse and emotion from leading action astray.

But where on such a line does the mean lie? Aristotle is very clear that it does not necessarily lie in the geometrical middle. The amount of training right for a beginner is not the right amount for a world-class runner. Aristotle distinguishes the mean relative to *the thing* from the mean relative to *us* and gives an example. Think about a trainer considering how much food to give her athletes. She may know that ten pounds is too much and two pounds too little. Does it follow that she should give them six (the mathematical mean)? Of course not. She has to consider each of the athletes and give *each one* an amount that is not too much and not too little *for him*.

So it is with the virtues.

In feeling fear, confidence, desire, anger, pity, and in general pleasure and pain, one can feel too much or too little; and both extremes are wrong. The mean and good is feeling at the right time, about the right things, in relation to the right people, and for the right reason; and the mean and the good are the task of virtue. (*NE* 2.6)

Think about bravery, or courage, surely one of the virtues. Aristotle's analysis says that bravery lies on a mean between extremes of fear and confidence. If we feel too much fear and too little confidence, we are paralyzed and cannot act rightly; we are cowards. If we feel too little fear and are overconfident, we act foolishly, recklessly. At each extreme, then, there is a vice, and the virtue lies in a mean between these extremes. But it doesn't lie exactly in the middle. What is courageous in any given circumstance depends on the facts.

Consider this example. I am walking down a dark and lonely street, and I feel a pointed object pressed into my back and hear the words, "Your money or your life." What would be the brave thing for me to do? Turn and try to disarm the thug? Try to outrun him? No. In my case, either action would be foolhardy, rash, stupid. There would be no taint of cowardice in me if I meekly handed over my wallet. Compare that with the case of a Green Beret or a Navy Seal in a similar situation, someone superbly trained in hand-to-hand combat. If such a person meekly handed over the wallet, one might suspect a sudden attack of cowardice. If he instead turned to disarm the attacker, that would not be rash or reckless. The trained combatant and I differ in relevant ways, so what is courageous for one of us may not be for the other. One can construct equally plausible examples of relativity to the time, to the things involved, and to reasons.

X: the mean for me
Y: the mean for a Navy Seal

Or let's think about being angry; again it is a matter of degree. You can have too much anger (like Achilles) or too little (simply being a doormat for everyone to walk over). Each of these is a vice, wrathfulness at the one extreme and subservience at the other. The virtue (which, in this case, may not have a clear name) lies at the mean between these extremes. But it is the mean *relative to us* in our *particular situation*. Aristotle doesn't intend to say that we should always get only moderately angry. About certain things, in relation to a given person, and for some specific reason, it might be the right thing to be very angry indeed. But in relation to other times, occasions, persons, and reasons, that degree of anger may be altogether inappropriate. We should always seek the mean, but what that is depends on the situation in which we find ourselves. All of the virtues, Aristotle says, can be given this sort of analysis.

Notice that this is not a doctrine of *relativism* in the Sophist's sense. It is clearly not the case that if Jones thinks in certain circumstances that it's right to get angry to a certain degree, then it *is* (therefore) right—not even for Jones. Jones can be mistaken in his judgment. True, there is a certain relativity involved in judgments about the right; and without careful thought, this might be confusing. But it is an *objective* relativity; what is right depends on objective facts—on actual facts about the situation in which Jones finds himself. It is those facts that determine where the mean lies, not what Jones thinks or feels about them.

> "The fact that a good and virtuous decision is context-sensitive does not imply that it is right only *relative* to, or *inside,* a limited context, any more than the fact that a good navigational judgment is sensitive to particular weather conditions shows that it is correct only in a local or relational sense. It is right absolutely, objectively, from anywhere in the human world, to attend to the particular features of one's context; and the person who so attends and who chooses accordingly is making . . . the humanly correct decision, period."
>
> *Martha Nussbaum (b. 1947)*

Finding the mean in the situation is the practical role of *reason* in ethics. The virtuous or excellent person is the one who is good at rationally discovering the mean relative to us with regard to our emotions, our habits, and our actions. How much, for instance, shall we give to charity? About these things we deliberate and choose. Because these are matters of degree and because the right degree depends on our appreciation of subtle differences in situations, being truly virtuous is difficult. As Aristotle says,

> going wrong happens in many ways . . . , whereas doing right happens in one way only. That is why one is easy, the other difficult: missing the target is easy, but hitting it is hard. (*NE* 2.6)

This is why it is a hard job to be good. It is hard to get to the mean in each thing. It is the expert, not just anybody, who finds the center of the circle. In the same way, having a fit of temper is easy for anyone; so is giving money and spending it. But this is not so when it comes to questions of "for whom?" "how much?" "when?" "why?" and "how?" This is why goodness is rare, and is praiseworthy and fine. (*NE* 2.9)

💎

> "Wickedness is always easier than virtue; for it takes the shortcut to everything."
>
> *Samuel Johnson (1709–1784)*

If you are good at using your reason to find the mean, you have *practical wisdom.* (The Greek word is *phronesis.*) Because virtue or excellence lies in the mean, and the mean is determined by reasoning, we can now also say that virtue is "disposition *accompanied* by right reason. Right reason, in connection with such matters is practical sense" (*NE* 6.13).

Aristotle does not give us a formula or an algorithm to use in making choices. He apparently thinks that no such formula is possible in practical matters pertaining to particular situations of choice. If a formula were possible, ethics could be a science rather than an art.* Nonetheless, there is a kind of standard for judging whether the right thing is being done. That standard is the virtuous and good person. The right thing to do in any situation is what the good person would do. In judging which are the best pleasures, for example, Aristotle's view is that

> the thing is as it appears to the good man. If this is true, as it seems to be and excellence and the good man, as good man, are the measure of each thing, then pleasures, too, will be the pleasures of the good man, and pleasant will apply to the things that please him. (*NE* 10.5)

Protagoras holds that "man is the measure of all things." We have seen how this leads to a kind

---

*We will see that some later writers on ethics, the utilitarians, for example, try to supply such a formula (p. 512). Kant also tries to find a single principle from which the right thing to do can be derived. See p. 449.

of relativism; if Jones thinks something is good, then it is good—to Jones. Aristotle disagrees and argues in this way: We do not take the sick man's word about whether the pudding is sweet, nor the word of someone who is color blind about the color of a tie; in the same way, not everyone is adept at judging the goodness of things. Protagorean relativism is a mistake because it is not everyone, but only the good person, who is the "measure of each thing." In every situation, virtuous and good actions are defined by the mean. The mean is discovered by "right reason" or practical wisdom. So the "measure" of virtue and goodness will be the person who judges according to practical wisdom.

You might still want to ask, but how do we recognize these practically wise persons? To this question Aristotle has no very clear answer.* Again, there is no formula for recognizing such persons. But that need not mean we cannot in general tell who they are. They tend to be those persons, we might suggest, to whom you would turn for advice.

RESPONSIBILITY

The virtues, as we have seen, are dispositions to choose and behave in certain ways, according to right reason or practical wisdom. If we have these dispositions, we are called good; if we lack them, we are called bad. It is for our virtues and vices that we are praised and blamed. But there are situations in which someone does a bad thing yet is not blamed. The presence of certain conditions can make praise and blame inappropriate. Let's call these "excusing conditions."

Aristotle is the first to canvass excusing conditions systematically, and so to define when persons should not be held responsible for their actions. This is an important topic in its own right, useful "for those who are laying down laws about rewards and punishments" (*NE* 3.1). It has, moreover, been discussed in a variety of ways by subsequent philosophers. So we must look briefly at the way Aristotle begins this conversation.

_____
*Compare Augustine, who does have a clear answer to this question, pp. 249–251.

Praise and blame are accorded to voluntary acts; but involuntary acts are accorded pardon, and at times pity. (*NE* 3.1)

Aristotle assumes that in the normal course of events most of our actions are voluntary. Occasionally, however, we do something involuntarily, and then we are pardoned or pitied. What conditions qualify an action as involuntary? He identifies two excusing conditions: compulsion and ignorance. Let us briefly discuss each.

When someone acts under compulsion we mean, says Aristotle, that

> the principle of action is external, and that the doer . . . contributes nothing of his own—as when the wind carries one off somewhere, or other human beings who have power over one do this. (*NE* 3.1)

Now, having your ship driven somewhere by a storm or being tied up and carried somewhere are particularly clear cases. If something bad should happen as a result of either of these, no one would blame you for it, for "the principle of action is external."

There are more debatable cases; for example, to save his ship a captain in a storm throws his cargo overboard. Here the action is one that we would normally blame a captain for. But it is not something a captain would ordinarily do; we might say that the storm forced him to do it. Yet we can't say that he contributed "nothing of his own." He did make the decision; in that respect, the action was voluntary. Still, because this is what "all people of sense" would do in those circumstances, the captain is pardoned. Aristotle concludes that though such actions are voluntary if considered as particular acts, they are involuntary when considered in context—for no one would ordinarily choose them. And that is the ground on which we excuse the captain from blame.

Again Aristotle insists that we not try to find a precise formula for deciding such cases. He stresses how difficult such decisions may be.

> There are times when it is hard to decide what should be chosen at what price, and what endured in return for what reward. Perhaps it is still harder to stick to the decision.

It is not easy to say if one course should be chosen rather than another, since there is great variation in particular circumstances. (*NE* 3.1)

This does not mean, of course, that anything goes. The application of practical wisdom to such situations helps us discriminate whether something was done by compulsion.

Let us consider the second condition. What sort of ignorance excuses us from responsibility? It is not, Aristotle says, ignorance of what is right. Those who do not know what is right are not ignorant, but wicked! We do not excuse people for being wicked. (Here is the source of the adage that ignorance of the law is no excuse.)

If ignorance of the right does not excuse, neither does ignorance of what everybody ought to know. But

ignorance in particular circumstances does—that is, ignorance of the sphere and scope of the action. . . . A man may be ignorant of *what* he is doing: e.g., when people say that it "slipped out in the course of a conversation"; or that they did not know these things were secret (like Aeschylus on the mysteries); or like the man with the catapult, who wanted "only to demonstrate it," but fired it instead. Someone, as Merope does, might think his son an enemy; or mistake a sharp spear for one with a button. . . . One might give a man something to drink, with a view to saving his life, and kill him instead. (*NE* 3.1)

It is ignorance about particular circumstances that makes an action involuntary and leads us to excuse the agent from responsibility. In such cases, a person can say: If I had only known, I would have done differently. The mark of whether that is true or not, Aristotle suggests, is regret. If someone does something bad through ignorance and later regrets doing it, that is a sign that she is not wicked. It shows that she would indeed have done otherwise if she had known. And in that case she can truly be said to have acted involuntarily and deserve pardon.

Again, there are difficult cases. What about the person who acts in ignorance because he is drunk and is not in a condition to recognize the facts of the case? Here Aristotle suggests that it is not appropriate to excuse him, because he was responsible for getting himself into that state. The same is true for someone ignorant through carelessness; that person should have taken care. Here is, perhaps, a harder case.

But perhaps the man's character is such that he cannot take care. Well, people themselves are responsible for getting like that, through living disorderly lives: they are responsible for being unjust or profligate, the former through evildoing, the latter through spending their time drinking, and so on. Activity in a certain thing gives a man that character; this is clear from those who are practicing for any contest or action, since that is what they spend their time doing. Not knowing that dispositions are attained through actually doing things is the sign of a complete ignoramus. (*NE* 3.5)

No one, Aristotle suggests, can be that ignorant.

There is further discussion of such cases, but this provides the main outlines of his views on **responsibility**. We can see that Aristotle assumes people must normally be held responsible for what they do, that compulsion and ignorance may be excusing conditions, and that he is rather severe in his estimation of when these conditions may hold. Although Aristotle does not explicitly say so, it is a fair inference that he considers the acceptance of responsibility and the sparing use of excuses as a part of the good life. By our choices and actions we create the habits that become our character. And so we are ourselves very largely responsible for our own happiness or lack thereof.

"Oh well," said Mr. Hennessy, "We are as th' Lord made us." "No," said Mr. Dooley, "lave us be fair. Lave us take some iv the blame ourselves."

Finley Peter Dunne (1876–1936)

THE HIGHEST GOOD

When Aristotle defines the good for human beings as "activity of soul in conformity with excellence," he adds that "if there is more than one excellence, it will be the best and most complete of these." We need now to examine what the "best and most complete" excellence is.

The best activity of soul must be the one that activates whatever is best in us. And what is that? Think back to Aristotle's discussion of the human soul. It incorporates the levels of nutrition and reproduction, sensation, and reason. At the very peak is *nous*, or mind: the nonpassive, purely active source of knowledge and wisdom. Can there be any doubt that this, which contains no potentiality at all, is the best, the most divine part of us?

But if that is so, the activity that is best is the activity of *nous*. And such activity should be not only the highest good but also the greatest happiness for a human being. This is just what Aristotle claims.

> This is the best activity . . . and also the most continuous. We are better able to contemplate continuously than to *do* anything. (*NE* 10.7)

The activity of *nous*—discovering and keeping in mind the first principles of things—Aristotle calls "**contemplation**." The life of contemplation is said to be the very best life partly because it is the exercise of the "best" part of us and partly because we can engage in it "continuously." But this life is also the most pleasant and the most self-sufficient. For these reasons it is the happiest life.

> We think it essential that pleasure should be mixed in with happiness, and the most pleasant of activities in accordance with virtue is admittedly activity in accordance with wisdom. Philosophy has pleasures that are marvelous for their purity and permanence. Besides, it is likely that those who have knowledge have a more pleasant life than those who are seeking it. Sufficiency, as people call it, will be associated above all with contemplation. The wise man, the just, and all the rest of them need the necessities of life; further, once there is an adequate supply of these, the just man needs people with and towards whom he may perform just acts; and the same applies to the temperate man, the brave man, and so on. But the wise man is able to contemplate, even when he is on his own; and the more so, the wiser he is. It is better, perhaps, when he has people working with him; but still he is the most self-sufficient of all. (*NE* 10.7)

Aristotle dismisses honor as a candidate for the good, you will recall, on the grounds that it is too dependent on others. What is truly good, it seems, must be more "proper to the person, and cannot be taken away." The same point is here used to recommend the life of contemplation as the very best life, for it is more "self-sufficient" than any other, less dependent on other people. The other virtues need the presence of other people for their exercise, while the wise man can engage in contemplation "even when he is on his own." And to Aristotle this seems to recommend such a life as the very best.*

Aristotle should not be taken to deny that there are good human lives that are noncontemplative. Ordinary men and women, not devoting themselves to science and philosophy, can also be excellent human beings—and therefore happy. But only those fortunate enough to be able to devote themselves to intellectual pursuits will experience the pinnacle of human happiness—that self-sufficient happiness which is most like the happiness of God.

Suppose we ask why the moral person acts morally. From what Aristotle says, we suspect that it is not because other people need the individual's just acts or are benefited by them; it is merely that he or she has come to see that this is the best way to live. This is the ground for Aristotle's recommendation of contemplation as well; it is the best way for an individual to live. "Best" always means "most self-sufficient" for Aristotle. So the life of contemplation is praised because it is a life independent of fortune—to the extent that is possible for a human being. We see clearly that Aristotle's ethics (and classical Greek ethics in general) is an ethics of self-perfection, or self-realization. There is not much in it that recommends caring for others for *their* sakes.†

---

*Contemplation, for Aristotle, is not what is often called "meditation" these days. It is not an attempt to empty the mind, but an active life of study to uncover the wonder and the whys of things.

†Such compassion, or caring, under the names of "love" and "charity" (*agape,* not *eros*) comes into our story with the Christians. See pp. 221–222 and 225.

This attitude underlies the rational justification for being virtuous in both Plato and Aristotle. They try to show that we should be just and moderate because, to put it crudely, it *pays*. True, neither argues that the consequences of virtue will necessarily be pleasing. Glaucon's picture of the perfectly moral and perfectly immoral men had ruled out that sort of appeal. Happiness is not related to virtue as a paycheck is related to a week's work. The relation for both Plato and Aristotle is internal; the just and virtuous life is recommended because it is *in itself* the happiest life (though they also believe that *in general* its consequences will be good). Although Aristotle always thinks of the good of a person as essentially involving the good of some community, and especially as involving friends, it remains true nonetheless that individuals are primarily interested in their own happiness. This may, we might grant, be a stimulus to achievement, but there is not much compassion in it.

Aristotle sums up his discussion of the contemplative life (the happiest of all) by *disagreeing* with Pindar's aphorism, "For mortals, a mortal lot is best." The contemplation of the wise person, he tells us, will

> be more than human. A man will not live like that by virtue of his humanness, but by virtue of some divine thing within him. His activity is as superior to the activity of the other virtues as this divine thing is to his composite character. Now if mind is divine in comparison with man, the life of the mind is divine in comparison with mere human life. We should not follow popular advice and, being human, have only human ambitions, or, being mortal, have only mortal thoughts. As far as possible, we should become immortal and do everything toward living by the best that is in us. (*NE* 10.7)

The activity of a truly wise human being, then, resembles the activity of God, the unmoved mover. Indeed, this is another case of God acting as a final cause, an ideal that draws all things, in this case the philosopher, to imitate its own self-sufficient activity as far as possible. Because the best and most pleasant activity for any living creature is what most fully realizes its nature, contemplation—the

life of reason—is the most happy life possible for human beings.

---

1. What *kind* of a thing is a virtue? Can virtue be taught? How?
2. Is virtue just one? Or are there many virtues?
3. Explain Aristotle's doctrine of the mean.
4. Why is it "a hard job to be good"?
5. What is practical wisdom?
6. What is "the measure of all things," so far as goodness goes?
7. What conditions, according to Aristotle, excuse a person from responsibility? Explain each.
8. Does having a bad character excuse a person? Explain.
9. What is the very best life?

FOR FURTHER THOUGHT

1. In your view, does Aristotle's logic do anything to undercut the relativism spawned by the Sophists' teaching of rhetoric? Explain your answer.
2. Keeping in mind Aristotle's doctrine of how soul and body are related, try to construct an Aristotelian account of *fear*. (Hint: You will have to consider both mental and physical factors, and how they are related.)
3. Write a short paragraph giving an Aristotelian account of the virtue of moderation.
4. We read that young people attracted to gang life are seeking "respect." Write an Aristotelian critique of this motivation.

KEY WORDS

terms	conclusion
statements	middle term
categories	valid
substance	first principles
primary substance	induction
secondary substances	*nous*
truth	nature
correspondence	material cause
argument	formal cause
syllogism	efficient cause
premises	final cause

teleology
entelechy
first philosophy
metaphysics
essence
unmoved mover
God
nutritive soul
sensitive soul

rational soul
eudaemonia
function
virtues
habits
practical wisdom
the mean
responsibility
contemplation

NOTES

1. Quoted from Ps. Ammonius, *Aristotelis Vita*, in W. D. Ross, *Aristotle* (New York: Meridian Books, 1959), 14.
2. I am indebted here to Marjorie Grene's excellent little book, *A Portrait of Aristotle* (Chicago: University of Chicago Press, 1963), 38–65.
3. Quoted in J. M. Edmonds, *Elegy and Iambus with the Anacreontea II* (New York: G. P. Putnam's Sons, 1931), 175.

4. All quotations from Aristotle's works are from *The Philosophy of Aristotle*, ed. Renford Bambrough (New York: New American Library, 1963), unless noted otherwise. Within this text, references to specific works will be as follows (numerical references are to book and section numbers).

    C: Categories
    I: On Interpretation
    M: Metaphysics
    PA: Posterior Analytics
    PH: Physics
    PS: Psychology
    NE: Nicomachean Ethics

5. As quoted in Grene, *Portrait of Aristotle*, 105.
6. I owe this example to J. L. Ackrill, *Aristotle the Philosopher* (Oxford: Oxford University Press, 1981), 42.

8

EPICUREANS, STOICS, AND SKEPTICS

Happiness for the Many

It is customary to discuss the development of philosophy in the Hellenistic and Roman periods after Aristotle in terms of three schools, or movements of thought. We will follow this practice, but without any claim to do full justice to these developments. We will look at only a few central tenets of these schools and show how they try to solve problems facing people of those times, problems not adequately addressed by the great systematic achievements of Plato and Aristotle.

To understand the appeal of these philosophies, however, we need to look at more than just their intellectual predecessors. A brief discussion of the altered social and religious climate will be useful. The era of the city-state was fading. After the war between Athens and Sparta, the regions of Greece engaged in a long series of struggles to achieve dominance, and some, Thebes and Macedonia for instance, managed it for a time (see Map 1). But the struggles with shifting alliances and continual warfare wore down the belief that a city could be an arena for living a good life. People lost confidence in it, retreating into smaller units and leaving the politics of cities to be settled by rather crude military types. (The Epicureans, as we'll see, are prominent among those who seek their happiness not as citizens but as members of a smaller voluntary community.) Under Philip of Macedon and his son Alexander, vast territories were conquered and unified politically.* And finally Rome established her dominance over the entire Mediterranean basin, bringing a kind of stability and enforced peace to the region. The Romans were good administrators and warriors and contributed much in the sphere of law but not much original philosophy.

With the loss of confidence in the cities went a loss of faith in the gods of the cities. In the era of empires, Athena seemed too restricted even for Athens. The Olympians had apparently failed, and their authority waned. It is true that the Romans took over the Greek pantheon and gave the old gods new names (Jove, Juno, Venus), but the vigor of the religion was gone. This didn't mean, however,

_____

*For Alexander, see http://en.wikipedia.org/wiki/Alexander_the_Great.

that religion was dead or dying—far from it. The old religions of the earth (religions of fertility, ancestor worship, and ecstasy), suppressed for a time by the Homeric gods of the sky, had never disappeared. Now they flourished with new vigor. To this was added a flood of religious cults and ideas from the East, all seeming to promise what the new age demanded. There was a proliferation of initiations into sacred and secret mysteries, of mediators and saviors, of claims to esoteric knowledge comprising fantastic systems, and of rites that promised a merging of the worshiper's very being with the being of some divinity.

Politicians, of course, made use of religion for their own ends, accepting (and encouraging) the accolades of divinity people laid upon them. Alexander was proclaimed a god; his successors liked the status it gave them and continued the practice.

The world seemed hostile and society brutal. People had lost control and grasped desperately at almost any promise to reestablish it. Fortune and Chance themselves came to seem divine and were worshiped and feared. Astrology, never a force in the Golden Age of Greece, "fell upon the Hellenistic mind," Gilbert Murray says, "as a new disease falls upon some remote island people."[1] The stars were thought to be gods, the planets living beings (or controlled by living beings).* Their positions in the heavens were consulted as signs of things happening and to happen on earth. The heavens were thought to be populated by myriads of spirits, powers, principalities, demons, and gods, and one never knew when they would cause some fresh disaster to overtake one.

The tradition established by Thales and his successors, never widespread, was impotent to stop all this. Rational criticism had not completely disappeared, but it must have seemed to many thinkers that they were in a new dark age. People were anxious and afraid, their confidence broken.

What could those who wished to carry on the enterprise of the nature philosophers, of Socrates, Plato, and Aristotle, do to stem the tide? Let us look first at Epicurus.

The Epicureans

> It is not possible for one to rid himself of his fears about the most important things if he does not understand the nature of the universe but dreads some of the things he has learned in the myths. Therefore, it is not possible to gain unmixed happiness without natural science. (*PD* 12.143)[2]

This passage strikes the key notes in the philosophy of **Epicurus** (341–270 B.C.). The aim of life is happiness. Happiness depends above all on ridding oneself of fears. And the basis for the removal of fear is science. We want to examine what fears Epicurus thinks stand in the way of happiness, what he thinks happiness is, why an understanding of the universe will help, and what kind of science will give us this understanding.

According to Epicurus,

> pleasure is the beginning and end of the blessed life. We recognize pleasure as the first and natural good; starting from pleasure we accept or reject; and we return to this as we judge every good thing, trusting this feeling of pleasure as our guide. (*LM* 129a)

The Greek word translated as pleasure is *hedone*, and the viewpoint expressed in the preceding passage is therefore called **hedonism**. As we have seen, Aristotle considers the view that pleasure is the good and rejects it.* He argues that something we share with the lower animals could not be the distinctively human good. But Epicurus is unmoved. Just look about you, he seems to be saying. Every living thing takes pleasure as a natural good; it is clearly one thing that is good not by convention but by *physis*. It is the ground of what we accept and reject, of what we pursue and avoid. And if we want to judge the goodness of some course of action, we ask whether there is more pleasure than pain involved in pursuing it.

---

*The philosophers were, perhaps, not altogether blameless in this. It was common to ascribe greater perfection to the heavenly bodies in their eternal course than to the changeable world we live in. And more than one philosopher spoke of them as divine. In Plato's later political thought, the supreme object of worship for the masses was to be the sun.

---

*See p. 185.

He does not claim that this is the way it should be but that this is how it is. Good and evil are measured by this standard of pleasure and pain. It is no use, Epicurus might say, to complain that this is unworthy of human beings; this is the way we are made—all of us. This fact levels things out and defeats the elitism of the philosophers. Perhaps only a few are capable of the tortuous dialectic that leads to the vision of the Form of the Good. Not many can live the life of divine contemplation that Aristotle recommends as the highest good. But a pleasant life is available to all.

It is in terms of pleasure and pain, then, that we must understand happiness.* The happy life is the pleasant life. And philosophy, Epicurus holds, is the study of what makes for happiness—nothing more, nothing less.

> Let no young man delay the study of philosophy, and let no old man become weary of it; for it is never too early nor too late to care for the well-being of the soul. The man who says that the season for this study has not yet come or is already past is like the man who says it is too early or too late for happiness. (*LM* 122)

But what, exactly, can philosophy do for us to make us happy? Note that contrary to Aristotle's view, the pursuit of philosophy is not in itself the recipe for the happy life. Philosophy is basically a tool for Epicurus. Though philosophical discussion with a group of friends is one of the great pleasures in life, Epicurus is not interested in philosophical speculation for its own sake. So only those parts of philosophy which serve the end of happiness are recommended. As he says,

> do not think that knowledge about the things above the earth, whether treated as part of a philosophical system or by itself, has any other purpose than peace of mind and confidence. This is also true of the other studies. (*LP* 85b)

There is a single-minded practicality about Epicurus' thought that brushes to one side all that does not serve the goal. So we should not expect much from him in the way of new developments

in science, logic, or epistemology; indeed, his contributions in these areas are mostly secondhand, as we will see. But in ethics he has some originality and has had some influence.

The study of philosophy can do two things for us. It can free us from certain fears and anxieties that spoil our happiness, and it can provide directions for maximizing pleasure in life. Let us look at each of these in turn.

There are pains and displeasures that are natural and cannot always be avoided, such as illness and separation from loved ones because of death. About these, however, Epicurus says that the intense pains typically do not last very long, whereas those that last a long time are usually not very intense; one way or another, these pains may be endured (*PD* 4; *VS* 4). But there are other pains that are due to certain *beliefs* we hold, and for these there is a sure remedy: change these beliefs. In fact, that is not only the expedient thing to do, he tells us, but also the right thing to do because the beliefs that cause us distress are *false*. So we can rid ourselves of these pains by a true apprehension of *the way things are*.*

What are these false beliefs that distress us? In the main, they fall into two categories: beliefs about **the gods** and beliefs about **death**. About the gods, people are misled by the "myths," as Epicurus calls them, which permeate the cults of popular religion. The heart of such myths is that the gods are always poking around in the universe to make things happen according to their whims and wishes, that they are interested in human affairs, and that they need to be appeased if things are not to go badly with us. Such beliefs fill us with dread, Epicurus believes, because we never know when some god or demon is going to crush us—perhaps for no reason we can discern at all. So we anxiously inquire of the diviners, prophets, augurs, soothsayers, astrologers, and priests about what went wrong or whether this is

---

*This theme is taken up in the nineteenth century by the utilitarians. See Chapter 19.

*In the first century B.C., the Roman poet Lucretius wrote a long poem popularizing the views of Epicurus. Its title in Latin is *De Rerum Natura* ("on nature"). I borrow the phrase "the way things are" from Rolfe Humphries' version of that title in his very readable translation (Indiana University Press, 1969).

a good time to do so and so and, if not, whether we can do something to make it a good time. (Usually, of course, we can, to the benefit of the "sage" in question.) Fear of the gods, then, is one of the most potent spoilers of contentment.

The other fear concerns death. It is the same anxiety that pulls Hamlet up short and prevents him from taking his own life:

> To die, to sleep;
> To sleep: perchance to dream: ay, there's the rub;
> For in that sleep of death what dreams may come
> When we have shuffled off this mortal coil,
> Must give us pause.[3]

Tradition was full of dreadful stories of the fates of the dead. Lucretius lists some of them: Tantalus, frozen in terror, fears the massive rock balanced above him; Tityos is food for the vultures; Sisyphus must forever roll his rock up the hill, only to see it crash down again; and so on (*WTA*, pp. 114–115).[4]

The good news Epicurus proclaims is that none of this is true. As Lucretius put it:

> Our terrors and our darknesses of mind
> Must be dispelled, not by the sunshine's rays,
> Not by those shining arrows of the light,
> But by insight into nature, and a scheme
> Of systematic contemplation.
>
> —*WTA*, p. 24

Now, of course, you want desperately to know what this "insight into nature" is that will dispel such terrors. It is nothing new; we are already familiar with it, but not exactly in this guise. What the Epicureans have in mind is the **atomism** of Leucippus and Democritus.* Why do they choose atomism as the philosophy that tells us "the way things are"? They never make that very clear. One suspects that Epicurus and Lucretius see atomism as particularly serviceable in the role of terror dispeller.

Let us remind ourselves of a few of the main points of atomism:

- Atoms and the void alone exist.
- The common things of the world, including living things, are temporary hookings together of atoms.
- The soul is material, made of very fine atoms, and is therefore mortal.
- Whatever happens is mechanistically determined to happen according to the laws by which atoms combine and fall apart again.

Epicurus accepts atomism as an account of the way things are, except for a slight but crucial modification to the fourth point. The universal determinism envisaged by Democritus is modified so that our free will to act can be salvaged.* After all, if we were not free, how could we follow the prescriptions for happiness Epicurus sets out? Although the atoms mostly follow strictly determined mechanistic paths, *sometimes*, he holds, they "swerve" unaccountably. Lucretius presents the argument:

> If cause forever follows after cause
> In infinite, undeviating sequence
> And a new motion always has to come
> Out of an old one, by fixed law; if atoms
> Do not, by swerving, cause new moves which break
> The laws of fate; if cause forever follows,
> In infinite sequence, cause—where would we get
> This free will that we have, wrested from fate,
> By which we go ahead, each one of us,
> Wherever our pleasures urge? Don't we also swerve
> At no fixed time or place, but as our purpose Directs us?
>
> —*WTA*, p. 59

With this alteration, the rest of atomist metaphysics is acceptable to Epicurus. This is the "insight into nature" that will dispel the terrors of religious myths. But exactly how will it do this?

The gods, Epicurus maintains, surely exist. But like everything else, they too are composed of atoms and the void. Nonetheless, they seem to be immortal, being composed of exceedingly fine atoms and dwelling between the worlds, unaffected by the grosser impingements of worldly things. (Epicurus thinks there must be many worlds because space is infinite, and our world is clearly limited.) Moreover, we must acknowledge that they

---

*You may find it helpful to review that philosophy, looking especially at pp. 32–38.

*Look again at p. 35 to see what problem atomism poses for free will.

dwell in unchangeable blessedness. It follows that they have no concern with the world, nor with human affairs:

> That which is blessed and immortal is not troubled itself, nor does it cause trouble to another. As a result, it is not affected by anger or favor, for these belong to weakness. (*PD* 1)

To be concerned about human affairs, Epicurus thinks, would be an imperfection in the gods. How could they be blessed if they had to worry about what Jones is going to do tomorrow? To poke around in the world, changing this and adjusting that, would mean the gods' immortality would be in jeopardy, for they could not help but be affected by their interventions; and such bumps and bruises are what shake the atoms loose and lead to disintegration.

There is no reason, then, to fear the gods. They have no interest in us and do not intervene directly. The heavenly bodies, moreover, are not demons or divinities that rule our destinies. Sun and moon, planets and stars are composed of atoms and the void just like everything else. Their behavior can be explained in exactly the same kinds of ways we explain familiar phenomena on earth. So it is inappropriate—ignorant—to look to the heavens for signs and portents, to go to astrologers for predictions, and try to read the riddle of the future in the stars. After summarizing some of the traditional stories of the gods, Lucretius says:

> All this, all this is wonderfully told,
> A marvel of tradition, and yet far
> From the real truth. Reject it—for the gods
> Must, by their nature, take delight in peace,
> Forever calm, serene, forever far
> From our affairs, beyond all pain, beyond
> All danger, in their own resources strong,
> Having no need of us at all, above
> Wrath or propitiation.
>
> —*WTA*, p. 70

So much, then, for fear of the gods. What of death? Remember that if atomism is correct, soul and body dissipate together in the event we call death. So there is no future life to look forward to. In what is probably Epicurus' best known saying, he draws the moral.

> Accustom yourself to the belief that death is of no concern to us, since all good and evil lie in sensation and sensation ends with death. . . . Death, the most dreaded of evils, is therefore of no concern to us; for while we exist death is not present, and when death is present we no longer exist. It is therefore nothing either to the living or to the dead since it is not present to the living, and the dead no longer are. (*LM* 124b–125)

Good and evil, of course, are pleasure and pain. These are the sources of happiness and unhappiness. Fear of death is predicated on the assumption that we will experience these sensations after death and perhaps be wretchedly unhappy. But that makes no sense at all, for when we are, death is not, and when death is, we are not. What, then, is there to fear? Death "is of no concern to us." Epicurus adds that it is also foolish to quake in *anticipation* of death. For what isn't painful when it is present should cause no pain when it is anticipated.

"After the game, the king and the pawn go into the same box."

Italian proverb

Such "insight into nature" can remove at least certain virulent strains of unhappiness from our lives. This is the negative benefit philosophy can confer, but it is not yet enough for happiness. We need also to know how to *live well*. And here too Epicurus gives guidance. The key point is clearly put in the following passage:

> For the very reason that pleasure is the chief and the natural good, we do not choose every pleasure, but there are times when we pass by pleasures if they are outweighed by the hardships that follow; and many pains we think better than pleasures when a greater pleasure will come to us once we have undergone the long-continued pains. . . . By measuring and by looking at advantages and disadvantages, it is proper to decide all these things; for under certain circumstances we treat the good as evil, and again, the evil as good. (*LM* 129b–130a)

The terms "Epicurean" or "hedonist" nowadays suggest someone who is a glutton for pleasures of every kind and indulges to excess in the satisfaction of every desire. This is a complete distortion of the philosophy of Epicurus; in his view, there is no better way to secure for yourself a life of misery than such sensual indulgence. If what you want is pleasure—the most pleasure—then you must be prudent in your pursuit of it.

> When we say that pleasure is the end, we do not mean the pleasure of the profligate or that which depends on physical enjoyment . . . but by pleasure we mean the state wherein the body is free from pain and the mind from anxiety. Neither continual drinking and dancing, nor sexual love, nor the enjoyment of fish and whatever else the luxurious table offers brings about the pleasant life; rather it is produced by the reason which is sober, which examines the motive for every choice and rejection, and which drives away all those opinions through which the greatest tumult lays hold of the mind. (*LM* 131b–132a)

To implement these general principles, we must make a distinction between different sorts of **desire**.

> You must consider that of the desires some are natural, some are vain, and of those that are natural, some are necessary, others only natural. Of the necessary desires, some are necessary for happiness, some for the ease of the body, some for life itself. (*LM* 127b)

The classification of desires, then, looks like this:

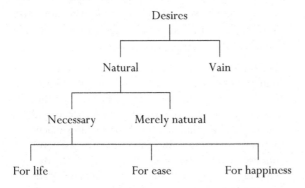

Let us fill in each of these categories with some plausible examples:

- Vain desires: luxuries of all kinds, designer clothing, being thin, keeping up with the Joneses

- Merely natural desires: sexual desire (natural but not necessary)
- Necessary for life: food, drink, shelter
- Necessary for ease: a bed
- Necessary for happiness: friendship

What philosophy can do for us is to make clear that not all desires are on a par and that satisfying some of them will cost more than it is worth. That is surely the case, Epicurus believes, with vain desires. It is likely to be the case with the merely natural desires; at least it is clear that following every sexual passion is a sure prescription for unhappiness. The point is that if we want to be happy, the crucial step is to control and limit our desires—if possible to those which are necessary. Epicurus recommends the simple life, as the following sayings make clear:

> Natural wealth is limited and easily obtained; the wealth defined by vain fancies is always beyond reach. (*PD* 15.144)

> Nothing satisfies him to whom what is enough is little. (*VS* 68)

> To be accustomed to simple and plain living is conducive to health and makes a man ready for the necessary tasks of life. It also makes us more ready for the enjoyment of luxury if at intervals we chance to meet with it, and it renders us fearless against fortune. (*LM* 131a)

> *"A human being has a natural desire to have more of a good thing than he needs."*
>
> *Mark Twain (1835–1910)*

So this hedonist, who finds pleasure to be the only natural good, values the old Greek virtue of moderation after all. Now, however, it is recommended on the grounds that it will give us the pleasantest life possible. What of the other **virtues**, of justice, for instance? Justice is not something good in itself, Epicurus argues, thus taking the view that Glaucon and Adeimantus urge against Socrates (*PD* 31–38).* Justice arises when

---

*See *Republic*, Book II and pp. 146–147.

people make a "compact" together not to injure one another, and it is reasonable to be just as long as that compact pays off—in increased pleasure, of course. Justice, then, is wholly a matter of *nomos* for the Epicureans. It is true that justice and the other virtues are praised, but only as means to a happy life for the individual (the "honesty is the best policy" syndrome).

We must say a word about **friendship**. The virtue of friendship is held in the highest esteem among the Epicureans. They are famous for it. Epicurus established in Athens a "Garden" in which his followers lived, sharing work, study, and conversation. In this Garden and in similar communities across the ancient world, men—including at least some women and slaves—cultivated this virtue. Friendship, they believed, is the key to the highest blessings this life holds. As Epicurus says,

> Friendship dances through the world bidding us all to waken to the recognition of happiness. (*VS* 52)

This blessing, Epicurus assumes, is open to all people—or at least to all who pursue their pleasures with prudence and moderation. So, he assures us, happiness is not restricted to the few. The many, too, may participate.

---

1. Why does Epicurus fasten on pleasure as the good?
2. For what kinds of pain is there a remedy? What is it?
3. What, according to the Epicureans, are the false beliefs about the gods, and how do these false beliefs distress us?
4. What false beliefs about death distress us, according to the Epicureans?
5. How is atomism "corrected"?
6. How does the wise person sort out and deal with desires?
7. What is the Epicurean view of moderation? Of justice? Of friendship?

The Stoics

Our treatment of the Stoic philosophers will be even more incomplete than that of the Epicureans because the Stoics work harder at developing all the major fields of philosophy. They make original contributions to logic, set forth a detailed theory of knowledge, and spend considerable effort on theories of the nature of the universe, elaborated over a period of five centuries by a succession of good minds. Although in many respects the Stoics are consciously opposed to the main principles of the Epicureans, the two schools share one belief: that philosophy is to serve the aim of promoting the best and happiest life a human being could live. We'll concentrate on the Stoics' views in this area, discussing their other philosophical contributions only to clarify their views about ethics.

The founder of **Stoicism** was Zeno from Citium, a city in Cyprus.* Like several other important figures in this tradition, he was not a native Greek, though he came to Athens as a young man (in about 320 B.C.), studied there, and taught there until his death, about 260 B.C. The fact that Stoic teachers came from areas that Plato and Aristotle would have regarded as barbarian is a sign that times had changed for philosophy. Stoic doctrines from the first had a universality about them that reached beyond the parochial concerns of any city or nation; in this way, they were both a reflection of the enlarged political situation and an influence on it. Socrates had thought of himself as a citizen of Athens. The Stoics considered themselves citizens of the world.

The universality of Stoicism is shown in another way. It appealed to members of all social classes. Among its leading figures was a freed slave, Epictetus (c. A.D. 51–135) and the Roman Emperor Marcus Aurelius (A.D. 121–180).

Let us begin with some reflections on happiness. Stoic ideas of **happiness** owe much to Socrates, Plato, and Aristotle, all of whom argue that what makes for a truly good life cannot depend on anything outside ourselves.† Stoics carry this ideal of self-sufficiency to the extreme by claiming that absolutely nothing that happens to the wise can

---

*Note that this is not the Zeno of the paradoxes, the associate of Parmenides.

†Socrates holds that a good person cannot be harmed (*Apology* 41c–d) and Plato argues that happiness is a condition of the harmonious soul. Aristotle claims that "the good is something proper to the person and cannot be taken away from him" (see p. 186).

disturb their calm happiness. This may seem a startling suggestion.*

How can this be? Epictetus puts his finger on the crux of the matter:

> What upsets people is not things themselves but their judgments about the things. For example, death is nothing dreadful (or else it would have appeared dreadful to Socrates), but instead the judgment about death that it is dreadful—*that* is what is dreadful. So when we are upset or distressed, let us never blame someone else but rather ourselves, that is, our own judgments. (*E* 5)[5]

What makes you unhappy? Suppose you learn that someone you trusted has been spreading untrue stories about you—vicious, nasty stories. This gossip is affecting your friendships. People are beginning to avoid you, act cool toward you. Would this make you unhappy? Most of us would probably say yes.

But, the Stoic urges, think more carefully. It can't really be these events as so far described that make you unhappy. What if you didn't care about such things? What if they meant nothing to you, if you thought this sort of thing was simply beneath your notice? Then they wouldn't make you unhappy.

This kind of thought experiment, the Stoic believes, proves that what happens to you can never *make* you unhappy. What makes you unhappy is "the judgment" you make on what happens to you: That this is important, terrible, and distressing. But if that is so, then your happiness and unhappiness are not beyond your control. Nothing can make you unhappy unless you allow it to do so. Your happiness is entirely up to you.

To understand this in depth, we need to appreciate a crucial distinction:

> Some things are up to us and some are not up to us. Our opinions are up to us, and our impulses, desires, aversions—in short, whatever is our own

doing. Our bodies are not up to us, nor are our possessions, our reputations, or our public offices, or, that is, whatever is not our own doing. The things that are up to us are by nature free, unhindered, and unimpeded; the things that are not up to us are weak, enslaved, hindered, not our own. So remember, if you think that things naturally enslaved are free or that things not your own are your own, you will be thwarted, miserable, and upset, and will blame both gods and men. But if you think that only what is yours is yours, and that what is not your own is, just as it is, not your own, then no one will ever coerce you, no one will hinder you, you will blame no one, you will not accuse anyone, you will not do a single thing unwillingly, you will have no enemies, and no one will harm you, because you will not be harmed at all. (*E* 1)[6]

This distinction between what is and what is not within our power makes possible the remarkable claims of the Stoic. When are we happy? When we get what we desire. Suppose now that we set our heart on the things that are beyond our power—a beautiful body, a fine estate, fame, being chairman of the board. Reflection will surely convince you that these things are at best only partly in our power; circumstances must cooperate if they are to be ours. If these are what we really want, disappointment is sure to follow. If we don't get them, we will be unhappy. If we do get them, we will be anxious lest we lose them. And neither disappointment nor anxiety is part of a happy life.

What, then, is within our control? "Your way of dealing with appearances" (*E* 6), Epictetus answers. What appears in the world is not in our control, but how we deal with it is. How we view appearances, our opinions about them, whether we desire or fear them—all this is within our power. This is our proper business, the area of our concern. Of all that lies beyond this sphere, we should be prepared to say, "You are nothing in relation to me" (*E* 1).

---

*Compare Aristotle, p. 187. As you study Stoicism, ask yourself: Is this an improvement on Aristotle, who holds that there is nonetheless some element of fortune in our happiness?

"The last of the human freedoms is to choose one's attitudes."

Victor Frankl (1905–1997)

What this means in practice can be gathered from several examples.

> When you call the slave boy, keep in mind that he is capable of not paying attention, and even if he does pay attention he is capable of not doing any of the things that you want him to. But he is not in such a good position that your being upset or not depends on him. (*E* 12)
>
> A person's master is someone who has power over what he wants or does not want, either to obtain it or take it away. Whoever wants to be free, therefore, let him not want or avoid anything that is up to others. Otherwise he will necessarily be a slave. (*E* 14)
>
> It is possible to learn the will of nature from the things in which we do not differ from each other. For example, when someone else's little slave boy breaks his cup we are ready to say, "It's one of those things that just happen." Certainly, then, when your own cup is broken you should be just the way you were when the other person's was broken. Transfer the same idea to larger matters. Someone else's child is dead, or his wife. There is no one who would not say, "It's the lot of a human being." But when one's own dies, immediately it is, "Alas! Poor me!" But we should have remembered how we feel when we hear of the same thing about others. (*E* 26)

Suppose now that we have, by dint of determination and long practice (for this is what it would take), gotten to the point where we always make the distinction. We never set our hearts on the things that are not in our power to control. It seems we have gotten ourselves into a serious difficulty. Having enough food to eat (to take just one example) is not something entirely within our control. People who live in lands stricken by famine are evidence enough for that. Are we not to desire food? And if not, how are we to live? At this point, it seems as though the Stoics are condemned by their principles to starve virtuously, but perhaps contentedly, to death. Is there a way they can solve this problem?

The key to the solution is found in the positive advice the Stoic gives: *to keep our wills in harmony with nature E* 4, 6, 13, 30; and (*M* 2.9). But to understand this, we have to explore what the Stoics mean by "**nature**." We need not go into the details of their nature philosophy, but the central idea is crucial.

Whatever exists, according to the Stoics, is material or corporeal. Our only certainties come from sense experience, and sense experience always reveals the material. But like Heraclitus, they hold that the material world is ordered by a rational principle, a *logos*.* That is what makes the world a world rather than a chaos. This principle, which (like Heraclitus) they sometimes call the fiery element, is not just a passive pattern in things; it is the ordering of the world by and for a reason.† As the ordering principle of the world, it is appropriately called divine.

Thus **God**, for the Stoics, is not like the gods of the Epicureans, separate from the world and unconcerned with it. Nor is the Stoic God like the unmoved mover of Aristotle, independent and self-sufficient, related to the world only as an ideal that the world tries to emulate. Neither of these divinities could be known through the senses. The Stoics conceive of God (whom, again like Heraclitus, they are willing to call Zeus) as *immanent* in the world.‡ Whatever material being you come across has a divine element within it. So the Stoics are committed to a version of **pantheism** (God is all and all is God), though the term "God" emphasizes the *ordering* and the term "nature" the *ordered* aspects of things. It is apparent that the Stoics are believers in Destiny or Fate. Whatever happens happens of necessity. But this is not a cause for despair, since Destiny is the same as Divine Providence. Whatever happens is determined by the divine reason, and so it must happen for the best.§ As Epictetus says,

> Just as a target is not set up to be missed, in the same way nothing bad by nature happens in the world. (*E* 27)

---

*See pp. 21–22.
†See p. 21.
‡See p. 22.
§Compare Heraclitus again, p. 22.

MARCUS AURELIUS

Marcus Aurelius (A.D. 121–180) was emperor of Rome for nineteen years. Late in life, while leading an army in the far north, trying to hold back the barbarian hordes, he recorded his most intimate thoughts in a journal. These often have the form of reminders to himself, but through the ages many have found that they speak also to them. The journal has come down to us as a small volume called *Meditations*, divided into twelve books, each made up of numbered paragraphs, often in no direct relation to each other. Marcus died in the army camp of an infectious disease. Here are a few samples of Stoic thought as filtered through the mind of an emperor.

A little flesh, a little breath, and a Reason to rule all—that is myself. (2,2)

Hour by hour resolve firmly, like a Roman and a man, to do what comes to hand with correct and natural dignity, and with humanity, independence, and justice. Allow your mind freedom from all other considerations. (2,5)

Remembering always what the World-Nature is, and what my own nature is, and how the one stands in respect to the other—so small a fraction of so vast a Whole—bear in mind that no man can hinder you from conforming each word and deed to the Nature of which you are a part. (2,9)

If the power of thought is universal among mankind, so likewise is the possession of reason, making us rational creatures. It follows, therefore, that this reason speaks no less universally to us all with its "thou shalt" or "thou shalt not." So then there is a world-law; which in turn means that we are all fellow-citizens and share a common citizenship, and that the world is a single city. (4,4)

What does not corrupt a man himself cannot corrupt his life, nor do him any damage either outwardly or inwardly. (4,8)

Your mind will be like its habitual thoughts; for the soul becomes dyed with the colour of its thoughts. (4,16)

Observe . . . how transient and trivial is all mortal life; yesterday a drop of semen, tomorrow a handful of spice or ashes. Spend, therefore, these fleeting moments on earth as Nature would have you spend them, and then go to your rest with a good grace as an olive falls in its season, with a blessing for the earth that bore it and a thanksgiving to the tree that gave it life. (4,48)

My own nature is a rational and civic one; I have a city, and I have a country; as Marcus I have Rome, and as a human being I have the universe; and consequently, what is beneficial to these communities is the sole good for me. (6,44)

All things are interwoven with one another; a sacred bond unites them; there is scarcely one thing that is isolated from another. Everything is coordinated, everything works together in giving form to the one universe. The world-order is a unity made up of multiplicity: God is one, pervading all things; all being is one, all law is one (namely, the common reason which all thinking creatures possess) and all truth is one—if, as we believe, there can be but one path to perfection for beings that are alike in kind and reason. (7,9)

Do not indulge in dreams of having what you have not, but reckon up the chief of the blessings you do possess, and then thankfully remember how you would crave for them if they were not yours. At the same time, however, beware lest delight in them leads you to cherish them so dearly that their loss would destroy your peace of mind. (7,27)

When you have done a good action, and another has had the benefit of it, why crave for yet more in addition—applause for your

(continued)

MARCUS AURELIUS *(continued)*

kindness, or some favour in return—as the foolish do? (7,73)

Universal Nature's impulse was to create an orderly world. It follows, then, that everything now happening must follow a logical sequence; if it were not so, the prime purpose towards which the impulses of the World-Reason are directed would be an irrational one. Remembrance of this will help you to face many things more calmly. (7,75)

Nothing can be good for a man unless it helps to make him just, self-disciplined,

courageous, and independent; and nothing bad unless it has the contrary effect. (8,1)

Despise not death; smile, rather, at its coming; it is among the things that Nature wills. (9,3)

The sinner sins against himself; the wrong-doer wrongs himself, becoming the worse by his own action. (9,4)

Quotations are from *Meditations*, Maxwell Staniforth, trans. (Middlesex, England: Penguin Books, 1964); numbers are to Book and Paragraph.

Although "whatever will be, will be," it does not follow that we can simply drift. Your attitude toward what happens makes an enormous difference, for on that your happiness or unhappiness depends.

> Do not seek to have events happen as you want them to, but instead want them to happen as they do happen, and your life will go well. (*E* 8)

If we are to be happy, then, we must keep our wills in harmony with nature. And we now can see that this is identical with keeping our wills in harmony with both reason and God, for nature is the sphere of events governed by the benevolent purpose of a rational deity. The Stoics sometimes speak of the soul as a *microcosm* (a little world) and compare it to the macrocosm of the universe. Our task, they hold, is to use our reason to order the microcosm in a way that mirrors the ordering of the macrocosm. This is possible because the reason within us is merely an aspect of the divine reason that orders the world as a whole. God is not only immanent in the macrocosm but is also present within each of us.

"Never does nature say one thing and wisdom another."

Juvenal (late first, early second centuries)

Now we can see how the Stoics address the problem raised earlier. Everything in nature contains its own ordering principle in harmony with the great order of the whole. In living things there is a natural tendency toward certain ends—self-preservation in particular, together with all that serves that end. This is part of the Divine Providence and is not to be despised. This is why animals seek food and shelter; and this is why they naturally seek to preserve their species. Denying these *natural* tendencies would certainly not keep one's will in harmony with nature!

So the Stoics eat when hungry, drink when thirsty, and do what is necessary to preserve themselves from the weather. It is in accordance with nature so to do. But, and this point is crucial, they pursue these natural goals with **equanimity**, not being disturbed if their quest for them is frustrated. In regard to what is natural to a living being, the Stoics distinguish what is *preferred*, what is *shunned*, and what is *indifferent*. We humans "prefer" not only food and shelter, but also skills, knowledge, health, reputation, and wealth. We "shun" their opposites, and we find many things "indifferent"; about them we simply don't care. The natural tendencies in human beings determine what falls in one class or another.

So there is nothing wrong with pursuing what is preferred. Where people go wrong, however, is in attributing some *absolute value* to all these things. And the mark of this wrong turn is their reaction when they do not get what they want: distress, despair, resentment, and general unhappiness. The wise person, by contrast, "uses such things without requiring them."[7] This attitude makes possible the equanimity of the Stoics, in which nothing that happens can destroy their calm. There is only one thing to which the Stoic attaches absolute value: that his will should be in harmony with nature. In comparison with that, even the things "preferred" seem only indifferent.

This means that the only true good is **virtue**: a life in harmony with nature, reason, and God. Stoics and Epicureans carry on a running battle over just this point. The Epicureans, of course, hold that the only good is pleasure, and everything else (including virtue) is good only in relation to that. Stoics typically respond in a most extreme fashion, denying not only that pleasure is the one true good, but also that it is even in the realm of the "preferred." Pleasure, according to the Stoics, is *never* to be pursued; it is not an appropriate end at all.

The Epicureans argue, as we have seen, that pleasure is the only natural good, the root of all our choosing. The Stoics reply that this is far from so. Our natural tendencies are for the acquisition of certain *things*, such as food, which is necessary for self-preservation. They do not deny that eating when hungry is pleasurable, but the pleasure is an *accompaniment* to the eating, not the end sought. Pleasure on its own won't keep you alive! People go wrong exactly here, in seeking the by-product instead of the end—a sure recipe, the Stoics think, for disaster. A virtuous person will in fact lead a pleasant life. But if she makes the pleasant life her object, she will miss both virtue *and* the pleasure that accompanies it!

There are two corollaries to the view that only virtue is the good. First, the only thing that counts in estimating the goodness of an action is the **intention** of the agent. You can see why this must be so. An action is an attempt to change the world in some way; whether the action succeeds depends upon the cooperation of the world; the world is not entirely in the control of the agent; and so the goodness or badness of the *person* or the *action* cannot depend on the action's outcome. But this means that a judgment on the agent must be a judgment on the agent's intention. Cleanthes gives the example of two slaves sent out to find someone. The one slave searches diligently but fails to find him. The other loafs about and runs into him by accident. Which is the better man? (*SES* 264). The Stoic has no doubt about the answer and takes it to show that results are to be considered indifferent. What counts is the state of your will; that is in your control, and that is what is absolutely good or bad. So the entire concentration of life must be put into the effort to set your will in harmony with nature. The outcome must be nothing to you.

This leads us to the second corollary. The important thing is to do one's **duty**. The notion of "duty" has not played a large role to this point. We hardly find it in Socrates or Plato, nor in Aristotle, nor Epicurus. These philosophers are asking: What is the best life for a human being to live? They never imagine that it might be a duty or an obligation to lead such a life. It is just a question of what the prudent or wise person would do. Why, we might wonder, does the notion of duty suddenly come to prominence in Stoic thought?

It has a natural home here because of the connection between the divine, rational principle that providentially guides the course of the world and the notion of *law*. It is law that shows us our duties. The principles governing the world are not only descriptions of how the world inevitably *does* go; they express how things, according to their natures, *should* go. So they take on for us the aspect of law reflected in civil law: they prescribe to us our duties and obligations. This notion of **natural law** (a concept we owe largely to the Stoics) is obviously a development of Heraclitean ideas about the *logos*. If we behave in certain ways, consequences—determined by the ordering principles of the world—necessarily follow. For example, if you smoke cigarettes for a while, you will become addicted. Since addictions are bad—they hand control of your life over to something "not your own"—understanding the order of the world is also understanding that you have a duty not to smoke.

The Stoics devote considerable attention to duties, distinguishing several classes of duties and examining particular cases. We need not explore the details, but we should note the one duty that is clear and always overriding: the duty to harmonize our intentions with the law of nature. This is the duty to be virtuous or to perfect ourselves. The microcosm of our soul *ought* to be in harmony with the order without. It is our first and most important task to see that it is. And this means that we must concern ourselves above all with the things in our power—with our beliefs, attitudes, and desires. Everything else must be, as Epictetus says, nothing to us in comparison. We began the discussion of Stoic thought by considering happiness. But now we can see that if we devote ourselves to virtue, to doing our duty, our happiness will take care of itself.*

"Happiness and moral duty are inseparably connected."

George Washington (1732–1799)

As you can see, Stoics believe that whatever city or nation we belong to, we are first of all citizens of the world. All men are brothers, for all are "children" of the same God. The consideration we owe to our neighbors is not different from that we owe to strangers. All of us, Greeks, Romans, and barbarians, are part of the same world and partake of the same divine reason.

Let Gilbert Murray have the last word.

The glory of the Stoics is to have built up a religion of extraordinary nobleness; the glory of the Epicureans is to have upheld an ideal of sanity and humanity stark upright amid a reeling world, and, like the old Spartans, never to have yielded one inch of ground to the common foe.[8]

---

*Compare this thought with what Jesus says in the Sermon on the Mount: "Seek first the Kingdom of God and his righteousness, and all these things will be added to you as well" (Matthew 6:33).

1. On what distinction does Stoicism rest? Explain how making this distinction is the key, for the Stoic, to both happiness and freedom.
2. How are God and nature related? What of evil?
3. What does it mean to keep one's will in line with nature?
4. Why doesn't a Stoic starve to death?
5. What is virtue, according to the Stoics?
6. Explain the Stoic critique of Epicurean philosophy.
7. Why does the Stoic believe intention is more important than results in evaluating the worth of a person?
8. What is it about the Stoic view of nature that makes duty an important notion?

The Skeptics

What has **skepticism** to do with happiness? We are apt to suppose that someone who doesn't know, or at least thinks he doesn't know, must on that account be *unhappy*. Aristotle, who holds that all men by nature desire to know, would surely think so. Moreover, we are almost all brought up as believers in something or other. Belief is as natural to us as breathing. What sense could it make to suspend all our beliefs, to get rid of that habit? And how could that make us happy? These are the perplexing questions we must now address. The ancient skeptics give some surprising answers.

Again we shall simplify, this time by focusing on the most radical group of skeptics, who call themselves by the name of a shadowy fourth-century figure **Pyrrho**, about whom little is known. From what we do know, it seems that Pyrrho is not interested in speculative or scientific philosophy, but only in the practical question of how best to live. But it is not sheer disinterest; it is what we might call principled disinterest. His pupil Timon is reported to have said that the nature of things is **"indeterminable,"** meaning that we cannot determine that things are more like this than they are like that.[9] But why not? Let us review a little of the story we have been telling.

From the time of Parmenides it is maintained that a distinction must be drawn between things as they appear to us and things as they are in themselves. The core insight is that things may not appear as they really are. The realm of appearance is generally agreed to be the world of the senses, which sometimes deceives us about reality: The straight oar in water looks bent; square towers in the distance look round; honey tastes bitter to a sick person; and so on. So the question forces itself upon thinkers: Is there some way to tell what things are really like? The usual answer is given in terms of intelligence or reason, and we have seen some of the results. Parmenides, following what he takes to be the best argument, asserts that reality is the One. Democritus holds that it is atoms and the void. For Plato, the independent world of eternally unchanging Forms constitutes the really real. And for Aristotle, reality is made up of individual substances that are composites of matter and form.

It is partly this diversity of answers that motivates the Pyrrhonists, who like to gather these and even more examples of disagreement among the philosophers. But sheer disagreement does not prove that nothing can be known about reality; some one of these views may well be correct and the others mistaken; or perhaps none of them are correct, but some future development of them might be. And we might come to know that. To support the claim that the nature of things is "indeterminable," we must say more.

The later Pyrrhonists systematize the arguments in favor of skeptical conclusions in a number of types or *modes* of reasoning. Our best source for these is a Greek physician, **Sextus Empiricus**, who lived in the second century A.D. Let us survey several of these modes.

The first mode stresses that the sense organs of animals differ from species to species. His arguments are rather primitive, since not much was known about the details of animal sense organs until recent times. But we can think of the registration of the world in the many-faceted eye of a fly, in the echolocation of a bat, and in what the frog's eye tells the frog's brain.[10] Cats and owls see much better in the dark than we do, and the olfactory world of the dog must be immensely rich compared to ours. In terms like these, we can understand what Sextus says:

> But if the same things appear different owing to the variety in animals, we shall, indeed, be able to state our own impressions of the real object, but as

to its essential nature we shall suspend judgment. For we cannot ourselves judge between our own impressions and those of the other animals, since we ourselves are involved in the dispute and are, therefore, rather in need of a judge than competent to pass judgment ourselves. . . . If, then, owing to the variety in animals their sense-impressions differ, and it is impossible to judge between them, we must necessarily suspend judgment regarding the external underlying objects.[11] (*OP* 1.59–61)

Here we have some of the key notions of skepticism. Because the nature of the "external underlying objects" appears differently to creatures with different sense organs, we cannot confidently judge that these objects are as they appear to us. If they appear one way to us and another way to the bat or fly or frog, it would be arbitrary to pick one of those ways rather than another and say that is how it really is. The result is that we must "**suspend judgment**."

The second mode concerns differences among human beings. These are particularly notable, Sextus tells us, with respect to objects of choice. He quotes poets and dramatists who exclaim about the variations in human preferences, and adds,

> Seeing, then, that choice and avoidance depend on pleasure and displeasure, while pleasure and displeasure depend on sensation and sense-impression, whenever some men choose the very things which are avoided by others, it is logical for us to conclude that they are also differently affected by the same things, since otherwise they would all alike have chosen or avoided the same things. But if the same objects affect men differently owing to the differences in the men, then, on this ground also, we shall reasonably be led to suspension of judgment. For while we are, no doubt, able to state what each of the underlying objects appears to be, relatively to each difference, we are incapable of explaining what it is in reality. For we shall have to believe either all men or some. But if we believe all, we shall be attempting the impossible and accepting contradictories; and if some, let us be told whose opinions we are to endorse. (*OP* 1.87–88)

The message is the same; we must suspend judgment. What does that mean? It means that we do not say either yes or no; we do not affirm or deny any proposition about the real nature of the underlying objects. We do not say, as the Stoics do, that they are part of the divine nature, nor do we deny that. We do not say, as the atomists do, that reality is composed of atoms and the void, but neither do we deny it. We do not say, as the Platonists do, that the things of sense are shadows of the eternal Forms, but neither do we deny it.

Note carefully that we *can* state what the object *appears* to be. We just refrain from making any further judgments. In terms of the appearance/reality distinction, the skeptic restricts himself to appearance. He is forced to this by the considerations in the "modes," of which we have examined only two. Some of the others concern the differences among our own organs of sense, the dependence of appearances on differing circumstances, and the differences in customs and laws.

There are also modes of a more formal character, standard ways of criticizing the arguments of the philosophers. A skeptic considers someone who affirms what is not evident *dogmatic;* and any claim about how things *really* are, independently of their appearance to our senses, is a claim about the nonevident. To be **dogmatic**, in this sense, is to claim to know something for which you have no evidence. So all the other schools of philosophy, with their theories about the reality beyond the appearances, are classified as dogmatic by the skeptics.

One of these more formal modes is based on an "infinite regress" argument and another on the charge of "circular reasoning." An **infinite regress** is generated when a claim *A* is supported by another claim *B* and *B* itself needs to be supported. If it is supported by *C*, the skeptic will ask how *C* is to be supported, and so on. **Circular reasoning** occurs when *A* is supported by *B*, *B* by *C*, and *C* by *A*. The argument goes in a circle.

Here is an example of Sextus making use of these modes. Suppose one of the "dogmatic" philosophers (a Platonist, perhaps, or a Stoic) has made some claim about the real nature of an object.

> The matter proposed is either a sense-object or a thought-object, but whichever it is, it is an object of controversy; for some say that only sensibles are true, others only intelligibles, others that some sensibles and some intelligible objects are true. Will they then assert that the controversy can or cannot be decided? If they say it cannot, we have it granted

that we must suspend judgement. . . . But if they say that it can be decided, we ask by what is it to be decided? For example, in the case of the sense-object . . . is it to be decided by a sense-object or a thought-object? For if they say by a sense-object, since we are inquiring about sensibles that object itself also will require another to confirm it; and if that too is to be a sense-object, it likewise will require another for its confirmation, and so on ad infinitum. And if the sense-object shall have to be decided by a thought-object, then, since thought-objects also are controverted, this being an object of thought will need examination and confirmation. Whence then will it gain confirmation? If from an intelligible object, it will suffer a similar regress ad infinitum; and if from a sensible object, since an intelligible was adduced to establish the sensible and a sensible to establish the intelligible, the Mode of circular reasoning is brought in. (*OP* 1.170–72)

The key question here is, "By what is it to be decided?" To use Protagoras' term, what is the "measure" we are to judge by? These modes attempt to show that the question cannot be satisfactorily answered, for the answer either will itself be subject to that very same question (infinite regress) or will assume what is to be proved (circular reasoning). The moral is the same: We must suspend judgment.

All of the various modes circle around a central point, which we must now explore more explicitly. It can be called the problem of the **criterion**. Claims to knowledge and truth are a dime a dozen; the Hellenistic world, as we have seen, is filled with them (just as ours is)—religious, popular, and philosophical. The problem we face is how to decide among them. By what mark or standard or criterion are we to decide where truth and knowledge really lie? This problem faces thoughtful people in an insistent way, and numerous attempts are made to solve it. The skeptics argue, however, that this is an insoluble problem: *No* satisfactory criterion is to be found. In a chapter called "Does a Criterion of Truth Really Exist?" Sextus Empiricus writes,

> Of those, then, who have treated of the criterion some have declared that a criterion exists—the Stoics, for example, and certain others—while by some its existence is denied, as by . . .

Xenophanes of Colophon, who say—"Over all things opinion bears sway";* while we have adopted suspension of judgement as to whether it does or does not exist. This dispute, then, they will declare to be either capable or incapable of decision; and if they shall say it is incapable of decision they will be granting on the spot the propriety of suspension of judgement, while if they say it admits of decision, let them tell us whereby it is to be decided, since we have no accepted criterion, and do not even know, but are still inquiring, whether any criterion exists. Besides, in order to decide the dispute which has arisen about the criterion, we must possess an accepted criterion by which we shall be able to judge the dispute; and in order to possess an accepted criterion, the dispute about the criterion must first be decided. And when the argument thus reduces itself to a form of circular reasoning, the discovery of the criterion becomes impracticable, since we do not allow them to adopt a criterion by assumption, while if they offer to judge the criterion by a criterion we force them to a regress ad infinitum. And furthermore, since demonstration requires a demonstrated criterion, while the criterion requires an approved demonstration, they are forced into circular reasoning. (*OP* 2.18–20)

Let us note several points in this passage. First, any claim that some principle is a criterion for truth itself needs to be supported. We shall need a criterion to decide whether that support is successful. And any attempt to provide such a criterion will either be forced into the infinite regress of criteria by which to decide criteria by which to decide . . . or it will be circular, begging the question in favor of some assumed criterion. We can represent the argument by a flow chart. (See the figure on page 213.)

No matter which alternatives we choose, the result is the same. And if we suspend judgment about a criterion, it follows that judgment is suspended about each and every claim to knowledge; for each claim to know depends on there being a criterion by which it is singled out as true knowledge. So if we cannot solve the problem of the criterion, we must suspend judgment generally.

---

*See pp. 17–18.

"I was gratified to be able to answer promptly. I said, 'I don't know.'"

Mark Twain (1835–1910)

Second, note that Sextus does *not* claim there is no criterion of truth; about that very question— is there or is there not a criterion?—the Pyrrhonian skeptic suspends judgment. There is a kind of skeptic who claims that nothing can be known. This kind is subject to a devastating counter: He can be asked how he knows *that*. But Sextus is careful not to make any such claim. He does not know whether anything can be known or not. If he is pushed back a step and asked whether he knows that he does not know, he will presumably confess that he doesn't. His attitude throughout is one of *noncommitment* to any knowledge claims that concern how things really are.

The argument about the criterion seems like a very powerful argument indeed. It sweeps the board clean.*

But this surely leads to a pressing question: How then can we live? If we make no judgments about the world we are in, won't we be paralyzed? To eat bread rather than a stone seems to depend on a judgment that bread will nourish you and a stone will not. *Can* we suspend judgments like that?

Here we must remember that skeptics do not deny **appearances**. Skeptics claim that we can live, and live well, by restricting ourselves to how things seem. Though there may not be a criterion to distinguish reality from appearance, there is a criterion for life and action. Sextus tells us that this practical criterion

denotes the standard of action by conforming to which in the conduct of life we perform some actions and abstain from others. . . . The criterion, then, of the Skeptic School is, we say, the appearance, giving this name to what is virtually the sense-presentation. For since this lies in feeling and involuntary affection, it is not open to question. . . .

---

*Compare Montaigne, pp. 303–306.

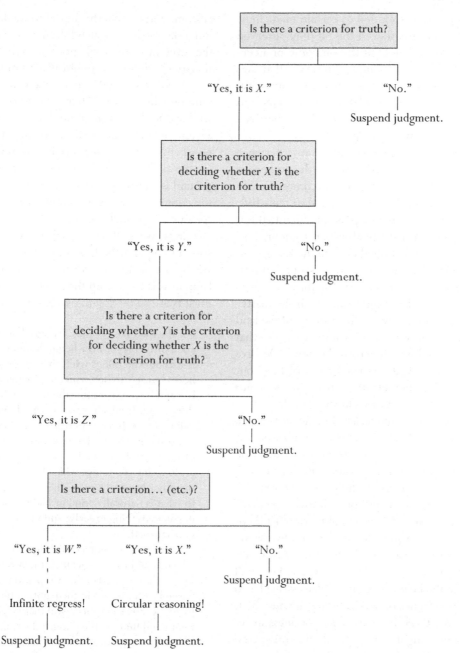

Adhering, then, to appearances we live in accordance with the normal rules of life, undogmatically, seeing that we cannot remain wholly inactive. (*OP* 1.21–23)

Sextus was a physician, a member of a school of medicine that followed similar principles.

These doctors were unwilling to speculate about the "real" nature of diseases, about underlying causes and unobservable entities—either physical or demonic—posited to explain illness. They wished to restrict themselves to what they observed, to appearances. If they observed that certain symptoms responded to certain medicines, they noted and remembered this. If they observed that diet positively affected the outcome of a certain disease, they had a rule to prescribe that diet for that disease. It was, we might say, empirical medicine rather than speculative. If medicine can be done in this way, then why can't life be lived according to the same principles?*

So if we are skeptics, we eat what experience has shown to be connected with health and behave in ways correlated with positive outcomes. We do not pronounce things to be truly good or truly bad, for about such claims we suspend judgment. But it is beyond question that bread *appears* to nourish us and scarcely less so that obedience to the law *appears* to be profitable. We do not worry about absolutes, either of truth or of goodness, for they are unattainable. But we follow appearances. In the matter of behavior, we conform to the customs of the land in which we live, for these customs express what appears to our fellow citizens to be good. We live "in accordance with the normal rules of life," but "undogmatically," not claiming that this is somehow the absolutely best or right thing to do.

As you can see, the relativism against which Plato struggles and which Aristotle thinks he has overcome is reborn. It is not reborn as a doctrine claiming to be the truth about matters, for no such claims are made. But since things may appear differently to different people or cultures, a *practical relativism* is the result. We might also note that skepticism tends to be a profoundly conservative view, for it will nearly always be the case that adaptation to customs and laws—whatever they may be—will appear to be the best way to live. Plato struggles to delineate the outlines of an ideal state, because he is convinced that there is an absolute goodness in reality that states might (and typically do) miss. And the Stoics think they have a criterion for correcting customs and laws in the appeal to the law of nature. But a skeptic has no such fulcrum on which to work the lever of reform. Skeptics are not great revolutionaries, religiously, politically, or morally.

On what grounds, then, could the skeptic recommend his views? There are two. One, which we have looked at in some detail, amounts to the argument that there really is no alternative. Every nonskeptical view founders in one way or another on the problem of the criterion. But the second ground is a more positive one and brings us back to the connection between skepticism and happiness. As long as we seek certainty about the true nature of things, we will be in doubt; if we are in doubt, we will be perturbed; as long as we are perturbed, we won't be happy. So the key to quietude and happiness is to give up the search for certainty. We must cease to be dogmatists and become skeptics.

> For the man who opines that anything is by nature good or bad is for ever being disquieted; when he is without the things which he deems good he believes himself to be tormented by things naturally bad and he pursues after the things which are, as he thinks, good; which when he has obtained he keeps falling into still more perturbations because of his irrational and immoderate elation, and in his dread of a change of fortune he uses every endeavor to avoid losing the things which he deems good. On the other hand, the man who determines nothing as to what is naturally good or bad neither shuns nor pursues anything eagerly; and in consequence, he is unperturbed.
>
> The Skeptic, in fact, had the same experience which is said to have befallen the painter Apelles. Once, they say, when he was painting a horse and wished to represent in the painting the horse's foam, he was so unsuccessful that he gave up the attempt and flung at the picture the sponge on which he used to wipe the paints off his brush, and the mark of the sponge produced the effect of a horse's foam. So, too, the Skeptics were in hopes of gaining quietude by means of a decision regarding the disparity of the objects of sense and of thought, and being unable to effect this they suspended judgment; and they found that quietude, as if by chance, followed upon their suspense, even as a shadow follows its substance. (*OP* 1.27–29)

---

*One might question, of course, how successfully medicine can be done on such a restricted empirical base. Modern medicine does not restrict itself to what is observable but makes use of the theoretical constructions of modern science. Does the same hold for principles of living?

This quietude, or tranquillity of soul, is what the skeptic means by happiness. Or, if happiness is more than this, it is at least a necessary condition for happiness; without it no one can be happy. Though no one can escape trouble entirely, most people are doubly troubled, once by the pain or suffering and once by two further beliefs: that this is something bad or evil they are undergoing, and that either they do not (in some absolute sense) deserve it, or—worse yet—that they do. The skeptic at least does not suffer these further agonies. So the skeptics recommend their attitude, the suspension of judgment about all claims to truth, on the grounds that doing so provides a basis on which a happy life can be built.

These may seem rather minimal claims and their kind of happiness rather a pale one. It seems to be a retreat of some magnitude from the "high" view of happiness expressed, for instance, by Aristotle: activity of soul in accord with excellence. But perhaps the times did not realistically allow for more—for most people. Furthermore, the problem of the criterion still remains; unless this can be solved, maybe no more can reasonably be expected. This is a very real problem with which numerous future philosophers struggle.*

---

1. What should we conclude from an examination of (a) differences in sense organs among animals; and (b) differences in taste among humans?
2. About what kind of thing does the skeptic "suspend judgment"? What does that term mean?
3. What is it to be "dogmatic"?
4. How does the skeptic use infinite regress and circular reasoning arguments?
5. What is the problem of the criterion? (Study the flow chart carefully.)
6. By what practical criterion does the skeptic live?
7. Why does the skeptic recommend suspending judgment as a key to happiness?

---

*See for example Augustine (pp. 232–234) and particularly René Descartes (*Meditation III*) and Hegel (pp. 459–462).

FOR FURTHER THOUGHT

1. Evaluate Epicurus' reasons for thinking that pleasure is the good for human beings in the light of (a) Aristotle's reasons for thinking that this could not possibly be correct and (b) the Stoic critique of this claim. Who do you think has the best of the argument here? Why?
2. Hot, sweaty, and dirty after an afternoon working in the yard, I came in and took a shower. My wife said, "I'll bet you feel better." I said, "Well, I'm clean, that's the main thing." Which of us is the Epicurean, which the Stoic?
3. Apply the problem of the criterion (with its considerations of infinite regress and circular reasoning) to Aristotle's theory of knowledge in terms of deduction, induction, and first principles. Can Aristotle survive such a critique? If you think he can, try to say how. If not, why not?
4. If you consider the popular culture of our day, would you say it is Platonistic, Aristotelian, Epicurean, Stoic, or Skeptical? Or is it just in large measure unwise?

KEY WORDS

Epicurus	virtue
hedonism	intention
the gods	duty
death	natural law
atomism	skepticism
desire	Pyrrho
virtues	indeterminable
friendship	Sextus Empiricus
Stoicism	suspend judgment
happiness	dogmatic
nature	infinite regress
logos	circular reasoning
God	criterion
pantheism	appearances
equanimity	

NOTES

1. Gilbert Murray, *Five Stages of Greek Religion* (New York: Doubleday, Anchor Books, 1955), 139. I am indebted to this source for numerous points in this section.

2. All quotations from Epicurus' works are from *Letters, Principal Doctrines, and Vatican Sayings*, trans. Russel M. Geer (Indianapolis: Library of Liberal Arts, 1964). Within this text, references to specific works will be as follows: *PD, Principal Doctrines; LM, Letter to Menoeceus; LP, Letter to Pythocles;* and *VS, Vatican Sayings*.

3. William Shakespeare, *Hamlet*, act 3, scene 1, lines 64–68.

4. Quotations from Lucretius, *The Way Things Are*, trans. Rolfe Humphries (Bloomington: Indiana University Press, 1969), are cited in the text using the abbreviation *WTA*. References are to page numbers of this edition.

5. Quotations from *The Handbook of Epictetus*, trans. Nicholas P. White (Indianapolis: Hackett, 1983), are cited in the text using the abbreviation *E*.

6. See also Marcus Aurelius, *Meditations*, trans. Maxwell Staniforth (New York: Penguin Books,

1964), 6.41. Quotations from this work are hereafter cited in the text using the abbreviation *M*.

7. Attributed to Chrysippus by Eduard Zeller in *Stoics, Epicureans, and Skeptics* (New York: Russell and Russell, 1962), 284–285. Subsequent quotations from this work are cited in the text using the abbreviation *SES*.

8. Murray, *Five Stages of Greek Religion*, 125.

9. Charlotte L. Stough, *Greek Scepticism* (Berkeley: University of California Press, 1969), 17.

10. There is a well-known study of interest in this connection: "What the Frog's Eye Tells the Frog's Brain," by J. Y. Lettvin, H. R. Maturana, W. S. McCulloch, and W. H. Pitts, *Proceedings of the Institute of Radio Engineers* 47 (1959): 1940–1951.

11. Quotations from Sextus Empiricus, *Outlines of Pyrrhonism* (Cambridge, MA: Harvard University Press, 1955), are cited in the text using the abbreviation *OP*.

CHAPTER

9

JEWS AND CHRISTIANS

Sin, Salvation, and Love

In Chapter One we sketched the religious and cultural traditions of the ancient Greeks. This was not philosophy, but the ground out of which philosophy grew. We noted then that another context, also prephilosophical, would have to be examined if we are to understand medieval and later philosophy. In this short chapter, we look at the Judeo-Christian tradition.

Background

Jesus, whom the Christians call "Christ" or "Messiah" (meaning "the anointed one"), was a Jew, as were all of his first followers; Christianity is a modification of the Jewish heritage. So if we want to understand the Christians, it is necessary to sketch something of the history in terms of which they understood themselves. Their history is the history of the Hebrew people. Let us outline, then, certain central convictions that grow out of that history and that the Christians take for granted.

Of the very first importance is the conviction that there is *one* **God**. We may be able to trace some development of this concept—from a kind of

tribal deity, to a God superior to the gods of their neighbors, to one having the exclusive claim to worship—but by the time of the great prophets from the eighth to the sixth centuries B.C., it was already clear to the Hebrews that all other "gods" were mere pretenders, "idols" that it was sinful to reverence.*

> Thus says the Lord, the King of Israel
> and his Redeemer, the Lord of hosts:
> "I am the first and I am the last;
> besides me there is no god. . . .
>
> "To whom will you liken me and make me equal,
> and compare me, that we may be alike?
> Those who lavish gold from the purse,
> and weigh out silver in the scales,
> hire a goldsmith, and he makes it into a god;
> then they fall down and worship!
> They lift it upon their shoulders, they carry it,
> they set it in its place, and it stands there;
> it cannot move from its place.
> If one cries to it, it does not answer
> or save him from his trouble."
>
> —Isa. 44:6, 46:5–7[1]

————

*Compare Xenophanes, pp. 15–16, who is writing at about this same time.

217

The one true god differs from idols in all these respects. He is not made by men; he cannot be seen or touched or carried; he is not restricted to any one place; and when you cry to him, he does help. He is, moreover, "the first and the last," meaning that he has no beginning and no ending. He is eternal. He alone is worthy of worship and reverence.

God is the creator of the entire visible universe. The world is not eternal, as Aristotle thinks; nor is it God or an aspect of God, as the Stoics believed. God precedes and transcends the world, which is, however, wholly dependent on his power. The first words in the Hebrew scriptures are

> In the beginning God created the heavens and the earth. (Gen. 1:1)

Moreover, God is entirely good, righteous, just, and holy. And this goodness is transmitted to the **creation**; on each of the "days" of creation, after God made light, the heavens, dry land, vegetation, animals, and human beings, we read that "God saw that it was good." Finding the world to be good, the Hebrews have a positive attitude toward it; the world is not something to flee or escape from; it is not just a shadowy image of true reality; and the body is not—as it is for Plato—a prison in which we are alienated from our true home. It is in this world that we have a home; it is here that God has put us; it is here that our tasks and purposes are to be accomplished and our happiness achieved. The shadowy existence in the underworld after death is not anything to desire.*

But this task and happiness are complicated by the fact of sin. In the well-known story of the first man and woman, we read that human beings have succumbed to the temptation to "be like God, knowing good and evil" (Gen. 3:5). Not content with their status, unhappy in obedience, wanting to play God themselves, humans have made themselves corrupt and find themselves outside the Garden. Of the first pair of brothers, one murders the other. And so it has been ever since.

_____

*See for instance Psalms 39:3 and 88:3–5, 10–12. Compare also Homer's Achilles on p. 8. Belief in a "resurrection of the body" grew among Jews in the several centuries before Jesus, however. In Jesus' time, one party, the Sadducees, held out against the belief. See Mark 12:18–27.

The story that occupies the rest of the Hebrew scriptures concerns a series of attempts to remedy this situation. It is the story of how God, sometimes directly and sometimes through representatives, acts to reestablish his rule in a community of righteousness and justice. It is often understood in terms of the concept of the "**Kingdom of God**." This story expresses the self-understanding of Jews and Christians alike. We sketch it briefly.

One tactic to clean up the unrighteousness of men would be to destroy them and start again. Something close to this is found in the story of **Noah**.

> The Lord saw that the wickedness of man was great in the earth, and that every imagination of the thoughts of his heart was only evil continually. And the Lord was sorry that he had made man on the earth, and it grieved him to his heart. So the Lord said, "I will blot out man whom I have created from the face of the ground, man and beast and creeping things and birds of the air, for I am sorry that I have made them." But Noah found favor in the eyes of the Lord. (Gen. 6:5–8)

The outcome is a great flood, from which only Noah and his family are saved, together with a pair of each kind of animal. But not many generations pass before wickedness again becomes widespread, and people become arrogant enough to think they can build a tower that reaches to heaven. This presumption is punished by the confusing of their languages, so that they cannot understand each other and cooperate in finishing that venture.

A crux comes when God calls a certain man, Abram (later called **Abraham**), to leave his home, his culture, his nation, and to venture out to a new land.

> Now the Lord said to Abram, "Go from your country and your kindred and your father's house to the land that I will show you. And I will make of you a great nation, and I will bless you, and make your name great, so that you will be a blessing." (Gen. 12:1–2)

It is in terms of this promise and burden that the Hebrew people identify themselves. They trace their heritage back to Abraham and believe that they have a special role to play in the history of the world: It is their privilege—and responsibility—to be agents for the reestablishment of God's kingdom on earth. They consider that they have entered into a covenant with God, the terms of which are to reverence him, obeying him only, establishing justice among themselves, and so be a blessing to the rest of corrupt mankind—who can learn from them the blessings of righteousness.

A second crux is the **Exodus**. After some generations, the children of Abraham, faced with famine in Palestine, move to Egypt. Eventually they are enslaved there and spend "four hundred years" suffering the considerable oppression of slaves. Against all odds, they leave Egypt under the guidance of **Moses** and establish themselves again in the land promised to Abraham. This remarkable occurrence, which leaves an indelible mark on the national character, is the sign and seal of their mission.

Corresponding to this deliverance from bondage and their establishment as a nation is the giving of **the Law** ("Torah"). It is the Law that marks the Hebrews as distinct and unique. It defines them as a people. What has distinguished the Jews to this day is the continuous possession of that Law, which begins with these words,

> "I am the Lord your God, who brought you out
> of the land of Egypt, out of the house of bondage.
> "You shall have no other gods before me."
> —Exo. 20:2–3

The Law goes on to forbid misusing God's name, killing, adultery, theft, false witness, and covetousness and to require keeping a Sabbath day holy and honoring one's parents. These statutes are well known as the Ten Commandments. But the Law also states in great detail how life is to be lived by the people of God, specifying dietary and health rules, principles of reparation for wrongs done, and regulations for religious observances.

The life of the Hebrew people in that continually troubled area of the Middle East is precarious. They achieve some years of security and prosperity in the time of David and Solomon.* But thereafter

it is a struggle to keep the community together. Surrounded by hostile nations, dominated for a time by the powerful Assyrians, exiled to Babylon, conquered by Alexander's armies, and finally made a province of the Roman Empire, they fight tenaciously for their heritage. They are constantly falling away from the Abrahamic covenant and the Law, if we are to judge by the succession of prophets who unsparingly condemn their waywardness and call them back again to God. Still, despite the people's "hardness of heart," as the prophets call it, there is truth in the boast of Josephus, the first-century A.D. Jewish historian:

> Throughout our history we have kept the same laws, to which we are eternally faithful.[2]

During the period of foreign domination there grows up an expectation that God will send someone who will act decisively to establish God's kingdom of righteousness among men. This agent of God is sometimes conceived in terms of a political liberator who will expel the oppressors and restore the ancient kingdom of David; sometimes he is conceived in more cosmic and apocalyptic terms, as one who will institute a general judgment and destruction of all the wicked, together with the rescue of the faithful few. This hoped-for figure is given a variety of titles: Son of David, Son of Man, Messiah.

Together with the insistent hope that God will not fail in his promise to create a holy people, a righteous kingdom, these expectations provide a rich context for understanding the life of Jesus. Jesus is called by all of these titles and often calls himself "Son of Man." Christians will look back particularly to Isaiah's prophecy about a "Suffering Servant" who will create the kingdom not by might, but by bearing the burdens of the people.

> He was despised and rejected by men;
> a man of sorrows and acquainted with grief;
> and as one from whom men hide their faces
> he was despised, and we esteemed him not.
> Surely he has borne our griefs
> and carried our sorrows;
> yet we esteemed him stricken,
> smitten by God, and afflicted.
> But he was wounded for our transgressions,

---

*This apex of the nation's power corresponds roughly to the time of the Trojan War.

he was bruised for our iniquities;
upon him was the chastisement that made us
    whole;
and with his stripes we are healed.
All we like sheep have gone astray;
we have turned every one to his own way;
and the Lord has laid on him the iniquity of us all.

                  —Isa. 53:3–6

These words, familiar to all who are acquainted with Handel's *Messiah*, are applied to the life, and particularly to the death, of Jesus. We must now turn to Jesus himself to see what leads so many to think of him in these terms.

---

1. How do prophets differ from philosophers?
2. What are the characteristics of God, according to the Judeo–Christian tradition?
3. What is the significance of God's call to Abraham? Of the Exodus?

Jesus

In the earliest Gospel* Mark introduces **Jesus**, after his baptism by John, with these words:

> Now after John was arrested, Jesus came into Galilee, preaching the gospel of God, and saying, "The time is fulfilled, and the kingdom of God is at hand; repent and believe in the gospel." (Mark 1:14–15)

That which the prophets foretold and apocalyptic seers envisioned is now "at hand." The "kingdom of God" is about to be established, and Jesus sees himself as the one to whom that task falls.

That the kingdom is indeed at hand is manifest in the healing miracles of Jesus. According to the gospel writers, Jesus cures leprosy, gives sight

---

*The word "gospel" means "good news." The four accounts we have of the life of Jesus (Matthew, Mark, Luke, and John) are called Gospels because they present the good news that God has fulfilled his promises to Abraham in the life and death of Jesus. It should be noted that each of these accounts is written from a Christian perspective by one who believes that Jesus is Lord, Savior, and the expected Messiah. We have no hostile or even neutral accounts of his life.

to the blind and hearing to the deaf, casts out demons, and even brings the dead back to life. These miracles are signs of God's presence and power and stimuli to repentance and faith.

The attitude and behavior of Jesus bears out his sense of a new beginning. He is absolutely without any class consciousness, associating with poor and rich, learned and ignorant, righteous and sinner alike. A common complaint among those who carefully observe the Law is that he associates with outcasts and undesirables. He does not do so, of course, to sanction their sin, but to lead them to righteousness, as the following parable illustrates.

> Now the tax collectors and sinners were all drawing near to hear him. And the Pharisees and the scribes murmured, saying, "This man receives sinners and eats with them."
>
> So he told them this parable: "What man of you, having a hundred sheep, if he lost one of them, does not leave the ninety-nine in the wilderness, and go after the one which is lost, until he finds it? And when he has found it, he lays it on his shoulders, rejoicing. And when he comes home, he calls together his friends and his neighbors, saying to them, 'Rejoice with me, for I have found my sheep which was lost.' Just so, I tell you, there will be more joy in heaven over one sinner who repents than over ninety-nine righteous persons who need no repentance." (Luke 15:1–7)

Absolute indifference to wealth and worldly goods is characteristic of both his life and his teaching. Of himself he says,

> "Foxes have holes, and birds of the air have nests; but the Son of man has nowhere to lay his head." (Luke 9:58)

And he emphasizes again and again that attachment to riches will keep one out of the kingdom.* A wealthy man asks him what he must do to inherit eternal life. Jesus replies that he must keep the commandments. The man says he has done so all his life. Then,

> Jesus looking upon him loved him, and said to him, "You lack one thing; go, sell what you have, and give

---

*Compare Socrates' voluntary poverty and the way he describes his divine mission in *Apology* 29d–30b.

to the poor, and you will have treasure in heaven; and come, follow me." At that saying his countenance fell, and he went away sorrowful; for he had great possessions.

And Jesus looked around and said to his disciples, "How hard it will be for those who have riches to enter the kingdom of God!" (Mark 10:21–23)

There are many sayings to the same effect. To be part of the kingdom of God requires absolute singleness of mind; care for possessions distracts one from that intensity.

And he said to him, "Take heed, and beware of all covetousness; for a man's life does not consist in the abundance of his possessions." (Luke 12:15)

No one can serve two masters; for either he will hate the one and love the other, or he will be devoted to the one and despise the other. You cannot serve God and mammon [riches].

"Therefore I tell you, do not be anxious about your life, what you shall eat or what you shall drink, nor about your body, what you shall put on. Is not life more than food, and the body more than clothing? Look at the birds of the air: they neither sow nor reap nor gather into barns, and yet your heavenly Father feeds them. Are you not of more value than they? And which of you by being anxious can add one cubit to his span of life? And why are you anxious about clothing? Consider the lilies of the field, how they grow; they neither toil nor spin; yet I tell you, even Solomon in all his glory was not arrayed like one of these. But if God so clothes the grass of the field, which today is alive and tomorrow is thrown into the oven, will he not much more clothe you, O men of little faith? Therefore do not be anxious, saying, 'What shall we eat?' or 'What shall we drink?' or 'What shall we wear?' For the Gentiles seek all these things; and your heavenly Father knows that you need them all. But seek first his kingdom and his righteousness, and all these things shall be yours as well." (Matt. 6:24–33)

What is this righteousness that is to take such an absolutely preeminent place in our aims? When a lawyer asks him what to do to inherit eternal life, Jesus answers,

"What is written in the law? How do you read?" And he answered, "You shall love the Lord your God with all your heart, and with all your soul, and with all your strength, and with all your mind; and your neighbor as yourself." And he said to him, "You have answered right; do this, and you will live." (Luke 10:26–28)

The key to the righteousness of the kingdom is **love**. But "love," as we have noted, is a word with many meanings.* What does it mean here? With reference to God, it clearly means a kind of undivided and absolute devotion; it is the appropriate response to the creator who provides for us and also for the birds of the air and the lilies of the fields. This devotion to God has a corollary: that we love our "neighbors" as ourselves. No better explanation of this requirement can be given than the one Jesus gives to the lawyer who asks, "Who is my **neighbor**?"

"A man was going down from Jerusalem to Jericho, and he fell among robbers, who stripped him and beat him, and departed, leaving him half dead. Now by chance a priest was going down that road; and when he saw him he passed by on the other side. So likewise a Levite, when he came to the place and saw him, passed by on the other side. But a Samaritan, as he journeyed, came to where he was; and when he saw him, he had compassion, and went to him and bound up his wounds, pouring on oil and wine; then he set him on his own beast and brought him to an inn, and took care of him. And the next day he took out two denarii and gave them to the innkeeper, saying, 'Take care of him; and whatever more you spend, I will repay you when I come back.' Which of these three, do you think, proved neighbor to the man who fell among the robbers?" He said, "The one who showed mercy on him." And Jesus said to him, "Go and do likewise." (Luke 10:30–37)†

Several things in this famous parable of the good Samaritan are worth comment. First, note that

*See the discussion of love in Plato's *Symposium* (pp. 137–138). The word the New Testament writers use for love is *agape*. It is interesting to compare the *eros* that Socrates extols with the *agape* that, Jesus holds, is the key to the kingdom of God.

†Note the three types and their response to the injured man. The priest represents the religious leadership; Levites were lay assistants to the priests; and Samaritans were foreigners who were despised by the Jews.

Jesus does not exactly answer the question he is asked, "Who is my neighbor?" Rather, he answers the question, "What is it to *act* as a neighbor?" The lawyer's reaction to the story shows that he knows enough about *how to be a neighbor* that putting off action until he has clarified the concept of *what a neighbor is* just constitutes rationalization and evasion of responsibility.* So the closing line directs the lawyer's attention to himself: Do likewise— see that *you* act as a neighbor. This redirecting of attention from externals to the condition of one's own heart is quite characteristic of Jesus.

Second, note that the key word here is "compassion." Jesus is explaining how he understands the second part of the Law. To love your neighbor as yourself is to have compassion, to "feel with" your fellow human being, and to act in accord with that feeling. Just as we feel our own desires, anxieties, cares, pains, and joys, so are we to "feel with" the desires, anxieties, cares, pains and joys of others. And as we act to fulfill the intentions that grow out of these self-directed passions, so, like the Samaritan, must we act to satisfy the needs of others.

> "And as you wish that men would do to you, do so to them." (Luke 6:31)

Love, understood in this way, strikes a new note in our story. It is a conception quite foreign to the Greek philosophers. For them the basic human problem focuses on the control of the passions; by and large, they ascribe the locus of control to reason. Plato sees it as a struggle to subjugate the beast within, Aristotle as a matter of channeling the passions by means of virtuous habits; the Stoics come close to recommending the elimination of feelings altogether.† For all of them, the goal is finding the best possible way to live. And though

it is true that the Platonic wise man will return to the cave to try to enlighten those still in bondage, none of them would say that the best way to live necessarily involves an equal concern for others— feeling for them just as we feel for ourselves. What Jesus recommends is not the control or extinction of passion, but its *extension*; it is in universal compassion that we will find the kingdom of God. Nor do the Greek philosophers recommend the universality of concern we find in Jesus, though the Stoics perhaps come closest in thinking of all men as brothers. But not even a Stoic would say this:

> "Love your enemies, do good to those who hate you, bless those who curse you, pray for those who abuse you." (Luke 6:27)

> "If you love those who love you, what credit is that to you? For even sinners love those who love them." (Luke 6:32)

We do seem to have something genuinely new here.

A corollary to this love is a new virtue: humility. **Humility** is conspicuously lacking from the Greek lists of virtues, but it is nearly the very essence of perfection according to Jesus. For humility is the opposite of pride, and **pride** is the very root of sin. It is pride—wanting to be like God— that leads to the sin of Adam. And it is pride that sets human beings against each other; the proud man, glorying in his superiority, cannot consider his neighbor equal in importance to himself and so cannot love as Jesus requires.

Pride, particularly pride in one's righteousness or goodness, is the attitude most at variance with the kingdom of God.

> He also told this parable to some who trusted in themselves that they were righteous and despised others: "Two men went up into the temple to pray, one a Pharisee and the other a tax collector. The Pharisee stood and prayed thus with himself, 'God, I thank thee that I am not like other men, extortioners, unjust, adulterers, or even like this tax collector. I fast twice a week, I give tithes of all that I get.' But the tax collector, standing far off, would not even lift up his eyes to heaven, but beat his breast, saying, 'God, be merciful to me a sinner!' I tell you, this man went down to his house justified

---

*Compare Augustine on the priority of will over intellect, p. 256.

†The Stoics, for example, oppose pity. In considering what behavior is appropriate when someone is weeping, Epictetus advises us not to be overcome; we should remember that his weeping has its source not in what has happened but in the view he takes of it. We may, perhaps, go as far as to moan with him, but Epictetus says, "Be careful not to moan inwardly" (*The Handbook of Epictetus* 16).

rather than the other; for every one who exalts himself will be humbled, but he who humbles himself will be exalted." (Luke 18:9–14)*

Jesus issues scorching denunciations of those— usually the wealthy and powerful—who consider themselves righteous but do not act as neighbors should act. Like Socrates, he thereby incurs hostility among those in a position to do him harm. Unlike Socrates, of course, he does not do so by asking questions. Like the prophets of old, Jesus thunders out condemnation; and it is not a claim to know that he tries to undermine, but pretensions to righteousness.† Here are two samples.

> "Woe to you, scribes and Pharisees, hypocrites! for you tithe mint and dill and cummin, and have neglected the weightier matters of the law, justice and mercy and faith; these you ought to have done, without neglecting the others. You blind guides, straining out a gnat and swallowing a camel!" (Matt. 23:23–24)

> "Woe to you, scribes and Pharisees, hypocrites! for you are like whitewashed tombs, which outwardly appear beautiful, but within they are full of dead men's bones and all uncleanness. So you also outwardly appear righteous to men, but within you are full of hypocrisy and iniquity." (Matt. 23:27–28)

His antagonism to mere outward observance leads him to deepen and internalize the Law. About the Law he speaks with authority, contrasting the *words* of the Law, which can be kept simply by behaving in certain ways, with the *spirit* of the Law, which requires an attitude of love. For example,

> "You have heard that it was said to the men of old, 'You shall not kill; and whoever kills shall be liable to judgment.' But I say to you that every one who is angry with his brother shall be liable to judgment." (Matt. 5:21–22)

> "You have heard that it was said, 'You shall not commit adultery.' But I say to you that every one who looks at a woman lustfully has already committed adultery with her in his heart." (Matt. 5:27–28)

> "You have heard that it was said, 'An eye for an eye and a tooth for a tooth.' But I say to you, Do not resist one who is evil. But if any one strikes you on the right cheek, turn to him the other also." (Matt. 5:38–39)

This attitude toward the Law, which the Jews hold so dear, brings him into severe conflict with the authorities. He seems to them to take the Law lightly; on several occasions, for example, they clash with him on the details of Sabbath observance. He is, moreover, popular among the common people and must seem to be undermining the authority of the Jewish leaders. They determine to put him to death.

Because of Roman law, they cannot execute Jesus themselves. So after a trial in the religious court in which he is convicted for blasphemy (putting himself in the place of God), the Jewish leaders bring him before the Roman governor, Pilate. Here he is accused of treason, of setting himself up as King of the Jews (a charge of blasphemy would not have impressed this cosmopolitan Roman). Pilate reluctantly accedes to their demands, and Jesus is crucified.

Each of the four Gospels ends with an account of the discovery, on the third day after Jesus' death, of an empty tomb and of numerous appearances of Jesus to his disciples. His followers come to believe that he has risen from the dead. And this is taken by them as a sign that he is indeed God's anointed, the suffering servant who takes upon himself in his death the sins of the world, thereby bringing in the kingdom of God in an unexpectedly spiritual way. Their response is to set about making disciples of all nations.

---

*The Pharisees claimed that they observed all the details of the Law. Tax collectors, working for the Roman occupiers, were generally despised; and it is true that many of them were corrupt. A "tithe" is one-tenth of one's income, which is what the Law required to be given for religious and charitable purposes.

†This difference, while significant, may be diminished by the observation that for Socrates virtue is knowledge. So one who claims to know what piety is, for example, would also—in Socrates' eyes—be claiming to be pious.

---

1. How, according to Jesus, are we to love God? Our neighbor?
2. Do the Christians present new virtues?
3. Christians accept as a fact that Jesus rose from the dead. What do they think that means for us?

The Meaning of Jesus

We have noted that all the Gospels are written by believers; they are shot through and through with the significance his followers attribute to Jesus after their experience of his resurrection. But it will be useful to discuss more explicitly some of the categories in terms of which his life and death are interpreted. For this purpose, we will look particularly at the Gospel of John and at some letters written by the greatest of the early missionaries, Paul.

John begins his Gospel with a majestic prologue.

In the beginning was the Word, and the Word was with God, and the Word was God. He was in the beginning with God; all things were made through him, and without him was not anything made that was made. . . .

And the Word became flesh and dwelt among us, full of grace and truth; we have beheld his glory, glory as of the only Son from the Father. . . . And from his fullness have we all received, grace upon grace. For the law was given through Moses; grace and truth came through Jesus Christ. No one has ever seen God; the only Son, who is in the bosom of the Father, he has made him known. (John 1:1–3, 14–18)

Notice the exalted conception of Jesus we have here. He is identified with the **Word**—the *logos*, the wisdom through which all things are made. This *logos* was "in the beginning" with God (a phrase meant to recall the first line of Genesis). Though this Word exists beyond the world, it comes into the world through Jesus, and in him makes known the grace and truth of God, enlightening all and bringing those who are willing into the family of God.

These remarkable claims are elaborated in a number of discourses that John attributes to Jesus. Jesus says, "He who has seen me has seen the Father" (John 14:9). He says, "I and the Father are one" (John 10:30). He calls himself "the light of the world" (John 8:12), "the bread of life" (John 6:48), and "the good shepherd" who "lays down his life for the sheep" (John 10:11).

If Jesus is the manifestation of God in the world, what do we learn of God from him?

For God so loved the world that he gave his only Son, that whoever believes in him should not perish but have eternal life. For God sent the Son into the world, not to condemn the world, but that the world might be saved through him. (John 3:16–17)

The God Jesus reveals is not Aristotle's unmoved mover, thinking true thoughts about himself. Nor is he akin to the gods of the Epicureans who live in blessedness, unconcerned with human beings. The message is that God is Love, that he cares for us, and will save us from our sinfulness through his Son Jesus, who took our sin upon himself in his death. The life and death of the Christ manifest the extremity of that Love and serve, in turn, as a model for life in the kingdom of God.

What is required is a "new birth," not of flesh and the will of man, but "of God."* And this new life—this is the gospel—is now available by trust in Jesus, the Christ.

Paul was a Jew, very strict about the observance of the Law, who was at first vigorously opposed to the new "sect" of Christians. While engaged in persecuting them, he saw a vision of Jesus and was converted, after which he devoted his life to spreading the gospel. He traveled extensively, establishing churches all over Asia Minor and Greece. He visited Athens and argued there with both the Jews and the philosophers, appalled by the "idolatry" he found there and preaching the one creator God and Jesus who rose from the dead.†

"The whole of history is incomprehensible without the Christ."

Ernest Renan (1823–1892)

---

*See Jesus' conversation with the Jewish leader Nicodemus in John 3:1–15.
†See Acts 17:16–34.

Paul comes to believe it is hopeless to try to attain the righteousness of the kingdom of God by observing the Law; no doubt this reflects in part his own zealous efforts before his conversion. All men, Paul holds, are inextricably caught in the web of sinfulness and cannot by their own (sinful) efforts "justify" themselves before the righteous judge. But what we cannot do for ourselves God has graciously done for us through Jesus.

> For no human being will be justified in his sight by works of the law, since through the law comes knowledge of sin.
> But now the righteousness of God has been manifested apart from the law, although the law and the prophets bear witness to it, the righteousness of God through faith in Jesus Christ for all who believe. (Rom. 3:20–22)

> There is therefore now no condemnation for those who are in Christ Jesus. For the law of the Spirit of life in Christ Jesus has set me free from the law of sin and death. (Rom. 8:1–2)

Having been freed from the burden of the Law and no longer needing to prove ourselves righteous, says Paul, allows us to participate in the Spirit of Christ, loving our neighbors and serving their needs. It really is Jesus, then, who has brought in the kingdom of God. Moreover, just as God raised Jesus from the dead, so will all who believe in him be raised to a blessed life with him.

Our consideration of Christian teaching can be brought to a close with these words from another author.

> We know that we have passed out of death into life, because we love the brethren. He who does not love remains in death. Any one who hates his brother is a murderer, and you know that no murderer has eternal life abiding in him. By this we know love, that he laid down his life for us; and we ought to lay down our lives for the brethren. But if anyone has the world's goods and sees his brother in need, yet closes his heart against him, how does God's love abide in him? Little children, let us not love in word or speech but in deed and in truth. (1 John 3:14–18)

1. What does it mean when John calls Jesus "the *logos*"? Relate this to Heraclitean and Stoic views.
2. How, according to Paul, can we be "justified" before God, the judge?
3. *Why* should we love our neighbors as ourselves?

FOR FURTHER THOUGHT

You should now have a fairly clear understanding of how Plato, Aristotle, Epicurus, and the Stoics envision the good life. Choose one of these philosophies, and work out a comparison (both similarities and differences) between it and the Christian view of the good life.

KEY WORDS

God	the Law
creation	Jesus
Kingdom of God	love
Noah	neighbor
Abraham	humility
Exodus	pride
Moses	Word

NOTES

1. Biblical quotations in this text are taken from the Revised Standard Version.
2. Josephus, *Against Apion* 200:20; quoted in C. K. Barrett, ed., *The New Testament Background: Selected Documents* (London: S.P.C.K., 1956), 202.

10

AUGUSTINE

God and the Soul

Augustine is not only a fascinating figure personally but also something of a turning point historically. He lived (A.D. 354–430) in the days of what we call "late antiquity," just as it began to merge into the medieval period. He brings together nearly four centuries of debate and consolidation concerning Christian doctrine. And he melds that with what he takes to be the best in the heritage of the Greek philosophers—the tradition stemming from Plato. Both of these traditions are given a unique stamp by Augustine's penchant for introspection, his passionate search for happiness, and the impress of his undeniably powerful mind. He would himself say that if he had contributed anything of value, it was due entirely to the grace of God. This would not be merely an expression of modesty, such as it tends to be today; Augustine believes it to be the literal truth. Whether we agree with that or not, we can fairly say that no one else did as much to shape the intellectual course of the next thousand years.

The views of some philosophers can be discussed independently of their lives, but Augustine's thought is so entangled with his life experiences that we need to understand something of that life.[1] There is no better introduction to his early years than his own *Confessions*, in which he reflects—before God but also before us all—on his youthful waywardness. By the time he wrote this reflective look at his life (in 397), he was forty-three years old, had been a Christian for eleven years, a priest for eight years, and a bishop for two. We cannot hope here to imitate the richness of these meditations but will try just to get a feel for how he saw his life from the point of view he had reached.

Augustine was born in northern Africa, which had been Roman for many generations but was always precariously perched between the sea and the barbarian interior. Christianity had taken root there but, despite its legitimation by the emperor Constantine in 325, was still in competition with the old pagan beliefs and ways. Augustine was the child of a Christian mother, Monica, and a pagan father who converted to Christianity before he died. Monica was the stronger influence, convinced all her life that her son would be "saved." But it was

Patricius, his father, who resolutely determined that Augustine should be educated; he studied literature and rhetoric and, for a while, the law. His education was intense but narrow, concentrating on the masters of Latin style and consisting of enormous amounts of memorization of, for example, Virgil's *Aeneid*. He read very little philosophy.

Meanwhile, he lived the life of pleasure. The bishop he became, looking back on those days, puts it this way:

> I cared for nothing but to love and be loved. But my love went beyond the affection of one mind for another, beyond the arc of the bright beam of friendship. Bodily desire, like a morass, and adolescent sex welling up within me exuded mists which clouded over and obscured my heart, so that I could not distinguish the clear light of true love from the murk of lust. Love and lust together seethed within me. In my tender youth they swept me away over the precipice of my body's appetites and plunged me in the whirlpool of sin. (C 2.2)[2]

It is not just sex, however, on which the bishop focuses in "the whirlpool of sin." He is almost more perplexed over a single act that comes to represent for him the puzzling nature of human wickedness. He, together with some companions, had shaken down an enormous quantity of pears from a neighbor's tree and had stolen them away. And why did they steal the pears? Did they need them? No. Did they eat them? No. They threw them to the pigs.

Why, then, did they steal the pears? This is what puzzles Augustine. In a judicial inquiry, he notes, no one is satisfied until the motive has been produced: a desire of gaining some good or of avoiding some evil. But what was the good gained here? What evil was avoided? He concludes: "our real pleasure consisted in doing something that was forbidden" (C 2.4). But why was that a pleasure? Augustine's reflective answer is that the act was, in a perverse sort of way, an imitation of God; it was an attempt to exercise a liberty that belongs to God alone: that of being unconstrained by anything outside himself (C 1.6). No one, Augustine felt, was going to make rules for *him* to live by. We come, then, even in this simple prank by a sixteen-year-old, to Augustine's analysis of the root of the human predicament: **pride**.

> "Perverseness is one of the primitive impulses of the human heart."
>
> *Edgar Allan Poe (1809–1849)*

He also notes that he surely would not have stolen the pears on his own.

> It was not the takings that attracted me but the raid itself, and yet to do it by myself would have been no fun and I should not have done it. This was friendship of a most unfriendly sort, bewitching my mind in an inexplicable way. For the sake of a laugh, a little sport, I was glad to do harm and anxious to damage another; and that without a thought of profit for myself or retaliation for injuries received! And all because we are ashamed to hold back when others say "Come on! Let's do it!" (C 2.9)

This power of the group to incite to evil deeds is expressed also in the following passage, in which Augustine sets out a very common experience of the young.

> I was so blind to the truth that among my companions I was ashamed to be less dissolute than they were. For I heard them bragging of their depravity, and the greater the sin the more they gloried in it, so that I took pleasure in the same vices not only for the enjoyment of what I did, but also for the applause I won.
>
> Nothing deserves to be despised more than vice; yet I gave in more and more to vice simply in order not to be despised. If I had not sinned enough to rival other sinners, I used to pretend that I had done things I had not done at all, because I was afraid that innocence would be taken for cowardice and chastity for weakness. (C 2.3)

It is clear that the Christian bishop at age forty-three does not take lightly the peccadilloes of his youth. It is not prudishness that accounts for this, however; it is a considered judgment that pursuing such desires is a sure way to miss true happiness. But the young Augustine had a long way to go before he would see things this way.

He took a mistress, to whom he was apparently faithful for many years. They had a son. Augustine completed his education and became a teacher of rhetoric and literature, first in the provincial north African town of Thagaste, then in Carthage, the great city of Roman Africa. He was an able teacher and earned a reputation, for which he was most eager.

But he was eager for something else as well. At nineteen, he read a (now lost) work by Cicero, the great orator, which contains an exhortation to study philosophy. Augustine was carried away:

> The only thing that pleased me in Cicero's book was his advice not simply to admire one or another of the schools of philosophy, but to love wisdom itself, whatever it might be, and to search for it, pursue it, hold it, and embrace it firmly. (C 4.4)

The young Augustine embraced this love of wisdom with a "blaze of enthusiasm." But where to look? He knew very little of classical philosophy, which is what Cicero surely had in mind. In Augustine's circle in late fourth-century Africa, it was Christ who was portrayed as "the wisdom of God"; so Augustine turned to the Bible. But he was greatly disappointed. Not only did it seem to lack the polish of the best Roman poets, its conceptions seemed crude and naive to him. In Genesis, after Adam and Eve had disobeyed God, we read that they "heard the sound of the Lord God walking in the cool of the day." What a way to think of God!

Moreover, Christianity seemed unable to solve a great puzzle, which was to perplex Augustine sincerely for many years. The Christian God was proclaimed to be both almighty and perfectly good. But if this is so, where does evil come from? If the answer is the devil, the question can be repeated: Where does the devil come from? If from God, then God is the source of evil. And if God is almighty, where else could the devil come from? But God is good; so how could he be the source of evil?

It may be useful to set the problem out in a more formal way.

1. If God is omnipotent (all powerful), omniscient (all knowing), and perfectly good, then there can be no evil, because
   a. being all-powerful, he *could do* something about any existing evil,
   b. being all-knowing, he *would know* about any existing evil, and
   c. being perfectly good, he *would want to eliminate* any existing evil.
2. But there is evil.
3. Therefore God is either
   a. not all-powerful (He *can't* do anything about the evil), or
   b. not all-knowing (He could do something if only he *knew* about it), or
   c. not perfectly good (He does know and could do something, but He *doesn't care*)—or
   d. some combination of a, b, and c.

Augustine could not see that the Christians had any satisfactory answer to this puzzle, traditionally called "the **Problem of Evil**." You should be able to see that it is quite a formidable problem. The argument looks valid; that is, if its premises are true, it looks as though the conclusion will have to be true. So that leads us to ask whether the premises are true. Obviously, there are two main possibilities here. We could argue that Premise 1 is false; or we could argue that Premise 2 is false. Roughly speaking, Augustine tries out each of these possibilities.

The first possibility was represented for him by a popular movement in his day, which has similarities to New Age thinking today. It was called "Manicheanism." Augustine was a "hearer" (more than an outsider, but less than a full member) among the Manichees for nine years.

Manicheanism was a sect founded by the Babylonian Mani in the third century. Mani was martyred (some say crucified) by the religious establishment in A.D. 277, and that fact helped spread the sect widely. Mani synthesized themes from the Persian religion of Zoroastrianism and Christianity. Manicheanism is often thought of as one of the many "heresies" prevalent during the first centuries of the Christian era, as the Church tried to sort out an orthodox view of revealed truth.

The doctrines of the sect are enormously complex, involving facets of astrology and half-digested bits of natural science, as well as borrowings from traditional religions. But the key beliefs are simple and provide a solution of sorts to the problem of evil. The reason there is evil in the world, say the

Manichees, is that there is *no omnipotent good power*. Rather, there are two equal and opposed powers, one good and one evil. It has always been this way, they say, and will always be so. So you can see that the Manichees deny the antecedent in the first premise.

This opposition, moreover, is not just "out there" in the world. It is resident within each of us, since we are ourselves a battleground between good and evil. That may not sound very profound; but the Manichees explain this dichotomy in a particular way. The good part of ourselves is the soul (composed of the light), and the bad part is the body (composed of the dark earth). A human being is literally part divine and part demonic.

> I have known my soul and the body that lies upon it,
> That they have been enemies since the creation of
> the worlds. (*MP*, p. 49)³

In fact, the entire earth is the province of the evil power, since evil resides in matter as such. We are, however, essentially *souls;* and as souls we experience ourselves to be under the domination of a foreign power—matter, the body, the world.

The "gospel" of the Manichees is that we can be saved from the domination of the evil power—matter—if we come to *know who we are*.

> A man called down into the world saying: Blessed is
> he that shall know his soul. (*MP*, p. 47)

The man was Mani, and this was the heart of his message.

Manicheanism, then, claims to solve the *theoretical* problem of evil by the postulation of the two powers—denying the infinite perfection of God—and the *practical* problem of evil by the doctrine that the soul is essentially good, untouched by the evil of the body. If only you can come to identify yourself with your soul, you will experience "salvation" from the evil. Augustine apparently felt that this solution freed him from his theoretical perplexities and allowed him to think of himself as "essentially good"—something he needed to be able to do. This, then, was the first "wisdom" that he embraced in his enthusiasm for the truth.

He noticed, however, that some of the doctrines were obscure and that others seemed to conflict with the best astronomical knowledge of the day. When one of the Manichean "Elect," a certain Faustus, came to Carthage, Augustine determined to inquire about these things. On examination it became obvious that Faustus was not wise.* So Augustine was disappointed a second time; neither Christianity nor Manicheanism seemed to offer the wisdom he was seeking.

Moreover, he found Manichean views unhelpful in a practical sense. Their key to salvation lay in knowledge, in a recognition of the true nature of the self as good. But this didn't seem to be of any help in actually changing one's life. It was too passive. (It may have been his experience as a Manichee that led to his later view that the root of sin lies not in the intellect but in the *will*.) The bishop he became reflects on his experience:

> I still thought that it is not we who sin but some other nature that sins within us. It flattered my pride to think that I incurred no guilt and, when I did wrong, not to confess it so that you [God] might bring healing to a soul that had sinned against you. (Psalm 41:4) I preferred to excuse myself and blame this unknown thing which was in me but was not part of me. The truth, of course, was that it was all my own self, and my own impiety had divided me against myself. My sin was all the more incurable because I did not think myself a sinner. (*C* 5.10)

These notions of pride, guilt, and a divided self we need to examine in more detail. But because of these intellectual and spiritual dissatisfactions, Augustine began to drift away from the Manichees.

He began to read the philosophers and found himself attracted to skepticism. He left Africa and went to Rome, where again he taught rhetoric and literature. He was recommended to the more attractive post of Professor of Rhetoric in Milan, where he was joined by his widowed mother; with her, he attended Christian services conducted by the Bishop of Milan, Ambrose. **Ambrose** was an immensely learned man, far more learned in the traditions of the Greek church fathers and Greek philosophy than Augustine (whose Greek skills were always imperfect). Ambrose was also an accomplished orator. At first, Augustine went simply

---

*Compare Socrates asking questions in Athens: *Apology* 21b–22c.

"I was in love with beauty of a lower order and it was dragging me down."

—St. Augustine

to hear him speak, but he soon found himself listening to the content as well as the style. And he began to discover the possibility of a Christianity that was not naive and crude but that could bear comparison with the best thought of the day.

What made the Christianity of Ambrose a revelation to Augustine, who had, in a sense, been familiar with Christianity since his childhood? There seem to have been three things. (1) There was the idea of God and the soul as *immaterial* realities. Augustine had found great difficulty in thinking of either as other than some sort of *body*, even if very ethereal bodies. (Recall that the Manichees thought of God and the soul as light.) But if God is a body, God cannot be everywhere present (and this idea fits with the Manichean dualism of two equal and opposite realities). If God is an immaterial spirit, however, then he is not excluded by the material world and he can be omnipresent. (2)

Ambrose was not afraid to plunder the Greek philosophical tradition for help in making Christianity intelligible. The category of immaterial reality was drawn from philosophy, particularly from that of Plato and his successors. (Remember the Forms, especially the Form of the Good.)* (3) Finally, there was the possibility of giving allegorical interpretations to Scripture, particularly to the Old Testament. Taken allegorically rather than literally, many passages ceased to offend and took on the aspect of conveying deep spiritual truths.

Augustine began to study the Bible seriously for the first time and to read philosophy. The Bible spoke of the Wisdom of God, and philosophers loved wisdom. Could Christianity contain the truth the philosophers were seeking? He began to suspect so. He grew more sure of it, then became virtually certain.

Yet he hesitated. What would happen if he became a Christian? In Augustine's view, this was a serious matter. His life would have to change drastically, for he was still preoccupied with worldly things: his career, his reputation, and sex. His mistress had returned to Africa, and marriage with an heiress was being arranged. Would he have to give all this up? Augustine was never one for half-measures, and it seemed to him that he would. But could he? He procrastinated. The bishop he had become expresses the agony of that time in the following way:

> I was held fast, not in fetters clamped upon me by another, but by my own will, which had the strength of iron chains. The enemy held my will in his power and from it he had made a chain and shackled me. For my will was perverse and lust had grown from it, and when I gave in to lust habit was born, and when I did not resist the habit it became a necessity. These were the links which together formed what I have called my chain, and it held me fast in the duress of servitude. But the new will which had come to life in me and made me wish to serve you freely and enjoy you, my God, who are our only certain joy, was not yet strong enough to overcome the old, hardened as it was by the passage of time. So these two wills within me, one old, one new, one the servant of the flesh, the other of the

_____

*See pp. 131–133.

spirit, were in conflict and between them they tore my soul apart. (*C* 8.5)

The *perversity of the will*, which leads to *lust*, which leads to *habit*, which becomes a virtual *necessity*, forms a chain that will play a crucial role in Augustine's analysis of what is wrong with human beings and how it can be cured.

"Nothing is stronger than habit."

Ovid (43 B.C.–A.D. 17)

In a dramatic experience, which Augustine relates in the *Confessions*, the chain of necessity was broken. After hearing from a traveler the stories of several others who had renounced the world and devoted themselves to God, Augustine rushed into a garden in a tumult. "My inner self," he says, "was a house divided against itself." "I was my own contestant. . . . "

> I felt that I was still the captive of my sins, and in my misery I kept crying, "How long shall I go on saying 'tomorrow, tomorrow'? Why not now? Why not make an end of my ugly sins at this moment?"
>
> I was asking myself these questions, weeping all the while with the most bitter sorrow in my heart, when all at once I heard the sing-song voice of a child in a nearby house. Whether it was the voice of a boy or a girl I cannot say, but again and again it repeated the refrain "Take it and read, take it and read." At this I looked up, thinking hard whether there was any kind of game in which children used to chant words like these, but I could not remember ever hearing them before. I stemmed my flood of tears and stood up, telling myself that this could only be a divine command to open my book of Scripture and read the first passage on which my eyes should fall. . . .
>
> So I hurried back to the place where Alypius was sitting, for when I stood up to move away I had put down the book containing Paul's Epistles. I seized it and opened it, and in silence I read the first passage on which my eyes fell: Not in reveling and drunkenness, not in lust and wantonness, not in quarrels and rivalries. Rather, arm yourselves with the Lord Jesus Christ; spend no more thought on nature and nature's appetites. (Romans 13:13,

14) I had no wish to read more and no need to do so. For in an instant, as I came to the end of the sentence, it was as though the light of confidence flooded into my heart and all the darkness of doubt was dispelled. (*C* 8.12)

Augustine had found the **wisdom** he had been searching for.

He gave up his career and his prospects for marriage. He retired for some months with some friends and his mother to a retreat where he studied and wrote. On Easter Day in 387, he was baptized by Ambrose, thus making his break with "the world" public. Not long thereafter, his mother having died, he returned to Africa, was made a priest (somewhat against his will), and in 391 was ordained bishop of Hippo, a city on the Mediterranean coast of Africa.

Thereafter he was engaged in practical affairs of the church: in serving as a judge (one of the tasks of a bishop in those days), in controversies to define and defend the faith, and in much writing. There are, of course, the sermons. But there are also letters and pamphlets and book after book in which Augustine explores the meaning of the faith he had adopted. In these the theme is—again and again—to try to *understand* what he has *believed*. For Augustine, faith must come first; understanding may follow (though on some difficult topics, such as the Trinity, even understanding will be only partial).* This order of things may seem strange to some of us. We may think that unless we understand first, we will not know what it is that we are believing. But it is a reflection of Augustine's conviction that will is more fundamental than intellect and that only if the will is first directed by faith to the right end will the intellect be able to do its job rightly.†

---

*Here is an analogy to Augustine's motto, *faith seeking understanding*. Suppose you are unable to solve a certain mathematical problem. Then you are given the answer. *Believing* that this is the correct answer, you are now able to work back and *understand* why it is correct.

†Think about Socrates. We said that in order to benefit from a conversation with Socrates, you had to be a person of a certain *character*. The arrogant, the proud, the self-satisfied would only be humiliated. (See pp. 66–67.) Augustine agrees that character is more fundamental than intellect. But whereas Socrates thinks of virtue or character as a matter of knowledge, for Augustine it is a matter of faith, or commitment.

With this point we are ready to leave the life of Augustine and focus on his philosophy. It is characteristic of Augustine's thought that we cannot do so without at the same time discussing his theology, or doctrine of God. For wisdom, Augustine is convinced, is *one*. And that means that philosophy and theology, understanding and faith, science and religion are inextricably bound together. What the lover of wisdom wants is the truth. And the truth is God. And God is most fully known by faith in Christ. We will not do full justice to this unity, but in selecting out certain themes that are of particular philosophical interest, we will try to keep in mind the whole context in which they play their part for Augustine. Part of Augustine's legacy is just this unity of thought. It sets the intellectual tone for a thousand years. Eventually, as we see, thinkers begin to take it apart again; the consequence is our largely secular modern world.

---

1. Explain what Augustine thinks we should learn from the adventure of the pears.
2. What advice of Cicero's shaped Augustine's life?
3. What problem made Augustine dissatisfied with Christianity?
4. How did the Manichees explain evil? Where is evil located? Where is good located?
5. For what reasons did Augustine become dissatisfied with the Manichees?
6. Describe the links in the chain leading to the bondage of the will.
7. What, according to Augustine, is the relation between belief and understanding?

Wisdom, Happiness, and God

Augustine simply takes for granted that philosophy, the pursuit of wisdom, has just one aim: happiness. This was the common assumption in late antiquity, shared by the Epicureans, the Stoics, and the Skeptics. Augustine was never greatly interested in nature philosophy and eventually turned away from it as resolutely as Socrates had done.* It could not make one happy.

What does interest Augustine intensely is the soul—his own soul first of all, then what that could teach him about the souls of all. For happiness and unhappiness are clearly conditions of the soul. How does Augustine understand **happiness**? That soul is happy which possesses what it most desires, *provided* that it most desires what wisdom approves.

> Just as it is agreed that we all wish to be happy, so it is agreed that we all wish to be wise, since no one without wisdom is happy. No man is happy except through the highest good, which is to be found and included in that truth which we call wisdom. (*FCW* 2.9.102–103)

You cannot be happy unless you have what you desire; yet having what you desire does not guarantee happiness, for you must desire the right things. Certain things, if they are desired and attained, will produce misery rather than happiness. Augustine knows this from bitter experience.

Moreover, the appropriate objects of desire must be things that cannot be taken away from us against our will, and they must be enduring.* If they could be taken away from us, we could not be secure in the enjoyment of them; and if they could fade or disappear on their own, we would fear their prospective loss even if we had them. What makes for happiness must *last*. These are among the truths that wisdom teaches.

But again we need to backtrack a bit. For, as we have seen, some philosophers—the skeptics—doubt whether any such truths can be known. Augustine himself had been attracted to **skepticism** for a time. He feels the strength of this objection. And he sees that unless it is met, nothing else can stand firm. So we must take another logical step backward.

Can the skeptical objections be met? Augustine believes they can be met, and decisively so. He admits that we can be deceived by the senses and that we can make purely intellectual mistakes. But there are three things we know with absolute certainty:

> The certainty that I exist, that I know it, and that I am glad of it, is independent of any imaginary and deceptive fantasies.

---

*See *Apology* 19c–d and pp. 131–132.

*This is by now a familiar point. See, for instance, p. 186.

In respect of these truths I have no fear of the arguments of the Academics.* They say, "Suppose you are mistaken?" I reply, "If I am mistaken, I exist." A non-existent being cannot be mistaken; therefore I must exist, if I am mistaken. Then since my being mistaken proves that I exist, how can I be mistaken in thinking that I exist, seeing that my mistake establishes my existence? Since therefore I must exist in order to be mistaken, then even if I am mistaken, there can be no doubt that I am not mistaken in my knowledge that I exist. It follows that I am not mistaken in knowing that I know. For just as I know that I exist, I also know that I know. And when I am glad of those two facts, I can add the fact of that gladness to the things I know, as a fact of equal worth. For I am not mistaken about the fact of my gladness, since I am not mistaken about the things which I love. Even if they were illusory, it would still be a fact that I love the illusions. (*CG* 11.27)

Skepticism, then, which doubts whether we can have knowledge at all, is an error. Knowledge and certainty are possible. Truth is available to us, at least to this small extent. And notice what this truth is about: his own existence, his thought, and his feelings. In short, the first thing we know for certain concerns ourselves and, in particular, the soul.†

The next question, obviously, is whether we can know *more* than this. In the spirit of the Platonic philosophers, Augustine turns to mathematics. He offers a number of examples, but the nicest one concerns a circle, from the center of which two radii are drawn to the circumference. Let the points at which the radii meet the circle be as close together as you like; it will still be the case that these two lines meet only at that point which is the center. You cannot draw it to look this way (Try!), but it is true nonetheless.‡ Furthermore, we know that between any two such lines, no matter how close together they are, innumerable other lines

can be drawn. Moreover, between any two such lines, no matter how close together, another circle can be inscribed! This is true, and we know it to be true (*SO* 20.35). And this truth is not something private to any one of us. It is knowledge common to all.

> Whatever I may experience with my bodily senses, such as this air and earth and whatever corporeal matter they contain, I cannot know how long it will endure. But seven and three are ten, not only now, but forever. There has never been a time when seven and three were not ten, nor will there ever be a time when they are not ten. Therefore, I have said that the truth of number is incorruptible and common to all who think. (*FCW* 2.7.82–83)

Augustine concludes that mathematical truth exists and we can know it.

Perhaps, however, we grant that there is mathematical truth but doubt that there is such a thing as practical truth—truth about what we should desire to be happy, about the highest good. But, Augustine asks,

> Will you deny that the incorrupt is better than the corrupt, the eternal better than the temporal, the inviolable better than the violable? (*FCW* 2.10.114)

Here is a truth that seems as secure to Augustine as the truths of mathematics. How could, for example, the beauty of a flower that lasts for a day be as good as an equivalent beauty that lasts for two days? And how could that be as good as the same beauty lasting forever? But this, notice, is a truth about what is "better," and so it has direct practical implications. Whatever is the highest good, whatever will actually fulfill the desire for happiness must be the best of all possible things —incorruptible, eternal, inviolable. Otherwise, even if we possessed it, it could be taken away from us without our consent. To settle for less than such a good is to resign ourselves to unhappiness.

But if this is *true*, then this **truth** is itself eternal—as unchanging a truth as seven plus three makes ten. And it is a truth common to all. These truths are not private possessions. I can know them, and you can know them; but their existence does not depend on either me or you. We do not *decide* their truth; we *acknowledge* it.

---

*The Academics were members of the Academy after Plato who turned to skepticism.

†At the beginning of modern philosophy in the seventeenth century, this theme will be picked up by René Descartes. See *Meditation II*.

‡Compare discussion of Socrates' sand drawings on pp. 122–123.

These truths are clearly superior to us and to the powers of our minds. This is shown in two ways. We do not make judgments *about* them, as we judge about sensible things or even ourselves; we make judgments *according to* them.

> When a man says that the eternal is more powerful than the temporal, and that seven plus three are ten, he does not say that it ought to be so; he knows it is this way, and does not correct it as an examiner would, but he rejoices as if he has made a discovery.
>
> If truth were equal to our minds, it would be subject to change. Our minds sometimes see more and sometimes less, and because of this we acknowledge that they are mutable. Truth, remaining in itself, does not gain anything when we see it, or lose anything when we do not see it. It is whole and uncorrupted. With its light, truth gives joy to the men who turn to it, and punishes with blindness those who turn away from it. (*FCW* 2.12.134–35)

Let us review. We want to be happy, and in order to find happiness we desire to be wise. Wisdom will tell us what the highest good is. Possession of this good will make us happy. Such a good must be eternal, available to all, and superior to ourselves. But we have now found something with precisely those characteristics: truth itself.*

> We possess in the truth, therefore, what we all may enjoy, equally and in common; in it are no defects or limitations. For truth receives all its lovers without arousing their envy. It is open to all, yet it is always chaste. No one says to the other, "Get back! Let me approach too! Hands off! Let me also embrace it!" All men cling to the truth and touch it. The food of truth can never be stolen. (*FCW* 2.14.145)

Truth is something we cannot lose against our will. And since it is superior to our minds, it is a candidate for being the highest good and the source of our happiness.

Now we have reached the point where we can *understand* (not just believe) why God must be brought into the picture. Think back to what Augustine claims to know: he exists, he lives, and he knows and feels. These facts are ordered in a kind of hierarchy. The latter facts presuppose the former; you cannot live unless you exist, and you cannot know and feel unless you are alive. Moreover, this is a hierarchy of value, for it is better to be alive than just to exist, and it is better to know and feel than just to live. These are the reasons we judge plants superior to rocks, animals to plants, and ourselves to all. At the top of this hierarchy is our own rational nature, by which we judge the rest and guide our own behavior. This is best of all among the things of experience. But what if there were something superior even to this? Would it not be right to acknowledge that as *God*, particularly if it were shown to be eternal and immutable?

But this is just what Augustine claims already to have shown! Truth itself exists. It is immutable and eternal. And it is superior to our reason. By definition, **God** is "that to whom no one is superior" (*FCW* 2.6.54).* So we can now say that, on the assumption that there is nothing superior to the truth, the truth itself is God. If there should exist something superior to the truth, then that is God. On either hypothesis, God exists! As Augustine puts it in a dialogue with a friend,

> You granted . . . that if I showed you something higher than our minds, you would admit, assuming that nothing existed which was still higher, that God exists. I accepted your condition and said that it was enough to show this. For if there is something more excellent than truth, this is God. If there is not, then truth itself is God. Whether or not truth is God, you cannot deny that God exists, and this was the question with which we agreed to deal. (*FCW* 2.15. 153–154)

> "Truth—is as old as God—
>   His Twin Identity
> And will endure as long as He
>   A Co-Eternity—"
>
>   *Emily Dickinson (1830–1886)*

---

*The common, public nature of truth is stressed also by Plato. See pp. 121–122.

*This idea is the root from which a much more sophisticated and complex proof will be drawn by Anselm of Canterbury. See Chapter 11.

Again let's set out the structure of the argument:

1. God is (by definition) that to whom there is nothing superior.
2. Truth exists and is superior to us.
3. If nothing is superior to truth, then God = truth and God exists.
4. If there is something superior even to truth, then God is that thing, and God exists.
5. Either 3 or 4.
6. So God exists.

To this demonstration his friend, Evodius, exclaims,

> I can scarcely find words for the unbelievable joy that fills me. I accept these arguments, crying out that they are most certain. And my inner voice shouts, for truth itself to hear, that I cling to this: not only does good exist, but indeed the highest good—and this is the source of happiness. (*FCW* 2.15.156)

Since his experience in the garden Augustine has believed this, and now he also understands it in a way that satisfies his reason. But one's reason is not unaffected by one's will and desires; without a will to truth, even the best rational demonstration may fail to convince. As we'll see, in a certain sense Augustine holds that *will* is basic.

---

1. How are wisdom and happiness related?
2. What is Augustine's argument against the Skeptics?
3. What shows that truth is superior to ourselves?
4. What is Augustine's argument for the existence of God?
5. What is the essence of God?

God and the World

Augustine has come to believe in the God of the Christians. Here, he is convinced, is wisdom and the path to happiness. But he needs also to understand what he has come to believe. He has discovered a rational proof that God exists. Could reason, employed in support of faith and enlightened by the divine light, also understand how this world is related to God?

Here too Augustine draws from the wisdom of the philosophers, especially from the Platonists.

For as Augustine reads them, they express in a perfectly rational way, without relying on the authority of revelation, ideas that mesh remarkably well with the Scriptures. His borrowings are not uncritical, but they are extensive. For this reason, it will be useful to take a detour to the views of Plotinus (A.D. 204–270), the main source for **Neoplatonism**. This tradition, within which Augustine himself must be counted a distinguished figure, lasted well into the eighteenth century.

The Great Chain of Being

The views of **Plotinus** are a blend of mystical insight and rational elaboration, the latter largely dependent on Plato. Mystical experience, which Plotinus is clearly familiar with, has certain characteristics that reappear in all ages and cultures. It is an experience of a particularly powerful and persuasive sort in which the focus is an absolute unity. The multiplicity of things disappears; one is no longer able even to distinguish oneself from other objects. Mystics talk of this experience in terms of identity of the self with "the All," with "the One," or with "God." It is accompanied by an absolutely untroubled bliss.

Plotinus knows such experience firsthand, so he is certain that there is another, better reality than the one we ordinarily experience. When he tries to express this reality, he speaks in terms of **the One**. About this One, Plotinus holds, we can literally say nothing; for to predicate any properties of it would be to imply some multiplicity in it, some division. It is "ineffable." We cannot even say that it *is*. It resides in a majesty *beyond being*.* Plotinus allows that it can be given names, but none of these are to be understood literally; they are at best hints that point in a certain direction. Some of these names are "Unity," "the Transcendent," "the Absolute," "the Good," and "the Source."†

Like Plato's Form of the Good, the One is the source of whatever else exists. But at this point, we must ask: why should anything else exist? The One

---

*Compare Plato on the Form of the Good, p. 133, and the emptiness of the Tao, from which, nonetheless, everything is born, p. 23.

†Compare the terminology in the *Star Wars* movies.

is absolutely self-sufficient; it needs nothing. But this is precisely the key. To make it clear, Plotinus uses a pair of analogies.

> Picture a spring that has no further origin, that pours itself into all rivers without becoming exhausted of what it yields, and remains what it is, undisturbed. The streams that issue from it, before flowing away each in its own direction, mingle together for a time, but each knows already where it will take its flood. Or think of the life that circulates in a great tree. The originating principle of this life remains at rest and does not spread through the tree because it has, as it were, its seat in the root. The principle gives to the plant all its life in its multiplicity but remains itself at rest. Not a plurality, it is the source of plurality. (*EP*, p. 173)[4]

The One is like the spring that, being itself full and lacking nothing, gives of itself without ever diminishing itself; or like the originating principle of life in a great tree that remains at rest in the root, though the whole tree pulses with life. Plotinus thinks of all reality as an **emanation** from the One. To use another analogy, it is like the light that streams from the candle, while the light of the flame remains undiminished.

Note that this is the old problem of the one and the many: whence this plurality of beings, this multiplicity all about us? The answer is, they originate in the One.* If we ask why there are so *many*, the answer is that there must be as many as possible, for the One is ungrudging in its giving.

> Every nature must produce its next, for each thing must unfold, seedlike, from indivisible principle into a visible effect. Principle continues unaltered in its proper place; what unfolds from it is the product of the inexpressible power that resides in it. It must not stay this power and, as though jealous, limit its effects. It must proceed continuously until

all things, to the very last, have within the limits of possibility come forth. All is the result of this immense power giving its gifts to the universe, unable to let any part remain without its share. (*EP*, p. 68)

Just as there are all possible degrees of brightness in the emanation of light from a candle, until it vanishes at last in the darkness, so there will be found all degrees of being, intelligibility, and life in the world. Reality is partitioned in graded steps, which are, however, infinitely close to each other. No degree can be lacking; every possible level of being is represented, from the complete self-sufficiency of the One to vanishingly small realities near absolute nothingness. In the world as we see it, being and nothingness are mixed in all degrees.

We get the picture of a **Great Chain of Being**, an image that is to be enormously influential for centuries.* It certainly has an impact on the thought of Augustine. How does he make use of these ideas in trying to understand what he has come to believe about God and the world?

First we must note that there is one aspect of Plotinus' thought that Augustine, as a Christian, cannot accept. For a Christian believes the world was *created*, and creation is a notion wholly distinct from emanation. Creation is a free act, voluntarily chosen; there is no necessity in it. Emanation, by contrast, is a necessary and continuous process. In the emanation picture, moreover, the *substance* of the world is not distinct from its source; the one flows indiscernibly into the other. Everything partakes of divinity. But in a creation scenario, there is discontinuity, not continuity; what is created does *not* have the same substance as the creator has. Augustine agrees with Plotinus that the world is not a self-sufficient reality, that it depends for both its being and character on a more fundamental reality. But the nature of that dependence is altogether different.

But how are we to understand the creation of the world? It could not be like the creation of buildings by stonemasons or of sculptures by artists. For in these cases people merely give new shape and form to realities that are already in existence. The

---

*See the earlier discussion of this same problem by Heraclitus (pp. 21–22), Parmenides (p. 30), and Plato (p. 127ff.). At the very beginning of the process of emanation, Plotinus holds, the One produces an image of itself in which it knows itself. He calls this reflective image "Intelligence." Intelligence in turn produces "Soul," the principle of life. Augustine reads this as a pagan version of the Christian Trinity: the One = the Father, the Creator; the Intelligence = the Word, Wisdom, the Christ; and the Soul = the Holy Spirit.

---

*For a fascinating study of the history of this idea, see Arthur Lovejoy, *The Great Chain of Being: A Study of the History of an Idea* (Cambridge, MA: Harvard University Press, 1936).

creation of the world must account for those very realities. That is exactly what we discover in Genesis 1:3, where we read, "God said, 'Let there be light,' and there was light."

> You did not work as a human craftsman does, making one thing out of something else as his mind directs. . . . Nor did you have in your hand any matter from which you could make heaven and earth, for where could you have obtained matter which you had not yet created, in order to use it as material for making something else? Does anything exist by any other cause than that you exist?
>
> It must therefore be that you spoke and they were made. (Ps. 33:9) In your Word alone you created them. (*C* 11.5)

Other than God himself, there is nothing but what he has made—again a rejection of Manicheanism, according to which the powers of light and darkness, good and evil, are equally eternal and uncreated. God "spoke" and the heavens and the earth *were*. Remember that in this context "your Word" represents not a spoken word but the *logos*, the Wisdom of God, the second person of the Trinity, who is "with God" and "is God," as John's Gospel tells us. It is through this rational, intelligent, and ultimately loving Word that God makes all things. And he makes them ***ex nihilo***, or *out of nothing*.

The world, then, is entirely, without any exception, dependent upon God.

Because the world is created through Wisdom (compare Plotinus' Intelligence, Plato's Forms), the world is a rational and well-ordered whole. Here again the philosophers confirm the biblical tradition. In the Genesis story we read that God looked at what he had made and "saw that it was good." How could it be otherwise, since God himself is good. For Augustine, as for Plotinus and Plato, there is a direct correlation between being and goodness. The more being something has (which means, of course, the more self-sufficient and eternal it is), the better it is. God, being completely self-sufficient and eternal, is completely good. The created world is less good than God. But still it is *good*. From the premise that the world is less good than God, one cannot conclude that it is therefore *bad*.

Here again Augustine parts company from the Manicheans. The source of evil is not to be found in body or matter, for these are creations of God and so are good. Not everything created is equally good, of course. As we have already seen, life is better than mere existence, and intellect better than mere life. In fact, Augustine follows Plotinus here and urges that there is a continuous gradation of goodness in things. The Great Chain of Being reaches from the most insignificant bits of

The Great Chain of Being

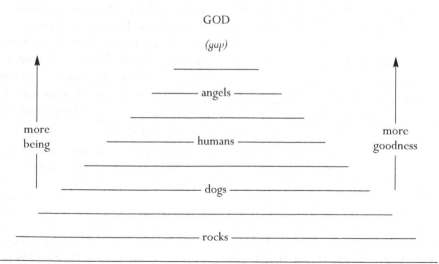

inanimate matter through primitive life forms, to rational creatures like ourselves, and beyond to the angels. That this is a chain of *being* the following examples may make clear.

A dog does not have language, but you do. So, compared to you, there is something lacking in the dog. You have an ability, the power to utter truths and falsehoods, which the dog just does not have. So there is *more to you* than there is to the dog; you have more of being, and the dog has less.

Or suppose I am standing before you in class, an eraser in my hand. Suddenly, I wheel about and hurl the eraser at the chalkboard! You are surprised—no doubt startled. You can't imagine why I have done this. But you don't think any the less of me or my character because of it. Then I say, "Imagine now, imagine that instead of an eraser in my hand it had been a kitten. . . ." The situation is altogether different, and my character has taken a precipitous drop in your estimation. Why? Because a kitten is higher on the Chain of Being than an eraser? Perhaps you, too, believe in the great chain.

The second example makes clear that the chain is not only a chain of being, but a hierarchy of value. So value and being correlate: the more being, the more goodness. And the great ladder reaches from sheer nothingness at the bottom (no being, no value) to God at the top (supreme being, supreme value). Even the lowest degree of existence, however, has its correlative degree of goodness. Nothing God has made is to be despised.

❦

"What is man in nature? Nothing in relation to the infinite, everything in relation to nothing, a mean between nothing and everything."

Blaise Pascal (1623–1662)

Perhaps one more word of explanation is needed. We are likely to think that the distinction between existence and nonexistence is *absolute* and, therefore, that Augustine's idea of *degrees* of being is suspect. But Augustine thinks he can have both. There is indeed an absolute distinction

between even the merest speck of being and nothing at all; however, among those things that are, he believes it is obvious that some have more of being than others.

Evil

As you should be able to see, this picture of things brings Augustine right back to the problem of evil. It was to solve this problem that he had embraced the dualism of the Manichees in the first place. But now, if God is good and the material world is good, he is faced again with the question, Where does evil come from?

The problem can usefully be divided into two parts, which we can call the problems of *natural* evil and *moral* evil. **Moral evil** is evil that depends in some way on the free choices of rational agents. We will postpone consideration of moral evil until we have a better understanding of Augustine's views on human nature. But we can now address the problem of **natural evil**. The heart of Augustine's solution can be simply stated: Natural evil does not exist! You can see that Augustine now proposes to solve the problem as we stated it on page 228 by denying the *second* premise. This allows him to continue to assert the first premise and to deny the conclusion.

Augustine does not wish to deny that we experience some things as evil. But he does want to deny that evil is a *reality*, that it *is*. If you were to make a list of all the things there *are*—solar systems, chairs, lobsters, volcanoes, enchiladas—evil would appear nowhere on that list. Nor would anything on the list be evil—insofar as it is. Being, remember, is goodness. Insofar as something is, then, it is good. What we *call* evil is just a lack of the being that something should have. Evil is the privation of good.

> For as, in the bodies of animate beings, to be affected by diseases and wounds is the same thing as to be deprived of health, . . . so also of minds, whatever defects there are are privations of natural good qualities, and the healing of these defects is not their transference elsewhere, but that the defects which did exist in the mind will have no place to exist, inasmuch as there will be no room for them in that healthiness. (*AE* 2.10–25)

There is a kind of primitive magic that "cures" by moving the disease or wound out of the body and into, for example, a tree. From Augustine's point of view, this is to misconceive the nature of the problem altogether. For a disease or wound is not a "thing," having some reality of its own, nor is healing "removing" that thing. Disease is just the privation of healthiness, and healing is restoring the body to that condition of health (of being and goodness) in which there will be nothing lacking, leaving "no room" for the defect.

Augustine is again making use of Plotinus here. For if we equate goodness and being, we must also equate evil and nothingness. And, as Parmenides already taught us, nothing *is not*. So ignorance is not a reality, but just the lack of knowledge; it is knowledge that is the reality and, therefore, good. Nor is weakness a reality, but simply the absence of strength; strength—that good thing—is the reality.

Since all created things are arranged in degrees of reality, they all participate to some degree in nothingness. Does this mean that they are all evil to some degree? True, they do not have the full degree of being and goodness that belongs only to God, but we ought not to call them "evil" on that score. It is irrational to complain that created things are not as good as God; to do so is tantamount to wishing that only God should exist and that there should be no created world at all! Created being is necessarily finite, inevitably limited. There is always much that any created thing *is not*. If it were not so, it would itself be God! For what makes the world distinct from God is precisely its admixture of nonbeing. The very *being* of created things, remember, is good to some degree; and isn't it better that the created world exist rather than not? It adds to the sum total of being and goodness in reality.

If, by contrast, you complain not that some created thing could have been perfectly good, but that it could have been better than it is, your complaint is equally irrational. For there is already in existence something better than that; and to wish the thing you complain about to be better is to wish it not to be what it is, but to be that other thing (see *FCW* 2.5).

The conclusion is that evil can exist only where there is good. To put it another way, evil depends

on good. Whatever is, insofar as it is, is good; and if there is evil in it, the reason is only that it—like all things less than God—has some part in nothingness as well as being. But no aspect of its nature can be evil per se.

TIME

It is not only the goodness of the world that Augustine is concerned to understand. He is also puzzled by its temporality. Creation is the realm of change and impermanence. Yet God is eternal, unchangeable. How comes the one from the other? There is an additional sting in the problem of time for Augustine because the Manichees target time as an irrational element in the orthodox notion of creation. They ask the Christians what they take to be an unanswerable question: What was God doing before he made the world? The supposition is that God must have chosen to create the world at some particular time. But why at that time rather than some other? There seems to be no answer to this question, no reason why God should suddenly, after ages of noncreation, decide to make the world; but without an answer, there seems to be something irrational about believing in creation (as opposed to belief in the *eternal* conflict of light and darkness).

Apparently there was a snappy answer in circulation.

> My answer to those who ask "What was God doing before he made heaven and earth?" is not "He was preparing Hell for people who pry into mysteries." This frivolous retort has been made before now, so we are told, in order to evade the point of the question. But it is one thing to make fun of the questioner and another to find the answer. So I shall refrain from giving this reply. (*C* 11.12)

Augustine's answer is, rather, a long and famous meditation on the nature of time and eternity. In it he establishes his view of God and God's relation to the created world. Let us see if we can follow his reasoning.

The first point is that God's **eternity** is not to be understood as everlastingness. God is not eternal in that he outlasts all other things; he is eternal in that he is not located in time at all. Those who imagine that God was idle through countless ages before engaging in the work of creation should think again.

> How could those countless ages have elapsed when you, the Creator, in whom all ages have their origin, had not yet created them? What time could there have been that was not created by you? How could time elapse if it never was?
>
> You are the Maker of all time. If, then, there was any time before you made heaven and earth, how can anyone say that you were idle? You must have made that time, for time could not elapse before you made it.
>
> But if there was no time before heaven and earth were created, how can anyone ask what you were doing "then"? If there was no time, there was no "then."
>
> Furthermore, although you are before time, it is not in time that you precede it. If this were so, you would not be before all time. It is in eternity, which is supreme over time because it is a never-ending present, that you are at once before all past time and after all future time. . . . You made all time; you are before all time; and the "time," if such we may call it, when there was no time was not time at all. (*C* 11.13)

So time was created along with the world. That is the way to answer the Manichees: Deny that God exists in time, and the question they asked simply cannot arise. God did not create the world at a given time, since before the creation, time itself did not exist.

What, then, is time? It is something we are all intimately familiar with. But in a much-quoted sentence, Augustine says,

> I know well enough what it is, provided that nobody asks me; but if I am asked what it is and try to explain, I am baffled. (*C* 11.14)

It is clear enough that there are three divisions to time: the past, the present, and the future. And yet these are profoundly puzzling. Think, for instance, of the **past**. The obvious thing about the past is that *it is no more*. There is a correlative fact about the **future**: *it is not yet*. Neither past nor future exists. The only aspect of time that has any existence, then, must be the **present**.

Consider, though, what we call a "long time." It seems evident that only what exists can be long.

What does not exist cannot be either long or short, any more than it can be white or sweet or smell of roses. When, then, is time "long"? Not in the past, for the past does not exist; nor in the future, for a similar reason. But this leaves only one alternative. A long time must exist in the present.

Let us, Augustine says, "see if our human wits can tell us whether present time can be long" (*C* 11.15). What would you call a long time? A century? Can that exist in the present? Suppose we are in the first year of the century; then ninety-nine years are still in the future—and these *are not yet*. Perhaps only a year, then, can be in the present. But suppose it is April. Three months have passed, and eight are yet to come; so most of the year either *is no more* or *is not yet*. Most of the year does not exist, and what does not exist cannot be long. Shall we count only the present month, then, as the present? But suppose today is the twenty-third day; most of the month is in the past and exists no more, while some of it is yet to come.

This thought experiment can be repeated, as you can readily see, for hours, minutes, seconds, until this conclusion is forced upon us:

> The only time that can be called present is an instant, if we can conceive of such, that cannot be divided even into the most minute fractions, and a point of time as small as this passes so rapidly from the future to the past that its duration is without length. For if its duration were prolonged, it could be divided into past and future. When it is present it has no duration. (*C* 11.15)

The present is just that knife edge where *what is not yet* becomes *what is no longer*, where the future turns into the past. The present itself "has no duration." So the present could not possibly be long. Where, then, does the time we call "long" exist? It cannot exist in the past or in the future, as we have seen. But now we see that it cannot exist in the present either. You can see why Augustine is baffled.

"Where is it, this present? It has melted in our grasp, fled ere we could touch it, gone in the instant of becoming."

William James (1842–1910)

Nonetheless, with prayers to God for help, Augustine presses on. It is evident that we are aware of different periods of time; and we can compare them in length to each other. How do we do this? We can see only what exists; that much is certain. So we cannot see the past or the future. We may predict the future on the basis of what we are aware of in the present, and we can make inferences about past facts. But since only the present exists, it is only the present we can be aware of. How, then, are we aware of times that do not exist? Augustine again looks into his soul.

> When we describe the past correctly, it is not past facts which are drawn out of our memories but only words based on our memory-pictures of those facts, because when they happened they left an impression on our minds, by means of sense-perception. My own childhood, which no longer exists, is in past time, which also no longer exists. But when I remember those days and describe them, it is in the present that I picture them to myself, because their picture is still present in my memory. (*C* 11.18)

Augustine concludes that though there are three times, they are not—strictly speaking—past, present, and future. If we speak accurately, we should speak of a *present of things past* (the memory), a *present of things present* (direct awareness), and a *present of things future* (which he calls expectation). Where do these times exist? The answer is clear: in the mind; nowhere else.

> It is in my own mind, then, that I measure time. I must not allow my mind to insist that time is something objective. . . . I say that I measure time in my mind. For everything which happens leaves an impression on it, and this impression remains after the thing itself has ceased to be. It is the impression that I measure, since it is still present, not the thing itself, which makes the impression as it passes and then moves into the past. When I measure time it is this impression that I measure. . . .
> It can only be that the mind, which regulates this process, performs three functions, those of expectation, attention, and memory. The future, which it expects, passes through the present, to which it attends, into the past, which it remembers. (*C* 11.27–28)

This clinches the argument. Time in its extension has no meaning apart from the mind, so it must have come into being along with creation. Our minds—vacillating and changeable—are not eternal. Minds are a part of creation. In possessing these powers of expectation, attention, and memory, our minds are the locale where time realizes itself. Our minds are in this respect a faint image of the mind of God, which also sees past, present, and future. But God does not see them fragmentarily, as we do. We cannot see it all; we must be selective. But to God, who lives in that "never-ending present," all time is known "at once."

> If there were a mind endowed with such great power of knowing and foreknowing that all the past and all the future were known to it as clearly as I know a familiar psalm, that mind would be wonderful beyond belief. We should hold back from it in awe at the thought that nothing in all the history of the past and nothing in all the ages yet to come was hidden from it. It would know all this as surely as, when I sing the psalm, I know what I have already sung and what I have still to sing, how far I am from the beginning and how far from the end. But it is unthinkable that you, Creator of the universe, Creator of souls and bodies, should know all the past and all the future merely in this way. Your knowledge is far more wonderful, far more mysterious than this. It is not like the knowledge of a man who sings words well known to him or listens to another singing a familiar psalm. While he does this his feelings vary and his senses are divided, because he is partly anticipating words still to come and partly remembering words already sung. It is far otherwise with you, for you are eternally without change, the truly eternal Creator of minds. (*C* 11.31; see also *CG* 11.21)

Time is indeed puzzling, and Augustine expresses the perplexities as well as anyone ever has. But his reflections on creation and time are not just an attempt to solve a theoretically interesting problem. The problem is urgent for Augustine because it concerns the relation between God and the Soul, the two foci of wisdom that bear on human happiness. Augustine's meditations on time reaffirm the sharp line of distinction between creation—even including its highest part, the mind—and

God who created it. We are not divine or parts of the divine.* We, together with the whole temporal order, are absolutely dependent upon God for our very being. Still, our relation to time is part of the image of God within us. Unlike God, we are in time; yet, like God to some degree, we are above it. God sees all time in a single moment. We cannot do that, but we do measure time and are aware of past, present, and future.

You should be able to see a correlation between being more like God in relation to time and our place on the Great Chain of Being. A stone, we think, has no temporal horizon at all, a honey bee is somewhat more open to past, present, and future, and a dog still more so, but less than we. (Wittgenstein once remarked that a dog can expect his master, but can he expect him *next week*?) Moreover, our relation to time, and particularly to our future, is the foundation for our free will, our responsibility, and our hope of happiness.

Time is significant not only for individuals but also for the human race. As a Christian, Augustine looks back to a sacred history (beginning with Adam, moving through Noah, Abraham, Moses, and the prophets to Christ) and looks forward to the culmination of God's kingdom in the future return of Christ as judge. To varying degrees, pagan thought diminishes the significance of time, often swallowing up the uniqueness of events in doctrines of circular eternal recurrence. The Socratic doctrine of reminiscence also fits this pattern: If learning is just recollecting what we have eternally known, then the moment of learning is not really very significant. It brings nothing new into being.† But for the Christians the course of events in history is tremendously significant; it occurs just once, and human decisions made in those never-recurring moments have a tremendous—an infinite—weight. For it is in time that our eternal destiny is settled. It is not surprising to find

---

*Here Augustine agrees with Homer (see p. 9) and disagrees with both the Manichees and more respectable philosophies such as Stoicism (see p. 205).

†This point of contrast between paganism and Christianity is focused on most insistently by Søren Kierkegaard in the nineteenth century. See pp. 492–495.

Augustine ending these meditations on time with expressions of awe and praise.

---

1. What are the characteristics of mystical experience?
2. What does Plotinus mean by "emanation"?
3. What is the Great Chain of Being? How are being and goodness related?
4. Explain what is meant by "creation *ex nihilo.*"
5. How does Augustine solve the problem of natural evil?
6. In what sense is God eternal, according to Augustine?
7. What is puzzling about past, present, and future?
8. How does Augustine resolve the puzzles about time?

Human Nature and Its Corruption

What is man? He is certainly a creature of God, but that does not yet distinguish him from any other creature. The Platonistic tradition on which Augustine draws so heavily is unequivocal: a person is an immaterial soul, who may for a time inhabit a body. If we look to the biblical story of creation, however, we get a view that seems to contradict this tradition, for we are told that God "formed man of dust from the ground, and breathed into his nostrils the breath of life" (Gen. 2:7). It seems obvious that human beings are here conceived as material beings—living bodies. Perhaps it is possible to understand the "breath of life" as the creation of an immaterial soul, but this seems strained.

Augustine's thought about human nature is thus pulled in two directions, and we can see an uneasy tension in his efforts to reconcile these traditions. In trying to remain true to the biblical tradition, he emphasizes that a human being is a unitary being: one thing. God did not create a soul when he took up the dust of the earth; he created *man.* But Augustine also believes in the soul and accepts Platonic arguments about its immateriality and its distinctness from the body. But if man is one thing, how can he be composed of two things? Aristotle solves this problem by considering the soul to be the form of a certain kind of living body; in the thirteenth century Thomas Aquinas will adapt this solution in his Christian Aristotelianism. But Augustine, drawing on the Platonic tradition, cannot take this line. And the result is an uneasy compromise. Man is one being, created by God, but he is composed of both body and soul, each a distinct created being.

How, then, are soul and body related to each other? Augustine tries to answer this question in the very definition of a soul.

> But if you want a definition of the soul, and so ask me—what is the soul? I have a ready answer. It seems to me to be a special substance, endowed with reason, adapted to rule the body. (*GS* 13)

So a soul is, by its very nature, suited to "rule the body" by virtue of possessing reason. One thing is clear, then. The soul and its powers are superior to the body. This fact is crucial to Augustine's view of the human predicament—of what stands in the way of our happiness and how we may after all attain it.

We are created by God and so, by nature, are something good. Yet on all sides we find ourselves involved in evil. We are created in the image of God's justice, yet we act unjustly. We are created for happiness, but we find ourselves miserable. Why? The biblical answer is that we have sinned. This seems precisely the right answer to Augustine. But, again, he wants to understand what that means. Augustine's analysis of **sin** and the way to blessedness draws heavily on his own experience. But to understand that experience he needs to come to terms with freedom and responsibility, with God's grace and foreknowledge, and above all with the nature of the will. These are perhaps the most original and penetrating parts of Augustine's philosophy.

Augustine takes the biblical story of the first human pair's sin quite literally. Adam and Eve—created good, happy, and dwelling in the Garden with all of their needs satisfied—are tempted by the serpent to disobey the commandment of God. And so they do. As punishment, they are made subject to death, driven out of the Garden, and forced into a struggle for survival. Their descendants inherit this status. They cannot "begin again" and take the position that Adam and Eve enjoyed before their

sin. This status, into which they are simply born, is **original sin**. Its characteristics are ignorance (i.e., lack of wisdom) and what Augustine calls "concupiscence," or wrong desire. If Augustine is right, we are in trouble from the very start of our lives. Look, he says, at infants.

> It can hardly be right for a child, even at that age, to cry for everything, including things which would harm him; to work himself into a tantrum against people older than himself and not required to obey him; and to try his best to strike and hurt others who know better than he does, including his own parents, when they do not give in to him and refuse to pander to whims which would only do him harm. This shows that, if babies are innocent, it is not for lack of will to do harm, but for lack of strength.
>
> I have myself seen jealousy in a baby and know what it means. He was not old enough to talk, but whenever he saw his foster-brother at the breast, he would grow pale with envy. . . . it surely cannot be called innocence, when the milk flows in such abundance from its source, to object to a rival desperately in need and depending for his life on this one form of nourishment. (*C* 1.7)

Innocence and guilt, it should be noticed, are to be found not in outward actions but in desires, in such things as jealousy and the "will to do harm." It is this condition of the heart, much more than the actions that flow from it, that is the essence of *sin*. We may call babies "innocent," but this is a very shallow judgment. They are innocent only in their lack of ability to do what they very much want to do. As Augustine allows, babies tend to grow out of crying and throwing tantrums. But this does not mean that their desires change; it may only mean that their concupiscence takes on more sophisticated and socially acceptable forms.

'In Adam's fall
We sinned all.'

The New England Primer

We need to understand the elements of sin more clearly. And we have to face the problem of how it could have originated in a world that was created good. What, then, is sin? It clearly has something to do with the motivation for action. So we need to understand motivation better. Whatever we do, Augustine says, is done from a desire for something. These desires Augustine calls "**loves**." We seek to delight in possessing the object of our love. If we think that wealth will make us happy, we love riches. We are sure that if only we can possess riches, we will delight in them, so we are moved by this love to acquire wealth.

Remember that reality is ordered in a Great Chain of Being, reaching from God to the merest speck of existence. This order is at the same time an order of value, for a thing's degree of being is an index to its degree of goodness. Clearly, things of higher value should be loved more and things of less value loved less. If our loves were rightly ordered, they would match the order of value in things themselves. In other words, there is an appropriate ordering of loves that matches perfectly the ordering of goodness in things. And this means that God, who is perfect being and goodness, should be loved most of all, and all the rest of creation in appropriate degrees corresponding to their goodness. In fact, the injunction of Jesus to love God absolutely, "with all your heart, and with all your soul, and with all your strength, and with all your mind," corresponds to the absolute value to be found in God. The rule to love our neighbors as ourselves also fits this ordering rule, for each of us has the same degree of value. Those who are perfectly virtuous—that is, righteous—have their loves rightly ordered. They love all things appropriately, in accord with their worthiness to be loved.

Sin, we can now say, is **disordered love**. It is loving things inappropriately, loving more what is of lower value and loving less what is of higher or highest value. Since we are motivated to act by our loves, these sinful desires produce wicked acts: murder, theft, adultery, deception, and so on. For example, Jane loves money and is willing to kill her aged aunt to get it. What this means is that she loves money (which is less valuable) more than she loves the person who has it (who is more valuable). Her desires are not ordered correctly, and the result is wickedness.

We have not yet plumbed the depths of sin, however. Two errors must be avoided. First, we may think that sin is just a *mistake*. We might think that vice or wickedness is simply not being aware of the true ordering of value in the world. This is akin to the view of Socrates, who holds that virtue is knowledge and vice ignorance.* The person who acts wrongly, according to this view, simply doesn't *know* what is right. Augustine agrees that there is a kind of ignorance involved in sin. But it is not *simple* ignorance, for he holds that the light of Wisdom has "enlightened every man,"† and the rules of righteousness are written in the human heart. So if we are ignorant, we are *willingly* ignorant. We don't *want* to see the truth. We obscure it and then complain that it is too obscure to make out. Sin, then, is not just ignorance. Socrates and Plato are on that score too optimistic; if the problem with human beings is not simple ignorance, there is no reason to hope that simple education will solve the problem. What is needed is not education alone, but *conversion*. And that concerns the **will**.

The second error is to suppose that sin might be something that just *happens* to us. Our environment and developmental history might just have produced certain loves in us rather than others. Our wickedness may be just bad luck—the luck of a bad upbringing, for example—and for luck no one is to blame. A key aspect of the notion of sin, however, is that we are to blame for it. For our sins we are punished, and justly so. Therefore something must be missing in this analysis.

We need to bring in the aspect of *will*. Augustine does this by offering an analysis of four basic emotions: desire, joy, fear, and grief.

> The important factor in those emotions is the character of a man's will. If the will is wrongly directed, the emotions will be wrong; if the will is right, the emotions will be not only blameless, but praiseworthy. The will is engaged in all of them; in fact they are all essentially acts of will. (*CG* 14.6)

---

*See pp. 69–70.
†John 1:9.

To desire something is not just to have a tendency to acquire it. To desire is to *consent* to that tendency, to acquiesce in it, to give in to it, to say yes to it—in short, to *will* it. In a similar way, to fear something is not just to be disposed to avoid something, perhaps with a feeling of panic added. To be afraid is to "disagree" that something should happen, and that disagreement is an act of will. What are joy and grief? They, too, are acts of will, joy being consent in the attainment of something desired and grief disagreement in the possession of something feared. In general, Augustine says that

> as a man's will is attracted or repelled in accordance with the varied character of different objects which are pursued or shunned, so it changes and turns into feelings of various kinds. (*CG* 14.6)

We noticed at various points the prominence that Augustine gives to the concept of will. Here we see why. It is the character of the human will that accounts for emotions and actions alike. We may be motivated by our loves, but in the last analysis, these loves come down to will. And for what we will we are responsible. The will is *free*.

Sin, then, for which we are properly held responsible, is a matter of the will having gone wrong. As Augustine puts it,

> When an evil choice happens in any being, then what happens is dependent on the will of that being; the failure is voluntary, not necessary, and the punishment that follows is just. (*CG* 12.8)

Note an important feature of this account of sin. Its root is not located in the body or anywhere in the material world. Its root is in the soul—precisely in that superior part of the human being which mirrors most clearly the image of God. The soul, which by means of reason is "fit to rule the body," consents instead to be the body's slave, preferring what is less good to what is better.

Again, of course, Augustine is rejecting the Manichean view of evil. If we really do manage to observe the injunction to know ourselves, what we will find is not the pure, unsullied soul that is part of God. What we will find is a rebel who has gone radically wrong by consenting to

a disordered love life. The miser loves gold, but there is nothing wrong with gold. What is wrong is that the miser consents to loving gold (which is worth less) more than justice (which is worth more). The lustful person loves beautiful bodies, but there is nothing wrong with beautiful bodies. What is wrong is that the love of sensual pleasures is preferred to the love of self-control "by which we are made fit for spiritual realities far more beautiful, with a loveliness which cannot fade" (*CG* 12.8).

But now we must face the question, How can this happen in a world created by a good God? Here we discover the second part of Augustine's solution to the problem of evil. The first part, you will remember, consisted in arguing that natural evil is not a reality but simply the privation of goodness. Whatever exists is good, simply in virtue of its *being*. The question now is whether this principle can be used in the sphere of moral evil, where it looks as though the bad will is itself a positive reality. Augustine is confident that it can.

The first thing to be established is that the will is itself a good thing. This is easily done, not only from the principle that all created things are good, but also from the reflection that without free will no one can live rightly. To live rightly is to choose to live rightly; no one can choose rightly without a free will; and since living rightly is acknowledged to be a good, the necessary condition for that good must itself be good (*FCW* 18.188–190).

There are, Augustine tells us, three classes of goods. There are great goods, such as justice, the mere possession of which guarantees a righteous life. There are lesser goods, such as wealth and physical beauty, which, though good, are not essential to the highest goods of happiness and a virtuous life. And then there are intermediate goods. Of these intermediate goods we can say that their possession does not guarantee either virtue or happiness, yet without them no one can be virtuous or happy. Such an intermediate good is free will. Whether it leads to happiness depends on what we do with it; and that is up to us.

Augustine thinks it obvious that the human race has made bad use of its free will; we have turned from the true and lasting good to lesser goods and have sought our happiness where it is not to be found. How are we to understand that?

> The will . . . commits sin when it turns away from immutable and common goods, towards its private good, either something external to itself or lower than itself. It turns to its own private good when it desires to be its own master; it turns to external goods when it busies itself with the private affairs of others or with whatever is none of its concern; it turns to goods lower than itself when it loves the pleasures of the body. Thus a man becomes proud, meddlesome, and lustful; he is caught up in another life which, when compared to the higher one, is death. (*FCW* 19.199–200)

The result of such "turning away" from the higher goods and "turning toward" the lower is *pride, meddlesomeness,* and *lust*. When we value most highly the goods we can all have in common—such as justice, love, and truth—peace reigns in our community. When our loves are fastened on lower goods—such as money, power, and fine possessions—the result is discord and strife; for if you have something of this sort, I do not have it—and often enough, I want it. Proud, meddlesome, and greedy individuals will never be at peace with one another.

Pride, however, is more than the result of sin. It is the very root of sin itself.* Why did the first couple disobey God's command? Augustine emphasizes that it was not because the command was difficult to obey; in fact, nothing was easier. They simply had to refrain from eating the fruit of one of the many bountiful trees in the Garden. In no way did they *need* to eat that piece of fruit. Why, then, did they disobey? The words of the serpent that tempted them suggest the answer. He said, "God knows that

---

*Note that in attacking pride Augustine is not recommending obsequiousness, or slavishness, or a groveling, fawning, or cringing attitude. There is a proper self-respect that each of us both needs and deserves. We are all creatures of God with a place on the Chain of Being; so each of us has an intrinsic value, and it is as bad to deny that as to claim more than is our due. Compare Augustine's pride to the Greek *hubris*, the sort of arrogance that puts oneself in the place of God. (See p. 8.)

when you eat of it your eyes will be opened, and you will be like God, knowing good and evil" (Gen. 3:5). This is the key. They wanted to be "like God." It is only because their wills had already "turned away" from a determination to be obedient to the truth that the temptation had any power over them.

> It was in secret that the first human beings began to be evil; and the result was that they slipped into open disobedience. For they would not have arrived at the evil act if an evil will had not preceded it. Now, could anything but pride have been the start of the evil will? For "pride is the start of every kind of sin." (Ecclesiasticus 10:13) And what is pride except a longing for a perverse kind of exaltation? For it is a perverse kind of exaltation to abandon the basis on which the mind should be firmly fixed, and to become, as it were, based on oneself, and so remain. This happens when a man is too pleased with himself: and a man is self-complacent when he deserts that changeless Good in which, rather than in himself, he ought to have found his satisfaction. . . .
>
> We can see then that the Devil would not have entrapped man by the obvious and open sin of doing what God had forbidden, had not man already started to please himself. That is why he was delighted also with the statement, "You will be like gods." In fact they would have been better able to be like gods if they had in obedience adhered to the supreme and real ground of their being, if they had not in pride made themselves their own ground. . . . By aiming at more, a man is diminished, when he elects to be self-sufficient and defects from the one who is really sufficient for him.
>
> This then is the original evil: man regards himself as his own light, and turns away from that light which would make man himself a light if he would set his heart on it. (*CG* 14.13)

Pride, then, is the cause of man's fall. Not content to live by the light God supplies, we aim to be our own light. Trying to lift ourselves above the place proper to us in the Chain of Being, we seek to become "like God," to be "self-sufficient," to make ourselves the "ground" of our own being. But in trying to rise above our place, we fall. For in this attempt at self-sufficiency we are catapulted at once into anxiety and concern for our own well-being, which we ourselves now have to guarantee. Not content with the true goods that are available to all, we find ourselves engaged in ruthless competition with others for the lower goods. Our loves settle upon the things of this world, and greed, lust, and covetousness reign among our desires. No longer are our wills ordered according to the worthiness of goods to be desired, the order implicit in the created world. As though we were God, we create our own order. But our order is in fact disorder, both within our souls and among one another.

The sin of pride shows itself also in the fact that the first couple, when confronted with their disobedience, make excuses:

> The woman said, "The serpent led me astray, and I ate," and the man said, "The woman whom you gave me as a companion, she gave me fruit from the tree, and I ate." There is not a whisper anywhere here of a plea for pardon, nor of any entreaty for healing. (CG 14.14)

One of the manifestations of sin is a refusal to admit that it is sin. Neither of the first humans would admit to sin; each tried to pin it on someone else.

The root of sin, then, is pride—setting ourselves up as the highest good when the highest good is rather something we should acknowledge as above us. Pride is the sixteen-year-old Augustine posing as the arbiter of right and wrong when stealing and trashing his neighbor's pears—ashamed to be less dissolute than his companions. Pride is the will turning away from God and to itself, resulting in a set of disordered loves.

Suppose we ask, what causes that? Why does that happen? God, after all, created us good. We have free will, to be sure, but why do we use our freedom in that way?

> If you try to find the efficient cause of this evil choice, there is none to be found. For nothing causes an evil will, since it is the evil will itself which causes the evil act; and that means that the evil choice is the efficient cause of an evil act, whereas there is no efficient cause of an evil choice. . . . It is not a matter of efficiency, but of deficiency; the evil will itself is not effective but defective. For to defect from him who is the Supreme Existence, to something of less reality, this is to begin to have an evil will. To try to discover the causes of such defection . . . is like trying to see darkness or to hear silence. . . .

No one therefore must try to get to know from me what I know that I do not know. (CG 12.6–7)

We can understand Augustine's argument in this way. Suppose that there were an answer to the question, Why do we sin? Suppose that we could find some X that is the cause of the will's turning away from the highest good. Then that X would—since it has being—be something good. But something good cannot cause something evil. So there cannot be such a cause in being.

Yet we must remember that created wills, living in time and subject to change, are a mixture of being and nonbeing. If the will, like God's will, were unmixed with nothingness, then it could not fall. So there is a "cause" for sin in the sense that the incomplete being of the will is a *necessary condition* for sin. This is what Augustine calls a "deficient" cause and compares to darkness or silence. Darkness is not a reality on its own; it is just the absence of light. Similarly, silence is the nonexistence of sound. A deficient cause is the absence of the fullness of being that would make sin impossible. The presence of such a deficient cause does not guarantee that the will turns away from God; it just makes that turning possible. So if we ask, then, what does cause the turning away of the evil will, the answer, literally, is *nothing*. The act is voluntary. For Augustine, this means that it cannot have an efficient cause. If it had an efficient cause it would occur necessarily and not be subject to just punishment.* Clearly Augustine is again relying on the Neoplatonic idea of the Chain of Being to solve this problem.

He has not yet solved it completely, however. Recall his doctrine of God. God exists "all at once" in a timeless eternity and "sees all things in a single moment." But that means that God knew—or foreknew—even before man was created that man would sin. So it was true that Adam was going to sin even before he chose to sin. And if that is so, did he really have any choice? Could he have refrained

---

*Here we meet for the first time a theme that will puzzle philosophers down to the present day: Does responsibility require exemption from the causal order of the world? Augustine thought the answer was an obvious yes. For other views, see David Hume ("Rescuing Human Freedom," in Chapter 15) and Immanuel Kant (pp. 452–454).

from sinning, even if he had wanted to? Doesn't God's foreknowledge take away man's free will?

Clearly Augustine needs to affirm both; free will is necessary for responsibility, and God's foreknowledge is a necessary consequence of his perfection. Can Augustine have it both ways? "It does not follow," he says,

> that there is nothing in our will because God foreknew what was going to be in our will; for if he foreknew this, it was not nothing that he foreknew. Further, if, in foreknowing what would be in our will, he foreknew something, and not nonentity, it follows immediately that there is something in our will, even if God foreknows it. Hence we are in no way compelled either to preserve God's prescience by abolishing our free will, or to safeguard our free will by denying (blasphemously) the divine foreknowledge. We embrace both truths, and acknowledge them in faith and sincerity, the one for a right belief, the other for a right life. . . . The fact that God foreknew that a man would sin does not make a man sin; on the contrary, it cannot be doubted that it is the man himself who sins just because he whose prescience cannot be mistaken has foreseen that the man himself would sin. A man does not sin unless he wills to sin; and if he had not willed to sin, then God would have foreseen that refusal. (CG 5.10)

If God foresees that I am going to freely will something, then I will undoubtedly will that thing freely. But it would be a crazy mistake, Augustine thinks, to conclude that this somehow robs me of my free will. How could it not be my will if what God infallibly foresees is that I am going to exercise my will? So Augustine does not see that there is any conflict between God's omniscience and individual freedom.

Augustine's analysis of the human predicament, then, reveals us to be in a pretty sorry state. We are proud, determined to be masters of our own destiny, turned away from the highest goods and anxiously devoted to the lower; our desires are not ordered by the order of value in things. Furthermore, we are continually engaged in turning away from the source of our being. And we cannot escape responsibility for this descent into evil, with all its consequences, both personal and social.

Is there any way out of this desperate plight?

---

1. How, for Augustine, are soul and body related?
2. What is "original" sin? We often say babies are "innocent." What does Augustine think?
3. What is "sin"? How is the will involved in it?
4. If the will is a good thing, why does it go bad?
5. In what way is pride the root of sin?
6. How does Augustine reconcile free will with God's foreknowledge?

Human Nature and Its Restoration

The result of sin is a diminution in the very being of human beings; they become smaller—more ignorant, weaker, and less in control of themselves. Their very will is divided. With one part of the mind they continue to acknowledge the truth of God and the righteousness of his law (since they cannot entirely put out the light that enlightens everyone); but with another part they love what is of lesser value. This was Augustine's own experience before his conversion. He often quotes a passage from Saint Paul to the same effect.

> I do not understand my own actions. For I do not do what I want, but I do the very thing I hate. . . . I can will what is right, but I cannot do it. For I do not do the good I want, but the evil I do not want is what I do. Now if I do what I do not want, it is no longer I that do it, but sin which dwells within me. (Rom. 7:15, 18–20)

Augustine is convinced that this condition is so desperate that none of us can rescue ourselves from it.*

> For by the evil use of free choice man has destroyed both himself and it. For as one who kills himself, certainly by being alive kills himself, but by killing himself ceases to live, and can have no power to restore himself to life after the killing; so when sin was committed by free choice, sin became victor and free choice was lost. (AE 9.30)

---

*See again Augustine's theory of the "chain" that sin forms, by which the soul becomes enslaved and loses its ability to do even what it truly wants to do (pp. 230–231).

Here, however, is the point where the distinctive "gospel" of Christianity comes into its own. What we cannot do for ourselves, God has done for us through his Son Jesus, the Mediator, who took upon himself the sins of the world. All that is required is to trust, by faith, that God has forgiven and received us, despite our turning away, and we will be healed.

This may seem simple enough. But once again there are problems in trying to understand it. We cannot save ourselves from our disordered loves, precisely because our loves are disordered. It would be as impossible as trying to lift ourselves off the ground by wrapping our arms around our own chests and lifting. The restoration of human nature—its re-creation—is no more possible for us than its original creation. So God has to do it. And he has in fact done it in Christ. All we need is to accept it by faith.

But is faith something we can do? This itself seems like an act of will. If our wills are divided against themselves, how can we wholeheartedly will to have faith? If we do not love God absolutely, what love that is actually present in us could lead us to do so?

Augustine writes treatise after treatise trying to clarify the situation and work out a satisfactory answer. Two things were never in doubt for him: Our wills are free, and our salvation is a gift of God's grace. That there is a tension between these ideas is undeniable. But he thinks they can be reconciled. Let us see how.

First it is important to realize that we can never free ourselves from dependence upon God. Remembrance of this will be the surest way to guard against pride, which is, as we have seen, the root of sin. "What have you that you did not receive? If then you received it, why do you boast as if it were not a gift?" (1 Cor. 4:7). Augustine applies this principle of Paul's to the free will: That in itself is a gift, one of God's creations. Whenever we will anything, we are but exercising a power we owe to God.

But that is not enough, for the question concerns merit. If I use my will to turn to God in faith, is that something I do on my own, for which God owes me a reward? The very idea is repugnant to Augustine, for it would let pride back in at the very place where it should be most firmly excluded. It is precisely that turning back to God for which we owe God himself the greatest thanks. For what gift can compare with that? But, then, is it something we have done? Or did God do it in us?

Augustine wrestles with this puzzle again and again. Perhaps his most developed thought on the matter is that *faith* (the turning of our loves back to God) is something in our power. But whether it will be exercised or not depends on whether there are certain "inducements or invitations" present in us or our environment. We do not, after all, choose to take a candy bar unless there is a candy bar presented for us to choose. These inducements are not in our power but are a gift of God. Apparently God makes an offer that some cannot refuse, which is too good to turn down; though when they accept it, they are making use of their own free will. But the grace offered is so great that it overwhelms any pride in its acceptance. We do not boast about possessing a candy bar when it has been offered to us. The appropriate response is gratitude (*SL* 52–60).

There is a section in the *Confessions* where Augustine is searching his soul for evidence of continuing sins and temptations. He sets forth his struggles to get his loves in order with respect to sex, food, pleasures of eye and ear, curiosity, the opinions of others, speech, and self-complacency. And in this section there is a phrase that is repeated again and again:

> Give me the grace to do as you command, and command me to do what you will! (*C* 10.29, 31, 37)

This phrase perfectly expresses that paradoxical combination of reliance on God's grace and determination to will the right that Augustine discovers when he tries to *understand* what he has come to *believe* in becoming a Christian. Our salvation—happiness, blessedness—is up to us. Yet it is wholly a product of God's grace; we have nothing that we have not received.

Let us say a bit more about the life in which Augustine claims to have found both wisdom and happiness. What is it like to live as a Christian? As we have seen, Augustine's theory of motivation holds that we are moved by our various "loves."

Our loves are expressions of the will as we desire a variety of presumed goods. Since it is the interior life that really counts, the quality of our lives will be determined by the nature of our loves.

As we have seen, things in the world are ordered in value according to the degree of being they possess (the Great Chain of Being principle). And the degree of value a thing possesses determines its worthiness to be loved. Happiness and virtue (which coincide as surely for Augustine as they do for Plato or the Stoics) consist in "**ordered love**," where our loves are apportioned according to the worth of their objects.

> He lives in justice and sanctity who is an unprejudiced assessor of the intrinsic value of things. He is a man who has an ordinate love: he neither loves what should not be loved nor fails to love what should be loved; he neither loves more what should be loved less, loves equally what should be loved less or more, nor loves less or more what should be loved equally. (*OCD* 1.27)

But we can now add two further distinctions.

Here is the first one. Some things are to be **used**, whereas others are to be **enjoyed**. And some may be both used and enjoyed.

> To enjoy something is to cling to it with love for its own sake. To use something, however, is to employ it in obtaining that which you love, provided that it is worthy of love. For an illicit use should be called rather a waste or an abuse. (*OCD* 1.4)

What is appropriately loved *for its own sake*? For Augustine there can be just one answer: only God alone. In loving the eternal truth, wisdom, and goodness of God we find blessedness. Here alone we can *rest*, content at last; for there exists no higher good to be enjoyed than the creator and restorer of our human nature. As Augustine says in a famous phrase,

> You made us for yourself and our hearts find no peace until they rest in you. (*C* 1.1)*

The enjoyment we seek is a never-ending delight in the object of our love, which nothing but the highest

and eternal good will provide. All other things are to be used in the service of that end so that we may find the blessedness of that enjoyment. Even other humans, though we are to love them as we love ourselves, are not to be loved *for their own sake*. To do so would be a kind of idolatry, an attempt to find our end, our "rest" in them rather than in the source of all good. Delight in friends and neighbors—or in our own talents and excellences—must be a delight that always turns to gratitude by being referred to the One who provides it all.

We can see now that Augustinian Christianity is totally different from that "trading skill" piety Socrates rejects in the *Euthyphro* (see 13a–15b and p. 85). Like much religious practice in our day, Euthyphro seeks to *use* the gods to attain what he *enjoys*. And he "turns away" from the question that Socrates says is the crucial one: What is that good *X* the gods accomplish through our service to them? Augustine absolutely rejects the notion that we can "use" what is highest for our own ends or "trade" our sacrifice and prayer for some blessings from on high. Whatever good we now have is a gift from God; we have nothing to trade with! God is to be sought not for the sake of some worldly advantage, but for his own sake alone. We don't treat God as a means to some further end. In God we "rest." God is to be *enjoyed*. And you can see that Augustine has an answer to Socrates' question. The good in question is the *transformation of our desire-structure* so that our ordered loves enjoy and use each thing appropriately. The point of piety is not to get what we want from God, but to allow God to change us so that we don't want the same things any more.

The second distinction corresponds to that between enjoyment and use. Augustine divides love into two kinds: charity and cupidity.

> I call "charity" the motion of the soul toward the enjoyment of God for his own sake, and the enjoyment of one's self and of one's neighbor for the sake of God; but "cupidity" is a motion of the soul toward the enjoyment of one's self, one's neighbor, or any corporeal thing for the sake of something other than God. (*OCD* 3.10)

From cupidity comes both **vice** (by which Augustine means whatever corrupts one's own soul) and

---

*Compare Plato on "traveller's rest and journey's end," pp. 130–131.

crime (which harms someone else). We try to enjoy what should only be used and destroy both ourselves and others. Greed, avarice, lust, and gluttony are all forms of cupidity. **Cupidity** is disordered love.

Charity, by contrast, is ordered love, directed toward enjoying God and all other things only in God. If charity is the motivation for one's life, all will be well. "Love, and do what you will," Augustine tells us.[5] You can do whatever you want, provided that your motivation is charity. Charity will motivate us to behave appropriately to all things (i.e., in accord with their actual value). From charity will flow all the virtues: temperance, prudence, fortitude, and justice.*

We must never assume, however, that what motivates us is pure charity. Augustine's own self-examination revealed the cupidity that remained in his life even as a Christian bishop. The Christian may be "on the way" toward the blessedness of truly ordered loves but cannot expect to find it entire until the resurrection of the dead.

---

1. Why, according to Augustine, can we not save ourselves?
2. What is virtue? How is it related to grace?
3. What can we properly enjoy? What can we properly use?
4. Contrast Augustine's notion of piety with the piety described in *Euthyphro* 13a–15b.
5. What are the two kinds of love?

Augustine on Relativism

As we have seen, Augustine argues against skepticism. And everything we have seen so far should lead us to conclude that he is completely opposed to relativism as well. No believer in God could accept Protagoras' saying that *man* is the measure of all things. There is indeed a "measure," a standard by which to judge. But it could not be any created thing, much less a human being whose valuations are determined by a set of disordered loves.* Moreover, if the doctrine of relativism is that (1) Jones can judge some particular action to be right, (2) Smith can judge that very same action to be wrong, and (3) both Jones and Smith are correct, then Augustine is certainly not a relativist.

Nonetheless, there is a sense in which Augustine can admit a good deal of what the relativist wishes to urge. Part of what makes relativism plausible are the differences in customs among the nations.† Another part of its plausibility is the conviction (which most people share) that it is usually wrong to lie, or steal, but not always. Augustine does justice to both these intuitions by recognizing that particular actions are always done out of particular *motivations* and in particular *circumstances*, which must both be taken into account when judging the goodness or badness, the rightness or wrongness of someone's act. Remember Augustine's rule: Love and do what you will. One crucial fact in the evaluation of all actions concerns the way they are motivated: Is the motivation charity or cupidity, a sound will or an evil will? A second crucial fact is an appraisal of what the circumstances require.

These principles give Augustine great flexibility with regard to outward behavior while rigorously constraining judgment about motives. Externally considered, one and the same act may be right in one circumstance and wrong in another. Think about a lie that consists simply in replying yes to a question. This may be wrong if it is said in order to

---

*Compare Aristotle on the unity of the virtues, p. 189. There is much similarity between his view and that of Augustine. But there is one great difference: For Augustine, charity (the source of the virtues) is a result of God's grace, not something we have in our control.

*Again, a comparison with Aristotle is instructive. Aristotle also disagrees with Protagoras; for him the "measure" is the good man (see p. 192), not just *any* man. Augustine might not disagree with this in principle, but he would ask, Where is this good man to be found? Among men, he would say, there is but one without sin—the Christ, the incarnation of the Wisdom of God, the *logos*. He can be the "measure." Aristotle's "good man" might have many virtues, but from Augustine's point of view, he is puffed up with pride—which undermines them all.

†Recall the example of the Greeks before Darius cited by Herodotus (see p. 47) and the judgment that custom is king over all.

gain an unfair advantage for oneself, but right if it is the only way to save a life. Without a full knowledge of both motivation and circumstances, we should be very cautious about pronouncing judgment. As we shall see in the next section, there is even one sense in which such judgment is reserved to God.

In pointing to these two factors, Augustine makes a significant contribution to the debate about **relativism**. While allowing considerable relativity to moral judgments, Augustine is saved from a complete relativism by (1) the Neoplatonic conviction that reality itself is ordered in value, corresponding to the degrees of being, and (2) the thesis about motivation. It is not merely by a conventional agreement that eternal things are of more value than temporal things. Nor is it just *nomos* to praise charity and condemn lust, greed, and hatred. Here we reach values that cannot be relativized. The command of Jesus to love God without reserve and our neighbors as ourselves is *absolute*. Augustine goes as far as to say, "Scripture teaches nothing but charity, nor condemns anything except cupidity, and in this way shapes the minds of men"* (*OCD* 3.10).

Similar considerations apply to justice. Some men, he says,

> misled by the variety of innumerable customs, thought that there was no such thing as absolute justice but that every people regarded its own way of life as just. . . . They have not understood, to cite only one instance, that "what you do not wish to have done to yourself, do not do to another"* cannot be varied on account of any diversity of peoples. When this idea is applied to the love of God, all vices perish; when it is applied to the love of one's neighbor, all crimes disappear. For no one wishes his own dwelling corrupted, so that he should not therefore wish to see God's dwelling, which he is himself, corrupted. And since no one wishes to be harmed by another, he should not harm others. (*OCD* 3.14)

In effect, then, Augustine makes two moves: (1) he breaks up the question about whether values are

relative by saying that some are and some are not; and (2) he locates those that are not in the realm of motivation. Augustine is certainly not a relativist, but neither is he a simple absolutist. The subtlety of his analyses of the interior life serve him in good stead in advancing the conversation at this point.

---

1. How can one and the same behavior be sometimes right and sometimes wrong?
2. Contrast Augustine's view of relativism with that of Protagoras.

The Two Cities

There is an old joke that there are just two kinds of people in the world: those who think that there are just two kinds of people and those who don't. Augustine is emphatically a member of the first group and in this displays his primary allegiance to the Christian heritage. The two kinds are the saved and the damned, those destined for eternal blessedness in heaven and those to be punished for their sins in hell.

But, as you might expect, Augustine's view is more sophisticated and subtle than that bare statement suggests. It is set forth in a book of more than a thousand pages that presents us with an entire philosophy of history. Augustine's intense interest in time and temporal progression is never merely speculative or introspective. In *The City of God* he brings together all he has learned in the forty and more years since first dedicating himself to the search for wisdom. Here he provides a unified interpretation of human history from creation to the end of the world.

The occasion for writing this magnum opus was the sack of Rome by a Gothic army under the leadership of Alaric in August of A.D. 410. The late Roman empire had been harried by barbarians from the north and east for some time, but for a barbarian army to take Rome, the "eternal city," was a profound shock to every Roman citizen, Christian and pagan alike. People asked: "How could this happen?" Jerome, who had translated the Bible into Latin, wrote, "If Rome can perish, what can be safe?"[6]

---

*Luke 6:31 and Matt. 7:12. See pp. 221–222.

Augustine's answer distinguishes "two cities," an **earthly city** and a **heavenly city**. The goal of each city is the same: peace. Members of the earthly city seek peace (harmony and order) in this life: such a peace is a necessary condition for happiness, the ultimate end of all men. For this reason states and empires are established, the noblest of them all (in Augustine's view) being the Roman empire. It is noblest in this respect: It succeeded in guaranteeing the earthly peace of its citizens better and for a longer time than any other state ever had.

Yet see to what a pass it had come! Why? To answer this question Augustine reaches back into his theory of motivation and applies its insights to Roman history. (Note again how everything is traced back to the soul and its relations with the highest good; God and the soul really do determine everything of interest in Augustine's world.) What motivated the founders of Rome and all its greatest statesmen? Like Homer's heroes, they wanted *glory*.*

> They were passionately devoted to glory; it was for this that they desired to live, for this they did not hesitate to die. This unbounded passion for glory, above all else, checked their other appetites. They felt it shameful for their country to be enslaved, but glorious for her to have dominion and empire; and so they set their hearts first on making her free, and then on making her sovereign. (*CG* 5.12)

The best among the Romans directed this quest for glory into the "right path"; it "checked their other appetites," and they were exemplars of virtue, "good men in their way," as Augustine puts it (*CG* 5.12). Those virtues (personal moderation and devotion to the good of their country) led to Rome's greatness. The passion for glory can yield magnificent results, and Augustine is ready to acknowledge them in full:

> By such immaculate conduct they laboured towards honours, power and glory, by what they took to be the true way. And they were honoured in almost all nations; they imposed their laws on many peoples; and today they enjoy renown in the history and literature of nearly all races. (*CG* 5.15)

And, Augustine adds (quoting from Matt. 6:2), "they have received their reward."

The passion for glory, however, is a peculiarly unstable motivation; it can lead as easily to vice and crime as to virtue. Since the glory sought is the praise and honor of others, what happens when the others honor wealth and domination more than moderation and justice? The result is obvious. In fact, the earthly city is always a mix of virtue and vice—precisely because it is an *earthly* city. The aim of its citizens is to *enjoy* what they should only *use*: earthly peace, possessions, and bodily well-being. Since these are exclusive goods (if I possess an estate, you necessarily do not possess it), any earthly city is bound to generate envy and conflict and to tend toward its own destruction.*

> We see then that the two cities were created by two kinds of love: the earthly city was created by self-love reaching the point of contempt for God, the Heavenly City by the love of God carried as far as contempt of self. In fact, the earthly city glories in itself, the Heavenly City glories in the Lord. The former looks for glory from men, the latter finds its highest glory in God, the witness of a good conscience. The earthly lifts up its head in its own glory, the Heavenly City says to its God: "My glory; you lift up my head." In the former, the lust for domination lords it over its princes as over the nations it subjugates; in the other both those put in authority and those subject to them serve one another in love, the rulers by their counsel, the subjects by obedience. The one city loves its own strength shown in its powerful leaders; the other says to its God, "I will love you, my Lord, my strength." (*CG* 14.28)

Pursuing earthly goods for their own sake is self-destructive, for it leads to competition, conflict, and disaster. And that is Augustine's explanation for Rome's fall. Rome was not, as some Christians held, particularly wicked; in fact, its empire was a magnificent achievement, characterized by the real, though flawed, provision of peace

---

*See pp. 7–8.

*It is the hope of Karl Marx and the communists that such envy and conflict can be overcome in *this* world; the key, they believe, is overcoming private property, so that the ground of envy is undercut. See Chapter 18. Augustine would have considered this naive.

and order for its citizens. But it reaped the inevitable consequence of earthly cities that set their loves on earthly glory.

Members of the heavenly city realize that here in this world they have no continuing home; they look for the fulfillment of their hopes in the life to come. Here they have a taste of blessedness, and through God's grace a beginning of true virtue can begin to grow on the ground of charity. But the culmination of these hopes lies beyond.

Nonetheless, citizens of the heavenly city duly appreciate the relative peace provided by the earthly city and contribute to it as they can. While on earth they consider themselves as resident aliens and follow the laws and customs of the society they are dwelling in, to the extent that doing so is consistent with their true citizenship. They *use* the arrangements of their society, but they do not settle down to *enjoy* them.

> However, it would be incorrect to say that the goods which [the earthly] city desires are not goods, since even that city is better, in its own human way, by their possession. . . . These things are goods and undoubtedly they are gifts of God. (*CG* 15.4)

So, with respect to laws that establish "a kind of compromise between human wills about the things relevant to mortal life," there is "a harmony" between members of the two cities. It is only when the earthly city tries to impose laws at variance with the laws of God that citizens of the heavenly city must dissent (*CG* 19.17).

There are, then, two kinds of people. They are distinguished by their loves. But this very fact—that it is motivation that makes the difference—removes the possibility that anyone can with certainty sort people into one class or the other. We might think Augustine would be tempted to equate membership in the Church with citizenship in the heavenly city, but he does not. The Church is, collectively, the custodian of the truth about God; individuals are another matter. We can tell who is on the church rolls, but we cannot tell for certain who is a member of the City of God. Only God can judge that.

Among the professed enemies of the City of God, Augustine tells us,

are hidden future citizens; and when confronted with them she must not think it a fruitless task to bear with their hostility until she finds them confessing the faith. In the same way, while the City of God is on pilgrimage in this world, she has in her midst some who are united with her in participation in the sacraments, but who will not join with her in the eternal destiny of the saints. . . .

In truth, these two cities are interwoven and intermixed in this era, and await separation at the last judgment. (*CG* 1.35)

This epistemological obscurity concerning the saints (for us, though not for God) is a direct consequence of the fact that it is motivation, desire, and the order of a person's loves that make the difference. Behavior is always ambiguous; once more it is the will that tells.

We shall not pursue the details of Augustine's interpretation of history in these terms. It is enough to say that *The City of God* understands human history as *meaningful*. It is not, as a distinguished historian once said, "just one damn thing after another." It has a narrative unity; there is plan and purpose in it; and the story found in the Christian Scriptures provides the key.*

Augustine believes that we can get a perspective on history only if we see it from the viewpoint of eternity—through God's eyes, so to speak. But just that viewpoint has been communicated by God himself through his prophets who prepared the way for the Christ; through the life, teachings, death, and resurrection of Jesus; and finally through the Church, which preserves and extends this "gospel." History is about God's calling citizens of a heavenly city out of the sinful world. These will eventually enjoy blessedness in perfect peace with one another and rest in enjoyment of the one eternal good. For Augustine, all of history must be seen in relation to that end.

---

1. What distinguishes the two cities from one another?
2. Why are we unable to tell with certainty who belongs to each city?

---

*Review the major "chapters" in this story by looking again at Chapter 9.

Augustine and the Philosophers

Augustine melds two traditions, the classical and the Christian. Certainly, tensions show up at various points in Augustine's work, but the degree of success he achieves makes him a peculiarly important figure. He is a culmination of the conversation that precedes him and one of the most influential contributors to the conversation still to come.

He is convinced that truth is one and that important contributions to our understanding of it have been made by both philosophers and prophets. But there is never any doubt which tradition has priority when there is a conflict: Augustine is first, last, and always a Christian, convinced that the one and only wisdom is most fully revealed in the Christ. He has put us in a good position to draw some broad contrasts between classical and Christian philosophy. These are suggestive rather than exact but point out certain patterns that tend to recur.

REASON AND AUTHORITY

Augustine is no despiser of reason. Not for him the *credo quia absurdum est* of some church fathers.* He wants to understand what he believes. He thinks that to a very large extent this can be done and so he must use his reason.

Nevertheless, belief has the priority. It must have, for rational understanding could never by itself discover the truth about the Word becoming flesh or about the Trinity. These things must be believed on the **authority** of the prophets and apostles who bear testimony to them. This authority is founded on eyewitnesses and is handed on in the Church. The key that unlocks the mystery of life is *revealed*, not *discovered*. Thus at the heart of wisdom Augustine finds a place for authority. This authoritative witness must be believed, and belief is a matter of giving one's assent by an act of will. As Augustine never tires of saying, unless you believe, you will not understand.

The following example may make this relation of belief and understanding clearer to you.

Imagine a young woman who has listened only to rock music. Now put her in a concert hall where Beethoven's violin concerto is being performed. She is not likely to get much out of it, but should she believe that there is something of great value going on in that hall? At that point she could accept that this is superb music only by relying on authority. But there is such authority—that of musicians, music critics, and music lovers over nearly two centuries. Augustine would say that it is reasonable for her to believe this on the basis of such authority. This belief not only is reasonable, but also may lead her to listen to the concerto again and again, until she eventually comes to the point where she understands for herself how magnificent it is.[7] Belief, Augustine holds, often properly precedes understanding.

Greek philosophy, by contrast, takes the opposite point of view: Unless I understand, the philosopher says, I will not believe. The extreme case is, of course, the skeptic, who, applying this exact principle, suspends judgment about virtually everything. But Xenophanes already set the pattern:*

> The gods have not revealed all things from the beginning to mortals; but, by seeking, men find out, in time, what is better.[8]

Having shaken themselves loose from their own tradition, from Homeric authority, philosophers on the whole are convinced that there is no alternative to trying to achieve wisdom on our own. And part of this pattern is the value they put on human excellence in the search for truth, on self-sufficiency, and on pride in one's attainments.

Here we have one of the great watersheds in the quest for wisdom: Is wisdom something we can *achieve*, or is it something we must *receive?* Augustine is convinced that we must receive it because of the absolute distinction between God and humans (we are too limited to discover truth on our own), sin (we are too corrupted to do it), grace (God provides it for us), and gratitude and humility (the appropriate responses to the situation).

---

*"I believe because it is absurd." This formula is attributed to Tertullian, a Christian writer of the second century.

*Review the discussion of the whole passage from which these words are taken, pp. 17–18.

INTELLECT AND WILL

Greek philosophers tend to see human problems and their solution in terms of ignorance and knowledge. This is particularly clear in Socrates, for whom virtue or excellence *is* knowledge. But the pattern is very broad, reflected in the importance of education for Plato's guardians, of practical wisdom and contemplation for Aristotle, and of knowledge of reality (in their different theories) by Epicureans and Stoics. Roughly, the pattern takes this form: Inform the intellect and the rest of life will take care of itself.*

Augustine, expressing both the Christian tradition and his own experience, disagrees. Intellect may well be impotent—or worse—unless the will is straightened out. The basic features of human life are desire and love, which are matters of the will. What is needed is not (at first) education, but *conversion;* not inquiry, but *faith.*

Again we have a watershed, which correlates fairly well with the first one. The Christian philosopher believes that we cannot rely upon reason alone; its use depends on the condition of the will, and the will is corrupted. On this view, our predicament is a deep one; we are not in a position to help ourselves out of it, but—this is also crucial—help is available. From the point of view of the Greek philosophers, the human predicament may be serious, but well-intentioned intellectual work will lead us out of it. (Even the skeptics think happiness is attainable.) Reason can master desire.

There is a sense, then, in which Christian thinkers are more pessimistic about humanity than the Greek philosophers.

EPICUREANS AND STOICS

We can cap this contrast by noting Augustine's criticisms of several pagan philosophies that may be serious rivals to Christianity's claim to wisdom. Platonism is the one Augustine thinks nearest the truth, but the Platonists go wrong in allowing worship of powers greater than human beings but inferior to God. Augustine concedes that there are such powers (whether called angels, demons, or gods) but insists that devotion, prayer, and worship belong only to God.

Augustine's interest in Epicurean and Stoic philosophers is sharpened because Saint Paul is alleged to have debated with them in Athens (see Acts 17:18). Moreover, between them they seem to cover neatly the this-worldly possibilities for happiness, the Epicureans seeking it in the pleasures of a material world and the Stoics in the virtues of the soul.

Recall that Epicurus and Lucretius hold that there is no sense in which we survive our physical death; the soul is as physical as the body and disperses when the body disintegrates. Augustine combines this view with their hedonism and concludes that they recommend nothing but the pursuit of bodily pleasures.* He ascribes to them the slogan, "Let us eat and drink, for tomorrow we shall die," which expresses a hedonist's determination to experience as much of bodily pleasure as possible before death extinguishes all sensation.

This doctrine, Augustine says, is "more fitting for swine than for men." Even worse, it is a doctrine that will inevitably lead to injustice and the oppression of the poor (*SS* 150). And the reason is by now a familiar one: They are trying to enjoy what should only be used and as a result are dominated by their disordered loves. But the key error is their neglect of life after death. Epicureanism in this life makes sense only if they are right about consciousness ending in the grave, and of course Augustine is convinced that cannot be right.

The Stoics, who locate happiness in the virtues of the soul, are considered more worthy opponents. Augustine cannot help admiring their courage and steadfastness. But the crucial question is whether the Stoics have indeed found the key to blessedness. Augustine is convinced that they have not. The Stoics' aim is to live in harmony with nature.† Recall the advice of Epictetus: "Do not seek to have events happen as you want them to, but

---

*The contrast, put this baldly, is overdrawn. We have to remember that for Plato's view of education, the *love* of the good is a crucial factor, and this isn't just a matter of intellect. Still, there is something essentially right about it.

*Is this justified? Compare Epicurus on pp. 201–202. Could it be that Augustine is (in part) responsible for the bad press the Epicureans have gotten?

†This concept is discussed on pp. 205–207.

instead want them to happen as they do happen, and your life will go well." Augustine caustically asks,

> Now is this man happy, just because he is patient in his misery? Of course not! (*CG* 14.25)

It is real happiness that we are interested in, not just contentment with what the world happens to dish out; the Stoic version of happiness is just a makeshift second best. True happiness is delight in the possession of the highest good, to which only the Christian has the key.

But, Augustine suggests, what else could you expect? The Stoic, like the Epicurean, "puts his hope in himself" (*SS* 150). This is simply another display of pride, which is the root of human trouble in the first place. From Augustine's point of view, even the virtues of the pagans are but "splendid vices."

Thus Augustine, though a great admirer of pagan learning, is also one of its most severe critics. He brings to the fore a number of "choice points" in which the Christian tradition differs from non-Christian rational philosophy. These traditions differ in their conceptions of God and of God's relation to the world; they differ about appeal to authority, about the priority of will or intellect in human nature, about whether pride is a virtue or a vice; and they differ in their conceptions of love. The general pattern on these issues that Augustine sets will dominate Western philosophy for a thousand years (although many variants are explored). But the fundamental questions that Augustine thinks he has settled will all come up for inquiry again at the beginning of the modern period.

---

1. What tension exists between reason and authority? Between intellect and will?
2. What is Augustine's critique of the Epicureans? Of the Stoics?

FOR FURTHER THOUGHT

1. Compare Socrates' view that no one ever knowingly does wrong with Augustine's contrary conviction. Which do you think is nearer the truth? Why?

2. State as clearly as you can Augustine's charge that the philosophers are guilty of pride. Then try to defend philosophy against that charge. Which position do you think has the stronger arguments?

KEY WORDS

pride	past
Problem of Evil	future
Manicheanism	present
Ambrose	sin
wisdom	original sin
happiness	loves
skepticism	disordered love
truth	will
God	ordered love
Interior Teacher	use
Neoplatonism	enjoyment
Plotinus	vice
the One	crime
emanation	cupidity
Great Chain of Being	charity
ex nihilo	relativism
moral evil	earthly city
natural evil	heavenly city
eternity	authority

NOTES

1. An excellent and readable biography is *Augustine of Hippo* by Peter Brown (London: Faber and Faber, 1967). A classic discussion of his philosophy is Etienne Gilson, *The Christian Philosophy of St. Augustine* (London: Victor Gollanz, 1961).
2. References to the works of Augustine are as follows:

   C: Confessions, trans. R. S. Pine-Coffin (Harmondsworth, Middlesex, England: Penguin Books, 1961).

   FCW: On Free Choice of the Will, trans. Benjamin G. Hackstaff (New York: Macmillan, 1964).

   CG: The City of God, trans. Henry Bettenson (Harmondsworth, Middlesex, England: Penguin Books, 1972).

   OCD: On Christian Doctrine, trans. D. W. Robertson, Jr. (New York: Macmillan, 1958).

   SO: The Soliloquies of St. Augustine, trans. Rose Elizabeth Cleveland (London: Williams and Norgate, 1910).

T: The Teacher, and *GS, The Greatness of the Soul*, in *Ancient Christian Writers*, ed. Johannes Quasten and Joseph C. Plumpe (Westminster, MD: Newman Press, 1964).

AE: Saint Augustine's Enchiridion, trans. Ernest Evans (London: S.P.C.K., 1953).

SL: The Spirit and the Letter, trans. John Burnaby, vol. 8 of *The Library of Christian Classics* (London: SCM Press, 1955).

SS: Selected Sermons of St. Augustine, ed. Quincy Howe, Jr. (London: Victor Gollanz, 1967).

3. Quotations from a *Manichean Psalmbook* in Brown, *Augustine of Hippo*, are cited in the text using the abbreviation *MP*. References are to page numbers.

4. Quotations from *The Essential Plotinus*, ed. Elmer O'Brien (Indianapolis: Hackett, 1980), are cited in the text using the abbreviation *EP*. References are to page numbers.

5. Quoted in Gilson, *Christian Philosophy of St. Augustine*, 140.

6. Quoted in Brown, *Augustine of Hippo*, 289.

7. The example is adapted from Jerry P. King, *The Art of Mathematics* (New York: Plenum Press, 1992), 138.

8. Quoted in John Manley Robinson, *An Introduction to Early Greek Philosophy* (Boston: Houghton Mifflin, 1968), 56.

11

ANSELM AND AQUINAS

Existence and Essence in God and the World

Augustine's influence in Western philosophy and theology was so great that when Peter Lombard, about A.D. 1150, collected notable sayings of the church fathers in the *Book of Sentences*, 90 percent of the quotations were from Augustine's writings.[1]

After the fall of Rome, intellectual work in the West was carried on largely within the Church. It was churchmen who preserved libraries, copied manuscripts, and wrote books. Over most of this work presided the Augustinian spirit, with its convictions that Wisdom is one, that Scripture and Reason are essentially in harmony, and that the interesting and important topics are God and the soul.

Later medieval philosophy, from the eleventh to the fifteenth centuries, is exceedingly rich and inventive. Notable contributions to the conversation are made not only by Christian thinkers, such as Abelard, Roger Bacon, Duns Scotus, and William of Ockham, but also by Muslims—Avicenna (Ibn Sinā) and Averroës (Ibn Rushd), among others—and by Jews, such as Solomon Ibn Gabirol and Moses Maimonides. For the purposes of this selective introduction, however, we focus on two examples: a famous argument put forward by Anselm of Canterbury and—at considerably more length—the Christian Aristotelianism of Thomas Aquinas. Anselm and Aquinas, both made saints of the Church after their deaths, exemplify some of the best, though by no means the only, philosophy of this period. The chapter closes by considering some doubts that were raised about the confident claim that reason and faith are harmonious, doubts that look forward to the birth of self-conscious modern philosophy.

Anselm: On That, Than Which No Greater Can Be Conceived

In about three pages, **Anselm** (A.D. 1033–1109) sets forth an argument concluding not only that God exists but also that he exists "so truly" that we cannot even *conceive* that he doesn't. This apparently simple, yet deeply perplexing argument is known to history as the **ontological argument**.*

Before formulating the argument, we should note something of the context Anselm is working in. Anselm was a priest and a bishop—the Archbishop of Canterbury, in fact. And from all accounts, his character and spirit were such as to merit his later sainthood. He is, moreover, steeped in the Augustinian tradition. The work in which the argument is found was first called *Faith Seeking Understanding*† (a concept that should by now be familiar). It is, in Augustinian fashion, a meditative work, the first chapter of which is a prayer. Here Anselm resolves to "enter the inner chamber of [his] mind" and "shut out all thoughts save that of God" (*Proslogium* 1).² As you can see, questions about God and the soul again predominate—the former to be known most clearly by a withdrawal into the recesses of the latter. God is not sought by exploring the *world*. Anselm acknowledges that he cannot fully comprehend God, but he says,

> I long to understand in some degree thy truth, which my heart believes and loves. For I do not seek to understand that I may believe, but I believe in order to understand. (*Proslogium* 1)

In the preface, Anselm notes that he had written an earlier work (*Monologium*, or *Soliloquy*), in which he had tried to see how far—setting Scripture aside—argument and reason could substantiate the central doctrines of Christianity. The answer was, pretty far—but not, of course, all the way. Because the arguments of this work were pretty involved, he began to wonder

> whether there might be found a single argument which would require no other for its proof than itself alone; and alone would suffice to demonstrate that God truly exists. (*Proslogium* preface, p. 1)

This argument he believes he has found—or has been taught by God himself.

The argument begins with a rather abstractly stated expression of the *idea* of God, a definition, if you like, of what we have in mind when we use the word "God." **God**, says Anselm, is *that, than which no greater can be conceived.** Let us think about this a moment. Why does Anselm use this strangely convoluted phrase, *that, than which no greater can be conceived?* Why not just say, more simply, that God is the greatest being we can conceive? There are two reasons, I think: (1) Anselm doesn't want the idea of God to be limited by what *we* may be able to conceive, and (2) he doesn't want to suggest that a positive conception of God may be entirely comprehensible to us. The strange phrase has this feature: It pushes us out beyond everything familiar by forcing us to ask again and again, Can something greater than this be conceived?

Suppose you imagine or conceive a certain being. Now ask yourself the question, Can I conceive of something that is in some way "greater" than this? If you can, then it is not yet God that you have conceived. Think, for instance, of an oak tree. Now an oak tree has certain powers and abilities but also some very definite limitations. It is not very hard to think of something "greater" than that—something, perhaps, that can move, that can seek nourishment and flee danger, rather than having to suffer whatever occurs at the spot where it is rooted. It follows that God is not an oak tree.

Suppose we think of a creature that does not have these limitations, a wolf, perhaps. Again, it is not hard to think of something "greater" than a wolf—a creature, for instance, that can plan

---

*The term "ontological" comes from the Greek word for *being*. The argument in question was given this name in the eighteenth century by one of its critics, Immanuel Kant, because (unlike the arguments of Aquinas) it does not begin from facts about the world, but goes straight from the idea of God to a conclusion about his being. Many thinkers find it important to distinguish two, or even more, distinct arguments because at least one form of the argument is pretty obviously invalid. Anselm himself does not do so, and we will interpret it as one argument. I will try to formulate this argument in its strongest form, while remaining fairly colloquial in manner. (Discussions of the soundness of this argument often bristle with technical-logical apparatus.)

†It was later titled *Proslogium,* or *A Discourse.* This is the title under which it is now known.

*Compare Augustine's formulation, p. 234.

ahead, build a shelter, heat and cool it, preserve food for the hard winter months. Because we can conceive something greater than a wolf, God is not a wolf.

What if we think of a human being? Is a human being something than which no greater can be conceived? Hardly. For one thing, human beings are mortal. Surely any being not subject to death would be greater than a human. Of two human lives, each of which is well worth living and equally happy, we judge the longer one to be preferable. And humans have many other limitations besides mortality; we can surely conceive a being that knows more than any human knows, is more powerful than any human, is not so dependent on other things, and is not subject to the moral failures of human beings. So when we think of God, we are not thinking of a human being, but of something much greater.

Until we reach the conception of *that, than which no greater can be conceived*, we have not yet thought of God. That is what we mean when we use the word "God." Although this conception is peculiarly abstract, it does seem to capture the crucial idea of God as the only being worthy of worship. Devotion to anything less would be idolatry.

Let us note one more thing about this conception of God before we move on to the argument that Anselm finds embedded in it. It is framed in terms of the Great Chain of Being.* This Augustinian notion is so much a part of Anselm's outlook that it is simply taken for granted. That the world is ordered by the degrees of being and value (greatness) in its various parts must seem to Anselm so obvious that it is beyond question. If you run up and down the chain, you find it easy to conceive of beings both lesser and greater; and your mind is inevitably carried to the idea of something that is not only actually greater than other existing things, but something than which you cannot even conceive a greater. And that, Anselm says, is what we mean by God.

But now the question arises: Is there a being answering to that conception? There really are oak trees and wolves and human beings. Is there a being than which nothing greater can be conceived?*

According to Psalm 14:1, "The fool says in his heart, 'There is no God.'" Let us consider this "fool." There are two ways he might think "There is no God." (1) He might just have these words in mind, without really understanding what they mean; in this case he is a fool only in a weak sense—he is ignorant of what he means by the words he is using. In this case we could easily explain to him what the words mean, and he would cease to be this kind of fool. (2) He might, however, understand what it is he is denying. This fool has the *idea* of God in mind, and presumably he understands the words "that, than which no greater can be conceived." It is this second way of saying or thinking these words that is of interest. Anselm's "discovery" is that such a fool necessarily convicts himself of error every time he thinks, "There is no God."

For suppose the fool were right. Then *that, than which no greater can be conceived* would exist only in his understanding and not in reality. It would exist in the same way, Anselm says, as a painting exists in the mind of a painter who changes his mind before putting brush to canvas. The painter has the painting "in his understanding," as Anselm puts it; but it does not exist also in reality.

It is easy to see how this might be the case with the painting. But can it be the case that *that, than which no greater can be conceived* exists only in the understanding? Anselm invites us to consider that it does. But then, he says, it is not after all *that, than which no greater can be conceived*. For you can certainly conceive of something greater than *that*. You can think that it exists both in the understanding and in reality.

---

*Review this Neoplatonic notion on pp. 236–237.

---

*Anselm, of course, does not doubt that there is. But he wishes to understand what it is that he so firmly believes. Though Anselm is writing at the request of (and primarily for the enlightenment of) his Christian brothers, there can be little doubt that he thinks the proof he has discovered is valid quite independently of any Christian assumptions. It should convince *anyone* who thinks about God at all. It should convince *you*.

Such a being will be "greater" in the sense that it has more powers and is less dependent on other things; it occupies a higher place on the Great Chain of Being. So it couldn't be true that *that, than which no greater can be conceived* exists only in our minds. God must exist in reality.

In fact, Anselm adds, this being exists so truly "that it cannot be conceived not to exist" (*Proslogium* 3). Most beings—trees, wolves, and humans, for example—you can imagine as never having existed. If a huge comet had collided with the earth several billion years ago, none of them would have existed. Could *that, than which no greater can be conceived* be like these beings? Could it be the sort of thing that we can conceive as not existing? Again let us suppose that it were; then it would depend on the cooperation or goodwill of other things for its existence—or maybe on sheer good luck!

But then it wouldn't be *that, than which no greater can be conceived*, for we can surely conceive a greater being than that. We can conceive of a being that is not so dependent on other things. In fact, we can conceive of a being that we cannot even *conceive* as not existing.

> Hence, if that, than which nothing greater can be conceived, can be conceived not to exist, it is not that, than which nothing greater can be conceived. But this is an irreconcilable contradiction. (*Proslogium* 3)

You cannot even conceive that God does not exist. You can, of course, say the words, "There is no God"; but, Anselm says, you cannot clearly think what they mean without falling into contradiction. What is contradictory cannot possibly be true. So what the fool says is necessarily false. It follows not only that God does exist but also that it is impossible that he does not.

Here is an analogy. You can *say* that one plus one equals three, but you cannot *conceive* that it is true. If you understand what one is and what three is, and if you understand the concepts of addition and equality, then you cannot possibly believe or even understand that one plus one equals three. To try to do so would be like trying to believe that three both *is* three and also *is not* three (but two). But

that is impossible, a contradiction. It is necessarily false that three both is and is not three. Just so, it is necessarily false that *that, than which no greater can be conceived* does not exist. To try to believe it is like trying to believe that *that, than which no greater can be conceived* both does exist (since it *is* that, than which no greater can be conceived) and does not exist. But you can't believe both. So, you must believe that it does exist. You cannot even conceive that God does not exist. That God should not exist is as impossible as that one plus one should equal three.

Why, then, does the fool (in the second sense) say in his heart, "There is no God"? Because he is a dim-witted fool who believes contradictions! The nonexistence of God is something that cannot be rationally thought.

It is little wonder that Anselm exclaims,

> I thank thee, gracious Lord, I thank thee; because what I formerly believed by thy bounty, I now so understand by thine illumination, that if I were unwilling to believe that thou dost exist, I should not be able not to understand this to be true. (*Proslogium* 4)

Even if Anselm *wanted* to disbelieve in God, he couldn't manage it. It would now be clear to him that the very sentence in which he expressed his disbelief is necessarily false.

Anselm's argument can be formulated in a variety of ways. Here is one way. See whether you can follow the steps, then see whether you can pick out a flaw in the argument. (Note that it is in form a **reductio ad absurdum**; look again at the discussion of this kind of argument in the section on Zeno, p. 320.)

1. God does not exist. (assumption)
2. By "God," I mean *that, than which no greater can be conceived* (NGC).
3. So NGC does not exist. (from 1 and 2)
4. So NGC has being only in my understanding, not also in reality. (from 2 and 3)
5. If NGC were to exist in reality, as well as in my understanding, it would be greater. (from the meaning of "greater")
6. But then, NGC is not NGC. (from 4 and 5)

7. So *NGC* cannot exist only in my understanding. (from 6)

8. So *NGC* must exist also in reality. (from 5 and 7)

9. So God exists. (from 2 and 8)

10. So God does not exist and God exists. (from 1 and 9)

11. So Premise 1 cannot be true. (by 1 through 10 and the principle of reductio ad absurdum)

12. So God exists. (from 11)

Note that this is an argument that moves from the **essence** of God to God's **existence**. That is, it moves from our grasp of *what* God is—the *NGC*—to the fact *that* God is. In a certain clear sense, the argument is a claim that the existence of God is *self-evident*. What that means is that it is enough to understand the conception of God to know that God must exist. Nothing else is required. God's essence *entails* God's existence. In this regard, if the argument is correct, knowing that God exists is like knowing that all bachelors are unmarried. Knowing what bachelors are (their essence) is sufficient for knowing that they are unmarried. That's entailed by the definition of "bachelor." You don't have to add anything else to get that conclusion. It's not like knowing (supposing this is true) that all bachelors are melancholy—a proposition for which evidence in addition to understanding the terms would be required. If Anselm is right, thinking clearly about the implications of the *NGC* concept is enough to guarantee the conclusion that there is a God. Just as it is necessarily false that there are married bachelors, so it is necessarily false that there is no God.

Is Anselm's argument a sound one? Should we be convinced by it? Or is it a tissue of confusions and ambiguities? Discussion since the eleventh century has been intense, beginning with Gaunilo of Marmoutier, a monk who was Anselm's contemporary. Gaunilo, writing "in behalf of the fool," notes that he has all manner of things in his understanding that have no existence in themselves. For instance, he says, he has the concept of a lost island filled with riches and delicacies, an island more excellent than any other island. This island he can conceive, and in that sense it is in his understanding. If we follow the principle of Anselm's argument, however, the island would be still more excellent if it were in reality as well. So, the island must exist. Otherwise, any actually existing island would be more excellent than it, and it wouldn't be the island more excellent than any other. But that is absurd.

Anselm replies to this criticism by acknowledging that it would indeed be absurd to infer the actual existence of such an island from the mere conception of it. But what holds for islands doesn't hold for the singular case of *that, than which no greater can be conceived*. You can't prove the existence of a perfect island, or of Zeus or Apollo either, from the concepts that designate them. But this concept, the NGC, is unique, pointing us out beyond any finite thing. If the argument works, it works only in this one case, only for that being described by this odd phrase, *that than which no greater can be conceived*. Neither Zeus nor perfect islands exist *necessarily*. But God does—or so Anselm means to convince us.

The argument has had both defenders and critics down to the present day. It is not only the conclusion that attracts attention—though if the argument were sound, the conclusion might be of the greatest importance. But it is interesting also because it involves the difficult notions of existence, conceivability, possibility, and necessity. And these are notions that run very deep in our conception of reality—whatever it might be like.

We will meet the argument again.*

---

1. What phrase does Anselm use to designate God? Why?

2. In what two ways may "the fool" say in his or her heart, "There is no God"?

3. Study carefully the steps in Anselm's argument. Write down questions you have about its correctness.

4. What is Gaunilo's objection to the argument? How does Anselm reply?

---

*See Descartes (*Meditation V,* Chapter 13) and Kant ("The Ontological Argument," Chapter 16).

Thomas Aquinas: Rethinking Aristotle

In A.D. 1225, **Thomas Aquinas** was born in a castle near Naples, the seventh son in a family belonging to the lower nobility. He was destined from an early age for a career in the Church, but not for the career he eventually chose. When he was five years old, his family sent him to Monte Cassino, one of the great and wealthy Benedictine monasteries, hoping that he would rise to become an abbot with a position of power and influence. After nine years of schooling with the Benedictines, he went to the newly founded university at Naples, where he became acquainted with the works of Aristotle. For centuries the only Aristotle available in the West had been the logical treatises, together with some commentaries on them. More works had been preserved by Arab scholars in the East, however, and the ethics, the metaphysics, the physics, and the treatises on the soul were now becoming available again.

In 1244, at the age of nineteen or twenty, much to his family's surprise and against their wishes, Thomas committed himself to becoming a friar in the newly founded Dominican order. Now friars were very different from settled, respectable, and often wealthy monks. Friars were itinerant preachers, going from town to town, begging for a living. They took literally Jesus' directions to his disciples in Mark 6:8, to take nothing with them except their walking sticks—"no bread, no bag, no money in their belts; but to wear sandals and not put on two tunics." Aquinas' family was so unhappy with this decision that the Dominicans decided, for safety's sake, to send him away from Italy to Paris. On the way north, however, his brothers kidnapped him and stole him away to a family castle, where he was kept for a year.

Nothing, however, would induce him to change his mind, not even the seductive wench his brothers sent to his room one night. According to the story, he drove her from the room with a burning brand snatched from the fire. After his family finally released him, he studied for some years in Cologne, Germany, with a man of vast learning and

Aristotelian persuasions, Albert the Great. Aquinas was rotund, a large man of slow movements, unusually quiet and calm. His fellow students began to call him "the dumb ox." His undoubted brilliance occasionally showed through, however, and on one such occasion, Albert is reported to have said, "This dumb ox will fill the whole world with his bellowing."

Aquinas was made a priest and studied to become a Master in Theology. He lectured on the Bible for several years and began to write. Meanwhile, he participated fully in regular *disputations*, as they were called. These were debates that took a more or less standard form. A question was announced for discussion—for instance, Is truth primarily in the mind or in things? Conflicting opinions were stated, often citing some authority. These opinions would then be critically evaluated, arguments for each and against each being put forward. Finally, a judgment would be given by a master or a professor. Much of what Aquinas wrote is structured in a similar way. This form of presentation, which came to be known (later, with scorn) as "scholastic," had certain advantages. It made for comprehensiveness and careful attention to detail. It depended absolutely on the ability of writers and readers to distinguish good arguments from bad. But it required enormous patience, and in the hands of lesser intellectuals than Aquinas it often degenerated into pedantry.

Aquinas spent time not only in Paris, but also in several places in Italy—and all the time, he wrote, or rather, he dictated to a secretary, and often to more than one. It is said that like a grand master at chess who can play numerous games at once, Aquinas could keep four secretaries busy writing separate texts. His collected works are enormous and touch every philosophical and theological topic.

In December of 1273, while saying mass, Aquinas seems to have had a mystical vision. He wrote no more. When urged to return to his writing, he said that he could not, that everything he had written to that point now seemed "like straw." He died in 1274 at the age of 49. Although there was continuing suspicion of Aquinas' reliance on Aristotle—that pagan thinker—and several of his

AVICENNA (IBN SINĀ)

Born in Persia, Avicenna (980–1037) was an important figure in the Islamic tradition that preserved and kept Greek philosophy alive when it had virtually disappeared in the dark ages of the West. A physician who wrote widely on medicine, the sciences, and philosophy, he produced a systematic vision of reality deeply indebted to Aristotle, but bent by pressures from Neoplatonism and Islam.

The most basic of all our notions is that of *being*, which cannot be defined (otherwise it wouldn't be basic), but with which we are intimately familiar because we ourselves and the things of common experience all manifest it. None of these things, when considered for what they are in themselves, exist necessarily. The essence of a horse, for example, does not carry its *being* with it. Horses are possible, but if there is to be an actual horse, some *cause* must supply its being. This cause—or some cause of that cause—must be more than merely possible; it must exist necessarily. In the final analysis, there must be a being that has its necessity in itself, not bestowed by another. And that being is God (Allah).

Contrary to Aristotle, then, Avicenna holds that God must be the *efficient* cause of the universe and not just its final cause or goal. Drawing on Neoplatonic thought, he posits a complex series of emanations that govern the heavenly spheres, and finally events here on earth. The world is not, as Augustine thought, created from nothing, but is eternally unrolling the necessary effects of its eternal and necessary cause. Things that are merely possible in themselves are therefore necessary in virtue of their causes, and everything that occurs (including human action) happens just as it must happen.

Avicenna imagines a "flying man" suspended in midair who, though unaware of his body or of anything impacting his senses, still knows that he exists. Since he does not need to know he even has a body to know his own existence, Avicenna concludes that he is essentially an incorporeal being—a soul.* Because the essence of one soul is indistinguishable from the essence of another (what makes me the particular individual I am is the body), I could not have existed prior to my birth. But will I survive my death? Yes, Avicenna answers. God will supply a principle of individuation when the body can no longer do it, although we do not know what that principle is.

He believes that truth is one, whether discovered by philosophers or announced by prophets. The prophet presents truth in an imaginative way, suited to those who are not able to engage in metaphysical contemplation. In its purity, however, truth is found in philosophical reflection.

_____

*This is a clear anticipation of Descartes' argument for the distinction of soul and body in *Meditation VI* (see p. 351).

---

theses were condemned by ecclesiastical authorities, on July 21, 1323, the pope declared Aquinas to be a saint. Because few miracles had been attributed to him, the pope is reputed to have said, "There are as many miracles as there are articles of the *Summa*."*

PHILOSOPHY AND THEOLOGY

Aquinas does not think of himself as a philosopher. When he talks about philosophers, he usually has in mind the ancients (Plato, Aristotle, and so on), but sometimes the more recent Muslim thinkers, such as Ibn Sīnā and Ibn Rushd. Philosophers are lovers of wisdom, Aquinas thinks, who lack the fullness of wisdom as it is revealed in Christ. Yet he has great respect for these philosophers, especially for Aristotle, whom he sometimes quotes as simply "the philosopher." He writes about the same topics as they do, discusses them frequently, borrows arguments from them, and is happy to acknowledge his debt to them. Yet he never uses them uncritically. Aquinas agrees with Augustine that (1) truth is one, (2) all men have been enlightened by the word or the wisdom of God, and (3) humans, in pride, have turned away from

_____

*The *Summa Theologica* (*Summary of Theology*) is the major work of Aquinas' maturity.

"As sacred doctrine is based on the light of faith, so is philosophy founded on the natural light of reason."

—Thomas Aquinas

God and from the truth. He concludes that the light of reason in sinful minds may be obscured, but it has not been wiped out. And intellect on its own can do a great deal.

> The divine rights of grace do not abolish the human rights of natural reason. (*ST*, 2a–2ae. x.10; *PT*, p. 31)[3]

Revelation, then, builds on reason but does not destroy it. Aquinas is very careful to discriminate what natural human reason can do from what must be learned from Scripture. You can compare the situation, as Aquinas sees it, to a three-story house. On the bottom floor, reason and natural experience do their work without the need of any supernatural aid. On the second floor, we find things

that are both revealed to us by God and demonstrable by reason. Among the truths that overlap in this way are the existence of God and the immortality of the human soul.

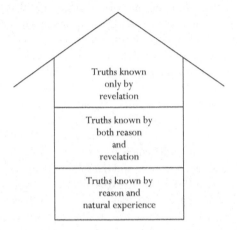

It is good, Aquinas thinks, that God has revealed such truths, even though reason can access them on its own,

> for otherwise they would have been arrived at only by a few, and after a long period, and then mixed with errors; more especially when we consider that man's entire salvation, which is God, depends on such knowledge. (*ST*, 1a.i.1; *PT*, p. 32)

The third floor contains truths that are beyond the capacity of natural intellect to discover, such as the internal nature of God as triune—as Father, Son, and Holy Spirit—and the historical fact of God's becoming incarnate in Jesus of Nazareth.

Though Aquinas always writes as a theologian, we can set out his contributions to the philosophical conversation by focusing our attention on the first and second stories of this house. We do, however, need to keep in mind his view that human beings have a supernatural end. He says,

> The happiness of human beings is twofold. There is an imperfect happiness in this life of which Aristotle is speaking, consisting in the contemplation of immaterial substances to which wisdom disposes us, an imperfect contemplation such as is possible in this life, which does not know what such substances are. The other happiness is the perfect happiness of the next life, when we will see the very substance of God himself and the other immaterial substances.

But what brings that happiness won't be any theoretical science, but the light of glory. (*DT*, question 6; *SPW*, p. 50)

EXISTENCE AND ESSENCE

Among the philosophers, it is Aristotle whom Aquinas thinks has the best arguments and the soundest overall vision. He wrote a number of careful commentaries on works by Aristotle, and when he speaks on his own behalf, Aquinas often sounds like a recording of Aristotle. As Augustine draws on the Platonists, Aquinas draws on the Aristotelians, including the Muslim commentators on Aristotle. But he also makes significant changes in Aristotle's outlook. Before we look at the ways Aquinas criticizes Aristotle, let's review some of the main features of Aristotelian metaphysics.*

We can remind ourselves of these features by considering an example. Think of a horse. According to the doctrine of Aquinas and Aristotle alike, a horse is a *substance*—that is, a complex item composed of form and matter. The *form* is what accounts for its being a horse rather than something else, and the *matter* is what makes it the particular horse it is. The form of the horse does not have any being outside of or beyond horses, as Plato had thought, but exists only in actual tangible, sensible horses. Its form as a horse is its *essence*—what it is, its defining characteristics. It is horses and the like—substances—that make up reality. This view is sometimes called **hylomorphism,** from the Greek words for matter (*hyle*) and form (*morphe*).

Such a substance does not, however, have only essential properties—its "horsiness," so to speak. A horse can be brown or black, fast or slow, daughter of Sparkplug or son of Trigger, in the barn or out at pasture, eating or sleeping. The medievals call these properties "accidents" or "incidental properties," to distinguish them from a horse's essential properties. Incidental properties are referred to by Aristotelian categories such as quantity, quality, relation, position, and so on. They are properties that can change without changing the essential nature of the horse they qualify. As a horse ages, it

*We do this briefly here. A more extended look back at pp. 168–178 might be helpful.

may grow grayer, thinner, and slower. If, by contrast, a horse should lose its essential properties, it would no longer be a horse. Like essential properties, accidental properties have their being only in some substance. No such thing as *black* or *fast* exists on its own, though there are *fast black horses*.

We can address the question of why horses and other substances are the way they are in terms of Aristotle's four causes: (1) the *formal cause* or the formula that makes it the kind of thing it is; (2) the *material cause*—the stuff making it up; (3) its *efficient cause*, or the trigger that brought it into being at a given time; and (4) the *final cause*, the end or goal it is driving toward. In addition, we can explain change in substantial entities in terms of the principles of *potentiality* and *actuality*. Any change is a shift from potentially being so-and-so to actually being so-and-so.

Matter is the principle of potentiality in the horse, form the principle of actuality. For instance, the fertilized egg of a mare is not yet a horse, but, Aristotle would say, it is matter for becoming a horse. Actually, it is an egg (embodies the form of an egg), but potentially, it is a horse. That bit of matter has within it a *telos*—a dynamism that, if all goes normally, will result in its coming to embody the form of a horse in actuality.

Aquinas shares all these metaphysical principles with Aristotle. You then might ask, Why should we pay any separate attention to Aquinas? Why not be content with the metaphysics of the ancient philosopher? Here is the reason: Because Aquinas sees, or thinks he sees, that Aristotle misses something—something fundamental, far-reaching, and extremely important. Strange as it may seem at first, what Aristotle overlooks is *existence*.

"A wise man's question contains half the answer."

Solomon Ibn Gabirol (c. 1021–c. 1058)

Perhaps it would be better to say that Aristotle takes existence for granted. Remember that when he is pursuing what he calls "first" philosophy, he notes that form is prior to substances; it is form that makes a substance real. Form is what *actualizes*, what transforms a potentiality into some existing, substantial thing. For that reason he calls form the substance of substance itself. Form brings existence along with it.

When Aristotle asks about how a particular substance comes into being, his answer is in terms of efficient causation by a prior actuality, an earlier substance, itself made what it is by form. And when Aristotle asks about the final cause of everything, he answers in terms of the unmoved mover, a pure form who is not the creator of the world, but its *telos*, its goal, its ambition. Notice that we don't have to ask whether this god exists; that he is form without matter settles the question.

Individual things within the world—this or that horse, for instance—require an efficient cause for their beginning to be at a certain time; but as a whole, no efficient cause is required for the world. It has its being eternally. It's just there. Why? Because of form. Existence (actuality) and essence (form) simply make a package. It follows from this, and from the fact that whatever exists has some form or other, that there could be no further question about existence.

Aquinas, however, looking at the world through Christian eyes, argues that it is the essence of a horse to be an embodied animal.* That is, when you think of *what* a horse is, you are not thinking just of its form; horsiness is not a horse. Only a substantial union of form and matter is a horse.

> Note that what composes composite substances is material and its form (humans, for example, contain body and soul), and neither of these by itself can be the thing's essence. . . . For a thing's essence, we have said, is expressed by its definition, and unless

the definition of a physical substance included not only its form but its material, definitions of natural objects wouldn't differ from those of mathematical objects. . . . Clearly then essence involves both material and form. (*BE*, 2; *SPW*, p. 93)

Now Aquinas notices that horses so considered might or might not exist.

> I can understand what humans or phoenixes are without knowing whether such things really exist; so clearly a thing's existence differs from its essence or whatness. (*BE*, 4; *SPW*, p. 104)

Even a phoenix, the mythical bird that rises again from the ashes of its own fiery destruction, must be conceived of as a union of form and matter. When we think of a phoenix, we are not imagining a disembodied form, but something substantial. It just so happens that it lacks something: existence. Existence, then, is not something to be taken for granted. Nor is it an automatic consequence of form. Existence, wherever we find it in the natural world, is *something added*.

The same is true of spiritual substances, beings that have no material stuff to be shaped by a form. If there are any such—and Aquinas is convinced that there are—these too are composite. Such substances are not composed of matter and form, of course, but of pure form and existence. Even in this case, form does not suffice for existence. Even with angels or human souls, existence is something added.

What this means is that the entire world, including ourselves, is contingent; in no way is its existence necessary. It could just as well not ever have been. But this entails a radical revision of what an efficient cause must be. For Aristotle, an efficient cause is an already actualized potentiality (a substance), the motions of which actualize some second potentiality—which already is an actuality of some kind or other. Rain and soil and sun (actualities) stimulate an actual radish seed (potentially a radish plant) to bring forth the (actual) plant. But if both such a cause and such an effect might or might not exist, then a true efficient cause must bestow existence—from the ground up! Or at least there must be a *first* such efficient cause—otherwise nothing at all would exist.

---

*We should not be misled by this phrase, "through Christian eyes," as though existence were something only a believer could see. It may be that it took theistic presuppositions, whether Christian or Muslim, to bring the phenomenon to our attention (Aquinas finds something similar in Ibn Sīnā). If it is a real phenomenon, however, it is there no matter what our other convictions are. We find it in atheistic form in Jean-Paul Sartre's 1938 novel, *Nausea*. The difference is that Sartre's protagonist finds existence repulsive, whereas Aquinas finds it an occasion for praise and thanksgiving.

AVERROËS (IBN RUSHD)

A Spanish Arab living during the time of Islamic domination there, Averroës (1126–1198) wrote numerous influential commentaries on the works of Aristotle, whom he admired extravagantly. In fact, he was often later referred to simply as "the Commentator."

Averroës was famous for—and attacked because of —the doctrine of "double truth," the idea that truths from Koranic revelation could contradict what philosophical reason could demonstrate, and yet both be true. It is puzzling how this view came to be attributed to him, since he explicitly denies it. Like Avicenna before him, he holds that the Koran was revealed so that even the humblest could participate in the truth, though in its purity that truth is available only to the philosopher. The Koran has a surface meaning suited to ordinary intellects, but a deep meaning for those capable of understanding it. If there seems to be a conflict, it is by understanding the sacred text philosophically that it should be resolved.

He opposes the hierarchical emanation doctrines of Avicenna and the distinction between essence and existence. God (Allah) is directly responsible for all the celestial spheres and their correlated Intelligences, together with the sublunar things of earth. The universe, being the product of an eternal being, is itself eternal (as Aristotle held).

Averroës is usually understood as denying personal immortality. The human soul is, as Aristotle says, the form of a human body and its active intellect (*nous*) is indeed a substance; but what makes me an individual person (distinct from other humans) is not this form but the particular matter it "informs." As form, this Intelligence is identical in all humans. When my body dies, then, *nous* continues on, but not as *mine*. Thus there is a kind of immortality, but it is strictly impersonal.

Here, however, is one of the points at which Averroës was suspected of holding the double truth doctrine. He also wrote that those who deny personal immortality are wrong and should be put to death. The resolution of this apparent inconsistency is found in his acceptance of the revealed doctrine of the resurrection of the body. If the body is resurrected, or if God supplies a celestial body to take its place, individuality can be preserved in immortality.

Now a thing's attributes are caused either from within its nature (like a human being's sense of the ridiculous) or by some extrinsic source (like light in the atmosphere by the sun). But the very existence of a thing can't be caused by its own form or whatness—I am talking of agent causality—because then something would be causing itself and bringing itself into existence, which is impossible. So everything in which existence and nature differ must get its existence from another. (*BE*, 4; *SPW*, p. 105)

Here Aquinas is clearly anticipating an argument for the existence of God. We turn to his five ways of proving God's existence in the next section, but for now we need to be certain that we understand the main point. Every finite substance, whether material or spiritual in nature, is composite. Material things are doubly composite, being a union of form and matter, this union joined to existence. Spiritual entities are simpler, not having a material component, but they are still a composite of form and existence. If there is to be anything at all, then, existence must be *added* to essence.

Aquinas begins his work *On Being and Essence* with a quote from Aristotle, to the effect that big mistakes grow from small beginnings. If Aristotle is mistaken here, at this fundamental metaphysical level, we can expect that error to have consequences throughout—and Aquinas thinks it does. Despite his undoubted respect for "the philosopher," Aquinas' philosophy turns out to be quite different from Aristotle's. For one thing, it radically changes the conception of God.

---

1. How does Aquinas understand the relationship between human reason and divine revelation?
2. What phenomenon does Aquinas think Aristotle has overlooked?

3. What is the double composition of material substances? In what way are purely intellectual substances simpler? Are they absolutely simple?

4. How does the recognition of a distinction between essence and existence necessitate a change in the notion of an efficient cause?

5. As Aristotle sees it, does the world need an efficient cause? How about Aquinas?

From Creation to God

Can we know, from the point of view of reason and experience, that God exists? And can we know anything about what God is, about his essence? We have seen that Anselm answered both questions at once with his conception of God as that, than which no greater can be conceived. If we understand what God is, he argued, we must know that God is. Aquinas is, of course, familiar with this famous argument, but he thinks it is not a good argument. Actually, he doesn't claim that the argument itself is flawed, but he says that we, as human beings, are not in a position to use it.

> A self-evident proposition, though always self-evident in itself, is sometimes self-evident to us and sometimes not. For a proposition is self-evident when the predicate forms part of what the subject means: thus it is self-evident that human beings are animals, since being an animal is part of what being human means. . . . But if there are people to whom the meanings of subject and predicate are not evident, then the proposition, though self-evident in itself, will not be so to such people . . .
>
> I maintain then that the proposition *God exists* is self-evident in itself, since its subject and predicate are identical: God, I shall argue later, is his own existence. But because what it is to be God is not evident to us the proposition is not self-evident to us. It needs to be made evident by things less evident in themselves but more evident to us, namely, God's effects. (*ST*, 1a.2.1; *SPW*, pp. 196–197)

Here, Aquinas is telling us that we cannot *start* where Anselm starts in his argument. Maybe we will end up in the same place, but we have to get there by another way. Why does Aquinas think that? Because he accepts the Aristotelian view of how humans acquire knowledge.* It may be appropriate for a Platonist such as Augustine or Anselm to think that we, being essentially souls, have direct insight into the essences of things (an immediate grasp of the Platonic Forms, if you will). For Aristotle and Aquinas, however, human beings are—as the quote shows—animals, and the knowledge animals have *begins* with sensation. Aquinas sometimes quotes Aristotle to the effect that our minds are like blank tablets until written on by our senses. What our physical senses disclose to us are material things in the world around us. We don't see God with our eyes or touch him with our fingers. Perhaps material things can be shown to be effects of a first cause. But the argument about God's existence has to start with things "more evident to us" than Anselm's definition of the essence of God.

Aquinas says that there are two kinds of arguments dealing with causes and effects. One begins from causes and shows why things are as they are. The other begins from effects and shows what must have been the case to bring these effects into existence. It is the latter kind of argument that we can use to prove the existence of God.

> Now any effect that is better known to us than its cause can demonstrate that its cause exists: for effects are dependent on their causes and can only occur if their causes already exist. From effects evident to us, therefore, we can demonstrate something that is not self-evident to us, namely, that God exists. (*ST*, 1a.22; *SPW*, p. 198)

Now Aquinas holds that the existence of God can be proved in five ways. Like the proof of Anselm, these "five ways" have been subjected to exhaustive logical scrutiny, often in a forbidding forest of technical symbols. I present Aquinas' arguments in his own words and then add some interpretive remarks. In these remarks I try to present the argument in as strong and sympathetic a way as I can. You may be inclined to try to criticize these arguments, and that's fine, but it is important that you first understand them.

---

*Human knowledge is discussed in more detail in the subsequent section, "Humans: Their Knowledge."

The Argument from Change

The first and most obvious way is based on change. For certainly some things are changing: this we plainly see. Now anything changing is being changed by something else. (This is so because what makes things changeable is unrealized potentiality, but what makes them cause change is their already realized state: causing change brings into being what was previously only able to be, and can only be done by something which already is. For example, the actual heat of fire causes wood, able to be hot, to become actually hot, and so causes change in the wood; now what is actually hot can't at the same time be potentially hot but only potentially cold, can't at the same time be actual and potential in the same respect but only in different respects; so that what is changing can't be the very thing that is causing the same change, can't be changing itself, but must be being changed by something else.) Again this something else, if itself changing, must be being changed by yet another thing; and this last by another. But this can't go on for ever, since then there would be no first cause of the change, and as a result no subsequent causes. (Only when acted on by a first cause do intermediate causes produce a change; unless a hand moves the stick, the stick won't move anything else.) So we are forced eventually to come to a first cause of change not itself being changed by anything, and this is what everyone understands by *God*. (*ST*, 1a.3; *SPW*, p. 200)

Change is understood to be an alteration in something, by which it becomes *actually* what it was only *potentially* until then. If the sun heats the sidewalk so that you can't stand on it with bare feet, this is a change from being actually cool (but potentially hot) to being actually hot. The world is full of such changes.

The next point is that each of these changes is brought about by something that is, in the appropriate way, *actual*. The ball thrown by the pitcher has the potential of being over the fence, but it doesn't have the power to realize that potentiality by itself. It takes an actual batter swinging an actual bat and actually hitting the ball to get it actually over the fence. In the same way, the wood does not actualize its potentiality for being hot on its own; it takes something actually hot to make the wood hot, too. Because nothing can be both actual and potential in the same respect, the wood cannot be at the same time merely potentially hot and actually hot, so it cannot make itself hot.

So, Aquinas tells us, nothing can change itself. Everything that is changed must be changed by another thing. But here you can see a question: What accounts for this second thing that actually brings the change about? Well, there are two possibilities. Either it is actualized by some third thing, or it is not. If it is not, then it is what Aquinas calls a "first cause of change"; it changes the thing in question without itself being actualized by another. If, however, it is made to be a cause of change by another, then the question repeats itself about this third thing.

Now the question arises, Could this series of changes go on to infinity? Might it be that there is no first cause of change at all, nothing that is the source of change without itself being changed by some other thing? Could it be that *everything* is changed by something else, which thing in turn is itself changed by something else? This is a tricky question, but on this question the soundness of the proof probably rests.

Aquinas answers no. His reason is that if this were true there would be no first cause of change. But if there were no first, then there would not be any secondary changers either, since each of them causes change only insofar as it is itself actualized by some prior cause. And, of course, if there were no secondary changers, there would be no change at all. But that is obviously false. We do see home runs hit and camp fires started, so the series cannot go on to infinity. There must be a point where change originates. This must be something that is not merely potential, but is fully and entirely actual. Otherwise, it would need something outside itself to actualize its possibilities.

"Something deeply hidden had to be behind things."

Albert Einstein (1879–1955)

It is important to guard against a misinterpretation here. Aquinas is not thinking of a first thing in a temporal series. His argument is not that one change precedes another, a second precedes that, and so on to the beginning of the world in time. In fact, Aquinas does not think that reason can prove that the world had a beginning in time. If it were not revealed to us by God that the world had a beginning, we could just as well conclude that the world is eternal, without beginning or end—as Aristotle in fact believes. For the purposes of proving the existence of God, however, this does not matter. An eternal world would need a first cause of change just as much as a temporally limited world does.

We must think, then, not of a temporal series, but of a nested set of necessary conditions. A necessary condition for the actualization of something is the reality of something that is not merely potential. Unless there were already something actual no actualization of any potentiality could occur. The set of conditions cannot be infinite, so there must be some condition that is itself *sufficient* to account for the rest. There must be something, then, that exists on its own, without requiring something else to bring it into existence. This would be a completely actual first cause of change. And that, says Aquinas, is what "everyone understands by *God*."

The Argument from Efficient Causality

In the observable world causes are found ordered in series: we never observe, nor ever could, something causing itself, for this would mean it preceded itself, and this is not possible. But a series of causes can't go on for ever, for in any such series an earlier member causes an intermediate and the intermediate a last (whether the intermediate be one or many). Now eliminating a cause eliminates its effects, and unless there's a first cause there won't be a last or an intermediate. But if a series of causes goes on for ever it will have no first cause, and so no intermediate causes and no last effect, which is clearly false. So we are forced to postualate some first agent cause, to which everyone gives the name God. (*ST*, 1a. 3; *SPW* pp. 200–201)

An efficient (or agent) cause, you will recall, is the trigger that sets a process going. Examples are the spark that produces the explosion, the stroke of the key that generates an alphabet letter on the computer's screen, and the wind of the hurricane that blows down the fence. What we find in the world is that these efficient causes are ordered

in series. We never find that something is the efficient cause of itself. The spark may cause the explosion, but it cannot be the cause of the spark. To be its own cause, it would have to preexist itself, and that is absurd. It cannot exist before it exists! The spark itself requires another efficient cause, perhaps a hammer striking a rock.

Another obvious fact is that if you take away the cause, you take away the effect: no hammer, no spark (or at least not this particular spark); no spark, no explosion (this particular explosion). What we find in the world, then, is that one cause depends on another for its existence. Again, this order need not be a temporal one, though it may be. Aquinas is not trying to prove that there was a temporally first event in the world's history. Even if the world is eternal, everything in it needs an efficient cause for its very existence. We can think of this as a hierarchically ordered set of dependencies, rather than a temporally ordered series of successive events.*

Again the question arises, Could this series of dependencies be infinite? Aquinas again says no. For if the series were infinite, there would be no cause that is "first." A "first" cause would be one on which the whole causal order depended, while it depended on nothing beyond itself. If there were no such cause, Aquinas says, there would be no intermediate causes and no ultimate effects. But there are causes and effects, so there must be a first cause. And that is what "everyone gives the name *God*."

One commentator gives a helpful analogy.[4] Suppose you are in your car, stopped at a red light, and are hit from behind. You want to know the cause of this unfortunate event. So you get out and see that the car that hit you had itself been stopped but was hit from behind. So you can't pin the collision on the driver of that car. As you look at the car behind that one, you notice that it, too, was hit from behind, and so on. Who caused your accident? Clearly, the driver of some car that hit a

---

*If you want an example of a causal relation of the efficient sort that is not temporally ordered, think of the depression of the sofa cushion, which is simultaneous with your sitting on it. Your sitting is the efficient cause of the depression in the cushion, but they happen precisely together.

second car, but was not himself hit, caused each of the other cars to cause an accident, ending in yours. He produced the whole series of causes. He is the "first" cause.

Suppose, however, that it were an infinitely long pileup. Then *no one* would have started the chain. But if no one started it, it would not have happened. Since it did happen, we can conclude that someone did start it. He is the first efficient cause.

The Argument from Possibility and Necessity

Some of the things we come across can be but need not be, for we find them being generated and destroyed, thus sometimes in being and sometimes not. Now everything cannot be like this, for a thing that need not be was once not; and if everything need not be, once upon a time there was nothing. But if that were true there would be nothing even now, because something that does not exist can only begin to exist through something that already exists. If nothing was in being nothing could begin to be, and nothing would be in being now, which is clearly false. Not everything then is the sort that need not be; some things must be, and these may or may not owe this necessity to something else. But just as we proved that a series of agent causes can't go on for ever, so also a series of things which must be and owe this to other things. So we are forced to postulate something which of itself must be, owing this to nothing outside itself, but being itself the cause that other things must be. (*ST*, 1a.3; *SPW*, p. 201)

This argument proceeds in two stages. To understand each stage, we must be clear about what Aquinas means by things that "need not be" and things that "must be." Both terms are applied to entities of various sorts, and he thinks we have examples of both sorts in our experience.

A thing that need not be can be generated (can come into being) and can be destroyed again (can pass away). The plants and animals of our experience are such beings. Mountains and rivers, too, are things that need not be. There was a time when the Rockies did not exist, and eventually erosion will wear them away. The mighty Mississippi, relatively stable though it has been for eons, will doubtless disappear some day, perhaps in the next ice age. Such beings, Aquinas would say, can suffer

essential changes. By this he means that they can come to be what they are—and they can cease being that again. Fido is essentially a dog, but when Fido dies, he ceases to exist.

Given that account, we can consider the first stage of the argument. Aquinas argues that at one time, whatever need not be was not (did not exist). This is certainly true of Fido. He asks us to suppose that everything were like that. Then there would have been a time when Fido didn't exist, the Rockies didn't exist, the Mississippi didn't exist, and so on. There would have been a time when nothing existed. But if there ever had been such a time, there would be nothing now. Why? Because from nothing you get nothing. But as every waking moment proves to us, something does exist. So there could never have been a time when there was nothing at all. But that means that there must be things that don't just have possible being; there must be some things that have necessary being, things that *must* be.

This, then, is the first stage of the argument. Not everything can have merely possible being, or nothing at all would exist. Some beings simply must be.

In the second stage, Aquinas admits that some of these necessary beings may owe their necessity to another necessary being. But, using the same reasoning as he used for agent causation, he argues that this series of necessary dependencies could not go on forever. So there exists something that simply *must be* (period!)— something necessarily existing that doesn't owe its necessity to another, but is the cause of whatever is necessary in other beings. This being is in itself eternal and necessary in the most proper sense of the word. And this being, "all men speak of as *God*."

The Argument from Grades of Goodness in Things

Some things are found to be better, truer, more excellent than others. Such comparative terms describe varying degrees of approximation to a superlative; for example, things are hotter the nearer they approach what is hottest. So there is something which is the truest and best and most excellent of things, and hence the most fully in being; for Aristotle says that the truest things are the things most fully in being. Now *when many things possess a property in common, the one most fully possessing it causes it in the others: fire*, as Aristotle says, *the hottest of all things, causes all other things to be hot*. So there is something that causes in all other things their being, their goodness, and whatever other perfections they have. And this is what we call *God*. (*ST*, 1a.3; *SPW*, p. 201)

This proof begins with the observation that the things we experience do not all have the same value. Some are better than others, some truer, some more excellent. All of these comparative judgments, however, make sense only if we assume that in each case there is something which exemplifies those characteristics to a superlative degree.

Aquinas uses the example, which he borrows from Aristotle, of hot things, which are judged more or less hot as they more or less resemble the hotness of fire. (Again, *we* know there are many things hotter than ordinary fire, but that just means we have a longer scale by which to make such comparative judgments; perhaps we would judge heat in comparison with the temperature of atomic fusion in the sun, and cold in comparison with absolute zero.) Something is better than another thing, then, to the extent that it more closely resembles the best. Something is truer if it is more like the truth, and so on.

But that is not the only point on which this argument rests. It is not just that the comparative degrees in such things are measured by the superlative; their very being depends on a superlative. As Aquinas says, fire is the cause of all hot things; and this must be actually existing fire. Again this is a *causal* proof. Aquinas is claiming that if there were not in existence a superlative degree of goodness, truth, and being, the existence of any lesser degree would be inexplicable. So there must be a maximum best, noblest, truest, and so on.

But since the lower degrees actually exist, the maximum must also really exist. This maximum is what explains the fact that we observe all these degrees of goodness in things: It is their cause. This maximum "best" of all things, Aquinas says, "we call *God*."

The Argument from the Guidedness of Nature

Goal-directed behaviour is observed in all bodies in nature, even those lacking awareness; for we see their behaviour hardly ever varying and practically always turning out well, which shows they truly tend to goals and do not merely hit them by accident. But nothing lacking awareness can tend to a goal except it be directed by someone with awareness and understanding: arrows by archers, for example. So everything in nature is directed to its goal by someone with understanding, and this we call *God*. (*ST*, 1a.3; *SPW*, pp. 201–202)

This proof is often called "the argument from design." It is probably the one that turns up most often in popular "proofs" of the existence of God, and it has a famous history.* The key idea is that intelligent beings act purposefully, arranging means suitable to achieve ends they have in mind. We plant and harvest and store, for example, so that we will have food in the winter when we know there will be none to gather. We can look ahead to a situation that does not now exist and take steps to meet it satisfactorily.

This capacity is none too surprising in intelligent beings; perhaps it is even the main thing that constitutes intelligence. But when we look at the nonrational part of the world, we see the same thing. And this *is* surprising. We can hardly suppose that my Newfoundland dog, Shadow, grew a thick coat in the fall and shed it in the spring because he foresaw that otherwise he would be uncomfortable and perhaps even in danger of not surviving! Yet it is just as if he had planned that rationally.

We see the same apparently rational planning wherever we look. Rabbits are quick so that they can escape foxes. Foxes are cunning so that they can catch rabbits. Moths are camouflaged to escape predators. And so on. Everything happens as though it were planned to happen that way. But we cannot believe that dogs, rabbits, foxes, and moths are doing that planning. Someone else must be doing it for them.

---

*See particularly the discussion by David Hume ("Is It Reasonable to Believe in God?" in Chapter 15). Many people think that Darwinian modes of explanation also tend to undermine the argument. A recent version of the argument is presented in *Darwin's Black Box,* a book by biochemist Michael Behe. See, for instance, www.arn.org/behe/behehome.html and www.cs.colorado.edu/~lindsay/creation/behe.html.

"Earth, with her thousand voices, praises God."

Samuel Taylor Coleridge (1772–1834)

Here is an analogy: People sometimes wonder whether computers are intelligent. Computers can certainly do some remarkable things: solve problems, rotate images in three dimensions on a screen, guide spacecraft. A standard reply is that though computers may look intelligent, the intelligence they display is not their own, but that of their designers and programmers. They have a "borrowed" intelligence.

Aquinas is claiming something similar for naturally existing beings. They do remarkable things, things that seem inexplicable in the absence of intelligence. We see their behavior "practically always turning out well." We cannot believe that they are themselves intelligent. So they must be directed to their goals "by someone with understanding."* This being, Aquinas says once more, "we call *God*."

Aquinas thinks, then, that by such reasoning from effects to causes we can prove the existence of God. In fact these five ways do not quite do that; they do not prove that there is one unique being who has all these traits: first cause of change, first efficient cause, a necessary being, a best being, and the intelligent designer of all the rest. But Aquinas thinks this is something reason can also prove. Such proofs provide a foundation on which Aquinas thinks all reasonable people should agree. If we think about the matter carefully, he contends, we should agree that atheism is irrational. This does not necessarily mean that the rational person will be a Christian, for some of the truths recognized in Christian faith cannot be rationally demonstrated. But the message of the Bible and the doctrines of the Church can rest on this foundation.

THE NATURE OF GOD

Let us suppose we are convinced. We know *that* God exists. How much do we know about *what* God is? Here Aquinas is quite cautious. This is representative:

> In this life we cannot see God's substance but know him only from creatures: as their non-creaturely and transcendent cause. So this is where our words for God come from: from creatures. Such words, however, will not express the substance of God as he is in himself, in the way words like *human being* express the substance of what human beings are in themselves. (*ST*, 1a.13.1; *SPW*, p. 215)

There is no way our finite minds can adequately grasp what God is. Still, we are not entirely ignorant. We do know that God is the cause of all the features of the world we live in, and we know that God is the source of the very existence of anything at all. So what can we say about God on that basis?

The first and most important truth we know about God is that God *is*. If we ask, "Is what?" the most fundamental answer is that God is existence, being, itself. Like Augustine, Aquinas harks back to God's answer to Moses before the burning bush, when Moses asks who is sending him back into Egypt. God there says (Exodus 3:14), "I AM WHO I AM. . . . Say to the people of Israel, 'I AM has sent me to you.'" But Aquinas thinks philosophical reason also must reach this conclusion. (Here we have something on the second floor of our house!)

> God's existing doesn't differ from his substance. To be clear about this, note that when several causes producing different effects have also, besides those differing effects, one effect in common, then they must produce that common effect in virtue of some higher cause to which it properly belongs. For the effect properly belonging to a cause is determined by the cause's own proper nature and form; so that effects properly belonging to causes of diverse nature and form must differ, and any effect produced in common must properly belong not to any one of them but to a higher cause in virtue of which they act. . . . Now all created causes, distinguished by the effects that properly belong to each of them, have also one effect in common, namely existence: heat, for example, causes things to be—or exist as—hot, and builders cause there to be—or

---

*Note the persistence of the Greek assumption that where there is order there is intelligence. See pp. 16–17.

exist—houses. So they agree in causing things to exist, but differ in this: that heat causes heat and builders houses. So there must be some cause higher than all of them in virtue of which they all cause existence, a cause of which existence is the proper effect. And this cause is God. Now the proper effect of any cause issues from it by reproducing its nature. So existing must be God's substance or nature. (*DPG*, 7.2; *SPW*, pp. 205–206)

Because existence is (as we saw earlier) something added to essence, it cannot be just by virtue of their essence that fires or house builders produce their effects. True, their effects differ because of the kinds of things they are. But that they both bring into being something that actually exists cannot be ascribed to those kinds. That is something

separate and requires a separate explanation. It must be that, in addition to being the kinds of things they are, they participate in being—which is not identical with either of them. This being, this existing, this energy or source of the existence of finite things cannot itself just be another finite thing. It is being itself. And that, Aquinas says, is the very substance of God. That's what God is—a great, unlimited, activity of existing. So Anselm is right after all: God's essence *is* his existence. But now we know that in a way appropriate to the kind of mind human beings have: as the cause of effects we are aware of through our senses.

Note how different from Aristotle's conception of God this is. God thought of in this way is not a pure form existing in isolated splendor,

---

MAIMONIDES (MOSES BEN MAIMON)

Like Averroës, his contemporary, Maimonides (1135–1204), was born in Spain. At the age of thirty, however, he fled rather than be forcibly converted to Islam and spent the latter part of his life in more tolerant (at that time) Cairo. There he was physician to the vizier of Saladin, ruler of Egypt. He wrote extensively on medicine and Jewish law, but his most influential work is *Guide for the Perplexed*.

The *Guide* is addressed to those intellectuals who are in perplexity over apparent contradictions between Scripture and the best science and philosophy of the day. The latter he takes to be represented by Aristotle, especially as understood by his Muslim interpreters. He agrees with Avicenna that being and essence are separable, but holds that the celestial spheres and the Intelligences governing them are created by God ex nihilo, not emanations from the very substance of God himself. This allows him to deny that everything happens necessarily in this world, thus making room for free will, evil, and miracles.

As to whether the universe is eternal or not, he holds that this cannot be proved either way, but that on either assumption the existence of

God can be demonstrated. We know God exists, but we know of his nature only what we can learn from his works. So the study of these works by way of natural science yields such knowledge as we can have of the divine nature. However, because all language is derived from our experience of the natural world, he holds that none of our words can apply literally to God, who infinitely exceeds his creation. We can, then, say what God is *not*, but never positively what God *is*. Thus Maimonides is one of the principal sources for the tradition of *negative theology*.

Maimonides believes that the highest perfection possible for a human being is to know God and to love him. Because we know God only through his works, the pursuit of science and metaphysics is, as Aristotle said, the best and happiest life. It also provides as much of immortality as is possible for us, since what will be preserved after death is the knowledge we have acquired. In the greatest human beings, however, this theoretical life can be combined with practical influence in the community, as is proved by the greatest of the prophets, Moses.

contemplating its own contemplation. God is an efficient cause, an agent continually bringing into existence all the many things that do exist. This is a God who is involved in the creation, a God who might well (though this has not been proved) know the number of hairs on a man's head and be aware of the fall of every sparrow, a God who might love human beings with a love beyond all comparing. Whether we can go that far or not, this is clearly a God on whose creative activity we absolutely depend; if for one moment God turned away from the creation, everything would disappear back into nothingness. Existence, remember, is something added to essence. And now we know that it is added by God, whose very essence is existence.

As for what else we might know about God, Aquinas says two things. First, we can know a great deal about what God is not. Drawing on a long tradition of "negative theology," Aquinas says that God is not, for instance, finite, material, potential, a tree or star, bad, and so on. We can pile on negatives, and this is useful. But no list of negative terms, no matter how long, will tell us what God *is*.

The second truth about God derives from the way we know of God at all: as the cause of effects in creatures. In the world around us, we observe many good things; in their fullness, we could call them "perfections." Life is such a perfection, for example, or wisdom, or power. All of these derive their being from the source of all being. But we don't merely want to say, Aquinas reminds us, that God is the *cause of life or wisdom or goodness.** We want to be able to say that in some sense, this great act of existing is itself alive and wise and good. How can we do that?

We have to acknowledge that what we mean by these terms is not derived from a direct acquaintance with God. We learn what "wise" means by experience with human or animal wisdom in this finite creaturely world, but we are also familiar with extensions of a word's meaning. For instance,

"healthy" is a term that belongs to people in its primary application, but because of cause and effect relations with other things, the term is extended. We call certain foods "healthy" because they contribute to health in humans. Or we call urine or blood healthy because they are a symptom or sign of health. Aquinas thinks something of the same sort is true of the words we use about God.

> So creatures having any perfection represent and resemble him . . . as effects partially resemble a cause of a higher kind though falling short of reproducing its form. . . . So the sort of words we are considering express God's substance, but do it imperfectly just as creatures represent him imperfectly.
>
> So when we say *God is good* we mean neither *God causes goodness* nor *God is not bad*, but *What in creatures we call goodness pre-exists in a higher way in God*. Thus God is not good because he causes goodness; rather because he is good, goodness spreads through things. (*ST*, 1a.13.2; *SPW*, p. 218)

Because the words we use of God get their original meaning from our experience in this world, they cannot mean exactly the same thing when they are applied to God. For instance, Socrates is wise and Socrates exists, but Socrates' wisdom is not the same thing as his existence. So

> words expressing creaturely perfections express them as distinct from one another: *wise* for example, used of a human being expresses a perfection distinct from his nature, his powers, his existence, and so on; but when we use it of God we don't want to express anything distinct from his substance, powers, and existence. So the word *wise* used of human beings somehow contains and delimits what is meant; when used of God, however, it doesn't, but leaves what it means uncontained and going beyond what the word can express. Clearly then the word wise isn't used in the same sense of God and man, and the same is true of all the other words. No word, then, is said of God and creatures univocally. (*ST*, 1a.13.5; *SPW*, p. 224)

A word is *univocal* when it is used with just one meaning. Aquinas denies that a word applied to both creatures and creator is used univocally. But it isn't used *equivocally*, either; that is, it's not the case that there is no connection between the meanings in the two cases, as there is between "bank" when used as a place to keep your money and

---

*Note that an atheistic materialist might want to acknowledge a cause for life or wisdom; she would, however, point to matter or the evolutionary process as that cause. What she would want to deny is that the cause is itself alive or wise.

"bank" as a place on which to stand while fishing. Rather,

> these words apply to God and creatures by **analogy** or proportion. . . .

> And this way of sharing a word lies somewhere between pure equivocation and straightforward univocalness. . . .

> Whenever words are used analogically of several things, it is because they are all related to some one thing; so that one thing must help define the others. . . . In the same way then all words used metaphorically of God apply first to creatures and then to God, since said of God they only express some likeness to creatures. Just as talking of a *smiling* meadow expresses a proportion: that flowers adorn a meadow like a smile on a man's face, so talking of God as a *lion* expresses this proportion: that God is powerful in his doings like lions in theirs. And so clearly we can't define what such words mean when used of God unless we refer to what they mean used of creatures. . . .

> But, as we have seen, such names don't simply express God's causality, but his substance, for calling God *good* or *wise* doesn't only mean that he causes wisdom or goodness, but that these perfections pre-exist in him in a more excellent way. (*ST*, 1a.13.5,6; *SPW*, pp. 224–227)

In this way Aquinas explains how we can talk intelligibly of God, while carefully preserving the ultimate mystery of God's being to creatures such as ourselves.

---

1. Why does Aquinas not accept Anselm's ontological argument for God?
2. According to Aquinas, from what basis must we argue if we are to prove God's existence?
3. Be sure to grasp the main points in each of the "five ways."
4. What is God's essence? How do we know?
5. How does analogy work in understanding God's nature?

HUMANS: THEIR SOULS

Aquinas takes for granted the basic concepts involved in the Great Chain of Being idea.* God, as perfect

---

*Review the development by Plotinus and Augustine of the idea of the Great Chain of Being, pp. 236–237.

being and goodness, freely creates a hierarchy of creatures, from angels to stones, varying in being and goodness. But Aquinas elaborates the higher reaches of the chain much more than Augustine did.

Between God and the highest of creatures there is an unbridgeable gap. But there are many levels of created substances higher than human beings. These angelic beings are pure intelligences, spiritual beings defined by a form or essence, but lacking any material substratum.

Two things must be noted about **angels**: (1) Lacking any matter, they also lack what individuates material things. (Remember that what makes this frog distinct from that frog is not its form, but the fact that it is composed of different matter.) Still, an angel is not, like God, a simple existence whose essence just is its existence. Like all created beings, angels are composite; they are made up of a form or essence plus existence—which here, too, is something added. (2) This lack of material stuff in spiritual intelligences means that there cannot be more than one angel of a given kind. To put it another way, each angel is an entire species in itself, every one differing from every other in essence—differing not as this dog differs from that dog, but as dogs differ from horses.

Human beings exist on the border between such pure intelligences and the material world, sharing something with beings both above and below them on the chain. This participation in higher and lower levels of being is already summed up, Aquinas thinks, in Aristotle's formula for humans: They are *animals* (material beings) whose distinctive characteristic is *rationality* (or intelligence).

Aquinas agrees substantially with Aristotle about soul and body. Because soul is the principle of life in things, there are various levels of soul. Plants have a kind of soul, which enables them to nourish themselves, grow, and reproduce. In addition to these powers, animals have sentient (sensitive) soul—that is, abilities to see and hear and so on, together with instincts and inclinations that draw them toward and move them away from things. Humans have rational soul, adding the abilities to abstract universals, think logically, and plan future actions in the light of goals. In all these ways, **soul** is the form of a body of a particular sort.

It is very important to Aquinas to insist that there are *not* three souls in a human being—vegetative, sensitive, and rational—as though we were composite beings made up of three substances.

If we hold that the soul is united to the body as its substantial form, then the co-existence of several essentially different souls in the same body cannot be entertained. To begin with, an animal having several souls would not compose an essential unity, for nothing is simply one except by one form. Form gives being and unity. Were man alive by one form, namely by vegetable soul, and animal by another, namely by sensitive soul, and human by a third, namely by rational soul, he would not be one thing simply speaking. (*ST*, 1a.76.3; *PT*, pp. 204–205)

But a human being *is* one thing, and the rational soul incorporates and governs all the rest. This kind of holism means that features we in some way share with the lower animals—emotion and desire, for instance—are transformed into *human* emotion and desire. In us, emotion and desire involve conceptualizations impossible for a nonrational creature. We can, but a cat cannot, fear damage to our reputation or hope to meet someone we admire. In fact, everything in us, even our bodily state, is affected by our dominant form, the rational form of a human soul.

We could put this point another way. The human body is not, in a living human being, a substance. Some philosophers—Plato comes to mind—have thought so and have thought of a human being as a kind of dual creature: a body to which a substantial soul has for a time been conjoined. But Aquinas will have none of this. At death we are not left with one of the substances in a human being (the body), while the other (the soul) departs. What we are left with is not, properly speaking, human at all, but an entity of a different kind: a corpse. We may call it human by extension or by analogy, but because the corpse has lost the form of a human being, it is no longer literally correct to call the corpse human. A human body is not a thing on its own, but *material* for a human being, made into one substance by the human soul, which is its form.

So the human soul is the form of the human body. Further, if soul inhabited body like a sailor his ship, it wouldn't give body or its parts their specific nature; yet clearly it does since when it leaves the body the various parts lose the names they first had, or keep them in a different sense; for a dead man's eyes are eyes only in the sense that eyes in a picture or a statue are, and the same goes for the other parts of the body. Moreover, if soul inhabited body like a sailor his ship the union of body and soul would be accidental, and when death separated them it wouldn't be decomposition of a substance, which it clearly is.* (*PDS*, art. 1; *SPW*, p. 188)

Despite this insistence on the unity of a human being, however, Aquinas also agrees with Aristotle that a rational soul is not *just* the form of a human body, the way the soul of a lobster is just the form of life in a lobster. There is something substantial about a human soul after all, something akin to angelic intelligences.† He agrees, moreover, for essentially the same reason: Reasoning souls

cannot share that special activity of theirs with any bodily organ, in the sense of having a bodily organ for thinking as an eye is the bodily organ for seeing. And so the life principle of a thing with understanding has to act on its own, with an activity peculiar to itself not shared with the body. And because activity flows from actuality, the understanding soul must possess an existence in and of itself, not dependent on the body. (*PDS*, art. 1; *SPW*, pp. 187–188)

You can see Aquinas, like Augustine, struggling to unify two strands of thought that are not easy to harmonize. On the one hand, a man or woman is one substance, and the soul is its form. On the other hand, a human soul, by virtue of its capacity to abstract universals and reason with them, its ability to know virtually anything, is an intellectual substance in its own right, able to subsist even when the body is destroyed.‡

On the one hand, a soul gets a content, becomes a determinate, individual soul only by virtue of its intimate relation to the body because whatever is in a soul is conveyed there by the specific

---

*Descartes, in the seventeenth century, uses this same figure, also denying that the soul is like a sailor in a ship. But he has an even harder time than Aquinas in making it stick, since he thinks the soul is a separate substance in its entirety. See pp. 347 and 351.

†See Aristotle on *nous*, pp. 181–183.

‡See the fuller discussion in the following section, "Humans: Their Knowledge."

bodily sense experience of some individual human. On the other hand, it is the soul's possible subsistence without the body that gives it immortality. Although Aquinas has rational arguments for each part of this view, in the end it may be a matter of faith that these demands can be reconciled. He calls on the Christian doctrine of the resurrection of the body to do the job.

> Firstly, if we deny the resurrection of the body it isn't easy—indeed it becomes very difficult—to defend the immortality of the soul. The union of body and soul is certainly a natural one, and any separation of soul from body goes against its nature and is imposed upon it. So if soul is deprived of body it will exist imperfectly as long as that situation lasts. . . . Secondly, what human beings desire by nature is their own well-being. But soul is not the whole human being, only part of one; my soul is not me. So that even if soul achieves well-being in another life, that doesn't mean I do or any other human being does. (CC, 15:17–19; SPW, pp. 192–193)

"My soul is not me." This definitive rejection of Platonism means that even if my soul is a substance capable of existing after my body dies, *I* may not survive. For *my* survival, that soul must be the form of a body—my body. And to buttress this hope of immortality, Aquinas looks not to reason, but to the resurrection of Christ. Just as Christ's body was transformed into a heavenly body, so, the Christian saint believes, will our bodies be also.

HUMANS: THEIR KNOWLEDGE

We have seen how humans can know something of God by (1) reasoning from effects to causes, and (2) using analogies from common experience to partially describe this cause of existing things. But how do we come to have knowledge of those effects in the first place? We need to pay some attention to Aquinas' theory of knowledge. As we have noted, knowing begins with sensing. How does sensing work? Take the eye, for example. An eye has the power to receive images of external things—their shape, color, texture, motion. It's not the substance being perceived that enters the eye, of course, but its sensible form.

Imagine you are stroking a cat that is purring contentedly on your lap. You see the cat stretch with pleasure, feel the softness of its fur, and hear the purr. Each of these sensible forms is received by the appropriate sense. Yet it is not three experiences you are having, but one. So these images must be united in what Aquinas (following Aristotle) calls your "common root sensitivity." The unified complex image formed in you is a particular item that mirrors a determinate, particular substance outside you: contented Tabby at a certain moment in time. When the cat jumps off your lap, your current sensory experience changes, but something is left behind in you. The proof is that you can later remember that experience, bring its images back into consciousness, and, as it were, run the experience again. So images are stored in you somewhere; Aquinas (again following Aristotle) calls this storehouse *the imagination*.

Thus far described, our minds do not differ much from the minds of the higher animals, which also have sensitivity, imagination, and (limited) memory. But we have an additional capacity called **intellect**. Using intellect, we can form *ideas* from the images stored in imagination. And ideas are not just more images, not copies of images, but what the medievals called "universals."* **Universals** are features of things that can be expressed in language and formulated in definitions. So while our senses can take in the sensible form of Tabby and the imagination can store that image, it is the intellect that can abstract the universal features of this cat and all other cats and formulate the *idea* of a *cat*.

> The senses are bodily powers and know singular objects tied down by matter, whereas mind [intellect] is free from matter and knows universals, which are abstract from matter and contain limitless instances. (ST, 1a.2ae. 2.6; PT, p. 231)

When this happens we have the form of the cat actually resident in the intellect itself. That's what a concept or idea of a cat is: the actual presence in the intellect of the very *form* that makes a cat a cat—only without making the intellect into a cat because the usual *material* for cats (flesh, bone, fur) is missing.

---

*Contrast David Hume, who thinks ideas just are faint copies of images. See pp. 397–398.

> "Knowledge is the conformity of object and the intellect."
>
> *Averroës (1126–1198)*

There might be a problem here. If our intellect deals in universals such as "small domestic feline" or "rational animal," which are true of limitless individuals, how is it possible for us to know particular things—Tabby or Socrates—that aren't pure forms? It is, after all the *matter* composing this cat or this human that make them the particular things that they are. But matter as such is unknowable; matter is what the intellect abstracts *from*. Aquinas solves this problem by noting that sensory images have two uses. They are the originals from which knowledge starts, but they are also needed when we think about particular things. We may be able to know a lot about cats-as-such in terms of forms or universals, but if we want to direct our thought to Tabby in particular, we need to recall an image of Tabby to tie our thought down to her. The image, remember, is as particular as the individual that produced it and will ensure that we are indeed thinking about that specific cat. Knowledge of particulars, then, is possible; it will involve both universals and images, as when we say that Tabby is gray or that Socrates is wise.

Intellect has two distinguishable operations. In the first of these the intellect enjoys a simple apprehension of some object; it grasps, more or less adequately, the *whatness of the object*, its *nature*, or what Aquinas calls its **quiddity** (from the Latin for "what it is"). So a child learns to identify a cat and distinguish it from a dog. The child's idea of a cat is not false to the reality, but it is pretty incomplete. An adult's idea is more adequate, and a biologist's concept more adequate still. Our idea of what a cat is can expand and improve; typically, it does improve with continued experience of cats. In such a simple grasp of a nature, there is, properly speaking, no truth or falsity. It's just there in the intellect. (Compare Aristotle on truth not being applicable to *terms*, but only to *statements*, p. 159.)

In the second operation, which Aquinas calls "making connections and disconnections," the intellect unites ideas to make judgments about the things apprehended. Such judgments may be affirmative or negative. So we say, "All cats meow," or "Socrates is not stupid." With respect to judgments the concept of **truth** is in place.

> For the meaning of true consists in a matching of thing and understanding, and matching presupposes diversity, not identity. So the notion of truth is first found in understanding when understanding first starts to have something of its own which the external thing doesn't have, yet which corresponds to the thing and can be expected to match it. Now when articulating what things are, understanding possesses only a likeness of the external thing, just as the senses do when they take in the appearance of what they sense. But when understanding starts to make judgements about the thing it has taken in, then those are the understanding's own judgements not found in the thing outside, yet called true judgements in so far as they match what is outside. Now understanding makes judgements about the thing it takes in when it says something about how it is or is not, and that we call understanding making connections and disconnections. . . . So that is why truth is found first in understanding making connections and disconnections. (*PDT*, 1.2; *SPW*, p. 59)

Truth, then, just as in Aristotle, is a matter of correspondence or matching between judgments made by the intellect and the thing being judged. To say "Socrates is wise" is true, provided Socrates is wise. Otherwise, the statement is false.*

There also seem to be two powers in the intellect: an active power and a receptive power. The former does the abstracting; the latter stores the abstract ideas, functioning for the active intellect as imagination does for the senses. There must be such a passive power, Aquinas argues, because we can bring back into active consideration ideas that have not been present to the conscious mind for some time; these ideas have not completely disappeared but are potentially present, ready once again to play a role in current thinking. It is the active power of intellect that Aquinas believes is not and cannot be tied down to any bodily organ. It is to this agent intellect that he looks when he searches for a proof

---

*See Aristotle's definition of truth, p. 161.

of the immortality of the soul. But the receptive intellect is equally important, lest our minds be restricted solely to awareness of the present moment.

It is very important to note that although intellect gets its material from the images stored in imagination, it is not those images that we know (at least not in the first instance). What we know are those hylomorphic objects that produced the images—the cat, the chair, the person sitting in the chair holding the cat. We know them by virtue of, or by means of, these images. But the images are not the primary objects of knowledge.* True, we can reflect on our own mental operations, draw back and pay attention to the image as such. In general, however, what we know is not limited to the contents of our minds. We know Tabby and Socrates and the fact that fire causes water to boil. None of these are mental phenomena.

This, then, is the account Aquinas gives of our knowledge of the material world. All our knowledge begins with what our senses reveal about it. This explains how we can know that the premises of his arguments for the existence of God are true. We begin from simple facts about the world—that things change, that one thing causes another, and so on. Starting there, Aquinas believes we can work back to that cause, which is its own existence, and the cause of whatever else there is.

---

1. In what way is the Psalmist right when he says we were created "a little lower than the angels"? (Psalm 8:5)
2. How does Aquinas explain the fact that a human being is one thing?
3. Is the soul (agent intellect) immortal? Why?
4. What are universals? Give some examples.
5. How does the intellect acquire universals?

HUMANS: THEIR GOOD

Following Aristotle again, Aquinas holds that every finite substance tends naturally toward its perfection, toward realizing its potential. Actualization

of a thing's potential is in fact the *good* for that thing. This natural teleology of final causes is present even in the inanimate world, but it is strikingly apparent in animals; they are always seeking something. This is especially true of human beings, who can scarcely sit still an hour without planning what to do next. We regard what we seek—rightly or wrongly—as good, as contributing to our perfection. We want dinner, or a movie, or exercise. These things are goals that move us to action, so we go to the kitchen or head toward the theater or change into our running shoes. Such actions are chosen as means to reach the goal, and we wouldn't engage in them if the goal didn't seem good to us.

This much seems mere common sense. But Aquinas pushes these thoughts in two directions. First, suppose we ask why we want exercise. We might answer, for the sake of health, which also seems good to us. Why do we want health? It must be for the sake of some further good. That such questions can be repeated leads us to ask, Is there any goal that we want simply for itself, not for the sake of something beyond it? Aquinas answers, yes, of course. Again following Aristotle, he identifies the goal as happiness (*eudaemonia*) or beatitude.* Whatever else seems good to us does so because it seems either to be a part of happiness or to contribute to our happiness. That it is good to be happy or blissful is beyond proving, but also beyond question.

Second, humans differ from other animals in being able to frame ideas in terms of universal concepts. We want dinner, but that concept can be filled out in a great many ways. Do we want steak, or chicken, or vegetables? Do we want to eat out or at home? Alone or with others? Simple or fancy? Dinner is good, but that rather empty concept cries out for a multitude of decisions. A sheep that is hungry and is put in a green pasture faces no such quandaries; it simply starts eating the nearest grass. The sheep's actions are pretty closely determined by what its senses reveal in its immediate environment. Human action is unlike that because our

---

*Contrast this "realism" about knowledge with the "empiricism" of John Locke, who says that the mind has "no other immediate object but its own ideas," p. 376.

*Note that happiness is no more just the *feeling* of happiness for Aquinas than it was for Socrates, Plato, or Aristotle. It is a condition of the person. Compare pp. 104, 148, 185.

universalizing intellect presents possibilities to us. Among these possibilities we must choose. And if you think "dinner" is a concept that can be filled out in numerous ways, consider "happiness."

We all want to be happy, then—to flourish, to fare well. This is a desire implanted in us by nature; whether that *should* be our goal is not up to us. (Though I have asked many students, I have never found a single one who confessed to having as a goal being unhappy in life!) Happiness is a natural good.* We don't have to consider whether to take happiness as a goal, but we do have to think about how to achieve that goal. This thinking eventuates in acts of will that produce actions.

> There is a desire for good in everything: good, the philosophers tell us, is what all desire. In things without awareness this desire is called natural desire: the attraction a stone has for downwards, for instance. In things with sense-awareness it is called animal desire, and divides into capabilities of affective and aggressive feeling. In things with understanding it is called intellectual or rational desire: will. So created intellectual substances have wills. (*SCG*, 2.47; *SPW*, p. 169)

Strictly speaking, a sheep does not have a will, though it does have desires. Nonetheless, Aquinas maintains, will is a species of desire. It is differentiated from desire in general by being rational desire, desire that is informed by intellectual knowledge and reason. True, like the sheep we may simply be attracted to food that is before us. But we can also apply universal concepts in reasoning about food; we can say, "That's filled with saturated fats, and though I'm sure I would like it, I will not eat it." Such a decision, made in the light of rational knowledge, in the light of some goal that reason approves (such as health), is an act of **will**. Humans, by virtue of their intellectual nature, have wills.

What that means is that human beings are not at the mercy of their desires. They can choose which desires to satisfy and which to leave unsatisfied—and that means the will is free.

Things lack freedom to decide either because they lack all judgement, like stones and plants which lack awareness, or because their judgements are fixed by nature, like nonreasoning animals. . . . But wherever judgement of what to do is not fixed by nature, there is freedom to decide. And all creatures with understanding are of this sort. For understanding takes in not only this or that good but the notion of good as such. . . . So all things with understanding have freedom of will deriving from understanding's judgement, and that is freedom of decision, which is defined as free judgement of reason. (*SCG*, 2.48; *SPW*, pp. 170–171)

Aquinas means that we can evaluate particular goods (such as this rich, dark, sweet, chocolate cake) in the light of "good as such" and decide in the light of our more general good whether *this* good is one that should be chosen. The fact that we can do this means we are responsible for our actions. Unlike sheep, we are not simply determined to act by our immediate surroundings.

Aquinas distinguishes between *acts of a human* and *human acts*. I do, in a sense, grow a beard every night. But whether I shave it off in the morning or let it grow is a matter for decision and the exercise of my will. Only the latter is properly called a *human act*. Why? Because only that is under the control of the form that makes me human: my rational nature. Suppose I really would like to have a beard but my wife just hates beards. Then I am faced with incompatible goods—having a beard or pleasing my wife—and I have to decide. I am free to decide either way. Whichever I do will be voluntary. What I decide will be willed in the light of intellectual reflection on overall goodness, and that will not only be something I am responsible for, but it will also be a revelation of my character.

Before we discuss character (virtue and vice), however, we should ask, What makes an individual action good or bad?

> We should judge actions good and bad in the same way we do things, since what things do reflects what they are. Now a thing's goodness is measured by how fully it exists; for . . . good and existent are interchangeable terms. . . . * Full human

---

*Compare Plato's argument for morality in the *Republic*, which depends on precisely this premise. See p. 148.

*This is, you will recall, one of the principles of the Great Chain of Being idea.

being, for example, demands a complex of soul and body endowed with every ability and organ needed for knowledge and movement, and if an individual lacks any of this he would not exist fully. As existing he would be good, but as not fully existing he would lack goodness and be called bad: thus for blind men it is good to be alive, but bad to be without sight. . . .

In a similar way then actions must be called good in so far as they exist, but in so far as they exist less fully than human actions should they will lack goodness and be called bad: if, for example, we don't do as much as we reasonably should, or do something out of place or the like. (*ST*, 1a2e.18.1; *SPW*, pp. 343–344)

What actions would "exist less fully than human actions should"? Clearly, actions would not exist as fully human if they were not under the control of our intellectual, rational faculties—because those faculties are what make us distinctively human. Those actions, then, would lack goodness and would be called bad. Good actions are actions that flow from our nature, fulfilling and perfecting that nature.

This principle allows Aquinas to formulate the notion of a **natural law**. Everything in the created world, of course, expresses the divine reason, according to which it was designed. God's reason can be called an **eternal law**, and nothing can happen that is not permitted to happen by God's eternal law. In creating the world, however, God brought substances into being that have natures or essences of their own, and these natures incorporate within themselves something of the eternal law. A stone, for instance, naturally falls to Earth. Sheep or wolves naturally act out their nature. Sheep eat grass, and wolves eat sheep; they have no choice. Human beings also have a given nature. But, as we have seen, our nature includes the capacity to formulate universals and to think about what to do in terms of them. This provides us with a freedom of action that stones and sheep and wolves lack. Unlike sheep and wolves, then, we can act in ways that are contrary to our nature, detrimental to it—and when we do, the saint tells us, we sin.

But we also have the capacity to know what the law of our nature is, together with a partial ability

(even apart from the special grace of God) to act in accordance with it. How do we know what the natural law says? Its first principle, Aquinas tells us, is this: "Good should be done and evil avoided." Now this is not something that can be proved from more general principles, or it wouldn't be first. It is a practical parallel to that principle of intellectual life in general, the principle of noncontradiction, which says that two contradictory propositions cannot both be true. Though it cannot be proved, there does seem to be something incoherent in its denial. Since I always act for the sake of some good, for me to say, "Let me do evil," is equivalent to saying, "Let evil be good."*

Can we know anything of natural law beyond this self-evident first principle? Yes. How? By observing the natural inclinations or propensities of things. For example, all human beings experience the drive to continue in existence. Our reason apprehends this universal drive as good. It is good to continue to live—so murder is wrong. And it is part of our nature to eat when hungry—so feeding the hungry is good. Humans have a natural tendency to mate and care for their children—so marriage, intended to provide a safe and lasting environment to meet these goals is a good thing. In general, law is what reason declares to be fitting in the light of the nature of something. By using our intellect, reflecting on the nature of human beings and other essences, we can discern the image of God's eternal law that is resident in the things he has created. Aquinas believes that in addition to murder and adultery, reason tells us that drunkenness, gluttony, suicide, lying, homosexuality, and the breaking of promises are contrary to nature. The argument is that all of these, in one way or another, violate the natural inclinations of a being with a nature like ours.

———————

*Notice that the first natural law does *not* say, "What I think is good should be done and what I take to be evil should be avoided." Aquinas does think that we have no alternative but to do the best we know, so if, after reflection, our conscience tells us to do something that is in fact wrong, that is what we should do. But that doesn't mean we are doing the right thing.

Now since everything subjected to God's providence is measured by the standards of his eternal law, as we have said, everything shares in some way in the eternal law, bearing its imprint in the form of a natural tendency to pursue the behaviour and goals appropriate to it. Reasoning creatures are subject to God's providence in a special, more profound way than others, by themselves sharing the planning, making plans both for themselves and for others; thus sharing in the eternal reasoning itself that is imprinting them with their natural tendencies to appropriate behaviour and goals. And it is this distinctive sharing in the eternal law by reasoning creatures that we call the law we have in us by nature. (*ST*, 1a2ae.91.2; *SPW*, p. 418)

In addition to the eternal law, which is part of the nature of God, and the natural law, which is resident in our own natures, Aquinas distinguishes two further kinds of law. The third kind is **human law**. This is law that is devised and promulgated by an authority in a community for the good of that community—or, at least, that is its essence. When human law is in accord with that goal, it also mirrors the eternal and natural law. But, as humans are subject to sin—rulers no less than the rest of us—human law may deviate from natural goodness and often does. Where human law deviates from natural law, Aquinas says, it is not truly law at all, but lawlessness. Why? Because it is not in accord with reason, which is the source of all law.

Human law, then, must meet four conditions to be true law: (1) It must issue from a legitimate authority that has responsibility for a community; (2) it must be promulgated publicly so that people can know what is and is not acceptable; (3) it must further the good of that community; and (4) it must be in conformity with reason. In terms of these criteria, Aquinas distances himself from any notion of law as simply what the sovereign declares, or whatever is customarily accepted.*

---

*Aquinas thereby aligns himself with those who claim that there is a criterion for judging human laws, from Heraclitus and Antigone, through Plato, Aristotle, and the Stoics. He sets himself against Sophist understandings of law and justice as wholly conventional, and against notions of law as simply what the ruler declares. Compare Hobbes, p. 367.

Finally, there is **divine law**. This is law that is beyond our natural capacities to discover but is revealed to us in the Scriptures. An example might be the New Testament commandment to believe in the Lord Jesus Christ in order to be saved. Reason cannot figure this out for itself; but, Aquinas holds, it is necessary to enable us to reach our final bliss. Here we have something on the third floor of the house.

We can now return to the issue of character. Like Aristotle, Aquinas holds that we shape our characters by developing habits or dispositions to act in certain ways. And we build such habits by actually acting in those ways. These habits of character are virtues and vices. *Virtues* incline us to act in ways that reason approves of; when you have a virtue, it is easy to do what otherwise is difficult. *Vices* are contrary habits, which incline us to ignore or neglect the discernment of good by our reason.

Virtues are important to us. The reason is that, though we are naturally oriented toward bliss or happiness, it is not so clear what contributes to that blessed state. Our rational faculties have (in addition to the task of finding truth) the practical role of choosing actions suitable to promoting our blessedness. But we are not, as the angels are, pure intellectual beings. We also feel the attractions of the senses and the pleasures of the body, and these animal propensities have some independence of our intellect. Thus, they need to be habituated to the good—trained, if you like, to obey their rightful master, reason. That's just what a **virtue** is: a habit of choosing wisely in light of the ultimate end of blessedness. Aquinas, again following Aristotle, says that the soul rules the *body* like a tyrant. He means that if I will to raise my arm, my arm (other things being equal) simply obeys and goes up. But our desires and emotions

don't obey my reason's slightest signal, but have their own ways of acting, which are sometimes at odds with reason: reason rules my affections and my aggressions, Aristotle goes on to say, *democratically*, like free people are ruled, who have their own will in certain areas. (*ST*, 1a2ae.56.4; *SPW*, p. 406)

As we see in this quote, Aquinas divides our desires and emotions into two large classes: the *affective* and the *aggressive*.*

> The object of our affective ability [is] anything sensed as straightforwardly good or bad, pleasurable or painful. But sometimes the animal has a hard struggle attaining such good or avoiding such bad things, because they are not within its immediate power, and then good or bad, seen as challenging or requiring effort, becomes an object of our aggressive ability. . . .
> . . . the function of aggressive feelings in animals is to remove obstacles preventing affective feelings from pursuing their objective, obstacles that make good difficult to attain or bad difficult to avoid. So all aggressive feelings end up in affective feeling, so that even aggressive feelings *are accompanied by* the affective feelings of *joy or sadness*. (*ST*, 1a2ae.23; *SPW*, pp. 163–164)

One function of virtue is to order these emotions and desires toward the good—that is, toward blessedness. So we have, Aquinas says, a virtue specific to the affective emotions, those that are immediately attracted by pleasure and repelled by pain. This virtue is **temperance**, which brings the impulse to pursue the pleasant and avoid the painful under the tutelage of practical reason. Temperance prevents us from indulging too much in pleasures, keeping us on an even keel and aimed at the blessed state.

With respect to the aggressive feelings, we have a second virtue: **fortitude** or *courage*. Fortitude makes us tenacious in pursuing what our reason determines to be truly good, so that we don't give up easily in the face of obstacles. It is firmness or resolve when temptations arise to distract us from our ultimate good by promising some minor gain. Fortitude is being steadfast rather than wimpy, determined rather than reckless. It keeps us from being overpowered by fear, on the one hand, or being rashly bold on the other.

In addition to these two virtues governing our emotional life, there is **justice**, which ensures that we are not inclined to take more than our share of

goods, or to favor ourselves in some distribution of such goods. Distributive justice does not apply so much to what we feel as to what we do. It has an intrinsic reference to others. To be just is to be fair and equitable in allotting to each person what is due to him or her. A just person, for instance, will not even be tempted to steal money lying in plain sight on someone's desk; to a just person, the possibility of stealing simply doesn't appear in the list of options for action. To truly have the virtue of justice is for it to be *easy* to leave the money there.

Finally, there is **prudence**, a virtue that pertains more directly to the intellect than do the others. Prudence involves habits that lead us to think again when we are being hasty and keep in mind the overall good when we are deliberating.*

These four (temperance, fortitude, justice, and prudence) do not exhaust all the virtues there are, but Aquinas calls them the **cardinal virtues**, the principal or most important of them. If human beings were simply animal beings, with no hope of immortality, these would be sufficient to produce whatever degree of happiness is attainable in this life. If we were restricted to the first two floors of the house, there would be nothing to add. But if it is rational to believe that our good is not exhausted by such bliss as this life offers, blessedness also requires the **theological virtues** of faith, hope, and love.

Here Aquinas self-consciously goes beyond Aristotle. He says that Aristotle understands perfectly well what we require for *eudaemonia* (happiness). But then, confined to this world, he resigns himself to making do with less. Happiness, Aristotle says, is activity of soul, in accord with reason, over an entire lifetime, which cannot be taken away from us, together with modest external goods—the most satisfying activity being that of intellectual contemplation. But Aristotle realizes that happiness in this world is fragile, as his reference to Priam makes clear.† In this life, we are ever subject to fortune, and though he rightly says our highest happiness is in contemplation, he acknowledges that even this cannot be continuously engaged in. So if this life

---

*The traditional terms for these are the *concupiscible* and the *irascible* desires and feelings.

*Compare Aristotle on "practical wisdom," pp. 191–192.
†See p. 188.

is all there is, we can at best approximate the goal that we all have.

What would true happiness consist in, then? It would have to be total immersion in absolute goodness forever—in the presence of and being suffused by that original energy or existence that *is* goodness and is the source of all good. Nothing else would do. That's what we all want, though we don't usually realize it. That's the goal of all our desiring. But we are talking of the mystical vision of God, perhaps of what Aquinas himself tasted briefly during that December mass, after which he could write no more. Philosophy can perhaps point to that bliss, but philosophy cannot supply it. That's a gift reserved for God's grace.

Because we are not self-sufficient in our existence, Aquinas writes, we have a "twofold ultimate goal." We are aiming at an internal perfection, which can only come when we deeply and whole-heartedly love God above all else and love our neighbors as ourselves. And we are aiming at unity with God, the source of all goodness and so also of that very perfection within.

> Bliss then, the ultimate human goal, will be twofold: one within, the ultimate perfection human beings can attain, a created bliss; and one without, union with which causes that bliss within, and this is God himself, an uncreated bliss. (*CPLS,* Bk. 4, 49; *SPW,* p. 328)

> Now the activity of seeing God, which we hold human bliss to be, cannot be measured by time: neither in itself, since it has no before and after, nor on the side of the seer or the seen, since both exist outside change, . . . for seeing God transcends the native power of all creatures and is something no creature can attain by nature. What properly measures it is eternity itself; and the seeing of God, bliss itself, is thus eternal life. (*CPLS,* Bk. 4, 49; *SPW,* p. 332)

---

1. What is the good for humans?
2. In what way does a human being have a will, rather than just a set of desires, like the lower animals?
3. Is the human will free? Why?
4. What distinguishes an act of a human being from a human act?
5. What does Aquinas mean by the natural law? How can we know what the natural law is?
6. Why are the virtues important to us?
7. Explain each of the four cardinal virtues. What does each put in order? And to what end?
8. What is the final source of blessedness for human beings?

Ockham and Skeptical Doubts—Again

Since Augustine rebutted skepticism in the late fourth century, there had been a broad consensus that human minds were capable of knowing the truth.* Thinkers disagreed, often sharply, about what constituted the truth, but these disagreements were almost always conducted on this epistemological common ground. God had created the world, and he created human beings in his own image. It would not have been suitable for God to mismatch reality and the mind. In any case, it was through Wisdom, the *logos*, the second person of the Trinity, that everything was created. So it was natural to suppose that the patterns in reality could be reproduced in the mind.

It is true that our minds are finite and limited. We cannot discover the whole truth on our own. But God has graciously come to our aid; he has revealed to us the truths necessary for our salvation, which are beyond our finite grasp. These revealed truths, which we accept on the authority of the Scriptures and the Church, are not in conflict with the truths we can discover on our own. How could they be, since both come ultimately from the same God? Revealed truth supplements our rational knowledge, completes it, and provides an overall framework within which all correct believing and knowing are carried on.

We must add two further notes to this happy picture.

1. Knowledge is understood in that very strong classical sense delineated by Plato when he distinguishes it from opinion.† In medieval philosophy, the requirement that knowledge "stays put" or "endures" is understood to mean that it involves

---

*Review his arguments on pp. 232–234.
†See pp. 119–121.

absolute certainty. If you *know* something, you are certain of it; you are not about to be shaken by any stray wind that might blow some doubts your way. As with Plato, this feature is correlated with the fact that knowledge is something for which reasons can be given. The reasons are sometimes based on logic, sometimes on experience, and sometimes on the Scriptures—often on a combination of them. But there is always "an account" that can be given.

2. Knowledge, and the certainty that goes with it, is crucially important. It is absolutely essential to get it right, because your eternal salvation depends on getting it right. That is why **heresy**—erroneous belief—is so terrifying. The difference between correct, or orthodox, belief and heresy is the difference between *heaven* and *hell*. So it is not just an attempt to satisfy Aristotelian "wonder" that motivates the medieval theologians and philosophers.* Getting it right has an intensely personal and practical aspect.

All this is common ground in the thirteenth century. On these foundations Thomas Aquinas builds a remarkably comprehensive system of thought. We can call it a system because it is cleanly ordered, its parts are interdependent, and it aspires to completeness. The kind of confidence in the intellect that Aquinas expresses has perhaps not been seen since the time of Aristotle himself.

It is surprising to learn that this systematic synthesis, so marvelous in its way, is being undermined already in the fourteenth century. Doubts raise their ugly heads once again: doubts not about some detail, but about the very foundation that has been taken for granted in the centuries since Augustine. It is even more surprising to learn that these doubts have their source not, as you might suspect, among some atheist or agnostic folks who can't accept the claims about revealed truth, but among theologians whose orthodoxy (at least on central issues) is beyond question.[5]

"I believe in one God, the Father Almighty," begins the Nicene Creed. What does this mean?

During the medieval period, God's **omnipotence** is understood to mean that he can do anything that is not self-contradictory. He cannot make a cube with only five sides, since by definition a cube has six sides. Nor can he make something that did happen not happen; for in this case it would be true of some event x that x both happened and did not happen—and that is contradictory. But since contradictory expressions do not describe real possibilities, this is no limitation on God's power. God can do anything that is possible. For any state of affairs that can be given a consistent description, then, God can realize that state of affairs. This doctrine is important partly because it protects the possibility of miracles.

Among those who derive some surprising consequences from this doctrine is **William of Ockham** (born in the 1280s and died about 1349). Ockham was English, taught at Oxford, and was embroiled in some nasty confrontations between his Franciscan order and the pope. Like all the major philosophers of the period, he thinks of himself first and foremost as a theologian. He is also a very acute logician who makes some important contributions concerning the status of logical principles and the structure of knowledge. Any adequate treatment of Ockham's thought would have to include his logic. But we will concentrate on what he says about the omnipotence of God—specifically, on the impact this doctrine has on views of the world and our knowledge of it.

Consider the following kind of case. You are sitting at a table, in good light, looking directly at a tangerine about three feet in front of your eyes. You are wide awake, not under the influence of any drugs, and are paying attention to what is before you. This seems to be the most favorable sort of case we can imagine for knowing something. We would ordinarily say that you know that there is a tangerine on the table.

But what does your knowledge consist in? It is clearly some state of yourself—what Ockham calls an "intuitive cognition." In standard cases, we think, this state is caused in part by the tangerine and in part by your sense organs and intellect. The first part of the cause is a matter of how the

---

*See Aristotle on wonder, p. 171.

world is—that there happens to be a tangerine on the table. The second part is a matter of how you are—where you are, whether your eyes are open, whether you have learned what a tangerine is, and so on. In the standard case, your "intuitive cognition" of the tangerine depends both on the actual existence of a tangerine on the table and on a suitable state within you. Ockham does not deny this.

But now consider the impact that the doctrine of God's omnipotence has on this case. God, remember, can do anything that is not self-contradictory. This means that he can cause to happen anything that does not have an inconsistent description. God has created a world that operates as we have described in the foregoing standard case. But could God *directly* cause you to have that "intuitive cognition" of the tangerine? In the standard case, your experience is caused by the presence of the tangerine, but could God cause this experience without the mediation of the actual piece of fruit?

To answer this question, we must ask whether that would be self-contradictory. And it is easy to see that it is not. The presence of that piece of fruit on the table neither entails nor is entailed by your "intuitive cognition" of it. Either, so far as logic goes, could exist without the other. So, God could cause you to have such an experience even in the absence of the tangerine.

What is the consequence of this line of reasoning? Evidently, our conviction that we *know* that the tangerine exists—even in this most favorable case—is mistaken. For knowledge, remember, involves absolute certainty that could not possibly be mistaken. But if God can produce in us the internal state that is usually caused by the tangerine even in the absence of the tangerine, there is a possibility that our "intuitive cognition" is mistaken.

At best, our belief that there is a tangerine in front of us is merely *probable* belief. It amounts to no more than what Plato calls "opinion." But since all our knowledge of the world rests ultimately on such favorable cases of "intuitive cognition," the claim to know is seriously undermined.

Ockham does not draw the completely skeptical conclusion that knowledge is impossible for us. But

these reflections deal a serious blow to confidence in our ability to find such absolute knowledge. And, as you can see, the blow comes from a consideration of what God's omnipotence implies.

A similar conclusion follows about the causality we claim to find in the world independent of ourselves. A piece of cloth is brought near a flame and starts to burn. How are we to explain the burning? It might be possible for God to cause it directly, so that our usual account in terms of the causal efficacy of the fire would be mistaken.* Again, the best we can do is to give probable explanations of why things happen in the world. It seems that our explanations might always be mistaken. And if that isn't skepticism itself, it surely seems to move us toward skeptical doubts, especially if one insists at the same time that knowledge must involve absolute certainty.

This produces a very interesting situation. For a thousand years thinkers assumed that reason and revelation are compatible, that reason can supply foundations—with certainty—for revelation to build upon. Philosophy, the pursuit of wisdom by our human wits, has been treated as the "handmaiden" of theology, which in turn is the "queen" of the sciences. And suddenly the suspicion arises that perhaps natural reason and experience are not well suited for this task!

Let us ask what effect this has on attempts to prove the existence of God. Such proofs are a main part of the service that philosophy is supposed to provide to theology. Ockham himself thinks that a certain form of proof is still possible, but let us consider some propositions put forward in the late fourteenth century by Pierre d'Ailly, a cardinal of the Church. He is discussing Aristotle's argument for a first mover (which was adapted by Aquinas in his "first way").† And he considers what a "captious debater" could say.

---

*We have here an anticipation of one of the most influential of all treatments of causality, that by David Hume in the eighteenth century. Hume does not depend on the doctrine of God's omnipotence; and the skeptical consequences are more determinedly drawn. See "Causation: The Very Idea," in Chapter 15.

†See again pp. 271–272.

1. It is not unqualifiedly evident that something is moved; movement may be only apparent. . . .
2. Even if we grant that an object is in motion, we do not have to grant that it comes from some other object.
3. Granted that all motion originates in another thing and granting that there is no infinite series of movers, we cannot infer a first unmoved mover, for the first mover might be unmoved for the present but not absolutely unmovable.
4. We cannot exclude the possibility that there is a circularity of causes and effects, i.e., A causes B, B causes C, and C causes A.
5. We cannot be sure that there is no infinity of essentially ordered causes. For God by His absolute power could create such an infinite series.
6. It is not evident that if something exists anew, it was produced.
7. It is very difficult to explain what it means for one thing to be effected or produced by another thing.[6]

This piling up of alternative possibilities that have not been definitively excluded seriously undermines our confidence in the "proof." At the very least, it shows us that a defender of the argument will have to do a lot more work if the argument is to succeed. It appears much less than certain that there must be a first mover, which all men call God.

It is important to note that d'Ailly does not intend to call the existence of God into question. Far from it. That God exists we know on the authority of the Scriptures and the Church. Rather, such reflections serve to undermine confidence in our natural ability to substantiate such truths apart from authority—at least with the certainty necessary for faith. (The cardinal allows that a *probable* argument for God's existence can be constructed.) Skepticism such as this, then, casts us more firmly than ever into the arms of the Church, which has such truths in its care. The moral is this: Aristotle and those who, like him, rely on our natural reason, should be approached with caution.

It seems then that the late Middle Ages is busily undoing what the earlier Middle Ages has done. It is engaging in a critique of the basic assumptions that have made the grand synthesis of classical and Christian thought possible. When several more ingredients are added to this furiously boiling pot—namely, the scientific revolution, the humanism of the Renaissance, and the impact of the Reformation on the Church—the modern era in philosophy will begin.

---

1. What assumptions about knowledge do thinkers in the late Middle Ages commonly make?
2. What Aristotelian views were condemned as heretical?
3. What effect did this condemnation have?
4. What impact does Ockham's reflection on God's omnipotence have on our claim to know something?
5. What impact does it seem to have on proofs for the existence of God?

FOR FURTHER THOUGHT

1. If you think Anselm's argument is faulty, write a brief explanation of what, exactly, is wrong with it.
2. What do you think about the prospects for proving that there is a God? (Don't just react. Give a reasoned explanation for your answer.)
3. Can God make a stone so heavy that he can't lift it? If he can't, does that mean his power is limited?
4. If our life is limited to this world, does that mean true happiness is impossible?

KEY WORDS

Anselm	will
ontological argument	natural law
God	eternal law
reductio ad absurdum	human law
essence	divine law
existence	virtue
Thomas Aquinas	temperance
hylomorphism	fortitude
analogy	justice
angels	prudence
soul	cardinal virtues
intellect	theological virtues
universals	heresy
quiddity	omnipotence
truth	William of Ockham

NOTES

1. Jasper Hopkins, *A Companion to the Study of St. Anselm* (Minneapolis: University of Minnesota Press, 1972), 17.

2. Quotations from Anselm's *Proslogium*, in *St. Anselm: Basic Writings*, trans. S. N. Deane (La Salle, IL: Open Court, 1962), are cited in the text by chapter number.

3. Quotations from Thomas Aquinas are from one of the following:

   St. Thomas Aquinas: Philosophical Texts, trans. Thomas Gilby (London: Oxford University Press, 1951), abbreviated as *PT*, or

   Aquinas: Selected Philosophical Writings, trans. Timothy McDermott (New York: Oxford University Press, 1993), abbreviated as *SPW*.

   References are first to the source in Aquinas, then to page numbers in these collections. References to the works of Aquinas are as follows:

   ST: *Summa Theologica*
   DT: *Commentary on Boethius' De Trinitate*
   BE: *On Being and Essence*
   DPG: *Disputations on the Power of God*
   PDS: *Public Disputations on the Soul*
   CC: *Commentary on St. Paul's First Letter to the Corinthians*
   PDT: *Public Disputations on Truth*
   CPLS: *Commentary on Peter Lombard's Sentences*
   SCG: *Summa Contra Gentiles*

4. Patterson Brown, "Infinite Causal Regression," in *Aquinas: A Collection of Critical Essays*, ed. Anthony Kenny (London: Macmillan, 1969), 234–235.

5. I am especially indebted in this section to Julius R. Weinberg's *Short History of Medieval Philosophy* (Princeton, NJ: Princeton University Press, 1964).

6. Cited in Weinberg, *Short History of Medieval Philosophy*, 287–288.

CHAPTER

12

MOVING FROM MEDIEVAL TO MODERN

It is not clear just when the modern era begins. But it cannot be denied that something of immense significance happens in the sixteenth and seventeenth centuries that changes life and thought startlingly. In philosophy the beginnings of modernity are usually attributed to René Descartes (1596–1650). Though there are other plausible candidates for the title of "father of modern philosophy," it is the work of Descartes that sets the agenda for most of what we call "modern" in philosophy. Despite the fact that he shares with medieval philosophers many concerns and convictions, Descartes sees clearly that a new beginning is required. He dramatically poses fundamental questions. And, although his own answers to these questions will satisfy few of his successors, they all see that an answer is required. Generations of philosophers will worry about solving the problems Descartes uncovers.

We can classify these problems under three heads.

1. Descartes, himself a distinguished mathematician and contributor to physics, sees with blinding clarity the need to assimilate the methods and results of the *new sciences* into our picture of the world. Copernicus, Kepler, and Galileo had reoriented thinking about both Earth and the heavens. Their new conceptions clash badly with the old, so some tearing down and rebuilding is called for.

2. Paradoxically, and to some extent accidentally, *skepticism* has arisen once more from its ashes—this phoenix that first Plato and then Augustine sought to slay.* Fueled by Reformation quarrels among the churches and lack of agreement among philosophers and scientists, the doubts of Sextus Empiricus spread rapidly among Renaissance intellectuals.† Descartes sees that skepticism cuts at the root of the claims made by science, philosophy, and religion alike. If we are going to rely on any one of them to tell us how things are, skepticism

---

*For Plato's attempt at refutation, see p. 121; for Augustine's, pp. 232–234.

†For a discussion of ancient skepticism, featuring the views of Sextus, see "The Skeptics," in Chapter 8.

will have to be taken on again—and this time killed for good.

3. Both of the first two problems mean that much closer attention will have to be paid to *knowledge*. Epistemological questions begin to take center stage. Can we know anything at all? And if so, by what means? Do the sciences give us knowledge of reality? If they do, how can we be sure of that? This preoccupation with epistemological questions is the principal heritage of Descartes. In ancient and medieval philosophy, questions about knowledge are just one sort of question among many others. But after Descartes they seem absolutely preeminent. *Unless you can solve these problems, no other problems can be solved.*

Those are Descartes' problems: the problems of modern philosophy. But to feel the force of them as problems we need to back up a bit and sketch the context. His age is intellectually, and in other ways as well, one of the most tumultuous we have ever lived through. Though we are interested primarily in the intellectual ferment, we cannot help but note some of the social, political, and economic factors that make this an age of change. It is useful to start with a review of the medieval picture of the world.

The World God Made for Us

Though there was by no means unanimity in the late Middle Ages about details, there was broad agreement about a certain picture of the world.[1] The universe, people thought, is a harmonious and coherent whole, created by an infinite and good God as an appropriate home for human beings, for whose sake it was made. It is difficult for us now to put ourselves into the place of medieval men and women and to see the world as they saw it. But let us try.

It will help if we try to set aside all we have learned in school about the structure of the universe and attempt to recapture a more direct and naive interpretation of our experience. Consider the sky as you see it on a clear day or night. If you look *at* it, rather than *through* it, as those with our picture of the world tend to do, you will almost certainly conclude that it has a certain shape. It is *something* (as our term "the sky" tends to suggest),

and it has roughly the shape of an upside-down bowl. It is the roof of the earth, the "firmament" of Genesis 1 that God created to separate the primeval waters and make a place for dry land and living creatures. This view of the heavens is very common among primitive people and among children, too. We have to *learn* that the sky is not a thing.

This primitive view of the sky undergoes a great deal of rather sophisticated development by the later Middle Ages, but two things remain constant. It is still considered a thing, and its nature is defined in terms of its relation to the earth. The development is largely due to the efforts of ancient philosophers (particularly Plato and Aristotle) and astronomers, especially an Egyptian astronomer of the second century A.D., named **Ptolemy**. How do they modify this primitive view?

For one thing, the earth is recognized to be roughly a sphere, so the heavens can't be completely analogous to the roof of a house or a tent. They, in fact, are spherical, too. The basic picture is of two spheres, the smaller one solid and stationary directly in the center of a much larger sphere, which is hollow and moving. The sphere in the center is, of course, the earth. And the outer sphere, composed of aether, a crystalline, weightless solid, is that of the stars, which revolve around the inner sphere once each day.

Astronomical observations complicate this picture considerably. Neither the sun nor the moon fits neatly into such a scheme, and they are given spheres of their own. Even more recalcitrant to neatness are those wanderers in the heavens, the planets. They seem to move in more complicated patterns, both speed and direction varying at irregular times. Much astronomical ingenuity had been devoted to the mathematical description of their paths; postulations of circles revolving around centers that are themselves revolving on circles are used to solve these problems. But the basic pattern is the same: Each planet is assigned an etherial sphere. Saturn occupies the sphere just below that of the fixed stars, and the moon occupies that nearest to the earth, with the sun and the other planets arranged between.

This universe is said to be finite. Aristotle holds that beyond the outer sphere there is literally nothing—no matter, no space, not even a void.* For medieval Christians, however, there is something beyond the sphere of the stars. It is often called simply heaven, but sometimes also the **Empyrean**, the place of perfect fire or light; it is the dwelling place of God and the destination of saved souls. (Note that heaven, in this view, has a physical location. From any place on earth, it is *up*.)

In this universe, everything has its natural place. The earth is the center toward which heavy objects naturally fall. The heavy elements, earth and water, find their natural place as near this center as they can. The lighter elements, air and fire, have a natural home between the earth and the sphere of the moon. But these four elements are continually being mixed up with one another and suffer constant change.

This change is explained by the motions of the heavens.† Aristotle supplies a mechanism to explain such change. The outermost celestial sphere rotates at great speed, as it must to return to the same position in only twenty-four hours. (Compare the speed at the inside of a merry-go-round with that at its edge.) This motion drags the sphere of Saturn (just inside it) along by friction; and this process is repeated all the way to the spheres of the sun and moon. These then produce changes in the air and on the earth: the tides, the winds, and the seasons, for example, and the generation of plants and animals. We may wonder, though: Why does the sphere of the stars move? Dante, whose *Divine Comedy* is a perfect expression of this view of the world, offers an Aristotelian explanation in terms of final causes.

Beyond all these [crystalline spheres], the Catholics place the Empyrean Heaven . . . , and they hold

it to be immovable, because it has within itself, in every part, that which its matter demands. And this is the reason that the *Primum Mobile* [or ninth sphere] moves with immense velocity; because the fervent longing of all its parts to be united with those of this most quiet heaven, makes it revolve with so much desire that its velocity is almost incomprehensible.[2]

The **celestial spheres** are quite different from anything on Earth. Here on Earth, all is subject to change, generation, and decay. But the spheres in which the heavenly bodies are located revolve in immutable splendor. Only one conclusion can be drawn: Terrestrial and celestial substances are made of different stuff and governed by different laws. Spiritual beings—angels, for instance, whom Aquinas holds to be pure forms without matter—have their home in these more perfect regions.

It is obvious—consider only the sun—that what happens in these spheres affects conditions on earth. Medievals drew the conclusion that signs in the heavens—comets and eclipses, for instance—are omens that need interpretation. What they mean is scarcely distinguishable from what the spiritual beings that dwell in those regions mean to convey. Virtually every astronomer is also an astrologer; as late as the seventeenth century, Kepler, recognized to possess unusually accurate astronomical data, is consulted for horoscopes, and reference to astrological phenomena is common in the work of Dante and Chaucer. Everything in the heavens is significant because it all exists for the sake of man.

Here we come to the heart of the medieval worldview. The earth is not only the physical center of the universe; it is also the religious center. For on this stationary globe lives the human race, made in the image of God himself, the summit of his creative work. Around human beings everything revolves, both literally and symbolically. The earth is the stage whereon is enacted the great drama of salvation and damnation. It is on the earth that human beings fall from grace. It is to the earth that God's Son comes to redeem fallen men and women and lead them to that heavenly realm in which they can forever enjoy blessedness in light eternal.

Nothing expresses this drama in its intimate connection with the medieval picture of the world

---

*Aristotle does not accept the atomists' conception of a *void,* that is, a space in which nothing exists. His reasoning depends on the notion of potentiality. Wherever there is space, there is potentially some substance. But potentiality is just the possibility of having some form; and what is formed into a substance is matter. So wherever there is space there is matter; matter never exists unformed; so the idea of empty space is a contradiction in terms. There could not be other worlds out in space beyond this world; this world is not just the only world there is, but the only world there *could be*.

†See the pre-Socratic speculations about the vortex, pp. 13–14.

better than Dante's great poem.* The journey on which he is led, first by Virgil and later by Beatrice, traverses the known universe. As we follow that journey we learn both physical and religious truths, inextricably linked. Let us trace the outline of that journey.

Dante begins his great poem by telling us that he had lost his way and could not find it again. (Suggestion: read the poetry aloud.)

> Midway life's journey I was made aware
> That I had strayed into a dark forest,
> And the right path appeared not anywhere.
> Ah, tongue cannot describe how it oppressed,
> This wood, so harsh, dismal and wild, that fear
> At thought of it strikes now into my breast.
>
> —*Inferno* 1.1–6[3]

The pagan poet **Virgil** appears and offers to lead him down through hell and up through purgatory as far as the gates of heaven. There he will be supplanted by another guide, as Virgil is not allowed into paradise. A vision of these moral and religious realities, embedded as they are in the very nature of things, should resolve Dante's crisis and show him the way again. It may also serve as a guide to the blessed life for all who read the poem.

We can read this complex allegory with an eye only to the values it expresses, but there is little doubt that Dante means its cosmology to be taken with equal seriousness. The point we need to see is that the cosmos, as envisaged by late medieval thinkers, is not an indifferent and valueless place; every detail speaks of its creator, and the "right path" is inscribed in the very structure of things.

We can do no more than briefly indicate that structure. There are three books in the poem: *Inferno, Purgatorio,* and *Paradiso.* In each a portion of the physical and moral/religious universe is explored. The first thing to note is that to get to hell (the inferno), one goes *down*—deep into the earth. Hell is a complex place of many layers; as one descends, the sins of its occupants become more serious, the punishments more awful, and the conditions more revolting. After an antechamber in which the indifferent reside (offensive both

to God and to Satan), Dante and Virgil cross the river Acheron and find hell set up as a series of circles, descending ever deeper into the earth. The first circle is limbo, in which are found the virtuous pagans, including Homer and Aristotle; this is Virgil's own home. Here there is no overt punishment; only the lack of hope for blessedness.

Descending from limbo, they find the damned in circles of increasingly awful punishments, corresponding to their sins:

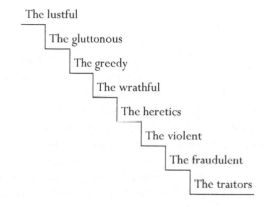

The lustful
The gluttonous
The greedy
The wrathful
The heretics
The violent
The fraudulent
The traitors

These last are frozen up to their necks in ice at the very center of the earth, guarded over by Satan—the arch traitor—in whose three mouths are the mangled bodies of Judas, Brutus, and Cassius.

Virgil and Dante climb down past Satan and climb up again through a passage in the earth until they come out on the opposite side from which they began. There they find themselves on a shore, facing a mountain that rises to the sky. This is the mountain of purgatory, where those who will ultimately be saved are purified of their remaining faults. Here there are seven levels (corresponding to the "seven deadly sins"), each populated by persons whose loves are not yet rightly ordered.* These have repented and will be saved, but they still love earthly things too much, or not enough, or in the wrong way. From the lower levels to the higher, the unpurged sins are ranked from more to less serious, those highest on the mountain being farthest from hell and closest to heaven. Let us list

---

*Dante's *Divine Comedy* was written in the first decades of the fourteenth century.

*For the concept of a proper ordering of one's loves, see Augustine, p. 250.

them in that "geographical" order, so that we can imagine Virgil and Dante mounting from the bottom of the list to the top:

Those who dwell at each level are purging their predominant passion by suffering penances of an appropriate kind. The proud, for example, are bowed down by carrying heavy stones, so that they can neither look arrogantly about nor look down on their fellows. It is worth noting that the "spiritual" sins of pride, envy, and anger are judged to be more serious (farther from heaven) than the "fleshly" sins of gluttony and lust; this ranking roughly corresponds to the evaluations of church fathers such as Augustine, for whom pride is the root of all sin.*

At the top of the purgatorial mountain, Virgil disappears, and **Beatrice**, who represents Christian love, takes his place. She transports Dante through the sphere of fire above the earth to the lowest celestial sphere, that of the moon. She answers Dante's question about why the moon seems to have shadows on it and in the process gives a fine description of the celestial realm, which looks roughly like this:

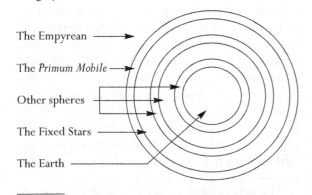

---

*For Augustine on pride, see pp. 246–247.

You can see that it conforms nicely to the Aristotelian/Ptolemic astronomical view we sketched earlier. Motion (energy) is imparted from outside toward the center, each of the spheres displaying in its own magnificent way the glory of God. This vision of the heavens as the visible image of the creator is summed up in the first canto of *Paradiso*.

> The glory of Him who moveth all that is
> Pervades the universe, and glows more bright
> In the one region, and in another less. . . .

> "All things, whatever their abode, [*Beatrice says*]
> Have order among themselves; this Form it is
> That makes the universe like unto God.

> Here the high beings see the imprint of His
> Eternal power, which is the goal divine
> Whereto the rule, aforesaid testifies.

> In the order I speak of, all natures incline
> Either more near or less near to their source
> According as their diverse lots assign.

> To diverse harbors thus they move perforce
> O'er the great ocean of being, and each one
> With instinct given it to maintain its course."
> —*Paradiso* 1.1–3, 103–114

The key notions in Dante's vision of the universe are order, harmony, justice, and, finally, love. The poem ends with Dante trying to describe, inadequately he admits, the vision of God. This vision is both intelligible and emotional. Its object both explains the universe and draws Dante's soul toward itself. In the end, imagination fails to communicate the glory.

> But like to a wheel whose circling nothing jars
> Already on my desire and will prevailed
> The Love that moves the sun and the other stars.
> —*Paradiso* 33.143–145

Such is the world for late medieval man: harmonious, ordered, finite, displaying the glories of its creator. Physics, astronomy, and theology are one in a marvelous integration of life and knowledge. Everything in the universe embodies a goal and purpose set within it by the divine love, which governs all. To understand it is to understand this purpose, to gain guidance for life, and to see that absolutely everything depends on and leads to God.

1. Describe the Aristotelian/Ptolemaic picture of the universe.
2. Why, given that picture of the universe, is it appropriate for Virgil and Beatrice to take Dante on a tour of the world in order to show him "the right path"?
3. What do the levels in hell and purgatory show us about virtue and vice?

The Humanists

That magnificent flowering of arts and letters we call the Renaissance is greatly influenced by the rediscovery of classical literature—poetry, histories, essays, and other writings—that followed the recovery of Aristotelian philosophy.* These Greek and Roman works breathe a spirit quite different from the extreme otherworldliness of monk's vows, on the one hand, and the arid disputations of scholastic theologians on the other. They present a model of style, both in language and life, that seems worthy of emulation. And a rather diffuse movement called **humanism** spreads gradually northward from Italy.

Some of the humanists are churchmen, but many are not. They belong to that aristocratic stratum of society that has leisure to cultivate the arts, paint, compose, or write. They are not, on the whole, antagonistic to the Church; nor do most of them pit the old pagan classical works against Christianity. On the contrary, they tend to see a profound harmony between Christianity and the classics. In this they are, of course, following in the steps of Augustine and Aquinas. But there is a difference. These theologians hold that pagan philosophy can be a servant to Christian understanding—but never its equal. Many humanists, however, equate faith with virtue and move toward a kind of universalism: The virtuous sage is blessed, whether he knows of Christ as savior or not.

In a dialogue called "The Godly Feast," printed in 1522, **Erasmus** (the "prince of humanists") has one of the characters say,

> Whatever is devout and contributes to good morals should not be called profane. Sacred Scripture is of course the basic authority in everything; yet I sometimes run across ancient sayings or pagan writings—even the poets—so purely and reverently and admirably expressed that I can't help believing their authors' hearts were moved by some divine power. And perhaps the spirit of Christ is more widespread than we understand, and the company of saints includes many not in our calendar.[4]

One of his partners in the conversation, on being reminded of Socrates' attitude at his death, exclaims,*

> An admirable spirit, surely, in one who had not known Christ and the Sacred Scriptures. And so, when I read such things of such men, I can hardly help exclaiming, "Saint Socrates, pray for us!"[5]

In another dialogue, "The Epicurean," Erasmus argues that those who spend their lives pursuing fine food, sex, wealth, fame, and power in a quest for pleasure actually miss the greatest pleasures: those of righteousness, moderation, an active mind, and a calm conscience. It is Epicurus, of course, who holds that pleasure is the one true good.† It follows that the *successful* Epicurean—the one who gets the most pleasure out of life—will live righteously and moderately, preferring the approval of God to the satisfaction of bodily appetites. But these are precisely the virtues cultivated by the Christian!

> If people who live agreeably are Epicureans, none are more truly Epicurean than the righteous and godly. And if it's names that bother us, no one better deserves the name of Epicurean than the revered founder and head of the Christian philosophy [Christ], for in Greek *epikouros* means "helper." He alone, when the law of Nature was all but blotted out by sins, when the law of Moses incited to lusts

---

*For the Renaissance, see http://en.wikipedia.org/wiki/Renaissance.

*Contrast this with Dante's vision two hundred years earlier, in which virtuous pagans are consigned—at best—to limbo. See *Inferno,* canto IV. For the last moments of Socrates' life, see *Phaedo,* pp. 115–117.

†See pp. 198–203.

rather than cured them, when Satan ruled in the world unchallenged, brought timely aid to perishing humanity. Completely mistaken, therefore, are those who talk in their foolish fashion about Christ's having been sad and gloomy in character and calling upon us to follow a dismal mode of life. On the contrary, he alone shows the most enjoyable life of all and the one most full of true pleasure.[6]

This gives us an insight into why these thinkers are called humanists.* Their concern is the development of a full and rich human life—the best life for a human being to live. Their quest is stimulated by the works of classical antiquity, which they read, edit, translate, and imitate with eagerness. They live, of course, in a culture dominated by Christianity and express that quest in basically Christian terms, but their interests focus on the human. To that end they recommend and propagandize for what they call "humane studies": an education centering on the Greek and Latin classics, on languages, grammar, and rhetoric. They are convinced that "the classics represent the highest level of human development."[7]

The ideal is a person who can embody all the excellences a human being is capable of: music, art, poetry, science, soldiery, courtesy, virtue, and piety. This renewed passion for human excellence is expressed in the art of Bellini, Titian, Tintoretto, Raphael, Holbein, Dürer, and Michelangelo. In these Renaissance painters and sculptors, one finds the ideal human form, often in an idealized natural setting—whether the subject is the Christian Madonna and child or Greek gods and heroes. And sometimes classical and biblical themes are found in the same painting.† The man who embodies this Renaissance ideal most completely is perhaps Leonardo **da Vinci**. His many accomplishments show what humans are capable of. He represents what humanists admired and worked for: a celebration of the human being as the central fact in all the created world.

---

*Note that Erasmus here follows the lead of much Greek thought, from Homer to Epicurus. Pursuit of virtue is recommended on basis of *self-interest*. Why be moral? Because you will be happier that way.

†We already find this unification in Dante, but there the classical is still severely subordinated to the Christian.

In the 1480s, a twenty-four-year-old Italian wrote a preface to nine hundred theses that he submitted for public debate. As it turned out, the debate was never held, but the *Oration on the Dignity of Man* by Giovanni **Pico della Mirandola** has seldom been equalled as a rhetorical tribute to the glory of being human. We could say it is the apotheosis of humanism. Pico finds the unique dignity of man in the fact that human beings alone have no "archetype" they are predetermined to exemplify. Everything else has a determinate nature, but it is man's privilege to be able to *choose* his own nature. He imagines God creating the world. All is complete, from the intelligences above the heavens to the lowest reaches of earth.

> But, when the work was finished, the Craftsman kept wishing that there were someone to ponder the plan of so great a work, to love its beauty, and to wonder at its vastness. Therefore, when everything was done . . . He finally took thought concerning the creation of man. But there was not among His archetypes that from which He could fashion a new offspring, nor was there in His treasure-houses anything which He might bestow on His new son as an inheritance, nor was there in the seats of all the world a place where the latter might sit to contemplate the universe. All was now complete. . . .
>
> At last the best of artisans ordained that that creature to whom He had been able to give nothing proper to himself should have joint possession of whatever had been peculiar to each of the different kinds of being. He therefore took man as a creature of indeterminate nature and, assigning him a place in the middle of the world, addressed him thus: "Neither a fixed abode nor a form that is thine alone nor any function peculiar to thyself have we given thee, Adam, to the end that according to thy longing and according to thy judgment thou mayest have and possess what abode, what form and what functions thou thyself shalt desire. The nature of all other beings is limited and constrained within the bounds of laws prescribed by Us. Thou, constrained by no limits, in accordance with thine own free will, in whose hand We have placed thee, shalt ordain for thyself the limits of thy nature. We have set thee at the world's center that thou mayest from thence more easily observe whatever is in the world. We have made

thee neither of heaven nor of earth, neither mortal nor immortal, so that with freedom of choice and with honor, as though the maker and molder of thyself, thou mayest fashion thyself in whatever shape thou shalt prefer. Thou shalt have the power to degenerate into the lower forms of life, which are brutish. Thou shalt have the power, out of thy soul's judgment, to be reborn into the higher forms, which are divine."

O supreme generosity of God the Father, O highest and most marvelous felicity of man! To him it is granted to have whatever he chooses, to be whatever he wills.[8]

Man as "maker and molder" of himself, able "to have whatever he chooses, to be whatever he wills." What a concept! Pico exclaims, "Who would not admire this our chameleon?"[9] With such possibilities open to them, it is no wonder that human beings should develop in so many different ways. Along with the theme of an essential unity that runs through humanity, the diversity of individuals comes to be valued more and more. **Individualism**, the idea that there is value to sheer uniqueness, begins to counter the uniformity of Christian schemes of salvation. Portrait painters strive to capture the unique character of each of their subjects, and variety and invention flourish in music and literature.

Finally, the humanists recapture some of the confidence that had characterized Athenians of the Golden Age. Human failings are more apt to be caricatured as foolishness (as Erasmus satirically did in *Praise of Folly*) than to be condemned as sins. And this reveals a quite different attitude and spirit. Though the humanists do not deny sin and God's grace, they tend to focus on our capability to achieve great things. As often happens in such cases, they thereby help to make great things happen.

---

1. What rediscoveries stimulate the movement we know as Renaissance humanism?
2. Describe the ideal human life, as pictured by the humanists.
3. In what feature of human beings does Pico della Mirandola find their "dignity"?

Reforming the Church

The worldview Dante expresses in his great poem was institutionalized in the Church. The Church was the keeper and protector of Christian truths and the harbor of salvation for those at sea in sin. But the institutional Church had strayed far from the precepts of humility and love enjoined by Jesus. It had become a means of securing worldly prestige, power, and wealth for those who were clever and ruthless enough to bend it to their will.

The Church in the West was dominated by the papacy in Rome, whose occupants had, through the centuries, succeeded in bringing under their control a great variety of incomes, privileges, and powers. Popes were continually engaged in political intrigues to establish and extend their power. More than one pope during this period exceeded in influence, wealth, and power any secular prince, king, or emperor. His court was more splendid, his staff more extensive, and his will more feared than theirs. For a king could, if need be, torture and kill the body; but the pope had the power to cast the soul into hell. If displeased with a monarch, the pope could put an entire land under the "interdict," which meant that no masses and no sacraments could be celebrated there—a dire threat indeed for those who depended on them for their eternal salvation.

No one doubts—and few doubted even then—that the Church had grown corrupt. Already in the fourteenth century Dante had set several popes, bishops, friars, and priests in the Inferno. There had been numerous attempts at reform. The establishment of new monastic orders by Saint Francis and Saint Dominic had been motivated by a desire to recapture the purity of Christian life by renouncing wealth and power. Unfortunately, their very success ensured the acquisition of wealth and power, with all the inevitable outcomes. Heretical groups, such as the Albigenses in southern France, mixed moral rigor with unacceptable theologies. (The Albigenses were exterminated after a twenty-year "crusade" called for by Pope Innocent III.)

The notorious **Inquisition** was established in 1231 under Pope Gregory IX, and heresy hunting gained official sanction. Heresy was considered "the greatest of all sins because it was an affront to the greatest of persons, God; worse than treason against a king because it was directed against the heavenly sovereign; worse than counterfeiting money because it counterfeited the truth of salvation; worse than patricide and matricide, which destroy only the body." If a heretic recanted under torture, he "might be granted the mercy of being strangled before being burned at the stake."[10]

Unless they could be assimilated into the structure of the Church, as the monastic orders were, reformers were harshly dealt with. The followers of John Wycliffe in England (the Lollards) were sent to the stake in 1401. Jan (John) Hus of Bohemia was burned in 1415. Savonarola of Florence was hanged and then burned in 1498. Meanwhile the Church, clutching its pomp and privileges, went from corruption to corruption. Here are a few examples. Pope Alexander VI had four illegitimate children (including Cesare and Lucrezia Borgia), though clerical celibacy was the rule. Pope Julius II led his own troops in armor to regain certain papal territories. And Leo X, made a cardinal through family influence at the age of thirteen, is said to have exclaimed after his election as pope, "The papacy is ours. Let us enjoy it."[11]

Albert of Brandenburg, already bishop of two districts, aspired to be also Archbishop of Mainz, which would make him the top cleric in Germany. The price demanded by the pope was high—ten thousand ducats. Because his parishes could not supply that fee, he paid it himself, borrowing the money at 20 percent interest from the banking house of Fugger. It was agreed that "indulgences" (more about these later) would be sold in his territories; half of the income he could use to repay the loan and half would go to Rome to help build Saint Peter's Cathedral.

Such examples, which could be multiplied indefinitely, called forth a steady stream of critical responses. In the eyes of many, they discredited the claim of the Church to be the repository of truth about God and man. But it was not until the protests of **Martin Luther** (1483–1546) that the situation was ripe for such moral objections to make a real difference. Luther's appeal for reform

coincided with a new assertion of the rights of nations against domination by the Church. Princes heard not only the cry for religious reform but also an opportunity to stop wealth and power from flowing interminably to Rome.*

Luther was a monk troubled about his sins and in mortal terror of God's justice. His sins did not in fact seem so terrible in the eyes of the world, for he was a monk of a most sincere and strict kind. But he had early seen the point that God looks not at externals, but at motivations; and he could not be sure that his motives were pure.† No matter how much he confessed, he was never confident that he had searched out every tinge of selfishness, greed, lust, and pride. And these sins the righteous God would judge. Luther did penances of a rigorous sort, going so far as to scourge himself. But he could never be sure: Had he done enough to make himself worthy of salvation? He suffered agonies of doubt and self-accusation.

> Though I lived as a monk without reproach, I felt that I was a sinner before God with an extremely disturbed conscience. I could not believe that he was placated by my satisfaction. I did not love, yes, I hated the righteous God who punishes sinners, and secretly, if not blasphemously, certainly murmuring greatly, I was angry with God.[12]

He was assigned by his superior to study the Bible and become a professor of theology. As he wrestled with the text of the Psalms and the letters of Saint Paul, it gradually dawned on him that his anxieties about sin were misplaced. He was, to be sure, a sinner. But the righteous God, whom Luther had so much feared, had sent Jesus, his Son, the Christ, precisely to win forgiveness for such sinners. This was an undeserved gift of **grace** and needed only to be believed to be effective. Even though one was not just, God "justified" the unjust person by means of the cross and resurrection of Christ, who

---

*For the Reformation, see http://www.newgenevacenter.org/west/reformation.htm.

†See the discussion of Jesus on pp. 222–224, and the similar point made by Augustine on pp. 243–244 and 250. It is perhaps significant that Luther was a monk of the Augustinian order.

had taken upon himself the sins of the world. Salvation did not have to be *earned!* It was a *gift!*

> I began to understand that the righteousness of God is that by which the righteous lives by a gift of God, namely by faith. And this is the meaning: the righteousness of God is revealed by the gospel, namely, the passive righteousness with which merciful God justifies us by faith, as it is written, "He who through faith is righteous shall live." Here I felt that I was altogether born again and had entered paradise itself through open gates. . . .
>
> Thus that place in Paul was for me truly the gate to paradise. Later I read Augustine's *The Spirit and the Letter,* where contrary to hope I found that he, too, interpreted God's righteousness in a similar way, as the righteousness with which God clothes us when he justifies us.[13]

With this insight, the Reformation was born. The power of this idea was first demonstrated in relation to the indulgences being sold under the authority of the pope and Archbishop Albert of Mainz. An **indulgence** was a piece of paper assuring the purchaser of the remission of certain penalties—perhaps in this life, perhaps in purgatory, and perhaps escape from hell itself. The practice of promising such spiritual benefits in return for worldly goods can be traced back to the Crusades. Popes offered heavenly blessings in return for military service in the Holy Land against the Turks. But for those who could not serve or were reluctant to go, a payment in cash to support the effort was accepted instead. This practice had proved so lucrative that, as we have seen, it was extended for other purposes—including the repayment of loans for the purchase of an archbishopric!

The set of indulgences sponsored by Albert were peddled in 1517 by a Dominican monk named Tetzel, who advertised his wares with a jingle:

> As soon as the coin in the coffer rings,
> The soul from purgatory springs.[14]

Although prohibited in Wittenberg, where Luther was both parish priest and teacher of theology, indulgences were sold near enough that his parishioners traveled to buy them. They came back boasting that they could now do what they liked, for they were guaranteed heaven. Luther was troubled. Was this Christianity—to buy salvation for a few gold coins? Didn't this make a mockery of repentance and the attempt to reform one's life? Indeed, didn't it make a mockery of God's grace, which was sold for worldly gain like any other commodity? On the eve of All Saints' Day, 1517, Luther posted **ninety-five theses** on the door of the Castle Church. He had drafted them quickly and meant them only to form the substance of a scholarly debate among theologians. But they caused a sensation, escaped his control, and were published and disseminated widely. Among the theses were these:

> 27. There is no divine authority for preaching that the soul flies out of purgatory immediately the money clinks in the bottom of the chest.
>
> . . .
>
> 36. Any Christian whatsoever, who is truly repentant enjoys plenary remission from penalty and guilt, and this is given him without letters of indulgence.
>
> . . .
>
> 43. Christians should be taught that one who gives to the poor, or lends to the needy, does a better action than if he purchases indulgences.[15]

Let us think about Thesis 27 for a moment. Here Luther says there is no "divine authority" for Tetzel's rhyme. What does he mean by this? There clearly was ecclesiastical authority for it, at least in the sense that the selling of the indulgences was sponsored by an archbishop and the pope. But for Luther, who had spent five years trying to understand the Bible and who knew well the works of the early Church fathers, particularly Augustine, this does not settle the matter at all. It didn't take a great deal of historical knowledge to discover that popes and councils of the Church had disagreed with one another and were often flatly in disagreement with the words of Scripture. So the fact that the practice was backed by the highest Church authority is just that for Luther—a fact. It does not make the practice *right*. Only a *divine* authority can determine that.*

---

*Compare the speech in which Antigone defends her action defying the king's command, p. 49.

What, then, does Luther mean by "divine authority"? Above all, he means the words and deeds of Christ. But secondarily, he means the testimony of the apostles who had known Jesus or of those (like Paul) to whom Christ had specially revealed himself. So Luther appeals to the Bible, that collection of the earliest records we have of the life and impact of Jesus. This was Luther's authority, against which the words of archbishops and popes alike had to be measured.

It is precisely here that his conflict with the established Church is sharpest. In a certain sense, the Church does not deny that Scripture is the ultimate authority; however, Scripture needs to be interpreted. And the proper interpretation of Scripture, according to the Church, is that given by the Church itself in the *tradition* that reaches back in a long, unbroken historical sequence to the apostles. Ultimately the authority to interpret Scripture resides in the pope, the successor of the apostle Peter, of whom Jesus had said, "You are Peter, and on this rock I will build my church" (Matt. 16:18).

In a great debate at Leipzig in 1519, Luther went as far as to say,

> A simple layman armed with Scripture is to be believed above a pope or a council without it.

His opponent in the debate replied,

> When Brother Luther says that this is the true meaning of the text, the pope and councils say, "No, the brother has not understood it correctly." Then I will take the council and let the brother go. Otherwise all the heresies will be renewed. They have all appealed to Scripture and have believed their interpretation to be correct, and have claimed that the popes and the councils were mistaken, as Luther now does.[16]

This exchange gives the tenor of the arguments that continued for about four years while the Church was trying to decide what to do about the rebel. Luther appeals to the Scriptures against the pope and the ecclesiastical establishment. They in turn point out the damaging consequences—heresy and the destruction of the unity of Christendom—if Luther is allowed to be right.

In 1521 Luther was formally excommunicated from the Church, and the split between "Protestants" and "Roman Catholics" became official. There is much more to this story, but we have enough before us to draw some lessons relevant to our philosophical conversation.

For more than a thousand years there had been a basic agreement in the West about how to settle questions of truth. Some questions could be settled by reason and experience; the great authority on these matters for the past few centuries had been Aristotle, whom Aquinas had called simply "the philosopher." But above these questions were others—the key questions about God and the soul and the meaning of life—which were answered by *authority,* not reason. And the authority had been that of the Church, as embedded in the decision-making powers of its clergy, focused ultimately in the papacy.

When Luther challenges this authority, he attacks the very root of a whole culture. It is no wonder that there is so much opposition. His appeal to the authority of Scripture sets up a standard for settling those higher questions that is different from the accepted one. And we can now see that the crisis Luther precipitates is a form of the old skeptical *problem of the criterion,* one of the deepest and most radical problems in our intellectual life.* By what criterion or standard are we going to tell when we know the truth? If a criterion is proposed, how do we know that it is the right one? Is there a criterion for choosing the criterion?

In the religious disputes of the following century, each side busies itself in demolishing the claims of the other side. On the one hand, Protestants show that if we accept the Catholic criterion, we can be sure of nothing because—as Luther points out—popes and councils disagree with one another. If there are contradictions in the criterion itself, how can we choose which of the contradictory propositions to accept?

Catholics, on the other hand, argue that reliance on one's individual conscience after reading Scripture could not produce certainty, for the conscience of one person may not agree with the conscience of another. Indeed, it is not long before the

------

*For a discussion of the problem about the criterion, see pp. 211–213.

Protestants are as divided among themselves as they are united in opposing the Catholics.

The consequence is that each side appeals to a criterion that is not accepted by the other side, but neither can find a criterion to decide which of these criteria is the correct one!

This quarrel, moreover, is not just an intellectual and religious debate. A series of savage and bloody quasi-religious wars ensues, in which princes try not only to secure territories, but also to determine the religion of the people residing in them.* Indeed, one outcome of these wars is that southern Germany is to this day overwhelmingly Catholic, whereas northern Germany is largely Protestant.

What the Reformation does, philosophically speaking, is to unsettle the foundations. Though the reformers only intend to call an erring Church back to its true and historical foundations, the consequences are lasting divisiveness, with those on each side certain of their own correctness and of the blindness (or wickedness) of their opponents. This unsettling of the foundations by the reformers is one of the factors that lies behind Descartes' attempt to sink the piles so deep that beliefs built on them could never again be shaken.

But these disputes of the Reformation are not the only source of Descartes' concern. We must consider next the revival of skeptical thought in the sixteenth century.

---

1. In what ways had the Church grown corrupt?
2. What does Luther find in the New Testament that leads to his objection to indulgences?
3. To what authority does Luther appeal?
4. How did the challenge posed by the Reformation raise again the problem of the criterion?

---

*Here you may be reminded of Socrates' point in *Euthyphro* 7b–d: The gods do not quarrel about length and weight and such matters, but about good and justice. Where there are accepted criteria (rules of measurement, for instance) for settling disputes, wars are unlikely. But where there are apparently irresolvable disagreements, involving appeal to differing standards, might may seem like the only thing that *can* make right.

Skeptical Thoughts Revived

As we have noted, the recovery of ancient scientific and philosophical texts (in particular, the works of Aristotle) was followed by the recovery of Greek and Roman poetry, histories, and essays. Somewhat later still, another rediscovery exerted an influence.[17] In 1562 the first Latin edition of a work by Sextus Empiricus was published, and within seven years all his writings were available.* Sextus calls his views "Pyrrhonism," after one of the earliest Greek skeptics, Pyrrho. In this period of divisiveness and strife between Catholics and Protestants, Pyrrhonism strikes a responsive chord in more than one thinker who considers that an impasse has been reached, but we will focus on just one man: Michel de Montaigne.

Montaigne (1533–1592) was a Frenchman of noble birth who, after spending some years in public service as a magistrate, retired at the age of thirty-eight to think and write. His essays are one of the glories of French literature. We are interested not in his style, however, but in his ideas—ideas that a great many people begin to find attractive in the late sixteenth and early seventeenth centuries.

His point of view comes out most clearly in a remarkable essay called *Apology for* **Raymond Sebond**. Sebond had been a theologian of the fifteenth century who had exceeded the claims of Augustine, Anselm, and Aquinas by claiming not only that the existence and nature of God could be proved by reason, but that rational proofs could be given for *all* the distinctive doctrines of Christianity. This is an astonishing claim; if true, it would mean that clear thinking alone would suffice to convince us all (Jews, Muslims, and pagans alike) that we should be Christians. No one had ever gone so far before. And, as you can imagine, Sebond attracted critics like clover attracts bees.

In his youth, Montaigne had translated Sebond's book into French, at his father's request. Much later, he set out to defend Sebond's thesis. ("Apology" here means "defense," as it does in the title of Plato's account of Socrates' trial.) It is an unusual

---

*For a discussion of the skeptical philosophy of Sextus, see Chapter 8.

defense, however; and Sebond, had he been alive, might well have exclaimed that he needed no enemies with friends like this!

Montaigne's strategy is to demonstrate extensively that Sebond's "proofs" of Christian beliefs are not in the slightest inferior to reasons offered for any other conclusion whatsoever. He claims that Sebond's arguments will

> be found as solid and as firm as any others of the same type that may be opposed to them. . . .
>
> Some say that his arguments are weak and unfit to prove what he proposes, and undertake to shatter them with ease. These must be shaken up a little more roughly. . . .
>
> Let us see then if man has within his power other reasons more powerful than those of Sebond, or indeed if it is in him to arrive at any certainty by argument and reason. (*ARS,* 327–328)[18]

Montaigne, then, is going to "defend" Sebond's claim to prove the doctrines of the faith by showing that his arguments are as good as those of his critics—because *none* of them are any good at all!

The essay is a long and rambling one, but with a method in its madness. It examines every reason that has been given for trusting our conclusions and undermines each with satire and skeptical arguments. Are we capable of knowing the truth because of our superiority to the animals? In example after example, Montaigne causes us to wonder whether we are superior at all. Have the wise given us insight into the truth? He collects a long list of the different conceptions of God held by the philosophers and then exclaims,

> Now trust to your philosophy . . . when you consider the clatter of so many philosophical brains! (*ARS,* 383)

He adds,

> Man is certainly crazy. He could not make a mite, and he makes gods by the dozen. (*ARS,* 395)

Can we not at least rely on Aristotle, the "master of those who know"? But why pick out Aristotle as our authority? There are numerous alternatives.

> The god of scholastic knowledge is Aristotle. . . . His doctrine serves us as magisterial law, when it is peradventure as false as another. (*ARS,* 403)

Surely, however, we can depend on our senses to reveal the truth about the world.

> That things do not lodge in us in their own form and essence, or make their entry into us by their own power and authority, we see clearly enough. Because, if that were so, we should receive them in the same way: wine would be the same in the mouth of a sick man as in the mouth of a healthy man; he who has chapped or numb fingers would find the same hardness in the wood or iron he handles as does another. . . .
>
> We should remember, whatever we receive into our understanding, that we often receive false things there, and by these same tools that are often contradictory and deceived. (*ARS,* 422–424)

Can't we at least depend on science? Haven't scientists discovered the truth about things? Montaigne reminds us that in old times most people thought that the sun moved around the earth, though some thought the earth moved.

> And in our day, Copernicus has grounded this doctrine so well that he uses it very systematically for all astronomical deductions. What are we to get out of that, unless we should not bother which of the two is so? And who knows whether a third opinion, a thousand years from now, will not overthrow the preceding two? (*ARS,* 429)

Well, maybe it is difficult or impossible to know the truth about the universe. But surely reason can demonstrate truth about right and wrong?

> Truth must have one face, the same and universal. If man knew any rectitude and justice that had body and real existence, he would not tie it down to the condition of this country or that. It would not be from the fancy of the Persians or the Indians that virtue would take its form. . . .
>
> But they are funny when, to give some certainty to the laws, they say that there are some which are firm, perpetual and immutable, which they call natural, which are imprinted on the human race by the condition of their very being. And of those one man says the number is three, one man four, one more, one less: a sign that the mark of them is as doubtful as the rest. . . .
>
> It is credible that there are natural laws, as may be seen in other creatures; but in us they are lost; that fine human reason butts in everywhere, domineering and commanding, muddling and confusing

the face of things in accordance with its vanity and inconsistency. . . . *

See how reason provides plausibility to different actions. It is a two-handled pot, that can be grasped by the left or the right. (*ARS*, 436–438)

Finally Montaigne gives us a summary of the chief points of skeptical philosophy. Whenever we try to justify some claim of ours, we are involved either in a *circle* or in an *infinite regress* of reason giving. In neither case can we reach a satisfactory conclusion.

To judge the appearances we receive of objects, we would need a judicatory instrument; to verify this instrument, we need a demonstration; to verify the demonstration, an instrument: there we are in a circle!

Since the senses cannot decide our dispute, being themselves full of uncertainty, it must be reason that does so. No reason can be established without another reason; there we go retreating back to infinity. . . . †

Finally, there is no existence that is constant, either of our being or of that of objects. And we, and our judgment, and all mortal things go on flowing and rolling unceasingly. Thus nothing certain can be established about one thing by another, both the judging and the judged being in continual change and motion. (*ARS*, 454)

Montaigne remarks that if the senses do not simply record external realities (as Aristotle assumes, using the image of a seal impressing its form on the wax), then our ideas may not correspond at all to those realities. Even worse, we are never in a position to find out whether they do or not. We may be in the position of having only pictures, without ever being able to compare these pictures to what they are pictures of. Here is that depressing and familiar image of the mind as a prisoner within its own walls, constantly receiving messages but forever unable to determine which of them to trust,

and utterly incapable of understanding what is really going on. This image plagues many modern thinkers, not least of all Descartes.

Like all radical skeptics, Montaigne is faced with the question of how to manage the business of living. To live, one must choose, and to choose is to prefer one course as better than another. But this seems to require precisely those beliefs (in both facts and values) that skeptical reflections undermine. Montaigne accepts the solution of Protagoras and Sextus Empiricus before him of simply adapting himself to the prevailing opinions. We see, he says, how reason goes astray—especially when it meddles with divine things. We see how

when it strays however little from the beaten path and deviates or wanders from the way traced and trodden by the Church, immediately, it is lost, it grows embarrassed and entangled, whirling round and floating in that vast, troubled, and undulating sea of human opinions, unbridled and aimless. As soon as it loses that great common highroad it breaks up and disperses onto a thousand different roads. (*ARS*, 387)

. . . since I am not capable of choosing, I accept other people's choice and stay in the position where God put me. Otherwise I could not keep myself from rolling about incessantly. Thus I have, by the grace of God, kept myself intact, without agitation or disturbance of conscience, in the ancient beliefs of our religion, in the midst of so many sects and divisions that our century has produced. (*ARS*, 428)

You can see that skepticism is here being used as a defense of the status quo. Montaigne was born and brought up a Catholic. No one can bring forward reasons for deserting Catholic Christianity that are any better than Raymond Sebond's reasons for supporting Catholic Christianity. Reason supports the Roman view just as strongly as it supports the Protestant view or, indeed, any other view—which is, of course, not at all! So to keep from "rolling about incessantly," the sensible course is to stick with the customs in which one has been brought up.* In one of his sharpest aphorisms, Montaigne exclaims:

---

*Note that Montaigne is making essentially the same point as Pico (p. 298). There are no determinate laws for human nature. But whereas Pico takes this to be the *glory* of man, Montaigne draws from it a *despairing* conclusion: The truth is unavailable to us.

†Here we have a statement of that problem of the criterion that was identified by Sextus. For a more extensive discussion of it, see pp. 211–213.

---

*Note how different this religiosity is from both that of the Catholic Dante (for whom the "indifferent" are rejected by both God and Satan) and the reformer Luther (for whom commitment and certainty are essential to Christianity). Can it count as being religious at all? What do you think?

The plague of man is the opinion of knowledge.
That is why ignorance is so recommended by our
religion as a quality suitable to belief and obedience.
(*ARS,* 360)

It is not knowledge, note well, that Montaigne
decries as a plague, but the opinion that one possesses it. If you are reminded of Socrates, it is no
coincidence.* He was known to his admirers as "the
French Socrates."

Such is Montaigne's "defense" of the rational
theology of Raymond Sebond. In an age when everyone's conscience seems to demand that those
who disagree are either blind or wicked, the view
has a certain attractiveness. While despairing and
pessimistic in one way, it seems at least to promote
tolerance. Someone who is a Catholic in Montaigne's sense is unlikely to have any incentive to
burn someone who differs. This is no doubt one,
but only one, of the reasons for the spread of Pyrrhonism among intellectuals and even among some
members of the clergy.

---

1. What is Montaigne's strategy in "defending"
   Raymond Sebond?
2. What does Montaigne have to say about depending
   on authority? Our senses? Science? Reason?
3. How does Montaigne try to show that we are
   involved either in a circle or in an infinite regress?
4. How does he recommend we live?

Copernicus to Kepler to Galileo: The Great Triple Play†

Renaissance humanism, the Reformation, and the
undermining of accepted certainties by the new
Pyrrhonists all contribute to a general sense of

---

*For the claim that Socrates is the wisest of men because
he knows that he doesn't know, see Plato's *Apology,* 20e–
23b. Socrates, however, is not a Pyrrhonian skeptic; he does
not doubt that knowledge is possible; he just confesses that
(with some possible few exceptions), he does not possess it.

†When your team is in the field, a triple play is a great
success.

---

chaos and lost unity. But there is also a spirit of expectation. Something new is in the air; the tumults
and controversies of the time are a testimony to it.
The newly invented printing press spreads the new
ideas. Imagination is enlarged by the discovery of
the New World, and a sense of excitement is generated by voyages around the globe. New wealth
flowing into Europe from America and the East
stimulates growth and a powerful merchant class.
The isolation of Europe is coming to an end and the
reverberations are felt on every side—not least in
the sphere of the intellect. The ancient authorities
had been wrong about geography. Perhaps they
were wrong about other things as well, and better
understanding might lie in the future rather than in
the past.

But nothing else can compare, in its long-term
impact, with the development of the new science. More than all these other factors combined,
this changes people's view of themselves, of the
world, and of their place in it. Before we examine the philosophy of Descartes, who was himself
a contributor to these new views, we need to
look briefly at one tremendously significant shift
in perspective—one that decisively overturns the
entire medieval worldview and undermines forever the authority of its philosophical bulwark,
Aristotle. It is traditionally called the Copernican
Revolution. Though there were anticipations of it
before **Copernicus**, and the revolution was carried to completion only in the time of Newton, it
is the name of Copernicus we honor. For his work
is the turning point. The key feature of that work is
the displacement of the earth from the center of
the universe.

We saw earlier how the centrality of the earth
had been embedded in the accepted astronomical
and physical theories. A stationary earth, moreover, had intimate links with the entire medieval
Christian view of the significance of man, of his
origins and destiny, and of God's relation to his
creation. If the earth is displaced and becomes just
one more planet whirling about in infinite space,
we can expect consequences to be profound. And
so they are, though the more radical consequences
are not immediately perceived.

"It [the scientific revolution] outshines
everything since the rise of Christianity and
reduces the Renaissance and Reformation
to the rank of mere episodes, mere internal
displacements within the system of medieval
Christendom."

Herbert Butterfield (1900–1979)

The earth-centered, multisphere universe had dominated astronomy and cosmology for eighteen hundred years. As developed by Ptolemy, with a complex system of epicycles to account for the "wanderings" of the planets, it was an impressive mathematical achievement, and its accuracy in prediction was not bad. But it never quite worked. And Copernicus (1473–1543) tells us that this fact led him to examine the works of previous astronomers to see whether some other system might improve accuracy. He discovered that certain ancient thinkers had held that the earth moved.

> Taking advantage of this I too began to think of the mobility of the Earth; and though the opinion seemed absurd, yet knowing now that others before me had been granted freedom to imagine such circles as they chose to explain the phenomena of the stars, I considered that I also might easily be allowed to try whether, by assuming some motion of the Earth, sounder explanations than theirs for the revolution of the celestial spheres might so be discovered.[19]

It is important to recognize that the heart of Copernicus' achievement is in the mathematics of his system—in the geometry and the calculations that filled most of his 1543 book, *De Revolutionibus*. As he himself puts it, "Mathematics are for mathematicians."[20] He expects fellow astronomers to be the ones to appreciate his results; from nonmathematicians he expects trouble.

We cannot go into the mathematical details. But we should know in general what Copernicus does—and does not—do. He does not entirely abolish the Ptolemaic reliance on epicycles centered on circles to account for apparent motion. His computations are scarcely simpler than those of Ptolemy. He retains

the notion that all celestial bodies move in circles; indeed, the notion of celestial spheres is no less important for Copernicus than for the tradition. And he accepts the idea that the universe is finite—though considerably larger than had been thought. Even the sun is not located clearly in the center, as most popular accounts of his system state.[21]

But his treatment of the apparently irregular motions of the planets is a breakthrough. The planets appear to move, against the sphere of the fixed stars, slowly eastward. But at times they reverse course and move back westward. This **retrograde motion** remains a real puzzle as long as it is ascribed to the planets themselves. But Copernicus treats it as merely an *apparent* motion, the appearance being caused by the *actual* motion of the observers on an earth that is not itself stationary. And this works; at least, it works as well as the traditional assumptions in accounting for the observed phenomena. Moreover, it is aesthetically pleasing, unlike the inexplicable reversals of earlier theory. Copernicus' view, though not less complex and scarcely more accurate in prediction, allows for a kind of unity and harmony throughout the universe that the renegade planets had previously spoiled. Until the availability of better naked-eye data and the invention of the telescope (about fifty years later) these "harmonies" are what chiefly recommend the Copernican system to his astronomical successors.

At first some of them simply use his mathematics without committing themselves to the truth of this new picture of the universe. Indeed, in a preface to Copernicus' major work, a Lutheran theologian, Osiander, urges this path. Copernicus' calculations are useful, but to give up the traditional picture of the universe would mean an overhaul of basic beliefs and attitudes that most are not ready for. So if one could treat the system merely as a calculating device, without any claims to truth, one could reconcile the best of the new science with the best of ancient traditions.*

---

*Here is foreshadowed one of the intense debates in current philosophy of science: Should we understand terms in explanatory theories in a "realistic" way, or take such terms as mere "instruments" for calculation and prediction?

Johannes **Kepler** (1571–1630), however, is not content with this restricted view of the theory. A lifelong Copernican, he supplies the next major advance in the system by taking the sun more and more seriously as the true center. Oddly enough, his predilection for the sun as the center has its roots not so much in observation, or even in mathematics, as in a kind of mystical Neoplatonism, which takes the sun to be "the most excellent" body in the universe.* Its essence, Kepler says

> is nothing else than the purest light, than which there is no greater star; which singly and alone is the producer, conserver, and warmer of all things; it is a fountain of light, rich in fruitful heat, most fair, limpid, and pure to the sight, the source of vision, portrayer of all colours, though himself empty of colour, called king of the planets for his motion, heart of the world for his power, its eye for his beauty, and which alone we should judge worthy of the Most High God, should he be pleased with a material domicile and choose a place in which to dwell with the blessed angels.[22]

It may be somewhat disconcerting to hear this sort of rhetoric from one we honor as a founder of the modern scientific tradition; but it is neither the first nor the last time that religious or philosophical views function as a source of insights later confirmed by more exact and pedestrian methods.

Part of Kepler's quasi-religious conviction is that the universe is fundamentally mathematical in nature. God is a great mathematician, and his creation is governed by mathematically simple laws. This view can be traced back through Plato to the Pythagoreans, who hold (rather obscurely) that all things are numbers. In the work of Kepler and his successors, this conviction is to gain an unprecedented confirmation. Mathematics must be devised to fit the phenomena, and the phenomena are given a mathematical description.

Drawing on more accurate data compiled by the great observer of the heavens, Tycho Brahe, Kepler makes trial after trial of circular hypotheses, always within the Copernican framework, but none of them exactly fit the data. He tries various other kinds of ovals without success. For the greater part of ten years he works on the orbit of Mars. At last, he notices certain regularities suggesting that the path of a planet might be that of an ellipse, with the sun at one of the two foci that define it. And that works; the data and the mathematical theory fit precisely.

This becomes the first of Kepler's famous three laws. The second offers an explanation of the varying speeds that must be postulated in the planets' movement around these ellipses: The areas swept out by a line from the sun to the planet are always equal in equal intervals of time. The third law is more complicated, and we need not bother about its details; it concerns the relation of the speeds of planets in different orbits. In fact, Kepler formulates a great many laws; posterity has selected these three as particularly fruitful.

The significance of Kepler's work is that for the first time we are presented with a simple and elegant mathematical account of the heavens that matches the data; and it is sun-centered. For the first time we have a really powerful alternative to the medieval picture of the world. Its ramifications are many, however, and will take time to draw out. Part of this development is the task of Galileo.

Galileo Galilei (1564–1642) was, in 1609, the first to view the heavens through a telescope. The result was a multitude of indirect but persuasive evidences for the Copernican view of the universe. New stars in prodigious numbers were observed. The moon's topography was charted; it resembled the earth remarkably, a fact that cut against the distinction between terrestrial imperfection and celestial perfection. Sun spots were observed; it was not perfect either! And it rotated—it was not immutable! The moons of Jupiter provided an observable model of the solar system itself. The phases of Venus indicated that it moved in a sun-centered orbit.

Encouraged by the successful application of mathematics to celestial bodies, Galileo sets himself to use these same powerful tools for the description and explanation of terrestrial motion. Previous thinkers, influenced by Aristotle, had

---

*In *Republic* 506d–509b, Plato uses the sun as a visible image of the Form of the Good (see p. 132). And in his later work *Laws,* he recommends a kind of sun worship as the heart of a state-sponsored religion.

asked primarily *why* bodies move. Why do objects fall to earth when unsupported? Aristotelian answers were at hand. A body falls because it is seeking its *natural place*. The significance of this answer can be seen by a thought experiment. Imagine that the earth is where the moon now is and that you let go of a rock some distance above the surface of the earth. What would happen? If Aristotle's answer were correct, the rock would not fall to the earth but would travel to the place where the center of the earth *used to be;* it would fly away from the earth.[23]

Place, not space, is primary in an Aristotelian world; place is a qualitative term, each place having its own essential character. The place at the center of the celestial spheres is the place of heavy elements. The concept of **space**, by contrast, which plays such a crucial role in the new science, is the concept of an infinitely extended neutral container with a purely mathematical description.

Note also that the Aristotelian explanation in terms of final causes gives no answer at all as to *how* an object falls; no specification of laws that describe its speed and trajectory is given.* But this is just what Galileo supplies in terms of a mathematical theory of motion. It is a theory that applies to *all* motion, terrestrial and celestial alike. For him, as for his two predecessors, the great book of nature is written in mathematical language. And we, by using that language, can understand it.

Let us set down some of the consequences of the new science. First, our sense of the size of the universe changes. Eventually it will be thought to be infinitely extended in space. This means it has *no center* because in an infinite universe every point has an equal right to be considered the center. As a result, it becomes more difficult to think of human beings as the main attraction in this extravaganza, where quite probably there are planets similar to the earth circling other suns in other galaxies. The universe no longer seems a cozy home in which everything exists for our sake. Blaise Pascal, himself a great mathematician and contributor to the new science, would exclaim a hundred years after

Copernicus, "The eternal silence of those infinite spaces strikes me with terror."[24]

Second, our beliefs about the nature of the things in the universe change. Celestial bodies are thought to be made of the same lowly stuff as we find on the earth, so that the heavens are no longer special—eternal, immutable, and akin to the divine. Furthermore, matter seems to be peculiarly *quantitative*. For Aristotle and medieval science alike, mathematics had been just one of the ways in which substances could be described. Quantity was only one of the ten categories, which together supplied the basic concepts for describing and explaining reality. Substances were fundamentally qualitative in nature, and science had the job of tracing their qualitative development in terms of changes from potentiality to actuality.*

But now mathematics seems to be a privileged set of concepts in terms of which to describe and explain things. Only by the application of geometry and mathematical calculation has the puzzle of the heavens been solved; and it is mathematics that can describe and predict the fall of rocks and the trajectory of a cannonball. Mathematics, it seems, can tell us what *really* is. The result is a strong push toward thinking of the universe in purely quantitative terms, as a set of objects with purely quantitative characteristics (size, shape, motion) that interact with each other according to fixed laws. It is no surprise that the implications of the new science move its inventors in the direction of atomism or, as they call it, "**corpuscularism.**"† We will see this at work in Descartes' philosophy.

In the third place, the new science does away with teleological explanations, or final causes. The question about what end or goal a planet or a rock realizes in behaving as it does is simply irrelevant. Explanations are framed in terms of mathematical laws that account for *how* it behaves. Why does it behave in a certain way? Because it is a thing of just this precise quantity in exactly these conditions, and things of that quantity in those conditions

---

*For a discussion of final causes, see pp. 169–171.

*See Aristotle's development of these ideas on pp. 168–171. For Aristotle's categories, see pp. 159–160.

†The key notions of ancient atomism are discussed on pp. 34–37.

necessarily behave in accordance with a given law. It is no longer good enough to explain change in terms of a desire to imitate the perfection of God.*

As you can see, this way of viewing the universe puts values in a highly questionable position. If we assume that the valuable is somehow a goal, something desirable, what we all want—and this is the common assumption of virtually all philosophers and theologians up to this time—where is there room for such goals in a universe like this? A goal seems precisely to be a final cause, something that draws us onward and upward toward itself. But if everything simply happens as it must in the giant machine that is the universe, how can there be values, aspirations, goals?

It looks as though knowledge and value, science and religion are being pulled apart again after two thousand years of harmony. Plato, and Aristotle after him, opposes the atomism of Democritus to construct a vision of reality in which the ultimate facts are not indifferent to goodness and beauty. Christian thinkers take over these schemes and link them intimately to God, the creator. But all this, expressed so movingly in Dante's *Divine Comedy,* seems to be in the process of coming unstuck again.

One more consequence of the new science will prove to be perhaps the most perplexing of all. Galileo sees that the quantitative, corpuscular universe makes the qualities of experience highly questionable. If reality is captured by mathematics and geometry, then the real properties of things are just their size, shape, velocity, acceleration, direction, weight: those characteristics treatable by numbers, points, and lines. But what becomes of those fuzzy, intimate, and lovable characteristics, such as warm, yellow-orange, pungent, sweet, and harmonious to the ear? It is in terms of such properties that we make contact with the world beyond us; it is they that delight or terrify us, attract or repel us. But what is their relation to those purely quantitive things revealed by Galilean science as the real stuff of the universe?

Our instinctive habit is to consider the apple to be red, the oatmeal hot, cookies sweet, and roses fragrant. But is this correct? Do apples and other such things really have these properties? Here is Galileo's answer:

> that external bodies, to excite in us these tastes, these odours, and these sounds, demand other than size, figure, number, and slow or rapid motion, I do not believe; and I judge that, if the ears, the tongue, and the nostrils were taken away, the figure, the numbers, and the motions would indeed remain, but not the odours nor the tastes nor the sounds, which, without the living animal, I do not believe are anything else than names, just as tickling is precisely nothing but a name if the armpit and the nasal membrane be removed; . . . having now seen that many affections which are reputed to be qualities residing in the external object, have truly no other existence than in us, and without us are nothing else than names; I say that I am inclined sufficiently to believe that heat is of this kind, and that the thing that produces heat in us and makes us perceive it, which we call by the general name fire, is a multitude of minute corpuscles thus and thus figured, moved with such and such a velocity; . . . But that besides their figure, number, motion, penetration, and touch, there is in fire another quality, that is heat—that I do not believe otherwise than I have indicated, and I judge that it is so much due to us that if the animate and sensitive body were removed, heat would remain nothing more than a simple word.[25]

Galileo is here sketching a distinction between two different kinds of qualities: those that can be attributed to things themselves and those that cannot. The former are often called **primary qualities** and the latter **secondary qualities**. Primary qualities are those that Galilean mathematical science can handle: size, figure, number, and motion. These qualities are now thought to characterize the world—or what we might better call the *objective* world—exhaustively. All other qualities exist only *subjectively*—in us. They are caused to exist in us by the primary (quantitative) qualities of things.

Heat, for example, experienced in the presence of a fire, no more exists in the fire than a tickle exists in the feather brushing my nose. If we try to use the term "heat" for something out there in the world, it turns into "nothing but a name"—that is, it does not describe any reality, since the

---

*Compare the teleological explanations of Aristotle (pp. 168–171) and Dante (pp. 293–296).

reality is just the motion of "a multitude of minute corpuscles." The tickle exists only in us; and if the term "heat" (or for that matter "red" or "sweet" or "pungent") is to be descriptive, then what it describes is also only in us. Take away the eye, the tongue, the nostrils, and all that remains is figure and motion.

Democritus, the ancient atomist, draws the same conclusion. He remarks in a poignant phrase, "By this man is cut off from the real."* The problem that Galileo's distinction between primary and secondary qualities bequeaths to subsequent philosophers is this: If, in order to understand the world, we must strip it of its experienced qualities, where do those experienced qualities exist? If they exist only in *us,* what then are *we?* If they are mental, or subjective, what is the *mind?* And how is the mind related to the corpuscular world of the new science? Suppose we agree, for the sake of the mastery of the universe given us by these new conceptions, to kick experienced qualities "inside." Then how is this "inside" related to the "outside"? Who is this man who, in Democritus' phrase, is cut off from reality? Galileo, concerned as he is with the objective world, can simply relegate secondary qualities to some otherwise specified subjective realm. But the question will not go away.

It is a new world, indeed. The impact of all these changes on a sensitive observer is registered in a poem by John Donne in 1611.

> And new philosophy calls all in doubt,
> The element of fire is quite put out;
> The sun is lost, and th' earth, and no man's wit
> Can well direct him where to look for it.
> And freely men confess that this world's spent,
> When in the planets, and the firmament
> They seek so many new; they see that this
> Is crumbled out again to his atomies.
> 'Tis all in pieces, all coherence gone;
> All just supply, and all relation:
> Prince, subject, father, son, are things forgot,
> For every man alone thinks he hath got
> To be a phoenix, and that then can be
> None of that kind, of which he is, but he.
> This is the world's condition now.[26]

Here is a lament founded on the new developments. Point after point recalls the detail we have just surveyed; Pyrrhonism, secondary qualities (why is the sun, source of light, heat, and color "lost"?), the moving earth, the expanding universe, corpuscularism, and in the last few lines, the new individualism, which seems to undermine all traditional authority. The medieval world has vanished: "'tis all in pieces, all coherence gone."

It did not go quietly, of course. The Roman Catholic Counter-Reformation tried to preserve as much as it could. The argument about Copernicanism, which seemed to be the key, was long and fierce; we all know the story of the Church's condemnation of Galileo's opinions and his recantation and house arrest. In 1633, the Church prohibited teaching or believing that the earth moved around the sun. And many Protestants were no more friendly, citing biblical passages that seemed to support the claim that the earth was stationary.* These conservative forces were not interested in the new science per se, but in the fact that it seemed subversive of the "coherence" Christian society had enjoyed for so long. It questioned everything and seemed to turn it all upside down. When one part of a coherent worldview is undermined, all the rest seems suddenly unstable.

But the new science proves irresistible, and in one way or another, religion, morality, worldview, and the structure of society would have to make peace with it. The question of what to make of this science is perhaps the major preoccupation of philosophers in the modern era.

If we wanted to sum up, we could say that the new science bequeaths to philosophers four deep and perplexing problems:

1. What is the place of mind in this world of matter?
2. What is the place of value in this world of fact?
3. What is the place of freedom in this world of mechanism?
4. Is there any room left for God at all?

---

*See p. 37.

*For example, Joshua 10:13, Ecclesiastes 1:4, 5, and Psalms 93:1.

Descartes, among others, sees the radical nature of these problems and sets himself to solve them.

---

1. How does Copernicus resolve the puzzle about the apparent irregularity in the motions of the planets?
2. What is the impact of a moving earth on Dante's picture of the world?
3. What does Kepler add to the Copernican picture?
4. Contrast Aristotelian explanations of motion with those of Galileo.
5. What impact does giving up final causes have on values?
6. What happens to the qualities we think we experience in objects? Explain the difference between primary and secondary qualities.
7. What questions does the new science pose to the philosophical quest for wisdom?

FOR FURTHER THOUGHT

Imagine that you are a philosopher living at the beginning of the seventeenth century. You are acquainted with the writings of the humanists, with Luther's reforming views of Christianity, with Montaigne's skeptical arguments, and with the new science. A friend asks you, "What should I live for? What is the point of life?" How do you reply?

KEY WORDS

Ptolemy	indulgence
Empyrean	ninety-five theses
celestial spheres	Montaigne
Virgil	Raymond Sebond
Beatrice	Copernicus
humanism	retrograde motion
Erasmus	Kepler
da Vinci	Galileo
Pico della Mirandola	place
individualism	space
Inquisition	corpuscularism
Martin Luther	primary qualities
grace	secondary qualities

NOTES

1. I am indebted for much in this chapter to the excellent book by Thomas Kuhn, *The Copernican Revolution* (Cambridge, MA: Harvard University Press, 1957).
2. Quoted in Kuhn, *Copernican Revolution,* 112.
3. Quotations from Dante, *The Divine Comedy,* in *The Portable Dante,* ed. Paolo Milano (New York: Penguin Books, 1947), are cited in the text by canto and line numbers.
4. Erasmus, "The Godly Feast," in *The Colloquies of Erasmus,* trans. Craig R. Thompson (Chicago: University of Chicago Press, 1965), 65.
5. Erasmus, "Godly Feast," 68.
6. Erasmus, "The Epicurean," in *Colloquies,* 549.
7. Ernst Cassirer, Paul Oskar Kristeller, and John Herman Randall, Jr., *The Renaissance Philosophy of Man* (Chicago: University of Chicago Press, 1948), 4.
8. Giovanni Pico della Mirandola, *Oration on the Dignity of Man,* in Cassirer, Kristeller, and Randall, *Renaissance Philosophy of Man,* 224–225.
9. Pico, *Oration,* 225.
10. Roland H. Bainton, *Christendom: A Short History of Christianity and Its Impact on Western Civilization* (New York: Harper and Row, 1964), 218.
11. Bainton, *Christendom,* 249.
12. Quoted in Dillenberger, "Preface to the Complete Edition of Luther's Latin Writings," in *Martin Luther,* 11.
13. Quoted in Dillenberger, *Martin Luther,* 11–12.
14. Quoted in Roland H. Bainton, *Here I Stand: A Life of Martin Luther* (London: Hodder and Staughton, 1951), 78.
15. Luther, "The Ninety-Five Theses," in Dillenberger, *Martin Luther,* 493–494.
16. Quoted in Bainton, *Here I Stand,* 117.
17. I rely here on Richard H. Popkin's *History of Scepticism from Erasmus to Descartes* (Assen, Netherlands: Van Gorcum, 1960).
18. Quotations from Michel de Montaigne, *Apology for Raymond Sebond,* in *The Complete Works of Montaigne,* trans. Donald M. Frame (Palo Alto, CA: Stanford University Press, 1958), are cited in the text, using the abbreviation *ARS.* References are to page numbers.

19. Quoted from Copernicus, *De Revolutionibus,* in Kuhn, *Copernican Revolution,* 141.

20. Quoted in Kuhn, *Copernican Revolution,* 142.

21. Kuhn, *Copernican Revolution,* 164–170.

22. Quoted in Edwin Arthur Burtt, *The Metaphysical Foundations of Modern Physical Science* (London: Routledge and Kegan Paul, 1924), 48.

22. Kuhn, *Copernican Revolution,* 86.

24. Blaise Pascal, *The Pensées,* trans. J. M. Cohen (New York: Penguin Books, 1961), sec. 91, p. 57.

25. Quoted in Burtt, *Metaphysical Foundations,* 78.

26. John Donne, "An Anatomy of the World," in *John Donne: The Complete English Poems* (New York: Penguin Books, 1971), 276.

13

RENÉ DESCARTES

Doubting Our Way to Certainty

When he is just twenty-three years old, René **Descartes** (1596–1650) experiences a vision in a dream. He writes down,

> 10, November 1619; I discovered the foundations of a marvellous science.[1]

This discovery decisively shapes the intellectual life of the young man. Before we focus on the philosophy of his *Meditations*, we need to understand something about that discovery and its importance for his method of approaching problems.

Descartes had received a good education, as he himself acknowledges. But he is dissatisfied. He had expected to obtain "a clear and certain knowledge . . . of all that is useful in life." Instead, he tells us,

> I found myself beset by so many doubts and errors that I came to think I had gained nothing from my attempts to become educated but increasing recognition of my ignorance. (*DM* 1.4, p. 113)[2]

Mathematics delights him "because of the certainty of its demonstrations and the evidence of its

reasoning," though he is surprised that more has not been done with it. As for philosophy, he says,

> Seeing that it has been cultivated for many centuries by the most excellent minds, and yet there is still no point in it which is not disputed and hence doubtful, I was not so presumptuous as to hope to achieve any more in it than others had done. (*DM* 1.8, pp. 114–115)

What is a serious young man, who has always had "an earnest desire to learn to distinguish the true from the false" to do? (*DM* 1.10, p. 115).

> I entirely abandoned the study of letters. Resolving to seek no knowledge other than that which could be found in myself or else in the great book of the world, I spent the rest of my youth travelling, visiting courts and armies, mixing with people of diverse temperaments and ranks, gathering various experiences, testing myself in the situations which fortune offered me, and at all times reflecting upon whatever came my way so as to derive some profit from it. (*DM* 1.9, p. 115)

A striking move! He does not give up learning, but he does give up "letters"—learning what other men had written. In this, Descartes is both a reflection of the age and an immense influence furthering the individualism we earlier remarked on. Where would he seek truth? Not in the writings of the ancients, but in *himself* and in *the great book of the world*. Because he concludes—echoing Socrates—that hardly anyone knows anything worth learning, he would have to *discover* the truth.* If he is going to "learn to distinguish the true from the false," he would have to look to himself.

He joins an army (a traditional way to "see the world") and in his travels meets a Dutchman interested in mathematics and the new physics. Descartes' interest is sparked, and he begins to think about using mathematics to solve problems in physics. While working on these problems, he has his dream.

What is this "marvellous science" that forms the content of his "vision"? Apparently it is analytic geometry.† Descartes sees in a flash of insight that there is an isomorphism between algebraic symbols and geometry. He sees, moreover, that this opens the door to a mathematical treatment of everything that can be geometrically represented. But nature seems to be something that can be geometrically represented, natural things having size, figure, volume, and geometrical relations to each other. Suppose that the things in the world were just objects having such geometrical properties; suppose that whatever other properties they have can in one way or another be reduced to purely geometrical properties; then the stunning prospect opens up of a science of nature—a physics—that is wholly mathematical. Mathematics, the only discipline that impressed him in his college days as clear and certain, would be the key to unlock the secrets of nature. Surely this is a vision fit to motivate a research program! And that is exactly what it does.

For the rest of his life Descartes works on this program, in constant communication with the best

minds at work on similar problems. In 1633 he is about to publish a *Treatise on the World*, when he learns of the Catholic Church's condemnation of Galileo and the burning of his books. He holds the treatise back, for in it he has endorsed the Copernican view of the moving earth. Four years later, however, he ventures to publish several works on light, on meteors, and on geometry. These are accompanied by a *Discourse on Method*, which we will examine in more detail shortly.

He writes on a wide variety of topics: on the sun, moon, and the stars; on comets; on metals; on fire; on glass; on the magnet; on the human body, particularly on the heart and the nervous system (for which he gathers observations from animal bodies at a local slaughterhouse). He formulates several "laws of nature." Here are two influential ones:

> that each thing as far as in it lies, continues always in the same state; and that which is once moved always continues to move.
>
> . . . . that all motion is of itself in a straight line; and thus things which move in a circle always tend to recede from the centre of the circle that they describe. (*PP* 2.37–39, p. 267)[3]

Newton will later adopt both of them, and so they pass into the foundations of classical physics; but they were revolutionary in Descartes' day. Both laws contradict Aristotelian assumptions built into the worldview of medieval science. It had been thought that rest (at or near the center of the universe) is the natural state of terrestrial things, while the heavenly spheres revolve naturally in perfect circles. To say that rest is not more "natural" than motion and that motion is "naturally" in a straight line is radical indeed. It could make sense only in a world of infinite space, where there is no such thing as a natural center. And it fits only with a moving earth.

Descartes applies these principles to a world that he takes to be geometrical in essence. He tries to do without concepts of weight and gravity, for these seem to be "occult" qualities like those in the nonmathematical science of Aristotle. To say that a body falls because it has weight or because it is naturally attracted to another body seems to him no explanation at all; it is just attaching a name to a phenomenon and supposing that we thereby learn something.

---

*Do you find it surprising that two thousand years after Socrates someone should still echo the same complaint? Could we say the same today? If not, why not?

†So-called Cartesian coordinates are, of course, named for Descartes.

For Descartes, bodies are sheer extended volumes. They interact according to mechanical principles that can be mathematically formulated. Given that a single body in motion would continue in that motion unless interfered with, and given the laws of interaction, the paths and positions of interacting bodies can be plotted and predicted. Since extension is the very essence of body, there can be no vacuum or void. (You can see that if bodies are just extended volumes, the idea of such a volume containing *no body* is self-contradictory.) So the universe is full, and motion takes place by a continual recirculation of bodies, each displacing another as it is itself displaced. The fall of bodies near the earth is due to the action on them of other bodies in the air, which in turn are being pressed down by others out to the edges of the solar system. This system forms a huge vortex tightly bound in by the vortices of other systems, which force the moving bodies in it to deviate from otherwise straight paths into the roughly circular paths traced by the planets.*

The key idea, as you can see, is that everything in the material world can be treated in a purely geometrical and mathematical fashion. Descartes is one of the most vigorous promoters of that "corpuscularism" noted earlier.† Although he criticizes Democritus and the ancient atomists (for thinking that atoms are indivisible, for positing a void, for believing in gravity, and for not specifying the laws of interaction precisely), it is clear that the general outlines of Descartes' universe bear a striking resemblance to that earlier theory.‡ In particular, the *mechanistic* quality of the picture is identical. He states explicitly that "the laws of mechanics . . . are identical with the laws of Nature" (*DM* 5.54, p. 139).

The radical nature of this conception can be appreciated by noting a thought experiment Descartes recommends. Imagine, he says, that God creates a space with matter to fill it and shakes it up until there is thorough chaos. All that God then adds is a decree that this matter should behave according to the laws of Nature. What would be the result?

> I showed how, in consequence of these laws, the greater part of the matter of this chaos had to become disposed and arranged in a certain way, which made it resemble our heavens; and how, at the same time, some of its parts had to form an earth, some planets and comets, and others a sun and fixed stars. Here I dwelt upon the subject of light, explaining at some length the nature of the light that had to be present in the sun and the stars. . . . From that I went on to speak of the earth in particular: how, although I had expressly supposed that God had put no gravity into the matter of which it was formed, still all its parts tended exactly towards its centre; . . . how mountains, seas, springs and rivers could be formed naturally there, and how metals could appear in mines, plants grow in fields, and generally how all the bodies we call "mixed" or "composite" could come into being there.
> (*DM* 5.43–44, p. 132)

Of course, Descartes does not actually succeed in demonstrating all that. No one yet has solved all these problems, and they are in fact insoluble with the limited resources that Descartes allows himself. But it is the conception and the daring it expresses that counts. This vision of a universe evolving itself in purely mechanistic ways has been enormously influential; and we haven't yet finished exploring its ramifications.

Descartes is quick to add that he does not infer from this thought experiment that the world was actually formed in that way, only that it could have been. Careful still about charges of heresy, he says it is "much more probable" that God made it just as it now is. But in either case, it is pretty clear that God is excluded from the day-to-day operations of the universe, which in Descartes' view proceeds as it must according to purely mathematical and mechanistic laws.

The Method

While working on these physical problems, and feeling certain that progress is being made virtually every day, Descartes asks himself why more

---

*The notion of a cosmic vortex, a huge, swirling mass of matter, is already found in the speculations of Anaximander; see pp. 13–14. Compare also Parmenides' arguments against the existence of a void, pp. 27–28.

†See p. 309.

‡For the views of the atomists, see Chapter 4. Descartes' criticisms may be found in Part IV, CCII, of *The Principles of Philosophy*.

progress hadn't been made in the past. It is surely not, he thinks, that he is more clever or intelligent than earlier thinkers. No, the problem is that they lacked something. And it gradually becomes clear to him that what they lacked is a *method*. They did not proceed in as careful and principled a way as they might have. Acceptance of obscurity, the drawing of hasty conclusions, avoidable disagreements, and general intellectual chaos are the results.

Descartes sets himself to draw up some rules for the direction of the intellect. It is of some importance to recognize that these **rules of method** formulate what Descartes takes himself to be doing in his scientific work. In particular, they are indebted to his experience as a mathematician. They are not picked arbitrarily, then, but are an expression of procedures that actually seem to be producing results. If only other thinkers could be persuaded to follow these four rules, he thinks, what progress might be made!

> The first was never to accept anything as true if I did not have evident knowledge of its truth: that is, carefully to avoid precipitate conclusions and preconceptions, and to include nothing more in my judgments than what presented itself to my mind so clearly and distinctly that I had no occasion to doubt it.
>
> The second, to divide each of the difficulties I examined into as many parts as possible and as may be required in order to resolve them better.
>
> The third, to direct my thoughts in an orderly manner, by beginning with the simplest and most easily known objects in order to ascend little by little, step by step, to knowledge of the most complex, and by supposing some order even among objects that have no natural order of precedence.
>
> And the last, throughout to make enumerations so complete, and reviews so comprehensive, that I could be sure of leaving nothing out. (*DM* 2.18–19, p. 120)

He says of these four rules that he thought they would be "sufficient, provided that I made a strong and unswerving resolution never to fail to observe them" (*DM* 2.18, p. 120). They are difficult to follow, as any attempt to do so will convince you immediately. But let us explore their content more carefully.

The first one has to do with a condition for accepting something as true. It is pretty stringent. You want to avoid two things: "precipitate conclusions" (hastiness) and "preconceptions" (categorizing something before you have good warrant to do so). How do you do this? By accepting only those things that are *so **clear and distinct** that you have no occasion to doubt them.* Descartes obviously has in mind such propositions as "3 + 5 = 8" and "the interior angles of a triangle are equal to two right angles." Once you understand these, you really cannot bring yourself to doubt that they are true. Can you?

What do the key words "clear" and "distinct" mean? In *The Principles of Philosophy* (PP 1.45, p. 237) he explains them as follows. Something is "clear" when it is "present and apparent to an attentive mind, in the same way as we assert that we see objects clearly when, being present to the regarding eye, they operate upon it with sufficient strength." Seeing an apple in your hand in good light would be an example. We are not to accept any belief unless it is as clear as that. Nothing obscure, fuzzy, dim, indefinite, indistinct, vague—only what is *clear!*

By "distinct" he means "so precise and different from all other objects that it contains within itself nothing but what is clear." An idea not only must be clear in itself but also impossible to confuse with any other idea. There must be no ambiguity in its meaning. Ideas must be as distinct as the idea of a triangle is from the idea of a square.

Ask yourself how many of *your* beliefs are clear and distinct in this way. Descartes is under no illusions about the high standard he sets. "There are even a number of people who throughout all their lives perceive nothing so correctly as to be capable of judging it properly." But the first rule of the method is to *accept nothing as true* that does not meet that high standard. In the first of the *Meditations* we shall see how much that excludes.

The second rule recommends **analysis**. Problems are typically complex, and an essential step in their solution is to break them into smaller problems. Anyone who has tried to write a computer program to solve a problem will have an excellent feel for this rule. Often more than half the battle is

"It is much easier to have some vague notion about any subject, no matter what, than to arrive at the real truth about a single question."

——RENÉ DESCARTES

to discover smaller problems we already have the resources to solve, so that by combining the solutions to these more elementary problems we can solve the big problem. We move, by analysis, not only from the complex to the simple, but also from the obscure to the clear and distinct, and so we follow the first rule as well.

The third rule recognizes that items for consideration may be more or less simple. It recommends beginning with the simpler ones and proceeding to the more complex. Here is a mathematical example. If we compare a straight line to a curve, we can see that there is a clear sense in which the straight line is simple and the curve is not; no straight line is more or less straight than another, but curves come in all degrees. If we know a line is straight, we know something perfectly definite about it; if we know it is curved, we do not. And it is in fact possible to analyze a curve into a series of straight lines at various angles to each other, thus

"constructing" the more complex curve from the simple straights.

For Descartes, this serves as a model of all good intellectual work. There are two basic procedures: a kind of **insight** or *intuition* of simple natures (which must be clear and distinct), and then **deduction** of complex phenomena from perceived relations among the simples. A deduction, too, is in fact just an insight: insight into the connections holding among simples. Geometry, again, provides many examples. Theorems are proved by deduction from the axioms and postulates. The latter are simply "seen" to be true; for example, through two points in a plane, one and only one straight line can be drawn. The same kind of "seeing" is required to recognize that each step in a proof is correct.

Deductions, of course, can be very long and complex, even though each of the steps is clear and distinct. That is the reason for the fourth rule: to set out all the steps completely (we all know how easily mistakes creep in when we take something for granted) and to make comprehensive reviews.

Descartes is extremely optimistic about the results we can obtain if we follow this method:

> These long chains composed of very simple and easy reasonings, which geometers customarily use to arrive at their most difficult demonstrations, had given me occasion to suppose that all the things that can fall under human knowledge are interconnected in the same way. And I thought that, provided that we refrain from accepting anything as true which is not, and always keep to the order required for deducing one thing from another, there can be nothing too remote to be reached in the end or too well hidden to be discovered. (*DM* 2.19, p. 120)

We will see this optimism at work when Descartes tackles knotty problems such as the existence of God and the relation between soul and body. But first we need to ask, Why does Descartes feel a need to address these *philosophical* problems at all? Why doesn't he just stick to mathematical physics?

For one thing, he is confident that his method will allow him to succeed where so many have failed. But a deeper reason is that he needs to show that his physics correctly describes the world, that it is more than just a likely story. In short, he needs to demonstrate that his physics is *true*. He is quite aware of the skeptical doubts of the Pyrrhonists, of the way they undermine the testimony of the senses and cast doubt on our reasoning. In particular, he is aware of the problem of the criterion.* Unless this can be solved, no certainty is possible.

Descartes thinks he has found a way to solve this problem of problems. He will outdo the Pyrrhonists at their own game; when it comes to doubting, he will be the champion doubter of all time. The first rule of his method already gives him the means to wipe the slate clean—unless, perhaps, there remains something that is *so clear and distinct that it cannot possibly be doubted*. If there were something like that (and, as we shall see, Descartes thinks that there is), the rest of the method could gain a foothold, deductions could lead us to further truths, and perhaps, from the depths of doubting despair, we could be raised to the bliss of certainty.

This is Descartes' strategy. And it is this attempt to justify his physics that makes Descartes not just a great scientist, but a great philosopher as well. We are now ready to turn to this philosophy as expressed in the *Meditations*.

Meditations on First Philosophy

Meditations is Descartes' most famous work. We focus our attention on the text itself, as we did earlier with certain dialogues of Plato. It is a remarkably rich work, and if you come to understand it, you will have mastered many of the concepts and distinctions that philosophers use to this day. So it will repay careful study. I cannot emphasize too much that in this section it is the *text*, the words of Descartes himself, that you must wrestle with. It is he who is your partner in this conversation, and you must make him speak to you and—as far as possible—answer your questions. What I do is offer some commentary on particularly difficult aspects, fill in some background, and ask some questions.

Though it is usually known just as the *Meditations*, the full title of the work is *Meditations on First Philosophy in Which the Existence of God and the Distinction of the Soul from the Body Are Demonstrated*. The title gives you some idea what to expect. But as you will see, his experience as a mathematician and physicist is everywhere present. It was first published in 1641.

Although not represented in our text, the *Meditations* are prefaced by a letter to "the Wisest and Most Distinguished Men, the Dean and Doctors of the Faculty of Theology in Paris." The motivation behind this letter is fairly transparent. It had been just eight years since the condemnation of Galileo's opinions, and, as we have seen, Descartes has allied himself with the basic outlook of Galileo. The Faculty of Theology in Paris had indeed been an illustrious one for some centuries. If he could secure their approval, he could almost certainly escape Galileo's fate. The *Meditations* was examined carefully by one of the theologians, who expressed his approval, but twenty-two years later it was placed on the *Index Librorum Prohibitorum* of books dangerous to read.*

Descartes had also asked one of his close friends, the priest and scientist Mersenne, to circulate the text to some distinguished philosophers, who were then invited to write criticisms of it. These criticisms, including some from his English contemporary Thomas Hobbes, were printed along with Descartes' replies at the end of the volume.†

In the letter to the theologians, Descartes refers to "believers like ourselves." He professes to be absolutely convinced that it is sufficient in these matters to rely on Scripture. But there is a problem. On the one hand, God's existence, he says, is to be believed because it is taught in Scripture.

---

*The *Index* was created in 1571 by Pope Pius V, after approval by the Council of Trent; the latter was a general council of the Roman Catholic Church, called to deal with problems created by the Protestant Reformation. It set in motion the Catholic Counter-Reformation, and the *Index* was one of its tools.

†We discuss the views of Hobbes in the next chapter. For his criticisms of the *Meditations*, see the "Third Set of Objections" in Haldane and Ross, *The Philosophical Works of Descartes*, Volume 2.

---

*For a discussion of this problem by the ancient skeptics, see pp. 211–213. For the impact of skepticism nearer to Descartes' time, see pp. 303–306.

Scripture, on the other hand, is to be believed because God is its source. Now it doesn't take a lot of thought to realize that there is a circle here, a pretty tight circle. It comes down to believing that God exists because you believe that God exists. (Recall skeptics such as Sextus and Montaigne, who maintain that all our claims to know are either involved in such circular thinking or are strung out in an infinite regress.)

To break into the circle, Descartes thinks it necessary to prove *rationally* that God exists and that the soul is distinct from the body. His claim that reason should be able to do this is no innovation; Augustine, Anselm, Aquinas, and others had said as much before. Descartes, however, claims to have proofs superior to any offered by these thinkers.

He refers to some thinkers who hold that it is rational to believe the soul perishes with the body. Aristotle seems in the main to think so (though he waffles).* Christian Aristotelians like Thomas Aquinas labor mightily, but inconclusively, to reconcile this view with the tradition of an immortal soul. Descartes thinks he has a proof of the soul that is direct, simple, and conclusive.† He claims, in fact, that his proofs will "surpass in certitude and obviousness the demonstrations of geometry." A strong claim indeed! You will have to decide whether you agree.

These are meditations on **first philosophy**. This is a term derived from Aristotle, who means by it a search for the first principles of things. First philosophy is also called *metaphysics*. Descartes uses a memorable image.

> Thus the whole of philosophy is like a tree; the roots are metaphysics, the trunk is physics, and the branches that issue from the trunk are all the other sciences.[4]

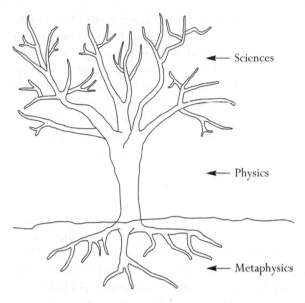

Metaphysics, then, is thought to be more fundamental even than physics. Physics and the other sciences give us detailed knowledge of material things; first philosophy inquires whether material things are the only things there are. What Descartes is seeking is a set of concepts that will give us an inventory of the *basic kinds of being*.* As it turns out, his inventory of what there is looks fairly simple. We can diagram it this way:

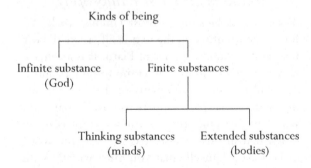

But by itself this chart isn't very informative. It is time to turn to the *Meditations* themselves, to see how Descartes fills in this schema and why it turns out just that way.

---

*For Aristotle's view of the soul as "the form of a living human body" see pp. 000–000.

†Descartes tends to use the terms "soul," "mind," and "spirit" interchangeably. They are all terms for "the thing that thinks." Some philosophers and theologians make distinctions among them.

---

*Aristotle calls such fundamental concepts "categories." See p. 159. It is interesting to note that in 1641 all the sciences are still counted as parts of philosophy, the love of wisdom.

The full text of Descartes' *Meditations* is represented here.[5] After each of the six sections, you will find commentary and questions. Read through each meditation quickly. (They aren't very long.) Then go to the discussion, moving back to the text to check your understanding. Write out brief answers to the questions. Descartes is a careful and clear writer and says exactly what he means. If you proceed in this way, you will not only learn some philosophy but will gain skill in reading a text of some difficulty—a valuable ability.

It may be helpful to have a preview of this dramatic little work. I offer an outline that sketches the progression from the first *Meditation* to the last.

Meditation I. The Problem:
   Can anything be known?
Meditations II–VI. The Solution: I can know
   II.   that I exist.
   III. that God exists.
   IV.   why we make mistakes and how to avoid them.
   V.   that material things *might* exist; and again, that God exists.
   VI.   that material things *do* exist and are distinct from souls.

Meditation I: On What Can Be Called into Doubt

For several years now, I've been aware that I accepted many falsehoods as true in my youth, that what I built on the foundation of those falsehoods was dubious, and accordingly that once in my life I would need to tear down everything and begin anew from the foundations if I wanted to establish any stable and lasting knowledge. But the task seemed enormous, and I waited until I was so old that no better time for undertaking it would be likely to follow. I have thus delayed so long that it would be wrong for me to waste in indecision the time left for action. Today, then, having rid myself of worries and having arranged for some peace and quiet, I withdraw alone, free at last earnestly and wholeheartedly to overthrow all my beliefs.

To do this, I don't need to show each of them to be false; I may never be able to do that. But, since reason now convinces me that I ought to withhold my assent just as carefully from what isn't obviously certain and indubitable as from what's obviously false, I can justify the rejection of all my beliefs if in each I can find some ground for doubt. And, to do this, I need not run through my beliefs one by one, which would be an endless task. Since a building collapses when its foundation is cut out from under it, I will go straight to the principles on which all my former beliefs rested.

Of course, whatever I have so far accepted as supremely true I have learned either from the senses or through the senses. But I have occasionally caught the senses deceiving me, and it's prudent never completely to trust those who have cheated us even once.

But, while my senses may deceive me about what is small or far away, there may still be other things that I take in by the senses but that I cannot possibly doubt—like that I am here, sitting before the fire, wearing a dressing gown, touching this paper. And on what grounds might I deny that my hands and the other parts of my body exist?—unless perhaps I liken myself to madmen whose brains are so rattled by the persistent vapors of melancholy that they are sure that they're kings when in fact they are paupers, or that they wear purple robes when in fact they're naked, or that their heads are clay, or that they are gourds, or made of glass. But these people are insane, and I would seem just as crazy if I were to apply what I say about them to myself.

This would be perfectly obvious—if I weren't a man accustomed to sleeping at night whose experiences while asleep are at least as far-fetched as those that madmen have while awake. How often, at night, I've been convinced that I was here, sitting before the fire, wearing my dressing gown, when in fact I was undressed and between the covers of my bed! But now I am looking at this piece of paper with my eyes wide open; the head that I am shaking has not been lulled to sleep; I put my hand out consciously and deliberately and feel. None of this would be as distinct if I were asleep. As if I can't remember having been tricked by similar thoughts while asleep! When I think very carefully about this, I see so plainly that there are no reliable signs by which I can distinguish sleeping from waking that I am stupefied—and my stupor itself suggests that I am asleep!

Suppose, then that I am dreaming. Suppose, in particular, that my eyes are not open, that my head is not moving, and that I have not put out my hand. Suppose that I do not have hands, or even a body. I must still admit that the things I see in sleep are like painted images which must have been patterned after real things and, hence, that things like eyes, heads, hands, and bodies are real rather than imaginary. For, even when painters try to give bizarre shapes to sirens and satyrs, they are unable to give them completely new natures; they only jumble together the parts of various animals. And, even if they were to come up with something so novel that no one had ever seen anything like it before, something entirely fictitious and unreal, at least there must be real colors from which they composed it. Similarly, while things like eyes, heads, and hands may be imaginary, it must be granted that some simpler and more universal things are real—the "real colors" from which the true and false images in our thoughts are formed.

Things of this sort seem to include general bodily nature and its extension, the shape of extended things, their quantity (that is, their size and number), the place in which they exist, the time through which they endure, and so on.

Perhaps we can correctly infer that, while physics, astronomy, medicine, and other disciplines that require the study of composites are dubious, disciplines like arithmetic and geometry, which deal only with completely simple and universal things without regard to whether they exist in the world, are somehow certain and indubitable. For, whether we are awake or asleep, two plus three is always five, and the square never has more than four sides. It seems impossible even to suspect such obvious truths of falsity.

Nevertheless, the traditional view is fixed in my mind that there is a God who can do anything and by whom I have been made to be as I am. How do I know that He hasn't brought it about that, while there is in fact no earth, no sky, no extended thing, no shape, no magnitude, and no place, all of these things seem to me to exist, just as they do now? I think that other people sometimes err in what they believe themselves to know perfectly well. Mightn't I be deceived when I add two and three, or count the sides of a square, or do even simpler things, if we can even suppose that there is anything simpler? Maybe it will be denied that God deceives me, since He is said to be supremely good. But, if God's being good is incompatible with His having created me so that I am deceived always, it seems just as out of line with His being good that He permits me to be deceived sometimes—as he undeniably does.

Maybe some would rather deny that there is an omnipotent God than believe that everything else is uncertain. Rather than arguing with them, I will grant everything I have said about God to be fiction. But, however these people think I came to be as I now am—whether they say it is by fate, or by accident, or by a continuous series of events, or in some other way—it seems that he who errs and is deceived is somehow imperfect. Hence,

the less power that is attributed to my original creator, the more likely it is that I am always deceived. To these arguments, I have no reply. I'm forced to admit that nothing that I used to believe is beyond legitimate doubt—not because I have been careless or playful, but because I have valid and well-considered grounds for doubt. Hence, I must withhold my assent from my former beliefs as carefully as from obvious falsehoods if I want to arrive at something certain.

But it's not enough to have noticed this: I must also take care to bear it in mind. For my habitual views constantly return to my mind and take control of what I believe as if our long-standing, intimate relationship has given them the right to do so, even against my will. I'll never break the habit of trusting and giving in to these views while I see them for what they are—things somewhat dubious (as I have just shown) but nonetheless probable, things that I have much more reason to believe than to deny. That's why I think it will be good deliberately to turn my will around, to allow myself to be deceived, and to suppose that all my previous beliefs are false and illusory. Eventually, when I have counterbalanced the weight of my prejudices, my bad habits will no longer distort my grasp of things. I know that there is no danger of error here and that I won't overindulge in skepticism, since I'm now concerned, not with action, but only with gaining knowledge.

I will suppose, then, not that there is a supremely good God who is the source of all truth, but that there is an evil demon, supremely powerful and cunning, who works as hard as he can to deceive me. I will say that sky, air, earth, color, shape, sound, and other external things are just dreamed illusions that the demon uses to ensnare my judgment. I will regard myself as not having hands, eyes, flesh, blood, and senses—but as having the false belief that I have all these things. I will obstinately concentrate on this meditation and will thus ensure by mental resolution that, if I do not really have the ability to know the truth, I will at least withhold assent from what is false and from what a deceiver may try to put over on me, however powerful and cunning he may be. But this plan requires effort, and laziness brings me back to my ordinary life. I am like a prisoner who happens to enjoy the illusion of freedom in his dreams, begins to suspect that he is asleep, fears being awakened, and deliberately lets the enticing illusions slip by unchallenged. Thus, I slide back into my old views, afraid to awaken and to find that after my peaceful rest I must toil, not in the light, but in the confusing darkness of the problems just raised.

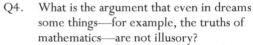

Commentary and Questions

Note the personal, meditative character of the writing. Descartes is inviting us to join him in thinking certain things through, asking us to mull them over and see whether we agree. He is not making authoritative pronouncements. Just as he reserves the right to be the judge of what *he* should believe, so he puts you on the spot. You will have to be continually asking yourself: Do I agree with this or not? If not, why not? This familiar first-person style is quite different from most of medieval philosophy; it harks back to Augustine's *Confessions* in the late fourth century. Descartes is, as it were, having a conversation with himself, so the structure of *Meditation I* is dialectical: proposal, objection, reply, objection, reply. . . . Try to distinguish the various "voices" in this internal dialogue.

Note that there are three stages in the "tearing down" of opinions, and one principle running throughout. The principle is that we ought to withhold assent from anything uncertain, just as much as from what we see clearly to be false. This is simply a restatement of the first rule of his method but is of the greatest importance.* The three stages concern (1) the **senses**, (2) **dreams**, and (3) the **evil demon** hypothesis.

Q1.   Aren't you strongly inclined to think, just like Descartes by the fire, that you can't deny that you are now reading this book, which is "right there" in your hands? Should you doubt it anyway?

Q2.   What do you think of Descartes' rule that we shouldn't completely trust those who have cheated us even once? Does this rule apply to the senses?

Q3.   *Could* you be dreaming right now? Explain.

---

*A brief look back at the four rules of the method will be of use at this point. See p. 317. Compare the principle Aquinas notes about big mistakes from small beginnings on p. 269. Once, when a friend of mine stumbled on an unusually high first step of a staircase, I formulated what came jokingly to be known as Norman's First Law: Watch that first step; it's a big one—good advice for appraising philosophical systems. For an alternative to Descartes' view, see the critique by C. S. Peirce on pp. 566–567.

Q4.   What is the argument that even in dreams some things—for example, the truths of mathematics—are not illusory?

Q5.   How does the thought of God, at *this* stage, seem to reinforce skeptical conclusions—even about arithmetic?*

"All that we see or seem
Is but a dream within a dream."

Edgar Allan Poe (1809–1849)

Here Descartes avails himself of the techniques of the Pyrrhonists, who set argument against plausible argument until they find themselves no more inclined to judge one way than another. But he acknowledges that this equilibrium or suspension of judgment is difficult to achieve. "Habit" strongly inclines him to believe some of these things as "probable." Like Descartes, you almost certainly take it as *very* probable that you are now looking at a piece of paper, which is located a certain determinate distance before your eyes, that you indeed have eyes, and that 2 plus 3 really does equal 5. And you almost certainly find it very hard *not* to believe these things. You probably find yourself so committed to them that you almost *can't* doubt them. (Ask yourself whether this is the case.) How can we overcome these habits of believing? We now know, if Descartes is right so far, that we *should* doubt them. As a remedy against these habitual believings, Descartes determines *deliberately* (as an act of will) to suppose that all his prior beliefs are false.

Q6.   How does the hypothesis of the evil demon help?

Descartes now thinks that he has canvassed every possible reason for doubting. We cannot rely on our senses; we cannot even rely on our rational

---

*Review the consequences William of Ockham draws from the doctrine of God's omnipotence (pp. 288–290).

faculties for the simplest truths of mathematics, geometry, or logic. All our beliefs, it seems, are dissolved in the acid of skeptical doubt.

Q7. Before going on to *Meditation II*, ask yourself the question, Is there anything at all that I am *so certain* of that I could not *possibly* doubt it? (Meditate on this question awhile.)

Meditation II: On the Nature of the Human Mind, Which Is Better Known Than the Body

Yesterday's meditation has hurled me into doubts so great that I can neither ignore them nor think my way out of them. I am in turmoil, as if I have accidentally fallen into a whirlpool and can neither touch bottom nor swim to the safety of the surface. I will struggle, however, and try to follow the path that I started on yesterday. I will reject whatever is open to the slightest doubt just as though I have found it to be entirely false, and I will continue until I find something certain—or at least until I know for certain that nothing is certain. Archimedes required only one fixed and immovable point to move the whole earth from its place, and I too can hope for great things if I can find even one small thing that is certain and unshakeable.

I will suppose, then, that everything I see is unreal. I will believe that my memory is unreliable and that none of what it presents to me ever happened. I have no senses. Body, shape, extension, motion, and place are fantasies. What then is true? Perhaps just that nothing is certain.

But how do I know that there isn't something different from the things just listed that I do not have the slightest reason to doubt? Isn't there a God, or something like one, who puts my thoughts into me? But why should I say so when I may be the author of those thoughts? Well, isn't it at least the case that I am something? But I now am denying that I have senses and a body. But I stop here. For what follows from these denials? Am I so bound to my body and to my senses that I cannot exist without them? I have convinced myself that there is nothing in the world—no sky, no earth, no minds, no bodies. Doesn't it follow that I don't exist? No, surely I must exist if it's me who is convinced of something. But there is a deceiver, supremely powerful and cunning whose aim is to see that I am always

deceived. But surely I exist, if I am deceived. Let him deceive me all he can, he will never make it the case that I am nothing while I think that I am something. Thus having fully weighed every consideration, I must finally conclude that the statement "I am, I exist" must be true whenever I state it or mentally consider it.

But I do not yet fully understand what this "I" is that must exist. I must guard against inadvertently taking myself to be something other than I am, thereby going wrong even in the knowledge that I put forward as supremely certain and evident. Hence, I will think once again about what I believed myself to be before beginning these meditations. From this conception, I will subtract everything challenged by the reasons for doubt that I produced earlier, until nothing remains except what is certain and indubitable.

What, then, did I formerly take myself to be? A man, of course. But what is a man? Should I say a rational animal? No, because then I would need to ask what an animal is and what it is to be rational. Thus, starting from a single question, I would sink into many that are more difficult, and I do not have the time to waste on such subtleties. Instead, I will look here at the thoughts that occurred to me spontaneously and naturally when I reflected on what I was. This first thought to occur to me was that I have a face, hands, arms, and all the other equipment (also found in corpses) which I call a body. The next thought to occur to me was that I take nourishment, move myself around, sense, and think—that I do things which I trace back to my soul. Either I didn't stop to think about what this soul was, or I imagined it to be a rarified air, or fire, or ether permeating the denser parts of my body. But, about physical objects, I didn't have any doubts whatever: I thought that I distinctly knew their nature. If I had tried to describe my conception of this nature, I might have said this: "When I call something a physical object, I mean that it is capable of being bounded by a shape and limited to a place; that it can fill a space so as to exclude other objects from it; that it can be perceived by touch, sight, hearing, taste, and smell; that it can be moved in various ways, not by itself, but by something else in contact with it." I judged that the powers of self-movement, of sensing, and of thinking did not belong to the nature of physical objects, and, in fact, I marveled that there were some physical objects in which these powers could be found.

But what should I think now, while supposing that a supremely powerful and "evil" deceiver completely devotes himself to deceiving me? Can I say that I have any of the things that I have attributed to the nature of physical objects? I concentrate, think, reconsider—but nothing comes to me; I grow tired of the pointless repetition. But what about the things that I have assigned to soul? Nutrition and self-movement? Since I have no body, these are merely illusions. Sensing? But I cannot sense without a body, and in sleep I've seemed to sense many things that I later realized I had not really sensed. Thinking? It comes down to this: Thought and thought alone cannot be taken away from me. I am, I exist. That much is certain. But for how long? As long as I think—for it may be that, if I completely stopped thinking, I would completely cease to exist. I am not now admitting anything unless it must be true, and I am therefore not admitting that I am anything at all other than a thinking thing—that is, a mind, soul, understanding, or reason (terms whose meaning I did not previously know). I know that I am a real, existing thing, but what kind of thing? As I have said, a thing that thinks.

What else? I will draw up mental images. I'm not the collection of organs called a human body. Nor am I some rarified gas permeating these organs, or air, or fire, or vapor, or breath—for I have supposed that none of these things exist. Still, I am something. But couldn't it be that these things, which I do not yet know about and which I am therefore supposing to be nonexistent, really aren't distinct from the "I" that I know to exist? I don't know, and I'm not going to argue about it now. I can only form judgments on what I do know. I know that I exist, and I ask what the "I" is that I know to exist. It's obvious that this conception of myself doesn't depend on anything that I do not yet know to exist and, therefore, that it does not depend on anything of which I can draw up a mental image. And the words "draw up" point to my mistake. I would truly be creative if I were to have a mental image of what I am, since to have a mental image is just to contemplate the shape or image of a physical object. I now know with certainty that I exist and at the same time that all images—and, more generally, all things associated with the nature of physical objects—may just be dreams. When I keep this in mind, it seems just as absurd to say "I use mental images to help me understand what I am" as it would to say "Now, while awake, I see something true—but, since I don't yet see it clearly enough, I'll go to sleep and let my dreams present it to me more clearly and truly." Thus I know that none of the things that I can comprehend with the aid of mental images bear on my knowledge of myself. And I must carefully draw my mind away from such things if it is to see its own nature distinctly.

But what then am I? A thinking thing. And what is that? Something that doubts, understands, affirms, denies, wills, refuses, and also senses and has mental images.

That's quite a lot, if I really do all of these things. But don't I? Isn't it me who now doubts nearly everything, understands one thing, affirms this thing, refuses to affirm other things, wants to know much more, refuses to be deceived, has mental images (sometimes involuntarily), and is aware of many things "through his senses"? Even if I am always dreaming, and even if my creator does what he can to deceive me, isn't it just as true that I do all these things as that I exist? Are any of these things distinct from my thought? Can any be said to be separate from me? That it's me who doubts, understands, and wills is so obvious that I don't see how it could be more evident. And it's also me who has mental images. While it may be, as I am supposing, that absolutely nothing of which I have a mental image really exists, the ability to have mental images really does exist and is a part of my thought. Finally, it's me who senses—or who seems to gain awareness of physical objects through the senses. For example, I am now seeing light, hearing a noise, and feeling heat. These things are unreal, since I am dreaming. But it is still certain that I seem to see, to hear, and to feel. This seeming cannot be unreal, and it is what is properly called sensing. Strictly speaking, sensing is just thinking.

From this, I begin to learn a little about what I am. But I still can't stop thinking that I apprehend physical objects, which I picture in mental images and examine with my senses, much more distinctly than I know this unfamiliar "I," of which I cannot form a mental image. I think this, even though it would be astounding if I comprehended things which I've found to be doubtful, unknown, and alien to me more distinctly than the one which I know to be real: my self. But I see what's happening. My mind enjoys wandering, and it won't confine itself to the truth. I will therefore loosen the reigns on my mind for now so that later, when the time is right, I will be able to control it more easily.

Let's consider the things commonly taken to be the most distinctly comprehended: physical objects that we see and touch. Let's not consider physical objects in general, since general conceptions are very often confused. Rather, let's consider one, particular object. Take, for example, this piece of wax. It has just been taken from the honeycomb; it hasn't yet completely lost the taste of honey; it still smells of the flowers from which it was gathered; its color, shape, and size are obvious; it is hard, cold, and easy to touch; it makes a sound when rapped. In short, everything seems to be present in the wax that is required for me to know it as distinctly as possible. But, as I speak, I move the wax toward the fire; it loses what was left of its taste; it gives up its smell; it changes color; it loses its shape; it gets bigger; it melts; it heats up; it becomes difficult to touch; it no longer makes a sound when struck. Is it still the same piece of wax? We must say that it is: not one denies it or thinks otherwise. Then what was there in the wax that I comprehended so distinctly? Certainly nothing that I reached with my senses—for, while everything having to do with taste, smell, sight, touch, and hearing has changed, the same piece of wax remains.

Perhaps what I distinctly knew was neither the sweetness of honey, nor the fragrance of flowers, nor a sound, but a physical object that once appeared to me one way and now appears differently. But what exactly is it of which I now have a mental image? Let's pay careful attention, remove everything that doesn't belong to the wax, and see what's left. Nothing is left except an extended, flexible, and changeable thing. But what is it for this thing to be flexible and changeable? Is it just that the wax can go from round to square and then to triangular, as I have mentally pictured? Of course not. Since I understand that the wax's shape can change in innumerable ways, and since I can't run through all the changes in my imagination, my comprehension of the wax's flexibility and changeability cannot have been produced by my ability to have mental images. And what about the thing that is extended? Are we also ignorant of its extension? Since the extension of the wax increases when the wax melts, increases again when the wax boils, and increases still more when the wax gets hotter, I will be mistaken about what the wax is unless I believe that it can undergo more changes in extension than I can ever encompass with mental images. I must therefore admit that I do not have an image of what the wax is—that I grasp what it is with only my mind. (While I am saying this about a particular piece of wax, it is even more clearly true about wax in general.) What then is this piece of wax that I grasp only with my mind? It is something that I see, feel, and mentally picture—exactly what I believed it to be at the outset. But it must be noted that, despite the appearances, my grasp of the wax is not visual, tactile, or pictorial. Rather, my grasp of the wax is the result of a purely mental inspection, which can be imperfect and confused, as it was once, or clear and distinct, as it is now, depending on how much attention I pay to the things of which the wax consists.

I'm surprised by how prone my mind is to error. Even when I think to myself non-verbally, language stands in my way, and common usage comes close to deceiving me. For, when the wax is present, we say that we see the wax itself, not that we infer its presence from its color and shape. I'm inclined to leap from this fact about language to the conclusion that I learn about the wax by eyesight rather than by purely mental inspection. But, if I happen to look out my window and see men walking in the street, I naturally say that I see the men just as I say that I see the wax. What do I really see, however, but hats and coats that could be covering robots? I *judge* that there are men. Thus I comprehend with my judgment, which is in my mind, objects that I once believed myself to see with my eyes.

One who aspires to wisdom above that of the common man disgraces himself by deriving doubt from common ways of speaking. Let's go on, then, to ask when I most clearly and perfectly grasped what the wax is. Was it when I first looked at the wax and believed my knowledge of it to come from the external senses—or at any rate from the so-called "common sense," the power of having mental images? Or is it now, after I have carefully studied what the wax is and how I come to know it? Doubt would be silly here. For what was distinct in my original conception of the wax? How did that conception differ from that had by animals? When I distinguish the wax from its external forms—when I "undress" it and view it "naked"—there may still be errors in my judgments about it, but I couldn't possibly grasp the wax in this way without a human mind.

What should I say about this mind—or, in other words, about myself? (I am not now admitting that there is anything to me but a mind.) What is this "I" that seems to grasp the wax so distinctly? Don't I know myself much more truly and certainly, and also much more distinctly and plainly, than I know the wax? For, if I base my judgment that the wax exists on the fact that I see it, my seeing it much more obviously implies that I exist. It's possible that what I see is not really wax, and it's even possible that I don't have eyes with which to see—but it clearly is not possible that, when I see (or, what now amounts to the same thing, when I think I see), the "I" that thinks is not a real thing. Similarly, if I base my judgment that the wax exists on the fact that I feel it, the same fact makes it obvious that I exist. If I base my judgment that the wax exists on the fact that I have a mental image of it or on some other fact of this sort, the same thing can obviously be said. And what I've said about the wax applies to everything else that is outside me. Moreover, if I seem to grasp the wax more distinctly when I detect it with several senses than when I detect it with just sight or touch, I must know myself even more distinctly—for every consideration that contributes to my grasp of the piece of wax or to my grasp of any other physical object serves better to reveal the nature of my mind.

Besides, the mind has so much in it by which it can make its conception of itself distinct that what comes to it from physical objects hardly seems to matter.

And now I have brought myself back to where I wanted to be. I now know that physical objects are grasped, not by the senses or the power of having mental images, but by understanding alone. And, since I grasp physical objects in virtue of their being understandable rather than in virtue of their being tangible or visible, I know that I can't grasp anything more easily or plainly than my mind. But, since it takes time to break old habits of thought, I should pause here to allow the length of my contemplation to impress the new thoughts more deeply into my memory.

Commentary and Questions

Descartes seems to have gotten nowhere by doubting. What to do? He resolves to press on, suspecting that the terrors of skepticism can be overcome only by enduring them to the end. The monster in the child's closet will disappear only if the child can muster the courage to look at it directly. If we avert our eyes in fear, we will not conquer.

The particular horror, of course, is that all our beliefs might be false—that nowhere would they connect at all with reality. If Descartes has carried us with him to this point, we know that we have lots of ideas and beliefs, but whether any one of them represents something that really *exists* must seem quite uncertain. Perhaps they are just webs of illusion, like those spun by a master magician—or the evil demon.

Descartes here presents a pattern of thought that deserves a name. Let us call it the representational theory of knowledge and perception, or the **representational theory** for short. The basic ideas of this theory are very widely shared in modern philosophy. We can distinguish five points:

1. We have no immediate or direct access to things in the world, only to the world of our ideas.*

---

*The American philosopher John Searle calls this view that we only perceive our *ideas* of objects "the greatest single disaster in the history of philosophy over the past four centuries." In *Mind: A Brief Introduction* (Oxford: Oxford University Press, 2004), 23.

2. "Ideas" must be understood broadly to include all the contents of the mind, including perceptions, images, memories, concepts, beliefs, intentions, and decisions.

3. These ideas serve as *representations* of things other than themselves.

4. Much of what these ideas represent, they represent as "out there," or "external" to the mind containing them.

5. It is in principle possible for ideas to represent these things correctly, but they may also be false and misleading.

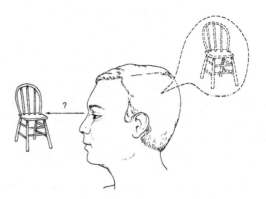

In *Meditation I*, Descartes draws a certain consequence of the representational theory. It seems that mind and world could be disconnected in a perplexing way, that even the most solid ideas might represent things all wrong—or maybe even not represent anything at all! This possibility, foreshadowed by the ancient skeptics and by William of Ockham in his reflections on God's omnipotence, provokes thinkers to try to find a remedy. What we need is a bridge across the chasm between mind and world, and it is clear that it will have to be built by inference and argument. We want *good reasons* to believe that our ideas represent the "external" world truly. But the good reasons must be of a peculiar sort. We have to start this construction project while isolated on one side, restricted in our choice of materials to those available there. It is from the vantage point of the mind that we try to stretch the girders of our argument across the gulf to the world.

We will examine Descartes' effort to build such a rational bridge. The difficulty of that task is emphasized in the dramatic rehearsal of skeptical worries about knowledge in *Meditation I*. And we can now see that these worries hover around the representational theory. The gulf between mind and external reality seems immense.* We might remember Archimedes, who says, "Give me a lever long enough, and a place on which to rest it, and I can move the earth." Descartes thinks that if he can find just one certainty, he might, like Archimedes, do marvels. He might just build that bridge.

Q8.   To what certainty does Descartes' methodical doubt lead? Is he right about that?†

The principle "I think, therefore I am" is often referred to as the *cogito*, from the Latin "I think" and we will use that shorthand expression from time to time. It is worth emphasizing that in the *cogito* Descartes has an example of *knowledge*, of knowledge about *reality*, and so of *metaphysical* knowledge. He has thrown the first plank of his bridge across the chasm.

Note that Descartes rejects the standard, long-accepted way of answering the question, What am I? (p. 324). According to a tradition that goes back to Socrates (and is codified by Aristotle), the way to answer such a question is to give a *definition*. The traditional way to define something will tell you (a) what *genus* it belongs to and (b) the *difference* between it and other things in that genus. Not surprisingly, this is called *definition by **genus and difference***. A human being is said to belong to the genus *animal;* and the difference between a human and other animals is that a human is *rational*. Human beings, Aristotle says, are *rational animals*.

Descartes objects to such a definition because it simply calls for more definitions; you need next

a definition of *animal* and a definition for *rational*. Then, presumably, you will require definitions for the terms used to define *them*. And so on.

This whole process has to come to ground somewhere. There must be some terms, Descartes thinks, that do not need definition of this sort, but whose meaning can just be "seen." These will be the *simple* terms. From them, more complex terms can be built up. We see in Descartes' rejection of the traditional definition procedure an application of the second and third rules of his method. He is searching for something so simple, clear, and distinct that it just presents itself without any need for definition. He is looking for something **self-evident**. If that can be found, he can use it as a foundation on which to build more complex truths.

Q9.   What, then, does Descartes conclude that he is?

Note that Descartes briefly considers the view that he may after all *be* a body, or some such thing, even though he does not *know* he is (p. 325).* But he does not try to refute it here; that proof comes in *Meditation VI*. Here he is interested in what he knows that he *is*—not in what he can infer that he *is not*.

Q10.   Why does Descartes rule out the use of the imagination in answering the question, What am I?

Q11.   What is included in "thinking," as Descartes understands the term? (See p. 325.) Note how broad the term is for him.

Q12.   Suppose I feel certain that I see a cat on the mat. Is it certain that there is a cat on the mat? What, in this situation, *can* I be certain of?

How difficult it is to stay within the bounds of what I know for certain! As Descartes says, his "mind enjoys wandering." And so it is with us. I, too, keep slipping back into the error of thinking that I know *sensible* things best—this desk, this computer keyboard, this hand. (Do you find that too?)

---

*Other thinkers after Descartes also wrestle with this problem. Locke recognizes the gulf but papers it over, Berkeley settles down on one side of it, Hume despairs of a solution, Kant redefines the problem so as to make the gulf (partially) disappear, Hegel denies there is a gulf at all, and Kierkegaard opens it up again. The problem is not dead today.

†Descartes' central idea here is anticipated by Augustine in his refutation of the skeptics. See pp. 232–233.

---

*This is the view that Thomas Hobbes urges against Descartes. See "Minds and Motives" in Chapter 14.

It is to cure this inclination to rely on the senses that Descartes considers the bit of wax. Read that passage once more (pp. 325–326). All the sensible qualities by means of which we recognize the wax can change. But we still judge that it is the same wax. What does that mean?

The distinction between *ordinary perception* and *judgment* is crucial for Descartes. It is illustrated by the hats and coats we see through the window. We say that we *see* men passing, but this is inaccurate, for they may be just robots dressed like men. What is actually happening in ordinary perception is that our intellect is drawing an *inference* on the basis of certain *data* (supplied by the senses) and issuing a judgment. Judging is an activity of the mind—indeed, as we'll see in *Meditation IV*, of the will.

Perceiving, then, is not a purely passive registration by the senses. Implicit in all perception is judgment, or *giving assent*. In ordinary perception, these judgments are apt to be obscure, confused, and just plain wrong. But fortunately they can be corrected by the application of ideas that are clear and distinct. (These points will be crucial in *Meditation IV*, where Descartes explains how it is possible for us to err.)

With respect to the bit of wax, the moral is that it is "grasped, not by the senses or the power of having mental images, but by the understanding alone." When based wholly on sense, our perception is "imperfect and confused." When directed, however, to "the things of which the wax consists" (the mathematically determinable simples of extension, figure, and motion), knowledge of the wax can be *clear and distinct*.

Now we can understand why Descartes introduces the wax example. If even here knowledge cannot be found in sensation, but only in a "purely mental inspection," then we should have less difficulty remembering that knowledge of *what we are* must also be approached in this way. Our tendency to think of ourselves as what we can *sense* of ourselves—these hands, this head, these eyes—is considerably undermined. Indeed, I must know myself "much more truly and certainly" even than the wax.

And there follows a remarkable conclusion: "I can't grasp anything more easily or plainly than my mind." (What would Freud have said to that?)

Q13. What qualities, then, belong to the wax essentially? (Look again at the basic principles of Descartes' physics on pp. 315–316.)

Q14. Why is our imagination incapable of grasping these qualities of the wax? By what faculty do we grasp it?

Q15. How does the wax example help to cure our habitual inclination to trust the senses?

Q16. How does our language tend to mislead us?

Meditation III: On God's Existence

I will now close my eyes, plug my ears, and withdraw all my senses. I will rid my thoughts of the images of physical objects—or, since that's beyond me, I'll write those images off as empty illusions. Talking with myself and looking more deeply into myself, I'll try gradually to come to know myself better. I am a thinking thing—a thing that doubts, affirms, denies, understands a few things, is ignorant of many things, wills, and refuses. I also sense and have mental images. For, as I've noted, even though the things of which I have sensations or mental images may not exist outside me, I'm certain that the modifications of thought called sensations and mental images exist in me insofar as they are just modifications of thought.

Both inferences seem to be correct. What reason is there to prefer Bridget's formulation?

That's a summary of all that I really know—or, at any rate, of all that I've so far noticed that I know. I now will examine more carefully whether there are other things in me that I have not yet discovered. I'm certain that I am a thinking thing. Then don't I know what's needed for me to be certain of other things? In this first knowledge, there is nothing but a clear and distinct grasp of what I affirm, and this grasp surely would not suffice to make me certain if it could ever happen that something I grasped so clearly and distinctly was false. Accordingly, I seem to be able to establish the general rule that whatever I clearly and distinctly grasp is true.

But, in the past, I've accepted as completely obvious and certain many thoughts that I later found to be dubious. What were these thoughts about? The earth, the sky, the stars, and other objects of sense. But what did I clearly grasp about these objects? Only that ideas or thoughts of them appeared in my mind. Even now, I don't deny that these ideas occur in me. But there was something else that I used to affirm—something that I used to believe myself to grasp clearly but did not really grasp at all: I affirmed that there were things besides me, that the ideas in me came from these things, and that the ideas perfectly resembled these things. Either I erred here, or I reached a true judgment that wasn't justified by the strength of my understanding.

But what follows? When I considered very simple and easy points of arithmetic or geometry—such as that two and three together make five—didn't I see them clearly enough to affirm their truth? My only reason for judging that I ought to doubt these things was the thought that my God-given nature might deceive me even about what seems most obvious. Whenever I conceive of an all-powerful God, I'm compelled to admit that, if He wants, He can make it the case that I err even about what I take my mind's eye to see most clearly. But, when I turn to the things that I believe myself to grasp very clearly, I'm so convinced by them that I spontaneously burst forth saying, "Whoever may deceive me, he will never bring it about that I am nothing while I think that I am something, or that I have never been when it is now true that I am, or that two plus three is either more or less than five, or that something else in which I recognize an obvious inconsistency is true." And, since I have no reason for thinking that God is a deceiver—indeed since I don't yet know whether God exists—the grounds for doubt that rest on the supposition that God deceives are very weak and "metaphysical." Still, to rid myself of these grounds, I ought

to ask as soon as possible whether there is a God and, if so, whether He can be a deceiver. For it seems that, until I know these two things, I can never be completely certain of anything else.

The structure of my project seems to require, however, that I first categorize my thoughts and ask in which of them truth and falsity really reside. Some of my thoughts are like images of things, and only these can properly be called ideas. I have an idea, for example, when I think of a man, of a chimera, of heaven, of an angel, or of God. But other thoughts have other properties: while I always apprehend something as the object of my thought when I will, fear, affirm, or deny, these thoughts also include a component in addition to the likeness of that thing. Some of these components are called volitions or emotions; others, judgments.

Now, viewed in themselves and without regard to other things, ideas cannot really be false. If I imagine a chimera and a goat, it is just as true that I imagine the chimera as that I imagine the goat. And I needn't worry about falsehoods in volitions or emotions. If I have a perverse desire for something, or if I want something that doesn't exist, it's still true that I want that thing. All that remains, then, are my judgments; it's here that I must be careful not to err. And the first and foremost of the errors that I find in my judgments is that of assuming that the ideas in me have a similarity or conformity to things outside me. For, if I were to regard ideas merely as modifications of thought, they could not really provide me with any opportunity for error.

Of my ideas, some seem to me to be innate, others acquired, and others produced by me. The ideas by which I understand reality, truth, and thought seem to have come from my own nature. Those ideas by which I hear a noise, see the sun, or feel the fire I formerly judged to come from things outside me. And the ideas of sirens, hippogriffs, and so on I have formed in myself. Or maybe I can take all of my ideas to be acquired, all innate, or all created by me: I do not yet clearly see where my ideas come from.

For the moment, the central question is about the ideas that I view as derived from objects existing outside me. What reason is there for thinking that these ideas resemble the objects? I seem to have been taught this by nature. Besides, I find that these ideas are independent of my will and hence of me—for they often appear when I do not want them to do so. For example, I now feel heat whether I want to or not, and I therefore take the idea or sensation of heat to come from something distinct from me: the heat of the fire by which I am now sitting. And the obvious thing to think is that a thing sends me its own likeness, not something else.

I will now see whether these reasons are good enough. When I say that nature teaches me something, I mean just that I have a spontaneous impulse to believe it, not that the light of nature reveals the thing's truth to me. There is an important difference. When the light of nature reveals something to me (such as that my thinking implies my existing) that thing is completely beyond doubt, since there is no faculty as reliable as the light of nature by means of which I could learn that the thing is not true. But, as for my natural impulses, I have often judged them to have led me astray in choices about what's good, and I don't see why I should regard them as any more reliable on matters concerning truth and falsehood.

Next, while my sensory ideas may not depend on my will, it doesn't follow that they come from outside me. While the natural impulses of which I just spoke are in me, they seem to conflict with my will. Similarly, I may have in me an as yet undiscovered ability to produce the ideas that seem to come from outside me—in the way that I used to think that ideas came to me in dreams.

Finally, even if some of my ideas do come from things distinct from me, it doesn't follow that they are likenesses of these things. Indeed, it often seems to me that an idea differs greatly from its cause. For example, I find in myself two different ideas of the sun. One, which I "take in" through the senses and which I ought therefore to view as a typical acquired idea, makes the sun look very small to me. The other, which I derive from astronomical reasoning (that is, which I make, perhaps by composing it from innate ideas), pictures the sun as many times larger than the earth. It clearly cannot be that both of these are accurate likenesses of a sun that exists outside me, and reason convinces me that the one least like the sun is the one that seems to arise most directly from it.

All that I've said shows that, until now, my belief that there are things outside me that send their ideas or images to me (perhaps through my senses) has rested on blind impulse rather than certain judgment.

Still, it seems to me that there may be a way of telling whether my ideas come from things that exist outside me. Insofar as the ideas of things are just modifications of thought, I find no inequality among them; all seem to arise from me in the same way. But, insofar as different ideas present different things to me, there obviously are great differences among them. The ideas of substances are unquestionably greater—or have more "subjective reality"—than those of modifications or accidents. Similarly, the idea by which I understand the supreme God—eternal, infinite, omniscient, omnipotent, and creator of all things other than Himself—has more subjective reality in it than the ideas of finite substances.

Now, the light of nature reveals that there is at least as much in a complete efficient cause as in its effect. For where could an effect get its reality if not from its cause? And how could a cause give something unless it had it? It follows both that something cannot come from nothing and that what is more perfect—that is, has more reality in it—cannot come from what is less perfect or has less reality. This obviously holds, not just for those effects whose reality is actual or formal, but also for ideas, whose reality we regard as merely subjective. For example, it's impossible for a non-existent stone to come into existence unless it's produced by something containing, either formally or eminently, everything in the stone. Similarly, heat can only be induced in something that's not already hot by something having at least the same degree of perfection as heat. Also, it's impossible for the *idea* of heat or of stone to be in me unless it's been put there by a cause having at least as much reality as I conceive of in the heat or the stone. For, although the cause doesn't transmit any of its actual or formal reality to the idea, we shouldn't infer that it can be less real than the idea; all that we can infer is that by its nature the idea doesn't require any formal reality except what it derives from my thought, of which it is a modification. Yet, as the idea contains one particular subjective reality rather than another, it must get this reality from a cause having at least as much formal reality as the idea has subjective reality. For, if we suppose that an idea has something in it that wasn't in its cause, we must suppose that it got this thing from nothing. However imperfect the existence of something that exists subjectively in the understanding through an idea, it obviously is something, and it therefore cannot come from nothing.

And, although the reality that I'm considering in my ideas is just subjective, I ought not to suspect that it can fail to be in an idea's cause formally—that it's enough for it to be there subjectively. For, just as the subjective existence of my ideas belongs to the ideas in virtue of their nature, the formal existence of the ideas' causes belongs to those causes—or, at least, to the first and foremost of them—in virtue of the causes' nature. Although one idea may arise from another, this can't go back to infinity; we must eventually arrive at a primary idea whose cause is an "archetype" containing formally all the reality that the idea contains subjectively. Hence, the light of nature makes it clear to me that the ideas in me are like images that may well fall short of the things from which they derive, but cannot contain anything greater or more perfect.

The more time and care I take in studying this, the more clearly and distinctly I know it to be true. But what follows from it? If I can be sure that the subjective reality of one of my ideas is so great that it isn't in me either formally or eminently and hence that I cannot be the cause of that idea, I can infer that I am not alone in the world—that there exists something else that is the cause of the idea. But, if I can find no such idea in me, I will have no argument at all for the existence of anything other than me—for, having diligently searched for such an argument, I have yet to find one.

Of my ideas—besides my idea of myself, about which there can be no problem here—one presents God, others inanimate physical objects, others angels, others animals, and still others men like me.

As to my idea of other men, of animals, and of angels, it's easy to see that—even if the world contained no men but me, no animals, and no angels—I could have composed these ideas from those that I have of myself, of physical objects, and of God.

And, as to my ideas of physical objects, it seems that nothing in them is so great that it couldn't have come from me. For, if I analyze my ideas of physical objects carefully, taking them one by one as I did yesterday when examining my idea of the piece of wax, I notice that there is very little in them that I grasp clearly and distinctly. What I do grasp clearly and distinctly in these ideas is size (which is extension in length, breadth, and depth), shape (which arises from extension's limits), position (which the differently shaped things have relative to one another), and motion (which is just change of position). To these I can add substance, duration, and number. But my thoughts of other things in physical objects (such as light and color, sound, odor, taste, heat and cold, and tactile qualities) are so confused and obscure that I can't say whether they are true or false—whether my ideas of these things are of something or of nothing. Although, as I noted earlier, that which is properly called falsehood—namely, *formal* falsehood—can only be found in judgments, we can still find falsehood of another sort—namely, *material* falsehood—in an idea when it presents what is not a thing as though it were a thing. For example, the ideas that I have of coldness and heat are so unclear and indistinct that I can't tell from them whether coldness is just the absence of heat, or heat just the absence of coldness, or both are

real qualities, or neither is. And, since every idea is "of something," the idea that presents coldness to me as something real and positive could justifiably be called false if coldness were just the absence of heat. And the same holds true for other ideas of this sort.

For such ideas, I need not posit a creator distinct from me. I know by the light of nature that, if one of these ideas is false—that is, if it doesn't present a real thing—it comes from nothing—that is, the only cause of its being in me is a deficiency of my nature, which clearly is imperfect. If one of these ideas is true, however, I still see no reason why I couldn't have produced it myself—for these ideas present so little reality to me that I can't even distinguish it from nothing.

Of the things that are clear and distinct in my ideas of physical objects, it seems that I may have borrowed some—such as substance, duration, and number—from my idea of myself. I think of the stone as a substance—that is, as something that can exist on its own—just as I think of myself as a substance. Although I conceive of myself as a thinking and unextended thing and of the stone as an extended and unthinking thing so that the two conceptions are quite different, they are the same in that they both seem to be of substances. And, when I grasp that I exist now while remembering that I existed in the past, or when I count my various thoughts, I get the idea of duration or number, which I can then apply to other things. The other components of my ideas of physical objects—extension, shape, place, and motion—can't be in me formally, since I'm just a thinking thing. But, as these things are just modes of substance, and as I am a substance, it seems that they may be in me eminently.

All that's left is my idea of God. Is there something in this idea of God that couldn't have come from me? By "God" I mean a substance that's infinite, independent, supremely intelligent, and supremely powerful—the thing from which I and everything else that may exist derive our existence. The more I consider these attributes, the less it seems that they could have come from me alone. So I must conclude that God necessarily exists.

While I may have the idea of substance in me by virtue of my being a substance, I who am finite would not have the idea of infinite substance in me unless it came from a substance that really was infinite.

And I shouldn't think that, rather than having a true idea of infinity, I grasp it merely as the absence of limits—in the way that I grasp rest as the absence of motion and darkness as the absence of light. On the contrary, it's clear to me that there is more reality in an infinite than in a finite substance and hence that my grasp of the infinite must somehow be prior to my grasp of the finite—my understanding of God prior to my understanding of myself. For how could I understand that I doubt and desire, that I am deficient and imperfect, if I didn't have the idea of something more perfect to use as a standard of comparison?

And, unlike the ideas of hot and cold which I just discussed, the idea of God cannot be said to be materially false and hence to come from nothing. On the contrary, since the idea of God is completely clear and distinct and contains more subjective reality than any other idea, no idea is truer *per se* and none less open to the suspicion of falsity. The idea of a supremely perfect and infinite entity is, I maintain, completely true. For, while I may be able to suppose that there is no such entity, I can't even suppose (as I did about the idea of coldness) that my idea of God fails to show me something real. This idea is maximally clear and distinct, for it contains everything that I grasp clearly and distinctly, everything real and true, everything with any perfection. It doesn't matter that I can't fully comprehend the infinite—that there are innumerable things in God which I can't comprehend fully or even reach with thought. Because of the nature of the infinite, I who am finite cannot comprehend it. It's enough that I think about the infinite and judge that, if I grasp something clearly and distinctly and know it to have some perfection, it's present either formally or eminently—perhaps along with innumerable other things of which I am ignorant—in God. If I do this, then of all my ideas the idea of God will be most true and most clear and distinct.

But maybe I am greater than I have assumed; maybe all the perfections that I attributed to God are in me potentially, still unreal and unactualized. I have already seen my knowledge gradually increase, and I don't see anything to prevent its becoming greater and greater to infinity. Nor do I see why, by means of such increased knowledge, I couldn't get all the rest of God's perfections. Finally, if the potential for these perfections is in me, I don't see why that potential couldn't account for the production of the ideas of these perfections in me.

None of this is possible. First, while it's true that my knowledge gradually increases and that I have many as yet unactualized potentialities, none of this fits with my idea of God, in whom absolutely nothing is potential; indeed, the gradual increase in my knowledge shows that I am *imperfect*. Besides, I see that, even if my knowledge were continually to become greater and greater, it would never become actually infinite, since it would never become so great as to be unable to increase. But I judge God to be actually infinite so that nothing can

be added to his perfection. Finally, I see that an idea's subjective being must be produced, not by mere potentiality (which, strictly speaking, is nothing), but by what is actual or formal.

When I pay attention to these things, the light of nature makes all of them obvious. But, when I attend less carefully and the images of sensible things blind my mind's eye, it's not easy for me to remember why the idea of an entity more perfect than I am must come from an entity that really is more perfect. That's why I'll go on to ask whether I, who have the idea of a perfect entity, could exist if no such entity existed.

From what might I derive my existence if not from God? Either from myself, or from my parents, or from something else less perfect than God—for nothing more perfect than God, or even as perfect as Him, can be thought of or imagined.

But, if I derived my existence from myself, I wouldn't doubt, or want, or lack anything. I would have given myself every perfection of which I have an idea, and thus I myself would be God. And I shouldn't think that it might be harder to give myself what I lack than what I already have. On the contrary, it would obviously be much harder for me, a thinking thing or substance, to emerge from nothing than for me to give myself knowledge of the many things of which I am ignorant, which is just an attribute of substance. But surely, if I had given myself that which is harder to get, I wouldn't have denied myself complete knowledge, which would have been easier to get. Indeed, I wouldn't have denied myself *any* of the perfections that I grasp in the idea of God. None of these perfections seems harder to get than existence. But, if I had given myself everything that I now have, these perfections would have seemed harder to get than existence if they were harder to get—for in creating myself I would have discovered the limits of my power.

I can't avoid the force of this argument by supposing that, since I've always existed as I do now, there's no point in looking for my creator. Since my lifetime can be divided into innumerable parts each of which is independent of the others, the fact that I existed a little while ago does not entail that I exist now, unless a cause "recreates" me—or, in other words, preserves me—at this moment. For, when we attend to the nature of time, it's obvious that exactly the same power and action are required to preserve a thing at each moment through which it endures as would be required to create it anew if it had never existed. Hence, one of the things revealed by the light of nature is that preservation and creation differ only in the way we think of them.

I ought to ask myself, then, whether I have the power to ensure that I, who now am, will exist in a little while. Since I am nothing but a thinking thing—or, at any rate, since I am now focusing on the part of me that thinks—I would surely be aware of this power if it were in me. But I find no such power. And from this I clearly see that there is an entity distinct from me on whom I depend.

But maybe this entity isn't God. Maybe I am the product of my parents or of some other cause less perfect than God. No. As I've said, there must be at least as much in a cause as in its effect. Hence, since I am a thinking thing with the idea of God in me, my cause, whatever it may be, must be a thinking thing having in it the idea of every perfection that I attribute to God. And we can go on to ask whether this thing gets its existence from itself or from something else. If it gets its existence from itself, it's obvious from what I've said that it must be God—for it would have the power to exist on its own and hence the power actually to give itself every perfection of which it has an idea, including every perfection that I conceive of in God. But, if my cause gets its existence from some other thing, we can go on to ask whether this other thing gets its existence from itself or from something else. Eventually, we will come to the ultimate cause, which will be God.

It's clear enough that there can't be an infinite regress here—especially since I am concerned, not so much with the cause that originally produced me, as with the one that preserves me at the present moment.

And I can't suppose that several partial causes combined to make me or that I get the ideas of the various perfections that I attribute to God from different causes so that, while each of these perfections can be found somewhere in the universe, there is no God in whom they all come together. On the contrary, one of the chief perfections that I understand God to have is unity, simplicity, inseparability from everything in Him. Surely the idea of the unity of all God's perfections can only have been put in me by a cause that gives me the ideas of all the other perfections—for nothing could make me aware of the unbreakable connection of God's perfections unless it made me aware of what those perfections are.

Finally, even if everything that I used to believe about my parents is true, it's clear that they don't preserve me. Insofar as I am a thinking thing, they did not even take part in creating me. They simply formed the matter in which I used to think that I (that is, my mind, which is all I am now taking myself to be) resided. There can therefore be no problem about my parents.

And I am driven to this conclusion: The fact that I exist and have an idea in me of a perfect entity—that is, God—conclusively entails that God does in fact exist.

All that's left is to explain how I have gotten my idea of God from Him. I have not taken it in through my senses; it has never come to me unexpectedly as the ideas of sensible things do when those things affect (or seem to affect) my external organs of sense. Nor have I made the idea myself; I can't subtract from it or add to it. The only other possibility is that the idea is innate in me, like my idea of myself.

It's not at all surprising that in creating me God put this idea into me, impressing it on His work like a craftsman's mark (which needn't be distinct from the work itself). The very fact that it was God who created me confirms that I have somehow been made in His image or likeness and that I grasp this likeness, which contains the idea of God, in the same way that I grasp myself. Thus, when I turn my mind's eye on myself, I understand, not just that I am an incomplete and dependent thing which constantly strives for bigger and better things, but also that He on whom I depend has all these things in Himself as infinite reality rather than just as vague potentiality and hence that He must be God. The whole argument comes down to this: I know that I could not exist with my present nature—that is, that I could not exist with the idea of God in me—unless there really were a God. This must be the very God whose idea is in me, the thing having all of the perfections that I can't fully comprehend but can somehow reach with thought, who clearly cannot have any defects. From this, it's obvious that He can't deceive—for, as the natural light reveals, fraud and deception arise from defect.

But before examining this more carefully and investigating its consequences, I want to dwell for a moment in the contemplation of God, to ponder His attributes, to see and admire and adore the beauty of His boundless light, insofar as my clouded insight allows. As I have faith that the supreme happiness of the next life consists wholly of the contemplation of divine greatness, I now find that contemplation of the same sort, though less perfect, affords the greatest joy available in this life.

Commentary and Questions

In the first paragraphs, Descartes resolves to explore more carefully his own mind. But then what alternative does he have, now that he has resolved to consider everything else "as empty illusions"?

A momentous step is taken: He *solves* (or at least he thinks he solves) the problem of the criterion! Here are the steps.

1. He is certain that he exists as a **thinking thing**.
2. He asks himself, What is it about this proposition that accounts for my certainty that it is true?
3. He answers, The fact that I grasp it so clearly and distinctly that I perceive it could not possibly be false.
4. He concludes, Let this then be a general principle (a *criterion*): Whatever I grasp with *like clarity and distinctness* must also be true.

He then reviews (yet again) the things he had at one time thought were true and reminds himself that no matter how sure he feels about them, he can't be absolutely certain.

Q17. Why does he feel a need to inquire about the existence and nature of God?

Descartes now tries to make clear a crucial distinction between **ideas** on the one hand and **volitions, emotions**, and **judgments** on the other (pp. 330–331). This distinction is embedded in an inventory of the varied contents of the mind (which is all that we can so far be certain of). You will find a schematic representation of that inventory below.

Q18. What is the key difference between ideas and judgments?
Q19. What is the key difference between judgments on the one hand, and volitions and emotions on the other?

Q20. What question arises with respect to the ideas that seem to be acquired from outside myself?
Q21. What (provisional) examples does Descartes give of each class of ideas?

We need to comment on the notion of **innate ideas**. In calling them "innate," Descartes does not mean to imply that they are to be found in babies and mentally defective adults, as some of his critics suppose. He merely means that there are some ideas we would have even if nothing existed but ourselves. These ideas do not require external causes for their existence in us; every developed rational mind will possess them from its own resources. Thus, the idea of a *thing* can originate with the *cogito*, which gives me the certainty that I exist as a thing that thinks—even if nothing else exists. Perhaps my idea of an antelope is caused in me by seeing antelopes in a zoo (though this remains to be proved). But we would have the ideas of thing, thought, and truth in any case.

Q22. Why do you think Descartes believes that the ideas of truth and thought are innate?
Q23. Why is he inclined to believe that some ideas do originate from objects outside himself? He gives two reasons (p. 330).
Q24. Are these two reasons conclusive?
Q25. What is the difference between being taught "by nature" and being taught "by the light of nature"? (See p. 331.) What is the **light of nature**?

We come now to a point of terminology. Descartes distinguishes **subjective reality** on the one hand from **formal** and **eminent reality** on the

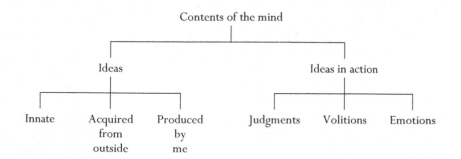

other. If we are going to understand Descartes' argument, we must be clear about how he uses these terms and keep his use firmly in mind.

It is easier to begin with formal reality. Something has formal reality if it is, in our terms, actual or existing. If there really are giraffes and angels, then giraffes and angels have formal reality. You also, because you exist, have formal reality. And when you form an image of a giraffe in your mind, that image also has formal reality—that is, it actually exists *as an image* in your mind. So any idea actually present in a mind is formally real. This means that (if there are giraffes) both the idea of a giraffe (when being thought) and the giraffe you are thinking of are formally real. They are distinct realities, but related: The one *represents* the other.

What you are thinking about when you entertain an idea has subjective reality, reality "for you." Giraffes and angels have subjective reality whenever you think of them, but there are ideas whose objects have *only* subjective reality: the tooth fairy, for instance, or unicorns. These, of course, are examples of ideas "produced by us." But if we look carefully, we can see that they have not been invented out of nothing. The idea of a unicorn comes from the ideas of a horse and a single horn. And (though Descartes has not proved it yet) it may be that horses and horns are formally real. Already he remarks (p. 331) that although one idea may be derived from others, this cannot go on to infinity: There must eventually be a cause for these ideas; and the reality of that cause must be more than "merely subjective." If this were not so, we would have gotten something "from nothing." And the light of nature assures us that this is impossible. There is an old Latin saying: *ex nihilo nihil fit*, or "from nothing, nothing comes."

Descartes does not, of course, make these distinctions for their own sake. There is a problem he is trying to solve: Given that I can be certain that *I* exist (together with all my ideas), can I be certain of the *formal* existence of anything else? Although thoroughgoing skepticism may have been refuted (we do know something in the *cogito*), we have not got beyond solipsism. **Solipsism** is a view that each of you (if there is anyone out there!) must

state for yourself in this way: "I am the only thing that actually (formally) exists; everything else is only real for me."

Another step in solving that problem is to note that there are *degrees of reality*: some things have more reality than others. This is the cardinal principle of the Great Chain of Being.* Descartes gives two examples, framed in terms of subjective reality (p. 331), though the same is true for formal reality, as well.

Q26.   Why does the idea of *substance* contain more subjective reality than that of *modification* or *accident?* (Think of a fender and the dent in it.)†

Q27.   Why does the idea of infinite substance have more subjective reality than that of finite substance?

On the basis of these distinctions, Descartes formulates a *causal principle*: There must be at least as much reality in the cause as there is in the effect. A cause is said to be *formally real* when it has the same degree of reality as the effect it produces; it is said to be *eminently real* when it has even more reality than its effect.

Q28.   What examples does Descartes offer to illustrate this causal principle?

Once more Descartes canvasses the various kinds of ideas he finds in himself as a thinking thing. He is looking for some idea of which he himself could not possibly be the cause. Such an idea must have a cause (since nothing comes from nothing). If (1) he is not the cause, and (2) there is a cause, then (3) he knows that he is not alone in the universe. Something else exists!

Descartes thinks his meditations to this point give him the materials with which to prove that

---

*See pp. 235–237.

†I owe this nice example to Ronald Rubin, the translator of these *Meditations*.

God exists. Let us see what the argument looks like:

1. I have an idea of an infinitely perfect substance.
2. Such an idea must have a cause.
3. *Ex nihilo nihil fit.*
4. So the cause of an idea must have at least as much *formal* reality as there is *subjective* reality in the idea.
5. Though I am a substance, I am not infinitely perfect.
6. So I could not be the cause of this idea.
7. So there must be a formal reality that is an infinitely perfect substance.
8. So God exists.

Q29. Is this argument valid?
Q30. Are there premises in the argument that are less than certainly true?

Meditation III contains two separate arguments for God's existence. The first one, which we have now examined, begins with the fact that each of us has an *idea* of God. The second one begins (on p. 333) with the fact that I exist. The argument then addresses whether I could exist if God does not. It is an argument by exclusion; it considers the other plausible candidates for the cause of my existence and shows in each case that it won't do. Note that both of these arguments are *causal* arguments. The first inquires about the cause of my *idea* of God, the second about the cause of my *existence*. Both make use of the causal principle Descartes has formulated.

Let us sketch the principal steps in this argument.

1. I exist.
2. There must be a cause for my existence.
3. The cause must be one of the following: (a) myself, (b) my always having existed, (c) my parents, (d) something else less perfect than God, or (e) God.
4. Not a, or I would have given myself perfections I now lack—because creating the properties of a substance is not as hard as creating the substance itself.

5. Not b, because my existing now does not *follow from* my having existed in the past.
6. Not c, for this leads to an infinite regress.
7. Not d, for this couldn't account for the unity of the idea of God that I have.
8. So e, and God exists.

Q31. Is there a weak point in this argument? Is there more than one?
Q32. Why does Descartes think his idea of God must be innate?
Q33. Explain why Descartes says we cannot "comprehend" God but can "reach" him in thought. (Compare touching an elephant and wrapping your arms around it.)*

At the end of the third *Meditation*, Descartes feels he has achieved his aim. He now knows that he is not alone. In addition to himself there is at least one other being—a substance infinite in intelligence and power, and perfect in every way. This latter fact will prove to be of very great significance, for Descartes will use it to defeat the hypothesis of the evil demon; a perfect being could not be a deceiver. Thus he thinks he can overcome the deepest ground for skepticism about knowledge of the external world. But that is a line of argument pursued in the remaining meditations.

Meditation IV: On Truth and Falsity

In the last few days, I've gotten used to drawing my mind away from my senses. I've carefully noted that I really grasp very little about physical objects, that I know much more about the human mind, and that I know even more about God. Thus, I no longer find it hard to turn my thoughts away from things of which I can have mental images and toward things completely separate from matter, which I can only understand. Indeed, I have a much more distinct idea of the human mind, insofar as it is just a thinking thing that isn't extended in length, breadth, or depth and doesn't share anything else with physical objects, than I have of physical objects. And, when I note that I doubt or that I am incomplete and dependent, I have a clear and distinct

---

*Compare the similar thought by Aquinas, p. 275.

idea of a complete and independent entity: God. From the fact that this idea is in me and that I who have the idea exist, I can clearly infer both that God exists and that I am completely dependent on Him for my existence from moment to moment. This is so obvious that I'm sure that people can't know anything more evidently or certainly. And it now seems to me that, from the contemplation of the true God in whom are hidden all treasures of knowledge and wisdom, there is a way to derive knowledge of other things.

In the first place, I know that it's impossible for Him ever to deceive me. Wherever there is fraud and deception, there is imperfection, and, while the ability to deceive may seem a sign of cunning or power, the desire to deceive reveals malice or weakness and hence is inconsistent with God's nature.

Next, I find in myself an ability to judge which, like everything else in me, I've gotten from God. Since He doesn't want to deceive me, He certainly hasn't given me an ability which will lead me wrong when properly used.

There can be no doubt about this—except that it may seem to imply that I don't err at all. For, if I've gotten everything in me from God and He hasn't given me the ability to err, it doesn't seem possible for me ever to err. Thus, as long as I think only of God and devote all my attention to Him, I can't find any cause for error and falsity. When I turn my attention back to myself, however, I find that I can make innumerable errors. In looking for the cause of these errors, I find before me, not just the real and positive idea of God, but also the negative idea of "nothingness"—the idea of that which is completely devoid of perfection. I find that I am "intermediate" between God and nothingness, between the supreme entity and nonentity. Insofar as I am the creation of the supreme entity, there's nothing in me to account for my being deceived or led into error, but, insofar as I somehow participate in nothingness or the nonentity—that is, insofar as I am distinct from the supreme entity itself and lack many things—it's not surprising that I go wrong. I thus understand that, in itself, error is a lack, rather than a real thing dependent on God. Hence, I understand that I can err without God's having given me a special ability to do so. Rather, I fall into error because my God-given ability to judge the truth is not infinite.

But there's still something to be explained. Error is not just an absence, but a deprivation—the lack of knowledge that somehow ought to be in me. But, when I attend to God's nature, it seems impossible that He's given me an ability that is an imperfect thing of its kind—an ability lacking a perfection that it ought to have. The greater the craftsman's skill, the more perfect his product. Then how can the supreme creator of all things have made something that isn't absolutely perfect? There's no doubt that God could have made me so that I never err and that He always wants what's best. Then is it better for me to err than not to err?

When I pay more careful attention, I realize that I shouldn't be surprised at God's doing things that I can't explain. I shouldn't doubt His existence just because I find that I sometimes can't understand why or how He has made something. I know that my nature is weak and limited and that God's is limitless, incomprehensible, and infinite, and, from this, I can infer that He can do innumerable things whose reasons are unknown to me. On this ground alone, I regard the common practice of explaining things in terms of their purposes to be useless in physics: it would be foolhardy of me to think that I can discover God's purposes.

It also seems to me that, when asking whether God's works are perfect, I ought to look at all of them together, not at one in isolation. For something that seems imperfect when viewed alone might seem completely perfect when regarded as having a place in the world. Of course, since calling everything into doubt, I haven't established that anything exists besides me and God. But, when I consider God's immense power, I can't deny that He has made—or, in any case, that He could have made—many other things, and I must therefore view myself as having a place in a universe.

Next, turning to myself and investigating the nature of my errors (which are all that show me to be imperfect), I notice that these errors depend on two concurrent causes: my ability to know and my ability to choose freely—that is, my understanding and my will. But, with my understanding, I just grasp the ideas about which I form judgments, and error therefore cannot properly be said to arise from the understanding itself. While there may be innumerable things of which I have no idea, I can't say that I am deprived of these ideas, but only that I happen to lack them—for I don't have any reason to think that God ought to have given me a greater ability to know than He has. And, while I understand God to be a supremely skilled craftsman, I don't go on to think that He ought to endow each of his works with all the perfections that He can put in the others.

Nor can I complain about the scope or perfection of my God-given freedom of will—for I find that my will doesn't seem to me to be restricted in any way. Indeed, it seems well worth noting that nothing in me other than my will is so great and perfect that it couldn't conceivably be bigger or better. If I think about my ability to understand, for example, I realize that it is very small and restricted and I immediately form the idea of something much greater—indeed, of something supremely perfect and infinite. And, from the fact that I can form the idea of this thing, I infer that it is present in God's nature. Similarly, if I consider my other abilities, like the abilities to remember and to imagine, I clearly see that they all are weak and limited in me, but boundless in God. My will or freedom of choice is the only thing I find to be so great in me that I can't conceive of anything greater. In fact, it's largely for this reason that I regard myself as an image or likeness of God. God's will is incomparably greater than mine, of course, in virtue of the associated knowledge and power that make it stronger and more effective, and also in virtue of all its greater range of objects. Yet, viewed in itself as a will, God's will seems no greater than mine. For having a will just amounts to being able either to do or not to do (affirm or deny, seek or avoid)—or, better, to being inclined to affirm or deny, seek or shun what the understanding offers, without any sense of being driven by external forces. To be free, I don't need to be inclined towards both alternatives. On the contrary, the more I lean towards one alternative—either because I understand the truth or goodness in it, or because God has so arranged my deepest thoughts—the more freely I choose it. Neither divine grace nor knowledge of nature ever diminishes my freedom; they increase and strengthen it. But the indifference that I experience when no consideration impels me towards one alternative over another is freedom of the lowest sort, whose presence reveals a defect or an absence of knowledge rather than a perfection. For, if I always knew what was good or true, I wouldn't ever deliberate about what to do or choose, and thus, though completely free, I would never be indifferent.

From this I see that my God-given ability to will is not itself the cause of my errors—for my will is great, a perfect thing of its kind. Neither is my power of understanding the cause of my errors; whenever I understand something, I understand it correctly and without the possibility of error, since my understanding comes from God. What then is the source of my errors? It is just that, while my will has a broader scope than my understanding, I don't keep it within the same bounds, but extend it to that which I don't understand. Being indifferent to these things, my will is easily led away from truth and goodness, and thus I am led into error and sin.

For example, I've asked for the last few days whether anything exists in the world, and I've noted that, from the fact that I ask this, it follows that I exist. I couldn't fail to judge that which I so clearly understood to be true. This wasn't because a force outside me compelled me to believe, but because an intense light in my understanding produced a strong inclination of my will. And, to the extent that I wasn't indifferent, I believed spontaneously and freely. However, while I now know that I exist insofar as I am a thinking thing, I notice in myself an idea of what it is to be a physical object and I come to wonder whether the thinking nature that's in me—or, rather, that *is* me—differs from this bodily nature or is identical to it. Nothing occurs to my reason (I am supposing) to convince me of one alternative rather than the other. Accordingly, I am completely indifferent to affirming either view, to denying either view, and even to suspending judgment.

And indifference of this sort is not limited to things of which the understanding is completely ignorant. It extends to everything about which the will deliberates in the absence of a sufficiently clear understanding. For, however strong the force with which plausible conjectures draw me towards one alternative, the knowledge that they are conjectures rather than assertions backed by certain and indubitable arguments is enough to push my assent the other way. The past few days have provided me with ample experience of this—for I am now supposing each of my former beliefs to be false just because I've found a way to call them into doubt.

If I suspend judgment when I don't clearly and distinctly grasp what's true, I obviously do right and am not deceived. But, if I either affirm or deny in a case of this sort, I misuse my freedom of choice. If I affirm what is false, I clearly err, and, if I stumble onto the truth, I'm still blameworthy since the light of nature reveals that a perception of the understanding should always precede a decision of the will. In these misuses of freedom of choice lies the deprivation that accounts for error. And this deprivation, I maintain, lies in the working of the will insofar as it comes from me—not in my God-given ability to will, or even in the will's operation insofar as it derives from Him.

I have no reason to complain that God hasn't given me a more perfect understanding or a greater natural light than He has. It's in the nature of a finite understanding that there are many things it can't understand, and it's in the nature of created understanding that it's finite. Indeed, I ought to be grateful to Him who owes me absolutely nothing for what He has bestowed, rather than taking myself to be deprived or robbed of what God hasn't given me.

And I have no reason to complain about God's having given me a will whose scope is greater than my understanding's. The will is like a unity made of inseparable parts; its nature apparently will not allow anything to be taken away from it. And, really, the wider the scope of my will, the more grateful I ought to be to Him who gave it to me.

Finally, I ought not to complain that God concurs in bringing about the acts of will and judgment in which I err. Insofar as these acts derive from God, they are completely true and good, and I am more perfect with the ability to perform these acts than I would be without it. And, the deprivation that is the real ground of falsity and error doesn't need God's concurrence, since it's not a thing. When we regard God as its cause, we should say that it is an absence rather than a deprivation. For it clearly is no imperfection in God that He has given me the freedom to assent or not to assent to things of which He hasn't given me a clear and distinct grasp. Rather, it is undoubtedly an imperfection in me that I misuse this freedom by passing judgment on things that I don't properly understand. I see, of course, that God could easily have brought it about that, while I remain free and limited in knowledge, I never err: He could have implanted in me a clear and distinct understanding of everything about which I was ever going to make a choice, or He could have indelibly impressed on my memory that I must never pass judgment on something that I don't clearly and distinctly understand. And I also understand that, regarded in isolation from everything else, I would have been more perfect if God had made me so that I never err. But I can't deny that, because some things are immune to error while others are not, the universe is more perfect than it would have been if all its parts were alike. And I have no right to complain about God's wanting me to hold a place in the world other than the greatest and most perfect.

Besides, if I can't avoid error by having a clear grasp of every matter on which I make a choice, I can avoid it in the other way, which only requires remembering that I must not pass judgment on matters whose truth isn't apparent. For, although I find myself too weak to fix my attention permanently on this single thought, I can—by careful and frequent meditation—ensure that I call it to mind whenever it's needed and thus that I acquire the habit of avoiding error.

Since the first and foremost perfection of man lies in avoiding error, I've profited from today's meditation, in which I've investigated the cause of error and falsity.

Clearly, the only possible cause of error is the one I have described. When I limit my will's range of judgment to the things presented clearly and distinctly to my understanding, I obviously cannot err—for everything that I clearly and distinctly grasp is something and hence must come, not from nothing, but from God—God, I say, who is supremely perfect and who cannot possibly deceive. Therefore, what I clearly and distinctly grasp is unquestionably true. Today, then, I have learned what to avoid in order not to err and also what to do to reach the truth. I surely will reach the truth if I just attend to the things that I understand perfectly and distinguish them from those that I grasp more obscurely and confusedly. And that's what I'll take care to do from now on.

Commentary and Questions

Note the transitional character of the first paragraph. Descartes sums up the argument so far, expresses his confidence that God's existence is more certain than anything else (except the *cogito*), and looks forward to further progress.

Q34. Is Descartes' assertion (p. 338) that deception is an evidence of weakness rather than power plausible? Explain your answer.

Before God's existence was proved, it was unclear whether any of our beliefs were true. Now there is a new puzzle: How can any of them be false? (Do you see why this puzzle arises?) So Descartes has to provide an explanation of the obvious fact that we can and do make mistakes.

For the basic framework he depends again on the idea of the Great Chain of Being. He finds that he is an "intermediate" between God and nothingness, having less reality than God, whose perfection excludes error, but more reality than sheer nonbeing. Error, in any case, is not a positive reality; it is only a defect, as weakness is only the absence of strength and cold the absence of heat. So it should not be too surprising that Descartes, and we, too, should be susceptible to error.

Two points he makes in passing are worth noting.

1. Why did God create me so that I could make mistakes? I don't know, he says, but if I could see

the world as God sees it, it is quite possible that I would judge it to be for the best.*

Q35. How does recognizing that I am only a part of a larger whole help answer this question?

---

2. Among the many things we do not know are God's purposes. It follows that Aristotelian final causes—the what for—are not appropriate in the explanations given by physics. Thus Descartes buttresses the mechanistic character of his (and the modern world's) scientific work. We can come to know *how* things happen, but not *why*.

A more detailed analysis of error can be given. It depends on another distinction: that between entertaining a belief, or having it in mind (which is the function of the **understanding**), and assenting to that belief, or accepting it (which is the function of the **will**).

Q36. How does this distinction between *understanding* and *will* explain the possibility of error?

Q37. In what way is the will more perfect than the understanding?

Q38. Can God be blamed for our errors?

Q39. How can we avoid error?

Meditation V: On the Essence of Material Objects and More on God's Existence

Many questions remain about God's attributes and the nature of my self or mind. I may return to these questions later. But now, having found what to do and what to avoid in order to attain truth, I regard nothing as

---

*Here is one expression of that attitude expressed in Leibniz and other later writers to the effect that "this is the best of all possible worlds." It is this optimism that Voltaire caricatures so savagely in *Candide*. These reflections of Descartes form part of a project known as *theodicy*—the justification of the ways of God to man. For another attempt at theodicy, see Hegel (pp. 478–481). You might also review the Stoic notion that evil does not exist in the world, but only in our perception of it (p. 205).

more pressing than to work my way out of the doubts that I raised the other day and to see whether I can find anything certain about material objects.

But, before asking whether any such objects exist outside me, I ought to consider the ideas of these objects as they exist in my thoughts and see which are clear and which confused.

I have a distinct mental image of the quantity that philosophers commonly call continuous. That is, I have a distinct mental image of the extension of this quantity—or rather of the quantified thing—in length, breadth, and depth. I can distinguish various parts of this thing. I can ascribe various sizes, shapes, places, and motions to these parts and various durations to the motions.

In addition to having a thorough knowledge of extension in general, I grasp innumerable particulars about things like shape, number, and motion, when I pay careful attention. The truth of these particulars is so obvious and so consonant with my nature that, when I first think of one of these things, I seem not so much to be learning something novel as to be remembering something that I already knew—or noticing for the first time something that had long been in me without my having turned my mind's eye toward it.

What's important here, I think, is that I find in myself innumerable ideas of things which, though they may not exist outside me, can't be said to be nothing. While I have some control over my thoughts of these things, I do not make the things up: they have their own real and immutable natures. Suppose, for example, that I have a mental image of a triangle. While it may be that no figure of this sort does exist or ever has existed outside my thought, the figure has a fixed nature (essence or form), immutable and eternal, which hasn't been produced by me and isn't dependent on my mind. The proof is that I can demonstrate various propositions about the triangle, such as that its angles equal two right angles and that its greatest side subtends its greatest angle. Even though I didn't think of these propositions at all when I first imagined the triangle, I now clearly see their truth whether I want to or not, and it follows that I didn't make them up.

It isn't relevant that, having seen triangular physical objects, I may have gotten the idea of the triangle from external objects through my organs of sense. For I can think of innumerable other figures whose ideas I could not conceivably have gotten through my senses, and I can demonstrate facts about these other figures just as I can about the triangle. Since I know these facts clearly, they must be true, and they therefore must be something rather than nothing. For it's obvious that everything true is something, and, as I have shown, everything that I know clearly and distinctly is true. But, even if I hadn't shown this, the nature of my mind would have made it impossible for me to withhold my assent from these things, at least when I clearly and distinctly grasped them. As I recall, even when I clung most tightly to objects of sense, I regarded truths about shape and number—truths of arithmetic, geometry, and pure mathematics—as more certain than any others.

But, if anything whose idea I can draw from my thought must in fact have everything that I clearly and distinctly grasp it to have, can't I derive from this a proof of God's existence? Surely, I find the idea of God, a supremely perfect being, in me no less clearly than I find the ideas of figures and numbers. And I understand as clearly and distinctly that eternal existence belongs to His nature as that the things which I demonstrate of a figure or number belong to the nature of the figure or number. Accordingly, even if what I have thought up in the past few days hasn't been entirely true, I ought to be at least as certain of God's existence as I used to be of the truths of pure mathematics.

At first, this reasoning may seem unclear and fallacious. Since I'm accustomed to distinguishing existence from essence in other cases, I find it easy to convince myself that I can separate God's existence from His essence and hence that I can think of God as nonexistent. But, when I pay more careful attention, it's clear that I can no more separate God's existence from His essence than a triangle's angles equaling two right angles from the essence of the triangle, or the idea of a valley from the idea of a mountain. It's no less impossible to think that God (the supremely perfect being) lacks existence (a perfection) than to think that a mountain lacks a valley.

Well, suppose that I can't think of God without existence, just as I can't think of a mountain without a valley. From the fact that I can think of a mountain with a valley, it doesn't follow that a mountain exists in the world. Similarly, from the fact that I can think of God as existing, it doesn't seem to follow that He exists. For my thought doesn't impose any necessity on things. It may be that, just as I can imagine a winged horse when no such horse exists, I can ascribe existence to God when no God exists.

No, there is a fallacy here. From the fact that I can't think of a mountain without a valley it follows, not that the mountain and valley exist, but only that whether they exist or not they can't be separated from one another. But, from the fact that I can't think of God without existence, it follows that existence is inseparable from Him and hence that He really exists. It's not that my thoughts make it so or impose a necessity on things. On the contrary, it's the fact that God does exist that necessitates my thinking of Him as I do. For I am not free to think of God without existence—of the supremely perfect being without supreme perfection—as I am free to think of a horse with or without wings.

Now someone might say this: "If I take God to have all perfections, and if I take existence to be a perfection, I must take God to exist, but I needn't accept the premise that God has all perfections. Similarly, if I accept the premise that every quadrilateral can be inscribed in a circle, I'm forced to the patently false view that every rhombus can be inscribed in a circle, but I need not accept the premise." But this should not be said. For, while it's not necessary that the idea of God occurs to me, it is necessary that, whenever I think of the primary and supreme entity and bring the idea of Him out of my mind's "treasury," I attribute all perfections to Him, even if I don't enumerate them or consider them individually. And this necessity ensures that, when I do notice that existence is a perfection, I can rightly conclude that the primary and supreme being exists. Similarly, while it's not necessary that I ever imagine a triangle, it is necessary that, when I do choose to consider a rectilinear figure having exactly three angles, I attribute to it properties from which I can rightly infer that its angles are no more than two right angles, perhaps without noticing that I am doing so. But, when I consider which shapes can be inscribed in the circle, there's absolutely no necessity for my thinking that all quadrilaterals are among them. Indeed, I can't even think that all quadrilaterals are among them, since I've resolved to accept only what I clearly and distinctly understand. Thus my false suppositions differ greatly from the true ideas implanted in me, the first and foremost of which is my idea of God. In many ways, I see that this idea is not a figment of my thought, but the image of a real and immutable nature. For one thing, God is the only thing that I can think of whose existence belongs to its essence. For another thing, I can't conceive of there being two or more such Gods, and, having supposed that one God now exists, I see that He has necessarily existed from all eternity and will continue to exist into eternity. And I also perceive many other things in God that I can't diminish or alter.

But, whatever proof I offer, it always comes back to the fact that I am only convinced of what I grasp clearly and distinctly. Of the things that I grasp in this way, some are obvious to everyone. Some are discovered only by those who examine things more closely and search more carefully, but, once these things have been discovered, they are regarded as no less certain than the others. That the square on the hypotenuse of a right triangle equals the sum of the squares on the other sides is not as readily apparent as that the hypotenuse subtends the greatest angle, but, once it has been seen, it is believed just as firmly. And, when I'm not overwhelmed by prejudices and my thoughts aren't besieged by images of sensible things, there surely is nothing that I know earlier or more easily than facts about God. For what is more self-evident than there is a supreme entity—that God, the only thing whose existence belongs to His essence, exists?

While I need to pay careful attention in order to grasp this, I'm now as certain of it as of anything that seems most certain. In addition, I now see that the certainty of everything else so depends on it that, if I weren't certain of it, I couldn't know anything perfectly.

Of course, my nature is such that, when I grasp something clearly and distinctly, I can't fail to believe it. But my nature is also such that I can't permanently fix my attention on a single thing so as always to grasp it clearly, and memories of previous judgments often come to me when I am no longer attending to the grounds on which I originally made them. Accordingly, if I were ignorant of God, arguments could be produced that would easily overthrow my opinions, and I therefore would have unstable and changing opinions rather than true and certain knowledge. For example, when I consider the nature of the triangle, it seems plain to me—steeped as I am in the principles of geometry—that its three angles equal two right angles: I can't fail to believe this as long as I pay attention to its demonstration. But, if I were ignorant of God, I might come to doubt its truth as soon as my mind's eye turned away from its demonstration, even if I recalled having once grasped it clearly. For I could convince myself that I've been so constructed by nature that I sometimes err about what I believe myself to grasp most plainly—especially if I remember that, having taken many things to be true and certain, I had later found grounds on which to judge them false.

But now I grasp that God exists, and I understand both that everything else depends on Him and that He's not a deceiver. From this, I infer that everything I clearly and distinctly grasp must be true. Even if I no longer pay attention to the grounds on which I judged God to exist, my recollection that I once clearly and distinctly knew Him to exist ensures that no contrary ground can be produced to push me towards doubt. About God's existence, I have true and certain knowledge. And I have such knowledge, not just about this one thing, but about everything else that I remember having proven, like the theorems of geometry. For what can now be said against my believing these things? That I am so constructed that I always err? But I now know that I can't err about what I clearly understand. That much of what I took to be true and certain I later found to be false? But I didn't grasp any of these things clearly and distinctly; ignorant of the true standard of truth, I based my belief on grounds that I later found to be unsound. Then what can be said? What about the objection (which I recently used against myself) that I may be dreaming and that the things I'm now experiencing may be as unreal as those that occur to me in sleep? No, even this is irrelevant. For, even if I am dreaming, everything that is evident to my understanding must be true.

Thus I plainly see that the certainty and truth of all my knowledge derives from one thing: my thought of the true God. Before I knew Him, I couldn't know anything else perfectly. But now I can plainly and certainly know innumerable things, not only about God and other mental beings, but also about the nature of physical objects, insofar as it is the subject-matter of pure mathematics.

Commentary and Questions

This brief meditation is a transition to the more important sixth meditation. Though Descartes says at the beginning that he wants to investigate whether anything can be known about material things (so far, only God and the soul are known), he doesn't solve that problem here. But he does take a significant step toward its solution. And, along the way, he discovers a third proof that God exists.

Again we find the typical Cartesian strategy at work. He wants to know whether **material things** exist independently of himself. How can he proceed? He can't just look to see because he has put the testimony of the senses in doubt. So he must consider more carefully the *idea* of material things, which is all that is available to him. And again he finds that some of these ideas are confused and obscure, while others are clear and distinct. The latter are those of extension, duration, and movement—the qualities that can be treated geometrically or mathematically. Material things, if there are any, are essentially extended volumes.* Once we are clear about their *essence*, it makes sense to inquire about their *existence;* and that is the subject of *Meditation VI.*

Note that these mathematical ideas are not just imaginary inventions. I cannot put them together any way I like, as I can construct fantastic creatures by combining heads, bodies, and hides at will. I may not yet know whether there are any triangular things outside myself, but the idea of a triangle "can't be said to be nothing" (p. 341). It has a *nature* that is "immutable and eternal." This nature does not depend on me.

The point can be put in this way. Suppose you imagine a creature with wings covered with scales, a long furry tail, six legs, and an elephantlike nose covered with spikes. Then I ask you, does this creature have a liver? You will have to *invent* the answer. You cannot discover it. But if you imagine a triangle and I ask you whether the interior angles equal two right angles, you do not have to invent an answer. Even if you had never thought about that question before, you could investigate and discover that the answer is yes. With respect to these geometrical properties, there are *truths*.† And these, remember, are the very properties that determine the essence of material things.

Since the idea of a material thing is the idea of something extended, and since extended things can be treated geometrically, it follows that the *idea* of a material thing is clear and distinct. Material substances have an essence or nature that would make a *science* of them a possibility—if only we could be assured that they exist. And we know that such a science is a possibility merely from an examination of their ideas. So, provided we can discover a proof that some *formal* reality corresponds to the *subjective* reality of our ideas of material things, we can have a science of material things. In this way, then, he hopes to give a metaphysical foundation to his mechanistic physics.

The discovery that certain ideas have a nature or essence of their own, quite independent of our inventions, also supplies Descartes with material for a third proof of God's existence.* If we simply pay close attention to what is necessarily involved in our idea of *what* God is (his essence or nature), we can discover, Descartes argues, *that* God is (that he exists). God's existence is included in his essence. Notice that, unlike the first two arguments, this is not a *causal* proof. In its bare essentials, it looks like this:

1. God, by definition, is a being of infinite perfection.
2. Existence is a perfection (that is, no being could be perfect that lacked it).
3. So God exists.

Q40.   Is the argument valid?
Q41.   Can the premises be questioned?

This last proof of God's existence allows Descartes to lay to rest a final worry that has been tormenting him. You really cannot help believing, he suggests, that your clear and distinct thoughts are true—while you are thinking them. But later you may not be so sure! You may then think you were dreaming what earlier seemed so certain. But now this worry can be dealt with. And *Meditation V* closes on a note of reassurance.

Q42.   How are the dream and demon worries finally disposed of?
Q43.   Can an atheist do science? (See the last paragraph.)

---

*Review the discussion of the bit of wax in *Meditation II* and on p. 329.

†Socrates thinks that we can never be taught anything other than what we in some sense already know; what we call "learning" is in fact just remembering. (See p. 141.) Descartes alludes to this doctrine here; in discovering the properties of a triangle I am "noticing for the first time something that had long been in me without my having turned my mind's eye towards it." Descartes is not, however, committed to the Socratic doctrine of the preexistence of the soul as an explanation of this phenomenon, since he thinks God's creation of a soul possessing certain innate ideas will suffice.

*This proof is a version of the ontological argument first worked out by Anselm of Canterbury in the eleventh century. See Chapter 11.

Meditation VI: On the Existence of Material Objects and the Real Distinction of Mind from Body

It remains for me to examine whether material objects exist. Insofar as they are the subject of pure mathematics, I now know at least that they can exist, because I grasp them clearly and distinctly. For God can undoubtedly make whatever I can grasp in this way, and I never judge that something is impossible for Him to make unless there would be a contradiction in my grasping the thing distinctly. Also, the fact that I find myself having mental images when I turn my attention to physical objects seems to imply that these objects really do exist. For, when I pay careful attention to what it is to have a mental image, it seems to me that it's just the application of my power of thought to a certain body which is immediately present to it and which must therefore exist.

To clarify this, I'll examine the difference between having a mental image and having a pure understanding. When I have a mental image of a triangle, for example, I don't just understand that it is a figure bounded by three lines; I also "look at" the lines as though they were present to my mind's eye. And this is what I call having a mental image. When I want to think of a chiliagon, I understand that it is a figure with a thousand sides as well as I understand that a triangle is a figure with three, but I can't imagine its sides or "look" at them as though they were present. Being accustomed to using images when I think about physical objects, I may confusedly picture some figure to myself, but this figure obviously is not a chiliagon—for it in no way differs from what I present to myself when thinking about a myriagon or any other many sided figure, and it doesn't help me to discern the properties that distinguish chiliagons from other polygons. If it's a pentagon that is in question, I can understand its shape, as I can that of the chiliagon, without the aid of mental images. But I can also get a mental image of the pentagon by directing my mind's eye to its five lines and to the area that they bound. And it's obvious to me that getting this mental image requires a special mental effort different from that needed for understanding—a special effort which clearly reveals the difference between having a mental image and having a pure understanding.

It also seems to me that my power of having mental images, being distinct from my power of understanding, is not essential to my self or, in other words, to my mind—for, if I were to lose this ability, I would surely remain the same thing that I now am. And it seems to follow that this ability depends on something distinct from me. If we suppose that there is a body so associated with my mind that the mind can "look into" it at will, it's easy to understand how my mind might get mental images of physical objects by means of my body. If there were such a body, the mode of thinking that we call imagination would differ from pure understanding in only one way: when the mind understood something, it would turn "inward" and view an idea that it found in itself, but, when it had mental images, it would turn to the body and look at something there which resembled an idea that it had understood by itself or had grasped by sense. As I've said, then, it's easy to see how I get mental images, if we supposed that my body exists. And, since I don't have in mind any other equally plausible explanation of my ability to have mental images, I conjecture that physical objects probably do exist. But this conjecture is only probable. Despite my careful and thorough investigation, the distinct idea of bodily nature that I get from mental images does not seem to have anything in it from which the conclusion that physical objects exist validly follows.

Besides having a mental image of the bodily nature that is the subject-matter of pure mathematics, I have mental images of things which are not so distinct—things like colors, sounds, flavors, and pains. But I seem to grasp these things better by sense, from which they seem to come (with the aid of memory) to the understanding. Thus, to deal with these things more fully, I must examine the senses and see whether there is anything in the mode of awareness that I call sensation from which I can draw a conclusive argument for the existence of physical objects.

First, I'll remind myself of the things that I believed really to be as I perceived them and of the grounds for my belief. Next, I'll set out the grounds on which I later called this belief into doubt. And, finally, I'll consider what I ought to think now.

To begin with, I sensed that I had a head, hands, feet, and the other members that make up a human body. I viewed this body as part, or maybe even as all, of me. I sensed that it was influenced by other physical objects whose effects could be either beneficial or harmful. I judged these effects to be beneficial to the extent that I felt pleasant sensations and harmful to the extent that I felt pain. And, in addition to sensations of pain and pleasure, I sensed hunger, thirst, and other such desires—and also bodily inclinations towards cheerfulness, sadness, and other emotions. Outside me, I sensed, not just extension, shape, and motion, but also hardness, hotness, and other qualities detected by touch. I also sensed light, color, odor, taste, and sound—qualities by whose variation I distinguished such things as the sky, earth, and sea from one another.

In view of these ideas of qualities (which presented themselves to my thought and were all that I really sensed directly), I had some reason for believing that I sensed objects distinct from my thought—physical objects from which the ideas came. For I found that these ideas came to me independently of my desires so that, however much I tried, I couldn't sense an object when it wasn't present to an organ of sense or fail to sense one when it was present. And, since the ideas that I grasped by sense were much livelier, more explicit, and (in their own way) more distinct than those I deliberately created or found impressed in my memory, it seemed that these ideas could not have come from me and thus that they came from something else. Having no conception of these things other than that suggested by my sensory ideas, I could only think that the things resembled the ideas. Indeed, since I remembered using my senses before my reason, since I found the ideas that I created in myself to be less explicit than those grasped by sense, and since I found the ideas that I created to be composed largely of those that I had grasped by sense, I easily convinced myself that I didn't understand anything at all unless I had first sensed it.

I also had some reason for supposing that a certain physical object, which I viewed as belonging to me in a special way, was related to me more closely than any other. I couldn't be separated from it as I could from other physical objects; I felt all of my emotions and desires in it and because of it; and I was aware of pains and pleasant feelings in it but in nothing else. I didn't know why sadness goes with the sensation of pain or why joy goes with sensory stimulation. I didn't know why the stomach twitchings that I call hunger warn me that I need to eat or why dryness in my throat warns me that I need to drink. Seeing no connection between stomach twitchings and the desire to eat or between the sensation of a pain-producing thing and the consequent awareness of sadness, I could only say that I had been taught the connection by nature. And nature seems also to have taught me everything else that I knew about the objects of sensation—for I convinced myself that the sensations came to me in a certain way before having found grounds on which to prove that they did.

But, since then, many experiences have shaken my faith in the senses. Towers that seemed round from a distance sometimes looked square from close up, and huge statues on pediments sometimes didn't look big when seen from the ground. In innumerable such cases, I found the judgments of the external senses to be wrong. And the same holds for the internal senses. What is felt more inwardly than pain? Yet I had heard that people with amputated arms and legs sometimes seem to feel pain in the missing limb, and it therefore didn't seem perfectly certain to me that the limb in which I feel a pain is always the one that hurts. And, to these grounds for doubt, I've recently added two that are very general: First, since I didn't believe myself to sense anything while awake that I couldn't also take myself to sense in a dream, and since I didn't believe that what I sense in sleep comes from objects outside me, I didn't see why I should believe what I sense while awake comes from such objects. Second, since I didn't yet know my creator (or, rather, since I supposed that I didn't know Him), I saw nothing to rule out my having been so designed by nature that I'm deceived even in what seems most obviously true to me.

And I could easily refute the reasoning by which I convinced myself of the reality of sensible things. Since my nature seemed to impel me toward many things that my reason rejected, I didn't believe that I ought to have much faith in nature's teachings. And, while my will didn't control my sense perceptions, I didn't believe it to follow that these perceptions came from outside me, since I thought that the ability to produce these ideas might be in me without my being aware of it.

Now that I've begun to know myself and my creator better, I still believe that I oughtn't blindly to accept everything that I seem to get from the senses. Yet I no longer believe that I ought to call it all into doubt.

In the first place, I know that everything that I clearly and distinctly understand can be made by God to be exactly as I understand it. The fact that I can clearly and distinctly understand one thing apart from another is therefore enough to make me certain that it is distinct from the other, since the things could be separated by God if not by something else. (I judge the things to be distinct regardless of the power needed to make them exist separately.) Accordingly, from the fact that I have gained knowledge of my existence without noticing anything about my nature or essence except that I am a thinking thing, I can rightly conclude that my essence consists solely in the fact that I am a thinking thing. It's possible (or, as I will say later, it's certain) that I have a body which is very tightly bound to me. But, on the one hand, I have a clear and distinct idea of myself insofar as I am just a thinking and unextended thing, and, on the other hand, I have a distinct idea of my body insofar as it is just an extended and unthinking thing. It's certain, then, that I am really distinct from my body and can exist without it.

In addition, I find in myself abilities for special modes of awareness, like the abilities to have mental images and to sense. I can clearly and distinctly conceive of my whole self as something that lacks these abilities, but I can't conceive of the abilities' existing without me, or without an understanding substance in which to reside. Since the conception of these abilities includes the conception of something that understands, I see that these abilities are distinct from me in the way that a thing's properties are distinct from the thing itself.

I recognize other abilities in me, like the ability to move around and to assume various postures. These abilities can't be understood to exist apart from a substance in which they reside any more than the abilities to imagine and sense, and they therefore cannot exist without such a substance. But it's obvious that, if these abilities do exist, the substance in which they reside must be a body or extended substance rather than an understanding one—for the clear and distinct conceptions of these abilities contain extension but not understanding.

There is also in me, however, a passive ability to sense—to receive and recognize ideas of sensible things. But, I wouldn't be able to put this ability to use if there weren't, either in me or in something else, an active power to produce or make sensory ideas. Since this active power doesn't presuppose understanding, and since it often produces ideas in me without my cooperation and even against my will, it cannot exist in me. Therefore, this power must exist in a substance distinct from me. And, for reasons that I've noted, this substance must contain, either formally or eminently, all the reality that is contained subjectively in the ideas that the power produces. Either this substance is a physical object (a thing of bodily nature that contains formally the reality that the idea contains subjectively), or it is God or one of His creations that is higher than a physical object (something that contains this reality eminently). But, since God isn't a deceiver, it's completely obvious that He doesn't send these ideas to me directly or by means of a creation that contains their reality eminently rather than formally. For, since He has not given me any ability to recognize that these ideas are sent by Him or by creations other than physical objects, and since He has given me a strong inclination to believe that the ideas come from physical objects, I see no way to avoid the conclusion that He deceives me if the ideas are sent to me by anything other than physical objects. It follows that physical objects exist. These objects may not exist exactly as I comprehend them by sense; in many ways, sensory comprehension is obscure and confused. But these objects must at least have in them everything that I clearly and distinctly understand them to have—every general property within the scope of pure mathematics.

But what about particular properties, such as the size and shape of the sun? And what about things that I understand less clearly than mathematical properties, like light, sound, and pain? These are open to doubt. But, since God isn't a deceiver, and since I therefore have the God-given ability to correct any falsity that may be in my beliefs, I have high hopes of finding the truth about even these things. There is undoubtedly some truth in everything I have been taught by nature—for, when I use the term "nature" in its general sense, I refer to God Himself or to the order that He has established in the created world, and, when I apply the term specifically to *my* nature, I refer to the collection of everything that God has given *me*.

Nature teaches me nothing more explicitly, however, than that I have a body which is hurt when I feel pain, which needs food or drink when I experience hunger or thirst, and so on. Accordingly, I ought not to doubt that there is some truth to this.

Through sensations like pain, hunger, and thirst, nature also teaches me that I am not present in my body in the way that a sailor is present in his ship. Rather, I am very tightly bound to my body and so "mixed up" with it that we form a single thing. If this weren't so, I—who am just a thinking thing—wouldn't feel pain when my body was injured; I would perceive the injury by pure understanding in the way that a sailor sees the leaks in his ship with his eyes. And, when my body needed food or drink, I would explicitly understand that the need existed without having the confused sensations of hunger and thirst. For the sensations of thirst, hunger, and pain are just confused modifications of thought arising from the union and "mixture" of mind and body.

Also, nature teaches me that there are other physical objects around my body—some that I ought to seek and others that I ought to avoid. From the fact that I sense things like colors, sound, odors, flavors, temperatures, and hardnesses, I correctly infer that sense perceptions come from physical objects that vary as widely (though perhaps not in the same way) as the perceptions do. And, from the fact that some of these perceptions are pleasant while others are unpleasant, I infer with certainty that my body—or, rather, my whole self which consists of a body and a mind—can be benefited and harmed by the physical objects around it.

There are many other things that I seem to have been taught by nature but that I have really accepted out of a habit of thoughtless judgment. These things may well be false. Among them are the judgments that a space is empty if nothing in it happens to affect my senses; that a hot physical object has something in it resembling my idea of heat; that a white or green thing has in it the same whiteness or greenness that I sense; that a bitter or sweet thing has in it the same flavor that I taste; that stars, towers, and other physical objects have the same size and shape that they present to my senses; and so on.

If I am to avoid accepting what is indistinct in these cases, I must more carefully explain my use of the phrase "taught by nature." In particular, I should say that I am now using the term "nature" in a narrower sense than when I took it to refer to the whole complex of what God has given me. This complex includes much having to do with my mind alone (such as my grasp of the fact that what is done cannot be undone and of the rest of what I know by the light of nature) which does not bear on what I am now saying. And the complex also includes much having to do with my body alone (such as its tendency to go downward) with which I am not dealing now. I'm now using the term "nature" to refer only to what God has given me insofar as I am a composite of mind and body. It is this nature that teaches me to avoid that which occasions painful sensations, to seek that which occasions pleasant sensations, and so on. But this nature seems not to teach me to draw conclusions about external objects from sense perceptions without first having examined the matter with my understanding—for true knowledge of external things seems to belong to the mind alone, not to the composite of mind and body.

Thus, while a star has no more effect on my eye than a flame, this does not really produce a positive inclination to believe that the star is as small as the flame; for my youthful judgment about the size of the flame, I had no real grounds. And, while I feel heat when I approach a fire and pain when I draw nearer, I have absolutely no reason for believing that something in the fire resembles the heat, just as I have no reason for believing that something in the fire resembles the pain; I only have reason for believing that there is something or other in the fire that produces the feelings of heat and pain. And, although there may be nothing in a given region of space that affects my senses, it doesn't follow that there aren't any physical objects in that space. Rather I now see that, on these matters and others, I used to pervert the natural order of things. For, while nature has given sense perceptions to my mind for the sole purpose of indicating what is beneficial and what harmful to the composite

of which my mind is a part, and while the perceptions are sufficiently clear and distinct for that purpose, I used these perceptions as standards for identifying the essence of physical objects—an essence which they only reveal obscurely and confusedly.

I've already explained how it can be that, despite God's goodness, my judgments can be false. But a new difficulty arises here—one having to do with the things that nature presents to me as desirable or undesirable and also with the errors that I seem to have found in my internal sensations. One of these errors seems to be committed, for example, when a man is fooled by some food's pleasant taste into eating poison hidden in that food. But surely, in this case, what the man's nature impels him to eat is the good tasting food, not the poison of which he knows nothing. We can draw no conclusion except that his nature isn't omniscient, and this conclusion isn't surprising. Since a man is a limited thing, he can only have limited perfections.

Still, we often err in cases in which nature does impel us. This happens, for example, when sick people want food or drink that would quickly harm them. To say that these people err as a result of the corruption of their nature does not solve the problem—for a sick man is no less a creation of God than a well one, and it seems as absurd to suppose that God has given him a deceptive nature. A clock made of wheels and weights follows the natural laws just as precisely when it is poorly made and inaccurate as when it does everything that its maker wants. Thus, if I regard a human body as a machine made up of bones, nerves, muscles, veins, blood, and skin such that even without a mind it would do just what it does now (except for things that require a mind because they are controlled by the will), it's easy to see that what happens to a sick man is no less "natural" than what happens to a well one. For instance, if a body suffers from dropsy, it has a dry throat of the sort that regularly brings the sensation of thirst to the mind, the dryness disposes the nerves and other organs to drink, and the drinking makes the illness worse. But this is just as natural as when a similar dryness of throat moves a person who is perfectly healthy to take a drink that is beneficial. Bearing in mind my conception of a clock's use, I might say that an inaccurate clock departs from its nature, and, similarly, viewing the machine of the human body as designed for its usual motions, I can say that it drifts away from its nature if it has a dry throat when drinking will not help to maintain it. I should note, however, that the sense in which I am now using the term "nature" differs from that in which I used it before. For, as I have just used the term "nature," the nature of a man (or clock) is something that depends on my thinking of the difference between a sick and a well man (or of the difference between a poorly made and a well-made clock)—something regarded as extrinsic to the things. But, when I used "nature" before, I referred to something which is *in* things and which therefore has some reality.

It may be that we just offer an extrinsic description of a body suffering from dropsy when, noting that it has a dry throat but doesn't need to drink, we say that its nature is corrupted. Still, the description is not purely extrinsic when we say that a composite or union of mind and body has a corrupted nature. There is a real fault in the composite's nature, for it is thirsty when drinking would be harmful. It therefore remains to be asked why God's goodness doesn't prevent *this* nature's being deceptive.

To begin the answer, I'll note that mind differs importantly from body in that body is by its nature divisible while mind is indivisible. When I think about my mind—or, in other words, about myself insofar as I am just a thinking thing—I can't distinguish any parts in me; I understand myself to be a single, unified thing. Although my whole mind seems united to my whole body, I know that cutting off a foot, arm, or other limb would not take anything away from my mind. The abilities to will, sense, understand, and so on can't be called parts, since it's one and the same mind that wills, senses, and understands. On the other hand, whenever I think of a physical or extended thing, I can mentally divide it, and I therefore understand that the object is divisible. This single fact would be enough to teach me that my mind and body are distinct, if I hadn't already learned that in another way.

Next, I notice that the mind isn't directly affected by all parts of the body, but only by the brain—or maybe just by the small part of the brain containing the so-called "common sense." Whenever this part of the brain is in a given state, it presents the same thing to the mind, regardless of what is happening in the rest of the body (as is shown by innumerable experiments that I need not review here).

In addition, I notice that the nature of body is such that, if a first part can be moved by a second that is far away, the first part can be moved in exactly the same way by something between the first and second without the second part's being affected. For example, if A, B, C, and D are points on a cord, and if the first point (A) can be moved in a certain way by a pull on the last point (D), then A can be moved in the same way by a pull on one of the middle points (B or C) without D's being moved. Similarly, science teaches me that, when my foot hurts, the sensation of pain is produced by nerves distributed throughout the foot which extend like cords

from there to the brain. When pulled in the foot, these nerves pull the central parts of the brain to which they are attached, moving those parts in ways designated by nature to present the mind with the sensation of a pain "in the foot." But, since these nerves pass through the shins, thighs, hips, back, and neck on their way from foot to brain, it can happen that their being touched in the middle, rather than at the end of the foot, produces the same motion in the brain as when the foot is hurt and, hence, that the mind feels the same pain "in the foot." And the point holds for other sensations as well.

Finally, I notice that, since only one sensation can be produced by a given motion of the part of the brain that directly affects the mind, the best conceivable sensation for it to produce is the one that is most often useful for the maintenance of the healthy man. Experience teaches that all the sensations put in us by nature are of this sort and therefore that everything in our sensations testifies to God's power and goodness. For example, when the nerves in the foot are moved with unusual violence, the motion is communicated through the middle of the spine to the center of the brain, where it signals the mind to sense a pain "in the foot." This urges the mind to view the pain's cause as harmful to the foot and to do what it can to remove that cause. Of course, God could have so designed man's nature that the same motion of the brain presented something else to the mind, like the motion in the brain, or the motion in the foot, or a motion somewhere between the brain and foot. But no alternative to the way things are would be as conducive to the maintenance of the body. Similarly, when we need drink, the throat becomes dry, the dryness moves the nerves of the throat thereby moving the center of the brain, and the brain's movements cause the sensation of thirst in the mind. It's the sensation of thirst that is produced, because no information about our condition is more useful to us than that we need to get something to drink in order to remain healthy. And the same is true in other cases.

This makes it completely obvious that, despite God's immense goodness, the nature of man (whom we now view as a composite of mind and body) cannot fail to be deceptive. For, if something produces the movement usually associated with an injured foot in the nerve running from foot to brain or in the brain itself rather than in the foot, a pain is felt as if "in the foot." Here the senses are deceived by their nature. Since this motion in the brain must always bring the same sensation to mind, and since the motion's cause is something hurting the foot more often than something elsewhere, it's in accordance with reason that the motion always presents the mind a pain in the foot rather than elsewhere.

And, if dryness of the throat arises, not (as usual) from drink's being conducive to the body's health, but (as happens in dropsy) from some other cause, it's much better that we are deceived on this occasion than that we are generally deceived when our bodies are sound. And the same holds for other cases.

In addition to helping me to be aware of the errors to which my nature is subject, these reflections help me readily to correct or avoid these errors. I know that sensory indications of what is good for my body are more often true than false; I can almost always examine a given thing with several senses; and I can also use my memory (which connects the present to the past) and my understanding (which has now examined all the causes of error). Hence, I need no longer fear that what the senses daily show me is unreal. I should reject the exaggerated doubts of the past few days as ridiculous. This is especially true of the chief ground for these doubts—namely, my inability to distinguish dreaming from being awake. For I now notice that dreaming and being awake are importantly different: the events in dreams are not linked by memory to the rest of my life like those that happen while I am awake. If, while I'm awake, someone were suddenly to appear and then immediately to disappear without my seeing where he came from or went to (as happens in dreams), I would justifiably judge that he was not a real man but a ghost—or, better an apparition created in my brain. But, if I distinctly observe something's source, its place, and the time at which I learn about it, and if I grasp an unbroken connection between it and the rest of my life, I'm quite sure that it is something in my waking life rather than in a dream. And I ought not to have the slightest doubt about the reality of such things if I have examined them with all my senses, my memory, and my understanding without finding any conflicting evidence. For, from the fact that God is not a deceiver, it follows that I am not deceived in any case of this sort. Since the need to act does not always allow time for such a careful examination, however, we must admit the likelihood of men's erring about particular things and acknowledge the weakness of our nature.

Commentary and Questions

We now know what the essence of material things is: To be such a thing is to be extended in space in three dimensions, to have shape and size, to endure, and to be movable and changeable in these dimensions. This is what a material thing would be—if there were any. At last we face the haunting question: Are there any?

The first thing to note is that they *can* exist.

Q44.   What is Descartes' reason for thinking this?

If, moreover, we examine our *images* of material things, it seems that the imagination produces these images by turning "to the body" and looking "at something there" (p. 345). It is as though a representation of a triangle were physically stored in the body (or brain); and imagination is looking, not at a real triangular thing, but at that stored representation. Because we can undoubtedly form mental images, it certainly seems as though some material things exist—namely, our bodies.

But to make this clearer, Descartes draws a sharp distinction between **imagining** something and **conceiving** it.

Q45.   How does the example comparing the triangle with the chiliagon help to clarify this distinction? (See p. 345.)

We still have no proof, of course, that there are any bodies. But again, progress has been made; for we now have an account of how one of the faculties of the mind works—on the assumption that there really are bodies. If we can find a proof of this assumption, it will "fit" with what we know about our mental capacities.

Descartes now turns from imagining to sensing. On pages 345–346, he reviews again his reasons for confidence in the senses and then his reasons for doubt.* At the end of this review he concludes

---

*In the course of this review he paraphrases one of the basic principles of Thomas Aquinas, who derives it from Aristotle: There is no idea in the intellect, which was not previously in the senses. This is, for instance, the foundation for Aquinas' rejection of the ontological argument (see p. 270). Descartes allows that this principle is superficially plausible, but in the light of his skeptical doubts he considers it naive. Not only do we know that we have ideas before we know we have senses, we know that some of these ideas must be innate—that is, they could not plausibly be derived from sensible experience. Such are the ideas of thing, thought, truth, and God.

again that what he is taught "by nature" does not deserve much credence.

However, the situation is now very different from that of the first *Meditation*. For now he knows that God exists and is not a deceiver. And in short order Descartes offers proofs that the soul is distinct from the body and that material things exist. Both of these depend on clear ideas of the essence of material things, which he arrived at in the fifth *Meditation*.

Here, in outline, is his proof for the distinctness of soul from body.

1. God can create anything that I can clearly and distinctly conceive—there being no impossibility in it.
2. If God can create one thing independently of another, the first thing is distinct from the second.
3. I have a clear and distinct idea of my essence as a thinking thing.
4. So God can create a thinking thing (a soul) independently of a body.
5. I also have a clear and distinct idea of my body as an extended thing—its essence.
6. So God can create a body independently of a soul.
7. So my soul is a reality distinct from my body.
8. So I, as a thinking thing (soul), can exist without my body.

Q46. How sound is this argument? What are the weak points, if any?

Q47. Is there a tension between the conclusion of this argument and Descartes' assertion (p. 347) that I am *not* in my body the way a sailor is in his ship?*

Descartes' proof for the reality of material things goes roughly like this:

1. I have a "strong inclination" to believe in the reality of the material (extended) things that I seem to sense. (To put it another way, their independent reality seems to be one of the things I am "taught by nature.")

---

*Compare the use that Aquinas makes of this same image, p. 279.

2. God must have created me with this inclination.
3. If material things do not exist independently, then God is a deceiver.
4. But God is not a deceiver.
5. So material things exist with those properties I conceive to be essential to them.

Q48. Evaluate the soundness of this argument.

At this point, Descartes has, he thinks, achieved his main objectives. Skepticism and solipsism have been defeated. The basic structure of reality has been delineated: God, souls, and material things. Reality, then, is composed of infinite substance and two kinds of finite substances—thinking and extended. The bridge has been built. Knowledge has been shown to be possible. Physics has been supplied with a foundation in metaphysics. And all this with a certainty that rivals that of geometry!

The rest of *Meditation VI* attends to a few details that are still left.

Q49. Compare what Descartes says on p. 348 with Galileo's view of "secondary qualities" (pp. 310–311).

Q50. If the senses present external things in such an inadequate way, what use are they?

Q51. How are we to account for certain errors the senses seem to lead us to—-such as the pain in an amputated limb or the desire of a person with dropsy (edema) to drink?

Q52. What is the final disposition of the problem arising from dreams?

What Has Descartes Done?

It is possible to argue whether Descartes is the last of the medievals or the first of the moderns. Like most such arguments about transitional figures, there is truth on both sides. But that both philosophy and our general view of the world have been different ever since is indisputable. Descartes develops a philosophy that reflects the newly developing sciences and, in turn, gives them a legitimacy they otherwise lack. A measure of his lasting influence is the fact that a significant part of philosophy since World War I has been devoted to showing that he was crucially wrong about some basic things (which would not be worth doing unless his influence was still powerfully felt).* Descartes is *our* ancestor.

Let us sum up several key features of his thought and then indicate where certain problems crop up.

A New Ideal for Knowledge

One commentator says of the Cartesian revolution that it "stands for the substitution of free inquiry for submission to authority, for the rejection of Faith without reason for faith *in* reason, and the replacement of Faith by Demonstration."[6] Though Descartes is far from trying to reject religious belief (indeed, he thinks he can rationally justify its two most important parts, God and the soul), in the last analysis everything comes down to what the rational mind finds clear and distinct enough to be indubitable. Nothing else will be accepted, regardless of its antiquity or traditional claims to authority. We each contain within ourselves the criterion for truth and knowledge. This radical individualism is qualified only by the conviction that rationality is the same for every individual (just as mathematics is the same for all). No longer can we put the responsibility for deciding what to believe on someone else, whether priest, pope, or king. It lies squarely on each of us.

Moreover, the ideal for such belief is the clarity and certainty of mathematics. Probability or plausibility is not enough. Being vaguely right is not enough. The habits of thought developed in us by nature are not enough. By analysis we can resolve problems into their simple elements; by intuition we can see their truth; and by demonstration we can move to necessary consequences. Knowledge has the structure of an axiomatic system. All this is possible. Anything less is unacceptable. To be faithful to this ideal is to free oneself from error and to attain truth.

In all this Descartes deserves his reputation as Prince of the Rationalists.* The ultimate court of appeal is reason—the light of nature. We ought to rely on intellect rather than sense, on intuition and deduction rather than imagination; "for true knowledge of external things seems to belong to the mind alone, not the composite of mind and body" (p. 348).

A New Vision of Reality

Descartes' metaphysics makes explicit and complete the worldview that was emerging already in the work of Copernicus, Kepler, and Galileo. Our world is a giant mechanism, not unlike a clock (see Descartes' analogy on p. 348). It was, to be sure, created by God. But now it runs on the principles of mechanics, and our science is mechanistic in principle. If we abstract from the fact of creation, the entire material universe, including the human body, is just a complex machine. The world has become a *secular* world. What happens can be explained and predicted without reference to any purposes or intentions of the creator. We are, we might say, worlds away from the intrinsically purposive, inherently value-laden, God-directed world of the medievals. Dante now begins to look like a fairy tale or, at best, a moral allegory with no literal truth value at all. It is, perhaps, no great surprise that the *Meditations* ends up on the index of forbidden books.

There are, to be sure, human minds or souls, and they are not caught up in the mechanism of the material world. They are, in fact, radically free. Even God does not have more freedom than a soul (see *Meditation IV*). But as we'll see, this disparity between soul and body is not so much the solution to a problem as it is a problem in itself.

Problems

Great as Descartes' achievement is, he bequeaths to his successors a legacy of unsolved problems.

---

*Among the critics are C. S. Peirce, Martin Heidegger, Ludwig Wittgenstein, Willard Quine, Richard Rorty, and Daniel Dennett. See the chapters on their philosophies.

*Though (almost) all philosophers try to reach their conclusions rationally, a rationalist is one who emphasizes the exclusive role of reason in the formation of knowledge. For one of Descartes' most distinguished predecessors in this tradition, see the discussion of the pre-Socratic thinker, Parmenides, in Chapter 2.

There are those who refuse to accept his radical beginning point and remain true to a more traditional approach, usually Aristotelian. But his methodological doubt has been powerfully persuasive to many, and the continued progress of physics seems to be evidence that his basic view of the world is correct. For the next hundred and fifty years, Cartesianism, together with its variants, will be the dominating philosophy on the European continent. As we'll see, different assumptions are at work in Britain, but even here the Cartesian spirit of independence is pervasive. Still, there are nagging worries. Let us note three of them.

The Place of Humans in the World of Nature

Descartes is intent on legitimizing the new science. And this he does. But what place is there for us in the universe of the new physics? Is it plausible to think that we, too, are just cogs in this universal machine? We assume that we have purposes and act to realize certain values. But where is there room for purposes and values in this mechanistic world? Is our assumption just an illusion? We assume that we can make a difference in the outcome of physical processes. But if the world is a closed mechanism, how can this be? We experience ourselves as conscious beings, aware of ourselves and the world around us. But can a machine be conscious? These are very contemporary questions, the sort cognitive science aims to sort out and solve.

All these questions force themselves on us once we take Descartes' vision of the universe seriously. Descartes is not unaware of them. His basic strategy for dealing with them consists in the radical split that he makes between mind and body. Bodies, he holds, are parts of the mechanical universe; minds are not. Physics can deal with the body, but not with the mind. We know that we are not merely automata because (1) we can use language, and (2) we are flexible and adaptable in a way no machine could be; reason, Descartes says, "is a universal instrument which can be used in all kinds of situations." It is quite possible, he says, that we could construct a machine that utters words—even one that utters words corresponding

to movements of its body. But it is not possible, he thinks, for a machine to "give an appropriately meaningful answer to whatever is said in its presence, as the dullest of men can do" (*DM* 6.56–57, p. 120).*

But merely dividing mind from body does not completely solve the problem. The question arises, How are they related?

The Mind and the Body

Descartes concludes that the mind is one thing and the body another; each is so independent of the other that either could exist without the other. They are, moreover, of a radically different character. The essence of a mind is thinking; minds are in no sense extended objects. The essence of a material thing is extension; but extended things such as bodies cannot think. Still, he says, mind and body are so intimately related as to form "a single unified thing" (p. 347).

But how can I be two things and yet one single thing? No explanation is given. Clearly he must insist that what happens to the body affects the mind, as when I get hungry, or am hurt, or open my eyes to a blue wall in daylight. And what the mind decides, the body may do, as when I choose to walk or eat an ice cream cone. There seems to be a two-way causal relation between mind and body. This view is called **interactionism**.

"What is matter?—Never mind.
What is mind?—No matter."

Punch

Yet it is completely puzzling how this can be. How can something that is not extended reach into the closed system of the mechanical world and work a change there, where all changes are governed by mechanical principles? And how can an alteration in the shape or position of certain material particles cause us to feel sad or think of Cleveland?

---

*This, of course, is precisely the aim of research on artificial intelligence. Will it be successful? Descartes bets not.

No explanation is forthcoming. It seems entirely mysterious. To save the integrity of his physics, Descartes pushes the mental out of the physical world entirely. But then it is inexplicable how physics itself can be done at all, since it seems to depend on interactions between nonphysical minds and physical bodies. Here is the problem that Schopenhauer would later call "the world knot." It is safe to say that a philosophy that does not solve the mind–body problem cannot be considered entirely acceptable.

God and the Problem of Skepticism

As we have seen, Descartes takes the skeptical problem very seriously. He pushes skeptical arguments about as far as they can be pushed, and he thinks that in the *cogito* he has found the key to overcoming skepticism. But even if we grant that each of us knows, by virtue of the *cogito*, that we exist, knowledge of the *world* depends on the fact that God is not a deceiver. And that depends on the proofs for the existence of God.

What if those proofs are faulty? Then I am back again in solipsism, without a guarantee that anything exists beyond myself. Are the proofs—or at least one of them—satisfactory? Descartes is quite clear that everything depends on that question; "the certainty and truth of all my knowledge derives from one thing: my thought of the true God" (p. 343). He is sure that the proofs are as secure as the theorems of geometry. But is he right about that?

THE PREEMINENCE OF EPISTEMOLOGY

In earlier philosophies there are many problems—the one and the many, the nature of reality, explaining change, the soul, the existence of God—and the problem of knowledge is just one among the rest. Descartes' radical skepticism changes that. After Descartes and until very recent times most philosophers have thought that epistemological problems are absolutely foundational. Among these problems of knowledge, the problem about knowing the external world is the sharpest and

most dangerous. Can we know anything at all beyond the contents of our minds? Unless this skeptical question can be satisfactorily answered, nothing else can be done. Epistemology is, for better or worse, the heart of philosophy for the next several hundred years.

These are problems that Descartes' successors wrestle with, as we'll see. Next, however, we want to look at a figure who is often neglected in the history of modern philosophy: Thomas Hobbes. Hobbes is more interesting to us than to previous generations, perhaps, because he presents an alternative response to the new science. Some recent thought about the mind—that associated with artificial intelligence—can be regarded as a struggle to replace the paradigm of Descartes with that of Hobbes.

FOR FURTHER THOUGHT

Descartes argues that there is no way you could tell that your ideas about the external world were correct unless there were a nondeceptive God to guarantee their basic rightness. Can you think of any way you might be able to know there is a world corresponding to your ideas? Try to construct a view that provides this reassurance without depending on God.

KEY WORDS

Descartes	volitions
rules of method	emotions
clear and distinct	judgments
analysis	innate ideas
insight	light of nature
deduction	subjective reality
first philosophy	formal reality
senses	eminent reality
dreams	*ex nihilo nihil fit*
evil demon	solipsism
representational theory	understanding
cogito	will
genus and difference	material things
self-evident	imagining
thinking thing	conceiving
ideas	interactionism

NOTES

1. Quoted in S. V. Keeling, *Descartes* (London: Oxford University Press, 1968).

2. Quotations from René Descartes' *Discourse on the Method of Rightly Conducting One's Reason and Seeking the Truth in the Sciences*, in *The Philosophical Writings of Descartes*, ed. John Cottingham, Robert Stoothoff, and Dugald Murdoch (Cambridge: Cambridge University Press, 1985), are cited in the text using the abbreviation *DM*. References are to part numbers and page numbers in the classic French edition, followed by page numbers in this edition.

3. Quotations from René Descartes, *The Principles of Philosophy*, in *The Philosophical Works of Descartes*, vol. 1, ed. Elisabeth S. Haldane and G. R. T. Ross (n.p.: Dover Publications, 1955), are cited in the text using the abbreviation *PP*. References are to the classic French edition, followed by the page numbers in this edition.

4. Quoted by Martin Heidegger in *The Way Back into the Ground of Metaphysics*, reprinted in *Existentialism from Dostoevsky to Sartre*, ed. Walter Kaufmann (New York: Merchant Books, 1957).

5. Trans. Ronald Rubin, *Meditations on First Philosophy* (Claremont, CA: Areté Press, 1641/1986).

6. Keeling, *Descartes*, 252.

AFTERWORD

This book is a history of the Western philosophical tradition whose home is in Greece and Jerusalem, Europe, Great Britain, and America. It is also an introductory book, touching only on highlights of this Western tradition. If anything is obvious these days, it is that there are other vigorous traditions as well. This edition gestures in that direction with brief discussions of the Tao, Zen, the Buddha, Avicenna, Averroës, and Maimonides, but these are mere hints of riches that lie beyond the scope of the book. There is no doubt that we have much to learn from other ways of thinking about the fundamental problems, just as others have much to learn from us. But we will only be shallow partners in cross-cultural conversations if we do not understand ourselves; and the way to understand ourselves is to understand our history.

The book also gives a very inadequate hint of the lively and interesting philosophical work being done today. New problems provoke novel thinking. New technologies bring new possibilities, and

these may promise good or threaten evil. Ethical problems are posed by genetic manipulation, cloning, and computing. Problems of global warming, terrorism, genocide, poverty, the environment, abortion, and euthanasia call for philosophical reflection about ends and means, and about human nature. The resurgence of religion keeps the tension with reason and science alive. Reflection continues on the challenges of skepticism and the extent and character of human knowledge. We can hardly say that Kant's four questions (What can we know? What ought we to do? For what can we hope? And what is man?) have been definitively answered.

Nor has the question about relativism been settled to the satisfaction of everyone. The rise of "multiculturalism" raises questions about the extent to which every culture deserves equal respect; are there some cultures that are better than others? If so, how would one tell? Is it all just a matter of opinion, as the ancient Sophists thought? Must might make right? Though the problem sometimes seems intractable, it is impossible to avoid taking up a point of view on the question. Some are struggling to see whether there is a way to acknowledge a truth in relativism without giving up the Socratic quest altogether.*

———————

*For a look at recent argument about relativism, see Norman Melchert, *Who's to Say? A Dialogue on Relativism* (Indianapolis: Hackett, 1994).

Philosophy isn't everything. Daniel Dennett has said that if the unexamined life is not worth living (Socrates), the overexamined life is nothing to write home about either. But philosophy has the peculiar characteristic of being inescapable for us all. So we should try to think about these matters with something approaching Aristotelian "excellence," remembering what my own little old German professor once said: "Whether you will philosophize or won't philosophize, you *must* philosophize."

APPENDIX
Writing a Philosophy Paper

It is not enough, when studying philosophy, to master the arguments of the philosophers. You must try your own hand at "doing philosophy," as the phrase goes, and the very best way to do that is to write a philosophical essay of your own. Here I give you some suggestions, and a few rules, for writing a good paper.

A philosophy essay is not a research paper, needing time spent in the library—or on the Internet. Your aim should not be to gain still more information, but to formulate and defend (at least provisionally, for now) an answer to some philosophical problem that you think important. What this requires is not research, but thinking—trying to figure out what can be said for and against a certain position. Is pleasure the good for humans, as Epicurus and Bentham think, or are the criticisms of Aristotle, Augustine, and Kant conclusive? Are our wills free? (Think of Democritus, Aquinas, Descartes, Hume, and de Beauvoir.) Is one or another argument for the existence of God cogent? Your aim should be to write a paper giving good reasons—*your* reasons—supporting *your* conclusion on some such problem.

In writing this paper, you need to have an audience in mind. Don't write it for your instructor. In particular, don't write it to please him or her; that will surely skew your results in a way that will be less than authentically you. I suggest that you keep in mind an intelligent person about your own age, someone not a philosophy major, but with an interest in the problem you are addressing—perhaps a brother or sister at another university. You want to convince this person that your conclusion on the matter in question is the most reasonable one.

You should begin with a statement of the problem you mean to address. Since you will not be writing a book, you need to narrow the problem down to something you can handle in five or ten pages. Don't try to answer the question "Does God exist?" but you might intend to show that Hume's critique of the design argument is fatally flawed. Don't address the question "Is human knowledge possible?" but you could try "Can I know that this apple exists independently of my perception of it?" Whatever your problem, it may require some clarification, perhaps including a summary of several ways other philosophers have answered it. Within the first few paragraphs, you should state clearly the view that you intend to support. Let us call this the *thesis* of the paper. You should give your audience an indication of this thesis early on so they can appreciate the relevance of the arguments you put forward in the body of the paper.

These arguments will present the premises that you believe make it reasonable to believe your conclusion. You should strive to set forth premises that are true, if possible, or at least plausible, keeping your target audience in mind. It may well be that some of your premises are not themselves obvious, and you may need to offer support for them. Thus you may need to develop sub-arguments for these premises, trying again to find reasons that are acceptable.

One persuasive tactic in argument is to consider objections to your thesis and show why they are not well founded. Here you should seek out the strongest objections; to consider only weak objections leaves your support for the thesis itself weak, since an opponent could easily cite the stronger objections. The way Plato deals with the Sophists is a good model; Thrasymachus and Callicles are not "straw men" that are easy to blow down, but worthy opponents whose defeat would indeed be a victory.

You may certainly get help from the philosophers you have studied, if you agree with some of their arguments. Here you need to be careful, though. You can't just borrow a philosopher's words without indicating that you are doing so. The way to do that is to use quote marks around the sentences you are borrowing, and indicate in a footnote the source from which they come. You may use the format for footnotes found in this text, or whatever format your instructor prefers. Even close paraphrases should be acknowledged this way. If you use sources other than this text (and your instructor will tell you whether that is desired or required), you should indicate that in a bibliography at the end.

You will find an outline a great help in writing a philosophy paper. Some experts recommend a full outline in complete sentences; they say that if you do this, the paper pretty much writes itself. I myself find a less full outline more helpful—a list of topics that need to be covered in more or less the desired order. In either case, you will find that continual revision will be necessary as you write. Perhaps Mozart could have a sonata completely in mind before he wrote down the first notes, but there are few Mozarts among us. Computers and word processors make moving text around, adding and deleting, deliciously easy, so make use of the technology. After you get a draft that you are fairly satisfied with, set it aside for a day or two. When you come back to it, you will certainly find things that can be improved. (This, of course, means that you shouldn't try to write the paper the night before it is due!)

The paper should close with a summary of the argument, recalling the problem to be solved, the solution proposed, and the main premises used to establish the conclusion.

Here are a few basic rules to observe:

1. Write clearly. Keep your sentences short and don't use fancy words. Write as simply as the subject allows. You are not out to impress anyone, but to convince your readers of your conclusion.

2. Don't use up space with obvious trivialities or broad generalizations. Don't begin by writing, "Since the dawn of time human beings have puzzled over the meaning of life."

3. Don't appeal to authority. If you are trying to prove that mind and body are distinct entities, it will not help to note that Descartes thought so. Descartes might be mistaken.

4. Don't fall back on "I believe" or "I feel." Your reader is not interested in your autobiography, but in the argument for your conclusion.

5. Avoid padding and repetitiveness. Saying the same thing six different ways will not strengthen your case.

6. Never make excuses. Don't say, "Of course, I'm only a college freshman. . . ." Just do your best. No one expects more.

7. If you write using a computer, run the spell-check feature, but don't depend only on that; if you type "buy" instead of "but," no spell checker will find the error. Proofread your paper carefully before turning it in. Sloppiness in spelling and grammar gives a bad impression of carelessness.

Your instructor will try not to evaluate your argument according to whether he or she agrees with your conclusion. You should pay no attention to the instructor's views on the topic in question—even if you know what they are. The important thing is the relevance, clarity, and strength of your premises relative to the conclusion you are supporting. The quality of the argument is what counts.

It should be unnecessary to stress that your paper should be your own work and represent the thinking that you have put into it. Plagiarism—passing off someone else's work as your own—is quite simply wrong. It involves lying, fraud, and cheating, and it undermines the trust that is the foundation on which a community of scholars can function. If these moral reasons do not convince you, you may want to remember that plagiarism is harshly punished in the academy. If you were discovered to have cheated in this way—a very real possibility—you would certainly be failed for this assignment, perhaps be failed for the course, and possibly even expelled from the school.

Writing a philosophy paper can be challenging, especially the first time you try it. But it is an excellent exercise for developing clarity of thought, self-criticism, and a sense for what rationality is really like.

GLOSSARY

Here you will find brief explanations of difficult or unfamiliar terms, sometimes followed in parentheses by the name or names of philosophers with whom the term is especially—though not solely—associated.

absolute knowledge A term in HEGEL's philosophy, designating the state of consciousness when everything "other" has been brought into itself and Spirit knows itself to be all of reality.

aesthetic KIERKEGAARD's term for the style of life that aims at avoiding boredom and keeping things interesting; the pursuit of pleasurable experiences. **Aesthetics** (also spelled "esthetics") is the theory of art and of the experience of the beautiful or sublime.

alienation HEGELian term appropriated by MARX to describe the loss of oneself and control over what properly belongs to oneself in capitalist social structures. One's work and the products of one's labor, for instance, are made alien to oneself and belong to another. Existentialism stresses the general feeling of alienation among modern human beings.

ambiguity A term applied to human reality, indicating its immanence and transcendence. (SIMONE DE BEAUVOIR)

analytic A term applied to statements the denial of which is a contradiction (for example, "All bachelors are unmarried"). (KANT, **logical positivists**)

anticipatory resoluteness HEIDEGGER's term for authentically facing the fact that one is destined for death.

a posteriori A term applied primarily to statements, but also to ideas or concepts; knowledge of the a posteriori is derived from (comes *after*) experience (for example, "Trees have leaves"). (KANT)

appearance The way things present themselves to us, often contrasted with the way they really are (for example, the oar in water appears bent but is really straight). KANT holds that all we can ever come to know is how **things-in-themselves** *appear* to our senses and understanding; appearance is the realm of **phenomena** versus **noumena.**

a priori A term applied primarily to statements, but also to ideas or concepts, that can be known *prior to* and independently of appeal to experience (for example, "Two and three are five," or "All bodies are extended"). (KANT)

argument A set of statements, some of which (the premises) function as reasons to accept another (the conclusion).

atomism From a Greek word meaning "uncuttable"; the ancient Greek view (by DEMOCRITUS and others) that all of reality is composed of tiny indivisible bits and the void (empty space). See also **logical atomism.**

attunement In HEIDEGGER's thinking, the term for a mode of disclosure that manifests itself in a mood; for example, the mood of anxiety discloses **Dasein's** not-being-at-home in the world of its ordinary concern.

authenticity Being oneself, taking responsibility for oneself in accepting the burden of having to "be here"— that is, thrown into this particular existence with just these possibilities. (HEIDEGGER)

autonomy Self-rule or giving the law to oneself, as opposed to *heteronomy,* being under the control of another. A key principle in KANT's **ethics.**

Being The fundamental concept of **metaphysics.** Doctrines of **categories** such as those of ARISTOTLE and KANT attempt to set forth the most general ways that things can *be.* The meaning of Being is the object of HEIDEGGER's quest.

Being-in-the world The most general characteristic of **Dasein,** according to HEIDEGGER; more fundamental than knowing, it is being engaged in the use of gear or equipment in a world functionally organized.

binary opposition A pair of terms, each of which lives on its opposition to the other. Examples are: appearance/reality, knowledge/opinion, one/many, speaking/writing, and good/evil. Often a target for deconstruction by postmodernists.

carceral society The character of current society, according to Foucault, where everything is formed by technologies analogous to those used in a prison.

Cartesian Theater The picture of experience as a display to a single observer in some central spot in the brain. (DENNETT)

categorical imperative The key principle in KANT's moral theory, bidding us always to act in such a way that the maxim (principle) of our action could be universally applied.

categories Very general concepts describing the basic modes of being. ARISTOTLE distinguishes ten, including "substance," "quantity," and "quality." KANT lists twelve, the most important of which are "substance" and "causality."

causation What accounts for the occurrence or character of something. ARISTOTLE distinguishes four kinds of cause: material, formal, efficient, and final. According to most recent theories, influenced by HUME, causation is a relationship between events, where the first is regularly or lawfully related to the second.

Chinese Room A thought experiment by John Searle constituting an argument that a computer program alone can not produce understanding or a mind.

compatibilism The view that human liberty (or freedom of the will) can coexist with determinism—the universal **causation** of all events. Classic sources are HOBBES and HUME.

conclusion That part of an argument for which evidence (in the form of the premises) is presented.

contingency What might be or might not be, depending; the opposite of necessity. RORTY, particularly, emphasizes the historical contingency of our language and point of view; neither is necessitated by the character of the world they are about.

convention The Sophists contrast what is true by nature (*physis*) with what is true by convention or agreement (*nomos*) among humans. The latter, but not the former, can also be changed by human decision.

correspondence A view of truth; a statement is said to be true, provided that it "corresponds" with what it is about—that is, it *says* that reality is such and such, and reality *is in fact* such and such. (ARISTOTLE, AQUINAS, LOCKE)

criterion A mark or standard by which something is known. The "problem of the criterion" is posed by skeptics, who ask by what criterion we can tell that we know something and, if an answer is given, by what criterion we know that this is the correct criterion. (SEXTUS EMPIRICUS, MONTAIGNE, DESCARTES, HEGEL)

Dasein HEIDEGGER's term for the way of being that is characteristic of humans. Literally meaning "being there," it designates that way to be in which one's own **Being** is a matter of concern.

deduction A kind of argument, aiming at validity, in which the premises purport to prove the conclusion; a successful or valid deductive argument.

determinism The view that there is a causal condition for every event, without exception, sufficient to produce that event just as it is. The philosophical relevance of determinism lies particularly in relation to human action. (DEMOCRITUS, EPICURUS, HUME, KANT)

dialectic A term of many meanings. For SOCRATES, it is a progression of questions and answers, driving toward less inadequate opinions. For PLATO, it is the sort of reasoning that moves from **Forms** to more basic Forms, and at last to the Form of the Good. For HEGEL, it is the progress of both thought and reality by the reconciliation of opposites and the generation of new opposites. MARXists apply the Hegelian doctrine to the world of material production.

différance DERRIDA's term for the destabilizing of meaning and reference by language as a system of differences; a word is what it is because it *differs* from other words, and it fails to *present* its signified meaning because it *defers* it to other interpretations.

dogmatism A term applied by philosophers to the holding of views for no adequate reason.

dualism The metaphysical view that there are two basically different kinds of things in reality; the most common dualism is that of mind and body, as in DESCARTES, for instance. (Compare **monism.**)

empiricism The view that all knowledge of facts must be derived from sense experience; a rejection of **rationalism,** the view that any knowledge of nature is innate or constructable by reasoning alone. Exemplified by HUME, LOCKE, BERKELEY, and the **logical positivists.**

entelechy A goal or end residing within a thing, guiding its development from potentiality to the actuality of its **essence.** (ARISTOTLE)

epiphenomenalism The view that consciousness is an effect of physical happenings in the body but has no causal powers itself. It is just "along for the ride."

episteme The term Foucault uses to designate the background assumptions of a given historical era.

epistemology Theory of knowledge, addressing the questions of what knowledge is, whether we have any, what its objects may be, and how we can reliably get more.

essence The set of properties that makes each thing uniquely the kind of thing that it is. (ARISTOTLE, AQUINAS, DESCARTES)

ethics The study of good and evil, right and wrong, moral rules, virtues, and the good life; their status, meaning, and justification.

ethnocentrism Judging everything by the standards current in one's own society.

eudaemonia Greek term for happiness or well-being. (PLATO, ARISTOTLE, EPICURUS, the Stoics, the Skeptics)

existentialism The philosophy that focuses on what it means to exist in the way human beings do—usually stressing choice, risk, and freedom. KIERKEGAARD is a main figure, as are HEIDEGGER and DE BEAUVOIR.

facticity The way of **Being** of **Dasein.** One aspect of our facticity, for instance, is our **Being-in-the-world;** another is our **thrownness**—simply finding ourselves in existence in some particular way. (HEIDEGGER)

fallibilism The view expressed by PEIRCE, and earlier by XENOPHANES, that though we may know the truth in certain cases, perhaps in many cases, we can never be certain that we do.

falling HEIDEGGER's term for the phenomenon of being defined by others. **Dasein** inevitably *falls-in-with* what "they" say and tends strongly to *fall-away-from* itself.

family resemblance WITTGENSTEIN's term for the way many of our concepts get their meaning. There is no set of necessary and sufficient conditions for an item to be a *game,* for instance, only overlapping and crisscrossing resemblances among instances of things we call games.

Forms Those ideal realities PLATO takes to be both the objects of knowledge and the source of the derived reality of the sensible world: the Square Itself, for instance, and the Forms of Justice and the Good. Used uncapitalized for the forms of ARISTOTLE and AQUINAS, which have no being apart from the particular things that exemplify them.

free spirit A term used by certain late-nineteenth-century thinkers, such as NIETZSCHE, to symbolize their freedom from the inherited tradition—particularly the religious tradition.

genealogy A search for the historical antecedents of current cultural assumptions. (NIETZSCHE, FOUCAULT)

Great Chain of Being The view that reality is stretched between God (or **the One**) and nothingness, with each kind of thing possessing its own degree of being and goodness. Found in PLOTINUS and AUGUSTINE; widespread for many centuries.

hedonism The view that pleasure is the sole objective of motivation (psychological hedonism) or that it is the only thing good in itself (ethical hedonism). (EPICURUS, BENTHAM, MILL)

hermeneutic circle The idea that any interpretation takes something for granted; for example, understanding part of a text presupposes an understanding of the whole, and vice versa. Every understanding lights up its objects only against a background that cannot at the same time be brought into the light. It follows that complete objectivity is impossible. (HEIDEGGER)

heterophenomenology A third-person method for investigating consciousness devised by Daniel Dennett. It yields descriptions of how things seem to a subject.

historical a priori What is so taken for granted at a time that it could hardly be imagined that one could question it. May change over time. (FOUCAULT)

hubris A Greek word meaning arrogance or excessive self-confidence, particularly of mortals in relation to the gods.

hylomorphism The theory that every material object is a composite of matter (*hyle*) and form (*morphe*); matter is the potentiality of a thing, form its actuality. (ARISTOTLE, AQUINAS—with qualifications)

idealism The view that objects exist only relative to a subject that perceives or knows them. There are many forms; in HEGEL's *absolute idealism,* for instance, mind or Spirit (the Absolute) is the only ultimate reality, everything else having only a relative reality. (also BERKELEY)

inauthenticity HEIDEGGER's word for **Dasein**'s fleeing from itself into the average everyday world of what "they" say and do; not being oneself.

induction A method of reasoning that infers from a series of single cases to a new case or to a law or general principle concerning all such cases.

innate ideas Ideas that any mature individual can acquire independently of experience. Defended in different ways by PLATO and by DESCARTES, attacked by LOCKE and the empiricists.

instrumentalism DEWEY's term for his own philosophy, according to which all our intellectual constructions (concepts, laws, theories) have the status of tools for solving problems.

language-games Comparing words to pieces in a game such as chess. What defines a rook are the rules according to which it moves; what characterizes a word are the jobs it does in those activities and forms of life in which it has its "home." Language is a game we play with words. (the later WITTGENSTEIN)

light of nature DESCARTES' term for reason, in the light of which things can appear so clear and distinct that they cannot possibly be doubted.

logical atomism A view expressed by the early WITTGENSTEIN, in which language is thought of as a logical calculus built up from simple unanalyzable elements called *names*. Names stand for simple objects, which are the substance of the world.

logical positivism A twentieth-century version of **empiricism,** which stresses the **tautological** nature of logic and mathematics, together with the criterion of **verifiability** for factual statements; if they are not verifiable by sense experience, the statements are not meaningful.

logical truth Truths that are true by virtue of logic alone. WITTGENSTEIN explains logical truths as **tautologies.**

logocentrism The view DERRIDA finds dominant in our tradition, where knowledge finds a foundation in its objects being present to consciousness and reason and logic are thought to be reliable avenues to the extension of truth.

logos Greek term meaning word, utterance, rationale, argument, structure. In HERACLITUS, the ordering principle of the world; in the Gospel of John, that according to which all things were made and that became incarnate in Jesus.

materialism The view that the fundamental reality is matter, as understood by the sciences—primarily physics; mind or spirit has no independent reality. (HOBBES)

metaphysics The discipline that studies being as such, its kinds and character, often set out in a doctrine of **categories.** Also called by some "first philosophy."

mirror A metaphor for the correspondence theory of truth, whereby the mind is supposed to "mirror" an independently existing reality. (RORTY)

monism The metaphysical view that there is only one basic kind of reality; materialism is one kind of monism, HEGELian idealism another. (Compare **dualism.**)

naturalism A view that locates human beings wholly within nature and takes the results of the natural and human sciences to be our best idea of what there is; since DARWIN, naturalists in philosophy insist that the human world is a product of the nonpurposive process of evolution.

natural law Law specifying right and wrong, which is embedded in the very nature of things; natural law is not based on custom or convention and therefore applies universally. (Stoics, AQUINAS, LOCKE)

nihilism The view that nothing really matters, that distinctions of value have no grounding in the nature of things; what threatens, according to NIETZSCHE, when God dies.

nominal essence An essence that is determined not by the true nature of things, but by the words we have for them. (LOCKE)

nomos The way things are insofar as they depend on human decision, custom, or convention. (Compare *physis*.) (Sophists)

normalization In Foucault, the goal and effect of disciplinary technologies; making all alike.

noumena KANT's term for things as they are in themselves, quite independently of how they may appear to us; he believes they are unknowable. (Contrasted with **phenomena** or **appearance.**)

nous Greek term usually translated as "mind." In ARISTOTLE, *nous* is the active and purely formal principle that engages in thinking and contemplation; he argues that *nous* is more than just the form of a living body; it is a reality in its own right and is eternal.

objective spirit That realm in which Spirit expresses itself externally, giving rationality to institutions, law, and culture. (HEGEL)

Ockham's razor A principle stated by WILLIAM OF OCKHAM, demanding parsimony in the postulation of entities for the purpose of explanation; often formulated as "Do not multiply entities beyond necessity."

One, the 1. In PLOTINUS and Neoplatonic thought, the source from which the rest of reality emanates. 2. A translation of HEIDEGGER's term "das Man," designating **Dasein** as not differentiated from the "Others," the crowd, the anonymous many who dictate how life goes and what it means.

ontic HEIDEGGER's term for the realm of ordinary and scientific facts. (Compare **ontological.**)

ontological 1. Having to do with **Being,** with what there is in the most general sense. 2. In HEIDEGGER, having to do with the deep structure of **Dasein's Being** that makes possible the **ontic** facts about average everydayness; disclosed in *fundamental ontology.*

ontological argument An argument for God's existence that proceeds solely from an idea of what God is, from his **essence.** Different versions found in ANSELM and DESCARTES; criticized by AQUINAS, HUME, and KANT.

phenomena What appears, just as it appears. In KANT, contrasted with *noumena*. The object of study by **phenomenology.**

phenomenology The attempt to describe what appears to consciousness; a science of consciousness, its structures, contents, and objects. (In HEGEL and later in HUSSERL and HEIDEGGER.)

physicalism The view that reality is through and through material in nature. (DEMOCRITUS, DENNETT)

physis The way things are, independently of any human decision; from it, our word "physics" comes. (Compare *nomos*.) (Sophists)

pictorial form What a picture and the pictured have in common, which allows the first to picture the second. (early WITTGENSTEIN)

possible experience In KANT, a term designating the extent to which sensibility and understanding can reach, structured as they are by the **a priori** intuitions of space and time, together with the **a priori** concepts or **categories.**

possible state of affairs In early WITTGENSTEIN, the way in which objects could relate to each other to constitute a fact.

power/knowledge Foucault's idea that knowledge and power are inextricably linked, as in technologies of discipline.

pragmatism A view developed by PEIRCE, JAMES, and DEWEY, in which all of our intellectual life is understood in relation to our practical interests. What a concept means, for instance, depends wholly on the practical effects of the object of our concept.

premise Statement offered in support of a conclusion; the evidentiary part of an argument.

present-at-hand A HEIDEGGERian term for things understood as bereft of their usual functional relation to our interests and concerns; what "objective" science takes as its object. A modification of our usual relation to things as **ready-to-hand.**

primary qualities In GALILEO and other early moderns, qualities that a thing actually has—for example, size, shape, location—and that account for or explain certain effects in us (**secondary qualities**), such as sweetness, redness, warmth. (DESCARTES, LOCKE, BERKELEY)

qualia The immediate qualities of experience, private and subjective. Sense data. Green, warm, loud, sweet.

quiddity Latin-origin term for *what* a thing is; its essence, in contrast to its actual existence. (AQUINAS)

rationalism The philosophical stance that is distrustful of the senses, relying only on reason and rational argument to deliver the truth. (PARMENIDES and DESCARTES)

rational psychology KANT's term for the discipline that attempts to gain knowledge of the self or soul in nonempirical ways, relying on rational argument alone; KANT thinks it an illusion that rational psychology produces knowledge.

ready-to-hand HEIDEGGER's term for the mode of **Being** of the things that are most familiar to **Dasein;** gear or equipment in its functional relation to **Dasein's** concerns.

realism A term of many meanings; central is the contention that reality is both logically and causally independent of even the best human beliefs and theories.

relativism A term of many meanings; central is the view that there are no objective standards of good or bad to be discovered and that no objective knowledge of reality is possible; all standards and knowledge claims are valid only relative to times, individuals, or cultures. (Sophists)

representational theory The view that our access to reality is limited to our perceptions and ideas, which function as representations of things beyond themselves; a problem associated with this theory is how we can ever know that there are things beyond these representations. (DESCARTES, LOCKE, BERKELEY)

rhetoric The art of persuasive speaking developed and taught by the **Sophists** in ancient Greece, whose aim was to show how a persuasive *logos* could be constructed on each side of a controversial issue.

secondary qualities Those qualities, such as taste and color, produced in us by the **primary qualities** of objects—size, shape, and so on. (GALILEO, DESCARTES, LOCKE, BERKELEY)

semantics Study of word-world relationships; how words relate to what they are about. (PEIRCE)

sense-certainty What is left if we subtract from sensory experience all interpretation in terms of concepts, for example, the sheer blueness we experience when we look at a clear sky; the immediate; where HEGEL thinks philosophy must start, though it is forced to go on from there.

showing Contrasted in WITTGENSTEIN's early philosophy with *saying;* logic, for instance, shows itself in every bit of language; a proposition *shows* (displays) its sense, and it *says* that this is how things stand.

skepticism The view that for every claim to know, reason can be given to doubt it; the skeptic suspends

judgment about reality (SEXTUS EMPIRICUS, MONTAIGNE). DESCARTES uses skeptical arguments to try to find something that cannot be doubted.

social contract The theory that government finds its justification in an agreement or contract among individuals. (HOBBES, LOCKE)

solipsism The view, which must be stated in the first person, that only I exist; the worry about falling into solipsism motivates DESCARTES to try to prove the existence of God.

Sophist From a Greek word meaning "wise one"; in ancient Greece, teachers who taught many things to ambitious young men but who specialized in **rhetoric.**

sound In logic a sound argument is one that is both valid and has true premises.

Stoicism The view that happiness and freedom are at hand for the asking if we but distinguish clearly what properly belongs to ourselves and what is beyond our power, limiting our desires to the former and thus keeping our wills in harmony with nature.

substance What is fundamental and can exist independently; that which has or underlies its qualities. There is disagreement about what is substantial: PLATO takes it to be the **Forms,** ARISTOTLE the individual things of our experience. Some philosophers (for example, SPINOZA) argue that there is but *one* substance: God. (also LOCKE, BERKELEY, KANT, HEGEL)

syllogism An **argument** comprising two premises and a conclusion, composed of categorical subject-predicate statements; the argument contains just three terms, each of which appears in just two of the statements. (ARISTOTLE)

synthetic A term applied to statements the denial of which is not contradictory; according to KANT, in a synthetic statement the predicate is not "contained" in the subject but adds something to it (for example, "Mount Cook is the highest mountain in New Zealand").

tautology A statement for which the truth table contains only T's. WITTGENSTEIN uses the concept to explain the nature of logical truth and the laws of logic.

teleology Purposiveness or goal-directedness; a teleological explanation for some fact is an explanation in terms of what end it serves. (ARISTOTLE, HEIDEGGER)

theodicy The justification of the ways of God to man, especially in relation to the problem of evil: What would justify an all-powerful, wise, and good God in creating a world containing so many evils? (AUGUSTINE, HEGEL)

things-in-themselves In KANT's philosophy, things as they are, quite independent of our apprehension of them, of the way they appear to us; *noumena.* Things-in-themselves are (for Kant) unknowable.

Third Man Term for a problem with PLATO's **Forms:** We seem to be forced into an infinite regress of Forms to account for the similarity of two men.

thrownness HEIDEGGER's term for **Dasein's** simply finding itself in existence under certain conditions, without ever having a choice about that.

transcendental Term for the conditions on the side of the subject that make knowing or doing possible. KANT's critical philosophy is a transcendental investigation; it asks about the **a priori** conditions for experience and action in general.

utilitarianism Moral philosophy that takes consequences as the criteria for the moral evaluation of action; of two alternative actions open to one, it is right to choose the one that will produce the best consequences for all concerned—for example, the most pleasure or happiness.

validity A term for logical goodness in deductive arguments; an **argument** is valid whenever, if the premises are true, it is not possible for the conclusion to be false. An argument can be valid, however, even if the premises are false.

verifiability principle The rule adopted by the **logical positivists** to determine meaningfulness in factual statements; if no sense experience can count in favor of the truth of a statement—can verify it at least to some degree—it is declared meaningless, since meaning is said to consist in such verifiability.

zombie An exact physical duplicate of a human being, but without conscious experience. (CHALMERS)

CREDITS

Text Credits

From Hesiod, "Theogony" in *Hesiod and Theognis,* translated by Dorothea Wender (Penguin Classics, 1973), copyright © 1973 by Dorothea Wender. Reprinted by permission of Penguin Books Ltd.

From *The Illiad* by Homer, translated by Robert Fagles, copyright © 1990 by Robert Fagles. Used by permission of Viking Penguin, a division of Penguin Group (USA) Inc.

From *The Odyssey* by Homer, translated by Robert Fagles, copyright © 1996 by Robert Fagles. Used by permission of Viking Penguin, a division of Penguin Group (USA) Inc.

From John Mansley Robinson, *An Introduction to Early Greek Philosophy,* copyright © 1968 by Houghton Mifflin Company. Used with permission of the publisher.

From Aristophanes, *The Clouds,* translated by William Arrowsmith, copyright © 1962 by William Arrowsmith. Reprinted by arrangement with New American Library, a division of Penguin Books USA Inc.

From Thucydides, *The Peloponnesian War,* translated by Rex Warner (Penguin Classics, 1954), copyright © 1954 by Rex Warner. Reprinted by permission of Penguin Books Ltd.

From Euripides, *Hippolytus,* in *Euripides I,* copyright © 1955 by University of Chicago Press. Reprinted with permission of the publisher.

From Plato, *Gorgias,* translated by Robin Waterfield. Copyright © 1994 by Oxford University Press.

From Xenophon in W. K. C. Guthrie, *The Greeks and Their Gods,* copyright © 1950 by Methuen & Company. Reprinted with permission of the publisher.

From Plato, *Symposium,* translated by Robin Waterfield. Copyright © 1994 by Oxford University Press.

From Plato, *The Trial and Death of Socrates,* trans. Grube (Hackett 1980). Reprinted by permission of Hackett Publishing Company, Inc. All rights reserved.

From Hamilton, Edith, *The Collected Dialogues, Including the Letters.* © 1961 Princeton University Press, 1989 renewed. Reprinted by permission of Princeton University Press.

From Plato, *Phaedo,* translated by David Gallop. Copyright © 1993 by Oxford University Press.

From Plato, *Protagoras,* translated by C. C. W. Taylor. Copyright © 1996 by Oxford University Press.

From Plato, *Meno,* translated by Robin Waterfield. Copyright © 2005 by Oxford University Press.

From Plato, *The Republic,* translated by Robin Waterfield. Copyright © 1993 by Oxford University Press.

From Renford Bambrough, *The Philosophy of Aristotle,* copyright © 1963 by Renford Bambrough. Reprinted by arrangement with New American Library, a division of Penguin Books USA Inc.

From Epicurus, *Letters, Principal Doctrines and Vatican Sayings,* translated by Russel M. Geer, copyright © 1964 by Prentice-Hall, Inc.

Photography Credits

INDEX

CPSIA information can be obtained
at www.ICGtesting.com
Printed in the USA
BVOW07s2039020416
442648BV00004B/4/P